D1203571

20th century the colum
century the columbia hist
the columbia history of the
columbia history of the 20
history of the 20th century
of the 20th century the col
the 20th century the colum
20th century the columbia
century the columbia hist
the columbia history of the
columbia history of the 20t
history of the 20th century
of the 20th century the col
the 20th century the colum
20th century the columbia
century the columbia hist
the columbia history of the
columbia history of the 20t
history of the 20th century

# the
# columbia
# history
# of
# the
# 20th
# century

RICHARD W. BULLIET, EDITOR

COLUMBIA UNIVERSITY PRESS

NEW YORK

Columbia University Press

*Publishers Since 1893*

New York    Chichester, West Sussex

Copyright © 1998 Columbia University Press

All rights reserved

Library of Congress Cataloging-in-Publication Data

The Columbia history of the 20th century / Richard W. Bulliet.

p.   cm

Includes index

ISBN 0–231–07628–2

1. History, Modern—20th century.    I. Bulliet, Richard W.

D 421.C57   1998

909.82—dc21                                        97–39426

*In memory of Eric Holtzman and William C. McNeil*

# Contents

# Contributors

*Richard W. Bulliet* is professor of history and director of the Middle East Institute at Columbia University. He has taught courses on Middle Eastern history and the history of domestic animals, as well as the "great books" courses on Western social and political thought, masterpieces of Western literature, and masterpieces of Western art in Columbia's noted core curriculum. His book *The Camel and the Wheel* won the Dexter Prize of the Society for the History of Technology. His most recent work is *Islam: The View from the Edge*. He is also coauthor of the world history textbook *The Earth and Its Peoples*, coeditor of *The Encyclopedia of the Modern Middle East*, and author of four novels, most recently *The Sufi Fiddle*.

*Ainslie Embree* is professor of history emeritus at Columbia University, where he was formerly department chair, director of the South Asian Institute, and acting dean of the School of International and Public Affairs. Born in Canada, he served as Counselor for Cultural Affairs at the American Embassy in Delhi (1978–1980) and as Special Consultant to the American Ambassador to India (1994–1995). His recent books include *Imagining India: Essays on Indian History* and *Utopias in Conflict: Religion and Nationalism in India*. He is editor-in-chief of the *Encyclopedia of Asian History*.

*Sheila Fitzpatrick* is the Bernadotte E. Schmitt Professor in History at the University of Chicago. Born in Australia and educated at the University of Melbourne and St. Antony's College, Oxford, she is coeditor of the *Journal of Modern History* and was president (1997) of the American Association for the Advancement of Slavic Studies. Her most recent books are *Accusatory Practices: Denunciation in Modern European History, 1789–1989*, edited with Robert Gellately; *Stalin's Peasants: Resistance and Survival in the Russian Village after Collectivization*; *The Russian Revolution*, second edition; and *The Cultural Front: Power and Culture in Revolutionary Russia*.

*Christopher Freeman* founded the Science Policy Research Unit (SPRU) at the University of Sussex in 1965 and was its first director until 1983. He is now professor emeritus at SPRU. Educated at the London School of Economics, after wartime service he became a researcher at the National Institute of Economics and Social Research, leading European projects on technical change in the world electronics industry, the chemical industry, and industrial research and development. In collaboration with Professor Luc Soete, he has recently written *Work for All or Mass Unemployment: Computerized Technical Change in the Twenty-first Century*; he has also completed the third edition of his textbook *Economics of Industrial Innovation.*

*Eric Holtzman*, professor of biological sciences and chair of the Biological Sciences Department of Columbia University, died in 1994 at the age of 54, not long after completing his chapter for this book. He made significant contributions to knowledge of cell membranes and cell communications and wrote two books on lysosomes, structures within cells that break down harmful substances. He was coauthor, with Alan Novikoff, of the widely used textbook *Cells and Organelles.*

*Akira Iriye* is Charles Warren Professor of American History and director of the Edwin O. Reischauer Institute of Japanese Studies at Harvard University. His recent books include *The Globalizing of America, Cultural Internationalism and World Order*, and *Japan and the Wider World.*

*Kenneth T. Jackson* is the Jacques Barzun Professor of History and the Social Sciences and former chair of the Department of History at Columbia University. He has been president of the Urban History Association and vice president of the Society of American Historians. His book *Crabgrass Frontier: The Suburbanization of the United States* won both the Francis Parkman and the Bancroft Prizes, and he is editor-in-chief of *The Encyclopedia of New York City.*

*Zachary Karabell* received his Ph.D. in history from Harvard University and has written widely on U.S. foreign policy and American culture. His publications include *Architects of Intervention: The United States, the Third World, and the Cold War, 1946–1962* and a forthcoming book on American universities in the age of universal higher education.

*William McNeil*, associate professor of modern European history at Barnard College, Columbia University, died in 1993 at the age of 46, shortly after completing his contribution to this volume. A specialist in European international relations and monetary policy, he was the author of *American Money and the Weimar Republic.*

*Joseph Paul Martin* is the executive director of the Center for the Study of Human Rights at Columbia University. Born in England, he joined a Catholic missionary order after completing national military service, and taught for three years at what was then the University of Botswana, Lesotho and Swaziland after studies in Rome. He earned his Ph.D. at Columbia University. His work in Africa continues through his support of annual regional human rights training programs in Burkina Faso, Uganda, and Zimbabwe and his editing of three collections of human rights documents.

*James Mayall* is professor of international relations at the London School of Economics and Political Science and chair of the Centre for International Studies there. He is the author of *Nationalism and International Society* and editor of and contributor to *The New Intervention: UN Experience in Cambodia, Former Yugoslavia and Somalia.*

*Robert L. O'Connell* is a senior intelligence analyst with the National Ground Intelligence Center and a contributing editor of *MHQ: The Quarterly Journal of Military History.* His books include *Of Arms and Men, Sacred Vessels,* and *Ride of the Second Horsemen.*

*Jean-Marc Ran Oppenheim* received his Ph.D. in history from Columbia University, where he serves as administrator of the Middle East Institute. Born in Egypt, he wrote his doctoral dissertation on the social history of that country's Alexandria Sporting Club. Formerly a professional horse trainer, he has been nationally ranked both as a three-day event rider and as a saber fencer.

*William N. Parker* is the Phillip Golden Bartlett Professor of Economics and Economic History emeritus at Yale University. He was educated at Harvard University and is a World War II veteran of the U.S. Army and the OSS. His most recent work has been on problems of European integration and the shape of the emerging set of international institutions, private and public, operating in the world economy in the 1990s. His research papers and interpretive essays have been collected in the two-volume work *Europe, America and the Wider World.*

*Mary Corliss Pearl* is executive director of Wildlife Preservation Trust International and associate director of the Center for Environmental Research and Conservation at Columbia University. She is also cofounder of the Center for Conservation Medicine, a consortium based at Tufts University School of Veterinary Medicine. Educated in physical anthropology at Yale University, she is coeditor of *Conservation for the* Twenty-first *Century* and editor of two book series, "Cases and Methods in Conservation Science" and "Perspectives in Conservation Science."

*Rosalind Rosenberg* is professor of history at Barnard College, Columbia University. A specialist in twentieth-century American women's history, she is the author of *Divided Lives: American Women in the Twentieth Century* and *Beyond Separate Spheres: Roots of Modern Feminism*.

*David Rosner* became professor of public health and history at Columbia University in 1997 after serving as University Distinguished Professor of History at Baruch College and the City University of New York Graduate Center. He is the author of *A Once Charitable Enterprise*, editor of *Hives of Sickness: Epidemics and Public Health in New York City*, and, with Gerald Markowitz, author and editor of numerous other books and articles on public health.

*Georges Sabagh* is professor of sociology emeritus and former director of the von Grunebaum Center for Near Eastern Studies at the University of California in Los Angeles. He has been involved in studies of population trends and characteristics in Los Angeles, Egypt, and Morocco and a consultant on similar projects in Tunisia, Senegal, and Mali. His most recent publications include book chapters entitled "Population Change: Immigration and Ethnic Transformation," "Middle Easterners: A New Kind of Immigrant," "The Analysis of Return Migration: The Experiences of the Maghrib and Mexico," and "Los Angeles, A World of New Immigrants: An Image of Things to Come?"

*Jahan Salehi*, a successful entrepreneur, is also a noted speaker and writer on issues concerning the Internet and telecommunications. Educated at Transylvania University and Columbia University, he is president of J2S2 Inc., an Internet production company that produces medical community-based forums online. He is the author of a forthcoming book *Searching the Internet: A Researcher's Guide*.

*John C. Spychalski* is professor of business logistics and chair of the Department of Business Logistics in the Smeal College of Business Administration of Pennsylvania State University. A specialist on transportation economics, public policy, management, and history, he is the editor of *Transportation Journal*, has advised private and public sector entities on transport issues, and is a board member of an urban transit system. He received the 1990 Distinguished Member Award from the Transportation and Public Utilities group of the American Economic Association and the 1996 Outstanding Transportation/Logistics Executive in North America Award from the American Society of Transportation and Logistics.

*B. F. Stanton* is professor of agricultural economics emeritus at the New York State College of Agriculture and Life Sciences, Cornell University, where he served as chair of the Department of Agricultural Economics. He has teaching and research experience in Finland, Belgium, Australia, and India, and his primary research interests have been related to the structure of agriculture and production economics. He was president of the American Agricultural Economics Association and is an Honorary Life Member of the International Association of Agricultural Economists.

*Neil De Grasse Tyson* is the Frederick P. Rose Director of New York City's Hayden Planetarium and a research scientist at Princeton University. After studying physics at Harvard University, he earned a Ph.D. in astrophysics from Columbia University. His research primarily addresses problems related to star formation models of dwarf galaxies, supernovae, and the kinematic and chemical evolution history of the Milky Way's galactic bulge. In addition to professional publications, he writes the monthly column "Universe" for *Natural History* magazine. His most recent book, *Universe Down to Earth*, contains essays exploring connections between cosmic science and everyday life experiences.

the
columbia
history
of
the
20th
century

# Introduction

RICHARD W. BULLIET

This book contains twenty-three chapters describing and analyzing the most important areas of thought and activity wherein basic aspects of human life underwent fundamental change in the twentieth century. Collectively, these changes accumulate to the greatest one-century period of change in human history.

Conventional histories of the twentieth century obscure this fact with event-charged narratives that propel the reader from the trenches of World War I, through the hardships of the depression and the grim struggle of World War II, to the nail-biting decades of the cold war with its enigmatic aftermath. By contrast, this history is infrastructural. It goes directly to the transformations that were taking place in the underlying foundations of human life while the century's various wars and crises daily filled the headlines of world newspapers. In so doing, it constructs a history of the century that puts broad currents of change at the forefront and thereby tells us how our lives got to be the way they are today.

In recent decades, historians have come to refer to broad notions about major past events that are generally known within a population as "master narratives." Without people being aware of them, or being able to say exactly where they come from, master narratives structure a society's thinking about the past and thus affect its thinking about the present and future.

Looking back, for example, to *Parley's Panorama, Or Curiosities of Nature, Art, History and Biography, a compendium of lore, historical and otherwise,* published in Cincinnati in 1856 for the edification of middle-class American families, we find this description of the first half of the nineteenth century:

> In comparing our continent, in 1850, with its condition in 1800, we may well be proud and grateful to observe what triumphs American labor, skill and capital, have effected in the interval. Was there ever a nation, that, in fifty years, felled such a world of forest, or opened to culture such

a breadth of soil—wove such an interminable length of broad and good roads over such a continent of wood, mountain and morass—built so many cities, towns and villages, mills, factories, docks, warehouses, churches, court-houses, alms-houses, hospitals, custom-houses—and connected them together, physically and intellectually, by such a complicated net-work of iron railroads and telegraphic wires! . . .

But we should take even wider views of the progress of our race during the eventful period which has just elapsed. What has been the result, in a political point of view, of the thousand battles which have stained, and the continual struggles which have signalized, the past fifty years? . . . [T]he peaceful triumphs of discovery and colonization, which have occupied the national energies which war had developed . . . are opening to industry and hope the interior of wretched Africa, by stationing powerful civilizing agencies upon her east, north, south and west . . . besides the efforts which have carried European civilization into the islands of the Pacific and China, Turkey, India and the wilds of Tartary and Siberia. . . .

A glance at the scientific aspect of the times shows us that the nineteenth century has been an age of scientific wonders, an age thus far distinguished above all ages for progress in all those sciences and arts which tend to mold nature and her powers to the use of man. . . . Steam navigation, canals, macadamized roads, railroads, electric telegraphs— balloon steaming may we not soon add?—have their entire history within the nineteenth century. To it also belongs, besides many other discoveries and inventions—those of Etherization, Animal Magnetism, Phrenology, Photography, Gun-cotton, Gutta Percha: the preparation of various abundant, but before unknown, esculents for food; Homeopathy, Hydropathy; teaching of the blind, deaf and dumb; cure of the insane . . .[1]

A century and a half later, dissection of a passage like this to extract its underlying assumptions and ideology would be an elementary assignment in a college history course. The master narrative of white Europeans and Americans, conceived of as a race, making unprecedented physical, cultural, and scientific progress and conferring the blessings of this progress and civilization upon the rest of the "wretched" and "wild" world manifests itself so often in nineteenth-century historical writing that it takes little effort to find it or to recognize its inherent biases. Yet it would be hard today to find a competent historian who would espouse the racism, imperialism, indifference toward the environment, and naive belief in scientific progress embodied in this passage.

Awareness that the master narratives of centuries past have become almost comical has prompted historians to scrutinize carefully the currently accepted ones. This scrutiny has given rise to the growing attention paid to the histories of groups or viewpoints generally excluded from these narratives: within the boundaries of American history alone, the histories of women, Native Americans, African Americans, Hispanic Americans, Asian Americans, gays and lesbians, and so forth. These new historical perspectives, in turn, have prompted concern in some quarters that the leading characters of the old master narratives are being deleted from history.

Disagreement over what constitutes the "mainstream" of history in the twentieth century (or any other time) goes beyond the historian's study or the book review columns of newspapers. No one can doubt that numerous master narratives are entertained in different sectors of our society, or that a large number of them can be found in other parts of the world.

The names of W.E.B. Du Bois, Marcus Garvey, Malcolm X, and the Reverend Martin Luther King, Jr. evoke among African Americans a master narrative of Jim Crow discrimination, assertion of racial identity and pride, and the struggle for equality. The names Theodore Herzl, Chaim Weizmann, Vladimir Jabotinsky, Louis Brandeis, and David Ben Gurion evoke for American Jews a master narrative of anti-Semitism and the Holocaust, achievement of statehood for Israel, and the struggle for survival against Arab enemies. And so it goes for every group that, in quest of, or from a desire to maintain, a sense of community identity, has knit its own master narrative from the yarns of the past, the bits of historical event and individual biography that everyone truly interested in that community's past must surely know.

Expand this perspective worldwide. The master narrative of twentieth-century Arab history rotates around the names of Sharif Husain, his sons Faisal and Abdullah, Abd al-Aziz ibn Saud, Michel Aflaq, and Gamal Abdul Nasser. Indian historians dwell on the thoughts and deeds of Mahatma Gandhi, Muhammad Ali Jinnah, Jawaharlal Nehru, and Subhas Chandra Bose; Mexican historians on Porfirio Díaz, Pancho Villa, Emiliano Zapata, and Lázaro Cárdenas. Hundreds of countries and self-conscious communities; hundreds of master narratives.

Therefore, the common feeling that *the* master narrative of the twentieth century is probably already known, at least in rough outline, to most people living at century's end has to be qualified. This century's vast expansion of education and literacy has, indeed, produced a broader knowledge of historical master narratives than ever before; but it has also multiplied the number of master narratives in circulation.

How, then, given this multiplicity of master narratives proper to different audiences, can a *History of the Twentieth Century* be written? How can any selection of past events be made without triggering charges that this so-called history pays disproportional attention to the master narrative of one particular group—for example, rich white folk of European descent? Certainly not by stirring up choice nuggets of information about everybody in the world and then pressing them tightly in hopes that they will adhere into a kind of historical fruitcake suited to every reader's taste.

This book's thematic or infrastructural approach takes as a premise the idea that the master narratives of all groups rest to some degree on foundations of historical development outside the arena of political drama, war, and revolution, and that all groups have been affected, to greater or lesser degrees, by the currents of changed described in each chapter. Some of these developments fall into the realm of social history, economic history, or technological history, all of which have become major areas of historical inquiry in the last third of the century. But the themes explored in this book were not chosen exclusively from these subdisciplines. Rather, the question was asked: In what areas of life have twentieth-century developments been so remarkable or revolutionary as to distinguish this century from any preceding era in human history?

A similar premise guided the historian Charles A. Beard when he compiled *Whither Mankind? A Panorama of Modern Civilization*, published in 1928.[2] He wrote in the introduction: "Underlying [this volume] is the assumption that science and the machine are two invincible facts with which all must reckon who write, teach, preach, lead, or practice the arts in our time." Then followed sixteen essays by noted authorities. Among the topics: Science, Business, Labor, Law and Government, War and Peace, Health, The Family, Race and Civilization, Religion, The Arts, Philosophy, Play, Education, and Literature. Beard's goal was to substitute the "visions of despair" stemming from modern science and industry with "a more cheerful outlook upon the future of modern civilization, without at the same time resorting to the optimism of the real-estate agent."

The crash of the New York Stock Exchange a year after *Whither Mankind?* was published put this sort of optimism on hold where, for many, it has remained ever since. Nor is it the intent of this book to look to the future with an optimistic heart. Its goal, rather, is to show how people of every condition, in every part of the world, have been strongly affected in one or several aspects of their lives by world technological, economic, social, and institutional developments. Though every chapter will not deal with every part of the world, each author has been asked to address his or her theme on a global basis to whatever degree possible.

The editor of this volume concurs with Beard's approach to his project: "Each writer was given a free hand. None of them was asked to assume any responsibility for the opinions of the others." Nor has the editor "taken on the duty of defending everything that appears in these pages." The intent has been to offer interpretive essays by highly qualified individuals, not with the idea that they would seamlessly blend together topically or stylistically, but with the hope that each author would reach beyond historical narrative for personal insights or conclusions.

Recruiting authors for this project was not an easy task. In an age of academic specialization, many scholars were reluctant to tread outside the spatial or chronological boundaries they were accustomed to. The mandate to give consideration to all parts of the century and all parts of the world seemed to many to be impossibly broad. Those who answered the call and whose essays are presented in this volume deserve particular thanks for shouldering the burden presented to them, and for doing so in a consistently excellent fashion. As a group, they embody no particular school of history or philosophical approach. Some are not primarily historians. Each of them, however, has worked to present his or her subject in a clear and forthright fashion with the average educated reader in mind.

Organizing a book of this sort reprised, on a smaller scale, the dilemma of avoiding master narratives. Collective volumes of history typically begin with politics, proceed to social and economic conditions, and end with culture. This sequence constitutes an implicit valuation of the subject matter and one that many historians would defend openly. World circumstances at the end of the twentieth century, however, call this convention into question. Which of today's political problems overshadows the world more than demographic increase or degradation of the environment? How many governments wield as much power internationally as the International Monetary Fund? What symbolizes the United States around the world? The Stars and Stripes? Or McDonald's, Coca-Cola, and Levi's jeans? At the present moment, culture, economics, technology, and social values seem at least as likely to shape the future of the world as political ideology or territorial conquest.

The essays in this book may be read in any order. The groups into which they are divided afford labels of convenience rather than real or conceptual boundaries. Taken as a whole, they tell the story of a world that has changed almost beyond recognition since the year 1900. In so doing, they provide the screen against which readers of any background or persuasion may project their own particular histories of the twentieth century.

ENDNOTES

1. S. G. Goodrich, ed., *Parley's Panorama, Or Curiosities of Nature, Art, History and Biography, a compendium of lore, historical and otherwise* (Cincinnati: Mack R. Barnitz, 1856), p. 607.
2. Charles A. Beard, *Whither Mankind? A Panorama of Modern Civilization* (New York: Longmans, Green and Co., 1928), p. v.

# 1 High Culture

RICHARD W. BULLIET

On December 9, 1889, President Benjamin Harrison dedicated the Auditorium Theater in Chicago, a building of architectural and acoustic excellence designed by the pioneer of functional architecture, Louis Sullivan. The next night, world-renowned soprano Adelina Patti sang Juliet in Gounod's *Romeo and Juliet*. Grand Opera, the epitome of nineteenth-century high culture, had arrived in the city of big shoulders.

Nevertheless, at the beginning, Chicago depended on New York's rival Metropolitan and Manhattan opera companies for performances. Oscar Hammerstein, the cigar maker, had founded the Manhattan company to challenge the Metropolitan, and pitted exciting new stars like Mary Garden and John McCormack against the older company's Arturo Toscanini and Enrico Caruso.

Chicago society, however, which had already established the Chicago Symphony, another benchmark of nineteenth-century high culture, was not satisfied with visiting productions. In 1909, John C. Shaffer, the socially ambitious publisher of the *Chicago Evening Post*, conferred with Mr. Hammerstein about building a new opera house and establishing a resident company with local financing. Getting wind of the enterprise, Otto Kahn of the Metropolitan outmaneuvered his rival with the enthusiastic support of Chicago "capitalists" (as the newspaper release called them)—men with names like Armour, McCormick, and Insull. Kahn bought the Auditorium Theater, hired away the Manhattan Company's director Cleofonte Campanini, and on November 3, 1910 staged a performance of *Aïda*, followed the next night by Debussy's *Péleas et Mélisande* with soprano Mary Garden singing the role of Mélisande, which Debussy had written for her.

For turn-of-the-century Americans, this sort of activity defined high culture, a zone of creative artistry where money, social elitism, publicity, stardom, and institution building converged. Some Chicago opera-goers undoubtedly enjoyed the performances and, as connoisseurs, savored their finer points. But three years later, when the Armory Show of "modern" art moved from New York to Chicago, raucous protesters paraded an effigy of Henry Hairmattress (alias Henri Matisse) and scoffed at cubist works by Picasso and Braque, and especially at Marcel Duchamps's *Nude Descending a Staircase*. Where grand opera floated on cushions of money and social respectability plumped up by nineteenth-century millionaire industrialists, "modern" art had to fight and claw for viewing space in competition with such coyly saccharine realist favorites as Paul Chabas's *September Morn*, with its demure nude timidly bathing in a sylvan pool.

The influential British critic Matthew Arnold defined culture as "the acquainting of ourselves with the best that has been known and said in the world, and thus with the history of the human spirit." Culture, in Arnold's sense, was a part of the dominant American credo in the first decade of the twentieth century, along with firm beliefs in morality and progress. But Arnold's "world" was understood to mean Western Europe, and England in particular, with its self-proclaimed cultural antecedents in classical antiquity and Judeo-Christian scripture. Most Americans and Western Europeans considered the arts and tastes of other parts of the world to be exotic, barbaric, or worse.

The odd few artists who were beginning to look outside of Europe for inspiration—Pablo Picasso to Africa, Paul Gauguin to Tahiti, Henri Matisse to Morocco—used local arts as sources of inspiration, much as the imperialists were exploiting non-Western lands for raw materials. However, Chinese opera, Japanese Noh drama, Iranian classical music, African sculpture, and Indonesian gamelan music would remain largely unknown and unappreciated beyond the parts of the world they originated in throughout the twentieth century, though by century's end genuine specimens could be viewed from time to time by conscientious devotees of educational television or university concert series. By contrast, symphony orchestras using European instruments, and for the most part playing European classical music, multiplied worldwide, along with such European cultural institutions as opera houses and art museums.

Arnold's high culture as "the best that has been known and said" (not to mention painted, sculpted, and composed) has included bygone monuments of creativity conserved in art and archaeology museums. But their twentieth-century continuations or transformations often remained in shadow until "recognized" by socially elite patrons. Nevertheless, the traditional patrons of high culture had limitations. Understandably, English-speaking literati who saw their tastes evolve from Tennyson in 1910, to T. S. Eliot in 1940, to Sylvia

Plath in 1980 might consider themselves mightily cultured despite a complete ignorance of modern masters using Western forms like Turkey's Nazim Hikmet, Lebanon's Adonis, or Greece's Constantine Cavafy. No one knows all languages in which poetry is written. The same holds true for novels and plays in different languages and music composed, performed, or sung according to different scales and aesthetic principles. Of the generally recognized major art forms, dance alone, perhaps because of its rhythms or the universality of human movement, seems translatable across cultural divides, which is part of the reason for its marked vitality, both in formal dance companies and as expressions of national identity, at the end of the twentieth century.

Recognizing the unbridgeable gaps between different world cultures and cataloging the where and when of who is best at what might suffice as a survey of twentieth-century high culture. But it would not explain the dominance of Western forms or address the question of what has become, or is becoming, of high culture within other traditions. The institutional layering of Western high culture and artistic taste over local preferences around the world testifies not so much to the eternal grandeur of a Johannes Brahms— whose *German Requiem* was played by the Teheran symphony orchestra in 1990 in memory of the Ayatollah Khomeini, who despised and prohibited Western music—as to the strength and pervasiveness of Western high culture as a complex of intellectual, institutional, economic, and political forces. An understanding of these forces is important to assessing the fragility and incipient dissolution of the concept of "high culture" at century's end, an outcome that it would have been impossible for pre–World War I Europeans and Americans to anticipate, or even imagine.

Patronage has always been at the heart of high culture. While royal patronage and religious patronage have long histories, they have been comparatively insignificant in the twentieth century. Their place has been taken by wealthy private citizens. And though Marxist theorists have argued that patronage by wealthy merchants is a peculiar feature of the later phases of Western capitalism, it is not unprecedented in other cultures. The wealthy salt merchants of Yangzhou, China, who maintained private theater troupes that evolved into the Beijing opera—a major manifestation of Chinese high culture—anticipated the Chicago industrialists who sponsored the advent of grand opera in their city by a century and a half.

Nevertheless, the burgeoning of private wealth derived from industry and commerce in the late nineteenth century enlarged the capacity of private, nonaristocratic patronage in the West beyond that of any previous economic system. Great wealth, of course, can turn in other directions than cultural patronage. In the Islamic world, society's elevation of piety to the level of the highest good has led generations of wealthy individuals to donate their surplus money to the building of mosques, religious schools, hospitals, fountains, and other public works in the name of religion. A parallel concern for piety and good works is evident in the history of private patronage in earlier European history, though the bankers of Renaissance Italy and the merchants of Flanders mixed their interest in religious art with a taste for female flesh, self-portraits, and, to a lesser degree, landscapes.

By the end of the nineteenth century, however, the progress of the Enlightenment had successfully divorced aesthetic taste from religious duty, and the preponderance of artworks in the areas of easel painting, sculpture, musical composition, and literature had become secular in subject matter and tone. This evolution away from religion and toward secular aesthetic taste reflects not so much the preferences of the creators of high culture as the markets in which they worked. Throughout the twentieth century artists willingly, on occasion, reverted to religious themes, and many of them executed commissions for religious institutions. However, the secular private art collector or subscriber to the opera, symphony, or ballet had become the primary consumer of artistic creativity in the realm these consumers designated "high culture" or "fine art."

Unlike earlier royal and noble patrons who fancied their own persons or allegorical glorifications of their might, or religious patrons—popes, bishops, abbots—who knew more or less what they wanted in the way of a crucifixion or a martyred saint, wealthy secular patrons of non-noble origin were not as a group drawn to any particular form or subject matter by virtue of their personal backgrounds. Their main concern was that the culture they patronized be generally accepted as excellent and appropriate for people of the highest social position. They could achieve this in one of two ways: either by buying artworks and patronizing cultural performances already associated with upper-class status, or by relying on experts and critics to tell them what works and performances currently being produced were "the best."

In the visual arts, the art critic, the gallery owner, the museum curator, and the academic art expert therefore came to play distinct roles in identifying "the best" pictures and sculpture for the art patron to purchase. It is not insignificant that none of these professions were well established before the nineteenth century, but all have flourished in the twentieth. In schematic outline the system works like this: critics, usually paid by a newspaper or magazine, visit galleries and museums and publish their opinions about what is good and why. The gallery owners place advertisements in the newspapers and magazines the critics work for, and depend in substantial part on the critics' favorable opinions of the works they have chosen to display. The gallery owners use those favorable opinions, along with their knowledge of what museums have acquired the works of the artist they are exhibiting, to help convince the buyer to make a purchase. Museum curators meet with artists, gallery owners, and critics in making decisions about what artworks to buy for their collections; but many museums receive most of their works as gifts from collectors. What particular works in their collections museum curators choose to display and what shows they choose to mount by currently active artists—consisting mostly of works the museum does not own—reinforces or informs the decisions made by gallery owners about what artists and styles to display, and gives critics something to write about in further reinforcement of the current market values. Finally, academic art experts, usually professors, certify the genuineness and provenance of artworks owned by museums, galleries, or collectors; amass and publish information about the lives and careers of artists they deem important; and associate with artists, critics, curators, gallery owners, and collectors, the latter of whom may grace their universities with gifts of art.

The art patron plays a central role in this schema because he or she buys from the gallery, donates to the museum, reads the art critic, and looks to books by the academic art expert to reinforce his or her choices. The money available to the patron for purchasing art touches the professional interests of all of the other groups. Indeed, some theoreticians have gone so far as to argue that the value of works judged to be "fine art," and therefore collectible, is entirely artificial—the product of this complex web of interests designed to separate private art patrons from their money. A corollary of this mode of thinking has gained a wide hearing in intellectual circles from the 1970s onward: that there is no meaningful distinction to be made between "high culture" and "popular culture" on the basis of quality, because quality is simply another term for market value, and market value is created essentially arbitrarily by groups that are directly or indirectly dependent on the largesse of art patrons, and hence inclined to assign value according to what they think they can "sell" more than any other criterion.

This sort of schematic analysis can be extended to other cultural areas: concert, ballet, and opera subscribers underwrite impresarios, conductors, music and dance critics, and academic musicologists, who establish standards of value in the field by what they choose to perform and write about. Buyers of "good literature" similarly underwrite the editors, book reviewers, and literature professors. Indeed, the argument can be extended to include the entire notion of "higher" education in the liberal arts. Students pay fees or governments underwrite them in order for them to learn what is intellectually valuable, but the standards of value are set by the university administrators and professors supported by the fees, except when they are challenged by voter groups (e.g. the Moral Majority) concerned with political bias in education, or wealthy university donors bent on achieving their own intellectual goals.

One illustration of this train of thought comes from the dada movement that began in Zürich in 1916, and was formally provided with a *Dada Manifesto* by the poet Tristan Tzara two years later. Appalled by the horrendous and seemingly pointless waste of human life during World War I, a small group of poets and artists declared that any succession of words or images was as meaningful or as meaningless as any other. Intoning "da da da da da" was as poetic as singing Friedrich von Schiller's "Ode to Joy" in the last movement of Beethoven's *Ninth Symphony*. The Romanian intellectual Peter Neagoe, in a pamphlet published in 1932 to explain the surrealist movement that evolved from dada, wrote:

> The young generation was aware of one thing—the only one commensurate with the colossal upstirring [of the war]—futility of effort. These young men did not formulate, did not articulate their feelings in generally comprehensive forms. Their feelings were too intense to permit coherent expression. They were aware of the parallel between organized art-expression and that other organized effort—the World War—and saw the futility of both.[1]

The dada artists had absolutely no intention of creating something of financial value, and few associated with the movement at its outset ultimately pursued art as a career. But the surrealist movement, christened by André Breton's *Manifeste Surréaliste* in 1924, took seriously the notion that totally accidental or unconscious creation could be accorded artistic value. By the time the movement reached London in June of 1936, through an International Surrealist Exhibition held at the Burlington Galleries, it was a sensation. The British art critic Herbert Read described the exhibition's reception in his book *Surrealism*, published in its aftermath:

> The press, unable to appreciate the significance of a movement of such unfamiliar features, prepared an armoury of mockery, sneers and insults. The duller desiccated weeklies, no less impelled to anticipate the event, commissioned their polyglot gossips, their blasé globe-trotters,

their old-boy-scouts, to adopt their usual pose of I know all, don't be taken in, there's nothing new under the sun—a pose which merely reflects the general lack of intellectual curiosity in this country.... When the foam and froth of society and the press had subsided, we were left with a serious public of scientists, artists, philosophers and socialists, and it is for the sake of this public, and in the confident hope of extending its membership, that we have prepared this definitive manifesto.[2]

Of the book's ninety-six illustrated works from the exhibit, twenty-four were owned by sixteen private collectors (four of them surrealist artists themselves) by the time the book appeared. None had yet become part of a museum collection, but many subsequently became famous in museums, such as Joan Miró's *The Harlequin's Carnival* in the Albright Art Gallery of Buffalo, New York. On the other hand, half of the forty-eight artists represented are virtually unknown today except by art historians.

Dada was not the only source of surrealism, of course, but the episode illustrates how even ideas that were avowedly antagonistic to the notion of "fine art" became valuable properties, and eventually major components of modern art, through the combined actions of galleries, critics, collectors, and museums.

The other side of the coin involved forgers who used the institutional nexus to ascribe value to works purporting to be by famous artists. In 1937, for example, the Dutch forger Han van Meegeren finished a painting, *Christ at Emmaus*, and brought it to a Paris lawyer for help in its sale. He claimed not to have painted it at all, but rather to have bought it from an impoverished French noble family that did not want its name revealed, and he asserted that it was by the seventeenth-century Dutch master Jan Vermeer. A noted professor certified it as genuine, and it was bought by an Amsterdam art dealer who sold it to the Boymans Museum in Rotterdam for £58,000. By the time he confessed to the forgery in court in 1947, Van Meegeren had sold more than £750,000 worth of "certified" Vermeers and Pieter de Hoochs, one of them to Nazi reichsmarschal Hermann Goering.

Piling up examples of collaboration between art critics or scholars and collectors—Bernard Berenson guiding the taste of collector Isabella Stewart Gardner, or Baroness Hilla Rebay von Ehrenwiesen that of collector Solomon R. Guggenheim—nevertheless falls short of proving that the generation of an institutional network for creating cultural value for the benefit of individual capitalist collectors has been the sole or even primary shaping influence in the maintenance and creative trajectory of "high culture" in the twentieth century. For even though individuals purchase books and artworks and attend operas, concerts, ballets, and dramas, architecture often reaches beyond the individual pocketbook, and museums and concert halls are often underwritten by public funds, as are individual artists, for that matter, in countries where government patronage extends to this level.

Some older museums originated as royal collections (the Prado, the Louvre, the Hermitage), while others were created purely for the public display of pictures (Amsterdam's Rijksmuseum in 1808, New York's Metropolitan Museum of Art in 1870, the Art Institute of Chicago in 1879, London's Tate Gallery in 1897). Most became, over time, publically financed institutions. The twentieth century has witnessed an explosion of museum building, however, not just in Europe and America, but worldwide. Some of it has been paid for by private wealth (the Getty Museum in Malibu Beach, California, the Frick Collection in New York City, the Phillips Collection in Washington, D.C.), but many of the larger edifices have come to rely on government support.

The history of the arts in the Soviet Union illustrates the influence governments can have over creative production. Stalin's preference for socialist realism over the abstractions of Vladimir Tatlin's abstract constructivism and Kasimir Malevich's suprematism, which had been leading avant-garde movements from 1913 to 1921, led to seven decades of Soviet artistic production that glorified the people and the state but failed to gain critical esteem or market value anywhere else. After the collapse of the USSR and associated communist regimes in Eastern Europe, truckloads of paintings and sculpture, the life achievements of thousands of skilled artists, were hauled off to dead storage and oblivion. Individual artists depended utterly on the favor of the state, as Dimitri Shostakovich discovered when his popular opera *Lady Macbeth of the Mtsensk District* was officially condemned in 1934. He did not recover his status as Russia's greatest composer until the premier of his *Fifth Symphony* in 1937.

The Nazi campaign against "degenerate art" (*entartete kunst*), which included cubism, abstraction, and expressionism, concentrated on the vilification of the Jews. But the overall impact of the Nazi regime on high culture was much more extensive. Compare the catalogs of the huge German Art exhibitions in Munich in 1930 and in 1937—when the Nazis had been in power for four years: only 15 percent of the 949 artists who exhibited in 1930 had works included in the later show, and almost three-quarters of the 557 artists admitted in 1937, when the show came formally under the patronage of Adolf Hitler, had not exhibited in 1930. Yet, among its 112 illustrations, the catalog of 1930 does not display a single piece of abstract or cubist "degenerate" art, and the works by expressionists are remarkably tame.

What the illustrations in the two catalogs do show is a major change in subject matter. Among the 72 works illustrated in 1937 are 13 of uniformed men or other military subjects, a similar number of scenes of village or farming life, and nine paintings and statues realistically displaying genitalia, presumably out of a concern for virility and naturalness. In the 1930 catalog, by comparison, no military scenes were shown, barely a half dozen village scenes, and distinctly fewer genitals. However, there were eight religious pictures. The 1937 catalog showed one portrait of a clergyman, one of a religious service in a village, and one of Hitler addressing a meeting entitled *In the Beginning was the Word.*

Stalinism and Nazism were extreme examples of totalitarian regimes, but they demonstrate both the importance of state cultural patronage or official taste in the twentieth century and the responsiveness of creative artists to the conditions of patronage under which they work. Milder forms of state patronage, such as the Works Progress Administration (WPA) in depression-stricken America or the U.S. military during World War II, did not have so strong an impact on style and subject matter, but institutional missions such as decorating public buildings and chronicling the war effort nevertheless encouraged the homey realism, often with a regional flavor, that dominated America's pictorial taste at the time.

The dilemma of regarding high culture in the twentieth century as an adventitious artifact deriving from changing patterns of patronage and the institutional structures they generated is that the role of the creative artist, as well as the idea that certain creative achievements truly are great achievements deserving of unstinting admiration, is reduced to insignificance. From this perspective, the composer, poet, painter, and architect become malleable functionaries, whose fame or failure depends less on their vision or craftsmanship than on their ability to respond to changing definitions of value and market demands.

However low critical estimation may currently be of Stalinist socialist realism or the Nazi exaltation of force, family values, and the youthful nude body, works dedicated to these themes defined the pictorial high culture of the USSR, not to mention most other communist countries, for almost 70 years, and that of Nazi Germany for a dozen years. The skilled and talented artists who produced these works had the hope and opportunity of becoming cultural icons, as the academic painters Bouguereau, Gérome, and Meissonier had in the 1860s under Napoleon III when Paul Cézanne was struggling resentfully and unsuccessfully for recognition. Though subsequent critical taste considered Cézanne a genius and Bouguereau a slick, boring purveyor of silky female flesh, the latter was generally considered the greater artist right up to the time of his death in 1905. Indeed, when Cézanne in 1895 heard that his own *Bather Resting* might be hung at the Luxembourg palace, he remarked, "At last I've shit on Bouguereau."[3]

Addressing the issue of quality and achievement in twentieth-century high culture outside the framework of patronage and market values means raising the question of "modernism" in the arts. Up to the 1950s discussions of Western culture in the twentieth century usually centered on the idea of the modern. Modern art, architecture, dance, music, and literature were praised, derided, defined, explained, misunderstood, and proclaimed as the best or worst of human aesthetic achievement.

In English literature, James Joyce, Virginia Woolf, William Faulkner, and a host of other daring writers found no end of detractors and admirers. In English poetry, T. S. Eliot, W. H. Auden, and Ezra Pound played similar roles. Architecture encompassed idiosyncratic creators like Frank Lloyd Wright and a legion of builders of minimally ornamented steel and glass office or apartment towers, following in the footsteps of Mies van der Rohe and the principles of design formulated by him and others at the Bauhaus design school in Weimar (until 1925) and Dessau, Germany, between 1919 and 1930. Modern dance began with Isadora Duncan at the turn of the century and proliferated into scores of innovative companies led by individualist choreographers like Martha Graham, Merce Cunningham, Alvin Ailey, and Twyla Tharp. "Art" music went in an eclectic direction with Igor Stravinsky and a rigorously planned direction with Arnold Schoenberg, eventually reaching the dense, difficult sound masses of Elliot Carter and the hypnotic repetitions of Philip Glass. And in painting and sculpture, new movements and styles proliferated like mushrooms in a damp forest: cubism, constructivism, suprematism, futurism, fauvism, dada, expressionism, surrealism—and that barely gets you to 1930.

What is striking about the names of the art movements is that each connotes something specific: cubists in pre–World War I Paris broke images into simple geometric forms; expressionists in contemporary Dresden and Munich used strong colors and distorted drawing to express emotions; futurists in contemporary Italy used multiple overlapping images of moving subjects to convey the frantic pace of a busy world. The word "modern," however, meant different things to different people. The "modern" was the style and look of here and now, as opposed to yesterday. It was what the avant-garde did, whether the main body of cultural troops followed along behind them or not. Yet beyond a general understanding that one had to innovate to be modern, the word did not have a consistent denotation across the artistic spectrum, or even within a particular art.

To take an example from painting, art critics from Amédée Ozenfant in 1931 to Herbert Read in 1974 have pointed to Paul Cézanne, who died in 1906, as the originator of "modern" art. But what did Cézanne do? Ozenfant:

> Nevertheless, one moment particularly pregnant with possibilities for the future was when Cézanne, deliberately and more ambitiously than ever before, dared break away from nature. . . . Yes, the point of departure must be Cézanne: without him there would be no meaning in Cubism.[4]

Read:

> There is no doubt that what we call the modern movement in art begins with the single-minded determination of a French painter to see the world *objectively.* . . . Cézanne wished to exclude [the] shimmering and ambiguous surface of things and penetrate to the reality that did not change, that was present beneath the bright but deceptive picture presented by the kaleidoscope of the senses.[5]

Then is modernism in art a matter of seeing nature objectively or of breaking away from nature? The word itself conveying so little meaning, multitudes of artists, critics, and scholars in every field of high culture have felt free to interpret or define it, and therefore to set limits that would demarcate not just its beginning but also its end. The Chicago art critic C. J. Bulliet (this author's grandfather) wrote in 1936, for example:

> The art movement that was excitedly and indignantly known, during the first quarter of the present century, as Modernism has run its course. It began with Cézanne and ended with Picasso. . . . Modernism will now go the way of its immediate predecessor, Impressionism, measuring time until some new impulse is born into the world. It may be for decades, if civilization slows down; it may be for even a boresome century.[6]

For many and perhaps most consumers of high culture in the twentieth century, the definition of modernism has been irrelevant. Whatever it is, they haven't much liked it. Even in New York in the 1990s, Antonin Dvořák's familiar and evocative symphony *From the New World* (1893) draws vastly greater applause than the premier performance of a cello concerto by Russian composer Alfred K. Schnitte; Peter Martins's reworking of choreographer Marius Petipa's ballet *Sleeping Beauty* (1890) more applause than Mark Morris's new choreography for the *Nutcracker* called *The Hard Nut*; an exhibit of paintings by Vincent Van Gogh (died 1890) more praise than one devoted to the contemporary master of figure painting Balthus. A survey of the one hundred poems most frequently selected by editors for inclusion in English-language poetry anthologies yields twenty-one twentieth-century poems by fourteen poets.[7] Arch-modernists Ezra Pound, T. S. Eliot, and W. H. Auden are represented by one poem each and Dylan Thomas by two, but less experimental poets dominate: William Butler Yeats with five; Robert Frost and Edwin Arlington Robinson (considered by many America's greatest poet at the time of his death in 1935) with two; and Thomas Hardy, A. E. Housman, Wilfred Owen, and Walter de la Mare with one each.

From the point of view of boldness of innovation, Pablo Picasso's excursion into synthetic cubism after 1912, Jackson Pollock's action painting in the 1940s, and Francis Bacon's grotesquely distorted men coupling in strange geometrical cages or arenas in the 1950s attest to the vitality of the avant-garde in painting throughout the first half-century. Parallel examples could be adduced for the other arts, but a long list of names is not needed to make the point that Western high culture in that fifty-year period did, indeed, see an explosion of inventiveness and personal idiosyncrasy. But it also saw armies of imitative, derivative artists, musicians, and writers diligently—if often dully—troop off in the footsteps of the most recent trailblazer. The artistic creators who have garnered the highest critical acclaim have largely defined modernism through their works, but the actual experience of high culture in the lives and minds of most people of European descent has consisted of roughly one part avant-garde (if that much), three parts imitators of the previous generation's avant-garde, and six parts time-honored traditional favorites.

But what of Western high culture in the century's second half? The first postwar decade exhibited strong continuity from the prewar period. Under the label the New York School, a loose agglomeration of artists working in New York City, abstract expressionism and action painting swept an American art world that had remained devoted to figurative painting throughout the war. The Museum of Modern Art's *Art in Progress* exhibit of 1944 did not include any American abstract art. The conceptual roots of the New York School lay in the prewar European surrealism of painters like the Spaniard Joan Miró and the Chilean Roberto Matta Echaurren rather than in American art. The

Armenian-born painter Arshile Gorky and the theorist-painter Robert Motherwell exemplified this transatlantic linkage.

At the same time, the International Style of modern architecture flourished in response to pent-up demand for new buildings during the wartime years and the need to rebuild Europe's shattered cities. Ludwig Mies van der Rohe had designed an all-glass skyscraper in 1921 and become director of the Bauhaus in 1930 after its 1925 move from Weimar to Dessau (the Nazi regime closed it in 1933). After emigrating to the United States, he collaborated with Philip Johnson in designing the elegant Seagram Building in New York in 1956–58. Johnson had started his own architectural firm in 1953. I. M. Pei, a similarly influential designer of grand projects like the John Hancock Tower in Boston (1973), opened his firm in 1955. Finnish-born Eero Saarinen established his reputation with the General Motors Technical Center in Warren, Michigan (1951–55), as Edward Durrell Stone did with his design of the American Embassy in New Delhi in 1958. New York's Lincoln Center for the Performing Arts, a showplace for the Metropolitan Opera, the New York Philharmonic-Symphony Orchestra (under modernist composers Leonard Bernstein from 1956 to 1969 and Pierre Boulez from 1971 to 1978), and the New York City Ballet (under the century's foremost ballet choreographer, Russian-trained George Balanchine, from 1948 to 1983), was designed in the fifties and built between 1959 and 1972. Among its architects were Philip Johnson and Eero Saarinen.

By the end of the 1950s, however, some critics and scholars were beginning to wonder whether the frenetic pace of modernist innovation was exhausting itself. Pop art, which had just begun in Britain and flourished in the United States with artists like Andy Warhol and Roy Lichtenstein, lightheartedly combined comic strip art, commercial icons, everyday objects, and references to popular culture in a manner far removed from Cézanne's, or Picasso's, or from Pollock's struggle for personal expression. By duplicating commercial or photographic images, Warhol undermined the individuality of the artist, which had been a hallmark of modernism.

Pop art was but one of a series of post-New York School developments, such as op-art, minimalism, conceptual art, and earth art. Contemplating a monumental work of the last-named school, Robert Smithson's piled dirt *Spiral Jetty* (1970) in Utah's Great Salt Lake, it is difficult, indeed, to sense an ancestral linkage to Cézanne. In the same way, the postwar creations of John Cage show little trace of his studying composition with Arnold Schoenberg. In "4'33" "(1952), a pianist sat at a piano for four minutes and thirty-three seconds doing nothing, allowing the ambient sounds of the concert audience to fill the demarcated temporal space. His later works entitled "Variations" incorporated chance, indeterminacy, banal sounds, and pictorial elements in what most listeners heard as cacophony.

Explicit utter rejection of all antecedent notions of art, except dadaist nihilism, came from a small group of Parisians in the 1950s who called themselves the *Lettrist Internationale* (LI). Filmmaker Guy Debord, a central figure in the group, produced a film in 1952 entitled *Hurlements en faveur de Sade* ("Howls in Favor of de Sade") that contained no images at all. When it was first presented in London in 1957, the program warned:

> OUTRAGE? The film . . . caused riots when shown in Paris. The Institute is screening this film in the belief that members should be given a chance to make up their own minds about it, though the Institute wishes to be understood that it cannot be held responsible for the indignation of members who attend.[8]

It sold out. Debord wrote of the LI attitude toward art:

> Capitalism grants art a perpetual privileged concession, that of pure creative activity, an alibi for the alienation of all other activities . . . but at the same time, this sphere reserved for "free creative activity" is the only one in which the questions of what we do with life and of communication are posed practically and completely.[9]

Elsewhere he remarked that "the image has become the final form of commodity reification."[10] The LI goal was to spark a revolution that would eliminate artistry and unite creative production with real social and political life and day-to-day experience.

Warhol, Cage, and Debord—the latter virtually unknown outside a limited circle of the avant-garde—challenged critics and theorists who had been educated in the tradition of modernism. At the same time, the awakening of a rebellious student political conscience broke out in 1968 in mass demonstrations and calls for revolution on the streets of Paris and the campus of Columbia University in New York City. It evolved its own counterculture of nihilism and idealism, confirming a feeling that an era was coming to an end. But if modernism, with its myriad sub-isms, was ending, what was coming to take its place? Hold on for postmodernism.

The problems of defining modernism are compounded when one confronts the term postmodernism. As early as the 1950s, a few sorrowful individuals made use of the term to describe a post-Western, post-Christian world they felt themselves to be on the threshold of. The entry of the term into general intellectual debate dates largely to the 1980s, however. Where earlier observers had lamented the apparent exhaustion of cultural forms, postmodernist theorists like American Fredric Jameson and Frenchman Jean-Jacques Lyotard saw, if not a phoenix rising from the ashes of modernism, at least some sort of strange fledgling with potential powers of flight. Another postmodernist pioneer, American Charles Jencks, wrote in 1987:

> The mood on board the ship of Postmodernism is that of an Italian and Spanish crew looking for India, which may, if it's lucky, accidentally discover America: a crew which necessarily transports its cultural baggage and occasionally gets homesick, but one that is quite excited by the sense of liberation and promise of discoveries.[11]

(Of course, if the crew doesn't discover America, it will die at sea.)

If modernism was perceived as a general human condition brought on by the industrialization and world domination of the capitalist West, and modernism in the arts was associated with specific styles or techniques somehow derived from this, then postmodernism was perceived in the 1980s as a general human condition brought on by the passage from an industrial society into a computer-dominated information society, and the passage from a dominant Western culture to a global culture of the masses. But where commentators on modernism made direct analogies with what they saw happening in the economic realm—maintaining, for example, that streamlining furniture and appliance design, a common practice from the 1930s to 1940s, reflected the efficiency of industrial processes, and releasing of unconscious dreams and passions in expressionism and surrealism reflected the Freudian neuroses of modern society—the effort to extract definitions from works considered by one or another critic (though not necessarily by the creators themselves) to be postmodern has yet to find a consensus.

Theorist Charles Jencks, commenting on the field of architecture—where postmodernism is best accepted as a legitimate concept—identifies the following rules of postmodernism: 1. dissonant beauty or disharmonious harmony; 2. pluralism, both cultural and political; 3. for architects, urbane urbanism, that is, integration of buildings with their urban surroundings; 4. subliminal anthropomorphism, that is, designed allusions to the building's human inhabitants; 5. anamnesis (the opposite of amnesia), that is, remembering and making allusion to styles of the past; 6. divergent signification, meaning a concern for content but a willingness for that content to be interpreted in various ways; 7. double-coding, meaning the deliberate use of irony, ambiguity, and contradiction; 8. multivalence, that is, interconnection of the building with multiple aspects of its environment; 9. tradition reinterpreted, as in the use of eighteenth-century cabinetmaker Thomas Chippendale's curvilinear broken pediment design for the roof line of Philip Johnson's AT&T Building in New York City (1984); 10. elaboration of new rhetorical figures, such as the double-coding and ambiguity already mentioned; and 11. return to the absent center, by which Jencks means the designing of a central space that nevertheless remains ambiguously unoccupied.[12]

Fredric Jameson, on the other hand, looking more at the art of Andy Warhol than the architecture of Robert Venturi or James Stirling, is struck by "the emergence of a new kind of flatness or depthlessness, a new kind of superficiality in the most literal sense" and "the end of the bourgeois ego or monad [which] brings with it the end of the psychopathologies of that ego as well—what I have generally here been calling the waning of affect."[13] How these criteria might be applied to the works of architecture that Jencks comments on may not be apparent, but clearly a mighty intellectual effort is under way at the end of the twentieth century to interpret an apparent unraveling or incipient transformation (depending upon whether one likes or dislikes the works that inspire the theorizing) of "modern" Western culture over the past four decades.

What is in question is not simply high culture, because postmodern theorists generally reject the significance of earlier distinctions between high culture and something lower that has been designated popular, mass, or consumer culture. In advocating social and political pluralism, discarding the assumptions that served to identify the masterworks of modernity, and alluding to and reinterpreting tradition without observing old distinctions between "great" and "minor" creative works, the theorists and practitioners of postmodernism embrace and validate the current and previous forms of representation that the last several generations of people of European descent who considered themselves cultured were schooled—formally or by social convention—to despise, disregard, or throw away: comics, snapshots, TV sitcoms, advertising, rock music, bygone crafts, kitsch trinkets, movie star memorabilia, pornography, and the written and visual works of feminists, gay men, lesbians, people of color, and non-Westerners in general. In other words, the high culture of Matthew Arnold that the Chicago industrialists underwriting the city's first resident opera company in 1910 took for granted had ceased to exist in the minds and writing of many of the West's leading intellectuals at century's end.

Other cultural commentators disagreed strenuously, and displayed nothing but contempt for the cultural relativism and jargon-laden obscurity of many postmodernist tracts. Hence the virulence of American debates in the 1990s over what should be considered a "great book" in a university curriculum, or whether public funds should be used to exhibit the homosexually explicit photographs of Robert Mapplethorpe. Adding an element of confusion, in some cultural areas the term postmodernism in itself seemed fragile. The 1960s postmodernism of choreographers Yvonne Rainer and Trisha Brown, for example, which relied on spare mathematical formulas, pedestrian movements, and a disdain for music and theatricality in general, had already been superseded by the post-postmodernism or "late" postmodernism of Bill T. Jones in the 1970s.

Taking leave of the shouts and harangues of a divided Western intelligentsia quarreling over what is becoming of its culture at the end of the twentieth century, let us return to the discussion broached earlier of the relationship of Western high culture to the rest of the world. The phenomenon of cultural imperialism is undeniable. Art patrons in non-Western countries oriented politically and economically toward Western Europe and the United States—such as Egypt, prerevolutionary Iran, and Japan—increasingly supported, as the century progressed, the efforts of indigenous artists working in modern European styles. Similarly, non-Western peoples associated politically and economically with the Soviet Union, or non-Europeans living within the Soviet Union, wholeheartedly adopted the socialist realism of the Stalinist era, and eschewed Western modernism.

By the end of the nineteenth century a few adventurous individuals in contact with Western influences had already begun to experiment with European-style novels, dramas, verse forms, and pictorial art. Up to World War II, however, the market for such products remained small. Western styles made stronger inroads during the first half of the century in popular genres that produced more immediate financial returns: cinema, where by 1930 Japan was producing as many movies as Hollywood; advertising; picture journalism; and so forth.

During the first two postwar decades, however, works inspired or informed by Western styles and sensibilities proliferated. This was the heyday of "development theory" in the West, a body of social scientific theorizing that extrapolated, from such material changes in the non-Western world as the spread of radios, electricity, and highways, a prediction of inexorable reorientation of political and social institutions—and eventually mental processes—in the direction of Western models. Large numbers of students from non-Western countries began to study in Europe, the United States, and the Soviet

Union, and vastly larger numbers enrolled in newly created or expanded state school systems structured, for the most part, around Western-style curricula. Graduates of new state universities or those returning with foreign degrees moved readily into elite social and economic positions.

Culturally, their tastes tended toward the West, as had the tastes of a smaller educated elite of the prewar period. To be sure, they still bought local products, but they did not usually think of them as high culture. Indigenous arts and crafts rooted in the traditions of earlier centuries often looked to the tourist or export trade for survival. This reorientation was usually accompanied by a loss in quality of production, as foreigners were less skilled in distinguishing good from mediocre and as the rug weavers, cloth dyers, bronzesmiths, miniature painters, jade and ivory carvers, and potters realized that their products were losing some of their appeal among wealthy people within their own society. To be sure, wealthy Iranians in the 1970s continued to invest in fine knotted rugs, but a millionaire's home with beautiful rugs on the floor might well have a nineteenth-century French bronze on the Louis Quinze sidetable, a "modern" painting on the wall, and a Mozart concerto playing from the stereo.

Ironically, as the quality of artistic production in traditional non-Western styles declined, a lively interest in those styles grew among a few collectors and scholars in the West. Traditional African woodcarving, for example, found a robust market, but one in which discerning dealers and collectors took pains to acquire "genuine" art objects—that is, older carvings originally intended for religious or other use locally, and not those produced solely for the tourist or export trade. Whether buying exotic art objects or viewing performances while traveling in distant lands, European and American patrons of non-Western culture were attracted in part because they thought of these art forms as vanishing, or as immutable classic expressions of otherwise lost traditions. And precisely among those Western patrons whose modernist attitude toward their own high culture put the highest premium on originality and innovation, too many signs of life in an exotic art raised concerns that classic forms were becoming corrupt.

In the 1960s, for example, the state rug factory in Ashkabad, the capital of the Soviet Socialist Republic of Turkmenistan, brought together dozens of Turkmen women and girls to practice skills they traditionally employed in villages and nomadic camps. Using time-honored methods, the factory produced excellent hand-knotted rugs featuring the distinctive geometrical patterns of the various Turkmen tribes. But it also turned out rugs featuring new designs based on the white boll of the cotton plant, since cotton was at that time a new cash crop in Turkmenistan, made possible by a long-distance canal that brought irrigation water to the desert. Though the Soviet cultural practice of extolling every economic advance doubtless made these rugs appealing to some buyers, Western visitors considered the new designs a betrayal not only of the traditional patterns, but of the entire pastoral way of life of the Turkmen.

The desire to see non-Western artistic creations as historically frozen exhibits in a universal Museum of Human Culture corresponded to the Western theoretical notion that the trajectory of global economic and political development, along either capitalist or socialist lines, would inevitably bring all the world's peoples into some sort of alignment with the cultural expressions of modern Western society in one of its forms. Each nation was viewed idealistically as being endowed with a particular artistic, cultural inheritance in which it could take pride and which would make its people distinctive within the emerging global society. But that inheritance was more often considered a relic of times gone by, at least at its best, than as something still evolving toward greater perfection. Arts that had been formally frozen for the longest periods of time, such as Japanese Noh drama, were particularly admired.

Under these circumstances, the crisis of Western high culture—assuming that a growing disinclination of people who regard themselves as cultured to wax ecstatic over newly produced "art" music, poetry, and art can be called a crisis—will inevitably have repercussions in other parts of the world. Postmodernism is still not a household expression, and in many intellectual households it is an expression uttered with contempt, but the sense that culture has been heading in a new and different direction since the 1960s is widely accepted even when it is being deplored. Whether, at century's end, a conservative reaction against cultural pluralism, relativism, and acceptance of popular culture as the truest expression of Western civilization will firmly set in, somehow reinvigorating or relegitimating the cultural forms of the nineteenth and first half of the twentieth century, cannot be determined. But even it this were to happen, the cachet of Western high culture in other parts of the world will have suffered a grievous blow.

With the collapse of the Soviet Union and its associated socialist regimes at the beginning of the 1990s, the rationale for people in other lands to orient themselves culturally toward Western socialist or capitalist models largely evaporated. For forty-five years after World War II, socialists and communists everywhere tried to embody their populist, internationalist, scientific, and humanitarian ideals in the very living of their lives. Where they stood in the world confrontation between socialism and capitalism influenced the novels, plays, and poems they read and wrote; the pictures and sculpture they viewed or created; and even the buildings they designed or lived and worked in. The same thing was true of people worldwide who saw their personal lives and fortunes deriving from the success of the Western capitalist model and the defeat of the socialist alternative. But with that battle concluded, and the core populations of the victorious side deeply uncertain of the continuing vitality of the artistic values and cultural forms that prevailed throughout most of the conflict, the way may have been cleared for an efflorescence of diverse cultures throughout the world.

Some observers believe that the culture of the future will lack a clear distinction between high and low. Depending upon their taste, they visualize it either as a wasteland of rock music, television, exploitation films, and mindless glorification of iconic superstars, or as a long-awaited elimination of the artificialities of cultural class division which taught a privileged elite to "appreciate" (and pay for) bogus cultural values and despise the unlettered masses for not sharing their refined tastes. Both of these lines of thought unwittingly perpetuate the myopia and self-regard of the West, however, in that they relegate the rest of the world to the role of observing the culinary mayhem in the Western cultural kitchen and then passively consuming whatever mess or delight it ultimately serves up. Given that the weight of world economic activity seems to be shifting irreversibly, or at least rebalancing itself, in the direction of Asia, it is imprudent to assume that cultural tastes—high, low, or otherwise—will not be affected along with everything else that engages market values.

Direct challenges to Western cultural imperialism represent one direction of change. Since 1979, the Islamic Republic of Iran has been at odds with the West in any number of ways. Ideologically, the implantation of an activist interpretation of Shi'ite Islam at the center of state and society has carried with it a specific rejection of cultural imperialism. Writer Jalal Al-e Ahmad, a key figure in the coalescence of an intellectual and political challenge to the Shah's regime, used the term *gharbzadegi* (West-struckness or Westoxication) to describe prerevolutionary Iranians who turned their back on their own culture, both religious and artistic, and aped Western tastes.

Putting Al-e Ahmad's ideas into practice in postrevolutionary Iran has meant establishing centers for teaching and developing traditional arts and crafts. For the most part, the fate of this effort is yet to be determined, but Iranian classical music is already experiencing a renaissance. In the 1970s, classical forms in Iranian music were clearly eroding, and Western instruments such as the guitar were gaining favor along with Western verse and melodic forms. *Musiq-e pop-e Irani*, or Iranian Pop Music, was enormously popular and continues to be so among exiled Iranians in Los Angeles and elsewhere. Within Iran, however, the Ayatollah Khomeini decreed a ban on inappropriate musical forms. As a consequence, Iranians inside the country and out now throng concerts given by musicians who adhere to the classic *dastgahs*, or modes, but who, in the Iranian tradition, also improvise during their performances. Instruments, too, have been affected: the *daf*, a broad, shallow drum, and the *kamancheh*, a small viol played vertically, have returned from near oblivion.

In lieu of political confrontation, money may be the key to the revival of world cultural diversity. In 1986, the International Commission for the Preservation of Islamic Cultural Heritage, an arm of the Organization of the Islamic Conference to which most of the world's oil-rich states belong, announced its first international Arabic calligraphy competition, since then repeated every three years. Calligraphers throughout the world's Islamic community compete for substantial cash prizes in fourteen different calligraphic styles— undoubtedly contributing to the revival of calligraphy in many countries. Similarly, in 1980 the Aga Khan, the leader of the world's Ismaili Shi'ites, began to sponsor a well-funded international competition in Islamic architecture intended not only to encourage new designs that would draw on traditional forms, but to address concretely the social situations of Muslims around the world.

Yet a third avenue to the restoration of world cultural diversity may be a heightened valuation of local popular art forms that have escaped the ossification of many of the traditionally more elite arts. *Lakhon Chatri*, for example, is a humorous and bawdy form of popular dance-drama from Thailand usually performed by groups who travel through the countryside. Though the costumes and movements are traditional, the dance has a strong improvisational element that allows the performers to update their humor—even to the extent, in the case of a troupe that played in New York City in 1994, of including a large plastic Coca-Cola bottle as a prop. A parallel case is that of Pakistani *Qawwali* music. Improvisation and a call-and-response format between the lead singer and the rest of the musicians, accompanied by a small harmonium and other instruments, makes for a lively and emotional performance that has long appealed to popular Pakistani audiences oriented toward Sufism, or Islamic mysticism. Despite these popular roots, however, Qawwali singers were enthusiastically received outside Pakistan in concerts in the 1990s.

Finally, it is possible that the debates over postmodernism underway in Europe and the United States will mark the boundary between a period when the force of modernism resided primarily in the West, and a subsequent period of flagging Western creativity when the cultural forms that originated in Europe are elaborated further primarily by non-Europeans. Already there can be no question that Latin American writers like Jorge Luis Borges (Argentina), Isabel Allende (Chile), Gabriel García Márquez (Colombia), Julio Cortázar (Argentina), and Octavio Paz (Mexico) have achieved broader international acclaim than prizewinning American writers like Donald Barthelme, John Barth, and William Gaddis, who similarly experimented with new narrative forms from the 1960s onward.

Whatever the future may hold, the history of high culture in the twentieth century has been tumultuous. At its beginning, the distinction between high and low was unquestioned, at least in Europe and America, and the canon of works and artists that cultured people could reasonably be expected to be familiar with was well-established, though it differed from country to country. At its end, for every highly educated postmodernist attempting to analyze an apparent sea change in culture (as well as in social life, politics, and economics) that first showed itself in the 1960s, there can be matched an equally erudite and refined individual who eschews television; reads no novelists later than Anthony Trollope (died 1882); considers serious music to have suffered a progressive decline after Mozart (died 1791); and dotes on impressionist painting (and perhaps also Van Gogh—who died in 1890).

In the United States a national debate erupted over the publication in 1987 of E. D. Hirsch, Jr.'s book *Cultural Literacy: What Every American Needs to Know.* Though the author broadmindedly included James Joyce, Igor Stravinsky, and cubism (though not Ezra Pound, Charles Ives, and dada) along with Jane Austen, Ludwig van Beethoven, and impressionism, the very idea that every high school graduate in the country, regardless of race, gender, national heritage, or social background, should be expected to know—much less esteem— the same set of cultural icons raised hackles. To Hirsch's critics, his views seemed little different from those articulated in John Franklin Brown's *The American High School* in 1909: "In no case should either the course of study or the spirit of the work in the high school be such as to subordinate the culture ideal to any other."[14] An alternative vision was adumbrated in 1991 by curator Kirk Varnedoe's presentation of the show *High and Low: Modern Art and Popular Culture* at the Museum of Modern Art in New York City. The exhibit (sponsored, one should note, by the AT&T Corporation) was devoted to showing the influence of graffiti, caricature, comics, and advertising on "fine art" in the twentieth century. It clearly demonstrated that whatever the canon of cultural importance inculcated in high schools and universities, artists in the twentieth century have been open to stimuli from every aspect of human life.

How and when the consensus of Western opinion on the subject of high culture came apart has varied from country to country. Nazism, communism, and other state ideologies strongly affected the course of the arts in some places. More broadly, however, the evolution of high culture has reflected the character of patronage for the arts, and this, in turn, has been affected by changes in educational indoctrination and the rise in importance—aided by technological innovations that had comparatively little impact on the established fine arts—of various forms of popular culture. At century's end, it seems extraordinarily unlikely that a new consensus on the standards of high culture will emerge anytime soon in the West. On the other hand, though some would argue that high culture as a concept is dead and not to be lamented, differences in wealth among individuals and nations will surely continue throughout the century to come, and it seems unlikely that well-heeled patrons, whether individuals, institutions, or public art commissions, will abandon the age-old human desire to distinguish oneself from less fortunate people by a display of "higher" taste.

The disarray of Western high culture may well redound to the benefit of the other peoples of the world, however. The twentieth century dawned with most of the world under the control of European imperialism. The twenty-first century begins with a multitude of independent states, some of which will have the means to patronize the arts quite lavishly. Though the worldwide dystopia of mass consumer culture predicted by some visionaries may well come into being, it is likely to be accompanied by a flowering of renewed non-Western cultural traditions.

ENDNOTES

1. Peter Neagoe, *What Is Surrealism?* (Paris: New Review Publications, 1932), p. 5.

2. Herbert Read, ed., *Surrealism* (London: Faber and Faber, 1936), pp. 19–20.

3. Ambroise Vollard, *Cézanne* (New York: Dover, 1984).

4. Amédée Ozenfant, *Foundations of Modern Art* (New York: Brewer, Warren and Putnam, 1931), pp. 49–50.

5. Herbert Read, *A Concise History of Modern Painting*, rev. ed. (New York: Oxford University Press, 1974), p. 13.

6. C. J. Bulliet, *The Significant Moderns and Their Pictures* (New York: Covici Friede, 1936), pp. v–vi.

7. William Harmon, ed., *The Classic Hundred: All-Time Favorite Poems* (New York: Columbia University Press, 1990).

8. Greil Marcus, *Lipstick Traces: A Secret History of the Twentieth Century* (Cambridge: Harvard University Press, 1989), p. 332.

9. Ibid., p. 211.

10. As quoted in Fredric Jameson, *Postmodernism, or The Cultural Logic of Late Capitalism* (Durham: Duke University Press, 1991).

11. Jencks, *Postmodernism* (New York: Rizzoli International Publications, 1987).

12. Ibid.

13. Jameson, *Postmodernism.*

14. As quoted in Henry F. May, *The End of American Innocence: A Study of the First Years of Our Own Time 1912–1917* (New York: Knopf, 1959; reprint, New York: Columbia University Press, 1992), p. 42.

SELECTED REFERENCES

Docherty, Thomas, ed. *Postmodernism: A Reader.* New York: Columbia University Press, 1993.

Giedion, Sigfried. *Space, Time and Architecture.* Cambridge: Harvard University Press, 1941.

Herdeg, Klaus. *The Decorated Diagram: Harvard Architecture and the Failure of the Bauhaus Legacy.* Cambridge: MIT Press, 1983.

Jameson, Fredric. *Postmodernism, or The Cultural Logic of Late Capitalism.* Durham: Duke University Press, 1991.

Jencks, Charles. *Postmodernism.* New York: Rizzoli International Publications, 1987.

Marcus, Greil. *Lipstick Traces: A Secret History of the Twentieth Century.* Cambridge: Harvard University Press, 1989.

May, Henry F. *The End of American Innocence: A Study of the First Years of Our Own Time 1912–1917.* New York: Knopf, 1959; reprint, New York: Columbia University Press, 1992.

Ozenfant, Amédée. *Foundations of Modern Art.* New York: Brewer, Warren and Putnam, 1931.

Varnedoe, Kirk and Adam Gopnik. *High and Low: Modern Art and Popular Culture.* New York: The Museum of Modern Art, 1991.

# 2    Popular Culture

RICHARD W. BULLIET

*you let me violate you. you let me desecrate you*
*you let me penetrate you. you let me complicate you*

From Kyrgyzstan to Kuala Lumpur to Kansas City, in 1994 MTV conveyed the sounds and words of Nine Inch Nails to the thrilled ears of mesmerized teenagers and the horrified ears of such of their elders as dared or deigned to listen. For most people for whom the end of the millennium has more or less coincided with plans for retirement, the acronym MTV stands for the utter demise of taste and standards, and the advent of a worldwide popular culture rooted in the basest of human instincts: sex, violence, and the commercialization of vulgarity.

Turning the calendar back to 1898, critic W. J. Henderson sang the same melody in *The New York Times Illustrated Magazine*:

> First of all, abolish the music halls in which the vulgar tunes set to still more vulgar words provide the musical milk upon which the young of the masses are reared. Abolish the diabolical street pianos and hand organs which disseminate their vile tunes in all directions and which reduce the musical taste of the children in the residence streets to the level of that of the Australian bushman, who thinks noise and rhythm are music.

St. Augustine said pretty much the same thing in the fifth century A.D. in his treatise *De Musica*. Elevated disgust with popular taste is constant; only the music changes.

From 1898 to 1930, M. Witmark & Sons was one of the most successful publishers of popular music in New York. However, a list of almost five hundred of their greatest hits issued during that period yields only a dozen or so titles—"Irene Goodnight," "Tip Toe Through the Tulips with Me," "My Wild Irish Rose," "Sweet Adeline"—that would be widely recognized in the United States a century later. "Ma Is Playing Mah Jong" and "I'm on the Water Wagon Now" are long forgotten. So, fortunately, are such race tunes, then popular with whites (though often composed by blacks), as "All Coons Look Alike to

Me" and "Mammy's Little Pumpkin Colored Coon." These latter would almost certainly offend sensitive ears at the end of the twentieth century as much as any rap music lyrics.

The most distinctive aspect of popular culture in the twentieth century, then, is neither a tale of civilized taste and sensitivity being gradually overcome by vulgar, commercialized junk, as some would hold, nor, as more recent devotees of cultural studies would have it, of an increasingly successful struggle of popular cultural forms, rooted in late-capitalist economic necessities, against an entrenched and institutionalized arts establishment bent on preserving the archaic and artificial standards that undergird its power. Though both of these scenarios are important, their analogues were written in the nineteenth century, if not before, when absinthe-drenched Parisian bohemians inveighed against the academy that disdained not just their paintings (now sometimes judged masterpieces), but their vulgar, dance hall lifestyle as well. This clash of perspectives simply continues.

What is new to the story of popular culture in the twentieth century is the tale of how this century's all-pervasive technological and economic changes have affected this ongoing clash as well, and in the process broadened it beyond Europe and America to encompass the entire world. Duplication, dissemination, preservation, and commercialization, along with the reductions in cost derived from all four, are the most obvious areas in which technology has had its impact.

Printed words began to be duplicated on a large scale in Europe in the fifteenth century, and in East Asia much earlier, and the techniques of etching and of engraving on wood and metal progressed in tandem so that books and broadsides could carry pictures as well as words. However, these earlier technological developments only marginally intruded on the domain of popular culture. So long as printed materials were expensive and populations remained largely rural and illiterate—as they did in most parts of the world up to the twentieth century—printed words were of considerably less importance in everyday life than oral communication. Performances by traveling players, musicians, and acrobats; recitations of tales and ballads dealing with current events and/or incorporating time-honored images and passages; design and decoration of domiciles and utilitarian objects; and participation in dances and musical entertainments, later termed "folk" or "ethnic," constituted the core of popular culture throughout the world. And all relied more on memory, custom, apprenticeship, and the spontaneous recomposition of generally known motifs than on printed matter or duplicated images.

Lithography, invented in Munich around 1796 by Aloys Senefelder, marked the first step in expanding the concept of visual duplication, and hence of broad dissemination. Since drawing or writing on lithographic stone was unconstrained by the cramped, laborious, and expensive processes of cutting wood or metal, and thousands more copies could be made without deterioration than could be printed from a fragile metal etching, the essentially unlimited reproduction of images became a reality. In Europe artists like Honoré Daumier and Henri de Toulouse-Lautrec popularized the artistic use of lithography, and it had a broad impact in such areas as newspaper illustration. In India, Iran, and the Arab world, it touched off an explosion in book publishing, since the elegant, cursive forms of the Arabic script favored in those countries could not then be attractively reproduced through typesetting.

Photography followed lithography, developed between 1816 and 1839 by Frenchmen Joseph Nicéphore Niepce and Louis Daguerre working together, and Englishmen William Talbot and John Herschel contributing independently. In 1881, photoengraving inaugurated the process of reproducing photographs in newspapers, which would improve by leaps and bounds in the twentieth century. In 1888, the American George Eastman introduced roll film and the simple box camera and, from that time on, photography split. Artists like Alfred Stieglitz fought successfully to get recognition for photography as a fine art, though one uniquely open to public appreciation because of its reproducibility and wide exposure in magazines like *Life* (founded in 1936) and *Look* (founded in 1937).

At the same time, however, steadily increasing numbers of people took to the camera as a device for preserving images and events of primarily personal meaning in slides and snapshots. This latter tendency accelerated with the introduction of color slide film in 1935, color prints in 1942, the Polaroid Land camera that developed film in a matter of seconds in 1947, inexpensive cameras with automatic focus and exposure in the 1980s, and the disposable camera in the 1990s.

On a parallel track, experiments with the illusion of motion created by rapidly alternating images yielded the motion pictures of the Frenchmen E. J. Marey and Emile Reynaud and the American Thomas Edison in the 1880s. In France, Louis and Auguste Lumière developed a projector in 1895, and on March 28 showed a fifty-foot film featuring behatted shop girls in *Lunch Hour at the Lumière Factory*. The first nickelodeon theater opened in Pittsburgh in 1905. Talkies arrived in 1927.

Sound reproduction kept pace with the visual media. Edison's carbon microphone in 1877 and phonograph in 1878 spelled the eventual doom of the popular sheet music industry and the itinerant piano salesman, ensuring that when commercial radio broadcasting began in 1922, music would become universally accessible instead of dependent on the capricious distribution of talent and live performance. Television, of course, marked the marriage of the moving picture and the radio broadcast. Though delayed by World War II, it boomed in the postwar years and received a further boost in 1956, when Ampex won the technological race to adapt the audio tape recorder—invented in wartime Germany and later perfected in the United States under the patronage of crooner Bing Crosby—to the recording of video pictures.

The 1980s saw the climax of this trajectory of technological development in the booming of VCR sales worldwide; massive increases in the availability and economy of xerography—electrostatic printing having been invented by American Chester Carlson in 1938 and offered commercially by Xerox in 1959—and the personal computer revolution that has promised to bring desktop publishing, photo editing, animation, and the retrieval of unlimited quantities of digitally stored sounds, pictures, and texts into every home equipped with a clever teenager. Then, in the 1990s, came the Internet.

The threat to long-held notions of high or elite culture posed by these developments materialized slowly in the early twentieth century, partly because the new technologies' initial high costs or demands on skill clouded the prospect of dissemination among the public at large, and partly because the moneyed classes who underwrote the institutional props of what they considered high culture could not conceive of snapshots, flickering motion picture pantomimes, and scratchy gramophone records as significant cultural competition. Though live performances of operas and symphony orchestras became a mainstay of radio broadcasting, and dramatic actors, particularly in Europe, initially fancied seeing themselves mutely mouthing the lines of their stage plays on film, lithography, photography, and other essentially unlimited visual reproduction techniques were long shunned by most serious artists because they diluted the financially potent concept of an "original," and acoustic amplification was eschewed for live performances of "art" music.

Each of the arts thought of as "fine" by turn-of-the-century European and American connoisseurs, of course, arose from and remained embedded in a continuum of creative performance or artisanship that, in varying manifestations, appealed to every social and economic stratum. At the turn of the century, traveling Shakespeare companies, such as Robert Bruce Mantell's, crisscrossed the United States and Canada playing to enthusiastic audiences of common folk. Composers of art music were intensifying their exploitation of melodies and rhythms from popular dance and balladry. And the self-taught

French artist Henri Rousseau achieved somewhat patronizing critical recognition with a painting style derived from what Museum of Modern Art curator Daniel Catton Rich later called the "retarded idiom of folk painting which, especially since 1800, had been practiced all over Europe and the New World."[1] Other "primitives" were to follow.

The prevailing assumption within Western culture at the turn of the century was that the distinction between the fine arts and mere folk crafts and entertainments was deeply meaningful, and that the melodies, rhythms, dance steps, comedic styles, and iconography of the common folk were best thought of as a kind of grab bag from which true artists of loftier vision could snatch occasional inspiration. But this distinction was not shared worldwide. To be sure, in some cultural regions, certain types of creative performance or production carried deeper meanings or enjoyed special regard. Religion, for example, imparted special significance to Hindu temple dancing and to the Shi'ite Iranian passion play reenacted every year in commemoration of the death of the Imam Husain ibn Ali. Similarly, a communal or tribal feeling informed group dancing and singing rituals in Africa and elsewhere; and sculptured totemic figures served symbolic functions in parts of the East Indies, the Pacific Northwest, and elsewhere.

But the association with religion or social ritual did not necessarily connote a difference in aesthetic quality. A person who sang or danced or sculpted in a non-Western symbolic context was not thereby felt to be intrinsically superior to a nonsymbolic performer or craftsperson in the way an academically trained portrait painter in England was felt by art patrons to be superior to a skilled painter of pub signs or theater backdrops.

Even in Japan, where the distinctions between popular and elite culture to some degree paralleled those in Europe, popular woodblock prints were not denigrated by the cognoscenti as artistically inferior, however vulgar their subject matter, in the way mass-produced Currier & Ives lithographs were in the United States. More than any other turn-of-the-century pattern of arts patronage, that of the West—as embodied in the formally expressed tastes of the most prosperous and educated social strata—was wedded to the concept of the artistic masterpiece, whether literary, dramatic, musical, or visual, and convinced that any creative activity that did not recognize and strive toward that empyrean designation was beneath the consideration of seriously cultured people.

This exaggerated conceptual gulf between the most elevated and the most common domains of creativity profoundly affected cultural and artistic responses to new technologies. For a critical half-century—until, roughly, the

1950s—popular culture embraced technology while high culture, with the exception of architecture, flirted with it and then shunned it. (The exception of architecture, where technological innovations like steel frame construction and reinforced concrete utterly transformed turn-of-the-century beaux arts styles, is illustrative of what might have happened in other artistic arenas if technology had been fully embraced. Yet even here, patrons of culture commonly expressed distaste for mass-produced, prefabricated structures, as opposed to unique monuments of architectural creativity.)

Photography provides an apt illustration. So long as photography remained expensive and difficult, artists felt both intrigued and threatened by its realism. Eugène Delacroix and Thomas Eakins were among those nineteenth-century painters who, without publicizing the fact, partially based paintings on photographs. At the same time, many photographers leaned strongly toward landscapes, portraits, and posed compositions that mimicked easel paintings. Toward the century's end, however, more and more easel painters turned away from realism, tacitly conceding the field to the camera. And an ever more extravagant taste for abstraction, distortion, unnatural colors, and drawing that struck viewers as being childish would soon dominate what came to be known in the twentieth century as "modern art."

As a consequence, photography seemed to have less and less to offer the ambitious artist, except for those few who adopted it as their medium. The number of artists in the interwar period for whom photographs were as important a medium as drawing or painting was negligible—Man Ray, Laszlo Moholy-Nagy, a few others. Occasionally a painter who remained wedded to precise realism, like Charles Sheeler, also worked in photography. Most photographers, however, related less to the world of art galleries, art critics, and museums upon which painters and sculptors depended than to a pyramid of activity that descended through fashion photography, advertising layout, and photojournalism to the everyday snapshot without significantly overlapping the world of fine art. When "commercial artists" experimented, sometimes brilliantly, with combining photography with drawing and typography, as became common in advertising, the art world declared that their work was not truly artistic.

The aversion to photography by painters and etchers throughout the first half of the century reflects not so much snobbishness on their part as the reluctance of the official art world of collectors, dealers, critics, curators, and academic art experts to accept as serious a medium that permitted unlimited reproduction. Only five of the 271 "contemporary" photographs in the landmark *Photography 1839–1937* exhibition at the Museum of Modern Art in New

York were owned by the museum, and none were loaned by other art museums. For the wealthy art collector, a high-quality reproduction of a woodcut or etching might look almost identical to a print pulled directly from the plate; but the artist's signature, the numbering of the edition, and the assurance that only a limited number of prints existed—all authenticated through the knowledge purveyed by dealers, critics, curators, and experts—justified a dramatically higher price. Artists were understandably loath to jeopardize their incomes by overproducing identical images.

By contrast, the collectors' market for photographs with limited numbers of signed prints competed with the far larger magazine and advertising market. Easel painters made their livings from gallery exhibitions, museum purchases, private patrons, and teaching, but photographers had more options. Though the number of galleries, museums, and private collectors interested in photography was smaller, the demand for advertising and magazine illustration was insatiable. Responding to that demand, however, confirmed the opinion of many people in the art world that photography was less than a fine art, except when practiced by famous figures like Richard Avedon or Margaret Bourke-White.

The casting-down of a new technology from the aesthetic heights of high culture recurred in the areas of music and theater. The records of Metropolitan Opera star Enrico Caruso, who died in 1921, were considered treasures by early owners of phonographs. No opera singer since has had so strong an impact on record sales. However, one did not need a voice capable of reaching the tenth balcony of an opera house to make an appealing phonograph record. Thus, as records, phonographs, and recording equipment became more common and less expensive, buyers indulged their taste for common pleasures to an ever greater degree, relegating the so-called "art" music to a diminishing part of the recording industry, and indirectly dictating the musical taste of radio broadcasting. "Art" musicians continued to depend primarily on live audiences drawn largely from the well-to-do. Popular musicians, however, from guitar-playing Mississippi field hands to Harlem blues singers to well-oiled big band crooners, depended proportionately more on recordings to reach their audience—or at least their agents and recording companies did.

Relations between live theatrical performance and motion pictures similarly moved from initial interest and even enthusiasm to growing distance. From the outset, all levels of the public were fascinated by the phenomenon of moving pictures, with their capacity to depict outdoor settings, cut from one scene to another, and show closeups of actors—all impossible in live drama. A few famous actors, such as Joseph Jefferson and Sarah Bernhardt, had bits of performance put on film as early as 1895–1900. But it was the initial 1908 screening in Paris of *The Assassination of the Duc de Guise* by the newly formed Film d'Art company that touched off a decade of European enthusiasm for cinema as a handmaiden of the stage. Eminent directors, actors, writers, and even composers eagerly contributed their efforts to artistic filmmaking that seldom ventured creatively beyond the bounds of theater performance.

In America, meanwhile, in 1909, Edison organized a handful of large producers of one-reel nickelodeon films into the Motion Picture Patents Company—the Trust, for short—for the purpose of monopolizing the new industry through exclusive licenses to his inventions. Given their monopoly position, Trust producers had little incentive to improve their product. But the smaller "outlaw" producers, who had to travel light and put up with goon intimidation and prudent sojourns outside U.S. jurisdiction (hence part of their attraction to Hollywood, which was conveniently near the Mexican border), felt the need to produce longer and more appealing films to entice exhibitors into defying the Trust's monopoly.

This rough and ready business climate was a far cry from the warm embrace given to Film d'Art by the Comédie Française. Many of the "outlaws" and their successors came from humble social origins: William Fox, of Twentieth Century Fox, had been a secondhand clothes dealer. Adolph Zukor, who became the central figure in forming Paramount Pictures, and Marcus Loew, whose company eventually became part of Metro-Goldwyn-Mayer, were both furriers. The latter company's namesakes, Samuel Goldwyn and Louis B. Mayer, were immigrants, from Poland and Russia respectively. And the four Warner brothers, whose late-forming company pioneered sound films, started out operating a string of theaters in Ohio.

Three thousand miles removed from the cultural centers of New York and Boston, these Hollywood movie moguls were more impressed by purely cinematic innovations—such as moving the camera to give the viewer multiple vantage points instead of the single one afforded by a seat at a live performance—than they were by Broadway stars. But they did not turn their backs on the stage. In fact, they made two-thirds of the plays that won Pulitzer Prizes between 1928 and 1943 into movies, and one of them, George S. Kaufman and Moss Hart's *You Can't Take It with You* (1937), won the Academy Award for best picture the following year. But they largely preferred to train (and control) their own actors, and a gulf steadily widened between performers and directors involved in stage productions and those who were part of the movie industry.

Flirtations between new technologies and established fields of high culture that cooled into disdain—the common experience of the first half of the century—protected the exclusivity of high culture and thereby the role that subscribing to operas, ballets, symphony orchestras, theaters, and museums played in maintaining or confirming membership in the rapidly growing middle class. However, this also had the effect of cutting off most artists and performers involved in high culture from the creative opportunities opened up by these same technologies. As a result, by the 1960s, when creative minds in the world of high culture—practitioners and patrons alike—finally began to turn seriously to new forms and techniques, they found that the world of popular culture had become so technically sophisticated and innovative that they felt constrained to take their cues from it despite what they considered its commercialization and vulgar taste. In short, the superiority of technique and performance that at the turn of the century had accompanied the well-entrenched sense that high culture was vastly more elevated than popular culture was now in substantial measure reversed.

The emotionally moving quality of certain small voices, hoarse voices, whispering voices, or falsetto voices had presumably always been known to small groups of people fortunate enough to know a gifted singer or speaker. But public performance voices—famous voices—had to have volume in the days before amplification. Whether opera diva or leather-lunged politician, the one who communicated best vocally was the one who could be heard in the back of the auditorium. Continuous improvements in amplification and recording removed this necessity. A late-twentieth-century operatic tenor like Luciano Pavarotti or lieder singer like Dietrich Fischer-Dieskau deploys vocal skills very like those similar stars had a century earlier. But singers like Billie Holliday, Pete Seeger, Ray Charles, Buddy Holly, Elvis Presley, Joni Mitchell, and Axl Rose could not have attracted devoted mass followings in the days before amplification and recording.

Amplification similarly affected instrumental music. The nineteenth century had witnessed myriad technical innovations in instrumentation, including the invention of the saxophone (by the Belgian Adolphe Sax, 1842), harmonium (by the Frenchman Alexandre Debain, 1840), and sousaphone (by the American J.W. Pepper, 1892) and greatly improved keying systems for the flute (by the German Theobald Boehm, 1830s) and clarinet (by the Frenchman Hyacinthe Klose, 1839). But performers of classical music in the twentieth century did not take easily to the next technological step, electronic amplification. The electric organ, invented in 1935, achieved glory in the Wurlitzer Company's extravagant movie organs rather than in concerts by the master of baroque music E. Power Biggs. The electric guitar, associated primarily with the pioneering developments of Les Paul around 1946, became the chosen instrument for acoustic experimentation by Jimi Hendrix, Eric Clapton, and scores of other blues and rock musicians, but was disdained by classical guitarists like the Spaniard Andrés Segovia. And Lionel Hampton, the foremost master of the vibraphone, an electronic marimba, was a jazz performer.

This is not to say that classical musicians never experimented with electronic music. From the late 1950s onward, Milton Babbitt, Karl-Heinz Stockhausen, and others composed extensively for the newly invented electronic music synthesizer, but their works were rarely performed in concert, and the synthesizer came to be used most extensively by popular musical groups and composers for movies and television. The Beatles and other rock groups also experimented brilliantly with overlapping different recorded sound tracks, including nonmusical noises, to produce a multilayered complexity of sound that could never be achieved in live performance. The art of mixing audio tracks to produce the best possible recording served, in the realm of "art" music, as a means of replicating the sound of the finest live performance. In popular music, more often than not, it went beyond performance verisimilitude to add new features.

The adoption, in 1983, of a standardized Musical Instrument Digital Interface (MIDI) for synthesizers and computers further expanded the potential for musical composition and recording. Anyone, however amateur or untrained, could now try to create music and preserve their creation. However, in the realm of "art" music, the 1980s also saw an intensifying interest in performing classical compositions on reproductions of the original instruments for which they had been written. This urge to go back in time, informed in large part by the scholarship of university music professors, was emblematic of the discomfort classical music devotees felt with an electronic technology that improved reproduction quality but seemed at the same time to be subverting traditional performance values.

Yet another important effect of technology on popular music was social. The turn-of-the-century aesthete's perception that anything he or she did not consider "fine" or "classical" was "vulgar" has been used here, for convenience's sake, as the boundary marker between high culture and popular culture. But even though aesthetes from St. Petersburg to San Francisco were probably of one mind concerning the supernal excellence of Tchaikowsky, Beethoven, Shakespeare, and Rembrandt, no such consensus was possible within the infinitely diverse realm of popular culture. New Orleans swells heard Jelly Roll Morton invent jazz on a whorehouse piano in the first years of the century. A decade later and not far away, on Will Dockery's plantation outside Jackson, Mississippi, Charley Patton, Tommy Johnson, and a handful of other rural black men invented blues guitar playing. But the audience for each was purely local; it is unlikely that any New Orleans swell ever made it to Dockery's plantation, or that any dirt-poor Mississippi sharecropper who heard Charley Patton also spent time in New Orleans whorehouses.

Unlike high culture, popular culture is intrinsically local and socially circumscribed. Barrelhouse piano was the music of lumberjacks and railroad tank towns; English music hall turns were little heard outside Britain; African rhythms followed separate courses of development in Cuba, Brazil, and Jamaica. Though historically it can be argued that opera, classical music, and theatrical drama all developed from the popular culture of sixteenth- and seventeenth-century Italy, particularly Venice, and absorbed other local traditions as they spread, it is highly unlikely, given the downtrodden state of the black populations of the Western Hemisphere in the early twentieth century, that jazz and blues music would ever have gained international acclaim and become America's greatest contribution to world culture without the recording industry. Nor would the later eclecticism of popular styles represented by the Beatles' combination of rhythm and blues with music hall balladry, Bob Marley's fusion of rock with Jamaican rhythm, or Paul Simon's combination of American songwriting and African drumming and choral singing ever have been possible without recording. Here again, despite many composers' earlier exploitation of folk melodies and rhythms, it is difficult to identify similarly successful eclectic experiments in the realm of "art" music, partly because its forms proved to be too rigid to accommodate "exotic" elements easily, but also because audiences for live performances much preferred the familiar to the unfamiliar.

The story of painting and sculpture in the twentieth century has a somewhat parallel plot line. The Museum of Modern Art's controversial *High and Low* exhibit of 1990–1991 documented both the evolution of styles in popular caricature, graffiti, comics, and advertising and the recurrent recourse "serious" artists have had to their imagery. Picasso's use of typography and newspapers in his cubist collages, Jean Dubuffet's and Cy Twombly's faux-infantile daubings and scrawlings, Roy Lichtenstein's fascination with gargantuan comic strip images made of enlarged Benday dots, and Andy Warhol's immortalizing of Campbell's Soup cans amply testify to this use of popular imagery as a reservoir for creative imaginations.

The emphasis of the exhibition and its erudite catalog written by the show's curator Kirk Varnedoe, however, was on the insights of elite artists.

The creativity embodied in the evolution of advertising, from cramped engravings to full-page marvels of photography and typography, or of comic-book art, from the crude drawing of Superman's creator, Joe Shuster, to the paintings of outstanding 1990s artists like Dave McKean, Bill Sienkiewicz, or Geoff Darrow, which display the highest levels of graphic sophistication in the comic book form, is relegated to a secondary level of interest. Duly acknowledged are the historic roles of artists like Rudolphe Töppfer, whose authorship of stories conveyed solely by caricature and caption in the 1820s excited the influential German philsopher-poet Goethe with the thought that an important new cultural form was being born; George Herriman, whose pre-World War I *Krazy Kat* brilliantly manipulated a set of archetypal images (strikingly similar to those in classic Persian Sufi poetry) against ever-changing abstract and surrealistic backgrounds; and Robert Crumb, whose characters published in "underground" comics became the icons of the 1960s counterculture in America. Yet Varnedoe's observation that "for the past twenty years, the comics as a popular form have been in what seems to be an inexorable decline"[2] flies in the face of the actual exuberance of the comic book industry and, even more, the publication in the 1980s and 1990s of brilliant works by Englishmen Alan Moore (*Watchmen*, *V for Vendetta*) and Neil Gaiman (*Sandman*, *Signal to Noise*), American Frank Miller (*The Dark Knight Returns*, *Sin City*) and numerous others.

Part of the difficulty with integrating late-twentieth-century comic books into a history of art seen from the perspective of high culture is that comic books are written and not just drawn—of the three authors cited above, only Miller both writes and draws, though even he also writes for other artists. The comic book, in other words, is a genre separate both from ordinary fiction writing and from graphic art, just as Goethe envisaged from Töppfer's early experiments. The potential of this form has thus far been differently realized in various parts of the world. In continental Europe, it has taken the form, in part, of elegant pornography—another form of popular culture that has taken advantage of every breakthrough in twentieth-century technology, including the Internet. In Britain, where associations of comic books with juvenile taste seem less entrenched than in the United States, it has become a bastion of nihilistic social critique—as in the works of Alan Moore and Neil Gaiman. And in the Arab world comic books have served the purpose of nationalist political indoctrination and moral instruction.

Japan, however, has surely been more affected by comic books, categorically known as *manga*, than any other society. A newsstand in a Tokyo train station will display a familiar-looking array of news, fashion, and special interest magazines on racks, but stacked four feet deep in front of the cash register will be a dozen or more of the most recent weekly black-and-white comic books, most approaching an inch thick. Commuters of all ages and both sexes buy them with alacrity, and they are broadly segregated into works for schoolboys, adult men, schoolgirls, and adult women. In comics oriented toward women, delicate heroines, literally with stars in their huge princess eyes, experience adventure and romance, but the stories stop well short of the panting prurience of the American seduction-abduction novels, usually called romances, marketed to a presumably similar audience in supermarkets. Male comics, on the other hand, feature real-life competitive situations, endless violence, and extravagantly strenuous sex wherein the artists skillfully work around the government's ban on full nudity.

Japanese comics, which pervade television and cinema as well as publishing, draw on a long tradition of humorous caricature in Zen Buddhism (*zenga*, or "Zen picture"), woodcuts portraying popular pleasures and pastimes (*ukiyo-e*, or "floating world"), and extravagant depictions of sexual congress (*shunga*, or "spring pictures"). Just as the styles of the nineteenth-century Japanese woodcuts that often arrived in the West as packing in tea boxes strongly affected impressionist artists such as Edgar Degas, so European narrative and satirical caricature affected Japan. Britain's Charles Wirgman published and drew in *The Japan Punch* starting in 1862, and Frenchman Georges Bigot did the same later in the century in his magazine *Tobaé*. In the first half of the twentieth century, Japanese comics generally paralleled those of the United States, and both countries used the medium for home propaganda and enemy demoralization during World War II.

The rebirth of Japanese comics in a new and distinctive form began in 1947, when Osamu Tezuka published his book-length *Shintakarajima* (New Treasure Island). Tezuka pioneered the unusual page layouts and picture cropping, creative sound depictions, and devotion of many panels to a single crucial action that became ever more sophisticated in later Japanese comics and inspired new departures by American comic artists in the 1980s. By the 1980s the combined weekly sales of the top four boys' comics approached 8.5 million. The most popular girls' comics and adult males' comics often sold a million copies a week. However, since the only Western artists who gained inspiration from Japanese comic book styles were themselves comic artists, such as Frank Miller, the remarkable success of this form, with its original and distinctive approach to visual narration, played no role in the portrayal of popular culture seen from above as presented at the Museum of Modern Art exhibition.

The evolution of the comic book speaks also to an aspect of twentieth-century popular culture not yet touched on: literature. Unlike other areas of artistic culture, technological advance—from handsetting through Ottmar Mergenthaler's linotype (1884) and Tolder Lanston's monotype (1887) machines to computerized printing today—had little direct impact on writers; nor did the transition from pen to typewriter to personal computer fundamentally alter their craft. Technology did have a role, however, in servicing the phenomenal expansion of literacy in the twentieth century and thereby in changing the audience for written poetry and fiction.

In turn-of-the-century America, Joseph Pulitzer and William Randolph Hearst pitted their New York newspapers, the *World* and the *Journal*, against each other in a readership war that featured sensational stories, banner headlines, lavish illustrations, cartoons, and publicity stunts. Their objective? To discover a level of vulgarity that would sell the most copies. Though elite newspapers, magazines, and publishing houses prided themselves on their more elevated tastes, the economics of massive editions targeted toward a mass readership increasingly influenced the publishing world as the century progressed, and especially after the popularity of television reduced the time the average American spent reading.

By 1979, survey results indicated that 73 percent of American poets earned less than $5,000 a year from writing. General adult fiction writers did a bit better, but more than half earned less than $10,000. Genre fiction writers, on the other hand, authoring westerns, thrillers, science fiction, historical romances, and gothic/occult novels, included only 42 percent below the $10,000 level and an impressive 23 percent earning over $50,000 a year. Though literature professors are prone to extol the accomplishments of pioneers in these genres—Bret Harte, Edgar Allen Poe, Jules Verne, Rudyard Kipling, Mary Shelley, Charlotte Brontë—few would speak as kindly of such late-twentieth-century inheritors as Louis L'amour, Robert Ludlum, Robert Heinlein, Stephen King, or Barbara Cartland. Yet the continuing disdain for genre fiction can not conceal the fact that *certain* genre writers of the late twentieth century—for example Elmore Leonard and P. D. James in crime, William Gibson in science fiction, and Art Spiegelman in comic books—have achieved tacit admission to the realm of high culture. Moreover, writers with reputations solidly anchored in serious fiction have been increasingly tempted by popular genres, most notably true crime in novels by Truman Capote and Norman Mailer, among others.

Since novels by American and British genre writers abound in different languages on airport paperback racks around the world, and the late-twentieth-century orgy of large corporations swallowing the best-known publishing corporations has led to an increasing insistence on sales blockbusters, it seems apparent that the self-declared literary novel, not to mention the serious poem, is becoming ever more confined to small print runs and limited audiences. Though this fact of literary life is presumed in the deliberately difficult prose of writers like William Gaddis and Donald Barthelme, younger writers at century's end, like younger composers and artists, are confronted by a cultural market in which, absent wealthy patrons, mass popular appeal is what puts bread on their tables.

This is not the case outside Europe and America, however. As imperialist world domination intensified during the first third of the twentieth century, Westernizing social strata everywhere looked upon Western-style education as a vehicle of social advancement and upon newspapers as an agency of protest or indoctrination. During the middle third of the century, decolonization gave birth to a multitude of independent states, all of which deemed mass public education the best way to catch up, compete, or enter into confrontation with the economically and politically dominant Western and/or Soviet blocs. Though cinema, newspapers, radio, and television were all commonly enlisted in the process of state and nation formation, writing and printing textbooks for the newly literate masses provided governments with their most effective tool.

However, once reading became commonplace—45 percent literacy in India in 1992, 75 percent in China—poets and authors of novels (a universally disseminated Western form) began for the first time to write for large, socially diverse audiences the same way Western writers had been for generations. With a wealth of Western styles a d motifs to add to their own traditions of literary form and imagery, non-Western writers captivated audiences that had never before been exposed to literature as a vehicle for political polemic, realistic depiction of common lives, portrayal of sexual relations, or confession of the author's inner emotions. While Europeans and Americans have devoted more and more of their reading time to genre fiction during the last third of the century, serious poems and novels have claimed larger and larger audiences in the Arab world, Latin America, East Asia, and elsewhere.

The paradox of increasing literacy winding up, in the West, with a flood of popular genre writing and the rampant miniaturization of magazine articles often to under one hundred words, while, in the rest of the world, there is an efflorescence of serious poetry and literature, is but one aspect of the geographically distorted evolution of popular culture in the twentieth century. Though the technological milestones discussed earlier in this chapter all originated in Europe and the United States, the earliest of them diffused rapidly to other parts of the world. Photographic cameras, gramophones, newspapers, and moving pictures were known in cultural centers everywhere in the world by World War I. Turkey, Egypt, India, Japan, and other non-Western countries developed significant film industries during the interwar years, Japan's film production rising to more than seven hundred films a year by the 1930s.

Regardless of social background, however, the devotees of the new popular culture technologies outside Europe and America during the first half of the century tended to associate them with Western styles and values. There was no equivalent of the American record producers who sought out hillbilly banjo pickers, Cajun fiddlers, and black jug bands to see what might tempt the record-buying public. To be sure, Egyptian and Indian popular singers have benefited from new technologies by cutting records and appearing in movies. But these performers mostly worked from well-established urban performance styles rather than from socially or geographically localized "folk" traditions. The latter tended to languish as the presentations of the former steadily improved in technological quality in response to the comparative standard set by the West.

This early cosmopolitan access to entertainment technology faded after World War II. From the 1960s on, American movies, jazz and rock music, and finally television gradually acquired larger and larger audiences worldwide (though, on the silver screen, Bombay musicals and Hong Kong martial arts films bucked the trend, along with Latin American television soap operas). Despite the disparagement heaped on Hollywood movies and television shows by the watchdogs of American high culture, their variety, abundance, technical excellence, and high production values—made possible by strong commercial underwriting in a self-regulated (and hence increasingly unregulated) industry—outclassed the products of state-controlled television systems and underfunded movie producers elsewhere. By the 1980s, when "serious" artists and writers in America were becoming resigned to the seemingly irreversible national fascination with popular culture, and in many instances turning to it for inspiration and personal profit, the rest of the world too seemed to be edging toward at least a partial Americanization of popular culture.

But limits to this scenario loomed. Even as MTV and CNN began broadcasting worldwide, other television prognosticators were concerned with the intractable problem of cultural difference. In 1985, before the curtailing of network censorship operations in the face of competition from uncensored cable television, the guardians of American popular sensibility and conscience were pondering the fact that a Canadian soap opera about professional hockey players was being aired in two versions in Montreal—a version in French that allowed the viewer to see an occasional bare breast, and a version in English that maintained "proper" decorum. Though no one truly believed that a knowledge of French *ipso facto* insulated a viewer from the morally corrupting influence of semi-nudity, there was a general feeling that much of American television was too violent and too prudish for the European market, but at the same time not violent enough and too risqué for the Japanese market. Marketers of American movies to international airlines reported similar cultural constraints.

A common denominator low enough to accommodate all dimensions of cultural diversity has not been found, and the post-cold war reassertion of cultural differences worldwide—the welter of Islamist movements provide a good example—suggests that the search for one has passed its high water mark. Even though some prophets declare they see the handwriting on the wall ("MTV, MTV, CNN, Hollywood" in this century's revised scripture), predictions of the absorption of serious artistic endeavor into the primal slime of commercial mass marketing and of a mortal withering of non-Western cultural traditions seem overly sanguine.

Through elitism, self-satisfaction, and the increasingly refined cultivation of a dwindling market of sophisticates, Western high culture gradually squandered much of the international cachet it enjoyed in 1900 and condemned itself to decades of stagnation by turning its back on revolutionary advances in technology. But at the century's end, Western popular culture has to a considerable degree acquired that same cachet. Michael Jackson in 1990 had become the equivalent of Sarah Bernhardt in 1900 in terms of international fame and artistic influence. And like the high culture it has superseded, Western popular culture in the non-Western world is as much—if not more—a mark of social status and aspiration as it is of aesthetic refinement. Its future depends not on ever more spectacular concert tours and commercial tie-ins, but on the longer-term working out of political and economic relations between the former imperialist West (both capitalist and socialist) and the rest of the world.

Leaving the future to write itself, consideration must now be given to the net impact of this century's complex interplay between high culture, popular culture, and technology. Four topics, among a possible larger number, serve to illustrate the depth of this impact and its likely permanent effect: volume of production, simplified codes of communication, an intercultural vocabulary of forms, and an expanded universe of reference (also called intertextuality).

More original drama is aired in a week of American network television programming than was produced by Shakespeare and all the other Elizabethan playwrights combined. Most of it is written in Los Angeles. The likelihood of something distinctively original reaching the public is limited not only by this overload of creative circuits, but also by a winnowing process that discards the great preponderance of program ideas presented and favors near-clones of existing successful shows. Writers put thousands of ideas before independent producers; producers advance hundreds of them to the attention of broadcasting executives; executives authorize and pay for scores of pilot films; and a handful are chosen for public viewing because they seem to fit a certain slot in terms of day, broadcast time, competition, and appeal to sponsors. All of this is analogous to the state of popular culture as a historical phenomenon. The ancient Greeks were capable of marvelous originality, but they were also held spellbound for centuries by only slightly varying stories about the Trojan War. Medieval Europeans could never hear enough about the evil lurking in dark forests. Arab listeners still revel in tales of tribal heros and magical travels. Repeating, with slight modification, well-known stories was the stock in trade of preliterate popular balladeers and storytellers.

But retelling familiar stories is also the stock in trade of late-twentieth-century crafters of screenplays, genre novels, and popular songs. Originality was an obsession of Western high culture during its century-long romance with the idea of modernism from roughly 1870 to 1970: works like *Finnegans Wake* or Picasso's early cubist canvases that few, if any, could understand were lionized for it. But high-volume creative production relies on formula more than originality, both out of necessity—there just aren't that many good new ideas—and out of inveterate audience desire to hear the same familiar and beloved themes over and over again. As technology has increased the size of audiences throughout the twentieth century and made possible novelties of a technical nature—movie special effects, multitrack recording, electronically altered or amplified sounds—cultural production has become more and more devoted to repetition of familiar themes and story lines. At century's end, the entire question of the nature and value of "originality" is being reexamined.

Turning to the phenomenon of code simplification during the second half of the twentieth century, it is obvious that formula entertainment and high-volume production lead in this direction. Corrupt heroes, all-pervasive badness, shady settings = film noir. Broken marriage, broken heart, lessons learned too late = country music hit. Laconic hero, braggart villain, showdown = western movie. Dead body, strangely isolated handful of suspects, you guessed wrong = Agatha Christie mystery. When elements of the formula are missing, the audience feels vaguely (or acutely) disappointed.

Such coded simplifications go well beyond these obvious formulae of cultural production, however. Language itself has been affected. Prior to World War II, "posh" (port out, starboard home—the best cabins for British voyagers to India) was one of the few acronyms in common use in English, though the Soviet Union was already well advanced in matters of word creation through abbreviation (NEP, Cheka, Comintern). The wartime efflorescence of shorthand codes (ETO, D-Day, GI), so convenient for telegraphic communication, did not fade with war's end, however. Combinations of syllables from two or more words and acronyms, either pronounced as words, e.g. NATO, or as sequences of letters, e.g. TV, have proliferated in alphabetically represented languages throughout the world. This fertile new source of word formation could be seen as representing a militarization of society, but it is perhaps more important to stress its role in simplifying understanding in a period of ever quicker and more abundant communication, both among speakers of the same language and between speakers of different languages.

Acronyms and standardized abbreviations, in turn, are but a subcategory in a more general growth of nonlingual iconic communication, particularly in the area of popular culture. Corporate logos and trademarks; international traffic and warning signs; iconic representations of cultural "stars" (or the stars themselves as icons, à la Madonna and Michael Jackson), particularly in advertising; icon-driven computer interfaces; and the electronic bar code (invented in 1949 by Bernard Silver and Norman Woodland but not perfected by RCA until 1974) are small parts of a complicated iconic environment that is a hallmark, well represented in comic books, of international popular culture.

The third area of impact, the spread of an intercultural vocabulary of forms, reflects the entire century's global evolution from imperialism-assisted domination by Western high culture to today's more ubiquitous but less coercive spread of Western-inspired, technologically mediated popular culture. The history of fiction, poetry, drama, music, and art worldwide abundantly demonstrates the tremendous influence during the first half of the twentieth century of cultural forms drawn from Western high culture. Novels began to be written where the novel form was previously unknown. Free verse intruded on local poetic traditions. European stage plays, symphonies, and modern art were performed or emulated in cultural capitals everywhere. And all of this at the cost, in varying degrees, of lessening vitality and even disappearance of indigenous cultural forms.

In the closing decades of the century, however, new international forms have emanated from popular culture. These have been mostly Western, but not exclusively—Asian martial arts have become so international that a hero who only uses his fists and doesn't kick in fights looks antique. In contrast with the forms derived from high culture, however, these newer forms are more technological and less tributary to the historic aesthetic presumptions of Western culture. Sitcoms (a good late-twentieth-century codeword), soap operas, news anchors, music videos, total abstraction in art, synthesizer music not dependent on set instrumentation, multitrack recording, photomontage, and a whole host of cinema techniques have entered the toolkits of creative people everywhere in the world. But unlike, say, the symphonic form, with its prescriptions regarding scale, key, instrumentation, and division into movements, these new Western-originated techniques are largely innocent of specific cultural orientation. An Iranian film of the 1990s looks different from a European or American film just as a tape of a Malagasy musical group sounds different even when they are singing a Western song.

Embedded in technological media, new forms and tools cross continents and oceans with the greatest of ease. However, instead of propagating the Western culture that spawned them, they constitute a set of potentials that can be adapted to any cultural setting. Moreover, their specific cultural contents can be more readily understood and appraised by people with differing cultural backgrounds precisely because their technological forms make them intellectually accessible. The medium may not be the entire message, as Canadian visionary Marshall McCluhan enigmatically suggested, but a culturally neutral and universally accessible medium enables messages to cross cultural boundaries.

The fourth area in which the technology of popular culture has had an indelible impact is in expanding everyone's universe of cultural reference. It is self-evident that photography permitted artists who could not afford to travel to museums and private collections to familiarize themselves with the history of art, that videotape made possible a parallel familiarization with the history of motion pictures and television, and that phonograph recordings freed listeners from the arbitrary selections of local concert musicians. Less apparent has been the cumulative effect of a seemingly infinite repetition of advertisements. Jingles, logos, trademarks, slogans, and styles became increasingly imprinted in people's memories as the century progressed. These indelible images thus became part of the referential vocabulary of artists, writers, and musicians.

Miguel de Cervantes and William Shakespeare did not use brand names in their writing, but they freely made use of other texts—chivalric romances for the former and Raphael Holinshed's *Chronicles of England, Scotland, and Ireland* for the latter—that they could assume their audiences were at least semiconsciously aware of. This sort of intertextual reference is well known. By the second half of the twentieth century, this vocabulary of reference had expanded far beyond literary texts. Brand names became essential tools for authors as diverse as Pulitzer Prize-winner William Gaddis and James Bond creator Ian Fleming. Advertising images appeared in abundance in serious art works just as well-known (through photography) art images abounded in advertising. Charles Ives put snatches of hymns and patriotic songs into his compositions; the Beatles put snatches of Bach in theirs. A conscientious exploration of the ever-expanding realm of cultural cross-reference would never end. Indeed, it has become so much a part of everyday life internationally—women's underpants emblazoned with the Marlboro cigarette pack for sale from a street vendor in Bishkek, Kyrgysztan; faux-University of Oklahoma football jerseys made in Taiwan on sale in Amman, Jordan—that it is difficult to conceive of yesteryear's essentially local arena of intertextual reference at the popular level, or near-universal convergence on a limited set of acknowledged masterpieces at the level of high culture.

Technology has not been the sole cause of the cultural transformations of the twentieth century. It could be argued that technology has simply been the mechanism through which deeper economic relationships within and among cultures have expressed themselves. But it has been essential to the process, whatever one conceives its underlying structure to be; and it has created potentials that economic dominance or subordination alone could never have brought about, at least in the course of one century. As we look toward the next millennium, our assumptions about the nature of cultural production and the prospects for renewed intercultural diversity—or, more dismally, for an ever-increasing cultural homogenization driven by commercial pandering to primal urges—must start from the premise of a technologically transformed cultural universe and a profound ambiguity regarding the intelligibility of the distinctions still being made between popular and high culture.

ENDNOTES

1. Daniel Catton Rich, *Henri Rousseau*, New York: The Museum of Modern Art, 1942, pp. 13-14.
2. Kirk Varnedoe and Adam Gopnik, *High and Low: Modern Art and Popular Culture*, New York: The Museum of Modern Art, 1991, p. 227.

SELECTED REFERENCES

Bardèche, Maurice, and Robert Brasillach. *The History of Motion Pictures*. New York: W.W. Norton and The Museum of Modern Art, 1938.

Douglas, Allen, and Fedwa Malti-Douglas. *Arab Comic Strips: Politics of an Emerging Mass Culture*. Bloomington: Indiana University Press, 1994.

Robinson, David. *From Peep Show to Palace: The Birth of American Film*. New York: Columbia University Press, 1996.

Schodt, Frederik L. *Manga! Manga! The World of Japanese Comics*. Tokyo: Kodansha International, 1983.

Varnedoe, Kirk, and Adam Gopnik. *High and Low: Modern Art and Popular Culture*. New York: The Museum of Modern Art, 1991.

Witmark, Isidore, and Isaac Goldberg. *From Ragtime to Swingtime: The Story of the House of Witmark*. New York: Lee Furman, 1939.

# 3    The "Woman Question"

ROSALIND ROSENBERG

In 1911 Japanese actress Matsui Sumako appeared in a play never before seen in Japan. The very presence of a woman on the stage of the Imperial Theater in Tokyo attracted attention, since, by tradition, women's roles were played by male actors. But what caused a still greater stir was the message that Matsui Sumako delivered. Playing an unhappy housewife, she declared that no woman should have to "become a man's plaything," that society should recognize women's "individuality," and that all women should "demand freedom." Theatergoers were stunned.[1]

Nowhere did the self-effacing deference of women seem more secure at the beginning of the twentieth century than in Japan. Whatever their economic station, Japanese families raised their daughters to serve the husbands that their fathers selected for them. But forces beyond the control of Japanese fathers were beginning to subvert that expectation. Ever since an American expedition forcibly opened the country to Western commerce in 1853, Japan had embarked on a path of rapid industrial development that included scientific and technological borrowings from the West. Despite the Emperor Meiji's success in resisting direct colonization, and despite efforts to preserve traditional society, Japanese officials found it impossible to control this process of Westernization. Along with capitalist enterprise came democratic ideas, including those expressed in the play in which Matsui Sumako appeared—Henrik Ibsen's *A Doll's House* (1879). Audiences raised to believe that life's one certainty was the subordination of women watched in amazement as Nora, the unhappy housewife-heroine, slammed shut her front door and ventured forth to find her own way.[2]

Wherever an educated middle class had emerged, as it had in most of the world by the beginning of the twentieth century, *A Doll's House* found an audience, and the character of Nora came to represent what was known as the "woman question." This question concerned whether women should have equal rights under the law, in education, and in employment. But it went beyond women's freedom to act outside the domestic sphere. When women sought the right to control their own earnings and to vote, they were demanding not simply the rights of men, but also the chance to rewrite the script they performed in response to the expectations of the communities in which they lived.[3]

No one could be sure where the "woman question" would lead, or what changes answers to it might bring. But women who were then beginning to call themselves feminists believed that freeing women from traditional constraints would affect everything. Questions about legal equality led to questions about economic rights, sexual freedom, the future of the family, and of society and politics more broadly. Nothing would remain unaltered, not even men's conceptions of themselves.[4]

Steeped in the progressive faith of late-nineteenth-century Western societies, feminists never doubted that their questioning, and the conditions that had given rise to it, would lead to a better world. And yet, the course of economic development in the twentieth century proved to be at best uneven, and, at certain times and in many places, positively harmful to women. While large numbers of urban, middle-class women gained increased prosperity, more advanced education, greater control over their fertility, and enhanced political influence within democratizing regimes, many others suffered reduced economic opportunities, declining political power under more totalitarian rulers, and decreased control over their reproductive lives. The problems of single mothers, the poverty of rural wives and mothers in developing regions, the fundamentalist backlash against women throughout the world, and even the complex issues that beset upper-middle-class women struggling to be both mothers and professionals developed out of the same historical transformation that brought such widespread success to *A Doll's House* at the turn of the century.

## Women in 1900

As of 1900, no one could either predict the victories women would win in the new century or forecast the defeats. Most women still lived in rural areas, where life revolved around the family unit, and where the economic and political forces that would transform women's lives had not yet penetrated.

Everywhere, women lived under a patriarchal rule reinforced by religious sanctions. In China, families crushed their daughters' feet and bound them to keep them small, supposedly enhancing the daughters' erotic appeal, but also ensuring their physical dependence. In India, although it was illegal to do so, families pressured widows to immolate themselves on their husbands' funeral pyres in a practice called "suttee." In parts of the Middle East and Africa, families subjected their daughters to clitoridectomies as a means of controlling their sexuality. In much of Asia, female infanticide remained a common method of population control. Everywhere, including the United States and Europe, women suffered from domestic violence. Lacking rights to their own property and having no official role in politics, women who sought to escape these conditions could rarely do so.[5]

Rural women's lives revolved around agriculture. In much of sub-Saharan Africa, where cultivators using little more than hoes tilled a few acres of land at a time and then moved on, women did most of the farming after men did the clearing. In Southeast Asia, where farmers engaged in intensive, wet rice cultivation, entire families labored in the fields. In most of northern Asia, Europe, and the Americas, by contrast, where farmers depended on extensive dry plowing, women participated much less. While they usually worked in family groups, daughters might also work as day laborers or domestics for other families. But wherever rural women lived and whatever responsibilities they shouldered outside their dwellings, they all shared common responsibilities at home. Laboring before the men arose and after they quit work, the women hauled water, cooked, sewed, laundered, traded food and other goods they produced at home, and cared for children.[6]

Virtually all women married, and while rural daughters in the United States enjoyed considerable freedom in deciding whom to wed, parents usually controlled marital decisions elsewhere. In Europe brides had generally reached their twenties, and nuclear families were the norm. In the Middle East and much of Africa and Asia, however, parents married their daughters off as early as possible—in some regions and economic groups, to men who already had several wives.

Rural wives typically bore between five and eight children, of whom half could be expected to reach adulthood. Inadequate sanitation, limited medical care, and poverty kept child mortality high, but cultural factors increased the dangers for daughters. In much of the world, families facing food shortages skimped on their daughters' nutrition and care, and therefore girls died in greater numbers than their brothers. Despite the pressures of poverty the rural birthrate remained high. Children, especially sons, were an important source of status and assistance in agricultural work when parents were young, and of social security in old age.[7]

For a small but growing number of women, however, the process of industrialization and urbanization was having a transformative effect. About half the population of Europe and the United States, pushed by declining agricultural prices (produced by more efficient farming techniques and the creation of a world market) and pulled by the prospect of employment in expanding businesses and industries, had moved into towns and cities by 1900.

Urbanization brought a marked improvement in standards of living. As officials came to recognize that diseases like cholera and tuberculosis observed no geographic or social boundaries in crowded cities, they embarked on civic improvement projects that included building sewage systems, paving streets and sidewalks, installing gas and electricity, regulating housing and food distribution, and constructing schools.[8]

These changes increased both life expectancy and literacy. In the United States, for instance, black women, who lived overwhelmingly in rural areas in 1900, experienced a dramatic increase in life expectancy as they and the country became more urbanized. In 1900 the average black woman's life expectancy was 34; by 1940 it had risen to 56, and by 1980 to 74. Their literacy followed a similar pattern: in 1900, 60 percent of black women could not read; by 1980 virtually all could.

Cities offered broader occupational opportunities for migrant families than did rural areas, but jobs rarely paid what was known in the United States as a "family wage," or enough for a man to support his wife and children. Most children worked also, as they had in rural areas; so too did many wives. Poor women worked in the proliferating low-wage, unskilled jobs that men would not take. They worked as domestic servants, factory workers, or in the expanding informal sector, taking in boarders, doing piecework for the garment industry at home, trading food, engaging in prostitution. Those women who were better off and had gained some education might find work as nurses, store clerks, grade school teachers, or clerical workers. An elite few attended college and entered professions.

There was nothing novel in all members of a family working. What was new was the fact that most urban employment allowed for greater independence from traditional family expectations than rural life had. Much of the intensity of the evolving "woman question" debate derived from the potential independence that these new opportunities offered to women. Although a woman rarely earned more than half what a man did (even on those rare occasions when she did the same work), a young woman wage worker was not under such intense pressure to marry and bear children as the daughter of farmers was. Many daughters spent at least some of their earnings on themselves, and when they married they bore fewer children than did rural women. Whereas in agricultural areas, each additional child meant much-needed help in farming, in cities (and in farming regions where land was scarce), every new child represented an economic liability. Families intent on guaranteeing the upward mobility of their offspring by keeping them out of the workforce to attend school strove to limit women's childbearing. Even before the widespread availability of the condom or the diaphragm, couples reduced the number of children they parented, relying on late marriage, withdrawal, abstinence, and, if necessary, abortion. In sum, urbanization brought many women real benefits: improved health, better education, greater economic opportunity, and less frequent childbearing.[9]

Urbanization also led, however, to new forms of exploitation, especially for poor women: low wages, frequent (and often extended) unemployment, sexual harassment, and the increased chance of being abandoned by a husband or lover. Moreover, the decline in fertility that accompanied urbanization led political leaders in Europe and the United States to worry about the consequences of women's increasing control over fertility. How was France to defend itself against Germany if women did not bear a new generation of soldiers? How were the Anglo-Saxons who had settled in the United States to maintain their cultural dominance if wives had fewer and fewer children, while immigrants from Italy and Eastern Europe produced as many offspring as ever before? In response to these worrisome questions, male politicians strove in the early twentieth century to limit women's possible independence. Contraception and abortion were outlawed; divorce made more difficult. In Europe, where anxiety over the declining birthrate seems to have been most pronounced, many countries enacted maternity benefits to make motherhood easier.[10]

Ironically, many of the reforms aimed at controlling women and promoting motherhood ultimately contributed to greater female autonomy. Male physicians, for instance, encouraged the new trend toward more physical exercise for urban women of all classes in the interest of better maternal health. Young women bicycled, hiked, swam, engaged in calisthenics, and played golf and tennis. All this exercise no doubt produced stronger mothers, but it also whetted women's appetite for greater freedom. In a related attempt to enhance young women's marital and maternal prospects, middle-class fathers offered their daughters increased education, while European and American church leaders sent women missionaries to Asia, the Middle East, and Africa to teach girls there how to be good wives for Westernized local men. But the more education women had, the more they learned about the rights being claimed by men, and the more they came to resent their own vulnerability in a world that did not recognize those same rights for women.[11]

## The Women's Movement

This growing resentment found expression as women began organizing groups to advance what they saw as their particular goals. Curiously, the sexual segregation that had long reinforced women's subordination throughout the world actually facilitated these organizational efforts. Everywhere women were accustomed to working together, whether within the domestic compounds of the Muslim harem, the religious groups of Christian and Jewish women, or the marketplace where women traded their produce and shopped. One of the oldest forms of women's organizing was the food riot, mounted to protest the high price of bread or other staples of people's diet. While these forms of organizing continued, new forms emerged at the end of the nineteenth and the beginning of the twentieth century. In the United States the largest women's group at the turn of the century was the Women's Christian Temperance Union, dedicated to outlawing alcohol consumption in the hope of preventing husbands from drinking up their wages and beating their wives and children. Throughout the world, middle-class women organized pacifist groups in the hope of stopping war, settlement houses to help the poor, working-women's unions to protect women from exploitative working conditions, and purity leagues to fight against what many women regarded as the sexual excesses of men.[12]

By World War I most European countries, the United States, and Japan had passed protective labor legislation for women that significantly shortened the hours that factory women worked. Given the resistance of male unionists to organizing women, this legislation proved critical to bettering working women's lives. But in many instances the protection of one group of women led to the exploitation of a new group. Japanese textile magnates, no longer able to employ women workers at night, moved their factories to southern China where no such restrictions existed. Rural Chinese families, impoverished by ruinous taxes, warlord fighting, and competition from foreign agricultural goods, sold their daughters to labor contractors for Japanese textile mills in Shanghai. In the United States, protective labor legislation in Massachusetts contributed to the decision of textile magnates to relocate to the South, where unions and reformers held little power.[13]

Early in the century, women reformers who tried, with such mixed results, to ameliorate the harsher aspects of industrial growth, generally accepted women's traditional roles as wives and mothers. They differed from prior generations only in seeking for themselves a stronger voice in determining public policy. For the most part, they believed in the unifying power of womanhood, a concept that transcended class, race, and even national boundaries. As mothers, or potential mothers, they believed they had a special role to play in politics, one that gave greater emphasis to morality, social welfare, and cooperation than men could be expected to provide.[14]

Increasingly, however, younger women came to believe that without greater sexual equality, especially in the political arena, women could not achieve their political goals. These younger women found it easiest to claim equal rights in countries with a tradition of liberal reform and Protestantism, both of which emphasized the power of individual conscience. Throughout the second half of the nineteenth century, the United States and England provided the most conducive climate to women's rights organizing, and leaders in these countries created models for other movements around the world. Writing in 1851, Harriet Taylor Mill, wife of liberal theorist John Stuart Mill, explained the movement's goals: "What is wanted for women is equal rights, equal admission to all social privileges; not a position apart, a sort of sentimental priesthood." Women's rights leaders demanded equal opportunities and access to education, property, earnings, divorce, child custody, and political participation. In 1898 the International Council of Women met in London to demand these basic rights for all women. Most representatives came from the United States and Western Europe, but observers also came from China, Persia, India, Argentina, Iceland, and Palestine. By the early twentieth century, in the United States, England, and France, married women gained control over their own property and earnings, and won the right to sue for the custody of their children in case of separation. But throughout the world women's suffrage remained an elusive goal.[15]

Frustration over their inability to achieve the franchise drove many suffragists to take militant action. Emmeline Pankhurst in England and her follower Alice Paul in the United States led mass marches, broke windows, and disrupted political meetings to support women's suffrage. By 1914 over 1,000 suffragists had gone to prison, where many embarked on hunger strikes and suffered forced feedings. "Votes for Women and Chastity for Men" became the militant suffragists' slogan, as they issued a concurrent attack on men's political and sexual exploitation of women. Yet victory continued to elude the suffragists. In countries where most men still could not vote, the idea of women's suffrage gained little support. Where democratic institutions were well-established, as in the United States, England, France, and Scandinavia, women made more progress, but most men continued to argue that granting the suffrage to women would have a corrupting effect on both women and the family.[16]

While suffrage leaders endured bitter disappointment, a growing number of socialist women dismissed the suffrage campaign as an essentially pointless battle. Poverty, not legal inequality, seemed to them to be at the root of women's problems. Inspired by the work of Karl Marx and especially Frederick Engels's *Origins of the Family, Private Property, and the State* (1884), they argued that women's subordination was rooted in the family, which under a system of private property concentrated economic and thus political power in the hands of men. Capitalism had brought greater opportunity to many middle-class, educated women, they conceded, but it had also brought greater poverty to many rural areas and the economic and sexual exploitation of women workers who had fled rural life for urban centers. Only a socialist revolution that abolished private property, they concluded, could liberate women.[17]

Some socialist women doubted that a political revolution alone would help women. Identifying serious limitations in the male-centered thinking behind both liberalism and socialism, they insisted that women's needs must be specifically addressed. In Germany the leading socialist feminist, Clara Zetkin, argued that women had specific problems that socialism alone did not address. "Just as the male worker is subjugated by the capitalist, so is the woman by the man, and she will always remain in subjugation until she is economically independent. Work is the indispensable condition for economic independence." By 1907, the Socialist Party supported women's suffrage, and Zetkin was pushing for equal pay and maternity insurance. But though Zetkin made real advances for feminism, in her view socialism always came first.[18]

Not all feminists who were sympathetic to socialist goals accepted the subordination of women's needs so quickly. American writer Charlotte Perkins Gilman argued that until women achieved economic independence and society took over the responsibilities of housekeeping and child care, women would remain subordinate to men and true social equality would remain elusive. Unlike many bourgeois (and even socialist) men who believed that the modern family served a necessary function in an urban, industrial society—providing men with a refuge in a tumultuous world and guaranteeing children the long years of shelter needed to prepare for the work of an advanced culture—Gilman argued that the modern family crippled women, who, in turn, enfeebled their husbands and children through suffocating attention, which rendered them unfit for the challenges of modern life. Gilman called for the establishing of community nurseries, kitchens, and laundries to free women to become economically self-sufficient.[19]

To still other women, socialism's principal failing lay not in its inability to alleviate women's economic subordination to men, but rather in its reluctance to recognize the central importance of reproduction in most women's lives. Both Margaret Sanger of the United States and Ellen Key of Sweden regarded reproduction as something over which women should exercise exclusive control. Sanger sought to advance women's autonomy by launching the modern birth control movement, while Key proposed governmental subsidies for all mothers, whether married or not. In speaking frankly about reproduction, Sanger and Key broke not only with conventional propriety, but also with the belief of most older women's rights leaders (including Gilman) that men should strive to be more chaste. Sanger and Key argued instead that women ought to have the right to a freer expression of sexuality, without fear of pregnancy or social reprisals.[20]

## World War I and Its Aftermath

In a few short years, World War I produced much that decades of political organizing had failed to accomplish. As women came to play a vital role in the wartime economy, replacing men in factories, caring for the wounded, and demonstrating their patriotism in countless other ways, politicians found it increasingly difficult to ignore their needs.

In Britain and France the need to maintain morale prompted governments to implement social welfare measures to protect the women and children left behind by soldier husbands and fathers. Ironically, the more liberal British, influenced by male labor leaders, produced the more conservative social policy (one that provided benefits to male "breadwinners" supporting their dependents), while the more conservative French, led by Catholic and business leaders, produced a more liberal program (one that, by granting benefits directly to women and their children, undercut men's economic control). Whatever form new welfare policies took, they gave women greater claim to the protection of the state than they had ever before enjoyed.[21]

Women's wartime contributions also gave new energy to the women's suffrage movement. In 1915 Denmark and Iceland granted women the franchise; in 1917 the Netherlands, Finland, and Russia did so. England, Germany, most of Central and Eastern Europe, part of Africa, and six provinces of China followed in 1918 and 1919. And in the United States women won the right in 1920, although as a practical matter most black women (like most black men) continued to be disenfranchised. In the Catholic countries of France and Italy, and throughout Latin America, however, the suffrage battle foundered. In these nations, nuns educated most girls well into the twentieth century, long after most boys were being educated by the state. Even liberal politicians, whose commitment to individualism might have made them the natural allies of suffragists, opposed extending the vote on the grounds that women were merely pawns of the Catholic Church.[22]

Feminism played a pivotal role and received its most ambitious support in Russia. In February 1917, 10,000 women in St. Petersburg marched to protest the government's decision to ration bread and demanded the abdication of the Czar. The government responded by ordering soldiers to attack the women, a decision that mobilized the workers, alienated the army, and touched off a revolutionary explosion that forced the Czar to abdicate in March. In July the new government gave all citizens over twenty the right to vote. In November the Bolsheviks took power, and Lenin appointed Alexandra Kollontai commissar for public welfare. In 1918 a new marriage law turned marriage into a civil ceremony and made divorce easy to secure. Kollontai guaranteed state protection for women and children and made maternity hospital care free. In 1920 the Soviet Union became the first country in modern Europe to make abortion legal. Lenin and Kollontai imagined a national system of kitchens, day-care centers, and laundries to free women from the labor of motherhood and housework. Attempts to revolutionize the family and housework foundered, however, in the face of the civil war that followed World War I. By 1922 Kollontai had fallen from favor, and two years later, Lenin died.[23]

Kollontai's legacy proved mixed. While women received better maternity care than ever before, enjoyed significant educational gains, and worked at most jobs, their lives were in many ways harder than ever. Saddled now with long hours of work outside the home, in addition to their traditional domestic responsibilities, many women experienced Soviet-style liberation as the vehicle for a new kind of exploitation.[24]

At the same time as the Great War was creating the opportunity for revolution in Russia, the Allies' rhetoric of national self-determination, combined with their practice of ignoring most nationalist aspirations at the Versailles peace table, gave renewed impetus to liberation movements throughout the world. Since these movements tended to be couched in the language of democratic, individual rights, they gave encouragement, in turn, to supporters of women's rights in countries from Latin America to Asia.

Women played only a small role in these movements. For the most part, those who supported the emancipation of women in Latin America, the Middle East, and Asia after World War I were middle-class, educated *men*, intent on modernizing, who believed that one key to their nations' economic and political development (and independence) was having educated, relatively emancipated women—like those in the West—who would become good, educated wives and mothers and a credit to their civilized (i.e. Westernized) men.

In China, for instance, where the British rewarded Japanese support during the war by reducing China to a Japanese protectorate, outraged, mostly male, Chinese students and intellectuals began a boycott of Japanese goods on May 4, 1919 and went on to form a nationalist movement that not only demanded freedom from Japan but also questioned many of the traditional values of Chinese culture, including its treatment of women. In that year more than 400 new periodicals appeared in China, and many of them dealt explicitly with the woman question. Following visits from both Margaret Sanger and Ellen Key, journals published articles on birth control and independent motherhood. And when a newspaper reported the suicide of a young woman forced to marry against her will, numerous articles, including a number by the future Communist leader Mao Zedong, appeared in the press condemning the practice of arranged marriages. During this same brief period, theaters across China began putting on A Doll's House, and in 1923 Lu Xun of the Beijing Women's Normal College gave a lecture entitled, "What Happens After Nora Leaves Home?" in which he concluded that women needed more than legal rights to survive apart from their families: they needed education and the chance to earn their own living.[25]

Although men led the Chinese independence movement, the events of 1919 led to the formation of women's groups in cities throughout China. These groups demanded an end to foot-binding, female infanticide, concubinage, child-marriage, and prostitution. And they called for women's suffrage, equal inheritance rights, education, the equal right to work, and women's freedom to choose their own husbands. Women won suffrage in six provinces, and divorce and inheritance rights in Hankow, but further reform proved impossible. The democratic and women's rights movements of the 1920s flourished mainly in urban areas with large middle-class populations but made little progress in the rural countryside, where traditional family structures and economic life remained tightly interdependent.[26]

A similar pattern of democratic-nationalist movements leading to greater freedom for women only in middle-class, urban areas occurred in parts of the Middle East. Democratic nationalism proceeded furthest in Turkey, where Mustafa Kemal, a captain in the Turkish army in World War I, capitalized on anti-imperial sentiment to drive European powers from Turkish soil, topple the Sultan, and establish a Turkish Republic. Kemal then set upon a course of modernization, during which he secularized the state, Latinized the alphabet, introduced Western dress, adopted civil marriage and divorce, banned polygamy, granted female suffrage (in 1935), and encouraged capitalist development. One of the foremost beneficiaries of Kemal's reforms was Halide Edip, a woman nationalist who served in Kemal's forces. Born to an influential family and given a European education, Edip became a prominent novelist, political activist, and women's rights advocate. Important though the top-down reforms imposed by Kemal proved for privileged women like Edip, they did not reach the great mass of Turkish women, most of whom remained tied to the land and under the direct control of the men in their families.[27]

In other Middle Eastern countries, where colonial domination proved stronger, the middle class weaker, and Islamic leaders more entrenched, winning rights for women proved even more difficult, and, when attempted at all, was more often rooted in the indigenous culture. In Egypt demands for greater freedom for women were based not on secularization but rather on a reinterpretation of Islamic texts. Building on the work of Qasim Amin, whose 1899 book *Women's Emancipation*[28] argued that female exclusion, the veil, arranged marriages, and divorce practices were not true to the original tenets of Islam, Egyptian feminists led by Huda Sharawi called in the 1920s for equality of the sexes. They made little headway, for their numbers were minuscule and religious leaders successfully opposed any deviation from traditional laws and practices.[29]

## The Rise of a Consumer Culture

Apart from political changes, the decade after World War I brought about an important economic and cultural transformation, especially in urban areas. In the United States, and to a lesser extent elsewhere, consumer goods, including cars, radios, movies, washing machines, and vacuums, flooded the market. Young women who in a prior generation would have entertained young men on the family's front porch now "dated" in cars. While the automobile was hardly the "house of prostitution on wheels" that one U.S. juvenile-court judge charged it with being, it did provide those who could afford one the opportunity for much greater freedom from parental supervision. Young women abandoned their corsets, bobbed their hair, hiked up their skirts, wore skimpy bathing costumes at the beach, started wearing makeup, and smoked in public. Sensuous film stars Greta Garbo, Marlene Dietrich, and Mae West gazed out on many audiences around the world each week.

Black female dancer Josephine Baker, born in the United States but achieving fame in Paris, celebrated female eroticism in her revealing costumes and fluid movements.[30]

Taking advantage of this more open and positive view of sexuality, Margaret Sanger in the United States Marie Stopes in Britain, and Theodore van de Velde in Holland published sexual manuals for married couples that rhapsodized about the joys of physical love. Translated into every European language, these books sold hundreds of thousands of copies. Buoyed by the greater sexual openness of the postwar years and the relative freedom of cities like New York and Paris, a few women began writing more openly about lesbianism. In 1928 British author Radclyffe Hall published *The Well of Loneliness*, a novel about a young woman who believes she should have been born a man, and falls in love with other women. Although Hall was prosecuted and her book banned in England, her writings were widely discussed.[31]

Sigmund Freud also turned to the issue of female sexuality in the 1920s. Breaking with the nineteenth-century view that women's psychology simply mirrored their biological nature, Freud argued that women, like men, achieve psychological maturity through a complicated set of developmental stages. At the heart of women's psychosexual development, Freud theorized, was their envy of the penis. As a little girl reached the Oedipal, or in her case Electral, stage of development, she rejected her mother for not giving her a penis. Whereas a boy established independence and a strong sense of self-control, because he feared castration from his father if he did not, a girl, having no such fears, never achieved the same level of autonomy. Indeed, she went through life longing for the penis she could not have, until she married and bore a child, which served as a substitute.[32]

A few women analysts, including German-born Karen Horney, faulted Freud for misunderstanding women. Horney turned Freud's theory on its ear by arguing that women's feelings of inadequacy stemmed ultimately from men's envy of women's reproductive ability, which prompted them to subjugate women in an effort to redress the sexual balance of power.[33]

American anthropologist Margaret Mead broke even more decisively with traditional American and European beliefs in the biological inevitability of female passivity and male aggressiveness in her studies of peoples of the South Pacific. These peoples' concept of sexual temperament, she reported, bore little resemblance to American or European notions of "natural sex differences." Among the Arapesh of New Guinea men and women seemed equally passive and nurturing, while among the Mundugumor both were aggressive. All of the people she studied proved far more comfortable with their sexuality than the typical American or European. To Mead so-called sex traits were largely the product of culture, and could be changed.[34]

Many older people, including some feminists, condemned what they saw as the risks of the new erotic consumer culture. To them the new self-absorption and flood of goods represented a shift—from a stable culture governed by saving and self-control to an uncertain one of spending and instant gratification. In Egypt, feminist writer Malak Hifni Nassef criticized those who urged revealing Western clothes on Muslim women. Giving up the veil, she argued, meant not greater freedom but the certainty of sexual harassment. In America Charlotte Perkins Gilman denied that sexual "indulgence" was an improvement over "repression" and predicted that the growing availability of contraception would not improve marriage, as Sanger, Stopes, and Van de Velde alleged, but would rather turn it into a site of "unromantic, dutiful submission to male indulgence."[35]

## Depression, Fascism, and World War II

Debates over sexuality and gender norms continued into the 1930s, but a worldwide depression quickly overwhelmed women's efforts to improve their lives. Those who followed Alexandra Kollontai's belief, that a strong modern state would serve as a vehicle for protecting women from exploitation, found that a strong state could oppress as easily as it could protect. In the United States, Congress restricted the right of married women to work in 1932, and opponents of the birth control movement blamed the depression on the country's declining fertility. At the same time, feminists' ability to fight back foundered over their inability to agree on what goals to pursue. While most continued to believe that women needed special laws to protect them from exploitation, a growing minority insisted that women and men were essentially the same and should be governed by the same laws. This latter group was led by Alice Paul, a young firebrand whose acts of civil disobedience on behalf of suffrage landed her in jail. With the vote won, she called for an Equal Rights Amendment, despite the objections of other women leaders that such an amendment would render unconstitutional all the protective laws they had fought so many decades to secure.[36]

In Germany, Spain, and Italy any discussion of equality was drowned out by fascists for whom the women's rights movement symbolized all that was wrong with modern morality, with its emphasis on the self and its rejection of traditional constraints. Whereas feminists demanded independence for women, fascists called for a renewed emphasis on maternity. Opposing recent advances in women's rights as a "product of the Jewish intellectual," Hitler promised women in 1934 "emancipation from emancipation." To encourage women to leave the workforce and bear children, the Nazis granted a Marriage Loan to married women who left their jobs. One-quarter of the loan was canceled with the birth of each legitimate child. The Nazis also closed sexual counseling centers and banned abortions, except for those deemed undesirable, like Jews and Gypsies. Under Mussolini the Italian government excluded women from government offices, doubled the fees of female secondary school and university students, and strove to prevent rural women from moving to urban areas. Together with Pope Pius XI, Mussolini condemned any form of birth control other than abstinence and called on women to bear more children. In China, Chiang Kai-shek ushered in a period of neo-Confucianism under which women's subordinate status was stressed. And in the Soviet Union, economic crisis killed off the last remaining vestiges of feminism, as concern over industrial production supplanted any interest in consumer goods or women's rights. Stalin called on women to produce more children and abolished the right to abortion (established under Lenin) to increase the likelihood that they would.[37]

Only in Latin America did women's rights movements continue to make gains. Allied with democratic movements and united through the Inter-American Commission of Women, Latin American feminists built on the democratic rhetoric of male leaders to argue that democracy could only succeed if women enjoyed the same basic rights as men and shared the same commitment to democratic freedom. Between 1929 and 1939, Ecuador, Brazil, Uruguay, Cuba, and El Salvador all granted women the vote.[38]

World War II challenged the belligerents to reconsider their commitment to pronatalism in order to staff war industries. For Germany, Italy, and Japan the cultural shift that such a reconsideration required proved too difficult, but in Britain and the United States governments quickly turned to "woman-power" in response to labor shortages. Throughout the war, U.S. and British women enjoyed greater occupational opportunity and higher wages than ever before. But the war did little to bring permanent change to gender relations. Men's absence increased their value in women's eyes, and the daily dangers of warfare made women's rights seem unimportant.[39]

## The Aftermath of World War II

More than 50 million people died in World War II. Twelve million perished in German concentration camps alone, another 20 million in Russia, and 10 million in China. Tired of war, seeking stability and a new affirmation of life, couples married and bore children. Indeed, marriage and birthrates soared as they never had in response to the pronatalist exhortations of Hitler, Stalin, or Mussolini in the 1930s. The United States, which had been relatively protected from the conflict, experienced a burst of prosperity as it found itself virtually without economic competition in the world. Europe, much of which had been devastated by the war, took much longer to recover: Western Europe, aided by U.S. funds, completed rebuilding by the end of the 1950s, but Eastern Europe, whose resources were depleted by the Soviet Union, lagged far behind. The devastation suffered throughout Europe, combined with the growing influence of labor and the fear that a depression would lead to a resurgence of fascism, led to the implementation of more generous social welfare policies in many countries. These policies made it possible for women to bear children while continuing to work. Conservative countries like France and Italy and socialist countries like Sweden and the Soviet Union provided supportive structures for working mothers that included pregnancy benefits, free health care, day care, and after-school programs.[40]

Protected from the ravages of war, the United States did not feel the same pressure to ease the lot of working mothers. And yet mothers worked as never before. Pent-up consumer demand fueled an economic boom that created new jobs, many of which women filled. In fact, though most women lost their high-paying war industry jobs in 1945, women's workforce participation rates were back up to the wartime high by the end of the 1940s, and women continued to enter new fields in the service and white-collar sectors in the following decades. By 1970, 43 percent of all U.S. women were engaged in wage labor, roughly the same levels as in France, Germany, and Britain.[41]

At the turn of the century the vast majority of women wage workers in the United States and Europe had been young, single women, with no more than a primary school education, who were working for a few years before marriage. By the 1940s, however, a new pattern had established itself: the majority of women workers from that decade forward would be married women over the age of 35. As younger women stayed in school longer, older women increasingly took their place in the work force. Driven by the need to replace the income children had once provided, lured by the prospect of being able to purchase a steadily expanding array of consumer goods, and freed by technological improvements from some of the heavier housework that had burdened their mothers, older women took jobs. Moreover, even as women bore more children in the decade after World War II, increasing use of birth control enabled them to concentrate their childbearing years in their twenties.

By their mid-thirties their youngest children were going off to school, and, with improved health care, women could look forward to another thirty years of productivity.

As women workers changed, so too did the jobs they took. The young woman worker in 1900 tended to work in domestic service, agriculture, or industry. By 1950 factory work remained, but domestic service and agriculture had been all but replaced by white-collar and service jobs. In Germany at the turn of the century, one-third of all women workers were engaged in agriculture and another third worked as domestics; by 1950 those occupations claimed only 8 and 12 percent of women workers respectively.[42]

Although World War II brought prosperity to the United States, and eventually to Western Europe, it destabilized the rest of the world, giving rise to civil war and wars of national liberation, especially in old European colonies. In all of these struggles women played an important role, and won new freedom for their sex as a result. In India, which won independence from Britain in 1947, women won equal political rights and a new emphasis on female education. In France, Italy, and more than a dozen Latin American countries women won the vote in the decade following the war.[43]

Nowhere did more dramatic change take place in the postwar years than in China. In 1949, the Communists took power and immediately passed laws meant to free women. According to the sixth article of the country's new constitution, "The People's Republic of China shall abolish the feudal system that holds women in bondage. Women shall enjoy equal rights with men in political, economic, cultural, educational, and social life. Freedom of marriage for men and women shall be put into effect." The following year the government issued the "Marriage Law," which prohibited bigamy, concubinage, and child-bride marriages; guaranteed men and women freedom to marry as well as to divorce; and granted widows the right to remarry. Immediately after passing the Marriage Law the Chinese government passed the Land Reform Act, under which 117 million acres were distributed to peasants without regard to sex. Not since the 1920s in the Soviet Union had any society tried to transform its gender system so completely, or so quickly. In urban areas the government enjoyed considerable success in undercutting parental control of marriage, discouraging through its housing policy the extended families of the past, and training women for a wide variety of jobs that had never been open to them before. Even those in rural areas experienced change. During the Great Leap Forward of the 1950s women's participation in collective labor reached its height, and rural brigades set up dining halls, nurseries, and sewing groups to free as many women as possible to work alongside men.[44]

But the ideal of gender equality exceeded the government's capacity to pay for these amenities. Bad planning and worse weather forced cutbacks and, as in the Russia of the 1920s, the programs meant to free women from domestic work were the first to go. Male leaders resisted granting women the same number of work points as men, even when the work being done was exactly the same, and they objected to training women in more technical skills. As a result women often retired from field work as soon as they had a daughter-in-law who could replace them. In fact, women could often make as much from raising vegetables and pigs as the men could make from the crops they grew. Nor did traditional families change as much as the government expected. While young people in urban areas gradually came to play an active role in arranging their own marriages, parents in rural areas continued to exercise considerable control. In the 1950s, young women who sought to make up their own minds regarding marriage or divorce were frequently beaten, tortured, and even killed for what their communities regarded as "loose behavior." A young man who defied his parents usually found that he no longer had a home to which he could bring his bride.[45]

The one area in which the government produced dramatic change, even in the countryside, was in birth control. By the end of the 1950s it was clear that socialism could not bring prosperity to the Chinese if the country could not control its birthrate. Taking aggressive action, Party leaders set birth quotas for each county or municipality, and established conditions that would allow the quotas to be met. The main features included an impressive distribution system of high-quality contraceptive devices, regulations against early marriage, economic incentives for having only one child, disincentives for ignoring the government's "call," a massive bureaucratic system with constant follow-up that did not allow the individual much choice, and abortion—coerced—if necessary. From a high of almost eight children per family in rural areas in 1963 and six in urban areas, the birthrate fell to less than three in the countryside and a little over one in the cities by 1980.[46]

Women clearly benefited physically from having fewer children than their mothers once had, but the new system had certain costs. The strong preference for male children led to a marked increase in female infanticide in rural areas, and women who would have liked to have had more children were barred by social pressure, or if necessary physical force, from doing so.

Women participated along with men in the revolution that brought socialism to power in the late 1940s, but during the 1950s economic crises prompted male leaders to narrow the revolution's goals to exclude the principal concerns of women. Those few feminists who sought to enlist women in a revolution of their own were either silenced or persuaded that their revolution would have to wait.[47]

## The Rebirth of Feminism

When feminism finally reappeared, it did so not in China or the Soviet Union, which had launched the boldest initiatives on women's behalf, but in the United States. Inspired by the civil rights movement of the 1950s and the worldwide wars of liberation of the 1960s, U.S. women asserted their own claims to equality and liberation.

Much had changed in the four decades since the first wave of feminism. In the United States and Europe women's educational levels had increased dramatically. Women were spending more of their life in the paid workforce. Improvements in health care extended women's life expectancy. And except for the temporary rise in the birthrate after World War II, women were spending less time raising children. Yet the opportunities available to women were not keeping pace with the other changes in their lives. Women college graduates were no longer content to take temporary jobs as secretaries until they married. They wanted careers. Working-class women who did the same work as men were no longer willing to be paid less for it, especially when a rising divorce rate increased the chance of their having to support both themselves and their children.

American author Betty Friedan galvanized many educated, middle-class women in 1963 with her book *The Feminine Mystique*,[48] in which she condemned the media, social scientists, psychoanalysts, and educators for telling women that they could only achieve happiness by dedicating their lives to full-time domesticity. The following year women gained a second boost, when Virginia Representative Howard Smith moved to amend a civil rights bill being debated in Congress. As drafted, the bill barred employers from discriminating on the basis of race; Smith added "sex" as a protected category. Whether Smith was motivated by a racist desire to scuttle the bill or a chivalrous impulse to give women the same rights as men was never clear, but the bill became the Civil Rights Act of 1964 as amended. When the federal government failed to enforce the act's sex provision, a group of women professionals led by Betty Friedan organized the National Organization of Women in 1966. Within a year the new organization was fighting for an equal rights amendment, day-care centers, and access to safe and legal abortions.[49]

By 1968 the new feminist movement had spread throughout Europe and was becoming radicalized. Its young members began demanding not just equal rights and economic equality, but also a full discussion of "sexism," by which they meant the tendency of men to stereotype all women as inferior. By 1970, some feminists were calling for the abolition of the family, while others were urging women to see lesbians as the true feminists, women whose loyalties were not vitiated by sexual relations with men.[50]

Whatever their particular approach, all modern feminists came to see "gender" as a central conceptual category. They particularly liked to quote French existentialist philosopher Simone de Beauvoir's observation in *The Second Sex* (1949) that "One is not born, but rather becomes, a woman." In other words, "sex" is a biological attribute, present at birth, but "gender" is a complex of attitudes and behaviors that individuals gradually absorb from their culture. De Beauvoir had struggled all her life to win success in a male world on male terms, and her writings implied that liberation would only come when women had succeeded in transcending the lives they led as wives and mothers and began thinking and acting like men. During the 1960s her approach won wide acceptance among feminists. By the 1970s, however, a younger generation began criticizing her idealization of men.[51]

Returning to a theme popular among women reformers at the turn of the century in Europe and the Americas, many younger feminists began arguing that the trouble with the world was not that women were not more like men, but that men were not more like women. For them men's reduction of half the population to a state of dependency had produced adverse consequences in every dimension of human relations, from sexual congress to foreign affairs.

Among feminists, lesbians in particular emphasized women's special strengths. Ever since a 1969 police raid on a gay bar at the Stonewall Inn in New York City's Greenwich Village ignited a riot in which gays and lesbians lashed back at their tormentors, homosexuals had been speaking out against traditional conceptions of gender and sexuality. Men as well as women, they argued, suffered from the straitjacket effect imposed by conventional norms of heterosexuality, and personal liberation required emancipation from those norms. One group, the Radicalesbians, proclaimed that such emancipation would only be complete when women freed themselves from male relationships altogether and identified with one another. "It is the primacy of women's relations to women," wrote one Radicalesbian, "which is at the heart of women's liberation and the basis of cultural revolution." In short, only women living and working with other women could envision a fundamentally new social order, freed of traditional patriarchal constraints that were harmful to men as well as women.[52]

## Changes in the Developing World

If the second wave of feminism began in the United States and Europe, it soon spread throughout the world. Especially as women began playing an important role in the United Nations in the 1970s and 1980s, and as indigenous women, profiting from improved education, began to speak for themselves, the particular concerns of non-Western women achieved wider expression. Increasingly, these women challenged the belief of those in developed countries that capitalist expansion had benefited women everywhere. In much of Africa, for instance, colonization had led to mass migration of men into urban areas. Since the jobs available to them never paid enough to support a family, women and children tended to stay behind to farm or were forced into the so-called informal market, where they traded goods. Far from improving women's lives, twentieth-century colonialism in Africa created greater hardship. Indeed, the biggest change in the lives of most African women over the course of the century was that their workday lengthened, as they struggled to produce and trade enough to feed their families in the absence of adult men. The imposition of European systems of private property aggravated their problems, because men gained title to the land that the women worked, making it difficult for them to secure loans to make improvements. For African women, in sum, the twentieth century brought a reduction in their customary rights to land, freedom of movement, and economic autonomy.[53]

In addition, the process of Westernization, which in the early twentieth century had fostered the first wave of feminism in Africa, the Middle East, and Asia, had elicited, by the 1970s and 1980s, a fierce backlash. In fact, because feminism had for so long been associated with the West and—in some cases—with leaders who imposed a Western ethos, late-twentieth-century political movements often, especially in Islamic countries, combined anti-colonialism with anti-Western-inspired feminism—frequently with the strong support of patriotic women. In Iran, where Reza Shah gained power through a military coup after World War I and imposed a policy of Westernization that culminated in his 1936 order that women no longer wear the veil, the long-simmering resentment of democrats and Islamic fundamentalists alike erupted in 1979. Reza Shah's son and successor was deposed and religious leaders gained control, reimposing religious rule, and ordering women once more to veil themselves. Many women resisted, but others welcomed the reassertion of Islamic, rather than Western, identity. Many young, urban women voluntarily readopted the veil, seeing it as a bulwark against both Western immorality and male aggression. In other Middle Eastern and Asian countries, civil codes granting all citizens equal rights coexisted with religious laws that severely restricted women's freedoms. Tensions between national law and religious law reached particular intensity in South Asia, where bitter divisions between Hindus and Muslims led to a renewed emphasis on the control of women as fundamental to the maintenance of group identity.[54]

In an effort to strengthen the position of women in non-Western countries, feminists began to advocate a combination of social, economic, and legal reforms. In the Middle East, feminists disagreed over whether to condemn veiling as oppressive or to endorse it as a valuable protection against sexual harassment in public life, but they shared a common commitment to legal reforms that would guarantee women equal rights in economic and family law. In Africa women leaders demanded educational programs geared to the needs of female subsistence farmers, health programs to combat high maternal and child mortality and to provide birth control, and campaigns to discourage the practice of genital mutilation. At the same time, grassroots organizers in India arranged for bank loans for women traders, campaigned against the practice of bride-burning (carried out by in-laws dissatisfied with the size of a new wife's dowry), and publicized the prevalence of rape.[55]

Not all women's organizing derived from explicitly feminist aspirations. In Latin America, for instance, women began to organize around issues having to do with care of home and family, seeking better health care, electricity, and running water in urban slums, and child care. Though they did not think of themselves as feminists, they organized along gendered lines and engaged aggressively in the political sphere on behalf of these gendered interests.[56]

## What Has Changed Since 1900?

In many ways, the changes that have taken place in women's lives throughout the world in the twentieth century are staggering. Economic growth and improvements in public health have brought increases in life expectancy to every region. In developed countries women's life expectancy now exceeds 75 years, and even in Africa it has risen to 54 years, thanks to the widespread reduction of infectious and parasitic diseases. At the same time women in developed countries are bearing fewer children, as improved family planning methods make it easier to limit fertility.[57]

Almost everywhere, women are working more outside the home and engaging in politics. As of 1990, 60 percent of all women in the United States, the USSR, and East Asia participated in the labor force. Women now make up more than half of most electorates, and in Scandinavian countries constitute about 30 percent of all legislators.[58]

Unfortunately, these striking gains are offset by continuing inequalities in every aspect of women's lives. Women only rarely hold top positions in unions or business, job segregation and wage discrimination persist, and everywhere women continue to shoulder primary responsibility for domestic labor. Even in the United States and Europe, where women now earn between 70 and 80 percent of what men do, women work longer hours than men each week. Women in the United States work about an extra month each year; in Africa more than two months. The economic crises of the 1980s hit women particularly hard. As heads of households they were more likely to be poor, and with cutbacks in social services they had fewer resources to fall back on. Because women lacked collateral and found it difficult to secure loans from most banks, they had to rely on informal lending institutions and pay high rates of interest.[59]

In politics women remain second-class citizens. They only rarely hold top positions in political parties or governments. Of the 159 United Nations member states in 1990, only six were headed by women. Only 3.5 percent of the world's cabinet ministers are women, and in 93 countries women hold no ministerial positions at all. As a consequence, government officials (along with business leaders) have been slow to understand the ways in which gendered assumptions have shaped economic and governmental policies, with serious consequences, both for women individually and for the world as it approaches the twenty-first century.[60]

Leaders have failed, in particular, to appreciate the degree to which some of the world's most serious problems are rooted in women's subordination. Perhaps the greatest danger for the future stems from the present surge in the world's population. This surge, which is concentrated in the poorer parts of Africa and South Asia, is leading to growing demographic imbalances between rich and poor countries, with political and environmental effects that could well threaten future human existence.[61]

Inattention to the needs of women, especially in developing countries, has played a critical role in producing this problem. While improvements in public health have led to reduced infant mortality throughout the world, women in poorer regions still bear large numbers of children, because they have benefited so little from the educational and economic changes that have improved the status of women elsewhere. In most countries in the developed world, decades of universal primary education have nearly eradicated illiteracy, and women have achieved parity with men in high school and college education. But in the Caribbean and Latin America 20 percent of all women are still illiterate, as are 40 percent in eastern and southeastern Asia and 70 percent in southern and western Asia and in sub-Saharan Africa. High rates of illiteracy go hand-in-hand with low rates of contraceptive use. Whereas in developed regions over 70 percent of all couples use contraception, in the developing world use averages only 30 percent and in parts of Africa and southern Asia the figure is much lower. According to the experience of richer countries, an improvement in the status of women in the developing world, through better education, economic opportunity, and access to birth control, would significantly reduce population growth, with benefits for the world as a whole.[62]

In the developed world, and especially among the middle classes and upper-middle classes, the challenge is different, but it still involves the position of women in society. In many developed countries fertility levels have fallen below replacement levels. Faced with the strain of caring for families and working outside the home, women throughout the developed world have simply been having fewer children. The danger in this decline is that these developed societies (unless they open their doors more widely to immigration) will soon not have enough people of working age to support elderly people no longer able to work. The only countries that have reversed this trend are those European countries, like Sweden, that have fashioned social policies to make childbearing more attractive to women. If developed countries are to reverse their declining fertility rates they would do well to look to those countries that have done so by providing paid maternity *and* paternity leave, child care, kindergarten, and housing, along with a significant degree of overall gender equality, measured, for example, by the number of female politicians and cabinet ministers.

Ironically, whether the goal is to raise fertility or to reduce it, changing gender roles in the interests of achieving greater gender equality appears to be a necessary precondition. Consciousness about gender will not eradicate the political or environmental challenges that the world faces in the next century, but inattention to gender will help guarantee poverty in much of the world, undercut efforts to control world population growth, and perpetuate the gender tensions that prompted Henrik Ibsen's Nora in *A Doll's House* to leave home.[63]

ENDNOTES

1.  Ono Kazuko, *Chinese Women in a Century of Revolution*, ed. Joshua A. Fogel (Stanford: Stanford University Press, 1989), p. 99; Brian Powell, "Matsui Sumako:

Actress and Woman," in *Modern Japan: Aspects of History, Literature and Society*, ed. W. G. Beasely (Berkeley: University of California Press, 1975), pp. 135–46.

2. Sharon Nolte, *Liberalism in Modern Japan: Ishibashi Tanzan and His Teachers, 1905–1960* (Berkeley: University of California Press, 1986), pp. 97–104.

3. Peter Filene, *Him/Her/Self: Sex Roles in Modern America*, 2nd ed. (Baltimore: Johns Hopkins University Press, 1986), pp. 6–7.

4. Nancy Cott, *The Grounding of Modern Feminism* (New Haven: Yale University Press, 1987), pp. 13–50.

5. Judith Stacey, *Patriarchy and Socialist Revolution in China* (Berkeley: University of California Press, 1983), pp. 40–41; Robin Morgan, ed., *Sisterhood Is Global* (New York: Doubleday, 1984), pp. 761–62.

6. Lynne Brydon and Sylvia Chant, *Women in the Third World: Gender Issues in Rural and Urban Areas* (New Brunswick: Rutgers University Press, 1989), pp. 69–120.

7. Bonnie S. Anderson and Judith P. Zinsser, *A History of Their Own: Women in Europe from Prehistory to the Present*, 2 vols. (New York: Harper and Row, 1988), 2:24–41; United Nations, *The World's Women: Trends and Statistics, 1970–1990* (New York: United Nations, 1991), p. 59.

8. Anderson and Zinsser, *A History of Their Own*, 1:284–85.

9. James Reed, *The Birth Control Movement and American Society: From Private Vice to Public Virtue* (Princeton: Princeton University Press, 1983), pp. 3–18.

10. Karen Offen, "Depopulation, Nationalism, and Feminism in Fin-de-Siècle France," *American Historical Review* (89) (June 1984): 648–76; Margaret Strobel, "Gender and Race in the Nineteenth- and Twentieth-Century British Empire," in Renata Bridenthal, Claudia Koonz, and Susan Stuard, eds., *Becoming Visible: Women in European History*, 2nd ed. (Boston: Houghton Mifflin, 1987), p. 386; Linda Gordon, *Woman's Body, Woman's Rights* (New York: Viking, 1976), pp. 136–58.

11. Bonnie Smith, *Changing Lives: Women in European History Since 1700* (Lexington, Mass.: D.C. Heath, 1989), pp. 317–30.

12. Karen Offen, "Liberty Equality and Justice for Women: The Theory and Practice of Feminism in Nineteenth-Century Europe," in Bridenthal, Koonz, and Stuard, eds., *Becoming Visible*, 2nd ed., pp. 335–73; Rosalind Rosenberg, *Divided Lives: American Women in the Twentieth Century* (New York: Hill and Wang, 1992), pp. 36–62.

13. Kazuko, *Chinese Women*, pp. 112–13.

14. Francesca Miller, *Latin American Women and the Search for Social Justice* (Hanover: University Press of New England, 1991), pp. 68–109.

15. John Stuart Mill and Harriet Taylor Mill, *Essays on Sex Equality*, ed. Alice Rossi (Chicago: University of Chicago Press, 1970), p. 120; Edith F. Hurwitz, "The International Sisterhood," in Bridenthal, Koonz, and Stuard, eds., *Becoming Visible*, p. 331.

16. Anderson and Zinsser, *A History of Their Own*, p. 366; Cott, *The Grounding of*

*Modern Feminism*, pp. 53–62; Susan Kingsley Kent, *Sex and Suffrage in Britain, 1860–1914* (Princeton: Princeton University Press, 1987), pp. 184–219.

17. Smith, *Changing Lives*, pp. 308–13.

18. Anderson and Zinsser, *A History of Their Own*, 2:387.

19. Charlotte Perkins Gilman, *Women and Economics* (Boston: Maynard and Co., 1898), pp. 225–69 and passim; Ann J. Lane, *To Herland and Beyond: The Life and Work of Charlotte Perkins Gilman* (New York: Pantheon, 1990), pp. 230–32.

20. Smith, *Changing Lives*, pp. 342–50; Ellen Chesler, *Woman of Valor: Margaret Sanger and the Birth Control Movement in America* (New York: Simon and Schuster, 1992), pp. 95–97, 124–25, 186–90.

21. Susan Pedersen, *Family, Dependence, and the Origins of the Welfare State, Britain and France, 1914–1945* (New York: Cambridge University Press, 1993), pp. 79–134.

22. Steven C. Hause with Anne R. Kenney, *Women's Suffrage and Social Politics in the French Third Republic* (Princeton: Princeton University Press, 1984), p. 253.

23. Richard Stites, *The Women's Liberation Movement in Russia: Feminism, Nihilism, and Bolshevism, 1860–1930* (Princeton: Princeton University Press, 1978), pp. 317–421.

24. Anderson and Zinsser, *A History of Their Own*, 2:297–300.

25. Kazuko, *Chinese Women*, pp. 93–105.

26. Ibid., pp. 105–11; Christina K. Gilmartin, "Gender, Political Culture, and Women's Mobilization in the Chinese Nationalist Revolution, 1924–1927," in Christina Gilmartin et al., eds., *Engendering China: Women Culture and the State* (Cambridge: Harvard University Press, 1994), pp. 195–225.

27. Kumari Jayawardena, *Feminism and Nationalism in the Third World* (London: Zed Books, 1986), pp. 27–42.

28. Qasim Amin, *The Liberation of Women: A Document in the History of Egyptian Feminism* (Cairo: American University Press, 1992).

29. Jayawardena, *Feminism and Nationalism in the Third World*, pp. 43–56.

30. Robert Lynd and Helen Lynd, *Middletown: A Culture in Transition* (New York: Harcourt, Brace, 1928), p. 114; Beth Bailey, *From Front Porch to Back Seat: Courtship in Twentieth-Century America* (Baltimore: Johns Hopkins University Press, 1988), pp. 1–12; Smith, *Changing Lives*, pp. 440–41; Mary Louise Roberts, *Civilization Without Sexes: Reconstructing Gender in Postwar France, 1917–1927* (Chicago: University of Chicago Press, 1994), p. 1.

31. Chesler, *Woman of Valor*, pp. 263–66; Smith, *Changing Lives*, pp. 448.

32. Sigmund Freud, "Some Psychological Consequences of the Anatomical Distinction Between the Sexes,"(1925) reprinted in Philip Reiff, ed. *Sexuality and the Psychology of Love* (New York: Colliers, 1963), 183–93.

33. Karen Horney, "The Flight from Womanhood: The Masculinity Complex in Women as Viewed by Men and by Women," *International Journal of Psycho-Analysis* 7 (1926): 324–39.

34. Margaret Mead, *Sex and Temperament in Three Primitive Societies* (New York: Morrow, 1935), pp. 310–39.

35. Gilman quoted in Nancy Woloch, *Women and the American Experience* (New York: Knopf, 1984), p. 413. Leila Ahmed, *Women and Gender in Islam* (New Haven: Yale University Press, 1992), pp. 169–88.

36. Rosenberg, *Divided Lives*, p. 103; Cott, *The Grounding of Modern Feminism*, pp. 137–42; Lois Scharf, *To Work and to Wed: Female Employment, Feminism and the Great Depression* (Westport: Greenwood, 1980), pp. 46–47.

37. Victoria de Grazia, "How Mussolini Ruled Italian Women," in Thebaud, *A History of Women in the West*, eds. George Duby and Michelle Perrot, vol. 5 (Cambridge: Belknap Press of Harvard University Press, 1994), pp. 120–148; Anderson and Zinsser, *A History of Their Own*, pp. 301–7; Smith, *Changing Lives*, pp. 458–72.

38. Miller, *Latin American Women*, p. 110.

39. D'Ann Campbell, *Women at War with America: Private Lives in a Patriotic Era* (Cambridge: Harvard University Press, 1984), pp. 101–38; Anderson and Zinsser, *A History of Their Own*, pp. 306–7; Smith, *Changing Lives*, pp. 482–87.

40. Gisela Bock, "Poverty and Mothers' Rights in the Emerging Welfare States," in *Toward a Cultural Identity in the Twentieth Century*, pp. 402–33; Smith, *Changing Lives*, pp. 512–17.

41. Linda Schmittroth, ed., *Statistical Record of Women Worldwide* (Detroit: Gale Research, Inc., 1991), p. 388.

42 Rosenberg, *Divided Lives*, pp. 157–57; Ute Frevert, *Women in German History: From Bourgeois Emancipation to Sexual Liberation* (New York: Berg, 1989), Table 8. See also Robert Moeller, *Protecting Motherhood: Women and the Family in the Politics of Postwar West Germany* (Berkeley: University of California Press, 1992), passim.

43. Jayawardena, *Feminism and Nationalism in the Third World*, pp. 95–108; Hause, *Women's Suffrage and Social Politics in the French Third Republic*, pp. 248–81; Miller, *Latin American Women*, p. 96.

44. Kazuko, *Chinese Women*, pp. 140–86.

45. Margery Wolf, *Revolution Postponed: Women in Contemporary China* (Stanford: Stanford University Press, 1983), pp. 79–273.

46. Judith Stacey, *Patriarchy and Socialist Revolution in China* (Berkeley: University of California Press, 1983), pp. 158–94.

47. Ibid.

48. Betty Friedan, *The Feminine Mystique* (New York: Norton, 1963).

49. Rosenberg, *Divided Lives*, pp. 180–92.

50. Ibid., pp. 192–208.

51. Simone de Beauvoir, *The Second Sex* (New York: Alfred Knopf, 1952), p. 267; Deirdre Bair, *Simone de Beauvoir: A Biography* (New York: Summit, 1990), pp. 379–95, 543–57, and 605–18.

52. Radicalesbians, "The Woman Identified Woman," in Anne Koedt, Ellen Levine, and Anita Rapone, eds., *Radical Feminism* (New York: Quadrangle, 1973), p. 245.

53. Lynne Brydon and Sylvia Chant, *Women in the Third World: Gender Issues in Rural and Urban Areas* (New Brunswick: Rutgers University Press, 1989), pp. 1–47 and passim; Kathleen Staudt, "The State and Gender in Colonial Africa," in Sue Ellen M. Charlton, Jana Everett, and Kathleen Staudt, eds., *Women, the State, and Development* (Albany: State University of New York Press, 1989), pp. 66–85.

54. Sattareh Farman Farmaian, *Daughter of Persia: A Woman's Journey from Her Father's Harem Through the Islamic Revolution* (New York: Crown, 1992), pp. 159–289; Deniz Kandiyoti, ed., *Women, Islam and the State* (Philadelphia: Temple University Press, 1991), pp. 4–7.

55. Ahmed, *Women and Gender in Islam*, pp. 208–48; Hay and Stichter, *African Women*, pp. 140–82; Leslie Calman, *Toward Empowerment: Women and Movement Politics in India* (Boulder: Westview Press, 1992), pp. 55–65.

56. Maxine Molyneux, "Mobilization Without Emancipation: Women's Interests, the State, and the Revolution in Nicaragua," *Feminist Studies* 11 (Summer 1985): 227–54.

57. United Nations, *World's Women: Trends and Statistics, 1970–1990*, p. 55.

58. Ibid., pp. 31–32.

59. Ibid., pp. 88–89.

60. Ibid., pp. 31–35.

61. Paul Kennedy, *Preparing for the Twenty-First Century* (New York: Random House, 1993), pp. 329–43.

62 United Nations, "Levels and Trends of Contraceptive Use as Assessed in 1988," *Population Studies* 110 (New York: United Nations, 1989), pp. 73–77; Bryden and Chant, *Women in the Third World*, pp. 188–212.

63. Kennedy, *Preparing for the Twenty-First Century*, p. 343.

# 4 Religion

ZACHARY KARABELL

If one were forced to summarize religion in the twentieth century in a sentence rather than a chapter, it might be said that the past hundred years have consisted of an extended struggle between organized religion and secular nationalism. Like two heavyweights lumbering through a long fight, these two have come to know each other intimately, and they have even learned from each other. Organized religion, particularly in the early decades of the century but continuing today, has often utilized the tools of secularism and nationalism, while the latter have developed many of the attributes of a religion.

Religion is at best an imprecise term. Wilfred Cantwell Smith, one of the deans of modern religious studies, once called for a moratorium on the word, saying that it was unintelligible. Professor Smith's frustration notwithstanding, "religion" remains firmly embedded in our vocabulary, even as its definition remains vague. At the very least, "religion" implies an allegiance to the nonmaterial, organizing forces of existence. The nature of these forces varies depending on one's creed. In the Western monotheistic traditions of Judaism, Christianity, and Islam, *the* force is God and the principles are God's commandments, God's revealed word, and the moral life of his prophets or—in the case of Christianity—of his son, Jesus Christ. In some Eastern traditions, particularly in Buddhism and in certain branches of Hinduism, the organizing force is the atman, the divinity within each individual. And in animist religions of Africa, the South Pacific, or in Japan's Shintoism, the guiding principle is found in nature.

Secularism rejects both the nonmaterial orientation of most religious traditions and the notion that order and meaning lie beyond the reach of man's reason. It elevates scientific knowledge and empirical experience above faith and the mystery of the divine. Given the vagaries of Western history, secularism in the modern world is closely tied to nationalism, another umbrella term best defined as an allegiance to the nation-state as the fount of order, law, and identity.

At times, nationalism harnesses religion in order to bind a group of individuals more tightly to the nation-state. Arab nationalism for much of the century has stressed that Arab culture is Muslim culture, and even Christian Arab nationalists such as the Syrian Michel Aflaq have tried to enlist Islam in the cause of Arab unity. Often, however, nationalism and religion are antagonistic, as the former supports the latter only insofar as it serves the interests of the nation-state while the latter asserts that the interests of the nation-state are ultimately secondary to the will of the divine.

Over the course of the century, the fortunes of religion have gone through extreme flux. In the early decades, religion was almost universally under attack by secular modernism and nationalism, and almost everywhere those concerned with it tried to halt the rapid retreat of religion from public and political life. Somewhat before mid-century, however, religion began to re-emerge as a potent factor in political life. Rather than primarily reacting to the assault of secular nationalism, religion began to offer alternatives, and by the last quarter of the century, its alternatives began to appeal to ever-larger proportions of people from the cities of North America to the plains of sub-Saharan Africa.

By New Year's 1900, Christianity had been under assault in Europe for more than a century. The rationalist movement of the 1700s known as the Enlightenment treated religion as the enemy of progress. The French Revolution raised the rights of man and loyalty to the state well above obeisance to God and the church. While in the past European monarchs and Christian prelates had competed for influence, neither had sought the eradication of the other. With the Enlightenment, the French Revolution, and the ascendancy of British liberalism, organized religion was denounced with vehemence and the church was stripped of land, influence, and power.

By the late nineteenth century, the turbulent forces of nationalism, the new doctrine of socialism, and the materialist philosophies of Karl Marx and the left-wing Hegelians had recast religion as the ally of traditional repressive societies bent on keeping the many enslaved to the whims of the few. Medical science made death less common, and with the gradual disappearance of random and frequent death, people's dependence on religion appeared to wane. As populations moved off the land and into industrializing cities, the social bonds of church and family were disrupted. And the rise of liberalism and its concomitant toleration allowed for a wide dissemination of ideas inimical to religion. Greater literacy gave more people access to materials that questioned traditional beliefs, and scientific discoveries in the fields of evolution and biology cast severe doubt on the historical accuracy of the Bible.

In largely Catholic southern Europe, the Church of the late 1800s was buf-feted by the humbling of the Pope by Italian nationalists, the organized cam-paign against the German Catholic Church by the new Prussian state and its chancellor Otto von Bismarck, and by the intense anticlericalism that erupted in France as a result of the Dreyfus affair (1894–1906). The affair culminated with the French government officially separating church and state, confiscat-ing church lands. In the Protestant north, religion was pushed out of the pub-lic realm and grudgingly allowed to continue its pastoral activities in private matters of morals and conscience. However, the British Anglican Church, the Swiss Calvinists, the Lutherans of Scandinavia, and Protestantism in general saw a steady decline of church membership and a steady erosion of respect.

In response to these setbacks, those unwilling to consign religion to the recess of private life attempted to modify it to suit the times. In the first decades of the twentieth century, a number of Christian Socialist parties made their appearance in Europe, including Germany and Switzerland, and theologians championed the notion of a Christianity that favored the "liber-ation" of the working class. In the 1920s, Pope Pius XI gave his imprimatur to a loose set of organizations known as Catholic Action. These societies, taking inspiration from thinkers such as Jacques Maritain of France, encouraged lay people to do the social work that had traditionally been done by priests. In Germany and Belgium, Catholic Action took the form of youth movements. In Spain, priests in Madrid founded Opus Dei in 1928—designed, like Catholic Action, to galvanize lay people to reintegrate the Church into soci-ety. Gravitating toward the Royalists in the Spanish Civil War (1936–1939), Opus Dei allied with conservatism and hierarchy, an allegiance that also char-acterized its activities in Latin America.

With the Russian Revolution of 1917 and the triumph of Marxist-Leninism, the Russian Orthodox Church faced intense persecution. In 1918, Vladimir Ilyich Lenin issued a seemingly innocuous decree calling for the separation of church and state that ushered in decades of hardship. Thousands of churches were closed and destroyed; priests were imprisoned or executed; and the met-ropolitan (bishop) of Petrograd refused to renounce his faith and was put on trial in 1922. Church icons were burned in public bonfires, and all monasteries were closed by the Soviet government. Still, millions nurtured their faith in private, either as acts of symbolic resistance to Soviet Communism or out of quiet conviction in God's existence. Within the non-Russian regions of the Soviet Union, religion was one of the few threads connecting Orthodox Ukrainians and the Muslims of Central Asia to their pre-Soviet identities.

What had begun as an internecine European struggle between religion and secular nationalism soon spread throughout the world. Borne on the wings of European colonialism and Western industrialism, the ideologies of modernity insinuated themselves into the most traditional societies. By 1900, the powers of Europe controlled virtually all of Africa and most of Asia. While the European presence in colonies was often minimal, most regions of the earth were exposed to at least some degree of colonial government with the concomitant introduction of European languages, laws, and culture. Accompanying colonialism were Christian missionaries, who established Christianity in sub-Saharan Africa and Asia.

When the missionaries set up schools and churches in China or Africa, they began to convert peoples from other religious faiths. In sub-Saharan Africa, French, German, Portuguese, and English missionaries won converts from the region's various animist religions and from Islam. In Asia, French Catholic missionaries made converts out of Indochinese Buddhists; the Dutch made minimal inroads into Indonesian Islam; and American and English Protestant missionaries saw limited success in China. Enjoying the protection of the colonial power, Christian missionaries contributed to the erosion of traditional faiths. Already weakened by the collapse of the indigenous state, the societies of Africa and Asia found their religions under siege as well.

Missionary Christianity was vibrant, but it was inseparable from a European colonial culture that celebrated a secular, scientific rationalism that undermined the universalist claims of religion. Just as Christian theologians in Europe attempted to formulate a response to secular modernity, so too Hindus in India and Muslims throughout the Near East tried to answer the challenge of the West.

In India, the response was as varied as Hinduism itself. Reacting to the claims of British administrators that Hinduism was a backward faith more steeped in superstition than the spirit, Hindu thinkers tried to isolate a "pure" textual Hinduism based on the ancient Vedic scriptures. Individuals such as M.N. Roy, Mohandas Gandhi (1869–1948), and the Bengali poet Rabindranath Tagore all sought to define Hinduism in terms of these scriptures and thereby to purge modern Hinduism of "corrupt" accretions such as rigid caste structure and idolatry.

However, these thinkers split over what role Hinduism was supposed to play in the political life of the country. With the formation of the Indian National Congress at the end of the nineteenth century and the growth of the Indian nationalist movement in the first decades of the twentieth, many believed that an India based on Hindu identity was doomed to failure. Not only was there a sizeable Muslim minority in India, but Hinduism was perceived by a goodly portion of intellectuals and nationalists as a regressive social force that would forever keep India subservient to the British. While Gandhi evoked images of Mother India and the Vedic tradition to galvanize Indian opposition to British rule, his colleague Jawaharlal Nehru opposed political Hinduism as incompatible with democracy. Until Indian independence in 1947, both strategies were followed, but with Gandhi's assassination in 1948, Nehru's secularism came to dominate Indian politics.

While Gandhi and others were concentrating on a reformed Hinduism that could be put to good use in the struggle for independence, Indian Muslims focused on Islam as a force of separatist nationalism. Comprising somewhat more than 10 percent of the subcontinent's population, the Muslims had ruled northern India before they were displaced by the British in the late eighteenth century. The Muslim League was created in 1906 in response to the Hindu patina of the Congress and, led by Muhammad Ali Jinnah (1876–1948), worked uneasily with Gandhi through the 1930s before Jinnah demanded the formation of a separate Muslim state. While Jinnah had been inspired by the great Indo-Muslim poet and mystic Muhammad Iqbal (1873–1938), his Islam was largely political, and the resulting creation of Pakistan represented an unusual fusion of religion and nationalism.

In the Muslim countries of North Africa and the Near East, there was, as in India, a series of attempts to reform Islam and harness it to nationalism. Faced with British and French economic, military, and political domination of their societies, the Arabs, Turks, and Persians tried to account for their failure to resist Western advances. Some found the answer in Western science and technology. The success of the Europeans, so this view went, was due to superior organization and superior military hardware, and those in turn stemmed from European science and modern government. Modernize the states and societies of the Muslim world, therefore, and soon European hegemony would be impossible to maintain.

Led by thinkers such as Muhammad Abduh (1849–1905), a generation of Muslim intellectuals asserted that Islam had originally fostered scientific inquiry and celebrated logic, reason, and technology. As a result, Muslims had almost overwhelmed European Christendom in the Middle Ages. But after that golden age, Muslims had departed from the true spirit of Islam and lost the inclination toward scientific progress. Only by embracing the essential compatibility between Islam and science could the societies of the Near East hope to compete with the Europeans.

Abduh's thinking influenced a generation of intellectuals and theologians. Some took from his work and championed Arab independence from European colonialism, while others expanded it into the realms of theology. According to Muhammad Rashid Rida (1865–1935), who championed the *salafiyya* tradition in the 1920s, all the knowledge essential to Islam in the modern world had been discovered by Muslims in the days of the Prophet Muhammad and his companions (seventh century A.D.). The task was to relearn what these ancients (*salaf*) had taught. While this was an inherently conservative agenda, in order to rediscover what the Muslim scholars of a millennium past had known, Muslims of the twentieth century had to employ many of the techniques of European scientific inquiry. Abduh and Rida thus represented one form of Muslim adaptation to the political and religious conundrum posed by European ascendancy.

Across the Atlantic Ocean, Latin Catholicism was not faring well. In country after country, the Catholic Church was disestablished by liberal reformist governments. While the church remained bound to the essentially conservative political structures of Argentina, Colombia, and Peru, elsewhere the church was stripped of many of its privileges and much of its vast landholdings. In Colombia, the church maintained a firm grasp over secondary education, but elsewhere secular universities and reform-minded liberal governments treated it as part and parcel of the "old order" that turn-of-the-century Latin American governments were eager to overturn.

Though Pope Leo XIII (1878–1903) had made a nod toward modern capitalism in his encyclical *Rerum Novarum* (1891), the church was often allied with the land-owning upper class that fought to preserve a system that kept peasants on the land and inhibited industrialization. While that social structure was not particularly in evidence in Argentina or Chile, it was very much the case in Peru, Central America, and Mexico. Disestablishing the church was one prong of a liberal, republican assault on a stagnant agrarian order that reformers believed was causing Latin America to fall drastically behind Europe.

The struggles between liberals and Catholics that stretched over the nineteenth century came to a symbolic head with the Mexican Revolution of 1910–1917. The Mexican Revolution was harshly anticlerical, and the 1917 Mexican Constitution even regulated the number of priests allowed in any one district. In the eyes of the revolutionary factions, the church's emphasis on heavenly rewards for suffering was simply liturgical pap designed to keep the peons on the land. Even after the fighting ended, the revolutionary government conducted a further pogrom against the church between 1926 and 1929, when many of the remaining church estates were confiscated. Church-state relations in Mexico began to thaw after 1940, when the dual threats of world war and communism led to an uneasy truce.

In North America, the situation was different. The United States and Canada are both multidenominational societies. Aside from Catholic Quebec, Canada is a Protestant nation, as is the United States. No Protestant denomination predominates, though Baptists and Methodists account for a significant portion of the Christian population in the United States Early in this century, the Catholic population in the United States was proportionally smaller than it became after mid-century, but it had achieved enough stature that Pope Pius X (1903–1914) terminated the mission status of the Catholic Church in the United States in 1908.

While anti-Catholicism was a staple of various nativist and populist parties in nineteenth-century America, the fissiparous nature of Christianity in the United States meant that the church did not come under the same fire by reformers and liberals as it did in Europe or Latin America. With the rapid expansion of business and capital in the early twentieth century, Protestant churches often allied with the social reformers of the period. The first decades of the century were dominated by the Progressive movement, which sought to humanize working conditions and improve the sorry state of American cities.

In response to the social Darwinism of the business class, church-minded souls turned to urban missions such as Jane Addams's Hull House in turn-of-the-century Chicago. Others were more explicit in their attempts to bring Christian morality into what appeared to be an increasingly acquisitive, amoral society. Walter Rauschenbusch (1861–1918) was a leading voice of the "Social Gospel," and his *Christianity and Social Crisis* (1907) addressed the problem of urban slums and the horrible living conditions that the working poor found themselves in. The stress was very much on creating a "kingdom of God on earth" and so harkened back to the early Puritan tradition of building in the New World "a city on a hill."

The Social Gospel was a white, middle-class sensibility that largely ignored or resisted examining the plight of blacks or women in industrial America. As an intellectual response to social conditions, it did not capture the spirit of believers. Though the harsh doctrines of predestination fell from favor in Baptist and Methodist circles at this time, there was a surge of new movements calling on believers to "be saved." From pulpits and pamphlets, Christians were told that they could and must exercise their free will and choose to surrender themselves to the infallibility of the Scripture and the divinity of Christ. Pentecostalism gained ground in the American heartland, and in the late 1910s, groups of Protestants began to espouse what they called the "fundamentals" of Christianity. In 1919, like-minded Protestants formed the

World Christian Fundamentalist Society, calling for a rejection of the liberal, modernist theology of Christians like Rauschenbusch.

The reaction against both secular society and those who tried to synthesize scientific rationalism with religion was not unique to the United States. While some religious reformers tried to harmonize religion and modernity, others focused on spiritual reawakening and on constructing a firm theological edifice to counteract secular nationalism.

In 1918, Swiss divinity professor Karl Barth published a commentary on the epistle of St. Paul to the Romans. Barth represented a conservative response to secularism, and over the next decades he led the charge against those who tried to modify faith to fit politics and society. A more ambiguous position was developed by Reinhold Niebuhr (1892–1970) in the United States, whose *Moral Man and Immoral Society* (1932) rejected the notion of social ethics because he rejected the notion that society could be moral. Along with other so-called neo-orthodox Christian thinkers, Niebuhr critiqued liberal notions of historical progress. With the rise of fascism and communism in Europe, Neibuhr became the most prominent Christian thinker in the United States.

In Europe in the 1920s and 1930s, Catholicism saw something of a Thomist revival, with thinkers such as Étienne Gilson and Jacques Maritain in France and G.K. Chesterton in England advocating a return to the medieval theology of St. Thomas Aquinas. European Christians also began to speak of Christian ecumenicalism. While in 1928 Pope Pius XI (1922–1939) refused to sanction church participation in the ecumenical movement, the drive toward greater unity among the Catholics, Protestants, and Orthodox was yet another attempt by the religious-minded to solidify their position in secular society.

In the western Muslim world, in addition to the more intellectual framework constructed by the *salafiyya*, there was a renaissance of Sufi movements. The Sufi tradition has succored the mystical and monastic aspects of Muslim society, and by the twentieth century, Sufi orders were the focus of popular religion. Sufis worshiped saints, celebrated magical powers, and practiced arcane rites. Most modernizers and intellectuals viewed Sufism with a mixture of disdain and dislike. Muhammad Abduh, though taking a more benign view of the religion of the countryside, sought through education to raise the consciousness of the masses above the primitive traditions (as he saw them) of the saints.

But Sufism was inseparable from textual Islam in large portions of the Muslim world. In the late nineteenth century and gathering steam in the twentieth, Sufi reformers tried to reinvigorate believers with the simple message that an individual could find God, that he could, through knowledge and submission to the shaikh, to the rules of the order, and above all to Allah, attain grace.

In Egypt, the Hamidiyya Shadhiliyya order was created at the turn of the century by Shaikh Salama al-Radi, who envisioned a Sufism that would respond to the needs of the urban poor, and provide them with a locus of support as well as an avenue for religion to play an active part in their lives. Under his son and successor, the order reached out to the middle class as well; an emphasis was placed on sobriety and hierarchical discipline. The Hamidiyya Shadhiliyya consciously rejected folk Sufism, but its founder understood the deep strength and importance of the Sufi message. His assiduous efforts at creating an order which would be acceptable to both the modernists and the *ulama* (clergy) came from the conviction that Sufism as a religious and social way was vital to the Islamic community.

Two of the most successful Sufi reformers were Ahmad ibn Idris and Ahmad al-Tijani. The Idrisiyya and the Tijaniyya orders created by these two found their most fertile ground in North Africa. Both were devoted to practical, daily life and rejected some of the more arcane forms of Sufism. A major sub-branch of the Idrisiyya, the Sanusiyya order, was centered in what is now Libya, and the Sanusi shaikhs led the resistance against the Italian invasion of Libya just before the First World War. Umar al-Mukhtar, leader of the Sanusi lodges in Cyrenaica, was one of the many victims of Italian colonialism, but his struggle made him a hero of the Libyan resistance. When Libya became an independent state after World War II, it did so under the aegis of the shaikh of the Sanusi brotherhood, Idris al-Sanusi, the king of Libya until overthrown by the nationalist army officer Mua'mmar al-Qadhdhafi in 1969.

In sub-Saharan Africa, Ahmad Bamba (1850–1927) founded the Muridiyya order in Senegal in 1886. Bamba directed the energy of his followers outward rather than inward. Doing away with most Sufi forms of meditation and asceticism, Bamba put his followers to work, literally, by having them farm peanuts. Using the money donated to the order by its members, Bamba bought vast tracts of land and brought them under the till for the first time in the waning years of French colonialism before World War II. The members were recompensed with their own land, and the order was transformed into a profitable business overlain with a religious ethic. It continues to thrive today.

In other parts of the "Third World," as opposition to colonialism grew, religion was often one method of resistance to the Western powers and one way for nationalists to reject the culture of the colonial overlords in favor of an indigenous identity based in part on religion. Egypt saw the formation of the

Muslim Brotherhood in 1928, led by Hasan al-Banna (1906–1949). The Brotherhood excoriated the liberalism of the British and vilified the Western-oriented Egyptian monarchy. In India, the Arya Samaj (founded 1875) was a movement composed of urban, educated Hindus that succored a reformed Hinduism. Out of the Arya Samaj came the Rashtriya Svayamsevak Sangh ("National Union of Volunteers," known as the RSS) in 1925. Where the former organization was grounded in doctrine, the latter was primarily a cultural organization, with a large following in the Indian northwest and in the southern state of Kerala. The RSS put forth the notion of India as a Hindu nation (*hindurashtra*) and advocated religious revival and communal solidarity to evict the British from India and prevent a multistate partition between Hindus and Muslims.

In addition, the Hindu Mahasabha (founded by Punjabi Hindu members of the Arya Samaj between 1915 and 1921) attacked the increasingly British character of Indian culture and called for a unified Hindu state that respected the rights of Muslim and other minorities. The RSS and Mahasabha attached Indian nationalism to Hinduism, and assailed the British for introducing the idea that India was not a nation. Hinduism, these groups posited, was the cohering force of Indian nationalism. While Gandhi in the 1930s and 1940s rejected the exclusivity of Hinduness espoused by groups such as the RSS and the Mahasabha, he gladly accepted their support.

Along with Jinnah's Muslim League, Maulana Abul Ala Maududi (1903–1979) established the Jam'at-i-Islami in 1941. Maududi was a dynamic orator and a charismatic organization leader. The Jam'at was created to "resacralize" political life and to work toward the formation of an Islamic state, with the Qur'an and the tradition of the Prophet as its constitution and Islamic law (*shari'a*) as the law of the land. While the Jam'at worked for similar ends as the Muslim League, once India was partitioned in 1947 and Pakistan became a state, it came into conflict with the Pakistani government. Jinnah and the Muslim League wanted to subsume Islam to the state, while Maududi wanted to subsume the state and civil society to divine law. Emerging as part of a nationalist movement, Maududi's Jam'at was also an early iteration of what would in time become known as Islamic fundamentalism.

Meanwhile, farther east in Asia, Chinese nationalism led to an outburst against Christian missionaries during the 1900 Boxer Rebellion. After Western residents and missionaries were killed, the European powers, with the cooperation of the United States, intervened to suppress the revolt. Though China was never formally colonized, Western influence helped erode the Manchu Dynasty, which finally collapsed in 1911.

The next years saw the rise of Western-educated reformers such as Sun Yat-Sen and China's ambassador to the west, Wellington Koo. With the ascendancy of the warlord Chiang Kai-shek in the 1930s and the concomitant growth of Chinese Communism under the aegis of Mao Zedong, neither the missionaries nor the traditional religious hierarchy of China thrived. Buddhist monasteries saw a decline in attendance, and with the collapse of the Manchu dynasty, Confucian systems of scholarship and bureaucracy were also weakened. In Tibet, however, largely independent of China's control, the Buddhist hierarchy led by the Dalai Lama continued to govern society in what was the closest approximation to a true theocracy anywhere in the modern world before the 1979 Iranian revolution.

Elsewhere in Asia, however, religion was more evident in the struggle for decolonization and independence. In Burma, the nationalist movement for independence from Britain was intimately supported by Buddhist monks such as U Ottama and U Wisara. Burmese Theravadan Buddhism was championed by the leader of postwar Burma, U Nu, who attempted to restore the central social position of Buddhism in political life. But the Buddhist monasterial organization (*sangha*) was weak in Burma, and though U Nu in many ways played the role of a traditional Burmese king who protected and patronized Buddhism, his religiosity and successful leadership of the nationalist struggle could not prevent the overthrow of the democratic Burmese government by the military in 1962.

In Sri Lanka (Ceylon until 1972), where the sangha was much stronger, Buddhism was one foundation of the political order. As with Burma, there was a revival of lay meditation in the first decades of the century, and in Sri Lanka, Buddhism was part of Sinhalese ethnic nationalism. In 1956, soon after independence from the British, S.W.R.D Bandaranaike was elected on a pro-Sinhalese, pro-Buddhist platform. This was the culmination of decades of Buddhist activism and reform during which Buddhism was reformed to reflect a scriptural purity. This new Buddhism emphasized the Noble Eightfold Path and the Four Noble Truths of the Buddha, and Buddhist schools, marriage registrars, and postwar government bureaucracies were set up to foster links between government and the sangha. For Bandaranaike, the struggle against colonialism was an earthly manifestation of the Buddhist struggle on the battlefield of truth.

In Thailand, which never fell under direct European rule, the monarchy drew legitimacy from the position of the king as symbolic head of the Thai sangha. That leadership was solidified by King Mongkut (Rama IV) in 1851, and over the next hundred years, the monarchy gradually helped build a civil society in which the ruler was integral to communal religion. The National Sangha Act of 1962 led to a highly centralized sangha, subservient to the king, which in turn bolstered a highly centralized state.

In Indonesia, Javanese Islam underwent Sufi reforms similar to Muslim Africa. Stressing piety and scriptural orthodoxy, *dawa* ("the call") movements eschewed Western medicine and science in favor of traditional healing, native clothing, and a certain degree of puritanical antimaterialism. The Muhammadiya, founded in 1912, was a pastoral movement dedicated to education and social services that avidly avoided politics and today boasts somewhere between five and ten million members. The Dar ul-Islam, on the other hand, represented activist, anticolonial, political Islam. Established to fight the Japanese occupation during World War II, the Dar ul-Islam then fought the Dutch and the first Indonesian government of Sukarno before it was defeated by the Indonesian army in 1962. The Dar ul-Islam, like Pakistan's Jam'at and Egypt's Muslim Brotherhood, survives as one of the grandfathers of modern fundamentalism.

In Japan, as the Japanese state became increasingly modern and Japan increasingly Westernized and militarized, a number of new religions sprang up before World War II. Sects such as Honmichi (1913), Soka Gakkai (1930), and Rissho Kosei-kai (1938) became centralized and began to use mass media to appeal to the lower middle classes and women. Shamanism, sorcery, and healing assumed a prominent role in these movements, and they complemented rather than opposed traditional Japanese Shintoism and Buddhism. As a force calling for Japanese to turn inward and away from the temptation of foreign—i.e. Western—cultures, the New Religions thrived after the war as well.

Religion as an adjunct of nationalism was especially evident in the Zionist movement, which emerged as one of many nationalist movements in eastern and central Europe at the end of the nineteenth century. Theodore Herzl (1860–1904) organized the First Zionist Congress in 1897 after witnessing the upsurge in anti-Semitism in France during the Dreyfus affair. The impulse toward Zionism was predicated on the feeling among educated European Jews that Jews would never be fully safe unless they possessed their own state. Until the establishment of Israel in 1948, the leaders of the Zionist movement were almost all secular Europeans whose Judaism was ethnic rather than religious. David Ben-Gurion (1886–1973) abjured any religious practice and was himself a socialist atheist. In fact, the nonreligious nature of Jewish nationalism alarmed many Orthodox Jews (*haredim*).

1901 saw the founding of the Orthodox Jewish Mizrachi in an attempt to infuse the spirit of orthodoxy into Zionism, and large numbers of haredim rejected Zionism and Zionist aims in Palestine as secular heresy. Agudat Israel, founded in Silesia in 1912, began as a movement to counteract reform, liberal Judaism. It soon took on many of the attributes of a political party, and after supporting the foundation of Israel in 1948, then joined successive government coalitions and became the voice of orthodox religious concerns. It forced, among other things, the Ben-Gurion government to pass laws that enshrined the Sabbath as a day of rest in the Israeli state.

The question of ethnicity as opposed to religion as the basis for the state of Israel was hardly resolved in 1948, and modern Israeli politics have often been deadlocked by religious questions like "What is a Jew?" that have polarized debate in the Israeli Knesset (parliament). Though Zionism gained the support of most Jews in the wake of the Holocaust, questions of religion, nationalism, and ethnicity continued to divide Israel in the decades after the war.

World War II had profound effects on religion throughout the world. The appalling loss of life and systematic killing not only raised severe doubts about secular nationalism in Europe, but also undermined European claims to be the sole representatives of civilization and progress. Postwar decolonization was not just the result of the economic or military weakness of the European powers. They were no longer morally capable of justifying the empire, though that did not stop imperialists in Britain, France, and Holland from trying. The failure of secular civilization to prevent the systematic slaughter of tens of millions of people invigorated the champions of religion who had until then been fighting something of a rearguard action against antireligious or areligious modern societies.

In addition, the division of much of the world into either capitalist or communist spheres during the cold war had the unintended effect of spurring a religious revival in the Christian West. Faced with a communist adversary centered in Moscow that was unabashedly antireligious, Europe, Latin America, and North America turned to Christianity as an ally in the struggle against "atheistic, godless communism." The fight against the Soviet Union became in the United States especially a religious crusade in which not just American freedom, but American religion seemed to be imperiled by the communists.

Church affiliation in the United States rose dramatically after 1945. In 1940, some 49 percent of Americans declared some sort of affiliation, in 1950 the figure was 55 percent, and in 1960 it reached a high of 69 percent. The money spent on new church construction rose from $26 million in 1945 to more than $1 billion in 1960. A tide of evangelism swept over the nation, and preachers such as Billy Graham, head of the Evangelistic Association, appeared at the sides of presidents throughout the cold war. The iconography was clear: God and the United States were allied in the fight against communism. That message was communicated in numerous ways by the quietly religious President Dwight D. Eisenhower and his Secretary of State John Foster Dulles, the son of a minister, throughout the 1950s. Reinhold Niebuhr, in turn, became the intellectual Christian spokesman of anticommunism, appearing on the cover of *Time* magazine on several occasions.

At the same time, Christian Democratic (CD) parties sprang up throughout Europe and Latin America. In postwar Italy and Germany, they came to dominate the government, and Christian Democracy made decent showings in France, the Netherlands, and Belgium as well. In 1937, Catholic intellectuals in Chile had formed the Falange Party, which concentrated on social reform with a strong element of Catholic theology. Led by Eduardo Frei, the Falange was folded into the new Christian Democratic Party in the late 1950s. A strong Christian Democratic movement took root to the north in Peru, and smaller parties were established in Guatemala and El Salvador.

At first the European CD parties in Italy and Germany embraced a limited socialism, but they soon became the representatives of the conservative political establishment. Christian Democratic rule in Italy did not end until the early 1990s, when the party was brought down by massive allegations of corruption. In Latin America, however, the parties remained on the moderate left, though in comparison to the radical movements of the 1960s and 1970s, they were proponents of gradual reform within the established order.

Meanwhile, the late 1950s saw the beginning of significant upheavals in the Catholic Church. These changes presaged and mirrored the religious syncretism that swept through the Western hemisphere and Europe in the 1960s and 1970s. In Europe, the erosion of faith following World War II led to a reevaluation within the Catholic Church. In particular, the prewar Catholic rebuff of ecumenicalism was reconsidered, and the church began to establish closer links with other Christian denominations. This trend culminated with the Second Vatican Council (also known as Vatican II) convened by Pope John XXIII in 1962.

Lasting from 1962 to 1965, Vatican II heralded Catholicism's "new opening" to the modern world. Part of the impetus was Pope John's desire to heal the rift between Western and Eastern (Orthodox) Christianity. But the council dealt with many other topics, ranging from human rights to the role of the clergy in politics to the plight of the poor and the rights of the individual. John XXIII had already initiated reforms designed to modernize the church, setting up a church office for television and news in order to utilize these new technologies for the benefit of Catholicism. Vatican II brought together church leaders from around the world, and was supported not just by John but by his successor Pope Paul VI (1963–1978).

Vatican II profoundly affected the lives of the hundreds of millions of Catholics around the world. In the late 1960s, Pope Paul enacted the council's policies and met with the archbishop of Canterbury in England and the Eastern Orthodox patriarch in Istanbul for symbolic reconciliations. The Catholic liturgy was reformed, and the clergy took a more active role in promoting peace and denouncing repression and dictatorship. The church did not, however, embrace all aspects of 1960s Western culture: it did not approve of the widespread availability of oral contraception, nor did it look with favor on radical political movements that denounced not only traditional governments but traditional social and familial arrangements. Like the Christian Democratic parties in the political sphere, the Catholic Church favored moderate reform but fought radical innovations.

But what the church said and what the clergy did were not always identical. In Latin America, some clergy adhered closely to dictates from Rome. The Argentine church supported the rule of Juan Perón (1946–1955), until Perón launched an anticlerical crusade in 1954 to divert public attention from his regime. When there were mass demonstrations against the church in 1955, the Vatican responded by excommunicating Perón. Over the next decades, however, the Argentine church rarely challenged the military juntas that ruled Argentina.

However, clergy elsewhere in Latin America often championed democracy and were in the vanguard of opposition against dictatorships. In Chile, the Christian Democratic Party was elected to office in 1964, and Eduardo Frei became president. In other countries, the clergy turned away from their allegiance with the conservative political order to a pro-reform, and at times oppositional, stance. In May 1957, the archbishop of Caracas denounced the dictator of Venezuela. In Guatemala, after the church supported the overthrow of the quasi-Marxist Jacobo Arbenz in 1954, it began in the 1960s to distance itself from the government and attend to the plight of the Indians and the poor. In a 1971 pastoral letter, the Guatemalan clergy spoke out against violence and repression, and by the 1980s, the Guatemalan military government led by Efraín Ríos Montt treated the Catholic Church as an ally of the insurgency and an enemy to the government. It was no coincidence that Ríos Montt himself was not a Catholic but an evangelical Protestant.

In aligning against the traditional order in Latin America, individual clergy sometimes drew the ire of the church establishment. In the late 1960s, the

Peruvian theologian Gustavo Gutiérrez and other priests developed what was popularly known as Liberation Theology, an eclectic combination of Marxism and traditional Catholic theology. Gutiérrez rejected the separation of the world into spiritual and material realms and declared that true salvation was to be found in the creation of just societies on earth. Liberation Theology became the spearhead of a radicalized, politicized Latin American Catholic clergy: in El Salvador, Archbishop Oscar Romero justified the use of violence to oppose repressive regimes; he was assassinated in 1980. In nearby Nicaragua, Archbishop Miguel Obando y Bravo distanced himself from the Somoza dictatorship and in 1979 declared his support for the Sandanista revolutionaries who came to power soon after.

These radical prelates were often not supported by the church. The church hierarchy in several countries did not take firm stands against human rights abuses in those countries, though many of the local clergy did. In 1979, Pope John Paul II denounced what he viewed as the excesses of Liberation Theology, but Liberation Theology was only one of many new challenges to traditional church authority. While Vatican II had taken major steps toward reform, the church hierarchy did not countenance the erosion of the nuclear family, the prevalence of divorce and abortion, and the loosening of sexual mores. It was also uncertain of how to incorporate the demands of women to play a more active role in pastoral and lay Christian life. The Catholic Church maintained that the clergy must be male and celibate, even while Protestant denominations throughout the world began to ordain women in the 1970s.

In the United States and Europe, the 1960s and 1970s saw not only a loosening of traditional social mores but the formation of syncretic religions. Often described as New Age movements, these religions fused Western psychoanalytic thought, Hindu and Buddhist mysticism, and Judeo-Christianity. While a small segment of educated elites in both Europe and the United States had been fascinated with Eastern religions since the late nineteenth century, in the 1960s young, educated, often well-to-do people turned to everything from Zen Buddhism to Transcendental Meditation to Wycca (witchcraft) and crystal healing. Zen came to the United States across the Pacific in the wake of World War II, while Transcendental Meditation (TM) owed some of its popularity to the journey of the hugely popular rock group the Beatles to India in the late 1960s to study with TM's guru Maharishi Mahesh Yogi. New Age movements shared a common belief in the divinity of mankind and many emphasized inner truth as the primary source of all truths. While New Age movements emerged out of the 1960s counterculture, they continue to thrive in the Western world.

While counterculture Americans were learning how to meditate, denizens of the Third World were finding that independence and secular nationalism tended to erode religion. In the Muslim Middle East, the 1950s and 1960s were dominated by nationalists such as Gamal Abdul Nasser. Nasser had little tolerance for the political Islam of the Muslim Brotherhood, and throughout the Middle East, Islam was visible in the private realm but hardly at all in the public. In India and Pakistan, the Hindu revivalist RSS, its political cousin the Jana Sangh, and the Jam'at-i-Islami remained active in the political life of their respective countries, but the general trend was toward secular modernization, whether undertaken by General Zia ul-Haq in 1970s Pakistan or by Nehru and his successors in India. In China, though the 1954 communist constitution established freedom of religion, Mao's Great Leap Forward of the 1950s and the Cultural Revolution of the 1960s showed that the only true freedom was the freedom not to believe. The Chinese Communist party attempted to indoctrinate Chinese Buddhist monks in the proper ways of communism, and both traditional Buddhism and Confucianism were treated as potential enemies of the communist revolution.

But as the promises of independence and nationalism went unfulfilled in many of these countries, religion often provided people with what the government could not. In ministering to the needs of the poor and politically disenfranchised, religious leaders at times became competitors for political power. In Southeast Asia in the late 1950s and 1960s, Buddhist monks of Tibet and Vietnam led the opposition against autocratic regimes. The Dalai Lama fled Tibet after the 1959 Tibetan revolt against Chinese domination and set up an exile Tibetan government in India. In Vietnam, Buddhist monks united in opposition to the dictatorial regime of the Catholic Ngo Dinh Diem, and it was the ritual self-immolation of Buddhist monk Quang Duc in Saigon in the summer of 1963 that led to the erosion of American support for Diem's government, and to his subsequent overthrow.

These movements hinted at the rise of political religion in the 1970s. As Third World nationalism and First World secular modernism in Europe and North America failed to enrich many countries and left the spiritual needs of even the rich nations untended, people turned to religion. The major manifestation of this shift was the rise of what is now known as religious fundamentalism. As Third World economies foundered, and as the first generation of charismatic independence leaders was replaced by military governments or successor regimes that seemed more intent on maintaining power and prestige than in developing their economies or addressing social problems, people looked to traditional religion as an alternative.

Fundamentalism was only one manifestation of a general religious revival, and it was one of several reactions to the effects of the cold war and nuclear weapons on international politics. The term "fundamentalism" is extremely broad, encompassing not just movements that utilize violence to achieve political ends, but other groups whose primary goals are to promote personal piety.

While groups such as the Jam'at in Pakistan and Dar ul-Islam in Indonesia had advocated a return to the mythic religious purity of early Islam, Islamic fundamentalism became an international force with the Iranian Revolution in 1979. Soon after the Shah fled the country, the Ayatollah Ruhollah Khomeini returned to Iran and within two years eliminated all rivals. Khomeini and the Shi'i Iranian clergy transformed Iran into a modern theocratic state. Khomeini also announced his commitment to spreading Islamic revolution throughout the Muslim world.

One of the characteristics of the Iranian Revolution was a demonization of the West. In the eyes of Khomeini, Western culture, with its emphasis on materialism and its attempt to sequester religion from public life, had corrupted Iran. The Iranian Revolution tried, unsuccessfully, to remove everything from Western music to Western clothing from Iran. Still, the anti-Western ideology of the revolution was adopted by other Islamic fundamentalists in the Middle East and Central Asia. To some degree, fundamentalism in the Islamic world channeled old grievances toward Western colonialism and imperialism in new directions. In other ways, political Islam was a radical innovation, offering a model of state unity with—and even subservience to— religion that had never existed in the past. Claiming to speak for a return to the days of early Islam, fundamentalists created as much of an imagined past as had the nationalists that the fundamentalists so excoriated.

In the 1980s and into the 1990s, fundamentalist groups became prominent in most countries in the Islamic world. In Algeria, the Islamic Salvation Front and the Armed Islamic Group (GIA) threatened to overwhelm the military government in a bitter civil war that erupted after an army coup terminated democratic elections in 1991. In Sudan, a military-fundamentalist alliance resulted in the most radical Islamic state besides Iran. In Saudi Arabia, the puritanical Wahhabi sect, which had been subservient to the Saudi monarchy since the 1920s, gained renewed strength as Saudi oil revenues stagnated and the lavish, un-Islamic lifestyles of the Saudi royalty became more widely known. In Egypt and Jordan, the Muslim Brotherhood was and still is the leading opposition group to the government, while in Israel and the Occupied Territories, Hamas and several smaller groups speak in the name of Islam to fight any Arab reconciliation with the Israelis. Even in secular Turkey, the 1990s have seen the resurgence of Islam in both popular culture and political life. In Afghanistan, the same confederations that fought the Soviet invasion with United States support turned toward the conquest of Afghanistan in the name of Islam after the Soviets departed.

Outside of the Muslim world, there have been fundamentalist movements in Judaism, Buddhism, Hinduism, and Protestant Christianity. The Gush Emunim and the Kach Party in Israel were both manifestations of political religion. The Gush Emunim was a post-1967 effort by ultra-Orthodox Jews to preserve Zionism within a religious framework. Espousing a Jewish messianism that called for the reconstruction of the ancient Jewish kingdom of Judea and Samaria, the Gush Emunim led the drive to annex the Occupied Territories.

In India, the Bharatiya Janata Party (the BJP or Indian People's Party) inherited the legacy of the Jana Sangh and the RSS and advocated an extreme form of Hindu nationalism for India. They achieved significant electoral success in the 1991 elections and remain a potent force in North Indian politics. To the south, in Sri Lanka, radicalized Buddhist Sinhalese nationalists fought both the government and Tamil Hindu insurgents in the northern part of the island throughout the 1980s and early 1990s. Even in the rapidly industrializing Pacific Rim, the 1980s saw an upsurge in Confucianist studies and Buddhist activism, while the New Religions of Japan, particularly the Soka Gakkai, attracted ever larger numbers of adherents.

And in the United States, Protestant fundamentalists took a more active role in national politics after the election of Jimmy Carter as president in 1977. With the presidency of Ronald Reagan, much of the Protestant fundamentalist agenda was adopted by the political establishment, including opposition to legalized abortion and the belief that a decline in traditional, Christian family values was at the heart of domestic problems.

At the end of the 1980s, as fundamentalism of all stripes attracted tens of millions of followers, the Catholic and Eastern Orthodox churches galvanized opposition to communist rule in Eastern Europe and the Soviet Union. Polish Catholicism had always been at the heart of Polish resistance to Soviet domination, and the election of the Polish Pope John Paul II in 1978 energized Polish resistance, both in the form of the Solidarity movement and in many unreported but no less significant acts of defiance. Similarly, the Ukrainian Orthodox (Uniate) church emerged as a bulwark of Ukrainian independence from the Soviet Union between 1989 and 1991. The revolutions in Europe in 1989 and the breakup of the Soviet Union in 1991 led to a widespread religious revival in the former Eastern bloc.

As the end of the twentieth century approaches, religion is very much in evidence in international politics. It is not just fundamentalism, but religious institutions and practices that have emerged as potent aspects of the last quarter of the century. While religion never "went away," for a time it seemed that institutional religion had lost a war to the secular nation-state. As both secularism and the nation-state have proven less solid than they once seemed, religion has moved once again to the center of public and private life.

The explanations for these developments are as varied as the variety of religious experience itself. Perhaps the Enlightenment and its nineteenth-century children erred in believing that the secular state could fulfill the same spiritual yearnings that the church had. Perhaps two devastating world wars, combined with the damages wrought by colonialism, imperialism, and industrialization, exposed the weakness of secularism and the dangers of nationalism and so reawakened religion as a competing force in international society. Perhaps the modern belief that the vagaries of human experience could be controlled and the needs of humanity satisfied by the modern technocratic state overlooked the more inchoate but undeniable spiritual needs of humankind.

In any event, religion has returned to the political spectrum, and in some cases, entered it as never before. Judging from the past hundred years, until secular nationalism satisfies the need for physical security and spiritual connection to the ineffable, religion will thrive. In 1900, many predicted it would soon be as safely ensconced in the past as the plague, but as the millennium approaches, more people than ever are fervent believers in that which secular society denies, in forces which modern science cannot detect, in gods which modern technology cannot find, and in movements which modern states cannot contain.

But while reports of religion's death may have been exaggerated, the attempts of certain groups to subsume public life to the dictates of religion seem as certain to founder as the attempts of the nation-state to remove religion from public life altogether. Ironically, the tools of modernity, and mass communications in particular, have allowed religion to spread its messages as never before. They also spread messages that directly contradict and indirectly undermine the claims of religion.

Many now predict that religion and secular nationalism are locked in a struggle from which only one will emerge intact. This forecast will of course be put to the test when Columbia publishes its history of the twenty-first century, but just to provide grist for the historical mill, consider another alternative: a synthesis of religion and secular nationalism, a hybrid guiding principle that looks to both the material and the spiritual. Somewhere out there is a neologism waiting to be born, one which will capture this synthesis, and sometime in the next fifty years, it will enter common parlance as surely as "secularism" and "fundamentalism" did in this century. This struggle between secular nationalism and religion is, as Kenneth Branagh remarked in the 1991 film *Dead Again*, "far from over."

# 5   Athletics: Play and Politics

JEAN-MARC RAN OPPENHEIM[1]

## Introduction

Sports and the games from which most derive have, throughout human history, reflected the structures and the aims of the societies in which they were practiced. This has been as true in the twentieth century as in any other. For sports the birth of the modern Olympiads in 1896 ought to be considered the century's starting point. So defined, this century has seen profound changes in how people compete societally through politics, economics, culture, psychology, technology—and sports. These changes have occurred at a pace dictated by the revolutions inherent in modern technology and social dynamics. Sports have, indeed, had a symbiotic relationship with twentieth-century society.

Most sports practiced in the twentieth century originated from earlier or traditional games and have been the contemporary athletic rituals that we believe represent our atavistic impulses. Thus, like their ancient counterparts, they have an abstract or symbolic aspect. Unlike ancient rituals, which were mostly expressions of collective religiosity, however, sports in this century have been largely secular activities, despite the strong emotions they foster in competitor and spectator alike. Twentieth-century sports rules are theoretically structured to apply in an egalitarian fashion to all participants who qualify according to democratic factors such as talent and skill. Like the societies by which they are fashioned, twentieth-century sports have functioned through bureaucracies whose goal is to ensure adherence to established rules and regulations and, when necessary, control inexorable changes. Modern science and technology, for instance, have affected most aspects of athletic training and given twentieth-century sports an element of rationalization. As society as a whole has embraced statistics, so too sports have generated systems of quantification to serve as barometers of athletic performance, though record-breaking as a form of achievement and fame is by no means an exclusively twentieth-century phenomenon. In the classical period, Greek city-states honored their victorious Olympian athletes with public statues and, just as we do today, with stipends.

Sports have been significantly affected by at least three of the major societal dynamics of the century: the influence of the West on the rest of the world has been reflected in sports primarily through the modern Olympic movement; the broad impact of the media on public perception has been reflected in the media enshrinement of athletic ritual; and lastly, the largely nationalist politicization and the commercialization of most human endeavor has clearly included sporting activity.

Because the modern Olympics originated in Europe at a time when its power was at an apex, the sports included in the Olympic Games naturally reflect traditions and rules generally regarded as "Western" or European, although not a few of these activities have been and continue to be practiced all over the world according to traditional indigenous structures. Indeed, over the course of this century, some sports that were previously exclusively European have become more identified with non-European athletes than with the heirs of their European originators, such as soccer.

By the eve of World War I, thanks to modern journalism, collective identity with sports heroes and their performances was the stuff of national pastimes and cultural phenomena. Sports writers consciously became cultural chroniclers, rather than mere conveyors of sports facts. After 1919 this sense of collective identity became politicized. Totalitarian movements especially, with their reliance on mass psychology, appreciated the impact that the politicization of sports could have on their citizens. Italian Fascists and German Nazis quickly began using sports as a vehicle for the transmission of their hallowed ideals of racial strength and beauty, while the Soviets projected the benefits of an idealized society through their athletes' successful performances. Sports-based national mythmaking is not, however, the exclusive province of totalitarian regimes—as any viewer of U.S. television coverage of recent Olympiads can attest.

Politicized nationalism in sports has become, indeed, a form of secular religion. In some instances it has served to repair, albeit temporarily, political, socioeconomic or ethnocultural ruptures in societies undermined by instability. For example, transnational pride is manifest in World Cup soccer when a South American team beats an opponent from Western Europe. On the other hand, sports can also spark hostilities between nations nominally at peace, such as in the famous Latin American soccer wars of the 1970s. Related to the rise of their mythopolitical uses sports have also become, on national and international levels, an extremely lucrative enterprise indeed, as indicated by the megabucks paid to athletic superstars.

## The Modern Olympics

Pierre de Coubertin's dream—a modern version of the classical games, encompassing gentlemanly competition to bring out a transcendent fraternal best in the participants—was doomed from the start. The Olympiads carried the seeds of politicization from the beginning and acted as a harbinger of the nationalist fervors that have characterized this century.

It was unrealistic for Coubertin to expect otherwise. The last third of the nineteenth century witnessed the unification of Italy and Germany as well as the demise of the heterogeneous Austro-Hungarian monarchy, the race for colonies all over the globe, and the increasing assertion of American power in the Western hemisphere and in the Pacific rim, to name but three indicative political developments.

In fact, the Olympiads were not the first forum to combine ideology and play. Starting in the 1820s, the *Turner* movement, aiming to rebuild the German national character after its Napoleonic trauma, had established a strong connection between gymnastics and Romantic nationalism. Moreover, by century's end the German Socialist Workers' movement had structured days of sports, games, and other festivities meant to foster an identity that combined political and social agendas. Whether romanticism, socialism, or nationalism, by the turn of the twentieth century sports were regularly being used to establish not only the primacy of the athletes but also, perhaps especially, the causes they represented.

Unlike their classical forebears, the Europeans did not even consider declaring a truce during wartime so that athletes could gather. When the illusion of a short war in August 1914 gave way to the reality of a long bloodbath, the 1916 Olympiad was canceled. The end of the war and resumption of the Olympiads with the 1924 Games in Paris did not in any way lessen the national passions that had already been in evidence in 1912 in Stockholm. On the contrary, athletes from the former Central powers and the new Bolshevik Russia were barred entirely from participation. And while the former were allowed to participate at the 1932 Olympiad in Los Angeles, the latter were quarantined until after the close of World War II.

The first show of unabashedly politicized sports was the 1936 Olympiad held in Berlin. Related to this, it was also the first Olympiad at which media had a privileged place—most notably the filmmaker Leni Riefenstahl, who memorably captured the Nazi Games in all their dulling glory in her masterpiece *Olympia*. With Hitler's rise to power in 1933, American as well as European officials had initially called for a boycott of the Games, citing the incompatibility of Nazi racial policies with the Olympic charter. The United States did not agree to participate until 1935, when Avery Brundage, then secretary of the American Olympic Committee, issued a favorable report after being given a personal fact-finding tour of Germany by German authorities. Non-Nazi German organizers of the Games were still skeptical: the regime's concepts of national and racial superiority were at odds with the ostensible internationalism and egalitarianism of the Olympics.

Despite these mutual apprehensions, the Games went on as planned. As the Nazi hosts had hoped, they became a showcase of German planning, efficiency, and persuasiveness. Brundage, for example, agreed to leave America's Jewish athletes at home. A Master Race sweep of medals was averted when non-Nordic athletes from other nations, most notably black American Jesse Owens, scored significant victories that became a focus not only of the international press, but for the Reich's propagandist Riefenstahl as well.

The 1940 Olympiad was awarded to Japan, then another authoritarian society with clearly articulated ideas of supremacy. Also significant in this decision was the nod it gave universalist principles by locating the Games outside a Western country for the first time in modern Olympic history. When Japanese militarist expansionism manifested itself in Manchuria in 1931 and in China in 1937, however, vehement international objections ensued. A potential crisis in IOC (International Olympic Committee) collegiality was only averted when Japan withdrew its original offer to host the Games—in order to pursue its military activities.

Like many institutions with a specific focus, the IOC encouraged a *sociabilité* among its members. The committee was made up largely of men with wealthy and/or aristocratic backgrounds who had the skills necessary to realize Coubertin's vision of the Olympics as a combination diplomatic enterprise and global village fete. In that light, the decision to award the 1940 Games to Japan and overlook its ideological and political transgressions is understandable. Japanese members of the IOC were all titled aristocrats, and their European counterparts were prone to overlook political reality in favor of personal regard for fellow members of their club.

This outlook was not immediately changed by World War II. Postwar representatives from Germany and Italy who had been aristocratic members of their nation's prewar fascist parties were allowed to rejoin the IOC in a shocking reaffirmation of that body's then commitment to confraternity over political morality. It is not unlikely that the Soviet Union was barred from IOC membership until 1951 at least in part because it could produce no aristocrats or wealthy industrialists to represent it in that exclusive and exclusionary club. Instead, it devised a proletarian answer to the Olympic Games in the form of the Red Sports International, a continuation of the pre-World War I German Socialist Workers' games and festivities.

Nonetheless, politically driven change did eventually come to the IOC. The cold war and the related phenomena of decolonization and Third World regionalism have infused the spirit of the Games and their management since 1948. The acceptance of the Soviet Union and its Eastern European satellite states in the Olympic movement in 1951, effectively a return to the concept of the Olympiads as an occasion of truce, meant that bloc voting—and hence acknowledged politicization—would become a regular feature of IOC meetings.

Throughout the period of East-West confrontation, intense competition between athletes from the Soviet and American blocs became a significant dimension of the cold war. Counting the number of medals garnered by each side acquired important symbolic value between the two camps. Each developed elite corps of athletes who dominated the Games throughout the era, and guaranteed that politics would never be far from the playing field.

Political censure of a nation by the exclusion of its athletes was occasionally applied in the pre-World War II period, most notably to athletes of the USSR. However, boycotts of sporting events by otherwise welcome participants were for social and cultural rather than political reasons—such as to protest the inclusion of bathing suit-clad women in a swimming event or other women athletes, even if "properly" attired, in a sport the boycotters viewed as a traditionally male activity. The Olympic Games, although occasionally faced with the threat of a boycott, had avoided such adversarial action in the interwar period. Once the cold war was imported into the IOC, however, boycotts or their threatened occurrence took place with a disturbing frequency. The political structure of the post-1945 world dictated the allegiance of most participating countries to one or the other superpower. The stadium had become a readily available field of surrogate battle.

As a consequence, nearly all Olympiads since 1951 have faced boycotts or other politically demonstrative actions. Issues sparking such activities have included the geopolitical dispute over which of the two Chinas—the People's Republic or the Taiwan-based Nationalist Republic—should be accepted as the "true" China. Pan-African, and ultimately international, agitation demanded that not only South Africa, but also any country maintaining sporting relations with it be excluded from Olympic competition so long as South Africa held to racial apartheid.

Even ostensibly domestic politics have found symbolic voice at the Olympics, most memorably when two African American track and field medalists at the 1968 Mexico City Games protested racial injustice at home by raising their clenched fists in a Black Power salute during the playing of the U.S. national anthem in honor of their victories.

Until 1980, it was the superpowers' proxies who participated in politically motivated boycotts. This changed when the United States led a boycott of the 1980 Moscow Games in response to the Soviet invasion of Afghanistan. The Soviets promptly returned the favor when the 1984 Olympiad was held in Los Angeles. Prior to the Soviet invasion, the United States and a number of Western nations had feared that the Soviet Union would use the Moscow Games to glorify its vision of Marxism and overshadow Western protests concerning Soviet treatment of dissidents; however, a United States boycott seemed unlikely. Once the invasion occurred, the United States had its excuse to boycott, and many nations with their own agenda followed suit. The Arabs, as defenders of Islamic struggle worldwide, found themselves strangely on the same side of a Cold War issue as the Israelis, whose solidarity with the United States dictated their support for the boycott. Ultimately, 62 nations boycotted the 1980 Olympiad while 81 participated, the largest political boycott in modern Olympic history.

While the end of the cold war obviated the need for ideological sparring between two opposed superpowers, it has not lessened the competition between national groups. Indeed, while nations such as China, with a political or ideological goal, continue to use the Olympic Games to fulfill an international agenda that will establish their relative prowess in sports and hence in other areas too, the United States and other nations whose economies are market-based continue to use the Games to showcase the advantages of the free enterprise system. Smaller nations draw significant prestige when their athletes succeed against, or even simply participate with, athletes from larger or more advanced nations, even when these athletes have trained in the very countries against which they are competing. The media, including commercial filmmakers, have made this one of the most visible aspects of the Olympics today.

Ideological or nationalist passions have not manifested themselves exclusively on the playing field or in IOC deliberations. Elements of ideology or nationalism also enter into scoring. The public, usually egged on by a less-than-impartial press, perceives the scores as reflections of ideological contests even when they are not. Moreover, at times it is clear that the judges' own nationalist agendas do influence their decisions. At the 1988 Seoul Olympiad this phenomenon was the focus of indignant attention, and the flagrantly partial scorers of the gymnastics events involved earned the dubious title "judging mafia." Moreover, two boxing judges were suspended for life after an investigation revealed that, prior to awarding a gold medal to a South Korean athlete who had been clearly outpunched by his American opponent, they had been wined and dined by their Korean hosts.

The most dramatic, and tragic, political use of the Olympic Games was the Palestinian terrorist action in 1972 in Munich. Here, the combat escalated from the purely symbolic to the actual. In an attempt to draw the world's attention to their political plight, armed Palestinians penetrated the Olympic village and took hostage members of the Israeli team. Efforts at negotiations were insincere, since, consistent with their stated policies vis-à-vis terrorists, neither the Germans nor the Israelis had any intention of acceding to the Palestinians' demands. When German sharpshooters, with the acquiescence of the Israeli government, tried to interdict the Palestinians and their hostages from boarding a plane, the result was the death of the Israelis and three of their captors. A horrified world watched on live television while the proceedings unfolded, as the media's dissemination of Olympic events became, as it has been ever since, more real that the events themselves.

In terms of immediate political impact, the tragedy backfired on the Palestinians' cause by eliciting greater world sympathy for the Israelis. In terms of the Olympics, it represented the final demise of Coubertin's naive dream of a reborn classical era. The death of the athletes at the hands of terrorists and of the terrorists at the hands of real soldiers fundamentally defied the ostensible purpose of the Games, and demonstrated that the surrogate battle could not completely displace actual lethal conflict. The trauma left the IOC literally speechless: a day of mourning was observed at Munich before the Games resumed. However, no official mention would be made of the tragedy at subsequent Olympiads for nearly 24 years, until the 1996 Atlanta Games were marred by an apparent act of terror as well. A homemade pipebomb detonated, killing one spectator at an Olympics-related concert; the FBI mistakenly suspected a security guard of comic-opera proportions, whose life became the target of unrelenting media attention.

## Modern Regional Games

As regional identity has become a factor in world politics and culture, a number of quadrennial games patterned on the Olympiads have emerged: the Asian Games, the Mediterranean Games, the Pan-American Games, and the African Games. Holding contests outside of Europe with participation limited to indigenous athletes had been discussed as early as 1923, when IOC-sponsored regional games were proposed.

The possibility of Latin American games was first raised in 1922, and revived in 1940 after the start of World War II and the cancellation of the Tokyo Olympiad. However, the Pan-American Games were not initially held until 1951. With the establishment of the Castro communist regime, and the resulting U.S.-Cuban rivalry for hemispheric influence, the Games represented Olympic-style U.S.-Soviet competition in the western hemisphere.

Continued politicization of the Olympic movement has manifested itself in sponsorship of other regional games as well: the first instance, the Mediterranean Games, was initially proposed in 1948 and held in 1951. However, the refusal of Arab countries to participate with Israel or even with some other Arab nations considered ideological foes, together with the failure of the Olympic movement to insist that its members abide by the charter and include all members in the regional games on penalty of exclusion from the Olympiads, ensured their eventual demise.

The Asian Games were an IOC project whose impetus came from India's first prime minister, Jawaharlal Nehru. They were initially held in 1954 and were truly pan-Asian. In 1963, however, the organizers of the 1964 Jakarta, Indonesia, event failed to invite the Israeli and the Nationalist Chinese teams and the IOC consequently withdrew its sponsorship. This led to a riot in the Indonesian capital, and the suspension of the Indonesian National Olympic Committee by the IOC. Indonesian president Sukarno renamed the event the Games of the New Emerging Forces (GANEFO) and proposed to hold them despite the loss of IOC sanction. The IOC in turn threatened to bar any athletes who participated in the GANEFOs from the next Olympiad. As the twentieth century draws to a close, the Asian Games are still a venue for sharp political and diplomatic maneuvering. The People's Republic of China, in particular, sees them as a venue for its own, often successful self-aggrandizement, as well as its largely unsuccessful efforts to thwart Taiwanese sovereignty.

Africa had been the focus of attention as early as the 1920s, when the IOC invited French and Italian colonial officials to advise on the feasibility of African games. Although such games for non-Europeans had been initially scheduled as early as 1925, the African games did not actually take place until 1965 when the politics of decolonization were palpable. The *Jeux Africains*, as the All-Africa Games were then called, excluded the still white- or European-controlled countries of South Africa, Rhodesia, Angola, and Mozambique. As these countries have gained their independence and, in the case of South Africa, ended apartheid, they have been allowed to participate. Whites, however, still make up a disproportionately large part of teams from South Africa and from former colonial societies such as Zimbabwe and Angola, which is due to the past devotion of training resources to mainly white, but not black, athletes.

In the late twentieth century, regional games such as the Asian or African Games have generated at least as much political friction as the Olympiads. However, they are also trying to become world-class sporting events as well as celebrations of cultural characteristics of the participants. The host countries, especially in Africa, make large financial investments in mounting these competitions—sometimes at the expense of more essential services—in order to impress visitors with the quality of their preparation for and presentation of these Games. Many of these attempts are, nonetheless, hampered by lack of funds, poor organization, and the absence of even Africa's own best competitors, who prefer participating in European and American meets where the competition is of higher caliber and the purses far more remunerative. Indeed, although Africa is the source of numerous world-class athletes, especially in track and field, almost all of them train at foreign universities, particularly in the United States, and compete almost exclusively abroad, donning their native countries' jerseys only for the Olympiads.

At least in Europe, traditional sports are also being revived. In the mid-1980s, moving away from the grandiosity and commercialism of the Olympiads and other games of world scope, the small nations of Europe—among them Monaco, Lichtenstein, Luxembourg, and Malta—began a contest called the *Jeux des Petits Etats d'Europe*. At about the same time, the First Inter-Island Games took place with competitors from Guernsey, Iceland, and St. Helena participating. Also in the mid-1980s the First Olympiad of the Minorities was held in order to gather European athletes belonging to ethnic groups considered marginalized in their nations of residence, such as the Welsh in Britain or the Bretons in France. As early as 1895, in conjunction with modern Zionism, European Jews created the Maccabi sports organization. Since the creation of the state of Israel in 1948, quadrennial Maccabean games for Jews of all nations are held there.

As the Olympiads become, increasingly, a circus of commercialism and media exploitation, it may fall more and more to people of different cultures, nations, and regions to have their own smaller festivals if they wish to use sporting events to celebrate individual traditions and cultural wealth.

## Women's Sports

The growth of women's participation in sports during the twentieth century parallels the growth in their prerogatives in society at large. As the

century comes to a close, we can look back on a chronicle of women's continuous but incomplete progress in all social and political contexts, including
sports. The factors which have contributed to the transformation of the
female athlete and to her net gain in participation at all levels of competition
are those which have transformed women's roles in society in general. They
include women's increasing contributions to their countries' nondomestic
economies, and their emancipation and acquisition of civic rights as a result
of more progressive social values arising out of political evolution or revolution. The progress of women's sports from Victorian games played separately
by upper-class girls or their proletarian sisters to the activities of highly paid
professional athletes and media-hyped world-record holders highlights the
trials and tribulations encountered by women in their quest for athletic
recognition.

As with men, women's progress in sports is reflected in the growth of the
modern Olympic Games. Unlike men's gains in that venue, however, women's
were rather gradual. In no small part this was due to Pierre de Coubertin's
view. He maintained that women could do all the sports they wished so long
as they did not do them in public; consequently, he tried to keep them out of
the Olympiads altogether. But his efforts at total exclusion were shortlived. As
early as the 1900 Paris Games, women were competing in golf and tennis. By
1912 in Stockholm, they participated as swimmers and platform divers, albeit
over the protests of those who objected strenuously to the idea of male spectators at women's events. Indeed, American women swimmers did not go to
Stockholm at all because the American Athletic Union (AAU) shared this
view.

Numerous national women's sports organizations sprang up in Europe
after World War I, partly as a result of women's wartime involvement in the
economy. These groups, modeled on working-class organizations that existed
prior to 1914, provided an outlet in a variety of sports for female athletes who
were still effectively barred from participating in the Olympics or in other
world-class events. To bring together the members of such organizations, the
*Jeux Internationaux Féminins* were first held in 1923 in Monaco and continued
into the 1930s, featuring competition by European women in track and field,
swimming, and basketball.

Under increasing pressure from socially progressive and women's sports
organizations to allocate a portion of the Olympics to female participation,
the aristocratic IOC's members relented and incorporated fencing, a sport
considered acceptable for their own wives and daughters, into the 1924 Paris
Games. This did not satisfy feminist sports organizations, which advocated

women's participation in the more plebeian track and field events. It was only when their influence persuaded powerful organizations such as the International Amateur Athletic Federation, which governed international track and field, to recognize women's organizations, and the IAAF prevailed upon the IOC to do the same, that women's sports on a broad basis, including gymnastics and track and field, were incorporated into the 1928 Amsterdam games. Women had finally scaled the heights and attained serious Olympic competition.

In the totalitarian societies that arose during the interwar period, women's sports acquired propagandistic significance. Such regimes were concerned with creating a mythical image for domestic and international consumption. Italian fascism emphasized the role of women as procreators of the race and hence resisted any efforts, including the public participation of women in sports, that would jeopardize this strategic social priority. This attitude was reinforced by an overwhelmingly conservative church hierarchy, which perceived such participation as little less than sinful debauchery.

Besides motherhood, National Socialism had an additional agenda: Aryanism, with its roots in the Germanic physical representation. The Nazi obsession with Aryanism reached cynical depths when German officials introduced young German women into the Olympic village at night for the pleasure of Nordic athletes who, it was hoped, would transmit their desirable physical traits.

From the interwar period to nearly the end of the cold war, the Soviet system paid lip service to a code of egalitarianism among its citizens. However, it overwhelmingly favored the participation of men rather than women in sports federations except where propaganda required featuring exceptional examples of Soviet female athleticism, either individually or en masse. This structure was dictated by economics since both sexes worked outside the home, while only the women had the domestic responsibility of raising families. The inescapable conclusion is that European totalitarian regimes of both the Right and the Left used women's participation in sports, as they did much else, for their own agendas.

While ideological concerns dictated the role of women in sports in totalitarian Europe, a combination of cultural mores and the media determined that of women in European and North American democracies. During the 1920s American advertising reshaped the projection of women and their role in society, showing women not only as symbols of domestic order, but also as independent flappers—physically boyish and participating equally with their male counterparts in the life of the "Jazz Age." While this reflects a transformation of the social, and especially the male, perception of women's roles, women's sports remained restricted, and women were largely prohibited from actually participating in competition on anything approaching equality with men.

Intercollegiate sports, the root of much of the twentieth-century metamorphosis in American athletics, were nonexistent for women in the interwar years. "Play Days" and "Telegraphic Meets" were the preferred form of competition for women: the former were quasi-spontaneous campus gatherings at which games were played in the context of other social activities; the latter involved individual female athletes recording the times of their best performances and exchanging them, via telegraph, with competitors from other schools. The common perception remained that women should not indulge in public in activities in which they might "forget themselves." Even after the introduction of women's track and field at the 1928 Olympics, the Women's Committee of the National Amateur Athletic Federation petitioned the IOC to drop the "dangerous experiment" of public competition.

Moreover, the vast majority of American women in the interwar years did not go to college. Their opportunity for sports came in the form of industrial leagues: teams organized by businessmen who saw female sports as a means to their own ends, such as the inherent benefit for the employer that workers would draw from playing games and the regional or national recognition that a team sponsor would gain from a successful team's efforts. Industrial leagues of a variety of sports were particularly successful in the midwestern United States.

The role of the media in the transformation of women's sports cannot be exaggerated. In the interwar years, a few strong-minded and strong-bodied— and exceptionally photogenic—women became celebrities in the realm of sports and adventure by an appeal that was crystallized in the popular press. Swimmer Gertrude Ederle, aviatrix Amelia Earhart, and tennis player Helen Wills made their mark through highly individualized and much chronicled careers. Their public appeal was due not only to their daring—Ederle swam the English Channel, Earhart flew solo across the Atlantic, and Wills won every major international tennis title—but also to their solid middle-class identity, their fortitude, and their looks. The 1920s French tennis player Suzanne Lenglen epitomized this phenomenon. In addition to playing a formidable game, Lenglen manipulated journalists and crowds through moods and antics that would be considered inappropriate in male athletes for at least another 50 years. Her public image was either self-projected or sharply intensified by a sensationalist media. The media's dissemination of images of this nature established the public's perception of female athletes as women first and athletes second, an assessment that would not be reversed until the feminist movement later in the century made it acceptable to admire women such as tennis star Martina Navratilova for pure athleticism.

For women in Western Europe and North America, the end of World War II served as a watershed. Their pivotal role in the war effort, both in uniform and in the factory, together with the ways in which postindustrial economies restructured traditional female roles, meant they could no longer be banished from the athletic field. The result was a novel emphasis on women's participation in sports. The 1948 Olympics in London led the way by introducing new track and field events for women, even as the IOC vetoed female participation in equestrian events, which were still dominated by male military officers. By 1952, when the Russians participated in the Olympics for the first time, women made up 10 percent of the competitors. Yet in spite of the quantifiable gains in records set and medals garnered, female athletes were still expected to act as females. Significant limits resulted. The gap between men and women participating in sports increased as the age of the participants increased, and women of working-class background were far less likely to participate in sports than were female members of the bourgeoisie. Nonetheless, during the 1960s and 1970s women's sports established themselves through the substantive combination of new women's Olympic events and outstanding performances by women. This long-awaited phenomenon was given wide-scale publicity by media eager to focus on trends with far-reaching social, cultural, and economic implications.

The women's liberation movement of this period in the United States positively and deeply affected women's sports. It took its cue from a variety of sources, including the much-publicized antics of professional superstars in various games, notably a tennis match between Billie Jean King and Bobby Riggs, and the spread of a new gospel: that women were quite capable of beating men at their own game. Once the taboo was broken, women challenged their exclusion from all sports. Although girls' efforts to join their brothers in baseball's Little Leagues attracted significant media attention, the impetus for fundamental change was most felt at the high school and college levels. Court challenges under federal legislation barring discriminatory policies for recipients of federal funding (including nearly all educational institutions, both public and private) resulted in a marked increase in funding for women's sports.

Public interest in female participation in professional sports was growing simultaneously. With subsequent media attention, women's participation in all sports, not just traditional activities like tennis and golf, increased. Even fashion consumerism began incorporating sports-garb designs, feeding the public interest in athletics through the popularization of the warm-up suit as unisex streetwear, and the male as well as female use of sports team names and logos or jersey numbers as decoration on caps, sweaters, shirts, and jackets. Indeed, stimulated by the fitness craze of the 1980s and 1990s, designers were producing clothing made to resemble athletic gear in keeping with a more popular athletic standard of feminine beauty.

In both Olympic and other world-class track and field events, women's performances now obtain as much attention from the media as men's, indicating growing interest in women's sports by the sports-watching public, a public that, according to commercial marketing surveys, remains, even as the century nears its end, predominantly male. Various studies carried on in the United States since the early 1980s have plotted a steady and consistent increase in both male and female acceptance of female athletes. Nonetheless, popular discussion of women's sports continues to suggest a dichotomy between ingrained cultural notions of traditional femininity and women's athleticism. These concerns sometimes take the form of sensationalist media attention to the actual or purported sexual orientation of individual women athletes. The same concern can be gleaned from the media's tendency to showcase a female athlete's life outside the sporting realm as a wife or mother. Male athletes garner attention of this nature far less frequently than women do.

It is difficult to gauge whether American feminist thinking has had the same impact on other societies. Certainly Western Europe has seen similar progress in women's sports participation and competition, though northern European women have led southern European and Iberian ones, for whom traditional and religious values and gender roles are more entrenched. Also, there continues to be a clear correlation between education, employment, class, socioeconomic status, and athletic participation. Women at the tops of these categories continue to be more likely to participate in a consistent fashion than their less fortunate sisters. Age, too, still plays a role, as with men, since the closer a woman is to her school days, the more likely she is to participate in athletic competition.

In Latin America, as in southern Europe, traditional cultural taboos have curtailed women's sporting activities to some degree. Even in Castro's ostensibly egalitarian Cuba, where occasional female achievement in international contests is heralded as the result of socialist structure, such success is still the exception rather than the norm.

Sports participation for women of Third World societies has not reached a level comparable to that of their European and American sisters. Traditional values and male-dominated social structures serve to stymie the athletic emancipation of non-Western women. Recently, with the help of former Soviet coaches, women from the Arab world have penetrated the upper reaches of track and field. Because their training is subsidized by the state, their publicized winning performances earn them extensive rewards back home. However, those from Islamic societies under fundamentalist pressure or influence have to contend, at best, with opprobrium back home.

Women are also now participating in the formulation of sports policies. As the end of the millennium approaches, the IOC has decreed that the 197 national Olympic committees, governing Olympic matters within their own countries, be at least 10 percent female by the year 2000 and 20 percent female by the year 2005, and has urged national and international sports federations to set similar goals. If these efforts succeed, the next century will undoubtedly see even greater public attention to women's athletics and even more lucrative commercial opportunities for women in sports.

## Imperialism

The fact that both the Olympiads and the non-European regional Olympic-style games discussed in the foregoing sections involve competition in sports originating in Europe or the United States is, of course, a product of the cultural dominance that characterized colonialism in the nineteenth and twentieth centuries, and continues to be influential in postcolonial cultures as well. Olympic sports are not, however, the only games whose diffusion has been driven by imperialism—especially Anglo-American imperialism—and the reaction to it. This phenomenon is demonstrated by the plethora of English-language terms in the world of modern sports not traditionally associated with the Olympiads. The universal use of terms like football, kick, goal, score, penalty, and halftime in soccer is only one example of this linguistic hegemony.

Regardless of how one theorizes imperialism, or whether one emphasizes colonialism, per se, or some other phenomenon of the era, such as capitalist development, industrialization, urbanization, or even anticolonial nationalism as the most significant factor in understanding imperialism, it is evident that dissemination of the colonizers' sports was as much an aspect of cultural imperialism as the influence of their literary or artistic traditions. Because Britain and, especially, the United States have been the most influential imperial powers of the twentieth century, it is not surprising that their sports have been successfully disseminated, often at the cost of actual or threatened extinction of traditional, indigenous sporting forms.

Some scholars have argued that games are culture-specific and that, there-fore, diffusion of sports during the colonial period depended on the intersec-tion of the inherent aspects of a sport and the group ethos of its practitioners. This approach, however, undervalues the appeal that some sports purportedly suited to a specific national temperament, such as baseball to American culture or judo to the Japanese ethos, have also held for other cultures. Witness the Japanese, Mexican, and Carribean enthusiasm for baseball; the Dutch and Israeli passion for judo. The transfer of sports activity appears to depend more heavily on the relative political, economic, and cultural power of the nations exporting the activity than on any inherent cultural predisposition. Hence the pastimes of wealthy, more developed nations are more likely to be transferred to lesser nations than vice versa. Although there are some exceptions, generally from the start of the colonial phase in modern world history, the vector of cul-tural influence has run along the same axis as vectors of political and economic power and, most often, at a directly proportional rate.

Although Japan has never been directly colonized, there was substantial Anglo-American commercial penetration during the latter half of the nine-teenth century. As a result, baseball—that quintessential American symbol—was introduced in Japan together with England's hallmark game, cricket, though the latter was largely displaced by the former when baseball became more popular with Japanese high school and university students. Though professional leagues were founded during the interwar years, Japan's military leaders banned the game on the eve of Pearl Harbor; the game was revived during the American occupation after 1945. Some analysts and historians attempting to explain baseball's appeal in Japan have pointed to its demand for perseverance, discipline, and self-restraint, together with its innate har-mony, as reflecting traditional Japanese activities. This, they suggest, made the game especially suited for the Japanese spirit. The more obvious parallels between modernization, industrialization, and the postwar Japanese percep-tion of American superiority might have contributed added appeal to the game. Some analysts have predicted that as American industrial and political power declines in Japan, the game will eventually lose its appeal to the Japan-ese; this, however, is unlikely to happen soon given the increasing globaliza-tion of mass culture and commerce. Indeed, GATT (General Agreement on Tariffs and Trade) may result in a day when Japanese teams become impor-tant components of U.S. major leagues, and international play will become routine, making the World Series truly global.

In colonial Africa and Asia, the European colonizers encouraged, as a mat-ter of policy, the adoption of Western sports. The ethos associated with team sports especially was often thought to be the best way to coopt indigenous elites into local administrative cadres.

Concurrent with political motivation during the period of colonial expansion was the religious zeal often referred to as "muscular Christianity," which entailed the active participation of missionaries and the educational institutions they established throughout the British empire. The French too, despite rigorous secular pedagogy at home, tended to conscript the church as an ally in their imperial schemes, especially when it came to colonizing and coopting indigenous populations. Schools throughout both the French and British imperial spheres actively promoted and even required the participation of students in Western forms of games and sports. Often, the adherents had to adjust to psychological and cultural requirements especially designed to impart a Western ethos by strictly adhering to the often arbitrary rules, regulations, vocabulary, and training of the Western sports practiced.

Cricket provides one of the clearest examples of ludic—that is, gaming—diffusion. Introduced in India by British missionaries, it was quickly appreciated by the colonizers as a vehicle likely to assimilate the ruling elites into a pro-British frame of mind. Cricket had to overcome indigenous cultural and religious resistance, such as Hindu objections to using a ball made of leather. However, the game ultimately proved itself to be an ideal vehicle for inculcating British culture into the elites of all the subcontinent's ethnocultural groups with teams of Hindu, Muslim, and Catholic Indian schoolboys faithfully—albeit imperfectly—replicating the playing fields of Eton on their own soil. As with many other cultural artifacts of empire, cricket survived India's independence in 1947. In postcolonial India and Pakistan, however, the game, originally the preserve of the elite, has become popular across the socioeconomic scale.

Soccer is another example of ludic diffusion in the colonial context, and has had an even wider diffusion than cricket. Originally carried the world over by British soldiers, missionaries, businessmen, and diplomats, it became popular in the colonies of other European powers as well, following the same pattern of assimilation as cricket, only on a larger scale. Like cricket, it was and remains an important cultural tool of social integration in both the colonial and postcolonial eras.

Occasionally, colonizers attempted to boost the qualities of their national teams by recruiting persons of talent and skill from among subject populations. Disappointing French results at the 1936 Berlin games motivated France to search its African colonies for black track and field talent in an effort to replicate the performances of Jesse Owens. The project foundered because the health of the indigenous populations was generally poor, French colonial administrators were uninterested in the leisure activities of their charges, and then World War II began.

By contrast, the British encouraged colonial athletes to compete in the names of their native lands. They furthered this intra-empire internationalism by structuring regularly held sports competitions and games such as the British Empire Games, which first occurred in 1930 in Edmonton, Canada. Many successful Empire Games athletes went on to represent their countries at more genuinely international meets.

In addition to using their educational institutions to foster a British games ethic throughout their empire, the British also introduced another vital institution: the sporting club. Originally conceived as an oasis of British culture for the benefit of colonial personnel, in time the sporting club became a place of cultural symbiosis. Recruited as club members, indigenous elites were taught and expected to conform to the fashion and structure of British sports. Even when the indigenous population was excluded from membership in the European clubs, the pattern in much of both the British and French imperial spheres, members of the native elites would often form their own, equally exclusionary clubs modeled after those of their colonizers. By the eve of decolonization, some of these institutions were hotbeds of anticolonial sentiment, where victories over European teams at the Europeans' own games could be hailed as refutation of claims of European superiority. It is ironic that membership today in many of these clubs—originally founded by the colonized as a democratic, egalitarian response to the exclusive and exclusionary colonizers' clubs, which were instruments of social filtration—is considered a sign of prestige and social attainment in much of the postcolonial world. Some of these clubs formed the nuclei of the national Olympic committees of a number of newly independent African and Asian nations in the period following decolonization.

Although most ludic diffusion went from colonizers to colonized, some forms of sports and games were transmitted in the opposite direction. Recognizable versions of polo, for example, were played on the Asian subcontinent long before the British established the East India Company, let alone direct imperial rule. Polo was introduced in Britain by returning army officers at the same time as Anglican missionaries were teaching cricket to uppercaste Indians. Now universally associated with royalty and the jet set, it is played by the rich and powerful the world over. Judo is another example of an apparently indigenous activity expropriated by the West. Developed by Japanese martial arts masters at the end of the nineteenth century to replace more complex and traditional martial arts, it became familiar to Americans and Europeans in the aftermath of Japan's defeat in 1945, and was brought home with them after their occupation of Japan. While the Japanese still dominate international competition, Western practitioners have successfully challenged this hegemony.

Sports have inherently dialectical characteristics which influence their historical metamorphosis. The historical record of the post-1945 period is replete with instances in which Third World teams have triumphed over their Western opponents in games introduced to them as instruments of colonial control and cultural domination. Indian, Pakistani, West Indian, and other former "colonial" cricket elevens routinely defeat British sides on the latter's turf in London. World Cup soccer play finds Latin Americans and other non-Western nations defeating European teams with as much regularity as Europeans beat them.

This kind of sporting victory often reinforces the self-esteem of the winners and provides an exultation rarely encountered in the spheres of politics, economics, or diplomacy. Indeed, one may argue that athletic contests in which the perceived political underdog triumphs are necessary to maintaining harmonious dynamics in international relations. Moreover, even where colonially imported sports such as soccer or tennis have displaced traditional forms of games, such as wrestling in Turkey, hammer-throw in Scotland, or kung fu in China, the cultural loss this has entailed has been, to some degree, offset by the integrating effect this has had in giving participants a commonality with other members of a diverse global community. In that respect, the sports of the colonial era now serve as agents for inclusion and even triumph by formerly excluded groups.

## Technology and Science

Athletes have always competed not only against each other, but also to surpass their own and other competitors' previous achievements. Speed has been a concern of athletes since the ancient Olympic games. It was also an element of games involving running in traditional and nonindustrial societies. However, only after electronic time measurement was introduced at the Stockholm Olympiad in 1912 could athletes be precisely timed and their records accurately preserved. Since then, the advent of sophisticated laser measurement technology has made it possible to measure elapsed time in hundredths of seconds, thus further refining and narrowing the gap between victory and defeat. This has also permitted instantaneous display of recorded time, thus increasing the level of anxiety in the athletes and excitement in the spectators. The former can monitor their own or their competitors' progress even as the competition is ongoing; the latter can and sometimes do watch the flickering numbers on the electronic timing boards more intently than the events themselves.

Imaging technologies such as still, laser, and motion photography have, as they have developed over the twentieth century, not only radically altered the means by which information about the events is disseminated, but also allowed performers to structure their training to more closely replicate actual competitive conditions. The expense of such aids has contributed to the transformation of athletics from pastime to professional endeavor and fostered the development of sports-related adjunct professions ranging from public relations to sports psychology. While Western athletes often have better access to state-of-the-art training support, competitors from the rest of the world are increasingly availing themselves of modern methods.

Progress in the technologies of transportation and communications have also contributed to the globalization of athletics. Even at the first modern Olympics in 1896 in Athens, most competitors came from far further than those who participated in the Ancient Games. Today, jet travel permits athletes to live, train, and compete wherever they choose.

The transmission of information from sporting events by wireless began as early as 1899 and did much to propagate public interest. Since then, revolutionary developments in travel and communications have exponentially increased mass involvement in sports events. Today, soccer's quadrennial World Cup competition is beamed via satellite to the entire planet, and billions of spectators are glued to monitors, cheering for teams whose victory or defeat is fraught with actual and symbolic significance for all of them.

Technological changes in the materials and manufacture of equipment, uniforms, and even playing surfaces have also transformed athletics. The use of lighter alloys and plastics permits players a greater and faster range of motion and new opportunities for maximizing performance. This, in turn, increases the pressure on trainers and coaches to use state-of-the-art equipment in order to produce winning performances.

This concern with achievement, always a hallmark of competition but especially emphasized in the period since World War II because of financial remuneration, has also introduced a new phenomenon: the use of performance-improving drugs to change the actual physical and metabolic structure of the athletes themselves.

Today, the illicit use of anabolic steroids has surpassed the issue of amateurism as the preeminent concern of the sports world, and specifically in the Olympics. Although the IOC had banned a number of substances for use by athletes as early as 1962, it was not until the 1976 Montreal Games that rumors of widespread steroid use by East German female swimmers and track and field athletes came to the public's attention, rumors that were confirmed by documents made available after the reunification of Germany in October 1990. A significant number of Soviet weight lifters were also disqualified for use of steroids then and in subsequent Games as well. However, the unprecedented media attention focused at the 1988 Seoul Games upon Canada's track star Ben Johnson confirmed that prohibited drugs were as widely used in the West as in the Eastern Bloc. The pressures of highly remunerative product endorsement contracts, coupled with the competitive will to win, encouraged world-class athletes to risk the use of drugs. Blood doping surfaced at the 1976 Montreal Olympiad as a performance-enhancing technique, involving athletes training at high altitude to increase their oxygen-carrying red blood cells. A portion of their blood would then be removed and preserved until just before the contest, when, returned in the form of a last-minute transfusion, it would enhance athletic endurance. Although blood doping involves no elements of a foreign substance, it is considered illegal since it violates the Olympic spirit through an "unnatural and unfair advantage" to a competitor.

Given the geopolitical significance often attached to athletic achievement by participants, their governments, and the public, it is not surprising that, beginning with the Nazi eugenics in the 1936 Games, there have been concerted, nationalistically inspired efforts to use science to produce—or reproduce—superior athletes.

Some countries have openly employed socio- or bioengineering techniques to achieve athletic victory. The People's Republic of China has been known to preselect parents in the hope of breeding children who will grow up to be athletes with desired features for particular sports. North Korea has sought to identify potential athletes at the tender age of 3 or 4, and then take over their upbringing to ensure the fulfillment of that potential, a practice that was also employed in the Soviet Union and its satellite states before its dissolution. Even in countries where the government does not have the authority to command mating or conscript toddlers, or eschews on moral or ethical grounds the notion of breeding human beings for particular purposes, scientific research in a wide array of areas is eagerly employed by the coaches, trainers, scouts, and parents who assist aspiring athletes to develop the talent that, it is hoped, will bring Olympic gold and prestige home to their national sponsors.

## Commercialism and Professionalization

For the founders of the modern Olympiads, amateurism reflected their initial concern with class differences rather than paid performances, since they excluded from participation athletes who received wages for manual labor. The definition of a professional athlete came on the heels of the Jim Thorpe controversy after the 1912 Olympiad. Because he had played professional baseball while still a student, his medals were taken away. Nonetheless, the IOC, ever class-conscious and ignoring the fact that military officers received all the emoluments of their commissions while training and competing, deemed them amateurs and therefore qualified to participate in Olympiads. It was not until 1952, after the march of Third World nationalism, decolonization, and the incorporation of the Soviet Union into the Olympic movement were having an impact on the social perspectives of even the IOC, that a similar exemption was accorded to noncommissioned officers and enlisted men. Other nonpatrician athletes the world over benefited from that development and from other techniques developed largely in Soviet-bloc nations to confer amateur status on subsidized professional athletes, techniques conveniently ignored by the IOC because of political sensitivities and expediency.

A more pragmatic definition of amateurism has evolved over the years to the point that it now permits the salaries, bonuses, endorsements, and other forms of financial and material rewards which world-class athletes receive for their athletic performances. It began with the commercial sponsorship of skiers at the 1968 Grenoble Winter Games, and continued apace thereafter, even though most of the skiers flagrantly violated an agreement made by their organizing body that they would not openly advertise their sponsors. By the late 1970s, the IOC rules were revised to allow athletes to openly display their sponsors' logos and otherwise earn money for their clubs, though personal gain was still frowned upon. In 1982, the rules were revised once more to allow the creation of a trust fund for individual athletes, ostensibly to meet their training and competition expenses. These funds, however, have now become sources of income long after the athletes' active careers and act as retirement funds of sorts indistinguishable from profit-sharing arrangements or pensions available from any other commercial enterprise.

In fact, contemporary remuneration for athletes is more reminiscent of the rewards given to the warriors of ancient times, such as Homeric heroes, than of the rewards to athletes who participated in the classical games. The latter received only olive wreaths and laurels for their victories. Homer's warriors had gold, silver, bronze, and captive women distributed to them from the booty of victory in proportion to both their skill on the battlefield and their status in the sociomilitary hierarchy. Substitute today's astronomical salaries, the profits from commercial endorsements, and high-priced automobiles, and you have modern Mycenean heroes.

The professionalization of sports and the increasing commercialism that transcends borders, cultures, and traditions, including the racial and gender integration of certain sports, has had the salutary effect of transforming the Olympic Games from the exclusive preserve of privileged groups to an endeavor involving all levels of society. A similar process has been evident in non-Olympic international sports like soccer and cricket, where, as the colonial powers withdrew, players of talent, regardless of their ethnoracial background, were conscripted into the games' ambitious clubs for national and especially for international competition.

The IOC itself has not been immune to the pressure of economic factors. At the 1960 Rome Olympiad, it inaugurated the practice of awarding "official" imprimatur to individual manufacturers and service providers for everything from the "official" timepiece to the "official" hotel chain, credit card, or potato chip. The electronic media are also charged a substantial sum for the privilege of transmitting telecommunications of the contests. Indeed, as the Olympics become more and more the object of commercial exploitation, one of the most dramatic effects has been the increase in the amount paid by television networks for the rights to broadcast the Games.

In 1976, the American Broadcasting Company won the rights to broadcast the Montreal games for a mere $25 million. By the 1980 Olympiad, in which the United States did not even compete, Moscow had managed to sell the rights to the National Broadcasting Company for $85 million. Each succeeding Olympiad reaches new heights, or depths, of sponsorship that would have been unimaginable only a few years before as commentators decry the plethora of commercial symbols. Significantly, television networks have begun to alter their coverage of the games to suit the habits and the schedules of their viewers and the selling needs of their sponsors. Since the largest portion of Olympic coverage rights are usually awarded to American television networks, this has guaranteed a very American-oriented dissemination of the Games in recent years.

## Conclusion

Although the transformation of athletics in the twentieth century is the result of a number of factors, all have come on the heels of urbanization and increased leisure time. The gradual shift from long rural workdays to a rhythm which permitted people to participate more conveniently and seriously in organized games paved the way for the popularization of sports. As the phenomenon of serious play spread, initially throughout Europe and North America, organizers conceived rational structures for the activities and the rules that covered them.

Like most aspects of twentieth-century society, sports acquired the parameters of regimentation and regulation. The most significant outcome of the process, with the benefit of a century's perspective, was its globalization. This was the result of European colonialism and of various forms of imperialism. Because colonizers introduced elements of their cultures among the colonized, the spread of games and their accompanying ethos was assured. This process was both overt and subtle, for the agents of Europeanization employed a variety of means to communicate their social and cultural priorities. Thus began the modern intersection of sports and politics.

Infused with ideological factors from their inception, the modern Olympic games have reflected the cycles of international politics. Nationalism inaugurated the process of politicization. The use of sports by all governments in their respective efforts to advance specific agendas continued unabated through two world wars, scores of revolutions and new nations, the cold war, and beyond. The process has been especially evident among Third World nations, especially when applied to regional emulation of the Olympics. Politics aside, the globalization of sports has substantially, though not completely, leveled the playing fields on which representatives of wealthy and poor societies meet.

Perhaps one of the most positive elements of sports in the twentieth century has been their symbolism as a social barometer. The progress of women in athletics has reflected their inclusion in the social and economic fabric of their respective societies. While this is certainly true for the liberated women of Western Europe and North America, it is less applicable for their sisters in other areas of the globe. However, there too, measurable progress is evident.

Originally participation in organized sports on a national, let alone an international, level was mostly the preserve of the privileged. Incremental changes due to the economic transformation of global society permitted the less privileged access to serious athletics. Also contributing to this emancipation were the ideological priorities of competing, hence sponsoring governments. As the century nears the millennium, commercialization and the spread of professional sports have substituted for political sponsorship and proffered to exceptional athletes careers unheard of on the eve of World War I.

The impact of most, if not all, of the aforementioned factors was magnified and ensured by the revolution in information technology. It is the thrill and the drama of competition, successful or not, as presented by the world media that, in the final analysis, has provided the inspiration to generations of budding athletes the world over to emulate the disciplined training and the competitive focus of victorious athletes.

ENDNOTE

1. This essay benefited from a reading by Alison R. Steiner.

SELECTED REFERENCES

Bailey, Wilford S. and Taylor D. Littleton. *Athletics and Academe: An Anatomy of Abuses and a Prescription for Reform.* New York: American Council on Education/Macmillan, 1991.

Eitzen, Stanley D. and George H. Sage. *Sociology of North American Sports.* 3d ed. Dubuque, Iowa: Wm. C. Brown, 1986.

Espy, Richard. *The Politics of the Olympic Games.* Berkeley: University of California Press, 1979.

Guttman, Allen. *Games and Empires: Modern Sports and Cultural Imperialism.* New York: Columbia University Press, 1994.

———. *The Olympics: A History of the Modern Games.* Urbana, Ill.: University of Illinois Press, 1992.

———. *Women's Sports: A History.* New York: Columbia University Press, 1991.

Mandell, Richard. *Sports: A Cultural History.* New York: Columbia University Press, 1984.

———. *The Nazi Olympics.* New York: Macmillan, 1971.

Mangan, J. A. *The Games Ethics and Imperialism: Aspects of the Diffusion of an Ideal.* New York: Viking, 1986.

van Schaik, Henri L. M. Interviews by author. Cavendish, Vermont, March 1989.

Touraine, Alain. "Leisure Activities and Social Participation," in Michael R. Marrus, ed., *The Emergence of Leisure.* New York: Harper & Row, 1974.

Rigauer, Bero. *Sports and Work.* Trans. Allen Guttman. New York: Columbia University Press, 1981.

# 6  Ethnicity and Racism

J. PAUL MARTIN

Nothing better illustrates the recurrent internecine travails of humanity than the complexities we label race and ethnicity. While religious and political ideologies as diverse as Christianity, Islam, Western Liberalism, and Marxism have preached against racism and hailed their own triumphs, the group consciousness and animosities stimulated by what are essentially inherited human physical and cultural diversities have reasserted themselves. As the twentieth century ends, the media bombard us daily with stories of interethnic violence from countries as varied as Armenia, Fiji, Guatemala, India, Iraq, Lebanon, Pakistan, Rwanda, South Africa, and Sri Lanka, as well as more incidental outbreaks on city streets around the world.

In the United States they are called bias crimes, in India communalism, but virtually every nation-state is burdened with profound social rifts along the lines of ethnic and religious consciousness. This has been a century marked by the high profiles of the killing of Jews by Nazi Germany, the legalized racism practiced in South African apartheid, and the recent "ethnic cleansing" in the former Yugoslavia, leaving us, as the century ends, with an acute awareness of the many festering ethnic tensions across the globe. The demise, over the course of the century, of the colonial and ideological forces that characterized its early to middle period destroyed the beginning of the century's prevailing patterns of social cohesion, and opened the way to fragmentation and primitive nationalisms. In the twentieth century, race has been a powerful motive and force both for struggles for freedom and for acts of oppression, the one enriching and the other impoverishing humankind.

Like many other twentieth-century phenomena, race and ethnic problems have been universalized. They now take place on a world screen and attract the involvement of international actors in the shape of other governments and intergovernmental or nongovernmental organizations. Not only do we all know about the ethnic problems of the world, we can also see how increasing ethnic conflagrations represent, in the wake of East-West tensions, the most dangerous ignition points for major violence and war, and one of the few common denominators of the wars at the end of this century. A February 7, 1993 report in the *New York Times* listed forty-eight different active ethnic wars: nine in Europe, seven in the Middle East and North Africa, fifteen in Africa, thirteen in Asia, and four in Latin America. The pervasiveness of the problems caused by ethnic diversity could not be better illustrated.

Throughout the century, the United Nations and the League of Nations before it have tried to develop legal instruments and institutions, such as the Convention, the Committee on the Elimination of Racial Discrimination, and the Sub-Commission on Human Rights, which would give sustained attention to the problems of indigenous peoples and minorities. National governments have created special administrative and judicial institutions to address diversity problems. Nevertheless there are few signs that these problems are diminishing, or that they are less likely to cause major conflicts in critical regions like the Middle East.

The span of the century emphasizes their recurrent nature. The former Yugoslavia, where until recently one perceived a sense of powerlessness on the part of the international community in the face of a vicious ethnic conflict, and today a fragile peace is observed, is the same region where, at the beginning of the century, ethnic forces unleashed by the Austro-Hungarian Empire's dissolution sparked the First World War. As the century opened, the Boers or Afrikaners were fighting the British for the power to develop their own race-based society. Today, nearly one hundred years later, apartheid is being dismantled, but ethnic conflicts are flaring up elsewhere, notably in Burundi and Rwanda. In the United States in the first half of the century, racism was still protected by standards set by the 1896 Supreme Court decision *Plessy v. Ferguson*, which allowed separate but equal public services for black and white citizens. Since its 1954 reversal in *Brown v. Board of Education*, the remaining part of the century has witnessed public debates, administrative ordinances, and judicial action seeking to redress the past and prevent continuing discrimination, leaving the country both proud of the enormous energy devoted to improving the situation of Americans of African descent, and embarrassed by the continued existence of an underclass closely linked to race. Overall the century is ending with increased global consciousness of racism, but without great vision or solutions.

The phenomena we call race and ethnicity are largely inherited, the given rather than acquired parts of each individual's makeup over which he or she has no control. These inherited characteristics, both physical and cultural, involve the social constructs of history and symbols that lead down the slippery slope of racism—leading, that is, to stereotyping, ranking, patterns of hegemony, and eventually, rationales that justify killing on the basis of race.

Inherited though they are, giving these particular characteristics the principal role in how we categorize human beings is a human construct in two senses: we could choose other characteristics such as intelligence or wealth, and we routinely attribute stereotypic, highly subjective attributes to profiles based on ethnicity. While contemporary academic and popular writing on ethnicity, race, and racism is extensive, it is difficult to find new insights and go beyond debates on definition and analytical theory. On our streets and in popular parlance, the problems of discrimination caused by race and poor race relations remain. The question is: what do we have to learn from the century's experiences as to where we go from here?

## The Growth of International Consciousness

The stage for internationalizing race and race relations in the twentieth century was set at two late-nineteenth-century conferences in Berlin, in 1878 and 1884. At the first, the European powers agreed on arrangements for the Balkans; at the second they decided on the partition of Africa, thereby establishing the "rules" for global hegemonies—ostensibly for the Europeans but also those for other colonial-minded powers, notably Japan. The history of the great powers' subsequent endeavors is riddled with the de facto racist principles then espoused, which treated other races as children incapable of looking after themselves and left many countries, notably black Africa, wholly unprepared to compete in the present world economy.

At the beginning of this century, the leaders of the European nations saw themselves as morally, politically, and economically superior to and in control of the rest of the world. In this sense their two wars beginning in 1914 and 1939 were indeed world wars whose consequences would be felt everywhere. In the peace negotiations after the first war through the Treaties of Paris and the founding of the League of Nations, the great powers paid special attention to Europe's ethnic minorities, whose problems were seen as a past and likely future cause of war. Their actions resulted in five treaties, four special chapters in the general treaties of peace, five declarations, and two conventions, by means of which fourteen states were placed under an obligation to observe specific standards designed to protect the some thirty million individuals belonging to racial, religious, and linguistic minorities within their individual jurisdictions. The principles incorporated in these treaties were designed to address the nationality problems raised by territorial redistribution after the war, by assuring these minority groups of individual and religious freedoms and equal treatment for all nationals within the same country, in law and in fact. The states also agreed to certain minority language rights, including primary instruction in minority languages. The general assumption on the part of the great powers, however, was that the minorities would eventually be assimilated into the general political life of their respective countries and the problems would pass away.

The League set up a Minorities Committee headed by the president of the Council (the League's executive body as opposed to its full Assembly), assisted by two other appointees. Between the wars the Council was called upon to address petitions from the different countries but acted only gently—as though undecided with regard to its powers. The postwar arrangements for European minorities, as well as the system of trusteeships devised for the former German colonies and Ottoman territories, including Palestine, reinforced the two-tier view of the world: those in power and those in need of protection. But the League's provisions were soon overtaken by the powerful ethnic and other forces unleashed by national socialism in Germany, followed by a further war and then renewed efforts, through the founding of the United Nations, to create a system for international peace. UN founders forged an institution based on a world composed of nation-states and individual persons. In so doing they completely ignored national minorities and other intervening groupings and launched a period of international politics submerged in the complexities of the cold war. But the forces could not be ignored. With the problems of South Africa in the vanguard and the Palestinian question close behind, documents and institutions began to be approved that affirmed the inadmissibility of racial discrimination. As the century ends, other than North-South relations, ethnic tensions are probably the major challenge on the agenda of the United Nations.

## The Colonial Legacy

As the twentieth century dawned, the European nations and Japan were busy consolidating their respective political and economic empires. Their presence was all but global: the only other major and truly international grouping of peoples were the Islamic countries ranging from Morocco in the West to the Dutch East Indies, but those were not unified politically, some being incorporated into the European colonial structures. Their common Islamic heritage, however, was a strongly defining factor in the eyes of Western governments, and certainly also for the Christian missionaries who sought to advance with the colonial powers. Throughout the century interaction between these forces of imperialism and religion created many points of political and religious tension, not the least of which was the creation and subsequent history of the state of Israel.

European colonialism's impact on Africa was especially massive. As well as subjugating Africa to an external power and fostering the prevalence of coercive political power and organization, the Europeans created extensive political units that bore no reference to local human geography or history. Their presence imposed new relationships among the existing traditional communities, and in some cases, an already dominant group like the Baganda in Uganda consolidated their power as subimperialists. Elsewhere subordinate groups used Western patronage to acquire new status and significant political power not only in their own region, but throughout the newly defined colonial units. Traditional ethnic cleavages took on new significance as the groups sought to respond to the European presence and to adjust their way of life to new economic and political opportunities. When the Europeans withdrew in the second part of the century, however, they left their former colonies with little in the way of political structures or trained personnel to run these states they had so arbitrarily created. Little provision was made for ethnic diversity within states and none for situations where ethnic groups were divided by the lines drawn in Berlin.

As did the colonial regimes, the cold war both suppressed and accentuated ethnic diversity. In countries such as the former Yugoslavia a common ideology as well as strong central power limited ethnic tension and violence. On the other hand, in regions like the horn of Africa internecine rivalries were repeatedly fueled by infusions of weapons from both Western and communist worlds to whichever sides they perceived as their surrogates. For complex and differing reasons, first the demise of colonial power and then the diminution of the cold war left many states less able to act to alleviate ethnic tensions, thereby creating millions of refugees around the world pushed out of their homelands on account of their ethnic identity. For colonial powers had imposed a political order which ignored earlier, more localized orders, and put forth the claim that the forces of modernization would bring about a new order that would transcend ethnic and tribal rivalries—under the guidance, of course, of the superior civilization represented by the colonial power. European and Japanese colonialism, and the means they had at their disposal, brought the peoples of the world closer together but did not provide the structures needed to recognize cultural and political diversity. Moreover, implicit in the whole process was the dominance of the colonizer over the colonized. This domination was based on a sense of racial superiority.

## Race and National Politics: The United States and South Africa

Among the many countries in the world where race has played a major political role, none competes with the United States and South Africa in the international visibility of their respective experiences. Race has been a constant theme in both American and South African history. In both cases, from the moment of their arrival, the colonizing forefathers of the dominant population had come to stay. They were not just traders. They were settlers looking for a new home. Both societies came to encompass peoples with vastly different cultural and historical experiences, and both groups of immigrants had to face initially more numerous indigenous inhabitants. Both brought in thousands of laborers from third countries, complicating the ethnic and cultural mix. From the beginning, relationships between the colonizers and the colonized were coercive, determined in all critical situations by the colonizers' superior firepower and resulting in the subordination of the native peoples. There were of course many variations within each society, most notably the quantity and quality of the immigrant groups that came to the States and South Africa from different parts of Europe. The latter organized themselves in ways that satisfied their need to retain their cultural heritage and yet adopt a lifestyle commensurate with that of their adopted home. For the States, early political independence and many highly trained immigrants unleashed great economic and political energy, making the country one of the major world powers by the beginning of the twentieth century. South Africa, on the other hand, relied heavily on extractive industries and cheap black labor for its wealth, and has yet to achieve the industrial diversity and size necessary to sustain well more than a minority of its population.

Given the United States' position as a world political and economic power throughout the century, its still-increasing dominance of the entertainment and mass communications media, and more overt and self-conscious attitude to its own behavior, it was perhaps inevitable that its historical experience and race-relations legacy in particular should become a worldwide reference point. Images of the South and the legacy of slavery, the conquest of the West and the treatment of Native Americans in the process, the achievements of Abraham Lincoln and, in the present century, the work of Dr. Martin Luther King, Jr. and Malcolm X are an integral part of global lore, communicated by literature but especially through distribution of the products of the American film industry.

Race relations have been a political preoccupation since America's origins. The American colonies were founded at a time of new social mobility. Never before had it been possible to transport so many so quickly and for such distances. Peoples were being thrown together in ways inconceivable in centuries past. European political ambition coupled with technical power first made control of the continent possible, and then created all manner of measures to subjugate preexisting inhabitants. By the beginning of this century, people had come to America from all over the world, often congregating in rural and urban ethnic enclaves. The entrepreneurs, the major professionals, and the managers were European, and the more menial labor was performed by the blacks and more recent immigrants, leaving a large transition space between rich and poor that would eventually be dominated by the unions and small entrepreneurs in all economic sectors. Relative to many other countries, the economic growth of the United States has enabled it to draw up, or at least give the belief that it could draw up, the majority of its immigrants along the scale of improved living standards. The popular media have always cultivated this image and still do. One example is the way in which virtually all current television stories starring African American characters portray them living in affluence and well-appointed living conditions. Only a very small proportion have attained such a status in real life.

At the beginning of the century the country was primarily concerned with absorbing European immigrants—Italians, Poles, Irish, Scandinavians, Hungarians, and others, almost all of whom were Christians or Jews. The immigrants initially gravitated to their own ethnic communities, where they enjoyed the support needed to adapt to American life. They found jobs with the help of their fellow nationals and eventually sent their children to the local public or parochial school. The parochial, religious schools were no less dedicated to helping immigrants' children integrate into their new country by reconciling their religious commitments with the civic ethic. Labor unions played an important role in raising their standard of living, but it was only late in this century, after extensive intervention by the federal government, that African Americans began to benefit from membership in the major unions.

The American union movement grew up in close conjunction with immigration and the immigrants' need for communities of shared religion, national origins, language, and culture. Ethnic communities used their control of the labor unions to provide their newly arrived members with jobs and therefore independence, stability, and integration into American society. In the nineteenth century, there is much detailed evidence to show this had meant excluding African Americans. A 1903 editorial in *The Colored American* noted: "The first thing they do after landing and getting rid of their sea legs is to organize to keep the colored man out of the mines, out of the factories, out of trade unions and out of all kinds of industries of the country."[1] The ethnic quality of the union movement was already visible in the mid-nineteenth century, so that by the beginning of the twentieth, it was possible to show how the numbers of African Americans were reduced in various trades. Excluding them and Asians from the unions restricted access to better-paid jobs and the chance of advancement to the lower-middle class. Many unions, especially the powerful railway unions, had specific exclusion clauses in their constitutions such as "a white free-born male citizen of some civilized country," "a white person of good moral character," or "of the Caucasian race."[2] The unions often achieved closed-shop status, completely excluding nonwhites from employment in individual industries. Even when these clauses were removed in the early part of the century, other mechanisms were used. Until mid-century those who did manage to join AFL (American Federation of Labor) unions were segregated into separate "auxiliary" units, often with provisions to ensure they remained segregated and excluded from the more skilled jobs. The work of A. Philip Randolph in organizing the black sleeping car attendants, which began when he was elected president of the Brotherhood of Sleeping Car Attendants in 1925, was an outstanding exception to the general pattern. Only later, with the advent of national affirmative action legislation and numerous lawsuits (whose documentation profusely illustrates the past patterns), did all unions have to move toward integration when hiring practices and seniority policies were gradually changed under court and legislative orders.

Looked at with foreign eyes, the African American experience is one of highs and lows. Increasing numbers of successful black Americans enjoyed fame and fortune: notably writers like James Baldwin and Maya Angelou, and athletes like Joe Louis, Jesse Owens, Althea Gibson, Jackie Joyner-Kersee, and Michael Jordan. Increasingly, black political leaders like Dr. Martin Luther King, Jr., Jesse Jackson, and David Dinkins have become internationally known figures, coming from the African American community with messages of heritage and renewal. Among their predecessors was Marcus Garvey, a Trinidadian immigrant who in the interwar years sought to inspire his fellow African Americans to take pride in their own culture and philosophies. Garvey therefore used a consciously racial formulation: "The time has come for the Negro to forget and cast behind him his hero worship and adoration of other races, and to start out immediately to create and emulate heroes of his own." This, as Garvey stated, would require freeing himself from his acceptance of the thoughts and opinion of the white race: "Any race that accepts the thoughts of another race automatically, becomes the slave of the other race."[3]

While he affirmed the equality of black and white, he urged Africans and African Americans to emancipate themselves by embracing something original—something racially their own—which he defined as African Fundamentalism, the Creed of the Negro Race. This view of life emphasized Africa as the cradle of civilization, with its own great leaders and heroes to inspire their modern-day descendants.

The second half of the century has been dominated by what came to be known as the civil rights movement, beginning with the 1954 Supreme Court case *Brown v. Board of Education*, climaxing during the 1960s with President Johnson's concept of the great society. There followed almost twenty years of trench warfare called affirmative action. Overall, the policy has lost ground and the relative condition of the underclass is debated. The evidence of pervasive race-conditioned discrimination remains, be it in the number of empty taxis that will pass a prospective black passenger or the increased likelihood of both conviction and a death sentence that black men have in the courts nationwide. African Americans have made some gains relative to the rest of the society in terms of income, educational attainment, health, housing, job status, and electoral politics. This is rightly attributed in part to antidiscrimination laws and the commitment to enforce them, but also to sustained national economic growth coupled with affirmative action programs and networks of individuals and organizations working to resolve friction. During the 1980s, however, African Americans gained little, as the economy weakened, civil rights enforcement lacked commitment, and social programs were being cut back. The community's problems remain symbolized by high unemployment among black youths—three to four times that of their white counterparts. We wait to see the effects of the strong economy of the 1990s.

Affirmative action's momentum slowed in the 1980s because numerical racial quotas came to be portrayed as unfair reverse discrimination, excluding white ethnics and ostensibly the most qualified in order to promote "less-qualified" African Americans, Native Americans, and women. Twelve years of the Reagan and Bush administrations brought little in the way of an affirmative action agenda, with the government even supporting court actions that weakened its effect. Most recently, in spite of an "inclusive" cabinet, the new Democratic agenda as enunciated by President Clinton has focused on economics, relegating what the vast majority of black Americans still see as the dominant factor in their daily lives, race and racism, to a minor role. It is beyond this essay to try to provide a bottom line on the end-of-the-century status of African Americans. But in general, while many black Americans have acquired substantial social status and acceptance, the vast majority of them and, more current data shows, Hispanic Americans as well, live the depressed life of an underclass, characterized by poverty, crime, poor health, and inefficient social services, and contrasting with more recent Asian immigrants who are moving up the economic scale ahead of both groups. On the political sidelines, virtually throughout the last two centuries, has been the United States' other major ethnic group, the Native Americans. They have tried to retain identity and community in those mostly desolate regions of the country defined as their homelands by their treaties with the United States government. It has been the discrimination drama of the African rather than the Hispanic or Native Americans, however, that has been played out on the world stage.

As pervasive as racial discrimination has been in the United States, its effect pales beside the experience of the subordinate nonwhite populations in South Africa. Although they now all call themselves black, they come from many different strands, including major groupings of African populations that moved from central Africa, earlier indigenous groups and, at the behest of the Europeans, Malay and Indian workers. Although the National (Afrikaner) Party only came to power in 1948, racial discrimination grew steadily as the dominant cleavage in South African life virtually from the moment the first Europeans from Holland settled there in 1652. The first military clash with the local inhabitants came in 1702 as the settlers, now including French Huguenots as well as the Dutch, ventured farther into the interior, setting up farms and towns. By the beginning of the twentieth century, when the Cape Colony had been under British rule for just over a hundred years, there also existed a group of two independent states formed by the Boers (Transvaal and the Orange Free States) and another British colony, Natal. Enclosed farms had rapidly taken over the high plateau, and the African population either remained as local labor or lived in informal reserves.

In the second part of the nineteenth century, the discovery of diamonds and then gold changed South Africa's place in the world irrevocably. While the extraordinary richness of the deposits was clear, both turned out to be highly expensive operations with little room for the independent digger, white or black. Ownership and management were white and the mines developed a two-tier, racially defined labor pattern, with the black population always paid significantly less and recruited and treated as transient workers. As there was no skilled local labor, white workers were initially brought from overseas, creating, by the beginning of the century, a large enough pool of white labor that black South Africans were excluded from all advancement opportunities. Skilled tasks and high wages became the unquestioned prerogative of whites throughout the South African economy; racial separation was a doctrine of the workplace long before it was legislated for the country as a whole. Cheap native labor made it possible for South Africa's mining, agricultural, and other industries to compete in world markets, at the same time providing a high standard of living for the white population.

Control of the huge gold deposits found in the Transvaal, then under the political sovereignty of the independent Boer republics, was undoubtedly the major cause of the Boer War (1899–1902), which saw British soldiers engage Boer guerrilla forces in two years of bloody skirmishes, leaving behind a desolate terrain. The war was certainly not brought about by racial concerns, but when it was over it was quite clear that the question of race in the form of a future native policy for South Africa was as important for the British government as creating a single political structure uniting all four units as a British colony. Strong humanitarian forces in Britain were concerned with the colonists' treatment of the African population, and, at the same time, the colonists, both Boers and those of English extraction, were seeking as the American colonies had before them greater control over their own lives in the form of local self-government. As the memories of the war Britain had won at great cost receded, the British government became more determined to create a political solution that would reconcile the Boers, and it began to provide them with large grants and loans to rebuild their economy. In the negotiations that led to the establishment of the Union of South Africa in 1911, the protection of the indigenous populations was reduced to a secondary consideration. The main guarantees of the Act of Union were for the white population, leaving native policy to the settlers. There was one "entrenched" clause to protect the right of the colored or mixed groups to vote, although not to be elected, in the Cape Colony. The provision remained until it was eliminated by the National government in 1956. As in the United States, white labor unions fought owners for their rights and for the exclusion of Africans from skilled jobs.

African resistance to the Act of Union was organized almost immediately, most notably through the formation of the African National Congress. The Pan-African Congress broke away from the ANC, and later there was the Black Consciousness Movement. The long history of this fight is beyond the scope of this essay. Suffice to say that a peaceful transition to a nonracial state has taken place. The process remains on the world's stage as South Africans seek to bring equality and redress to a society where ethnic identity once defined political and economic power.

Elsewhere in the world, state responses to racial tensions have run the spectrum from attempts at homogenization, integration, separation, special protection, special status, and national pluralism to affirmative action programs. Less laudable responses have included forms of victimization, scapegoating, genocide, and other coercive measures designed to suppress both culture and political aspirations. Law has often failed to be an effective integrating force when its legitimacy and ability to assure fairness have been questioned and it has become seen by the disenfranchised as the instrument of the powerful. More recently, affirmative action laws have been resisted by the enfranchised. With law no longer a guiding force and many political ideologies so generally discredited today, the question becomes what other social forces can assure harmony between ethnically diverse groups with consciously differing interests. Law, however, functions best if it is truly an expression of social consensus on common behavior. In an increasingly democratic world, the consent of the governed has become more important. Racial harmony is harder for the powers-that-be to legislate insofar as minority group interests are now seen to be legitimate by bodies of the United Nations, and therefore as requiring reconciliation rather than the subordination that has typified the relationships among many ethnicities in the twentieth century. Few are the national institutions that recognize ethnic group consciousness and facilitate legislative and administrative processes of conflict resolution.

## Racism and International Law: The United Nations

Throughout the cold war period and until the past decade, the anti-apartheid movement dominated the United Nations' race agenda. 1948 saw both the signing of the Universal Declaration of Human Rights and the accession to power in South Africa of the Nationalist Afrikaner party under prime minister Dr. Daniel François Malan, followed by years of detailed legislation aimed at preserving the ethnic identities of that nation's variously defined groups under the guidance of the National Party. South Africa gradually became the showcase of common racial concern in a world otherwise dominated by bipolar international politics, and there have been numerous special anti-apartheid initiatives on the part of the United Nations and its various bodies.

An organization of nation-states, the UN has always sought to preserve the interests of its member states in the face of claims by their national minorities. The fear is that claims to self-determination might result in secession or claims to secession. International law has left the right to self-determination vague, though it is in the first article of both the Covenant on Civil and Political Rights as well as Economic, Social and Cultural Rights. There is no generally accepted body of law that addresses distinctions between autonomy and sovereignty with regard to national minorities.

One of the UN's early attempts to deal with racism's consequences was the 1951 Convention on Genocide, dedicated to identifying and preventing acts intended to destroy, in whole or in part, a national, "ethnical," or religious group. Proscribed acts included killing or harming group members, imposing conditions of life designed to bring about their physical destruction, and preventing births or forcibly transferring children. In 1965 the General Assembly approved a more detailed Convention on the Elimination of All Forms of Racial Discrimination, which in its preamble condemned any form of racial superiority as scientifically false, morally condemnable, socially unjust, and dangerous. Racial discrimination was defined as "any distinction, exclusion, restriction or preference based on race, color, descent or national or ethnic origin which has the purpose or effect of nullifying or impairing the recognition, enjoyment or exercise, on a equal footing of human rights and fundamental freedoms in the political, economic, social and cultural or any other field of public life." The document also prohibited all propaganda and all organizations based on ideas or theories of the superiority of one race or group of persons of one color or ethnic origin, or which attempted to justify racial hatred or discrimination.

The Convention on the Elimination of Racial Discrimination entered into force in 1969 and has now been ratified by more than 80 percent of the world's states. However, the Committee composed of eighteen experts charged with monitoring the implementation of its provisions has always been poorly staffed and able to do little more than hear the reports prepared by those few states that care to file them. Reports from most states are now overdue.

In June 1989 pressure from advocacy groups resulted in the International Labor Organization (ILO) completely rewriting its own 1957 convention on indigenous and tribal peoples. The ILO removed the assimilationist and paternalistic orientation of the earlier document, and set out to "recognize the aspiration of these peoples to exercise control over their own institutions, ways of life and economic development and to maintain and develop their identities, languages and religions, within the framework of the states where they live." In addition to emphasizing a state's obligation to ensure the protection of the rights of indigenous and tribal peoples, and the elimination of socioeconomic gaps, states are enjoined to preserve their social identity, customs and traditions, and institutions. Self-identification, land and environment issues, and religion and language play an important part in the conceptualization of these populations and their rights.

As the century ends, the United Nations' work on race, racism and ethnicity is most energetic in the Sub-Commission on the Prevention of Discrimination and the Protection of Minorities, a subsidiary body of the Commission on Human Rights. In 1993 the General Assembly approved the declaration on the rights of persons belonging to national or ethnic, religious, and linguistic minorities, and the subcommittee has since been working on a draft declaration of the rights of indigenous peoples. Recent meetings have seen the broadening of its interest to address forms of racial discrimination other than South Africa's apartheid. Also worthy of special attention is the Sub-Commission Working Group on Indigenous Peoples, which is developing new standards and enjoys the participation of hundreds of representatives of indigenous peoples, many of whom face massacres, kidnappings, cultural deprivations, and forced evictions at the hands of others interested in their land or services. An especially difficult question is the impact of discrimination on the control and ownership of the cultural property of indigenous peoples, such as artifacts or medicines. The varied situations of these groups make both consensus on the standards and effective protection difficult. The working group is examining varying degrees of self-determination as a means to preserve identity and culture from political and cultural assimilation, new ways to approach their respective governments, and the use of special rapporteurs to monitor conditions. These problems and situations such as that in the former Yugoslavia have pushed the United Nations to develop new mechanisms for fact-finding, peace-keeping, and surveillance, as well as for actual intervention.

The central problem now facing the United Nations is inherent in the topic of this essay, namely, drawing the lines that define a people, especially those without traditional territory, as a religious or ethnic minority to be protected, and, one can add, defining—and considering the consequences of so doing—each individual's ethnic identity or race. There are many ambiguities. Although some groups' leaders are happy to define themselves in racial terms—leaders of the Zulu, the Khosa, etc.—the world abhorred South Africa's attempt to classify everyone in terms of a specific race group because of the implied racial stratification. On the other hand, many ethnic groups seek more protection than can ultimately be given by ascribing to them special rights. The United Nations has been unable to achieve consensus on the definition of an ethnic or cultural minority or an indigenous group, let alone use it as grounds for a claim to self-determination. In the definition of a group, a number of overlapping considerations come together: ownership and use of land, geographical location, culture, religion, language, economic way of life, self-identity, common traditions and ancestry, and form of government. In defining themselves different groups place a different emphasis on different elements, making a common definition impossible. In a world of communications without boundaries and of increasing flows of labor, capital, and goods, few groups enjoy the uniqueness and isolation necessary to make them a legally definable ethnic group, and even they will find it hard to remain so. On the other hand, ethnic consciousness, racial discrimination, and racism exist, and as their consequences are often so detrimental to world peace, they cannot be ignored by the international community.

The importance of the UN conventions and declarations is that they define common standards and build consensus in the world community. Their limitation so far is that they are not provided with the power to invoke and act in response to situations such as in Nagorno-Karabakh, Serbia, or any other point of ethnic conflict. Indeed the United Nations' preoccupation with legal instruments and procedure is seen as an exercise in procrastination if not cynicism, avoiding the real problems. And as the century ends, the international actors are multiplying. In addition to the United Nations and its agencies, the Conference on Security and Cooperation in Europe, beginning with its basic document, the 1975 Helsinki Final Act, has moved steadily toward substantial provisions for the rights of minorities, most recently to focus on the rights of the Roma or Gypsies in Eastern Europe. Domestic ethnic groups readily seek international support, and the handful of early nongovernmental organizations concerned with race and ethnicity is expanding rapidly—joined most notably by associations of leaders of indigenous organizations.

## Defining Race and Racism

The language of race only began to change in mid-century. The 1946 edition of the *Encyclopaedia Britannica* used earlier physical concepts to depict race as a problem of classification and of identifying two forms: one which used studies of the skull and the other external characteristics such as skin and hair. A combination of these measurements, namely cranial capacity, the ratio of length to breadth, and the angle the most projecting part of the jaw makes with the forehead, was proposed in the article as the way to identify a person's race. The article went on to categorize the world's peoples into three main groups: the straight-haired, the woolly-haired, and the curly-haired. These were then broken down into subcategories on the basis of the other criteria. On the United States Government census forms we are accustomed to other equally ambiguous forms of classification. Likewise, at birth, on their certificates children are identified in terms of their race. An appropriate definition of race and ethnic identity, especially when it is needed to form criteria for group identity, has proved elusive throughout the century.

There are a number of terms in current use. The term "minority" is used primarily to describe any racial, tribal, linguistic, religious, caste, or nationality which, within a nation-state, is not in control of the machinery of state and which is normally less numerous than those who are. "Nationalities" is used to describe large, complex but homogeneous minority groups which have the territorial space necessary for a degree of independence. "Indigenous people" describes peoples with centuries-long ancestral territory and their own self-contained political and social structures; "ethnic identity" describes a person's inherited biological and cultural characteristics; and "race" adds to ethnicity a more precise categorization, and begins, in its usage, to connote the forms of political, cultural, or at least attitudinal subordination associated with racism. These terms are implicitly relational, defining the identity of one group over and against that of another or others. Competitive, dominate-or-be-dominated characteristics can easily condition such relationships, especially when there is also a question of land resources and culture. Conflicts arise between the traditional occupiers of the land and those from outside who would take control. This classic issue of colonization has been acted out throughout the ages, the occupation of the Americas being the most massive example; but it continues today for the Yanomami in Brazil, the Inuits in Canada, the peoples of the southern Sudan, and the Tibetans. The United Nations continues to wrestle with the definition of the struggles of these various groups and the nature of their legal claims for protection through the international system. Each group presents unique characteristics in terms of geographic boundaries and homogeneity of language, culture, and religion as the basis of its identity and claim to self-determination. Even similar terms rarely reflect similar conditions on the ground. Amidst these life and death conflicts, definition of group ethnicity has been impossible.

Short of territory, race is probably the way that groups of human beings most commonly define themselves in relation to others, presumably because of its association with the physical characteristics that are most visible and, in their more extreme variations at least, the most "objective" ways to distinguish groups from one another. This categorization is based on physical and cultural characteristics which, on closer scrutiny, are pervious, ambiguous, or little more than mental constructs. Group categorization often reflects little more than an individual's choice to be so labeled or to label others as belonging to a specific collectivity with certain shared inherited characteristics. One only has to think of the grounds that a black and white couple, on the one hand, and the society in which they live, on the other, might use to designate their child.

There are, of course, many qualities other than racial features to distinguish a human being. This act of classification, which seems deeply rooted in the human psyche, is the starting point of many other social constructs that lead to racism in all its forms; it could also lead to an appreciation of the beauties of human diversity. Ethnic identity provides some with a sense of roots and history, and with a sense of inherited loyalties as well as clues for the future. For others it opens the door to discrimination and subordination. The modalities of racially defined discrimination vary in terms of form, intensity, and duration, making generalizations too facile. The subject of discrimination can feel anything from the sense of being a nonperson or even a nonentity vis-à-vis the dominant group to being the object of massive opprobrium and hate, and the object of an immediate threat of annihilation.

One of twentieth-century academia's preoccupations has been wrestling with definitions of race and racial groupings, including ways to count and identify them. An estimated 575 to more than 5,000 different ethnic and national groups would be further expanded if religious and linguistic minorities were added too. On closer inspection, we find that designation as a group results from a combination of indicators—physical features, cultural practices, language, religious beliefs, political allegiance, etc.—each of which will not necessarily receive the same weight in defining different groups. In China, geographic location is more important than language, ancestry, or physical features. For others a history of de facto self-determination might be important. Many self-defined groups, however, rely on disputed historical accounts. From the beginning of the colonial enterprise and in various ways, anthropologists from Europe have educated the metropolitan populations about the peoples their governments have subjugated, providing first a sense of the diversity of their customs, but soon also an understanding of the rationality of these other societies, followed by a sense of moral obligation to protect them and their culture, and more recently of the need to decolonize and not exploit their land and resources.

## The Legacy of the Twentieth Century

Both the interpretation of and the attempts to ameliorate the problems caused by race and race relations have proved to be moving targets. International migration is increasing, impelled by political and economic factors; the United States, for instance, accepts about a million immigrants each year.

Migrations all over the world bring millions of people with very different customs into contact with one another, where the less powerful are forced to accept the mores of the dominant group and the latter suppress the freedoms and culture of the newcomers, such as in the case of migrant workers from Southeast Asia in oil-rich Arab states. When challenged by others, some groups retreat into the ethnic chauvinism of the skinhead nation or the Ku Klux Klan. For them and many others, race has an aura of objectivity, in that it embodies the appeal to roots and the symbols and rituals of ancestral allegiance, and seems to satisfy their search for protection from the insecurities of a changing world and fear of domination by another racial group.

The protection of infranational groups is fraught with ambiguity in the sense that providing extra protection (as compared with that provided to other citizens) easily leads to either privileges seen to be at the expense of others or controls unacceptable to the group. Politicians glibly call for the protection of the rights of minorities without being explicit as to what these rights are. Cultural groups seem to need more support in order to protect their language, customs, and social identity when they live within a larger dominant society. Protection requires some degree of recognition of the group and of the group's special claims to land, language, appropriate education, and the like. The white South African government long sought to classify all its citizens in terms of their race or ethnic group; and as an opposition group, the same individuals are seeking to perpetuate group identity in a South Africa under majority rule. The African National Congress is, however, adamant that there will be no racially or culturally defined group protections in the new South African constitution. Few governments in fact are willing to make special provisions for ethnic minorities if they lack territorial definition and must rely on other, less tangible qualities to distinguish them as a separate group.

The evolving relationships between state and internal minorities as well as the increasing number of problem cases on the roster of the United Nations raise frequent appeals for a redefinition of the modern state and the modern system of states. Both Europe's current search for new interstate relationships and Africa's attempt to live with territorial lines largely drawn by a group of Europeans in Berlin in 1885 illustrate the clear need for new ways to recognize groups with a strong sense of identity. In becoming more aware of both the diversity within states and the inequalities in their relationships, it is harder to live with the illusion of a worldwide democracy where the vote of one state is equal to that of another. At the same time we have witnessed the growth of an international consciousness espousing universal values, setting international standards, and now permitting intervention by the international community to prevent serious violations of these common values and norms. Nation-states are no longer able to treat their own citizens with impunity, but they also cannot fully control other processes, such as the drug trade and some banking practices, that operate in the interstices between states beyond their individual and collective control. The result has qualified concepts of national sovereignty and brought about new forms of international regulation. States are increasingly less self-contained economically, as labor markets and capital flows become internationalized.

The implications of these processes for racial minorities are complex. The century has seen the disintegration of the unities formed by many empires— Austro-Hungarian, German, Ottoman, Japanese, British, French, Belgian, Portuguese, Italian, and most recently, Russian—resulting in the formation of many new states little prepared to reduce their internal ethnic animosities. And, as the century's political systems and experience in nation-building have not produced new ideas for resolving the claims of the minority groups, ethnic conflict remains a major danger to peace and international security. On the other hand, populations now mingle more freely, fostering both ethnic homogenization and the search for ethnic and religious identity to help cope with the encroaching anonymity or at least homogeneity of the modern *homo economicus.*

In preventing ethnic violence, mitigating ethnic tensions, and healing the wounds we hear little about successes. These achievements are less dramatic and newsworthy than the crises. The rules against racial discrimination are generally clear. Missing still are effective means of enforcement.

## Conclusion

The blind spot of liberal thought, with its emphasis on the individual, has been its nonrecognition of the de facto degree to which human minds aggregate human beings, notably on the basis of certain inherited characteristics, and then make multiple other assumptions. On the other side, in practice, we are seeing many peoples seek refuge in accentuated ethnic identity in order to attain more general political and economic goals that in other circumstances would not require an ethnic base. Ethnicity, with all its ramifications, seems to be the most instinctual form of grouping. As the number of the world's nation-states grows and political groupings fragment, future world orders as well as nation- and state-building must seek political models that recognize diversity and discourage secession and the type of aggression by which one ethnic group moves others and modifies borders in the pursuit of ethnic purity. Given the number of current ethnic conflicts, ethnicity is central to world security. Many other factors, however, are necessary to bring it to the point of, and define the nature of, resulting physical conflict. Racism adds to ethnicity the defining of a group in terms of certain characteristics that are ostensibly neutral, but in fact imply a relationship of subordination to another, mostly one's own group.

The history of the century has been a move from a world carved up among great powers to one of fragmenting states, where lines of political power increasingly correspond to group associations based not on interest, class, or geographic lines, but on certain physical and cultural, largely inherited characteristics. During this century the world has become more ready to accept the right of subnational groups to control their own institutions and to protect their unique ways. In practice, however, many other global forces—notably economic development, tourism, and the mass media—are eroding their independence and separate identities.

The general move toward democracy and popular sovereignty, which has brought greater legitimacy to the claims of subordinate groups, has also forced once-dominant groups to adjust laws and attitudes that could be called racist. Judging by the extent of ethnic conflict at this point in the century, however, few states have been successful in devising institutions that value ethnic identity and routinely reconcile conflicts arising from the resultant groupings.

ENDNOTES

1. Herbert Hill, "Race and Ethnicity in Organized Labor: The Historical Sources of Resistance to Affirmative Action," *The Journal of Intergroup Relations* 12 ( 4) (1984): 11. Published in Washington, D.C. by the National Association of Human Rights Workers.
2. Ibid., pp. 22–23.
3. Robert A. Hill, ed., *The Marcus Garvey and Universal Negro Improvement Association Papers* (Berkeley: University of California Press, 1983), p. 7.

SELECTED REFERENCES

For Current Debates on Law and Ethnicity

Gellner, Ernest. *Nations and Nationalism.* Oxford: Basil Blackwell, 1983.

Horowitz, Donald L. *Ethnic Groups in Conflict.* Berkeley: University of California Press, 1985.

Shapiro, Ian, and Will Kymlicka, eds. *Ethnicity and Group Rights. Nomos 39, Yearbook of the American Society for Political and Legal Philosophy.* New York: New York University Press, 1997.

# 7   Imperialism and Decolonization

AINSLEE EMBREE

Had there been a United Nations at the beginning of the twentieth century, it would have included about fifty nations instead of the one hundred and eighty that constituted its membership in the last decade of the century. The remarkable difference in numbers is due in large measure to the fact that in 1900 much of Africa, South and Southeast Asia, the Caribbean, and Oceania had been brought under the control of European powers, and these areas were composed of colonies, which became independent states at the end of the century. In 1939, at the beginning of the Second World War, the Western European powers and the United States controlled, outside their own homelands, about a third of the world's area and population. Most of these acquisitions had been made during the great outward expansion of European power that, by the end of the nineteenth century, had became known—at times pejoratively, at times as an expression of national pride—as imperialism.

At the end of the twentieth century, the European powers have lost control of most of these territories through decolonization—that is, due either to armed revolt or an agreed transfer of power, usually under pressure from nationalist leaders in the colonial areas. More than a hundred new states have emerged in a little over twenty years. As to what these changes have meant in terms of quality of life for the approximately 750 million people affected, it is impossible to generalize.

Imperialism and decolonization are not, of course, unique to the modern era: one could use both as unifying themes for a history of the world. Roman imperialism provided much of the legacy that would define the imperial powers of Western Europe, just as Persian imperialism had shaped Western Asia. The polities that Spain destroyed in Central and South America were themselves imperial structures built on the cultures of conquered peoples. On the Indian subcontinent, imperial powers from the fourth-century B.C. Mauryas to the sixteenth-century Mughals conquered and subdued other ethnic and cultural groups. When the imperial centers of power weakened, either old political entities that had been conquered reemerged, or new ones were formed out of the empire's administrative units in ways that clearly bear resemblance to modern decolonization. Decolonization is, then, not so much a reversal of imperialism as an aspect of the same process. While one flag may indeed be lowered over an administrative building and another raised, the work that goes on inside the building may not show any such symbolic change.

Limiting a survey of imperialism and decolonization to the nineteenth and twentieth centuries is certainly questionable, since overseas territories were acquired by European powers, notably Spain and Portugal, in the early sixteenth century in the Americas and Asia, and England and France established colonies in seventeenth-century North America. Decolonization also occurred: the British colonies on the Atlantic seaboard revolted in the eighteenth century; the Spanish and Portuguese ones in Latin America in the nineteenth century. But these were, in a very real sense, the "old" European empires, part of a different political and economic world. There are, of course, continuities with the former period, but a quite new phase of territorial acquisition began at the end of the nineteenth century, lasting to the beginning of the twentieth century, which constituted new kinds of empires.

In those last years of the nineteenth century, imperialism became more dramatic—and more dangerous—as the Germans, Belgians, and Italians challenged the older entrants in the race for territory, most notably in what was known as "the scramble for Africa." At the very end of the century, the Americans, having completed the conquest of the lands to the west and southwest of their original territories, took control of large segments of the old Spanish empire in the Philippines and the Caribbean.

Another fundamental difference between the old imperialism and the new is that no indigenous civilizations were really destroyed in the nineteenth century, as had been the case in the earlier period of European expansion. The vigorous persistence of such civilizations throughout the period of European colonization gives the twentieth-century version of decolonization its special quality. To put it simply: the people who had overthrown the British in the Atlantic colonies were British, not indigenous people; in India, the indigenous people overthrew the British.

The explanations for European imperialism have been many and varied, but most of them can be subsumed under four intertwined headings all relevant to the process of decolonization. Perhaps the most commonly accepted explanation in the past, both in scholarly and popular writing, has been that the European powers sought overseas territories for economic reasons—that colonies had been acquired in order to supply the raw materials on which the·

development of Western capitalism depended and to supply the colonizers with a ready market for manufactured goods. This argument is undoubtedly valid, but it prevents an understanding of the process if other factors are ignored and too much emphasis is placed on the economic value of colonies to the nation as a whole, rather than to segments of it.

Related to the economic argument is the strategic one, stressing that the overseas possessions were key counterweights in the European balance of power in the nineteenth and twentieth centuries. That this was still a concern to imperial powers at the end of the Second World War is suggested in an interesting exchange of memoranda in 1946 between Prime Minister Clement Attlee and his Foreign Secretary, Ernest Bevin. Is it clear, Attlee asked, that the benefits Britain receives from the control of the Mediterranean and the Indian Ocean are worthwhile? The socialist Bevin's reply was a curious restatement of nineteenth-century positions. If Britain gives up control, its place will be taken by the Russians and the Americans, Bevin replied, and "It is our way of life as against the red tooth and claw of American capitalism and the Communist dictatorship of Soviet Russia."[1] Decolonization would have to contend with new versions of imperial prestige and strategic necessity.

The third explanation for nineteenth-century imperial expansion emphasizes that very often expansion was not the product of national policy but of the activities and ambitions of individuals and groups. Cecil Rhodes's activity in Africa is a striking example of personal ambition driving territorial conquest. More frequently, territories were acquired by a chartered company, with the profit of shareholders being the acknowledged goal. When particular moments of expansion are considered, very often the stated policies of the home governments seem to have been devised afterward to explain and justify actions taken by "men on the spot" for quite other reasons, as was true of much of Britain's expansion in India.

A fourth explanation is frequently encountered in the literature of the time, perhaps best summed up in the expression borrowed from American history: Manifest Destiny. Through much nineteenth-century imperialist rhetoric runs a sense that the forces of history require the world beyond Europe and North America to be brought into the orbit of a higher civilization. This seemed reasonable in a century when the Western world's self-confidence was justified by its increasing mastery of the physical world through science and technology and of the political world by democracy and constitutionalism. When the Philippines were taken, the governing body of the U.S. Presbyterian Church heard "by the very guns of our battleships" that God has "summoned us to go up and possess the land."[2]

To emphasize the imperialism and decolonization of the Western powers' overseas empires is not to deny analogous movements in non-Western nations, but certain differences make comparison difficult. The Ottoman Empire lost vast territories after the First World War, and in some areas, such as Syria, there had been a strong nationalist movement, but even there Western powers—especially France and Great Britain—played a decisive role. Thus Syria's historical development in the twentieth century displays a continuing admixture of Ottoman and Western imperialism. Russia also built up a vast empire from territories contiguous to itself in Central Asia, just at the time the Western European powers were expanding overseas. This empire underwent enormous changes in the 1980s and 1990s, but the process can best be described as the disintegration of a weak nation-state rather than decolonization. Nor should it be forgotten that at the very end of the nineteenth century, Japan emerged as an aggressive and successful imperial power in Korea and Manchuria, but the loss of empire was very largely the result of its defeat in World War II rather than from decolonization.

While the processes of imperialism and decolonization can be defined in terms of the polarities of conquest and liberation, both differ strikingly from area to area, and an understanding of these differences must begin with recognizing their individual determining factors. The primary one, obvious enough, but perhaps for that reason often ignored, is the historical experience of the region before the period of imperial conquest. The decolonization of the Portuguese territories in Africa, for example, bears little real resemblance to the process that took place in Portugal's Indian possessions because of the different natures of the two societies before the imperial conquest. And that the indigenous religious and cultural structures of New England were quickly destroyed by the British while those in India were little changed is surely more an indication of the nature of the indigenous societies than of the conquerors.

A sketch of imperialism and decolonization is, therefore, best organized in broad geographic regions—Africa, Asia, the Americas—but with attention given to the forms in which the Western powers expressed their hegemony. Furthermore, within these continental limits, one has to distinguish very clearly between the historical experiences of, say, North Africa and Central Africa or South Asia and Southeast Asia.

A second determining factor for differences in decolonization, and one closely related to the emphasis on an area's past history, is the nature of the nationalist movements that developed during the period of imperial domination. Differences between such movements are quite startling, from the revolutionary Marxism of the Vietnamese to the bourgeois, liberal nationalism of India—with its almost unquestioning acceptance of British models—to the appeal in Algeria of a nationalist ideology that claimed to be based on Islam.

Somalia represents the complexity—and the tragedy—that imperialism and decolonization inherently bring to bear on the identity of an indigenous people. The formal process of decolonization received little attention in the 1940s and 1950s, but the consequences of its failures dominated the media in the early 1990s as petty warlords battled for control of starving Somalis. This strip of coastal territory was largely inhabited by a pastoral people who, if accounts by foreign observers are to be trusted, had an awareness of a shared culture that might have become the basis for a nationalist movement. By the beginning of the twentieth century, however, the region had been divided between three European governments—Britain, Italy, and France. And there was no simple way to decolonize the region, as the creation of the Republic of Somalia in 1960 and the departure of the European powers prompted Ethiopia to demand part of its territory because of boundary disputes left unsettled by the European powers. Soviet military aid to Somalia alarmed the West in the days of the cold war, and finally the authority of the government was destroyed by warring factions. This led to American military intervention, under United Nations auspices, at the end of 1992. An American army officer involved encapsulated the dilemmas of imperialism and decolonization in his complaint that it was impossible to create a government "when every Tom, Dick, and Harry" claimed that he had a right to a piece of the country.[3]

To stress the primary importance of the indigenous cultural and political situation for understanding imperialism and decolonization is not, of course, to deny the formative role of the imperial power. It is necessary, however, to keep in mind the changing political, economic, and cultural conditions of the imperial power at different times and how these interacted with the local society. Witness the collaboration of Spanish religious and secular authorities in transplanting Spanish culture to the territories conquered by Spain in the New World and the Philippines, symbolized by religion and language. Compare with this the frequent hostility of British colonial officials in Africa and India to missionary activity, and their mocking contempt for natives who spoke English or became Christians, "trying to be like us." Trade and administrative control were almost always the aims of British imperialism. For the British and the Dutch, the "white man's burden" was the necessity of ruling—not, as for the Spanish, the French, and the Americans—"a civilizing mission."

In the linked processes of imperialism and decolonization, the extent to which the occupied territories were settled by European immigrants is another key determinant. In North America white settlers had utterly submerged the indigenous peoples, in terms not only of numbers but also of their cultures. India presents a complete contrast: the numbers of European immigrants were so minuscule as to leave no statistical trace, while the pre-colonial cultures remained vigorous, and the indigenous peoples greatly increased in numbers. In South America, large numbers of immigrants dominated the colonized areas, and in the nineteenth century their descendants struggled for independence from Spain and Portugal. Elsewhere, immigrants played a different role, as in Algeria, where, while large numbers of French settlers had made it their permanent home and had transplanted many of the artifacts of their culture, they were in the presence of a much larger indigenous population with its own vibrant culture. Decolonization here faced rigorous opposition not only from the imperial power but from the European colonists. In a few areas, as in the Philippines, while there was not a very large European immigration, European or at least Europeanized culture became dominant. South Africa represents a sui generis case, where white immigrants, without strong ties to a European country, passionately identified themselves with a South African territorial homeland, even while living in the midst of a much larger black population, many of whom were themselves migrants from other territories.

These, then, are some of the factors relating to imperialism and decolonization that in varying degrees determined the political, economic, and cultural developments of the third of humanity—about 750 million people—that in 1939 lived in territories controlled by European powers or the United States. Even within continents, however, the diverse regional cultures, with few unifying elements, have had very different historical experiences. These regional cultures combined with the cultures of imperialist powers, which themselves varied according to times of conquest, to produce contrasting patterns of decolonization.

Examples of imperialism and decolonization are, therefore, best drawn from a number of regions, although scarcely representative: Southeast Asia (Philippines, Vietnam, and Indonesia); South Asia (India); North Africa (Egypt and Algeria); and Central Africa (the Belgian Congo). Nearly a hundred other nations were created by the process of decolonization, but this selection illustrates both commonalities and differences. Latin America is omitted from consideration because the processes of both imperialism and decolonization were in a much different time frame.

## Southeast Asia

Oddly enough, many studies of decolonization scarcely mention the Philippines, perhaps because the United States is not usually classified with the European imperial powers, but the islands that comprise the modern nation of the Philippines demonstrate the ambiguities and contradictions of imperialism and decolonization. In 1521, when the Spanish arrived there, they found, unlike their experience in Mexico, no flourishing cities, no well-articulated elite cultures, no centralized form of government, and no precious metals. In the course of the next two centuries, however, Manila became the center of a great entrepot trade on the sea lanes between China and Mexico, emigration of Spaniards was encouraged, and Roman Catholicism largely replaced the indigenous religions. Despite attempts to Hispanicize the population, however, Spanish was spoken by only a small percentage. Resistance to Spanish rule developed at the end of the nineteenth century, and when the Spanish-American war broke out in 1898, the Filipino leaders supported the Americans. When they declared the establishment in 1898 of the first Philippine republic, the American government, however, refused to recognize it, defeating it in the Philippine-American War (1898–1901). Unlike most other imperial conquerors, the Americans promised self-government leading to independence, but the process was slow and tortuous, depending on the American authorities' certainty that a stable government could be assured. In 1935, what is often referred to as the first example of freely given decolonization took place: a ten-year period of self-rule was begun with the establishment of a semi-independent form of government, to lead to subsequent independence. Before the ten years were up, the Japanese conquered the islands, but after an American reconquest in 1944, the Republic of the Philippines was declared in 1946. The conditions the Americans imposed, and that the Filipinos accepted, were surprisingly onerous, such as the free admission of American goods, with Americans having equal access with Filipinos to the country's natural resources and being given ninety-nine year leases on important military bases. One reason why, in contrast to other decolonized areas, the nationalist leaders acquiesced in the foreign demands was that the nation was so devastated by the war that they were willing to pay a heavy price for aid. Another very important one, familiar in most imperial situations, was the existence of a prosperous elite, with whom the Americans had forged alliances soon after they had annexed the Philippines, and through whom they exercised a form of indirect rule.

Social inequalities led to communist-led peasant uprisings, known as the

Huk rebellions, in Luzon from 1949 to 1953, against the landlords who owned vast estates. These were put down with massive American assistance, and in the 1970s new protests against the government led to President Ferdinand Marcos assuming dictatorial power with American support. He was finally overthrown by a popular movement led by Corazon Aquino, again with considerable American support. Here as elsewhere, looking at decolonization requires what John King Fairbank referred to as "a triple focus"—on each of the cultures, and then on their effects on each other.[4]

Such a triple focus is as difficult as it is necessary when one turns to the region of Southeast Asia that became known to Europeans as Indochina after the French conquest of the three regions of Laos, Cambodia, and Vietnam between 1858 and 1893. That the three, distinct in history and culture, were given a new identity by the West is a useful symbol of the functioning of imperialism, as is the fact that the components of the new name attributed the culture of the region to two other great civilizations—India and China. The area did in fact owe much to Chinese and Indian influences, but the use of "Indochina" erases for outsiders, but not, of course, for the peoples of the three countries, the individuality of each of them. Thus an important aspect of their decolonization involved a reassertion of their cultural particularities, which included ancient enmities against each other, and, especially in the case of Vietnam, against the Chinese as well as the French. By the 1700s the modern Laos was really three kingdoms, harassed in the nineteenth century by neighboring Siam, Burma, and China, as well by each other, and then by the French. Cambodia had been the center from about 800 to 1400 of a powerful kingdom whose monarchs sought to immortalize their greatness in the magnificent Hindu temples at Angkor Wat. In the nineteenth century, its rulers came under Vietnamese control, and, through them, under the French.

Early in the nineteenth century, the territory now known as Vietnam was an expansionist state under the Nguyen dynasty (1802–1845), controlling Cambodia and part of Laos, but the region had long been of interest to the French, who had engaged in trade and missionary activity since the second half of the seventeenth century. In the 1840s its ruler became increasingly hostile to both the French missionaries and their converts, who numbered perhaps a tenth of the population. Anti-French activity, including the persecution of Vietnamese Christians—combined with the desire of the government of Napoleon III to have a share in imperial expansion—led to a French invasion of the area in 1858 that met with great resistance. Not until 1883 did the whole of what is now Vietnam come under French control. Laos was also taken over, as was Cambodia, and after 1893 the three regions were made into the Indochinese Union. As with other areas that came under European rule, the subsequent history of Indochina needs two summaries—one from the point of view of the imperialist rulers, the other from that of the nationalist leaders who opposed them. The French speak of irrigation projects that quadrupled rice production, of roads, bridges, schools, and hospitals constructed and a centralized administrative system established. The nationalists—and many Western historians—speak of France's exploitation of the region's raw materials for their own factories, of the impoverishment of the peasants, and of the creation of a new class of Vietnamese who collaborated with the French for their own advantage. In 1939, 80 percent of the population were said to be illiterate, while the nationalists alleged that of the pre-conquest population, most had some degree of literacy. This second reading of French rule in Indochina led U.S. President Franklin D. Roosevelt to give a simplified—but not unreasonable—version of French imperialism in Indochina: "Why was it such a cinch for the Japanese to conquer the land? The native Indo-Chinese had been so flagrantly downtrodden that they thought to themselves: Anything must be better than to live under French colonial rule."[5]

There had always been opposition to French rule, but a new kind of leader appeared in the person of a young man who later adopted the name of Ho Chi Minh, who had joined the Communist Party of France in 1920. Five years later he founded the Revolutionary League of the Youth of Vietnam, and his leadership of the communist groups before the Second World War and during the Japanese occupation of Indochina from 1940 to 1945 was crucial to the complex and tortured history of decolonization. This was a curious period, without exact analogy elsewhere in the colonial world, for French administrators, loyal to the Vichy government in France, continued to rule under the Japanese until the war ended. Then, on September 2, 1945, Ho Chi Minh proclaimed Vietnam's independence, signaling the beginning of a long struggle for decolonization, at first against the French and then against the Americans.

In postwar Cambodia the French tried to exercise their power through King Sihanoukh, the representative of the monarchy they had preserved as a façade for their power. Instead he initiated a campaign against them, however, and in 1953 France granted Cambodia its independence. In Laos, a number of parties struggled with each other and with the French, until the Pathet Lao, under communist leadership, gained the upper hand, proclaiming a People's Democratic Republic in 1975. The great struggle with the French, however, took place in Vietnam, where the French fought a bitter and very costly war against Ho Chi Minh that ended with their defeat in 1954.

France's leaders apparently believed that the resources of Vietnam might still be used to rebuild France after the devastation of World War II. And the psychological appeal of empire, as personified in General Charles de Gaulle, can't be discounted as an important factor in the French decision to fight to maintain its power in Indochina. Added to these reasons was the support France received from the British and Americans to prevent the region from falling under the control of Ho Chi Minh and his Communist Party.

The third region of decolonization in Southeast Asia that demands attention is Indonesia, an immense territory of thirteen thousand islands, covering about five thousand square kilometers of land and sea, with a late-twentieth-century population approaching two hundred million. The borders of the modern state are largely the product of Dutch imperialism in the nineteenth century, but the whole region has been linked throughout a long historical experience by many indigenous empires, trade routes, and overlapping cultural influences. The nature of those influences has been much disputed by historians, but there is general agreement that the islands have been inhabited for many thousands of years, and that such skills as metallurgy, wet-rice cultivation, and techniques for maritime navigation enabled large empires such as that of Srivijaya in Sumatra and Mataram in Java to develop. These centers were much influenced by the Indian social, religious, and political thought transmitted by Buddhism and Hinduism, as witnessed by the monuments at Borobudur and the Hinduized culture of the island of Bali. Traders carried on actively with China, bringing cultural elements as well as material artifacts to the islands. Islam was brought to the islands by traders and missionaries as early as the twelfth century, and its spread was sporadic and uneven for some centuries; but by the sixteenth century there were a number of important kingdoms with Muslim rulers and sizable Muslim populations. These foreign influences all combined with the strong indigenous cultures to produce a distinctively Indonesian culture.

The early-sixteenth-century arrival of Portuguese traders and the Dutch arrival at the beginning of the seventeenth century marked a new stage in the history of Western expansion. In the seventeenth century, the Dutch East India Company successfully ousted its Portuguese and British trading rivals through a ruthless use of force against both foreigners and indigenous peoples, symbolized by the treatment of the people of the island of Banda in 1621, who had resisted the Dutch attempts to control their trade. Thousands were killed in a massacre whose brutality prompted a Dutch East India Company official to remark that "We must realize that they fought for the freedom of their land just as we expended our lives and goods for so many years in defense of ours." Such comments do not often appear in the accounts of imperial conquest and of decolonization.[6]

The Dutch East India Company controlled the trade and commerce of the islands with the outside world, and not until 1799 was its rule replaced by the direct rule of the Netherlands government. From 1820 to 1906 almost all of the islands were brought under Dutch control. In 1830 a new form of economic control was instituted in Java, the main center of Dutch power, that is often considered typical of colonial rule but was in fact quite different from methods of extraction of revenue tried elsewhere. This was the cultivation system, known as *kultuurstelsel*, by which, in lieu of taxes, the peasants were compelled to use a fifth of their land to produce crops such as coffee, sugar, and indigo for export to the Netherlands. From 1840 to 1880 the estimated profits from the system amounted to a quarter of the budget of the Netherlands—unmatchable by any of the other imperial powers and their colonial possessions.

Protests against this economic system fueled the independence movement during the 1930s. Its best-known leader, Sukarno (1901–1970), united various factions under his vision of a new Indonesian nationalism. The Japanese occupation of the islands unwittingly strengthened the movement, as the Japanese made use of many of its leaders, including Sukarno, in positions of authority they could not have enjoyed under the Dutch.

When the Japanese surrendered to the Allies on August 17, 1945, Sukarno declared Indonesia independent and himself president, but the Dutch, assisted by British forces, reasserted their authority. Their proposal for decolonization, which involved setting up a federation of Indonesian states in partnership with the Dutch Kingdom, was unacceptable to the Indonesian nationalists. Urged by the United Nations, the Dutch agreed to the complete independence of Indonesia on January 1, 1950 with Sukarno as president. But the parliamentary form of government that was set up imposed checks on Sukarno's authority that he claimed prevented him from taking the necessary steps to maintain stability and develop the economy, and in a move that would be duplicated in many newly independent countries, he forged an alliance with the army and superseded the authority of the parliament, establishing an authoritarian regime he called "Guided Democracy." He was deposed in 1968, as his economic policies, dependence on the Communist Party, and grandiose building schemes seemed to be weakening the nation. Sympathetic critics suggest, however, that he made a necessary contribution to a difficult process of decolonization by giving the people a sense of pride in their national identity.

## South Asia

The term South Asia is itself a product of decolonization. It was devised to replace the term India as a designation for the whole of the subcontinent after the 1947 division of the British Indian empire into the new states of India and Pakistan. In all the long history of imperialism, no comparable area with such a vast population had ever been controlled so long—almost a century and a half—by such a distant power. The British East India Company began trading with the area in 1600, when the Mughal Empire was the dominant power. But not until the second half of the eighteenth century, roughly from 1765 to 1775, did the company become a territorial power through the acquisition of Bengal, one of the largest and richest of the Mughal provinces, with a population of perhaps forty million. To British politicians in London and to the shareholders and officers of the East India Company as well, this seemed to be more than enough territory. Even Robert Clive, a leading actor in the combination of war and chicanery that won this vast prize, declared that "to go farther was a scheme so extravagantly ambitious that no government in its senses would ever dream of it."[7] They did, of course, go farther, driven by the many motivations of imperialism as noted above—a search for security from hostile neighboring states, the exclusion of European rivals, the desire to expand trade, and the personal ambition of the officials involved in the Company's trade and governance in India. By 1850, the entire subcontinent was under British control.

The conquest was neither easy nor sudden, and a number of Indian rulers fought very stubbornly, such as Haider Ali and Tipu Sultan, the rulers of Mysore; the Marathas in Central and Western India; and the Sikhs in the Punjab. The last major assault on British rule came in 1857, in the great uprising known to the British as "The Mutiny," and to later Indian nationalists as the "First War of Independence." In addition, there were many local uprisings in rural areas against what was regarded as excessive taxation. The well-trained, efficient army, with British officers but a majority of Indian soldiers, was, as Commander-in-Chief Lord Kitchener once pointed out, unlike armies elsewhere, as it was intended more for internal security than for protection against foreign invasion. A modern school of historians, who style themselves "subalterns" because they emphasize the contributions of the masses to the long process of decolonization, point out that the nationalist leaders depended very often on ideas, methods, and institutions of the British, whereas the peasants, relying on "the traditional organization of kinship and territoriality," depended more frequently upon violence.[8]

Popular accounts of British rule in India give the impression that the British were convinced their control was permanent and unshakable, but behind the bombast of imperialistic rhetoric was always the awareness of those most deeply involved of just how fragile their rule was, and how tenuous the supports that held it in place. It was not the former Mughal rulers, however, who threatened British rule. Sir John Malcolm, who had a leading role in bringing many of the princes of Central India under British suzerainty, identified the source of danger quite accurately as early as 1922. The Brahmans, the old Hindu elite, he wrote,

> have for ages been the nominal servants, but the real masters of the turbulent and the bold, but ignorant and superstitious, military tribes of their countrymen. Their knowledge of how to wield dangerous power has been rendered complete by frequent exercise; and when we consider what they have lost by the introduction and extension of our dominion, it would be folly to expect exemption from their effort to subvert it.[9]

The subversion of British power by an indigenous elite was by no means straightforward, and the complex story of decolonization climaxed not with an armed struggle, as in the Philippines, Vietnam, Indonesia, or elsewhere, but with a negotiated transfer of power by the British legislature to Indian politicians who had been elected under established constitutional procedures. Behind this process, however, were complex economic, political, and cultural interactions between the rulers and the Indian elites that explain the nature of both imperialism and decolonization in India. The British had become rulers of a society with well-established trading and commercial activities, a functioning legal system, large urban centers, and a formal revenue system. In all these spheres of activity there were indigenous elites who continued much of their activities under the British, though the forms of these activities were often greatly modified.

A central charge of Indian nationalists was that India's poverty was due to British rule, which prevented industrialization in order to exploit the agricultural resources of the country and maintain it as a market for British goods.[10] Against this view, the economic historian Morris D. Morris has persuasively argued that industrialization and economic modernization did not occur because preconditions in terms of capital, markets, and political infrastructure were not available in nineteenth-century India. Most economic decisions were made by both Indian and foreign private capitalists who invested their money where it would bring the highest returns, which generally meant in trade and not industry. Their interest did not lie in solving poverty. The government itself had a hands-off policy in regard to the economy.[11]

There can be little doubt that since India was a free-trade economy without any protective tariffs or real governmental encouragement of industrial development, it was very difficult for industries to develop in competition with the rest of the world, particularly with British industries. At the time of independence in 1947, India remained overwhelmingly agricultural. Eighty-five  percent of its population of more than 400 million lived in rural areas, the majority scarcely above subsistence level, with a 15 percent literacy rate, and a reliance on low-productivity techniques. India, like many other colonial areas, illustrated the point of John Stuart Mill's dictum that "the government of a people by itself has a meaning and a reality; but such a thing as government by another does not, and cannot exist."[12]

Of the second category of interaction, the political, the most obvious result the intrusion of British power in India had was the unification of the subcontinent under one central authority. This was a point the British never wearied of making, and they made it with great force in 1930 in the official report on India's readiness for a measure of responsible government. The British, it stated, had taken a congerie of warring kingdoms and transformed them into a unitary India, and if there was now a growing sense of nationality, "it has been only the existence of British rule in India that has rendered such a development possible."[13] Indian nationalists naturally rejected this reading of their history, arguing that such unification had always been central to the Indian historical experience, and the British account of Indian history was a self-serving justification of their conquest.

Cultural developments, the third category of India's interaction with the West, are closely related to the economic and political changes that linked it to the world system in the nineteenth century. While many regions of India shared in the changes, Calcutta, its economic and political capital, best demonstrated how cultural confrontation and adaptation took place. One sees in Calcutta a lively, self-confident intelligentsia, secure in their ancient culture, reaching out to extract from the West the knowledge that could be of benefit to them. What they wanted from the West was defined for them by Ram Mohan Roy (1772–1833), the most famous of that group: "Mathematics, Natural Philosophy, Chemistry, Anatomy, and other useful sciences, which the natives of Europe have carried to a degree of perfection that has raised them above the inhabitants of the rest of the world."[14] Such useful sciences and not armed rebellion, he and others argued, could give India its rightful place as a free nation. The vehicle for the transmission of this knowledge was the English language. Probably not more than 2 percent of Indians are fluent in English, but it is mainly from this group, who are, on the whole, representatives of the traditional elites, that those who exercise power of all kinds are drawn.

The Indian nationalist movement, which had its formal beginning with the establishment of the Indian National Congress in 1885, was the product of cultural, political, and economic forces in the nineteenth century interacting with the complex factors of the Indian historical experience. The many centuries of Islamic rule, the imposing presence of British power, the diversity of languages and religions, and the poverty and illiteracy of the masses, contrasted with a prosperous and sophisticated elite, guaranteed a struggle for autonomy and independence that would be strikingly distinctive. One of its differing characteristics was that the nationalist leaders were not nativists. None argued for a return to Indian patterns of government, but instead insisted that their goal was attaining a representative, parliamentary government, on the British model, which would guarantee British freedoms to the people of India. Another characteristic was that the leaders were almost always men and women who had won professional distinction, and who were as respected by the British as they were by their own country. Almost without exception they came from the traditional regional elites; there were few "new" men or women—for women played a large part in the Indian decolonization process—among them.

All of this meant that the nationalist movement did not call for social revolution or the transformation of society, but rather for a transfer of the control of the existing political and economic system from British to Indian hands. This was true even in the period after 1920 when Mahatma Gandhi dominated the Indian National Congress, for while he had a radical social vision, the change he desired was to come not through an armed attack on the existing system but through the transformation of the individual psyche. Though his strategy of nonviolence was a potent weapon against the British, his great gift to the nationalist movement was to persuade Indians that his method of nonviolence was deeply rooted in Indian civilization, marking it off from the violent cultures of Islam and the West. He was able to make his ideas part of a coherent ideology formulated in the vocabulary of Indian religion, which made a very deep appeal to many levels of society.

Although the Indian National Congress was clearly the most articulate voice for Indian political aspirations, its stated goal of a democratically elected representative government was increasingly questioned throughout the twentieth century by Muslim leaders. What they began to formulate was, in effect, an alternative Indian nationalism that denied the Indian National Congress's vision of a constitutional structure based on Western-style majority rule. By the 1930s Muhammed Ali Jinnah, leader of the Muslim League, had begun to express what became known as "the two nation theory"—that India, was not, as the Congress insisted, a unitary state with a single national identity but was instead two nations, one Hindu and the other Muslim. Jinnah desired independence from the British as fervently as the Indian National Congress did, but he argued that the unified India of which the Congress spoke was an artificial one, created and maintained by British bayonets. His argument was important to the process of decolonization, not just in India but elsewhere, where imperialism had created unitary, authoritarian states. The solution, he insisted, was to divide the Indian Empire of the British into autonomous states, based on religion and ethnicity, linked in a loose federation.

After the Second World War it was clear that the British neither could nor would attempt to maintain their position in India by force. By 1947 it was also clear that transferring power to a single national entity with a strong central government, as the Congress demanded, presented insuperable difficulties in view of the Muslim League's position. With great reluctance, the leadership of the Indian National Congress agreed to partition the subcontinent between India, as the successor state of British India, and the new state of Pakistan. It was the only solution. As it worked out, the Muslim leaders were not happy with the partition, for Pakistan got far less territory than they had hoped for, and what they did get, West Pakistan and East Pakistan, were separated by a thousand miles of Indian territory. Nor was Pakistan by any means a home for all the Muslims of the subcontinent: at the time of partition, more than fifty million remained in India.

The final stages of decolonization in 1947, with the deaths of half a million people and the movement of more than 13 million refugees from one country to another, were, in terms of human suffering, surely the most horrendous to mark the formal end of imperialism anywhere. Relations between communities which increasingly identified themselves in religious terms remained one of the most intractable problems related to decolonization in plural societies where the unitary state had its origin, as Jinnah had insisted, in the bayonets of the conqueror.

## North Africa

A history of all the varieties of imperialism and decolonization from antiquity to the present could be written using the southern littoral of the

Mediterranean, but for a sketch focused on the nineteenth and twentieth centuries, two areas must suffice: Egypt and Algeria. At the beginning of the nineteenth century, both were provinces of the Ottoman Empire, with the Ottomans themselves being successors to other great imperial powers—Arab, Byzantine, and Roman.

Egypt should perhaps be described as a quasi-colony of a European power rather than as a colony, yet in many respects it provides a paradigm for both imperialism and decolonization. Because of its very long history as a definable geographical, cultural, and political unit, it maintained a measure of independent sovereignty even after the British occupation in 1882, just as it had maintained its identity after its conquest by the Ottomans in 1517. Napoleon's appearance with his army in 1798 signaled the beginning of modern European involvement, for although the Ottomans soon reasserted their authority, from this time on Egypt became enmeshed in the imperial rivalries of France and Great Britain. The Ottoman governor, Muhammad Ali (1805–1849), instituted a series of economic and administrative reforms that laid the foundation for the modern Egyptian state, but under his successors heavy expenditures on infrastructure, including railways and the Suez Canal, led to an increasing debt owed to European countries. Faced with bankruptcy, the ruler was forced by his creditors to place the government's revenues and expenditures under joint British and French control in 1875.

Strong nationalist sentiment had built up against foreign intervention, and in 1881 Ahmad Urabi, an army officer, led an attempt to establish an independent parliamentary government. To prevent this, the British, acting without French participation, sent in an army the following year, thus beginning an occupation that would last until 1922. They defended this action on the grounds of the need, in the interests of both the European powers and the Egyptian people, to maintain financial control. They also stressed the necessity of securing the sea routes to India via the Suez Canal, so indicating the interplay of imperial interests that had become a characteristic feature of nineteenth-century international relations. Foreign merchants from all over the Middle East, as well as from France and Great Britain, dominated the economy.

Britain remained in control of Egypt, acting through its kings, until 1922, when independence was declared as a result of mounting nationalist pressures. Decolonization was, however, far from complete, with Britain retaining control of foreign policy, the army, and the large southern province of Sudan. While Egypt had a modern bureaucracy and a large intelligentsia anxious for economic and political reform, conflicting forces prevented the formation of a stable democratic regime. The British used their influence to prevent parties that would threaten their commercial and imperial interests from coming to power, while factions manipulated by both the king and the British divided the major nationalist political party, the Wafd.

The poverty of the Egyptian masses, the government's inability to solve economic and social problems, and Britain's increased dominance during World War II led to subsequent unrest. The challenges came from two sources that would play major roles in many parts of the colonial world: religious revitalization movements and the military. In the 1930s the Muslim Brotherhood, whose leaders espoused a return to Islamic principles based on the Qur'an and the application of Shari'a, or traditional Islamic law, to create a more just economic order, made a wide appeal to students, lower-middle-class urban dwellers, and others who felt that the Westernized elites had betrayed Egypt. The other group dissatisfied with the continued dominance of the British and the incompetence of the ruling class—symbolized by Egypt's defeat by the new Israeli state in 1948—was a faction in the army known as the Free Officers. In 1952, under the leadership of Gamal Abdul Nasser, Anwar Sadat, and Muhammad Naguib, they forced King Farouk to abdicate and established a republic. Since the Muslim Brotherhood, with its well-organized cadres and its aggressive Islamic ideology, posed a threat to this new republic, it was soon banned.

Under the leadership of President Nasser, Egypt moved swiftly to seek the place in the world it felt it had so long been denied by Western imperialism. Along with Josip Broz Tito in Yugoslavia and Jawaharlal Nehru in India, Nasser claimed a special place for what became known as the nonaligned movement, made up mainly of newly decolonized countries. Egypt also challenged the European countries, especially France and Britain, by the nationalization of the Suez Canal in 1956, and Nasser's defiance of Israel and the United States gave Egypt a special place in the Arab world. Finally, although its economic problems remained largely unsolved, 1954 to 1956 fairly clearly marked Egypt's emergence from the long period of Western imperialist domination.

Algeria's experience of Western imperialism and decolonization had a markedly different character from Egypt's. British occupation of Egypt in 1882 came after years of economic penetration, and was basically concerned with financial and military control. In Algeria, the French almost from the beginning of their intrusion had a fairly consistent policy of bringing Algeria into close economic, political, and cultural relations with metropolitan France. The guiding ideas of this policy are suggested in a remarkable document drawn up at a 1944 meeting of representatives of General de Gaulle's Free French forces at Brazzaville in French Equatorial Africa to consider relations with "La France Outremer" (France Overseas) after the war. The preamble reads: "The ends of the civilizing work accomplished by France in the colonies exclude any idea of autonomy, all possibility of evolution outside the French bloc of the Empire; the eventual dissolution, even in the future, is denied."[15] This represents an important aspect of French thinking about their colonial empire, often summed up as an assimilationist model—of making France Overseas an integral part of European France. Algeria was the test case for working out the policy.

French involvement had begun in 1830 when a government force landed near Algiers, the capital, declaring that it had to redress insults to their citizens. France's stated intention was only to control the coastal areas, leaving the interior in the hands of the Algerians, but Algerian opposition soon developed. The first to lead it was Abd al-Qadir, whose appeal to an Islam-based nationalist pride became the hallmark of opposition to European conquest in other areas where Islam was strong. But in the 1840s the French gained the upper hand and began a campaign to make room for French settlers. Revolts continued, often led by local religious leaders, but the greatest of these, which took place in 1870–1871, were crushed by the French, who then demanded an indemnity of 36 million francs and confiscated 11 million acres of land.

Confiscation and defeat led to increased European settlement, and by 1885 nearly four hundred thousand settlers were living permanently in Algeria, dominating its economic and social life, following a European lifestyle, and maintaining close contact with metropolitan France. Education was in French, and while readily available to the settlers, only a small proportion of Algerians had access to it or to the social services the French provided. The settlers were allowed to send deputies to the French legislature after the 1870–1871 revolt, and in 1898 Algeria was given a legislative body of its own; but here, as in all the municipal bodies, the settlers had full control. After the First World War, the French government undertook modest reforms, such as making it possible for more Algerians to be elected to the various assemblies, but there was strong opposition to these measures from the settlers, whose voices were heard in Paris.

It was difficult, in this situation, for an Algerian nationalist movement to find a voice, but when it did, it had a strong component of Islamic social thought, with an emphasis on the great legacy of Arab culture and a growing rejection of the French intention of assimilating the elites into their own culture. In 1947, after the Second World War, in recognition of the support Algerians had given to the Free French, the French Assembly recognized Algeria as "a group of departments endowed with a civic personality," but unrest was growing despite French repression of nationalist movements. A decisive change came in 1954 with the founding a new organization, the Front de Libération Nationale (FLN), whose stated aim was complete decolonization and the creation of a socialist, democratic state, based on Islamic principles, with full citizenship for all residents of Algeria, but no special privileges for the European settlers. Despite the advantage of guerrilla warfare tactics, they could not defeat the half-million-strong French army sent to Algeria, but in 1958, the exiled FLN leaders declared the establishment of the Algerian republic. The war in Algeria played a decisive role in bringing General de Gaulle back to power in a France bitterly divided over the question of Algerian independence, and the settlers continued to resist de Gaulle's attempt to negotiate an agreement. Not until 1962 was this achieved, when a referendum was held in which a massive majority of Algerians voted for independence. Of the nine hundred thousand European settlers, only about a tenth elected to stay.

Creation of a viable state after decolonization was not easy in any of the colonial empires, and Algeria was no exception. At that time and since, the question has often been asked: Why did the French struggle so long and so bitterly to maintain power there? Why did so many apparently believe, in the words of the Brazzaville report, that "the ends of the civilizing work accomplished by France exclude any idea of autonomy," even when, as in the case of Algeria, it seemed so inevitable? Part of the answer seems to be that politicians in all parties, both left and right, had come to believe, as one historian has put it, that "the existence of France as a nation depended on its empire."[16] Furthermore, many people accepted the settlers' argument that they should not and could not be abandoned. The British could give up India so easily precisely because it had no British settlers and no one thought of it as part of Great Britain.

## Central West Africa

The Belgian historian Jean Stengers has summarized Belgium's experiment in imperialism and decolonization with this comment: "Leopold II had created the Congo from his Brussels palace without ever going to Africa. It was unmade by a small number of policy-makers, the majority of whom were from the metropole."[17] While the bizarre history of the Belgian Congo (renamed Zaire between 1971 and 1997) is atypical of either nineteenth-century imperialism or decolonization, by its very distortions of both processes it highlights many of their salient features—economic imperatives, national prestige, personal ambitions, international rivalries, and nationalism. In the Belgian Congo one sees what Edward Said has called "the images of Western imperial authority," symbolized in novelist Joseph Conrad's Kurtz, alone "in the center of Africa, brilliant, crazed, doomed, brave, rapacious, eloquent."[18] Leopold II, king of Belgium, probably saw in the Dutch success in Indonesia with their kultuurstelsel a model for establishing a profitable commercial enterprise in the heart of Central Africa, using the Congo River as a trading route and the peoples of the interior for labor. The company that he established, the Association Internationale du Congo, was a private enterprise, not an activity of the Belgian state; and when the vast territories to which he laid claim by right of exploration were recognized by the world powers in 1885 as the Congo Free State, it was as an independent state of which he in his own person, not as king of Belgium, was the sovereign. Rubber derived from trees growing wild became the economic basis of the Congo Free State; and as demand increased, the means for obtaining it through forced labor became increasingly brutal, and accounts of the way the native people were being treated began to reach Europe.

The result of such publicity was that in 1908 the Belgian government formally annexed the Free State, and began an administration generally regarded in Europe and the United States as among the better colonial regimes in Africa. In terms of social service, the Belgians could claim, apparently with good reason, that the public health schemes touched a large proportion of the population. As for education, the record is more ambivalent. While primary and elementary education was fairly widespread, there was very little secondary education that would make training possible for the professions, the humanities, or the social sciences. Since few Congolese went abroad to study, the number of évolués—literally, people who had evolved to a higher stage of civilization—was very small. In 1960 as independence was granted, there were said to be only sixteen Congolese college graduates out of a population of 14 million. This is undoubtedly a major reason why a nationalist movement was so late beginning in the Congo, and why, when decolonization took place, it had so many disastrous consequences, since the Congolese had no experience of administration in government or business. Also lacking in the Congo was the kind of strong religious tradition, allied with an indigenous culture, that had been important in giving ideological shape and providing a base for mass mobilization for nationalist movements in many other colonial areas. Islam, so major a factor in the development of a nationalist base in North Africa, was represented by only two hundred thousand members. The first important nationalist leader, Patrice Lumumba, who came from a Christian background, stated the aims of his new party, the Mouvement National Congolais, in 1958 in phrases resonant of the anticolonial nationalism that had shaken imperialist regimes throughout the world:

> We wish to bid farewell to this old regime, this regime of subjection which deprives our nationals of enjoyment of the acknowledged rights of any individual and any free citizen. . . . Africa is irresistibly engaged in a merciless struggle for its liberation against the colonizer.[19]

There were riots in Leopoldville, the capital, early in 1959, and the Belgian authorities acted swiftly. Aware of what was happening in Vietnam and Algeria, and doubtful of the value of a struggle to hold on to the territory, they announced in January 1960 that the Congo would become independent by June 30. By going in good grace they hoped Belgians could still play an important economic role in an independent Congo.

Decolonization unfortunately led to renewed foreign involvement in the Congo. Soon after independence, an army mutiny broke out and Katanga, the richest of the Congo's provinces, seceded with Belgian aid. The government of Patrice Lumumba, who had become prime minister, was unable to control the spreading violence and appealed to the United Nations for assistance, which was given in the form of a UN force with strong United States backing, though it was also opposed by the Soviet Union. The Congo was thus caught in the bitter struggles of the cold war, and in the end, Lumumba, disappointed with the UN and the United States, appealed for Russian aid. External and internal groups deposed him that same year and he was subsequently murdered, though by whom it is not clear. UN forces remained until 1964, and with economic and military help from the United States, General Mobutu, who had supported the UN operations, established a one-party government after a military coup.

## Conclusion: Patterns in Imperialism and Decolonization?

"The organizing theme of human history," William H. McNeill, the world historian, reiterates, is, and ought to be, the story of "the advances of human power over nature and over one another."[20] This generalization is peculiarly apt as a summary of imperialism and decolonization. Imperialism was surely made possible by the use of new forms of power to control nature and the peoples of remote areas, but just as surely decolonization was made possible as the colonized gained mastery over those same sources of power. As used by the colonized in their liberation struggles, power came not only from guns, but from modern means of communication, universities, industrialization, and new forms of political organization—all the artifacts of the domain of modernity. The great issue at the time of decolonization was the ability of the new leaders to use these artifacts to provide viable and stable governments.

One conclusion a survey of imperialism and decolonization leads to is that, in the final analysis, the primary importance of both was their contribution to the making of modern nation-states. This was not, of course, the aim of the imperial powers, who had been concerned with expanding their power for economic advantages from trade and commerce, new opportunities for their citizens, shifts in the balance of international power through control of strategic areas of the world, and unquantifiable but real gains in national prestige. But the realization, or the attempted realization, of all these things meant the creation of new forms of political entities. Many nationalist leaders seemed to have been unaware of how heavy a price decolonization would exact from their people as they adjusted to the new reality. Jawaharlal Nehru, at the time of the formal transfer of power from Britain to India, said that "after a period of ill-fortune India discovers herself again."[21] Such a statement was often echoed by other leaders, but what was lacking even in Nehru's eloquence was an awareness that the India of the past could not be the India of the age of nation-states.

Another conclusion one draws from the writings of the leaders was that very few of them recognized how severely constrained the new nations would be by the actions, not so much of their old masters, but of two powers, the United States and the Soviet Union, with whom they had not had much direct contact before independence. This and other complexities and contradictions of imperialism and decolonization may lead one to the conclusion that Augustine came to as he surveyed the decay of imperial Rome, remembering what it had done, for good and evil, to the conquered people and to Rome itself. Bad men, he concluded, would see the process of imperialism as felicity, while good men might see it, and what followed from it, as the "necessity of history." Marx had said much the same thing about the British in India: they were greedy and ruthless, but without intending to, they brought about a social revolution.[22]

ENDNOTES

1. Prime Minister to the Secretary of State, memorandum, 2 March 1946, and Secretary of State to the Prime Minister, memorandum, 13 March 1946, in A. N. Porter

and A. J. Stockwell, eds., *British Imperial Policy and Decolonization* (London: Macmillan, 1987), pp. 240, 247.

2. As quoted in H. W. Brands, *Bound to Empire: The United States and the Philippines* (New York: Oxford University Press, 1992), p. 73.

3. World Service of the BBC, broadcast, 10 January 1993.

4. Ibid.

5. As quoted in Raymond F. Betts, *France and Decolonization, 1900* (London: Macmillan, 1991), p. 57.

6. As quoted in D. G. E. Hall, *A History of Southeast Asia* (London: Macmillan, 1964), p. 287.

7. J. C. Marshman, *The History of India* (London: Longmans, Green, 1871), 1:311.

8. Ranajit Guha, *Subaltern Studies I: Writings on South Asian History* (Delhi: Oxford University Press, 1982), p. 4.

9. Sir John Malcolm, memorandum, 12 April 1922, *House of Commons, Parliamentary Papers*, vol. 8 (London: HMSO, 1834).

10. Bipin Chandra, *The Rise and Growth of Economic Nationalism in India* (New Delhi: Peoples Publishing House, 1966).

11. Morris D. Morris, "The Growth of Large-Scale Industry to 1947," in Dharma Kumar and Meghnad Desai, eds., *The Cambridge Economic History of India* (Cambridge: Cambridge University Press, 1983), 2:553–676.

12. As quoted in R. C. Dutt, *The Economic History of India* (Delhi: Publications Division, Government of India, 1963), 1:xxxi.

13. *Report of the Indian Statutory Commission* (London: HMSO, 1930), 2:10–12.

14. Ram Mohan Roy, "Letter on Education," in Steven Hay, ed., *Sources of Indian Tradition* (New York: Columbia University Press, 1988), 2:31.

15. As quoted in Prosser Gifford and William Roger Louis, eds., *The Transfer of Power in Africa: Decolonization, 1940–1960* (New Haven: Yale University Press, 1982), p. 89.

16. Ira M. Lapidus, *A History of Islamic Societies* (Cambridge: Cambridge University Press, 1989), p. 694.

17. Jean Stengers, "Precipitous Decolonization," in Gifford and Louis, *The Transfer of Power*, p. 328.

18. Edward W. Said, *Culture and Imperialism* (New York: Alfred A. Knopf, 1993), p. 10.

19. Ibid., p. 325.

20. William H. McNeill, "Advancing History Education in American Schools," occasional paper, September 1996 (Westlake, Ohio: National Council for History Education), p. 3.

21. Jawaharlal Nehru, *Independence and After* (Delhi: Ministry of Information, Government of India, 1949), pp. 3–4.

22. Saint Augustine, *De civitate Dei* (City of God), bk. 4 (413–26); and Karl Marx, "The British Rule in India," in Karl Marx and Freidrich Engels, *The First Indian War of Independence, 1857–1859* (Moscow, 1959).

SELECTED REFERENCES

The literature on imperialism is very large, with many books dealing in a general way with both theoretical issues and historical developments. It tends to romantic glorification or to harsh condemnation. The literature on decolonization deals mainly with specific areas or with single colonial powers. What appears below should be considered in addition to those sources that are cited in the Endnotes.

Brands, H. W. *Bound to Empire: The United States and the Philippines.* New York: Oxford University Press, 1992.

Cohen, William B., ed. *European Empire Building.* St. Louis: Forum Press, 1980.

Gifford, Prosser and William Roger Louis. *The Transfer of Power in Africa: Decolonization, 1940–1960.* New Haven: Yale University Press, 1982.

Kahin, George. *Nationalism and Revolution in Indonesia.* Ithaca: Cornell University Press, 1952.

Pandey, B. N. *The Break-up of British India.* London: Macmillan, 1969.

Sarkar, Sumit. *Modern India, 1885–1947.* Delhi: Macmillan, 1983.

Smith, Tony. *The Patterns of Imperialism: The United States, Great Britain, and the Late-Industrializing World Since 1815.* Cambridge: Cambridge University Press, 1981.

Thornton, A. P. *Doctrines of Imperialism.* New York: John Wiley, 1965.

# 8 Nationalism

JAMES MAYALL

I

In the twentieth century it became possible, for the first time, to speak intelligibly of world history.[1] Before 1900, political, economic, military, and cultural developments in one part of the world had profound, if sometimes delayed, repercussions in all other parts. No doubt, over the very long term, it was always so. After 1900 the speed with which these multiple repercussions were felt increased—slowly at first, although from mid-century, exponentially. More important, the process of interaction began to be understood, however imperfectly. But not everyone has been touched equally by the forces of world history. Here and there, in the shrinking rain forests of the Amazon or Borneo, it is still possible to find areas where life is governed according to a traditional pattern beyond the reach of modern technologies and tastes, but even these societies are threatened with extinction once they come in contact with the outside world. Elsewhere, most people have been conscious, however dimly, of their common predicament: how to prosper in, or at least survive, the remorseless advance of modernity.

The dawning of world history did not, unhappily, imply the ending of conflict or the triumphant assertion of human solidarity. Indeed, if the story sounded different in different parts of the world, this is also because it has almost invariably been told—not always consciously—with a national bias. "Nationalism," in Elie Kedourie's celebrated phrase "is a doctrine invented in Europe at the beginning of the nineteenth century."[2] It asserts that humanity is naturally divided into nations, and on this basis "pretends to supply a criterion for the determination of the unit of population proper to enjoy a government exclusively its own, for the legitimate exercise of power in the state, and for the right organization of a society of states."[3] The doctrine says nothing about who or what constitutes a nation—an omission which has seldom worried nationalists. For those who speak in its name, the nation is a self-evident category.

For most, the nation is a group which shares a common culture, inhabits an ancestral homeland, has been (or is in the process of becoming) shaped by common experiences of peace and war, and can be enjoined to share a vision of its collective destiny. One does not have to accept Kedourie's negative interpretation—he regarded nationalism as one of the disastrous excesses of European romanticism—to acknowledge its seductive appeal. It can be used as a rallying slogan by any group that feels itself oppressed by an alien power or betrayed by a home-grown tyranny. By the same token, control of the symbols of national unity has always been jealously guarded by governments as an essential prop to their own legitimacy.

It is thus less the European origins of nationalism that are important for understanding its impact on twentieth-century history than its ability to mobilize people wherever traditional patterns of life are being eroded. Nationalists habitually appeal to the past—the more distant and golden the better—but their appeal is to populations buffeted by forces beyond their control. While most of the great theorists of nationalism—Johann Gottfried Herder, Johann Gottlieb Fichte, Joseph Mazzini, John Stuart Mill, Ernest Renan—died before the end of the nineteenth century, their ideas achieved apotheosis only in the twentieth. As a political doctrine, nationalism is quintessentially modern.

Despite its universal appeal, nationalism betrays its European origins in two ways. Historians have devised several typologies and subtypologies to account for its varieties. The most important distinction is between those who define the nation as a historically framed political and civic community and those who view it, by analogy, as an extended family of kin. The two interpretations overlap, but for the first the essential characteristic is citizenship, not social or ethnic determination; for the second it is a predetermined and inescapable ethnic identity. This distinction approximates Hans Kohn's Western and Eastern nationalism,[4] and Hugh Seton-Watson's contrast between the old continuous nations such as the English, French, or Russians and the "new" nations of Serbs, Croats, Arabs, Indians, and Africans.[5]

The second way nationalism betrays its European origins is in its inability to stand alone as a self-sufficient political ideology. If nationalism's strength lies in its appeal to deeply embedded—even if ultimately invented—traditions,[6] its weakness lies in the almost complete lack of substantive content in nationalist theory. Except in colonial situations, it is impossible to derive a program of action from nationalist thought, and even in this case, while nationalism can determine the end—i.e., the overthrow of alien rule—it has nothing to say about which means should be employed. Liberalism, Marxism, and fascism, the contending dogmas which have mapped the twentieth century, all came from Europe. Unlike nationalism, these ideologies were able to generate large-scale social programs, but they could only achieve power in alliance with nationalism.

For this reason, the impact of nationalism on history cannot be understood except in conjunction with the other major forces that have shaped the modern world, just as these in turn cannot be deciphered if the way in which they have forged national loyalties, appealed to nationalist sentiment, or evoked a nationalist response is ignored. People all over the world now identify themselves with nations, and—although not all these have achieved statehood—wherever possible, with a nation-state. But whatever we may think, these identities are not primordial. The nations we inhabit, and the stories we tell each other about them, have been constructed from the more dramatic and far-reaching episodes of twentieth-century history. Let us consider four of them: imperial expansion and anticolonialism; war and the rise of the military; revolution and ideological conflict; and the repeated attempts to fashion a world order based on the principle of national self-determination.

## II

Nationalism and imperialism are often seen as opposites, the first a doctrine of self-rule, the second one of political domination. However, nation and empire are locked in a more complex symbiosis than this juxtaposition suggests. Nationalists may believe their homelands have always belonged to them, but it is the empire-builders who have drawn the political map. On one account there are over 8,000 distinct linguistic communities in the world; yet in 1996 there were still under 200 independent states. Clearly if political independence is the principle goal of nationalists, their success record is unimpressive.[7] From the withdrawal of the Spanish and Portuguese from Latin America early in the nineteenth century to the breakup of the Soviet Union at the end of the twentieth, the vast majority of "nation-states" have been created as the result of imperial withdrawal, within borders determined by the imperial authorities. These were sometimes adjusted at the time of withdrawal to take account of the claims of rival national communities, as in central Europe after 1919 or the partition of the Indian subcontinent into India and Pakistan after 1947, but more often the successor government simply took over a preexisting administrative and territorial unit.

The symbiosis operates not merely at the level of the structures that the nationalists inherited but also at the deeper level of the ideas on which the modern nation is allegedly founded. During the nineteenth century the values of the previous century's French Revolution, and more generally of the Enlightenment—a commitment to liberal democracy, fundamental human rights, and self-determination—were initially accepted by European nationalists, though many subsequently rejected them in favor of cultural particularism. Even more paradoxically, the same values were spread around the world primarily as a result of Britain's and France's national imperialism. Both countries had been politically centralized and socially integrated within a single political culture prior to the rise of nationalism as a political doctrine. Their mercantilist rivalries had also led to the establishment of colonial possessions in Asia and the Caribbean during the seventeenth and eighteenth centuries.[8] But it was as national democracies, i.e., states in which the principle of popular sovereignty was firmly established, that they completed the "enclosure" of the world during the nineteenth and early twentieth centuries.

Prior to 1991, there were two waves of state creation in the twentieth century. First, in the immediate aftermath of the First World War, the political map of Europe and the Middle East was redrawn broadly along national lines following the collapse of the Hapsburg, Ottoman, and Romanov empires; second, the process was extended to Asia, Africa, the Caribbean, and the Pacific upon the European powers' withdrawal after 1945. The contrasting nature of these empires—dynastic, in the Hapsburg, Romanov, and Ottoman cases, and national, in the British and French—meant that the patterns of anti-imperial nationalism which they provoked also differed. It is nonetheless worth noting certain structural features that are common to both.

First, while nationalism is a doctrine of popular sovereignty, claiming to mobilize the citizenry in defense of its historic rights, twentieth-century nationalist movements were almost invariably led by intellectuals, lawyers, or businessmen. Politicians need a constituency, and in a period when imperial rule was the enemy, the appeal of the nation proved by far the most potent means of conjuring one into existence. It is not difficult to understand why: the other contenders for people's political affections—individuals joined only in defense of property and individual rights, and social and economic class— are associated with internal social divisions, whereas the appeal to the nation is to a form of solidarity that transcends these divisions. As empires habitually tend to exploit social and ethnic cleavages as a way of maintaining order, liberals and socialists are equally at a disadvantage in dealing with imperialism unless they can successfully monopolize the nationalist movement. In this respect, the nationalist opponents of the European dynastic empires had more in common with later African and Asian anticolonial nationalists than is generally supposed.

Secondly, nationalism alone was seldom strong enough to break the grip of imperial rule. In both twentieth-century waves of state creation—after 1919 and after 1945—nationalists were presented with a window of opportunity that had been pried open by war. Prior to both world wars, nationalist agitations had been regular occurrences, at least in those parts of the European and overseas empires that had acquired a measure of political self-consciousness; but while these may have loosened the hold of imperial legitimacy, they failed to undermine it. After each of the two wars, nationalists won statehood even on the farthest frontiers of empire, where traditional society had been scarcely touched by modern ideology or technology, and where popular national consciousness barely existed.

Thirdly, nationalism was not merely weak politically in comparison with the imperial states against which it was arrayed, it was also intellectually parasitic. It is true that the overthrow of alien rule provided nationalists with an unambiguous objective, but it did not tell them how to achieve it, or on what principles to base their national state once it had been achieved. For this reason, they sought ideological allies among those, whether rationalist or historicist, who claimed to possess a program tailored to the needs and aspirations of modern society. And in this sense, despite the sharply contrasting contexts in which they operated, both European and Third World nationalists were heirs to the same tradition.

Throughout the nineteenth century, nationalists had identified with the progressive struggle against privilege, aristocratic rule, and prescriptive right. Those who confronted the British, French, and other European overseas empires did not have to contend with dynasticism, but they had to combat racism—which implicitly undergirded the doctrinal accommodation European democrats made to justify the expansion of their power worldwide. Whether it was expressed, in its pathological form, as a belief in a natural racial hierarchy, or more benignly in terms of the conviction that European nations had a duty to extend the benefits of their own civilization to "lesser breeds without the law," as Rudyard Kipling wrote in his poem, "Recessional," European imperialism erected formidable obstacles to local political participation.

Despite these similarities, there were two major contrasts in the nationalist responses to empire in Europe and further afield. The first concerned the relationship of ethnic to national identity; the second the means by which the transfer of power was effected. Traditional empires were personal or dynastic;

as strong or weak as their rulers, when these empires finally collapsed they also disappeared—their lands divided according to the spoils of war or swallowed up in a new imperial dispensation. The disappearance of the Hapsburg, Ottoman, and Romanov empires followed this pattern, except that the dynastic principle was itself a victim of the First World War. No new empire that claimed title by right of conquest and legitimacy by hereditary descent could arise in Europe. The old empires broke up into their constituent ethnic parts, or in a few cases such as Yugoslavia, into unstable federations of related, even if hostile, ethnic communities.

In President Woodrow Wilson's vision of a new world order, the successor states to the old empires were to be based on democratic principles. Wilson's ideas had been widely disseminated during the Great War and formed the basis of the United States' position at the Paris Peace Conference. Indeed, it was his conviction that a world made safe for national states would also be a world made safe for democracy. But this assumption was notoriously mistaken. It overlooked the extent to which the peoples of Eastern and Central Europe had become so intermingled that it was impossible to redraw the map of Europe without entrapping ethnic minorities in virtually every state. The political culture of much of the area was also profoundly undemocratic. As early as 1861, John Stuart Mill had noted the difficulty of combining two nations within a single state under a democratic constitution.[9] Not only was his insight still valid in the 1920s (as it is arguably in the 1990s) but the fact that as one moved eastward from Vienna, the proportion of the population accounted for by the peasantry increased, reduced the chances of a civic nationalism taking root—at least in the short run.

Nationalist politicians in search of a constituency had no alternative but to appeal to ethnic sentiment rather than democratic principle. After 1918 plebiscites were held in regions of mixed national composition, sometimes with surprising results—as when Poles voted to stay in Germany rather than live in a reborn Poland, or Slovenes preferred Austria to the new Yugoslavia.[10] But the refusal of Britain and France to test national sentiment in Ireland or Alsace robbed the plebiscite of its general validity. In practice, as Alfred Cobban wryly pointed out, no sooner had the principle of national self-determination been elevated to the status of an international norm than it was freely interpreted as a principle of national determinism.[11] Under this reformulation, the element of choice was effectively removed from the determination of a person's political identity.

Many European colonies were also ethnically heterogeneous. To take only the most extreme example, the territorial division of Africa had been agreed upon at the Congress of Berlin in 1884. Borders—mostly straight lines drawn on a map to prevent conflict between the competing imperialists—frequently cut through ethnic communities such as the Yoruba, divided between Dahomey and Nigeria; the Ewe, between Togo and Ghana; or the five-way division of the Somali between the Somali protectorates, Ethiopia, Kenya, and Djibouti. Yet at the beginning, ethnic as opposed to racial consciousness played only a minor role in African nationalism. Much the same held for Asia.

The European empires had been built up by strong national states. When the British and French withdrew from their overseas possessions after 1945, they remained immeasurably more powerful than even the strongest of the successor states. For Asian and African nationalists, this was undoubtedly a problem. If, as the historian Isaiah Berlin suggests, the rise of nationalism was an "automatic psychological accompaniment of foreign rule—a natural reaction . . . against oppression or humiliation of a society that possesses national characteristics," [12] the transfer of power was only a partial therapy. The emperors did not conveniently vanish as they had in Europe, to become suitable subjects for nostalgic films and romantic fiction; they remained stubbornly influential, reduced in power and prestige compared with the new superpowers, but still occupying two of the five permanent seats on the United Nations Security Council. Great power attracts as much as it repels: indeed, the former metropolitan states acted as much as models for emulation as targets for nationalist fury or scapegoats for national failings.

Toward the end of the century, ethnic conflicts have proliferated over much of Asia, Africa, and Oceania. They also returned with a vengeance to Europe after the end of the cold war. From the perspective of the 1990s, it is difficult to recapture the optimism that was associated with decolonization and the nearly universal conviction in Asia and Africa that nationalism was a doctrine of liberation. A few movements—for example Subhas Chandra Bose's Indian National Army, or the Afrikaner National Party in South Africa—had supported the Third Reich on the ancient principle of making a friend of their enemy's enemy, but most anticolonial nationalist parties had little in common with the cultivated irrationalism that was the trademark of Nazism and European Fascism.

Fascism was the pathological heir of that strand of European romanticism which rejected the universalism of both the French Enlightenment and British classical political economy. After Germany's humiliating defeat in the 1918 war, as after the Napoleonic invasions a century earlier, they responded, in Berlin's phrase, "like the bent twig of the poet Schiller's theory, by lashing back and refusing to accept their alleged inferiority." [13] What interested the

National Socialists (Nazis) was what had interested the romantics before them: not what they shared with the rest of humanity, but what distinguished them and placed them on a higher plane. By contrast, most anticolonial movements in the British, French, and Dutch empires enthusiastically accepted the idea of a single humanity and universal values. If they too lashed back against European domination, it was seldom in the name of some precolonial ethnic or political identity, but in protest against their exclusion from colonial society.

Elie Kedourie vividly documents the process by which, once the initial resistance of the traditional leadership had been overcome, a second generation of notables and intellectuals enthusiastically endorsed the professional ambitions, lifestyle, and world view of their conquerors.[14] Their aspirations were cosmopolitan, not nationalist. Only when they returned home from education in London, Paris, or Berlin to discover that they could not practice as engineers, teachers, lawyers, or doctors on equal terms with the Europeans did their political attitudes change. Even then their cultural cosmopolitanism often lingered on: Motilal Nehru, the father of India's first prime minister, is said to have had his shirts laundered in Paris throughout his adult life, while Leopold Senghor, Senegal's first president and the inventor of the philosophy of negritude, was only willing to postpone his annual vacation in Normandy for a day in order to accommodate the inaugural meeting of the Organization of African Unity's Council of Ministers in August 1963.

It may be argued that such men were not "real" nationalists, that they had been co-opted by the imperial powers to facilitate their continued control after the formal transfer of power. This was Stalin's view, also sometimes favored by Third World radicals such as Kwame Nkrumah of Ghana, Gamal Abdul Nasser of Egypt, and Fidel Castro of Cuba, who were determined to maintain the anti-imperial struggle at the center of the Nonaligned Movement. But none of these leaders were cultural nationalists, and their attacks on their political opponents were based on their ties with the West, not their cosmopolitanism.

Both European and Afro-Asian nationalism were reactions to humiliation at the hands of foreign rulers. However, in Europe this manifested itself at the level of national cultures, most of which were defined by common language, while over much of the former colonial world it was felt at the level of political exclusion on racial rather than ethnic or linguistic grounds. The mass political parties formed to agitate for independence had no difficulty in accepting the structures and definition of the nation-state that had been established by the colonial powers. Ethnicity and religion, of course, were never far below the surface—Indonesia was predominantly a Javanese state just as India was a Hindu one—but awareness of their social diversity reinforced the outward commitment of most African and Asian governments to the rationalist values of secular modernization and human rights. Whether they had opted for a liberal or a socialist development strategy or a mixture of the two, once the nationalists achieved power they needed to "build" nations which often had very little or no preexisting social reality. If for no other reason than to obtain international support for this project, anticolonial nationalists clung to their internationalist and rationalist credentials.

At least they did so wherever there was no significant European settler population. The speed of the collapse of European imperial power was partly the result of the democratic pressure on the colonial question within metropolitan societies. In areas where the interests of their own citizens were not involved, the British and French were confronted not merely by nationalists in the colonies demanding independence, but by a fifth column of liberal supporters at home. But in Algeria, which had a population of over a million French settlers or "pied-noirs"; in Kenya, where the settlers had taken over the best farming land; and in Southern Rhodesia, where the settler population had enjoyed de facto independence from Britain since 1922, the fifth column operated on the side of the settlers. Where two intransigent nationalisms confronted one another, the settlers' appeal to their kith and kin at home proved initially a far more effective influence on colonial policy than liberal support for the local nationalists. In each case the transfer of power was preceded by a prolonged insurgency.

The same was true of the Portuguese empire. Just as the Portuguese population itself was denied democratic rights until the revolution of April 1974, African nationalists had no realistic opportunity of achieving their objectives without resorting to armed rebellion. A similarly all-encompassing confrontation between white and black nationalism took place in South Africa, which had achieved its independence from Britain in 1910, and was governed from 1948 by the Afrikaner National Party under a constitution which disenfranchised the majority nonwhite population. In 1962 the government drove the African National Congress (ANC) into exile. Many of its leaders, including Nelson Mandela, were imprisoned, while those that got away spread across the world. The ANC was the oldest nationalist organization in Africa, but until 1960 it had pursued a policy of peaceful protest. When it finally changed its tack to advocate armed resistance, the government banned it, along with the breakaway Pan-African Congress and the South African Communist Party.

In all these cases the civic character of anticolonial nationalism was an early victim. The settler populations defended their interests with a passionate but often arrogant assertion of their rights, often after suppressing their opponents with a brutality that belied their claims to represent a superior civilization. (The ease with which they were able to mobilize support from their kith and kin in the metropolitan countries also revealed the extent to which ethnic and cultural identities underpinned even the securely anchored civic nationalisms of France and Britain.) The African nationalist movements responded in kind, revealing, in their turn, how thin was the secular rationalism in which their leaders dressed their programs and pronouncements.

Guerrilla insurgencies, which take a high toll in human lives in return for the promise of a very uncertain prize, depend on the maintenance of morale and discipline. Loyalty is at a premium but often hard to come by, which is why nationalist forces often call on the "irrational" superstitions of the local people among whom they operate, or on their fears of reprisal, to keep them in line. In Kenya, the aims of the Mau Mau rebellion included the recovery of land, the abolition of Christianity, and the restoration of ancient customs: the rebellion was sustained by a secret society whose members were initiated by taking bloodcurdling oaths designed to compel obedience. In Rhodesia, ZANU, the more successful of the two nationalist movements, made extensive use of local witch doctors. In Algeria, both sides resorted frequently to torture. In these conflicts between settler and indigenous nationalisms the issue of ethnic identity also surfaced much earlier than elsewhere. The Mau Mau was a Kikuyu rebellion; no sooner had the Front de Libération Nationale (FLN) secured the withdrawal of France from Algeria in 1962 than it faced a rebellion from the Berber population; ZANU was a predominantly Shona breakaway from the Ndebele-dominated ZAPU; the political succession in Angola in 1975 was contested by three largely ethnically based parties. And so on.

With the partial and ambiguous exception of Afrikaans-speaking white South Africa, settler nationalisms everywhere were defeated not on the battlefield, but by a combination of abandonment by the metropolitan power and international pressure. But despite the excesses to which these conflicts gave rise, the withdrawal of European imperial power was carried out in the name of the civic form of nationalism that the West European states themselves espoused. By 1960, the General Assembly of the United Nations had ruled that all colonial peoples had a right to independence and that lack of preparation for self-rule could not be used as an excuse for prolonging colonial government.[15]

The new world order created by decolonization was thus one of nation-states, territorially but not ethnically defined. Indeed, while the nationalism of governments was widely applauded, there was a rare east/west and north/south consensus in favor of the territorial status quo. Throughout the 40-year cold war, secessionist nationalists found the international environment inhospitable to their aspirations. The collapse of communism in 1991 led to a new wave of state creation in the former Soviet Union and Yugoslavia, although this time, as after 1919, the criteria were largely ethnic. Czechoslovakia split peacefully into its component parts in January 1993 and in April, Eritrea, which had fought a 30-year war with Ethiopia, voted in a referendum, judged "free and fair" by international observers, for independence. How widely the demonstration effects of these events will be felt remains to be seen. Nor is it yet clear whether they will displace official nationalism as the basis of the international order.

## III

The triumph of an official, theoretically civic form of nationalism was largely the result of two developments, the nationalization of empire and the ideological conflict between the United States and the Soviet Union that dominated world politics after 1945. Regarding the first, the French and British empires were great national projects, widely supported within society (even though in both countries there were vigorous opponents of imperialism) and offering careers and opportunities to all classes.

Ever since Napoleon had introduced the *levée en masse*, it had been axiomatic that the armed forces of a modern state existed to defend the people and protect their interests. The outbreak of World War I in 1914 had also shown how deeply the idea of the nation-in-arms had taken root in European societies: patriotic fervor was so great that none of the belligerents initially had recourse to conscription. This sense of national pride, widely diffused among the population at large, was an integral part of the ethos of the professional armed services. Moreover, their patriotism was intimately bound up with empire: Algeria and Indochina were to a large extent creations of the French army, which was one reason why it proved so difficult for France to disengage, just as the idea of the British nation was inseparable from the history of the Indian Civil Service and the British army in India. However, nationalism at the center provoked counternationalisms on the colonial periphery.

Anticolonial nationalisms often professed to be antimilitary—Nehru kept India's armed forces starved of resources until after their defeat by China in a border conflict in 1962, and Julius Nyerere, Tanzania's first president, initially hoped to do without an army altogether—but an army, if not always a navy and an air force, turned out to be as indispensable to the modern state as a central bank or national anthem.

In many new states, the sense of civic patriotism did not long survive the transfer of power. In both Asia and Africa, as earlier in Latin America, civilian governments were frequently toppled by the army. Once in power the military found it difficult to stand above the social and ethnic divisions of society, but it was common practice for the conspirators to justify their seizure of power in the language of national redemption. In their eyes, the army was the only national institution capable of reversing the damage done by corrupt and self-seeking politicians. Thus, for example, Colonel Gamal Abdul Nasser overthrew the Egyptian monarchy in 1952; Field Marshal Ayub Khan took power in a bloodless military coup in Pakistan in 1958; Kwame Nkrumah, the first president of Ghana, was overthrown in 1966. In 1971, in a grotesque parody of military purification, General Idi Amin ousted President Milton Obote of Uganda and plunged his country into more than a decade of repressive and brutal government and intense ethnic conflict.

The officers who so argued took over the self-image of the European armies they replaced; but they also inherited another legacy, that of the modernizing reformer. During the 1950s and 1960s the officers who toppled the Egyptian monarchy, Ahmad Ben-Bella's government in Algeria, Sukarno's in Indonesia, Nkrumah's in Ghana, and many more, hoped to achieve the kind of social transformation that Mustafa Kemal Ataturk had aimed for in Turkey during the 1920s. Nation-building, like the maintenance of empire, was a task for which the armed forces felt themselves peculiarly suited.

From the mid-1950s, the nation-building projects of the new states were also encouraged by the United States and the Soviet Union. Though both were anti-imperialist, the conflict that developed between them was between competing forms of universalism rather than nationalism. The founding fathers of liberalism and communism had been profoundly antipathetic to nationalism, with liberals regarding it as irrational and romantic, and Marxists as false consciousness—like religion, an opiate with which the bourgeoisie prevented the masses from understanding their true class interest.

It was not self-evident, therefore, that the international system over which they presided would be made safe for nationalism, whether of the civic or ethnic variety. This apparently paradoxical outcome was largely a consequence of the nationalization of socialism, and the parallel socialization of liberalism. The nationalization of socialism was occasioned by the need to defend the

Bolshevik Revolution against the surrounding capitalist powers, and subsequently against Nazi Germany; the socialization of liberalism by the need to defend liberalism from its own inner contradictions during times of economic depression, and to adapt it to the needs of a modern war economy. On both sides, the idea of social engineering forged an alliance with nationalism that later carried over into the foreign policies of the two superpowers.

Soon after the 1917 October Revolution, Lenin concluded that it would be necessary to appease the nationalists if the Bolshevik victory was to be secured. Much of the opposition to the czarist empire had come from the oppressed nationalities, and those that had obtained their freedom—the Azerbaijanis, Armenians, Belorussians, Ukrainians—opposed the reimposition of rule from an imperial center, regardless of its ideological complexion. Lenin's solution was to create a federal structure based on the formula "national in form, socialist in content." This concession was intended to be transitional, since in the end all nationalities would be assimilated into the new socialist society. In the meantime the union was defined in terms of national identities even where, as in Central Asia, there was no evidence of nationalist sentiment. Despite including a right of secession in the constitution, the Bolsheviks were able to take over the czarist empire and maintain it virtually intact for 70 years. The historian Ian Brenner explains the tortuous reasoning by which this constitutional sleight of hand was achieved: [16]

> Given a right to secession, the republics would pledge to fully acknowledge and participate in a union under Soviet leadership; in return for such a pledge, nationalities would not choose to enact their right to secession. National institutions would be constrained by the popular feeling of a freely entered contractual arrangement, thus providing a justification for empire that lies at the foundation of Soviet nationalities policy.

With the collapse of communism in 1989, it became clear that by nationalizing it, Lenin and his successors had offered up a dangerous hostage to fortune. But viewed from the outside, this was far from clear at the time. Josef Stalin pursued the policy more ruthlessly than Lenin, treating the Russians as the greatest nation and punishing others—most notably the Chechens, Germans, Kalmyks, and Crimean Tatars—who were deported en masse to Central Asia and Siberia for so-called crimes against the Soviet Union. Simultaneously there was a policy of sustained Soviet indoctrination, backed by extensive Russian migration into non-Russian areas. During the Second World War, Stalin appealed to Great Russian nationalism rather than socialism in rallying Soviet citizens to fight for the motherland. Sergei Eisenstein's films, which had previously celebrated the Revolution, now appealed with spectacular historical imagery to a glorious Russian past. No one could seriously doubt that Stalin was the inspiration for his film *Ivan the Terrible*.

In its own terms the nationalities policy was not wholly unsuccessful. Local elites in the predominantly ethnic republics were co-opted so that the Party Secretary would generally be a national even if his immediate subordinate was almost invariably a Russian—as was the local chief of the KGB. Under the system of central economic planning, peripheral economies were kept dependent on Russia, although they also attracted higher levels of investment than they had under the czars. Throughout the Soviet period, secessionism was successfully contained, and had it not been for the catastrophic failure of the Soviet economic system during the 1980s, it is doubtful whether nationalist agitation alone would have made a serious impact on the Soviet state.

For the Chinese Communists in 1949, nationalism was not the problem it had been for the Bolsheviks after 1917, partly because the Han ethnic group are so dominant in the Chinese population that major challenges to the Chinese state have generally arisen because of divisions among the Chinese themselves rather than because of disaffection on the part of ethnic minorities. But it was also because, from the start, the Communists pursued their objectives within an unambiguously Chinese cultural framework. Unlike the Bolsheviks, they had no internationalist commitments; indeed, their enthusiasm for social revolution was as a solution to a national problem. In 1919 both Communists and Dr. Sun Yat-Sen's Kuomintang had been led by young intellectuals both attracted to Western liberal ideas of self-determination and impressed by the Bolshevik Revolution. When the united front between the two groups finally split in 1927, the government of the right-wing faction under General Chiang Kai-shek was recognized by the Western powers, and after the Second World War, it took China's seat as one of the five permanent members of the Security Council.

However, it was the Communists under Mao Zedong who proved more successful both strategically and in mobilizing the Chinese population. During the civil war, Mao had followed Lenin in using the appeal of national self-determination as a way to attract ethnic minorities away from the Nationalist government. A resolution of the first All-China Congress held in South China in 1931 went into the issue of minority self-determination in detail:[17]

. . . in districts like Mongolia, Tibet, Sinkiang, Yunan, Kweichow and others where the majority of the population belongs to non-Chinese nationalities, the toiling masses of these nations shall have the right to determine for themselves whether they wish to leave the Chinese Soviet Republic and create their own independent state, or whether they wish to join the Union of Soviet Republics, or form an autonomous area inside the Chinese Soviet Republic.

This tolerance of minorities did not survive the Revolution. In 1949 Chiang Kai-shek's government was driven from the mainland to the island of Taiwan, where it established, under American protection, a successful free-enterprise economy. On acquiring power, Mao's first public speech was titled "The Chinese people have stood up."[18] Succession, rather than self-determination, was to define the new China, a move which Mao accomplished by endorsing Sun Yat-Sen's doctrine of China's five races: the Han, Tibetans, Uighurs, Mongols, and Manchus. The Communists also wove the concept into the Red Flag of the People's Republic, which has a large star for the Han and smaller stars for the other four races. To drive the point home, they proceeded to annex Sinkiang and Tibet. The forceful incorporation in 1950 of Tibet—the one minority homeland where nationals outnumbered Han—caused an international outcry, but it was not challenged at the United Nations because Britain and India, the two powers most immediately concerned, had always accepted Beijing's theoretical sovereignty over the territory.[19]

The nationalists harbored irredentist dreams of returning to the mainland until 1972,[20] encouraged by the Americans, who continued to insist that the Taiwanese government was the rightful government of China. But to the rest of the world the irredentism of the People's Republic seemed more plausible. In the end, the Beijing government successfully resisted Western proposals under which both countries would have been represented at the United Nations and in 1979 took China's seat on the Security Council.

The specter of a successfully nationalized socialism in the Soviet Union and China encouraged the socialization of the civic nationalisms of Western Europe. Prior to the 1930s the governments of the Western democracies had taken the loyalty of the national citizenry for granted. Nationalism was a useful resource in war, and indeed had stood them in good stead in 1914, but in peacetime such enthusiasm might develop into a threat to the established order. It apparently never occurred to the French and British governments that their populations, who had so heroically answered the call to arms in 1914—thus proving that Marx's prediction about international proletarian solidarity was false—might feel betrayed once peace returned by being treated as mere labor, a commodity like any other traded in a free market.

The economist John Maynard Keynes, who had resigned from the Paris Peace Conference in 1919 in protest of the imposition of punitive reparations on Germany, sensed the danger that might befall liberal society if it did not reform itself.[21] As a rationalist, he saw the problem as essentially technical, the impossibility of operating a harmonious international economy without an adequate supply of credit. Others, like Ortega y Gassett, the Spanish philosopher and minister of culture in the Spanish Republic, argued that the breakdown of traditional ties and obligations had not only awakened the masses but also confronted European societies with an identity crisis.[22] His short-run forebodings were dire; in the longer term, he believed, the only solution was to introduce the nation as a whole to the high culture of the elite and to educate the mass in the values of liberal civilization. Neither Keynes's analysis nor Ortega y Gassett's warnings were capable of shaking the liberal democracies out of their complacency. However, gradually and in response not to intellectual prodding but to mass unemployment during the 1930s, they edged toward acceptance, in principle, of positive entitlements, the concept which after 1945 was to underpin the welfare state.

In saving liberalism from both its ideological enemies—communism with its sacrifice of individual liberty and human rights to the principle of equality, and fascism with its demand that both liberty and equality give way to the needs of the state as interpreted through the will of its leader—Western governments made major concessions to nationalism. They were slower than either the communists or the fascists to understand that retaining power required the loyalty of the people, but in the end they reached the same conclusion. Looking back on the first half of the twentieth century, the historian David Thomson summed up the logic of the new nationalism in 1954:

> It was thus no accident that the Hitlerite movement in Germany clung to its title of National Socialism, and made much of its efforts to relieve unemployment by schemes of public works and rearmament. The mainspring of the demand for socialism was the discovery that Germans made during the currency crash of 1923, and most other peoples made during the economic crisis, that the individual or the family is helpless in the face of economic slump.[23]

When the postwar welfare state emerged in Britain and Western Europe, it was more nationalist than its founders might have wished. Citizens were now able to look to it for substantial entitlements ranging from free secondary education to health care and unemployment pay. This expensive extension of its traditional prerogatives had predictable results. In the second half of the twentieth century, all the Western democracies operated restrictive immigration policies, albeit with varying degrees of success. Their explanation was straightforward: in deciding who had the right to the new benefits, the easiest principle of discrimination was between nationals and aliens.

The United States, arguably the only successful manufactured nation, was only partially affected by the socialized nationalism that established itself elsewhere in the industrial world. In 1945 the American economy was so strong, and the attachment to free enterprise so deeply embedded, that the American government considered it neither necessary nor desirable to construct a welfare state on the European pattern.

Even so, American nationalism had a decisive impact on the second half of the twentieth century, partly because the Americans were widely regarded by other peoples as having devised a uniquely successful formula for "nation-building," through industrial and technological innovation and the creation of economic opportunity. This perception was generally shared by the Americans themselves, and informed much of their foreign policy particularly in Asia and Africa. American nationalism was also an active ingredient in sustaining the cold war: indeed, at times anticommunism seemed virtually synonymous with American ideology and identity. During the Vietnam War in the 1960s, the identification was so close that for a time it prevented the government from understanding either the strength of the nationalist forces arrayed against it, or the depth of the political crisis that the war had provoked in the United States itself. For liberal Americans, the Vietnam War came to symbolize the folly of American triumphalism but also, often with scant regard to the evidence, the legitimacy of nationalism everywhere else. There were many, particularly in the Third World, who agreed. The global reach of the United States and its zealous attachment to the capitalist free market ensured that America became the prime target for much anti-Western xenophobia, and therefore the active agent that kept anticolonial nationalism alive.

The alleged "artificiality" of many new Asian and African states had more to do with the character and duration of the colonial experience than with their multiethnic nature. A short period of imperialist government—in Africa little more than seventy years—undermined traditional precolonial societies but did not provide the new states with the resources from which to fashion a civic political culture. In this respect India, although deeply divided on religious, ethnic, and linguistic grounds, was more fortunate. The Indian business and professional class had grown up over the previous hundred years; by 1947, the year of India's independence, it was both numerous and committed to liberal values.

There was, it is true, something illusory about this commitment. The Indian National Congress adopted a secular ideology and a modernizing development strategy, but its mass support—in 1947, out of a population of around 700 million, more than 90 percent were rural peasants—remained overwhelmingly Hindu and traditional. Moreover Gandhi brilliantly succeeded in adapting traditional cultural and ideological symbolism to nationalist purposes, thus obscuring the extent to which Congress had inherited not merely the administrative structures of the British Raj but many of its attitudes toward government as well.

The imperial outlook became evident soon after independence, when the Naga people on the northeastern frontier rose in revolt against Delhi. The rebellion was vigorously suppressed and its leaders imprisoned, although the government let it be known that once the territorial integrity of the country had been accepted, it was prepared to allow a substantial measure of regional and ethnic autonomy. This formula of autonomy within the Union established the precedent by which the Indian authorities dealt with numerous centrifugal pressures. India's success in containing separatism influenced the pattern elsewhere; it established early on that territory, not culture, was to determine national identity, allowing the government, which alone had access to the international community, to monopolize and propagate an official version of Third World nationalism. Roughly speaking, this amounted to the continuation of the anticolonial struggle into the independence period, and by international means.

The international environment thus helped to shape the nationalism of the former colonial world. Except where local enmities dictated otherwise, as in Pakistan, the governments of most new states were determined to stay out of the cold war, which they believed threatened them with a new form of domination. In the second half of the 1950s, the Nonaligned Movement was thus established under Indian, Egyptian, and Yugoslav leadership as an institutionalized expression of Third World solidarity.

Nonalignment had a number of advantages for Afro-Asian nationalists. It allowed them a measure of independence from the Western network of military alliances; at the same time, by accepting economic assistance from both sides in the cold war, they were able to maximize the economic resources available to them for nation- and state-building and to minimize the political costs. It sometimes provided them with a means of mediating in conflicts among themselves.

African nationalists found nonalignment particularly useful in this regard.[24] Largely for contingent reasons—the contacts in Europe between the first generation of African political leaders and the "detribalized" founders of the pan-African movement from North America and the Caribbean—the language of African nationalism was always continental. At the time of independence in the early 1960s, all African leaders were committed to unity, a principle that proved as elusive in practice as had fraternity during the French Revolution. It sounded good, but what, in practice, did it mean? A few governments, under the radical influence of Ghana's Kwame Nkrumah, maintained that their independence required continental political and economic institutions. A second group of former French colonies, whose independence was disputed by the radicals, argued for a continuation of close economic, military, and political links with France, while a third group rejected both the implicit Euro-Africanism of the francophone states and the radicals' integrationism.

Onto these arguments were grafted others concerning the nature of African socialism, the appropriate relationship between Africa and the newly formed European Community, and the pan-African commitment to confronting white racism in Southern Africa. Between 1960 and 1963 governments engaged each other in bitter political warfare in the name of pan-Africanism. Before long, as opposition politicians fled across the border, often to seek support from their kinsmen or from a government adhering to a different faction, governments began to recognize their common vulnerability to subversion. Beyond the rhetoric of solidarity, they needed an authorized version of African nationalism; as a consequence, the Organization of African Unity (OAU) was created. Its charter set out the agreed compromise among the three groups, based on a common commitment to antiracism and liberation, territorial integrity and nonalignment—a concession to the radicals that cost their opponents nothing. As an editorial in the Algerian journal *Jeune Afrique* remarked at the time, African governments had set up a trade union of leaders, thus ensuring that for the time being African nationalism, like Asian nationalism, would remain an elite rather than a mass phenomenon.

## IV

During the 1970s a relative relaxation in the cold war's intensity shifted the focus of African and Asian nationalism from the east-west to the north-south conflict. For many Third World elites, for whom political independence was no longer at issue, this shift reflected their resentment at continuing to be economically dependent on the industrial west. The enemy thus remained outside the state itself. For the most part, ethnic rebellions, of which there was no shortage, had no more success in challenging the state authorities or disturbing the established pattern of world politics than they had at the height of the cold war.

The nation- and state-building strategies adopted by Third World governments during these years bore a superficial resemblance to those adopted in Western Europe after 1945. Just as European governments had found it necessary to manage the national economy in the interests of full employment, so in the postcolonial world, governments defined the modernization of the colonial economy as their central political task. But whereas in Europe, the socialization of liberalism had mostly been adopted as a result of popular pressure from below, the socialization of Third World nationalism was top-down—an imposition by the political elite on the population of their countries, some of which lacked an entrepreneurial middle class, and all of which lagged far behind the affluent West in terms of their material standard of living.

There was nothing new in the idea of using state power to help bring about national unification and economic development: in the nineteenth century, it was the method adopted by the United States, Germany, and Japan—who became, in the twentieth century, by far the most successful economies. Moreover, for thirty years after the Second World War the aid policies of the major Western powers, international financial institutions such as the World Bank and the International Monetary Fund (IMF), and, although admittedly with a different ideological end in view, the Soviet Union, had encouraged Third World governments to engage in national economic planning. The problem was that by the 1970s, there was little evidence that the strategy worked except in a few ethnically homogenous and culturally integrated countries, mostly in east Asia.

Official nationalism habitually operates in alliance with some other ideological program. Since the early 1960s, Third World nationalists had attempted to use state power, not merely for purposes of economic development at home, in this respect following in the well-trod footsteps of Alexander Hamilton and Frederick List, but also more novelly to change international trading rules in their own favor.[25] This campaign, carried out within the General Agreement on Tariffs and Trade (GATT), the United Nations Conference on Trade and Development (UNCTAD), and the United Nations itself, failed. The Western powers made token adjustments but refused to engage in any major structural reform. If militant nationalism is often fueled by a perceived hurt or rejection, the events of 1973–1974 should have been taken as a warning by Third World governments that a price would have to be paid for economic failure. They were not. The dramatic quadrupling of world oil prices by the Arab oil-producing countries indeed produced a nationalist reaction in the Third World, but the lessons that were drawn from it were the wrong ones. A tight supply situation in the crude oil market, coinciding with the disruption caused by the 1973 Arab-Israeli War, allowed the governments of the oil-producing countries to seize control of the market from the private oil companies, the seven most important of which (the majors) were Western corporations.

The drama was played out on the world stage rather than in the relations of governments with their own people. Even a cursory assessment of the likely impact of the new oil prices on the economies of most African, Asian, and Latin American countries would have suggested that the Arab and other oil-producing states had inflicted major damage on their development prospects. Very few of them had oil reserves or refinery capacity of their own, and most were already facing chronic balance of payment problems. Yet no such assessment was made. Indeed, while the industrial powers reacted nervously, fearing that they were entering a new era in which they would be held to ransom by the producers of other commodities, similarly driven by national resentments rather than by economic rationality, most Third World leaders were enthusiastic about the Arab *coup de main*. Just as Japan's victory over Russia in 1905 had been welcomed throughout the colonial world as providing evidence that Europeans were not, after all, invincible, so the Arab success in apparently effecting a major shift in the world's financial resources was regarded as a victory over the West on behalf of the Third World as a whole. [26]

The euphoria was short-lived. Recession in the industrial world quickly revealed the fact that oil was a unique commodity. And although the Arab oil producers emerged as major aid donors, they pursued their own national interests and showed no inclination to make their newly acquired wealth freely available to other developing countries. The idea of collective Third World solidarity faded predictably in the face of traditional forms of national assertiveness. The immediate consequence was that most Asian and African countries were locked into the Western-dominated international economy even more securely than before. By the end of the decade, many countries were hopelessly in debt, a condition which during the 1980s allowed the international financial institutions to exercise enormous influence. Even where countries initially resisted IMF pressures for reform out of resentment at being dictated to, or fear of the likely domestic repercussions, as at different times, for example, the Nigerian, Tanzanian, and Zambian governments all did, they subsequently introduced reforms of their own which differed little from the new international orthodoxy.

The erosion of official nationalism by economic forces beyond the control of all but the most disciplined and self-confident governments was temporarily masked by the international repercussions of the 1974 Portuguese revolution. The military coup, which overthrew the dictatorship of Marcelo Caetano in April of that year, was quickly followed by the granting of independence to the remaining Portuguese colonies of Angola, Mozambique, and Guinea Bissau. The fact that the successor governments in Angola and Mozambique declared themselves to be Marxist/Leninist states, signing treaties of friendship and cooperation with the Soviet Union, seemed to indicate the continued possibility of an alternative ideological alliance for African nationalists. However, though the Soviet authorities tried to enforce ideological orthodoxy on countries they had made a significant military investment in, by the mid-1970s domestic difficulties left them in no position to underwrite the economies of their new allies.[27] Indeed, they refused to sponsor African membership in the Council for Mutual Economic Assistance (CMEA), as they had earlier done for Cuba and Vietnam. Instead they encouraged the African nations to sign the Lomé Convention, making them eligible for European loans and thus effectively consigning them to the European Community's sphere of influence.

By the mid-1980s, states in many parts of the former colonial world were in deep trouble, and some, such as Chad, Lebanon, or Somalia, were barely functioning as states at all. Others, including the former Portuguese colonies, had drifted into disastrous civil wars that belied their governments' claims to speak on behalf of all the people. Many countries had been forced by the IMF and the World Bank to adopt structural adjustment policies that committed them to reducing the role of the state in direct economic management. By the same token, such adjustments also reduced the resources available to the political class, ostensibly for "nation-building," more often for patronage to secure their own positions. The economic crises of the 1970s and 1980s did not destroy the international economy in the way that the Great Depression of the 1930s destroyed it; nor was there any wholesale revival of fascist ideology. Nonetheless, the stage was set for an intensification of ethnic and religious conflict in Asia, Africa, and after 1989, in Europe.

With hindsight, the Soviet failure to preside over a socialist international economy can perhaps be seen as an early warning that its own system—always more imperial than truly national—was about to collapse. At the time it caught almost everyone by surprise.[28] The end of communism was in some respects a similar phenomenon to the demise of official Third World nationalism: in both cases, the authority of central government and its self-justifying ideology was—widely and increasingly—openly held in contempt.

In very few of the threatened Third World states was the opposition genuinely national. Eritrea and the Tamil insurgency in northern Sri Lanka were among the exceptions; but in most, resentment against those in power cut across divisions within society without transcending them. By contrast, in Eastern Europe and western parts of the Soviet Union (the Central Asian republics had more in common with other parts of the Third World), the collapse of the Soviet economy and political authority was accompanied by the organization of national parties simultaneously claiming their right of national—by which they mostly meant ethnic—self-determination, the restoration of democratic government, and the establishment of an open market economic system.

These seemingly contradictory demands threatened to overwhelm the new nationalist politics. In the first half of the century, liberalism had been salvaged by its socialization, a process that by the 1950s transformed Western politics into a debate about social democracy—that is, about the appropriate mix between private and public power. Socialism was saved, and its appeal internationally widened, by nationalization. By such measures, the subversive appeal of popular nationalism was held in check. There were periodic ritual outlets for national sentiment, such as the Olympic Games, the World Cup, and other modern equivalents to Roman gladiatorial contests, but until the mid-1980s it seemed that both the division of the world into two differently organized economic systems, and the political and territorial map, had been fixed once and for all.

With the collapse of communism in 1991 these certainties gave way to a much more confused and paradoxical outlook. On the economic side, nationalists regularly professed the values of civil society and the open market, although how long their enthusiasm for liberalization would survive the realization that it also involves a loss of national control was uncertain. On the political side, the end of the cold war meant not only that nationalists could operate openly and bid for power, but that the territorial question would inevitably be reopened. If in the past, states were created out of the debris of empires, how were they to be established in the postimperial world of the twenty-first century?

## V

As the last decade of the twentieth century nears its close, there is depressingly little evidence to suggest that international society has devised a satisfactory answer to this question. Historically, the rise and fall of states was usually the result of conquest or dynastic marriage. Once the idea of popular—as opposed to dynastic—sovereignty gained ground, states emerged from the disintegration of empires. But having inherited the international system in 1919, nationalists themselves were unable to unravel the enigma that lay at the heart of their legacy.

Wilsonian liberals who were largely responsible for drawing up the League of Nations Covenant had originally assumed that the demands for national self-determination were an accurate reflection of national realities. Unhappily, this proved not to be the case. Throughout the twentieth century the number of nationalists always exceeded the supply of nations, however the nations were defined. When it proved impossible to redraw the political map to coincide with the national map, the peacemakers tried to reconcile state to nation by negotiating treaties guaranteeing minority rights under the League of Nations. This attempt to limit sovereignty was unsuccessful, and the concept of minority or group rights fell into disrepute after Hitler invoked it to justify German aggression in Central and Eastern Europe.

After the end of the Second World War, the victorious powers again had to decide which nations had a right to statehood. And again, the task was beyond them. Indeed, from the vantage point of national or ethnic minorities, the Charter of the United Nations represented a retreat, since it made no attempt to provide them with legal protection. The Charter rests on the twin principles of sovereignty and inalienable human rights—the latter the subject of the Universal Declaration of Human Rights, which includes the right of all peoples to self-determination. But deciding who was a people entitled to exercise this right proved as problematic as deciding who or what was a nation.

The political scientist Walker Connor has suggested that this is the wrong question and that we should ask instead, "when is a nation?"[29] Even in Western Europe, a self-conscious, collective sense of national identity emerged much later than is generally imagined, and the difference in this respect between Europe and the Third World has also been greatly exaggerated. If the process of national formation is really as protracted and incomplete as Connor's argument indicates, it is not surprising that governments have been wary of endorsing any substantive criteria for the establishment of nation-statehood.

Between 1945 and 1991, state practice rather than philosophical or legal argument gave rise to a conventional interpretation of the principle of national self-determination. It came to be defined, very narrowly, as meaning no more than European decolonization and the establishment of black majority rule in South Africa. This equation, not merely of state with nation, but of nation-state with colony, was a reasonable compromise, at least from the point of view of those whose primary concern was preserving international order. Insofar as it was the European colonial powers who had created the political and economic structures through which the new states were introduced to international society, the conventional interpretation also reflected the political—if not always the cultural—reality at the time of decolonization.

Moreover, in most postcolonial societies, access to the goods offered by the modern world could only be obtained through a Western, albeit colonial-style, education, and by mastery of one or another of the metropolitan world languages. Those who saw in independence not merely liberation from alien rule but opportunities to widen their experience of the world had no reason to quarrel with the conventional view—at least so long as they did not perceive themselves to be systematically discriminated against on racial, ethnic, or religious grounds. For the losers in the battle for state power—including such groups as the Nagas engulfed in India; the Ibos in Nigeria; the Kurds in Turkey, Iran, and Iraq; the Timorese in Indonesia; the Karens in Myanmar; and many more—this definition of self-determination was so obviously a fiction that they were bound to challenge it whenever opportunity offered.[30] Nor were the potential national challenges all located in the Third World. By the end of the 1970s, there was a general ethnic revival in Europe on both sides of the iron curtain and even in North America.[31]

Nonetheless, the conventional interpretation survived all but one of the violent challenges that were thrown at it between the partition of India in 1947 and the reunification of Germany in 1990. Secession was proscribed. After a crisis that threatened to introduce the cold war into the heart of Africa, Katanga was reincorporated into the Congo (the former Belgian Congo and from 1971 to 1997 Zaire) by the United Nations in 1964. In 1970, at the end of three years of civil war in Nigeria, the breakaway Ibo Republic of Biafra's surrender was greeted by the UN Secretary-General, U Thant, with the promise that the United Nations would never preside over the partition of a member state.

A year later Bangladesh was "liberated" by the Indian army, and subsequently admitted to the United Nations. But although this act proved the Secretary-General wrong, the breakup of Pakistan was not followed by other successful national secessions, or even by a renewed debate on the criteria for self-determination and international recognition. In both the Sudan and Ethiopia, civil wars persisted with only brief interludes for more than thirty years, and with only laconic and largely ineffective international efforts to intercede. India, despite its instrumental role in breaching the national self-determination norm in 1971, remained adamantly opposed to its own militant separatists in Punjab and Kashmir twenty years later. Many other examples could be cited of similar state intransigence in the face of ethnic or religious revolt, ranging from Bougainville in Papua New Guinea to Basque or Irish separatism in Europe.

Yet the end of the cold war and the collapse of communism reopened the national question in ways whose final implications it is impossible to foresee. The Western powers continued to resist recognizing new states on the basis of their claims to self-determination. Right up to the abortive Soviet coup in August of 1991, they were more concerned with supporting the process of Soviet reform than with recognizing even the Baltic Republics, whose incorporation in the USSR they had never formally accepted, let alone condoned. Similarly, they persisted well into 1992 in encouraging the Yugoslavs to pursue democratic reform within the existing frontiers of the Federation, despite the mounting evidence that the situation had already disintegrated into a ferocious territorial conflict between Serbs and Croats.

Still, with the collapse of communism the state monopoly of nationalism had been broken. Since no governments—and very few observers—had foreseen the first of these developments, governments were unprepared for the second. A series of dramatic events at the beginning of the 1990s forced their hand: the reunification of Germany; the Soviet coup; the dismemberment of the USSR into its constituent republics; Germany's insistence in forcing through international recognition of Slovenia and Croatia; and the subsequent fateful recognition of Bosnia, a state whose territory was occupied and/or coveted by Serbs, Croats, and the Bosnian Muslims, who were unhappily caught in the middle of the Serb/Croat conflict without regional allies.

The end of the cold war led to a brief period of triumphalism, particularly in the West.[32] A vision opened up of a world at last made safe for democracy, the open economy, and collective security. When President Saddam Hussein of Iraq used a border dispute as a pretext for annexing Kuwait in August 1990, he was repelled by an American-led coalition, acting under a Security Council Resolution and with the active participation of most Arab states. Sadly, the optimism was short-lived. No sooner had it formed than the vision began to fade. It was obscured by the recognition that, on the one hand, in a disintegrating world the costs of policing the new world order were likely to be beyond the will and resources of even the United States; and on the other, at the end of the century as at the beginning, nationalism retained its power to destroy as well as to liberate.

The evidence supporting these conclusions was genuinely ambiguous. Sometimes hope elbowed out despair. In April 1993 the Eritreans conducted their referendum in a carnival atmosphere during a three-day voting spree that recorded 99.8 percent of the population for independence from Ethiopia. One international observer recorded that the Eritreans had "never lost their sense of ethnic identity even though 40 percent were Muslims and 60 percent Christians, and despite intermarriage with their neighbors, the Tigrayans; they maintained their own language, Tigrinya, and their distinctive culture."[33]

Here was nationalism as liberation. John Stuart Mill, one feels, would have given the new state his blessing. The Eritrean referendum also suggested a way in which the question of recognizing new states could be reconciled with the demands of international order. Eritrea had been independent de facto for two years prior to the referendum; but it was agreed at the time of the overthrow of the communist regime in Ethiopia that international recognition would be dependent upon a democratic test of opinion. Whether Eritrea will be able to sustain a civic form of nationalism remains to be seen. Not only cynics might question the motives of the Eritrean People's Liberation Front (EPLF) government in outlawing political parties organized along racial or religious lines. Their liberal logic is impeccable, but the element of coercion suggests a gap between political aspiration and social reality.

In the former Yugoslavia and over much of the former Soviet Union, on the other hand, hope gave way to despair. As the old political system crumbled, life took on an increasingly Hobbesian aspect, with communities that had previously coexisted—if not always amicably, at least in relative peace—turning on one another in an orgy of violence and atrocities. In 1991, between 10 and 25 percent of the population was said to be Yugoslav, i.e. the product of mixed marriages, yet these people were powerless to stop the headlong retreat from one another into ethnic ghettos. Nor did the outside world know what to do. The basic problem was that while the United Nations could keep a peace that had already been negotiated, and even on occasion help to negotiate one, the organization had not been designed for peace enforcement in civil and ethnic conflicts.

In this respect the significance of the Gulf War was to expose the limitations of the post-1945 international system. The resolutions under which the American-led coalition acted were carefully drafted to avoid threatening Iraqi sovereignty once the independence of Kuwait had been restored. It is true that Western leaders subsequently called upon the Iraqi people to overthrow Saddam Hussain, but since the concept had no force behind it, it merely encouraged Shi'ite and Kurdish revolts which he ruthlessly suppressed. Public opinion, rather than any change in official views of self-determination or minority rights, forced the Western powers to impose safe havens for the Kurdish and Shi'ite minorities.[34] And even then they were not prepared to commit ground troops. Similarly, in Croatia and Bosnia, public opinion forced governments to send forces to protect humanitarian relief supplies for the victims of Serbian "ethnic cleansing" and the atrocities committed by all three communities. Inevitably, this put the United Nations in the invidious position of presiding, in the full light of day, and under the glare of the world's television cameras, over a process of forced population movements which had previously been associated with totalitarian dictatorships.

Will the nationalist politics of the twenty-first century follow the pattern of Eritrea or of Bosnia? In other words, will nationalist parties and movements opt for a civic nationalism based on the rights and obligations of all citizens, or will they insist on building exclusive ethnic communities? No doubt the answer will vary with time and place as it has over the last hundred years. However, one somber reality must be acknowledged: if states, like Bosnia, where there are deep ethnic and religious divisions and no dominant political culture, are to survive the intertwined unleashing of internal communal passions and the predations of their neighbors, there will have to be international guarantees, and probably military intervention, of a kind and scale never previously envisaged. One thing seems certain: the need to belong, to locate oneself within a community whose identity can be traced backward and forward, will not easily be transcended, particularly in hard times. Despite the technological and economic integration of the world—perhaps even because of it—nationalism, in either its benign or malignant forms, will continue to dominate world politics into the new century.

ENDNOTES

1. See David Thomson, *World History, 1914–1950* (London: Oxford University Press for the Home University Library, 1954) pp. 1–11.
2. Elie Kedourie, *Nationalism* (London: Hutchinson, 1960), p. 9.
3. Ibid.
4. Hans Kohn, *The Idea of Nationalism: A Study in its Origins and Background* (New York: Macmillan, 1961),pp. 572–76.
5. Hugh Seton-Watson, *Nations and States: An Enquiry into the Origins of Nations and the Politics of Nationalism* (London: Methuen, 1977).
6. On this theme, see Benedict Anderson, *Imagined Communities: Reflections on the Origin and Spread of Nationalism*, 2d ed. (London: Verso Press, 1992); and E. J.

Hobsbawm and Terence Ranger, eds., *The Invention of Tradition* (Cambridge: Cambridge University Press, 1983). For a less skeptical view see Anthony D. Smith, *National Identity* (London: Penguin Books, 1991).

7. Ernest Gellner, *Nations and Nationalism* (London: Oxford, Blackwell, 1983), pp. 43–50.

8. See, for example, C. A. Bayley, *Imperial Meridian: The British Empire and the World* (London: Longmans, 1989).

9. J. S. Mill, *Representative Government* (London: 1861, numerous subsequent editions), chap. 14.

10. E. J. Hobsbawm, *Nations and Nationalism Since 1780* (Cambridge: Cambridge University Press, 1990), p. 134.

11. Alfred Cobban, *Nationalism and National Self-Determination* (London: Oxford University Press, 1969), pp. 53–54.

12. Isaiah Berlin, "The Bent Twig: On the Rise of Nationalism," in Henry Hardy, ed. *The Crooked Timber of Humanity, Chapters in the History of Ideas* (London: John Murray, 1990), p. 251.

13. Ibid.

14. Elie Kedourie, *Nationalism in Asia and Africa* (New York: The World Publishing Company, 1970), pp. 71–91.

15. United Nations, General Assembly Resolution 1514 (New York: United Nations, 1960).

16. Ian Brenner and Ray Taras, eds., *Nations and Politics in the Soviet Successor States* (New York: Cambridge University Press, 1993), p. 10.

17. As quoted in Walker Connor, "Ethnology and the Peace of South Asia," *World Politics* 22 (1) (October 1969): 51–86.

18. Speech, 21 September 1949, in *Selected Works of Mao Tse-Tung*, vol 5. (Beijing: 1977).

19. See Alistair Lamb, *The China-India Border: The Origins of the Disputed Boundaries* (London: Oxford University Press, 1964), chap. 3.

20. The Shanghai Communiqué of February 1972 recorded the change in the American position: "Chinese on both sides of the Taiwan Straits affirm that there is one China. The United States does not challenge that position."

21. See J. M. Keynes, *The Economic Consequences of the Peace* (London: Macmillan, 1920).

22. José Ortega y Gassett, *The Revolt of the Masses* (London: Allen and Unwin, 1932).

23. Thomson, *World History*, pp. 142–43.

24. See James Mayall, *Africa: The Cold War and After* (London: Elek Books, 1971); and I. W. Zartman, *International Politics in the New Africa* (Englewood Cliffs, N.J: Prentice-Hall, 1966).

25. James Mayall, *Nationalism and International Society* (Cambridge: Cambridge University Press, 1990), chaps. 7 and 8.

26. See Kenneth Dadzie, "The United Nations and the Problem of Economic Devel-

opment," in Adam Roberts and Benedict Kingsbury, eds., *United Nations, Divided World* (Oxford: Clarendon Press, 1988), p. 144.

27. See Margot Light, "Moscow's Retreat from Africa," in Arnold Hughes, ed., *Marxism's Retreat from Africa* (London: Frank Cass, 1992), pp. 21–40.

28. Two notable exceptions were Daniel Moynihan and Helen Carrère d'Encausse. See D. P. Moynihan, *Pandaemonium: Ethnicity in International Politics* (London: Oxford University Press, 1993); and H. Carrère d'Encausse, *Decline of an Empire: the Soviet Socialist Republics in Revolt* (New York: Newsday Books, 1979).

29. Walker Connor, "When Is a Nation?," *Ethnic and Racial Studies* 13 (1) (January 1990).

30. Mayall, *Nationalism and International Society*, chap. 4.

31. On the links between ethnicity in the politics of multicultural states and international politics, see Moynihan, *Pandaemonium.*

32. See, in particular, Francis Fukuyama, "The End of History?," *The National Interest* (Summer 1989): 3–18.

33. Colin Legum, "Eritrea: The Newest Sovereign Nation-State," *Third World Reports* (28 April 1993).

34. See James Mayall, "Non-Intervention, Self-Determination and the New World Order," *International Affairs* 67 (3) (July 1991): 421–29.

SELECTED REFERENCES

Anderson, Benedict. *Imagined Communities: Reflections on the Origin and Spread of Nationalism.* 2d ed. London: Verso Press, 1992.

Bremmer, Ian and Ray Taras, eds. *Nations and Politics in the Soviet Successor States.* New York: Cambridge University Press, 1993.

Cobban, Alfred. *The Nation-State and National Self-Determination.* London: Collins: 1969.

Gellner, Ernest. *Nations and Nationalism.* Oxford: Blackwell, 1983.

Hobsbawm, E. J. *Nations and Nationalism Since 1870.* Cambridge: Cambridge University Press, 1990.

Horowitz, Donald L. *Ethnic Groups in Conflict.* Berkeley: University of California Press, 1985.

Kedourie, Elie . *Nationalism.* London: Hutchinson, 1960.

———. *Nationalism in Asia and Africa.* New York: World Publishing Company, 1970.

Kohn, Hans. *The Idea of Nationalism: A Study in its Origins and Background.* New York: Macmillan, 1961.

Mayall, James. *Nationalism and International Society.* Cambridge: Cambridge University Press, 1990.

Moynihan, Daniel. *Pandaemonium: Ethnicity in World Politics.* Oxford: Oxford University Press, 1993.

Seers, Dudley. *The Political Economy of Nationalism.* Oxford: Oxford University Press, 1983.

Seton-Watson, Hugh. *Nations and States: An Enquiry into the Origins of Nations and the Politics of Nationalism.* London: Methuen, 1977.

Smith, Anthony D. *National Identity.* London: Penguin, 1992.

———. *The Ethnic Revival in the Modern World.* Cambridge: Cambridge University Press, 1981.

Thomson, David. *World History 1914–1950.* London: Oxford University Press for the Home University Library, 1954.

# 9    Socialism and Communism

SHEILA FITZPATRICK

Socialism has many meanings. *The Oxford English Dictionary*[1] offers the following definition: "A theory or policy of social organization which aims at or advocates the ownership and control of the means of production, capital, land, property, etc., by the community as a whole, and their administration or distribution in the interests of all." But what is that "community" (a nation-state? a region or municipality? a self-selected group of like-minded persons?), and how does it attain ownership and control of the means of production? Is socialism a necessary stage in the development of human societies? Is it a free moral choice made by popular consensus, and if so, is that choice reversible? Who determines what "the interests of all" are, and who adjudicates claims arising from the conflicting interests of individuals and groups? How are the common assets "administered," and what control do other members of the socialist community have over the administrators? Socialists have given many different answers to these questions. Moreover, the answers given by socialist theory have often been different from the answers given by socialists' practice.

My task in this chapter will be to describe the variety of meanings that socialism as a practice has had throughout the world in the twentieth century.[2] Several aspects of this statement of intention need to be emphasized. In the first place, I am focusing on socialist practice, not socialist theory. The doctrinal disputes that so preoccupied many Marxist groups will receive little attention in this essay. In the second place, in writing of a "variety of meanings," I am taking the position that for the historian there is not and cannot be one "true" practice of socialism, by comparison to which all other practices of socialism deviate or fall short. For my purposes, there is no *Ur-Sozialismus*. The range of socialisms that will be discussed extends from German Social Democracy to Soviet Communism in the first half of the twentieth century and from the postwar British and Scandinavian "welfare states" to the Maoist-inspired national liberation movements in the Third World in the second half of the century.

This broad-church approach means that, generally speaking, I accept as socialist those social movements, political parties, and state regimes that describe themselves as socialist and are recognized as such by other (but not necessarily all other) socialist groups. Of course, recognition is not always a straightforward matter. It has been standard practice for Marxists to accuse each other of being "renegades," "apostates," "deviationists," or "capitalist-roaders" at the slightest provocation; but from my standpoint such accusations may be understood as a backhanded affirmation of kinship. The German National Socialists pose a more complex problem in terms of my criteria, as their name identified them as "socialist." I exclude them from consideration, however, since this claim was not seriously pursued by the Nazis themselves, and they were regarded as alien (*not* as apostates or deviationists) by socialists of virtually all persuasions. Regimes whose claims to a socialist identity appeared dubious or opportunistic to contemporaries, such as Nasser's in the United Arab Republic in the 1950s or Sukarno's in Indonesia in the 1960s, pose another problem. I grant them a place, but only a marginal one, in the history of socialist practice.

Another definitional question that must be dealt with before proceeding further is the relationship of "socialism" to "communism." Once again, I am not interested in essential meanings,[2] but in the meanings established by twentieth-century usage and practice. In some contexts, the two terms were used almost synonymously. In another established usage, the distinction between socialism and communism was a matter of degree, communism being considered a more extreme or advanced form of socialism. The most salient twentieth-century distinction between socialism and communism, however, was based simply on the existence in most European nations in the interwar period (and subsequently in many nations in other parts of the world) of two competing parties of the left, a Socialist Party (democratic, parliamentary-based, reformist) and a Communist Party (revolutionary at least in rhetoric, and affiliated with the Moscow-based Communist or Third International Party).

For all the variety of socialist theory and practice in the twentieth century, some generalizations may still be offered. It is notable, first of all, that, despite the internationalist principles of most socialists, the nation-state has almost always been central to the practice of socialism in the twentieth century. This is the "state power" that socialist parties have aspired to seize by revolution or win by parliamentary means. For the bureaucracy of the state (or, in the case of communist regimes, the party-state) has been the implementing mechanism of social change when power is won. In all socialist and communist regimes, branches of the central state bureaucracy have become the instruments of public ownership and management, economic planning, redistribution of wealth, and administration of social welfare.

Marxism (including derivatives such as Marxism-Leninism and Maoism) has unquestionably been the most influential form of socialism in the twentieth century. Of course, Marxism itself is far from a unitary phenomenon. Important traits of "classical" Marxism include:

1. understanding of socialism as the antithesis of capitalism (meaning that capitalism is "the other" for socialists),
2. a theory of history that holds that capitalism will inevitably collapse and be succeeded by socialism,
3. the belief that political regimes represent the rule of a dominant class and that conflict between exploited and exploiting classes provides the basic dynamics of politics,
4. the view that the industrial proletariat is the class whose natural interest is socialism.

Several of these traits have undergone radical metamorphosis in the course of the twentieth century. In the first place, the capitalist "other" of the era before the Second World War became the imperialist "other" of the postwar period, imperialism being understood by Marxists as an outgrowth or final stage of capitalism. This was part of a shift of the central arena of socialist contestation from the industrialized world to the economically backward, ex-colonial Third World. In the second place, as a consequence of the same shift, Marxist socialism lost the identification with a particular socioeconomic class—the industrial proletariat, and by extension the urban labor movement—that had been central to both its theory and its practice in Europe before the Second World War. In the third place, the idea of socialism as the designated heir of a collapsing capitalism, which was widely accepted during the Great Depression, lost credibility in the Western economic boom after the Second World War. By the 1990s, few socialists still held to the idea that history was on their side.

Socialism has been a dominant presence in the internal and international politics of the twentieth century. But in the understanding of most observers, it has not been *the* dominant presence. The twentieth century is rarely labeled "the age of socialism," on the pattern of the nineteenth-century "age of liberalism." This no doubt reflects the fact that, from a Western perspective, socialism/communism has characteristically been perceived less as an actuality than as a powerful *alternative*—externally, a threat or a model; internally, more often the party in opposition than the party in power. If there is something of an "always a bridesmaid, never a bride" flavor to the history of twentieth-century socialism, however, socialist rhetoric must bear part of the blame. Its insistent claim that the future belonged to socialism implied (perhaps incorrectly) that the present did not.

The drama that will be related in the following pages can be divided into two acts. In the first act, set in industrialized Europe, socialist movements develop in close association with labor movements, and the great events are the First World War and, arising out of it, the Russian Revolution of 1917. In the second act, for which the Second World War serves as prelude, much of the action takes place outside Europe in a context of postwar decolonization and the cold war division of the world into socialist and imperialist (or totalitarian and democratic) camps. Russia, representing itself at the beginning of act 1 as a developed nation ripe for proletarian revolution, appears in a different light in act 2, when its historical experience is reinterpreted in terms of its relevance to the general problem of underdeveloped nations, namely, how to escape foreign economic domination and catch up with the developed West. By the middle of the second act, however, the role of exemplar to the Third World is increasingly passing to China—communist since 1949, and a competing center of world Communist leadership since the late 1950s—and, in a different way, Cuba. The United States, almost absent from act 1, assumes a central role in act 2 as the chief enemy of socialism, leader of a worldwide anticommunist crusade. The climax and finale of the play is the abrupt collapse of communist power in Eastern Europe in 1989 and the demise of the Soviet Union at the end of 1991, 74 years after Russia had experienced the world's "first socialist revolution" in October of 1917.

## Socialism in the Early Twentieth Century

At the beginning of the twentieth century, the socialist movement was gaining strength in Western Europe. Most countries had recently acquired or were in the process of acquiring socialist (labor) political parties with a base of support in the industrial working class and the trade unions. There was already an international organization, the Second International, espousing Marxist socialist principles (though the influence of Marxism on labor parties in the English-speaking world was much less than on the Continent). The German Social-Democratic Party dominated the International and was the most powerful in Europe, but in Britain and Sweden the labor (socialist) parties had also achieved a strong parliamentary presence. To be sure, none of the

European socialist parties had yet won a parliamentary majority and set up a government. Only in distant Australia had a labor party won a national election and formed a government before 1914—and the Australian Labour Party had an even more ambiguous relationship to socialism than its relative, the Labour Party in Britain.

To many people within the socialist movement, and to an increasing number outside it in the years before the First World War, socialism seemed the wave of the future. This perception was related to the socialists' rapid rise to political prominence over the past decades, the strength in both numbers and resentment of the industrial workers who supported the socialist parties and trade unions, and the sense of impending crisis associated with the danger of a general European war. For socialism's supporters, its apparently inexorable advance demonstrated the simple justice of its cause: who but the privileged few could reject the argument that wealth, privilege, and opportunity were inequitably distributed in society, and that these wrongs should be righted? For the opponents of socialism, its organizational and parliamentary successes underlined a threat to the established order that was even greater than that of war—the threat of revolution.

In Marx's analysis, formulated half a century earlier, capitalism polarized society, generating an ever poorer and ever larger proletariat that would finally realize its strength and overthrow the capitalists in a socialist revolution. The necessity of workers' revolution remained an article of faith in the Second International in the early twentieth century, but at the same time the socialists' own successes were undermining it. If socialist parties could win power by parliamentary means, would it not be possible to use the existing governmental structure to redress social inequities? Was this not already happening in Germany and England, even before the socialist parties achieved a majority position? Were there not signs of improvement in the condition of the working class, rather than the progressive immiseration Marx had predicted? When Eduard Bernstein raised these questions in the 1890s, the German Socialists rejected them as heresy. All the same, as more and more evidence came in to support the "reformist" position, revolution became an increasingly abstract and remote concept for the leaders of European socialism.

In the early twentieth century, socialism was primarily a European phenomenon, though its members included parties from the United States, Japan, Australia, South Africa, and several Latin American countries. The Second International was predominantly an association of European socialist parties. Though in India, China, and elsewhere, a few intellectuals were becoming interested in socialism—which they often first encountered as students in Europe—this had no immediate practical consequences. Economic backwardness—the absence of industrial development, urbanization, a strong urban proletariat, labor organizations—seemed an insuperable obstacle to the development of socialism. There was, however, one partial exception to this rule: Russia, that slovenly giant on the fringe of Europe, which was still mainly a backward, peasant country, but from the 1890s had experienced rapid industrial growth in a few major cities and regions of the country.

Russian intellectuals, westward-looking, alienated, and inclined to socialism since the mid-nineteenth century, began reading Marx in the 1880s, before Russia had any of the prerequisites of the socialist revolution he described. A splinter group of Marxists detached itself from the populist mainstream of the Russian intelligentsia, arguing that capitalist industrialization was inevitable in Russia and that the peasant commune, on whose socialist potential the populists relied, was bound to disintegrate under its impact. No sooner had the Marxists made this prediction than it started to come true, albeit with a much larger dose of state sponsorship and foreign investment than the processes of capitalist industrialization observed by Marx in Western Europe. Industrialization generated a new class of urban industrial workers, volatile and uprooted, with which the Marxist intellectuals made tentative contact; its strength was manifested in the revolution that engulfed Russian towns and villages in 1905, almost but not quite overthrowing the old regime. The Russian Social-Democratic Labor Party, formed at the turn of the century, split into Menshevik and Bolshevik factions a few years later. Its leaders, including Trotsky (a Menshevik in the prewar period) and Lenin (leader of the intransigent Bolshevik party), were reasonably prominent participants in the politics of the Second International, though the turbulent and faction-prone Russians were treated with some condescension by the dominant German socialists.

In the context of international socialism, the United States was also an anomaly, though of the opposite kind from Russia. Here was a developed, industrialized society with powerful capitalists, a large urban working class, and even a trade-union movement—that is, a society possessing all the prerequisites for socialism—that yet stubbornly refused to move in a socialist direction. "Why is there no socialism in the United States?" was the title of a widely read study by the German sociologist Werner Sombart, published in 1906.[3] Sombart's answer was that workers in America, unlike those in Europe, were not attracted to socialism because of the greater flexibility of the class structure, the opportunities for upward mobility, the open frontier, and the greater material benefits available to workers under American capitalism. In addition, Sombart remarked in wonder, "I believe that emotionally the American worker has a share in capitalism: I believe that he loves it."[4]

## The First World War and the Russian Revolution

The outbreak of the First World War was an enormous blow to the international socialist movement. Instead of workers of different countries realizing their class solidarity and refusing to fire on each other, almost all were swept up in the waves of patriotism that engulfed the belligerent countries in August of 1914. The same thing happened to the major socialist parties, which abruptly abandoned their internationalist and antiwar positions and voted full support for their governments. Socialist leaders such as Jules Guesde in France, Emile Vandervelde in Belgium, and Arthur Henderson in Britain were co-opted into wartime cabinets. Some socialists whose countries were not yet involved in the war protested, but dissidents in the belligerent countries were exceedingly few. One of the few was Lenin, whose Bolshevik party not only opposed the war but also stated that it was in the interests of the Russian revolutionary movement that Russia be defeated.

The enormous carnage of the war and misery of the trenches produced great war-weariness in the soldiers and civilians of the belligerent countries. But it was Russia—"the weakest link in the capitalist chain," as Trotsky put it—that snapped. In March of 1917 (February, according to the old Julian calendar that remained in use in Russia until 1918), a revolution took place that led to the abdication of Emperor Nicholas II and the formation of a Provisional Government; initially led by liberals but supported by most socialists, it was hailed as a triumph for democracy in the Allied camp. This in turn survived only a few months until the Bolsheviks, acting with substantial support in the streets but virtually no support from other Russian socialist groups, overthrew it in the October Revolution and proclaimed a "dictatorship of the proletariat" that would lead the new Soviet Republic through the transitional period between capitalism and socialism.

The Bolshevik Revolution terrified Western governments, which feared that it would set off a string of mutinies and rebellions elsewhere as well as causing Russia's unilateral withdrawal from the war. The leaders of European socialism were scarcely less appalled, not only because of their commitment (on the Allied side) to the war effort and emotional stake in the Provisional Government, but also because they saw the Bolsheviks' action as an irresponsible putsch in a country still too undeveloped in orthodox Marxist terms to have earned a socialist revolution. Lenin and Trotsky (a recent convert to Bolshevism) naturally disputed this reading of Marxism. But the Bolsheviks nevertheless took for granted in the early years that the long-term survival of their revolution depended on its providing the spark to set off European social revolution. They attached particular importance to the success of revolution in Germany, the advanced, industrialized country that had historically provided the leadership of the international socialist movement.

In 1918–1919, it did indeed seem possible that, as in 1848, the flames of revolution would sweep all over Europe. As the European war ended with the defeat of Germany and Austria-Hungary, Kaiser Wilhelm and the new Hapsburg emperor, Karl, abdicated, and governmental order collapsed. Workers' and soldiers' councils, on the model of the Russian soviets, sprang up in many German cities; Bavaria for a few months proclaimed itself a Soviet Republic. The Austro-Hungarian Empire disintegrated into factious chaos as the newly independent states of Poland, Czechoslovakia, Austria, Hungary, and Yugoslavia struggled into being. In the Austrian capital of Vienna, socialists dominated; in Hungary, the left socialist Bela Kun headed a short-lived Soviet Republic. The victorious allies, Britain and France, never came so close to revolution, despite isolated mutinies in their armed forces, but the governments' fear of such an outcome was acute.

In the turmoil of these years, most of the leaders of the now-defunct Second International found that their instincts were overwhelmingly on the side of law and order and against "irresponsible" revolutionary attempts, despite the Marxist doctrine on socialist revolution to which they all, in principle, subscribed. This was particularly obvious in Germany, where the Social-Democratic Party was closely involved in the crushing of revolution and the establishment of a new parliamentary regime, the Weimar Republic.

The Bolsheviks, fighting for survival in a civil war in which the Western powers were actively supporting their opponents, observed this cutting of their revolutionary lifeline with horror. From their standpoint, the renegade leaders of the old Second International had betrayed the socialist cause and thrown in their lot with the capitalists. Their bitterness was intensified when the European socialist leaders accused them of betraying democracy by embracing dictatorship; Karl Kautsky's reproach that the Bolshevik terror of the civil war period represented a setback to the progress of world civilization brought an angry response from Trotsky. The capitalist bourgeoisie (or any other ruling class), Trotsky answered, would never relinquish power without a fight, and "history [shows] no other way of breaking the class will of the enemy except the systematic and energetic use of violence."[5]

After the events of 1917–1919, a lasting split between Europe's reformist and revolutionary socialists was almost inevitable. Still, the Bolsheviks did their best to facilitate it, first by creating a new Communist International, whose First Congress was held in Moscow in 1919, and then by demanding that any party desiring entry into the Comintern should demonstrate its revolutionary credentials by demonstratively splitting with or expelling its moderates. Almost no European socialist party escaped a traumatic and acrimonious breakup, which usually left a majority of members in a "reformist" Social-Democratic Party and a minority in a "revolutionary" Comintern-affiliated Communist Party. The reformist parties formed their own Labor and Socialist International, headquartered in London, but this never enjoyed the prestige or influence of the Second International. The Comintern, based in Moscow and dominated by the Soviet Communist Party,[6] provoked great fear in the governments of Europe but proved inept, and after a while uninterested, in fomenting revolution in the West.

## The Interwar Period (1918–1939)

The interwar period was a disappointing one for socialists in Europe. Although socialist and labor parties were a significant political force in almost every country of Western Europe, as well as in Australasia and some Latin American countries, their electoral successes were relatively few and their achievements unimpressive.[7] Acrimonious squabbling between social-democratic and communist parties occurred almost everywhere, but perhaps most notably in Germany, where the Left's preoccupation with internal feuding weakened its ability to react effectively to the threat from the Right. After Hitler came to power in 1933, both the social-democratic and communist parties were outlawed. As dictatorships of the Right multiplied, especially in Eastern Europe, socialist parties were banned or restricted in an increasing number of states.

Although the Great Depression of the 1930s appeared to confirm the Marxist prediction that capitalism was prone to recurrent crises which would finally destroy it, the most decisive and effective responses to the Depression—those of the Nazi regime in Germany and Roosevelt's New Deal in the United States—did not come from the socialist camp. In Europe in the 1930s, the fascist governments of Germany and Italy dominated the political scene, inheriting the socialists' prewar role as pacesetters and innovators. The Popular Front, a belated alliance between socialists and communists to resist the advance of fascism, provided emotional solace to the Left but failed to alter the course of the Spanish Civil War, the most significant locus of conflict in the prewar years.

Isolated diplomatically, politically, and economically from the West in the 1920s, the Soviet Union was partially reintegrated into the network of European and international diplomacy in the 1930s but at the same time closed its frontiers and retreated into an even deeper economic, cultural, and psychological-political isolation. Some of the characteristics of Soviet-style socialism were already delineated—though by no means easy to decipher from afar— by the end of the first decade after the Bolshevik Revolution. The Soviets had become bureaucratic institutions, losing their initial significance as manifestations of grassroots democracy. The "proletarian dictatorship" was to all intents and purposes a party dictatorship, connected with the proletariat only by virtue of the party's zeal in recruiting workers as members and promoting them into managerial positions; and the regime was intolerant of political opposition or internal dissent. The civil war had left its mark on the Communist Party, which had developed a belligerent macho ethos, an intense suspicion of "class enemies" (ranging from prosperous peasants and priests to former aristocrats and "bourgeois" intellectuals), and more than a touch of xenophobia.

At the end of the 1920s, the Soviet regime launched the ambitious industrialization drive of the First Five-Year Plan; outlawed private businesses and trade; forcibly collectivized peasant agriculture, at the same time deporting several million kulaks (prosperous peasants); closed down about half the churches in the country; and arrested many "bourgeois" engineers and other members of the old intelligentsia as traitors and saboteurs. This was the beginning of a new phase in Soviet development characterized by Marxist-Leninist theorists as "the construction of socialism," but perhaps more appropriately seen as an experiment in state-directed, forced-pace economic modernization. With it came an abrupt drop in urban and rural living standards and the establishment of the Gulag system of convict labor; and collectivization was an unadmitted disaster. But Stalin justified the costs in terms of the Soviet Union's vulnerability to attack by hostile capitalist powers as long as the country remained economically backward.

Although the leaders of European social democracy remained suspicious, rank-and-file socialists and trade-unionists tended to have a more sympathetic attitude to the Russian Revolution and the Soviet Union. The Soviet regime did its best to foster this, tirelessly publicizing "Soviet achievements" in the economic, technological, and cultural realms; stressing Soviet commitment to peace, disarmament, education, and women's rights and its opposition to fascism, colonialism, and racism; and providing foreign visitors with carefully supervised tours of assorted Potemkin villages. The more alarming the threat of fascism became, the stronger was the desire on the part of the Left to believe that a successful "socialist experiment" was in progress in the Soviet Union. Many prominent European and American intellectuals, including George Bernard Shaw, Romain Rolland, and John Dewey, made the pilgrimage to the Soviet Union and reported favorably on what they saw. Such "fellow-travelers" usually discounted reports of famine, labor camps, and purges as disinformation put out by the Soviet Union's enemies.[8]

The fly in the ointment for intellectuals of the Left was Trotsky—"the prophet outcast," as his biographer called him, wandering the world like Ishmael after his struggle with Stalin and expulsion from the Soviet Union in 1930. Although only a minority of intellectuals on the Left embraced Trotsky's cause or accepted his characterization of Stalin's regime as the triumph of a new bureaucratic ruling class and the Thermidor of the Russian Revolution, many had twinges of uneasiness at the implausibility of the accusations made against him at the Moscow show trials of 1936–1938 and the violence, both rhetorical and physical, with which the Stalinists pursued him. In European communist parties with some base of popular support, the defection of a few Trotskyists made comparatively little impact. But in the United States, among the New York intellectuals whose attraction to socialism in the 1930s was perhaps related to its historic status as an "un-American" creed, Trotskyism played a larger role. When the Trotskyist Fourth International was founded in 1938, its U.S. affiliate was the largest group. Trotsky also had supporters in Mexico, where he was given asylum by President Lázaro Cárdenas and spent the last years of his life.[9]

The Comintern (the Moscow-directed Third International) continued to pay lip service to revolution, and was still regarded with great fear by Western governments. The Comintern of the 1930s was indeed a sinister organization because of its cloak-and-dagger style and connections with Soviet security and espionage agencies. But it constituted a serious threat not so much to the powers of Europe as to Communist "renegades" and former Comintern and Soviet operatives, who were in real danger of being assassinated, as Trotsky was in Mexico City in 1940. The "Popular Front" policy of cooperation among all parties of the Left in the effort to avert war and prevent the spread of fascism, adopted by the Comintern in 1935, had nothing to do with revolution (or, for that matter, socialism). It served what the Soviet Union had decided were its diplomatic interests, namely, containment of Nazi Germany and avoidance of war, particularly of German aggression against the Soviet Union.

Outside Europe, however, in the European colonies and quasi-colonies of Asia and Africa, the Comintern had a different role. Right from the beginning, the Comintern and Soviet leaders were interested in what would later be called the Third World. This was related to Lenin's theory of imperialism,[10] which implied that colonial peoples were as much the victims of capitalist exploitation as was the industrial proletariat at home, as well as to the Comintern's desire to go one better than the old Socialist International by casting its net outside Europe. Moreover, Russia had its own complex imperial legacy, having been in Marxist eyes both a victim of Western economic imperialism and an imperialist in its own right in the East; and the Soviet Union included within its boundaries the mainly Islamic peoples of Central Asia and the Caucasus, nineteenth-century acquisitions of Imperial Russia who now had to be somehow fitted into the Marxist intellectual framework. The Baku Conference of Toilers of the East, held under Comintern auspices in 1920, was intended to convey Soviet solidarity with the worldwide cause of the liberation of colonial peoples from the imperialism of the great capitalist powers.

Although liberation from imperialism was the ultimate objective of Comintern activity in the colonial world, Marxism did not provide much hope that such liberation would occur in the near future. What communists could do, however, was stir up trouble in the colonies. Within a year of the Comintern's creation, it was sending emissaries to such promising trouble spots as China, India, the Dutch East Indies, Singapore, Mexico, South Africa, Egypt, and Latin America. Some of its emissaries, such as the young Indian socialist, M. N. Roy, had been engaged in similar activity on their own account—in Roy's case, in Mexico—even before before they became "Comintern agents."

The Comintern's great hopes for the non-European world in the 1920s lay in China, not strictly a victim of political imperialism, but an economic victim whose central governmental system had disintegrated early in the twentieth century. Many Chinese intellectuals welcomed and were inspired by the Russian Revolution. A communist party was established and made considerable headway in the cities in the 1920s, though it was competing with an energetic nationalist movement in the form of Chiang Kai-shek's Kuomintang. In 1927, in an egregious error that became legend in the communist movement, the Comintern instructed the Chinese Communists to enter into an alliance with the Kuomintang—which then promptly turned on the Communists in Shanghai and Nanking, executing thousands and effectively destroying the party.

In the wake of this disaster, Chinese Communists fled the cities and organized guerrilla groups in the countryside. Mao Zedong emerged as the new

Communist leader, despite the disapproval of the Comintern Executive Committee, building up his Red Army with peasant support and establishing first one regional base and then, under pressure from the Kuomintang and after the famous Long March to the north, another centered in Yan'an. These experiences laid the foundation for Mao's theories, later enormously influential in the Third World, that a communist liberation movement could be rural-based and dependent on peasant mobilization. In the 1930s, however, the Chinese Communists' struggle with the Kuomintang and Japanese occupation forces, despite its successes, was conducted out of sight of the rest of the world, which saw Chiang Kai-shek rather than Mao as the key player in the Chinese national liberation effort.

The Comintern was by no means the only conduit of socialist ideas to the colonial world in the interwar period. Such ideas were also picked up in radical circles in London or Paris by young men from the native elites who had been sent from India, China, or any one of dozens of colonial outposts to study in the metropolis.[11] While national independence was their primary interest, the students almost invariably accepted socialist principles as well, partly because European socialists were most sympathetic to their aspirations for national independence, and partly out of a high-caste disdain for commerce and capitalism. India's Jawaharlal Nehru, Sri Lanka's S. W. R. D. Bandaranaike, Vietnam's Ho Chi Minh, Kenya's Jomo Kenyatta, and Tanzania's Julius Nyerere were among the many future national independence leaders who learned socialism as students in Britain or Europe. The London School of Economics, particularly in the person of the socialist scholar, Harold Laski, acquired a special reputation in this regard, but any Western exposure might have a similar effect on a young colonial—J. P. Narayan, the future Indian communist leader, became a revolutionary Marxist at the University of Wisconsin in the 1920s. With rare exceptions, the colonial intellectuals who became socialists under Western influence in the 1920s and 1930s had little immediate impact in their own countries. Their hour was to come after the Second World War and decolonization.

## The Second World War and the Cold War

In August 1939, Germany and the Soviet Union signed a Non-Aggression Pact stating that neither power would attack the other, and (in an unpublished Secret Protocol) recognizing the rights of both parties to act as they saw fit in their respective spheres of influence in the lands lying between the two countries, namely Poland and the Baltic states. Socialists and communists all over the world received news of the pact with incredulity, since it was a betrayal of the antifascist commitment that in the late 1930s many had come to see as the very essence of socialism; and their distress was all the greater when Germany immediately occupied its portion of Poland, leading Britain and France to declare war. Within a few weeks, the Soviet Union, which was not yet a belligerent in the new war, quietly followed Germany's example and occupied eastern Poland. These developments were perceived differently inside the Soviet Union than they were by socialists outside: Soviet Communists hoped (without really believing) that Stalin would succeed in avoiding the war, or at least in buying time to prepare for it, by these maneuvers.

The Soviet Union managed to stay out of the war for almost two years, entering only when Germany launched a massive military attack on it in June of 1941. This made life easier for the socialists of the world, though not for Soviet citizens. Once the Soviet Union had become a co-belligerent on the Allied side, socialists were once again able to see the war as a clear-cut struggle between democracy (including socialism) and fascism; while the Allied leaders—even such a dyed-in-the-wool anti-Bolshevist as Winston Churchill, the British Prime Minister—suspended their hostility to communism and emphasized Russian bravery and suffering in the face of the German attack. Stalin, for his part, dropped the rhetoric of socialism for the duration of the war and shifted to a more universal banner of Russian patriotism and the defense of the native land against foreign invaders. As a gesture to the Allies (which included the United States from December of 1941), the dreaded Comintern was formally dissolved in 1943. These moves might have caused more unhappiness in the Soviet Communist Party had it not been that the Great Purges of 1937–1938 had recently decimated the party's top echelons, including the Old Bolshevik and civil war cohort, thus destroying much of the party's collective memory and sense of continuity with the revolutionary past.

By the end of the war in 1945, the wartime alliance was wearing very thin, partly because the Allies could not agree on the terms of a postwar settlement for Eastern Europe, especially Poland. In practice this issue was settled (at least for the next four decades) by the unilateral actions of the Soviet Union, whose armies liberated the region from German control in 1944–1945 and remained in occupation, meaning that the Soviet Union was in a position to determine the postwar political outcome. In Stalin's view, it was natural that the victorious Allies should impose their own social systems on the areas under their control; thus, Western Europe and Japan would get Anglo-American-style democracy, and Eastern Europe would get Soviet-style communism. Not long after the end of the war, Stalin upset the Western leaders by reintroducing a Marxist definition of the "two camps" that were emerging in the postwar world, identifying the one led by the United States as "capitalist" and "imperialist," and the one led by the Soviet Union as "socialist."

The state of hostile nonbelligerence between these two camps came to be known as the cold war. Each superpower regarded the other as filled with hubris, ideologically rigid, dangerously expansionist because of its crusading sense of mission, and extremely strong. The postwar Western view of the Kremlin's menace of international communism and the Kremlin's designs on the Free World are sufficiently well known not to need rehearsal here. But consider the picture—almost a mirror image of the Western one—sent back to Moscow in 1946 by Nikolai Novikov, the Soviet ambassador in Washington. "The foreign policy of the United States, which reflects the imperialist tendencies of American monopolistic capital, is characterized in the postwar period by a striving *for world supremacy*," Novikov wrote to Foreign Minister Vyacheslav Molotov (who underlined the last three words). "This is the real meaning of the many statements by President Truman and other representatives of American ruling circles: that the United States has the right to lead the world."[12]

The establishment of Soviet-type regimes in postwar Eastern Europe provided an occasion to judge just how the Soviets conceptualized their social system.[13] In Soviet-style socialism, nationalization of industry and trade was an essential element, as was collectivization (in countries with small-farming peasantries). Old elites had to be suppressed and new elites created by "promoting" workers and peasants and their children. Religion was repressed and sometimes persecuted. Nationalism was stigmatized as "bourgeois," and the schools tried to inculcate internationalist principles. Citizens were encouraged to denounce wrongdoers to the state authorities. Education and medical care was free and organized by the state. Like the Soviet Union itself, the new East European regimes were welfare states, though the level of expenditure on social services was much lower (with education a partial exception) than that of the richer nations of Western Europe.

In Western Europe, both social-democratic and communist parties had substantial popular support in the postwar years. The latter caused considerable alarm to the United States, which, in its capacity as leader of the Western (capitalist, democratic) camp, shared some of Stalin's concern about maintaining the appropriate social system. But perhaps the most noteworthy development from our perspective lay elsewhere, in the shift toward welfare-state policies and other forms of state intervention (including selective nationalization) that occurred throughout Western Europe after the war. Such policies were part of the prewar socialist agenda; and in some cases, notably the British, they were introduced by a socialist government. But this was not always the case. Even nonsocialist governments found themselves introducing extensive social insurance and national health schemes, broadening educational access, and building low-cost public housing.

As the welfare-state principle became accepted in Europe, and indeed in much of the industrialized world, it lost much of its early identification with socialism—except in the United States, where (despite the welfare policies introduced during the New Deal) "socialized medicine" was still an ideological bugbear. In general, however, the state's responsibility to ensure a basic level of welfare for all its citizens (implying, of course, considerable expansion of the state bureaucracy and increased taxation to cover the costs) was not seriously challenged after the war, even by conservatives, until the emergence of Thatcherism and the ideologies of the New Right in the 1980s.

In the postwar United States, fear of communism at home and abroad dominated political discourse. The American public and politicians believed that the communist ideology of the Soviet Union meant that it sought world domination regardless of the cost. Eastern Europe was the prime demonstration of Soviet expansionist intentions. The victory of the Chinese Communists (seen in the United States as Moscow's agents) provided further confirmation in 1949; and the North Korean attack on South Korea in June 1950 was similarly interpreted as part of a global strategy of communist aggression directed from the Kremlin. Each side demonized the other during the cold war: in American postwar thinking, the concept of international communism became a conspiracy theory, just as the concept of imperialism was on the Soviet side.

American fears of communist subversion reached their height in the new Red Scare of the early 1950s, epitomized by the investigations of communist subversion conducted in a blaze of publicity by Senator Joseph McCarthy and the House Committee on Un-American Activities. This episode differed from its precursor, the Red Scare of 1919–1920, in focusing primarily on elites, especially intellectuals and the members of the federal bureaucracy, and involving a theatrical element of public self-criticism that bore a strange resemblance to the rituals of the Communist purge practiced in the Soviet Union. In one of the mirror images characteristic of the period, the American anticommunist witch-hunt was matched by the Soviet "anticosmopolitan campaign," whose targets were Jews, intellectuals who had been overinfluenced by Western culture, and other "agents of American imperialism."

The adjective "totalitarian" came into journalistic as well as intellectual discourse in the United States in the cold war period.[14] The original (prewar) model for a totalitarian political system—that is, a dictatorship with aspirations to total control over its citizens, à la George Orwell's *1984*, with a mobilizing party, an explicit ideology, and a vigilant secret police—was Nazi Germany. While there were good intellectual reasons for applying the totalitarian model to the Soviet Union, there were also good cold war political reasons (just as there were for the Soviet analysis of the postwar United States as imperialist). The totalitarian label put the Soviet Union in the same category as the recent hated wartime enemy. In an analytical realignment that involved repudiation of the prewar political antithesis of left and right, totalitarian became an antithesis for democracy. This opened up future possibilities for socialists who were not Moscow-oriented communists to extricate themselves from the old "Left" continuum linking reformist socialism to communism. In the immediate postwar years, however, "socialism" was still almost as pejorative a word in popular American usage as "communism."

## Third World Socialism and National Liberation Movements

For the great powers in the postwar world, socialism (communism) scarcely had meaning outside of their confrontation. But it was a different matter in the rest of the world, most dramatically in those countries emerging from colonial status with the collapse of the British, French, and Dutch empires in the wake of the Second World War. In almost all of these emerging countries in the Third World, a small class of native intellectuals, usually educated in the West, provided an ideology for the new postcolonial state regime that combined nationalism, anti-imperialism, and socialism. In this context, "socialism" meant primarily an anti-imperialist ideology for the independence struggle and, after independence, for extensive state control and intervention in the economy.

From the perspective of the decolonizing Third World, the value of Soviet socialism was primarily as a model for rapid economic modernization without dependence on foreign capital in a backward country. This was in many ways a more realistic interpretation of Soviet experience than the one prevalent in European socialist circles before the war, which treated the Russia of 1917 as roughly on a par with other modern, industrialized European states, and accepted at face value Bolshevik claims about the strength and so-called maturity of the Russian proletariat. To some Western scholars, it suggested a new reading of the historical significance of Marxism as an ideology of modernization.[15]

China, however, had an even greater appeal than the Soviet Union as a developmental model for the Third World. It was a more recent example of state-directed socialist modernization, and, unlike the Soviet Union, was neither integrated into a Euro-American geopolitical world nor bashful about acknowledging that it was a predominantly peasant country whose experience had much in common with that of colonial Asia and Africa. The Chinese Communists who took power in 1949 had just emerged from a national liberation struggle against the Japanese, in addition to the country's earlier experience of competing Western imperialisms at the turn of the century, and they were eager to encourage others on the same path.

The common context of Third World socialism may be summarized as follows: a colonial heritage; a low level of urbanization, industrial development, and labor organization (which made the classical Marxist emphasis on the proletariat irrelevant); and a small native elite, including some Western-educated intellectuals, that tended to view private entrepreneurship with suspicion and assumed that the state had to take the lead in economic life as well as in building a sense of nationhood.

For a large number of newly emergent nations after the Second World War, primarily those that had been under British rule, independence was achieved as a result of the imperial power's decision to depart. In this context—for example, India under Nehru, Sri Lanka (formerly Ceylon) under S.W.R.D. Bandaranaike, Ghana under Kwame Nkrumah, or Tanzania under Julius Nyerere—the socialism of the new regimes had little revolutionary content and focused on state economic planning, selective nationalization, control of foreign investment, and social welfare policies.

Where Third World countries had to fight for independence, socialism had a different meaning, with a much sharper anti-imperialist and revolutionary thrust. The most familiar example is Vietnam, where the Vietminh—led by Ho Chi Minh, whose Marxism went back to Paris circa 1920 and whose revolutionary experience started in the Comintern—fought first the French and then the Americans in a war that lasted three decades. The term "national liberation movement" came into use in the 1970s for independence movements emphasizing armed struggle, strongly hostile to the West and Western imperialism, using mobilization techniques similar to those of the Chinese Communist Party in its revolutionary struggle, and advocating some form of socialist transformation of society as a revolutionary goal. In addition to the Algerian FLN (one of the few national liberation movements that was not explicitly Marxist), such movements included the MPLA in Angola, FRELIMO in Mozambique, SWAPO in Southwest Africa, and the ANC in South Africa.

The same term came to be used for Latin American guerrilla movements in countries that already had political independence but sought both to overthrow a reactionary government at home and to escape from foreign economic imperialism. These movements espoused different variants of socialism, ranging from the Sandinistas in Nicaragua to the "Shining Path" in Peru, but hostility to "Yankee imperialism" was a common thread. Fidel Castro's Cuba was an inspiration for such movements (though Castro's socialist ideology and strong Soviet connections were acquired only *after* the 1959 Revolution), as was Che Guevara, the Argentine-born hero of the Cuban Revolution, who was killed in 1967 while leading a guerrilla movement in Bolivia.

Third World socialism, especially in its more revolutionary guise, became closely linked with the cold war rivalries of the superpowers. Its anti-imperialist component had a strongly anti-American tinge, since the United States was seen in the Third World as assuming the "white man's burden" laid down by the declining European powers; and the United States for many years saw national liberation movements purely as Moscow's (or possibly Beijing's) pawns in the global advance of world communism.

The Soviet Union, though not really very interested in national independence movements even after Stalin (who had ignored them almost completely), started trying to exploit the opportunities inherent in this situation in the second half of the 1950s. Two well-known early examples, the flirtation with Nasser in Egypt and Sukarno in Indonesia, ended badly and left the Soviet Union with a skeptical attitude to the socialist pretensions of Third World nationalist leaders. By the 1970s, however, the Soviet Union had acquired some enthusiasm for playing games with Third World clients, not out of any belief in their socialist potential, but because it was felt to enhance the Soviet Union's status as a superpower. In most Third World conflicts of the 1970s and 1980s, the contending parties established themselves as clients of the two superpowers (for example, India/Pakistan; Somalia/Ethiopia; Israel/the Arab states of the Middle East), adopting a rhetoric of "socialism" or "democracy" that suited the patron but otherwise often had little relation to reality.[16]

More ideologically fervent support for national liberation movements came from China and Cuba, which helped to the best of their ability with men and matériel, especially in Africa. These countries, and the Soviet Union as well, also provided various forms of training, ranging from general education at institutions like the Lumumba "Friendship" University in Moscow to guerrilla warfare camps, for Third World sympathizers and revolutionaries.

### "Socialism Has Become Banal"

In the First and Second Worlds, socialism had different trajectories in the 1960s and 1970s. In the communist bloc, Nikita Khrushchev's denunciation of Stalin at the Twentieth Party Congress in 1956 set off shock waves, even though his criticism was directed mainly at the Great Purges and Stalin's personality cult, leaving untouched the basic institutions of the Stalin period, including collectivization, and acquitting the Communist Party of any responsibility for Stalin's crimes. The Hungarian revolt of 1956 was put down by Soviet troops, but for Eastern Europe as a whole this was the beginning of a gradual process of extrication from Soviet cultural controls and the economic exploitation that had characterized the early postwar years. The limits of this liberalization were indicated in 1968, when Soviet tanks were sent into Czechoslovakia to crush Alexander Dubcek's experiment with "socialism with a human face." But at the beginning of the 1980s, a much more significant challenge from Poland's Solidarity movement passed without military intervention.

In the Soviet Union itself, attempts to revitalize the economy and make the clumsy central planning apparatus more flexible proved largely unavailing; living standards rose, but not as fast as expectations; and the cultural liberalization and reopening to the West that many educated Russians were waiting for failed to materialize. As the Chinese never tired of pointing out after the acrimonious Sino-Soviet split in the late 1950s, socialist convictions had become a deficit commodity in the Soviet Union. The Communist Party still paid lip service to Marxism, but it was harder to find a serious Marxist in the Soviet Union than in virtually any other country in the world. While Lenin remained a national hero, the Second World War had almost displaced the October Revolution in national mythology by the 1980s, and the aging war veterans who dominated the party had as little in common with the Bolsheviks of 1917 as they had with the coming generation of cautiously Westernizing blue-jeans wearers. Political dissidents made their appearance and were repressed, but in a halfhearted manner, and to the accompaniment of maximum publicity in the West that trickled back to the Soviet Union via samizdat and foreign radio broadcasts.

Among Western intellectuals of the Left, disenchantment with Soviet-style socialism took hold with Khrushchev's Secret Speech in 1956 and increased greatly after the 1968 invasion of Czechoslovakia. By the end of the 1970s, Alexander Solzhenitsyn's *Gulag Archipelago* had become the dominant trope for Soviet socialism—even, or perhaps especially, in Paris, where leading intellectuals like Jean-Paul Sartre had previously cultivated a rather perverse attachment to the Soviet Union. At the same time, however, Third World socialism was making its way back to the First World via the student revolution of 1968, the rise of the New Left, and the mounting opposition to the Vietnam War in the United States. While the New Left undoubtedly owed much to the Old Left,[17] it was the Third World that provided many of its heroes and theorists, including Che Guevara, Fidel Castro, Mao Zedong, and Frantz Fanon.

In the mid-1970s, Eurocommunism made a brief appearance on the historical stage when the leaders of the Italian, Spanish, and French communist parties decided to cast off Moscow's tutelage, drop the "obsolete" notions of the necessity of revolution and the dictatorship of the proletariat, and seek "a democratic path to socialism." This was accompanied by a critique of Soviet socialism that in many respects echoed those made by Trotsky in *The Revolution Betrayed* (1937) and the Yugoslav Communist Milovan Djilas in *The New Class* (1957).[18]

The waning of the cold war, the waxing of the welfare state, the political reappraisals associated with Vietnam, and, finally, Eurocommunism all contributed to a revised view of socialism in the United States. The old North American aversion to socialism now seemed an idiosyncratic prejudice, as a *New Yorker* commentator wrote in 1978, for in Europe socialism was not a millenarian dream but a mundane reality. In Western Europe, the piece read, "No-one resists Socialism. There is no moral opposition. Socialism has become banal, like democracy."[19]

## The End of Socialism?

In 1989, Mikhail Gorbachev's energetic efforts to revitalize and democratize the Soviet system led him to indicate to Eastern Europe that there, too, radical reform was permissible. The effect was dramatic: within months, communist regimes all over Eastern Europe had fallen, the Berlin Wall was down, and Germany was reunified. Back in the USSR, the Communist Party formally renounced its monopoly of power. As the center's grip weakened, demands for republican and regional autonomy (coming as much from local political elites as populations) multiplied. The Baltic States, following Eastern Europe's lead, were the first Soviet republics to achieve independence. At the end of 1991, Gorbachev was overthrown, and the 74-year-old Union of Soviet Socialist Republics was pronounced dead. The new leaders of Russia and the other successor states (former communists almost to a man) swiftly repudiated socialism and declared their allegiance to capitalism, nationalism, and democracy.

As of March 1997, the socialist camp (that is, countries with communist regimes) had shrunk to a pitiful handful: China (apparently taking its own capitalist road, but with the old regime still in charge), Cuba, Laos, North Korea, and Vietnam.[20] By universal agreement, the cold war was over. In the opinion of many, moreover, its end also marked a decisive ideological victory for capitalism and democracy that amounted to the end of socialism. One excited Hegelian called it "the end of history."[21] Vaclav Havel, first post-communist leader of Czechoslovakia, described it as "the end of the modern era"—that "era of belief in automatic progress brokered by the scientific method" in which truth seemed objectively knowable, and the advancement of the human race could be rationally planned.[22]

The astonishing geopolitical upheavals of 1989–1991 are the main reason for the recent spate of announcements of the end of socialism. But several secondary causes should be noted. At the end of the 1970s, for the first time since the Second World War, the expansion of welfare states throughout the industrialized world was halted by recession, and the spiraling costs and bureaucratization of social services were widely criticized. In Britain, the Thatcher government, in power for most of the 1980s, set about dismantling many of the policies put in place by Clement Attlee's Labour government forty years earlier. The whole principle of state intervention came under sustained attack from the New Right in the United States, Britain, and elsewhere throughout the decade; privatization was its buzzword. Current economic thinking was strongly in favor of the market and against government intervention, and few economists were willing to defend the economic rationality of public ownership, even of railroads, postal services, and utilities. Not only in North America and Western Europe, but also in countries as diverse as Japan, Turkey, New Zealand, Malaysia, Argentina, Singapore, Mexico, and Brazil, public assets were being sold off by governments at a rapid clip, basically for ideological reasons.[23]

If there are many arguments in favor of the "end of socialism" hypothesis, there are also arguments against it. In the first place, it is essentially a First and Second World picture, which has little to do with the state of socialism in the Third World. From the standpoint of guerrilla fighters in Latin America, the collapse of the Soviet Union is not a highly significant event, though it no doubt ranks above the pruning of welfare-state budgets in Northern Europe. For intellectuals in Latin America, as in most of the non-Islamic regions of the Third World, Marxism is still the dominant discourse.

In the second place, the claim that socialism is dead, for all its apparent universal sweep, has to be understood partly in parochial terms as a product of conflicts within American academia. Whatever has been happening to Marxism elsewhere in the world, for the last ten to fifteen years it has been flourishing as never before on American university campuses, primarily among faculty members in the humanities and social sciences. In this new "postmodern" version of Marxism, a key concept (drawn from the Italian socialist Antonio Gramsci rather than directly from Marx) is cultural hegemony. It is more often applied in the context of gender or ethnicity than in the traditional context of class; the focus of "class struggle" has shifted to the resistance to white male dominance in academia and the society at large. Proponents of the "death of socialism" view are at least partly reacting to (and against) this phenomenon.

The proposition that socialism is dead obviously has a partisan political aspect. Yet its appeal has been wider than that, primarily because of the very widely held impression that the events of 1989–1991 signified the end of an era.[24] Of course, "the end of an era" and "the end of socialism" are two different concepts (all the more since, as noted earlier in this article, few people in the West ever characterized the twentieth century as an age of socialism). But apocalypses are easy to conflate, especially by those who have just lived through them, and the apocalyptic mood makes it easy to overgeneralize. If it is reasonable to assert, for example, that the belief in state ownership of the means of production as a mechanism for achieving social justice has been widely discredited, the broader claim that the aspiration for social justice itself has been discredited must be treated much more cautiously.

Has the end of what historian Eric Hobsbawm called the "short twentieth century" marked a definitive collapse of socialism as a widely held ideal and generator of practices? That question has no simple answer. Socialism is one of those powerful but amorphous phenomena, capable of multiple and ingenious mutations, whose death tends to be proclaimed frequently but not usually persuasively. Generally what has been noticed is the withering of a part, not the extinction of the whole. Nevertheless, death—or exhaustion of the ability to mutate—does occur: for example, a religion may disappear, or an institution such as monarchy lose its vitality. This may happen gradually, or it may occur as the result of a cataclysmic event, the equivalent of the great meteorite that some scientists think wiped out the dinosaurs. It is possible that socialism (in its twentieth-century guise) has suffered that kind of massive assault; it is also possible, perhaps even likely, that once again the news of its death has been exaggerated. But these are judgments better left to twenty-first century historians. The great lesson to be learned from history is that history has more imagination than we have, and may still have a trick or two up its sleeve.

ENDNOTES

1. Second edition, 1989. My thanks to Jonathan Bone for his indefatigable and imaginative research assistance in the writing of this article.
2. The *Oxford English Dictionary*, 2d ed. (1989) gives the following definitions of communism:

   1a. A theory which advocates a state of society in which there should be no private ownership, all property being vested in the community and labor being organized for the common benefit of all members; the professed principle being that each should work according to his capacity, and receive according to his needs.
   b. A political doctrine or movement based on Marxism and later developed by Lenin, seeking the overthrow of capitalism through a proletarian revolution.

3. W. Sombart, *Warum gibt es in den Vereinigten Staaten keinen Sozialismus?* (Tübingen: 1906). Translated by Patricia M. Hocking and C. T. Husbands as *Why Is There No Socialism in the United States?* (White Plains, N.Y.: International Arts and Sciences, 1976). This question has since been addressed by several generations of American sociologists and labor historians. See, for example, John M. Laslett and Seymour Martin Lipset, *Failure of a Dream? Essays in the History of American Socialism* (Garden City, N.Y.: Anchor Press, 1974).
4. Sombart, *Why Is There No Socialism*, p. 20.
5. Leon Trotsky, *Terrorism and Communism: A Reply to Karl Kautsky* (1920; reprint, Ann Arbor: University of Michigan Press, 1961), p. 55. Karl Kautsky's similarly titled work was written in 1918–1919.
6. The Bolsheviks adopted the name of the Russian (later Soviet) Communist Party in 1918.
7. An exception should be made for the social welfare legislation enacted by socialist/labor governments in Sweden and New Zealand in the second half of the 1930s.
8. See Sylvia R. Margulies, *The Pilgrimage to Russia: The Soviet Union and the Treatment of Foreigners, 1924–1937* (Madison: University of Wisconsin Press, 1968); and Paul Hollander, *Political Pilgrims: Travels of Western Intellectuals to the Soviet Union, China, and Cuba, 1928–1978* (New York: Oxford University Press, 1981).
9. Isaac Deutscher, *The Prophet Outcast: Trotsky, 1929–1940* (London: Oxford University Press, 1963). For Trotsky's characterization of Stalinism, see Leon Trotsky, *The Revolution Betrayed* (Garden City, N.Y.: Doubleday, Doran, 1937).
10. V. I. Lenin, *Imperialism—The Highest Stage of Capitalism* (written 1916).

11. See Edward Shils, "The Intellectuals in the Political Development of the New States," *World Politics* 12 (1960):3.

12. "The Novikov Telegram (Washington, September 27, 1946)," in *Origins of the Cold War. The Novikov, Kennan, and Roberts "Long Telegrams" of 1946* (Washington, D.C.: U.S. Institute of Peace, 1991), p. 3.

13. For some fascinating insights into the first stages of imposition of a Soviet-type system, see Jan Tomasz Gross, *Revolution from Abroad: The Soviet Conquest of Poland's Western Ukraine and Western Belorussia* (Princeton: Princeton University Press, 1988).

14. See Abbott Gleason, *Totalitarianism: The Inner History of the Cold War* (New York: Oxford University Press, 1995).

15. See Adam B. Ulam, "The Historical Role of Marxism," in *The New Face of Soviet Totalitarianism* (Cambridge: Harvard University Press, 1963).

16. On Soviet attitudes to Third World socialism, see Jerry F. Hough, *The Struggle for the Third World: Soviet Debates and American Options* (Washington, D.C.: Brookings Institution, 1986).

17. See Maurice Isserman, *If I Had a Hammer . . . The Death of the Old Left and the Birth of the New Left* (New York: Basic Books, 1987).

18. Milovan Djilas, *The New Class* (New York: Praeger, 1957). For a classic statement of Eurocommunist principles by the leader of the Spanish Communist Party, see Santiago Carrillo, *Eurocommunism and the State* (Westport, Conn.: L. Hill, 1978).

19. William Pfaff, "The European Left," *The New Yorker*, 7 August 1978, p. 58.

20. From *World Almanac and Book of Facts 1996* (New York: 1996). China is classified as a "Communist Party-led state" rather than a communist state. Azerbaijan and Bosnia & Herzegovina are categorized as regimes "in transition."

21. Francis Fukuyama, *The End of History and The Last Man* (New York: Free Press, 1992).

22. Vaclav Havel, "The End of the Modern Era," *The New York Times*, 1 March 1992, p. 15.

23. See John D. Donahue, *The Privatization Decision: Public Ends, Private Means* (New York: Basic Books, 1989), p. 6.

24. See, for example, Eric Hobsbawm, *The Age of Extremes: A History of the World, 1914–1991* (New York: Pantheon, 1994), whose image of the "short twentieth century" gives the collapse of the Soviet Union a significance as an epoch-closing event comparable to that of the outbreak of the First World War.

SELECTED REFERENCES

Aguilar, Luis E. *Marxism in Latin America*. New York: 1968.

Aspaturian, Vernon V., Jiri Valenta, and David P. Burke, eds. *Eurocommunism Between East and West*. Bloomington: 1980.

Braunthal, Julius. *History of the International*. Trans. Henry Collins and Kenneth Mitchell. 3 vols. New York and Boulder, Colo., 1967–1980.

Cohen, Stephen F. *Bukharin and the Bolshevik Revolution*. New York: 1983.

Cole, G. D. H. *A History of Socialist Thought*, 5 vols. in 7 parts. London: 1953–1960.

Desfosses, Helen and Jacques Levesque, eds. *Socialism in the Third World*. New York: 1975.

Diggins, John P. *The Rise and Fall of the American Left*. New York: 1992.

Friedmann, R. R., N. Gilbert, and M. Schere, eds. *Modern Welfare States*. New York: 1987.

Johnson, Chalmers A. *Peasant Nationalism and Communist Power*. Stanford: 1962.

Lewin, Moshe. *The Making of the Soviet System*. New York: 1985.

McFarlane, S. Neil. *Superpower Rivalry and Third World Radicalism: The Idea of National Liberation*. Baltimore: 1985.

Paterson, W. E., and I. Campbell. *Social Democracy in Post-War Europe*. London: 1974.

Rakowska-Harmstone, Teresa and Andrew Gyorgy, eds. *Communism in Eastern Europe*. Bloomington: 1979.

Rose, Saul. *Socialism in Southern Asia*. Oxford: 1959.

Schwartz, Benjamin. *Chinese Communism and the Rise of Mao*. Cambridge: 1951.

# 10   The International Order

AKIRA IRIYE

## International and Regional Orders

At the beginning of the twentieth century, the international order was essentially definable as an interplay among the European powers. As the century draws to its close, the global order is much less unitary. It is constituted, at one level, by the advanced industrialized nations (collectively known as the "G-3 World," or the United States, Western Europe, and Japan) and, at another, by the increasingly self-assertive "Third World," as well as by countries that until recently formed the socialist bloc. It is far from clear whether the earlier European-dominated international order or the more diverse situation today is more conducive to global stability. At least it should be recognized that the twentieth century has witnessed various definitions of international order. To trace them is to become aware of the forces that shape a given world community—or that undermine it and bring about an alternative order. This essay will first briefly outline changing definitions of world order that have appeared in this century and then look more closely at the development of internationalism, a force that has contributed to shaping some of the more enduring definitions.

The history of twentieth-century international affairs began with what would prove to be the last stage of the age of European domination. The international order was then defined by the European powers not simply through their military force but also through their economic and cultural resources. Together they accounted for more than two thirds of the world's manufacturing output, nearly three quarters of trade, and virtually all of capital export. Among them the European powers divided much of the rest of the world into their colonies and spheres of influence, linking these areas to Europe economically as well as politically. Scientific discoveries and technological innovations originating in Europe spread all over the world in the form of railways, transoceanic cables, cameras, and bicycles as well as modern schools and hospitals. European ideas of nationalism, equality, human rights, social justice, and myriad others influenced people elsewhere. In war and in peace, it was the great powers that defined the terms of interstate behavior: military strategy, international law, arbitration, peace making, treaties, diplomatic etiquette. It was to Europe that men and women in other parts of the world went to study specialized subjects, to train as artists and musicians, to travel and marvel at products of modern civilization.

That era of European dominance ended with the great powers' fratricide during 1914–1918, when they squandered their resources in mutual slaughter and destruction that they were not able to put an end to until the United States intervened. That, more than anything else, heralded the coming of the age of American power. To be sure, the United States had always constituted part of the West, and economically and technologically had already caught up with the most advanced European nations. In international affairs, however, the nation had functioned essentially as a junior partner before the war, willing to take the initiative in imposing regional order only in the Caribbean. The First World War changed the picture, with the United States not only contributing to the military victory of one side but also taking the initiative in the postwar peace conference to emerge as the major creditor and trading nation in the world. It was not that the European powers were now eclipsed in the international scene. Despite the war, many of them still retained their empires, rebuilt their armed forces, and continued to wield tremendous cultural influence over the rest of the world. Nevertheless, they now had to share their role as definers of international order with the United States.

In a sense as a harbinger of later developments, the First World War also brought Japan to the international arena. Hitherto its role had primarily been to fit into the European-defined system of big-power politics. The war enabled Japan to extend its influence in Asia and the Pacific at the expense of European powers, and to try to impose its own definition of regional order. It is also noteworthy that, with the declining prestige of Europe and the rise of radical anticolonialism emanating from the new Bolshevik regime in Russia, some colonial or semicolonial countries (China, Korea, Vietnam, India, Indonesia, Turkey, Egypt, etc.) began to agitate for a greater measure of autonomy, challenging the control exercised by the powers. In this sense, too, the First World War forevisaged subsequent developments.

The global order that had prevailed before the war may be said to have become regionalized in its aftermath. If the United States had joined the League of Nations, and if the depression had not put a temporary halt to the capacity of American financial resources to develop an interdependent global economic order, the nation might then have emerged as the new world hegemon. In reality, however, during the interwar years (1919–1939) there grew a tendency toward the establishment of regional orders. International relations in Europe were first defined by the Locarno treaties (1925), then by their breakdown following the Nazi seizure of power in Germany (1933), by the antagonism between the fascist and antifascist states (the latter led by the Soviet Union), and eventually by a Nazi-Soviet rapprochement (1939) that led to the German invasion of Poland and the outbreak of the Second World War. In most of this drama of the European regional order, the United States had little direct involvement. But it was quite active in the Western Hemisphere, where it promoted a new principle (the good neighbor policy) for regional order, and in the Pacific, where an attempt at regional stability first bore fruit in a series of disarmament agreements (1921–1922, 1930) which ultimately broke down, discarded by Japan in the 1930s. In the meantime on the Asian mainland, Japan sought to establish a new order, combining Asia's people and resources in a conscious challenge to Western influence. The regionalist tendencies had an economic dimension in that, at least during the 1930s, each region tended to develop as a closely interconnected trading bloc or, as in the case of Europe, to become divided into sub-blocs. Culturally, too, there grew an emphasis on regional, national, and racial distinctiveness, as exemplified by Germany's Aryan racism, the Soviet Union's Russian nationalism, and Japan's pan-Asianism. The situation at this level was not so much international order as international chaos. The only possible "order" might have been a world defined in terms of two confronting blocs, one consisting of the Axis (Germany, Italy, Japan, Spain) and the other of the democracies (the United States, Britain, Western Europe), with the Soviet Union possibly joining the former.

In this context, the Second World War signaled the collapse of such a possible ordering. Instead of joining the Axis, the Soviet Union found itself at war with them, and the anti-Axis forces transformed themselves into a United Nations alliance, envisaged as a new structure of international order. The victory of the allies was thus to have been translated into a postwar structure of international affairs, though in reality, of course, the world then was just as divided as it had been in the 1930s. Here again, the role of the Soviet Union was crucial. Instead of joining the United States and other wartime allies in establishing a new order, it chose to stay out, distancing itself from the Western powers and consolidating its own spheres of influence.

The confrontation between the two groups of nations, or the cold war, thus defined the postwar international order. It was a situation neither of war nor of peace. We may argue whether the bipolar structure generated insecurity and uncertainty in all parts of the globe, or whether it developed its own system of stability. That some stability emerged—at least in the sense that there would be no third world war—was due in part to the possession by the United States and the Soviet Union of nuclear weapons. The "balance of terror" became translated into the "long peace" as neither superpower wished to destroy itself and its allies in a nuclear war, the only type of warfare imaginable between the two hostile camps.

In the drama of world affairs from the Second World War to the cold war era, Europe (outside of the Soviet Union) and Japan inevitably lost their influence. Once again the European powers had to turn to the United States to help bring their war to an end and promote their postwar reconstruction and security, whereas in Asia Japanese ambitions for an alternative structure of regional order had been dashed. Japan became, after 1945, a minor part of the U.S.-defined Asian-Pacific alliance system, which pitted itself against the Soviet-Chinese combination after China came under communist domination.

As there had been earlier, there were economic and cultural dimensions to the evolving international order. The Second World War, of course, mobilized all the economic and cultural resources the two alliance systems could marshal, and the victory of the United Nations implied that their economic interests and cultural influences would determine the nature of the postwar order. Because of the preeminence of the United States during and after the war, this would mean a world in which the American policies of open, interdependent economic exchanges and cross-cultural relations would be vigorously promoted. Indeed, the Atlantic Charter (August 1941) enunciated these principles, and during the war the United States energetically pushed for a postwar system of unrestricted economic transactions as well as cultural interchanges of the kind associated with the Fulbright programs for student and scholarly exchanges. The onset of the cold war meant, on the other hand, that these instruments for creating a unified international order would not be universally applied. Soviet-bloc countries did not participate in the global economic organizations such as the International Monetary Fund or the World Bank, nor did they associate themselves with American-initiated cultural exchanges. Rather, they developed their own trading arrangements and organized international ideological initiatives through the Cominform.

The international order defined by the cold war lasted for nearly a quarter century. Around 1970, however, it began to be significantly transformed. A number of factors contributed to this. The bipolar confrontation still defined one aspect, the geopolitical dimension, of international affairs, but it was no longer the only definition of international order. Indeed, even this bipolarity changed its character as the superpowers were unwilling to use their arsenals to engage in war; it was bound to happen sooner or later that they would determine to relax tensions and reduce the level of their armament, which was costing them enormous sums of money. Starting in the 1970s, Washington and Moscow entered into various agreements to limit their nuclear and conventional arms. With cold war tensions easing, the Soviet Union steadily lost its powerful status in the world, leaving the United States as the sole superpower by the early 1990s. In the meantime, economically relentless forces were creating a more integrated world order. Different regions of the globe were more interconnected than ever before through trade, investment, and other activities that cut across cold war divisions. The economic performances of Western European countries and Japan were particularly impressive, and their expanding trade and investment activities were truly worldwide.

The years following the late 1960s also witnessed the emergence of regional orders. Of course, various parts of the world had developed their uniquely local issues that had little to do with the cold war, but during the 1970s and the 1980s well-defined regional orders outside the bipolar framework began to emerge. In Europe, forces for closer regional integration crystallized in the successful functioning of the European Community. It was as if Europe, which had lost its centrality in international affairs after the First World War, was regaining some of the lost ground. Asia, in the meantime, was for the first time developing its own regional identity. Not the kind that Japan had sought to impose during the 1930s, this new Asian order was more a product of impressive economic performances by China (both the mainland and Taiwan), South Korea, and the countries belonging to the Association of Southeast Asian Nations. Although much less cohesive politically and ethnically than Europe, Asia's rise nevertheless indicated that not just Japan but other countries in the area were now ready to define their own position in world affairs. The fact that Asian countries had their own distinctive cultural traditions was significant, for it meant that the international order was becoming culturally diverse. This was even more the case in the Middle East, where the Islamic religion defined its culture, oil its economy, and the Arab-Israeli confrontation its politics. None of these had much to do with the U.S.-USSR confrontation; in fact, the superpowers were quite helpless in coping with the challenges of Islamic fundamentalism, increases in oil prices, or Arab hostility toward Israel.

Such complex developments at the regional level, however, should not obscure another significant phenomenon: with the easing of cold war tensions, there emerged a sense of global unity and order for the first time since the end of the Second World War. This is evidenced in the participation of the People's Republic of China, the two Germanys, and the two Koreas in the United Nations; the world organization's peacekeeping operations with full backing from all members of the security council; and the activities of many international agencies under the aegis of the United Nations—such as the International Atomic Energy Agency, the World Intellectual Property Organization, the Stockholm conference on the human environment (1972), and the ongoing conference on the law of the sea (first convened in 1958 but meeting more regularly since 1973). As will be noted below, forces promoting such instances of international cooperation have existed throughout the twentieth century, but in the recent decades they have become more visible and more effective.

This brief summary suggests that the century has witnessed various patterns of international order: one defined by the European powers, the interwar regional system, the world divided into two contesting blocs (Axis vs. the United Nations; the United States and its allies vs. the Soviet Union and its allies), and, more recently, the as yet insufficiently characterizable post-cold war system, which combines the military might of the United States as the sole superpower, economic expansion in many lands, and Third World self-consciousness. Through all these processes of transformation, forces of internationalism, oriented toward cross-national endeavors, have played a conspicuous role. It is to an examination of these forces that we must now turn.

## Nationalism and Internationalism

International order by definition supposes the prior existence of nations. The crudest definition of international order, therefore, is simply a given world system consisting of a multiplicity of nations, each pursuing its own power and interests. The sum total of these pursuits constitutes a given state of international affairs. That is why, since the seventeenth century when modern nation-states made their appearance in Europe, nationalism has often appeared to be the only durable framework for understanding international relations. At the same time, however, nations do enter into agreement with one another to stabilize their interrelationships and, by implication, to contribute to establishing some semblance of order in the world. Without those agreements, there would only be "laws of the jungle" in international relations. Realizing this, seventeenth-century European statesmen and jurists developed concepts of international law, a set of certain principles and codes that should guide the behavior of nations in war and peace. Whether international law was to be regarded as an equivalent of natural (and therefore universally applicable) law or simply as a set of expedient rules to serve specific purposes in particular circumstances was never resolved, but at least by the late eighteenth century the idea of international law as holding primacy over domestic law had become accepted in principle. In other words, even as sovereign nations sought to protect and expand their interests, they were expected to abide by certain codes governing the conduct of a multiplicity of nations. To accept such a commitment presupposed a view of the world which was not all chaos but, on the contrary, contained elements of order. That is to say, international order would mean not any given state of interrelationships among sovereign nations but a conscious creation, a normative state of affairs among nations. Here were the origins of internationalism. It is clear that the idea of international order is inherent in, and requires, an internationalist proposition.

A remarkable development of international relations in the twentieth century has been the growth of internationalism. This may seem strange at first sight, given the century's calamitous world wars resulting in millions of casualties as well as costly arms races endangering the whole of humanity. Perhaps because of these very tragedies, however, efforts have been made to strengthen internationalism as a better alternative to war, destruction, and disorder. By definition, internationalism aims at transcending national interests as the only framework for international relations and seeks to link nations so that together they may promote the well-being of the whole world, or at least of larger units than independent national entities. For this reason, the best expressions of internationalism are agreements among nations to pursue common objectives as well as international organizations and agencies that serve the shared interests of member nations. In both these instances, the twentieth century has recorded a remarkable history.

Neither international agreements nor organizations are unique to the century, to be sure. Even if we exclude peace treaties and commercial accords, because they pertain essentially to adjustments of differences among sovereign nations, we may point to such significant instances of nineteenth-century internationalism as the 1856 agreement on neutral rights, the Red Cross's founding during the Crimean War, numerous international expositions (or world's fairs), the 1899 Hague conference to explore limitations on armaments, and various worldwide organizations aimed at universalizing certain modern services (e.g., the mail, telegraphic communication) and activities (e.g., associations of scientists and doctors). One should also add to the list various peace organizations (e.g., the World Peace Congress, headquartered in London) which coalesced the religious pacifism of several countries; similarly religious but more socially oriented YMCAs and YWCAs; businessmen's philanthropic associations like the Rotary Club; and, on the part of workers, the Socialist International, a worldwide activity of Marxists who believed that only through their combined solidarity could war be prevented.

One can see in these beginnings various types of internationalism. First there was legal internationalism, with its emphasis on international agreements to promote a more stable world order. Second, traditional religious pacifism continued to contribute to the idea of the unity of humanity, transcending parochial differences. Third was economic internationalism, whether capitalist or socialist, both alike promoting the cross-national solidarity of social classes. Fourth, what may be termed "cultural internationalism" comprised many activities dedicated to the proposition that cultural pursuits across national boundaries, in scientific, medical, communication, or other fields, would engender better understanding among peoples and thus enhance chances for a more peaceful world order.

The twentieth century has made use of this legacy and further enriched it. It should be noted that internationalism prior to the First World War was essentially a European phenomenon. Most international agreements, organizations, and activities were promoted by European governments and individuals, and others were hardly more than invited guests or bystanders. International cooperation often meant intra-European cooperation. Americans, to be sure, were part of the picture, but most initiatives for international organization and cooperation originated across the Atlantic. American internationalists wanted first and foremost to establish national organizations dedicated to the promotion of world order, such as the American Society of International Law, founded in 1905, or the Carnegie Endowment for International Peace, established in 1910. Few international associations had their headquarters in the United States. As for the rest of the world, whether Asia, the Middle East, or Latin America, most countries were not even invited to international congresses. Several did participate in world's fairs, but primarily in order to exhibit their exotic wares and artifacts. It is perhaps significant that the 1904 St. Louis Exposition, the last major event of the kind before the war, was predominantly a European and American affair. A world congress of arts and science that was held simultaneously in the same city brought together the world's leading artists, writers, and scholars, but among the hundreds of participants was only one from Japan, and none from any other country in Asia, the Middle East, or Africa.

Important beginnings for more comprehensive internationalism had to wait till after the European powers, in their act of fratricide, demonstrated the need for going much beyond the nineteenth-century legacy if the world were to be spared another such tragedy. After 1919, internationalism came to mean much more than intra-European cooperation. The United States would now play a central role, and other countries would become steadily drawn into the endeavor. The League of Nations, of course, was the most graphic example, not least because the participation of forty-four nations, including countries from Latin America, Asia, the Middle East, and North Africa, made the world organization look more like the real world than had any international association established earlier. Moreover, although neither the United States nor the Soviet Union joined the League, at least the former participated in the activities of such adjunct organizations as the International Labor Organization, the Permanent International Court of Justice, and the Intellectual Cooperation Organization.

These various bodies, especially the ILO and the ICO, were particularly significant as they reflected the then widespread conviction that matters such as capital-labor relations and the promotion of medical, scientific, artistic, and other cultural pursuits knew no national boundaries and that international cooperation in these spheres constituted a vital part of postwar world order. Cultural internationalism in this broad sense was viewed as the indispensable foundation of a stable international system. As the League of Nations Council asserted in 1921, "no association of nations can hope to exist without the spirit of reciprocal intellectual activity between its members." It was believed, in the words of the French poet, Paul Valéry, that the League of Nations at one level must be a league of intellect in which intellectuals of all countries would cooperate with one another to enhance their interaction and contribute to mutual understanding. Intellectual cooperation assumed that scholars, doctors, artists, literary figures, journalists, filmmakers, musicians, and many others could and should work together for common ends, serving as agents for internationalization—a term that gained its currency at that time. Specifically, they would organize multinational cultural conferences and exhibits, publish open letters addressing urgent problems of the day, exchange students and faculty among universities of different countries, collect information on the study and teaching of international relations, jointly produce educational movies, and try to influence the education of each country so as to promote better knowledge and understanding among peoples. These were ambitious projects, but enough individuals and groups in all parts of the world dedicated themselves to intellectual cooperation that the international order of the 1920s developed a distinctively cultural coloration.

To take one of the most important examples, under the League's Intellectual Cooperation Organization a committee on intellectual cooperation was established to function as the center of worldwide multinational cultural endeavors. It held annual meetings in Geneva, each time with a full agenda of activities. Many countries organized their own national committees on intellectual cooperation, including, besides Western European nations, the United States, Mexico, Venezuela, Brazil, Japan, China, India, Egypt, Poland, Czechoslovakia, and Hungary. Indeed, the records of ICO meetings indicate that countries such as India, Brazil, and Poland were among the most interested in the affairs of the organization, their governments contributing significant portions of its budgets. That they seriously believed in the need for developing cultural underpinnings for international order may be seen in their successful attempt at having the League put the question of "moral disarmament" on the agenda of the 1932 world disarmament conference. The idea was that no arms control agreement would be tenable unless sustained by peoples' and nations' psychological and moral preparedness for peace. Therefore, a disarmament agreement must be accompanied by specific educational programs for changing their attitudes on international issues. Nothing came either of arms limitation or moral disarmament at that time, but this example shows the degree to which cultural underpinnings of international order were taken seriously during the interwar years.

The League of Nations, of course, was but one instance of international organization. It was backed up by support groups (League of Nations associations) in many countries consisting of prominent citizens. The number of international bodies dealing with cultural matters mushroomed; in addition to medical, scientific, and technological societies that had existed earlier, hundreds of new ones were now created, ranging from a world congress of folk artists to a society of contemporary music. They held frequent world conferences, all equally dedicated to the proposition that such instances of intellectual cooperation should provide a solid foundation for international understanding and peace. One should also note in this connection student exchange programs that began to be promoted as an integral part of postwar internationalism. Not simply as individual endeavors, but through the sponsorship of government or newly established cultural-exchange organizations, students from universities and even schools would be sent abroad to train them to become "world citizens," a term that then gained currency. It is perhaps significant that the United States, even as it reversed its traditional open-immigration policy during the 1920s, welcomed more foreign students, especially from East Asia and Latin America, than ever before. There were also initiatives for the countries in those regions to bring in American students. The network was clearly expanding.

There was another sort of internationalism after the First World War—the Communist International, with its headquarters in Moscow and branches all over the world. Whatever impact Comintern activities had on international order—it must be admitted that, at least initially, their aim was to undermine the world order defined at the Paris Peace Conference—they may be viewed as part of the wider phenomenon of network-building. Just as the League of Nations and other agencies were establishing close ties among nations, the Comintern, through local communist parties and their sympathizers, contributed to creating a sense of crossnational solidarity transcending nationalistic concerns. At least for intellectuals in many lands, the Comintern seemed to offer an attractive alternative to traditional world politics, one that transcended—indeed aimed at demolishing—national boundaries and connected revolutionaries and common people in all countries together. By the late 1920s, however, it was evident that the new international order envisioned by the global revolutionaries was no nearer to realization than that being promoted through the League of Nations. If anything, by espousing "socialism in one country" and joining the capitalist nations in signing the Treaty of Paris (the Kellogg-Briand Pact) of 1928, which renounced war as an instrument of foreign policy, the Soviet Union under Joseph Stalin may in fact have begun to move closer to the League-promoted internationalism.

The League of Nations was weakened not by the Soviet Union but by Japan, which, in attacking China's Northeast (Manchuria) in 1931, violated the Kellogg-Briand Pact and then when censured by the League withdrew from it. Internationalism in the 1930s was much shakier than in the preceding decade as Japan was followed by Germany, then by Italy and Fascist Spain, in terminating association with the world organization. The world was becoming divided, with these fascist, "revisionist" powers openly challenging the international order that had been defined for the 1920s and proclaiming their own: Japan's in East Asia, Germany's in Central and Eastern Europe, Italy's in the Mediterranean. These regional orders were connected through the revisionist ideology stressing racial and national solidarity as against individualism, corporatism as against democracy, and Volkgeist against materialism. The combined new order was opposed by the Western democracies and by the Comintern—the latter proclaiming the strategy of the popular front to coalesce these two against the revisionist world order. But then, when the Soviet Union reversed its position and entered into partnership arrangements with Germany (1939) and Japan (1941), it seemed as if the globe was becoming divided into two camps, the aggressive, totalitarian nations and the democratic powers. Internationalism was a casualty of such ominous developments.

And yet it would be wrong to say that internationalism merely died an ignominious death during the 1930s. On the contrary, internationalists in many lands, even in Germany or Japan, kept their faith. Of course, particularly in totalitarian countries, their task was not easy, and many of them were forced into silence, went underground, or migrated, joining the large number of refugees who became a familiar sight in the decade. It is interesting to note that one activity the League of Nations continued to carry on was the settlement of these refugees. In cooperation with other relief organizations, the League undertook to help them find a new home. But this was not all. Even as late as 1937, the League's Intellectual Cooperation Organization was meeting to discuss "the future of letters," as if to demonstrate that despite the gathering cloud on the world horizon, cultural pursuits were to continue. Moreover, at the organization's meeting (which was attended by Japanese delegates, indicating that Japan's withdrawal from the League had not ended its association with the latter's intellectual activities), the participants drafted a treaty of intellectual cooperation. The draft read that the signatories were conscious of their "common interest in preserving mankind's heritage of culture and in promoting the further development of the sciences, arts and letters" and believed that "the cause of peace would be served by the promotion of cultural relations between peoples through an intellectual body having a threefold character of universality, permanence and independence." In reality, of course, no such treaty was ever ratified, and these noble expressions of cultural internationalism remained but a dream. Still, the very existence of such a gathering and such a draft reveals that efforts were being maintained to continue intellectual cooperation to the extent possible so that, when peace returned, they could be resumed.

And that was exactly what happened. Thanks in no small degree to the internationalist endeavors of the 1930s, during the Second World War specific plans were made to prepare for a postwar world of political, economic, and cultural interdependence. This wartime "new" internationalism may have been more "realistic" than Wilsonian internationalism: after the experiences of the 1930s, it was difficult to eliminate considerations of military power from a vision of durable world order. Geopolitics would now have to play a role in any definition of internationalism. Yet at the same time, precisely because military force, balance of power, and eve-present dangers of aggression had to continue to be taken seriously, efforts would have to be redoubled to ensure the cooperation of nations in nonmilitary spheres as well. It is to be noted that the United Nations, the new world organization, went a step beyond the League of Nations in envisioning international cooperation not only to prevent aggression but also to promote the economic welfare and social justice of all countries. One specific achievement was the Bretton Woods (New Hampshire) conference of 1944, which laid the groundwork for postwar economic cooperation. The conferees proposed the establishment of an International Monetary Fund and a World Bank. The former was unprecedented as a cooperative undertaking in which its member nations would be willing to abide by certain rules about rates of exchange and currency conversion. The World Bank, in the meantime, was an innovation: a huge sum (initially $10 billion) was to be set aside for developmental assistance. No such international program had ever existed; earlier, economic development in dependent areas of the world had been undertaken by the colonial powers. What was now visualized was a world in which colonies would steadily gain autonomy, giving rise to a situation where many independent nations would be economically underdeveloped. It would be a major task of more developed countries to help them, and to do so in an international framework. It may be noted, in this connection, that China's membership in the UN security council was a symbol of the growing importance of the non-Western part of the world in postwar international affairs. As world was conceived as having more and more non-Western countries, one key question that arose was how to accommodate their nationalism into the new internationalism.

One fundamental way was to recognize aspirations for freedom and human rights as universal. Both the promising beginnings of cross-cultural dialogue in the 1920s and the tragedies of mass slaughter in the 1930s and 1940s brought home the realization that no international order would survive unless it were based on essential regard for the unity of humanity. Racial equality, religious tolerance, freedom of expression, democratic self-government—these had to be universally applied if the postwar world were to be truly international. This idea found its expression in the United Nations' Universal Declaration of Human Rights (1948) and in the founding of the United Nations Educational, Scientific, and Cultural Organization (1945). (During the war, education ministers of various allied governments, including Chinese and Soviet as well as U.S. and European, had met periodically in London to reestablish educational and cultural exchange programs, and there was a great deal of continuity in the personnel of these meetings, the ICO, and UNESCO.) In addition to UNESCO, the United Nations established such other agencies as the World Health Organization (founded in 1948), the World Meteorological Organization (1950), the United Nations

International Children's Fund (1953), and the Food and Agriculture Organization (1945).

The world order after 1945, however, did not exactly proceed along the lines envisaged by these wartime plans and postwar organizations. The international order came to be defined by the geopolitics of the cold war, based on a balance of military power between two camps. International cooperation that included countries in both camps was extremely difficult to undertake. The onset of the cold war meant the failure of the new internationalism. Instead of a politically cooperative, economically and culturally interdependent international order, the world became divided economically and ideologically as well as geopolitically. The world order defined by the cold war, however, contained large areas that did not quite fit in. For the postwar period saw the emergence in the international arena of the Third World, consisting of less developed countries and areas, many of which had been colonies. As they gained their independence one after another and undertook the task of "nation-building," several, such as India, Egypt, and Indonesia, began to develop their own conception of international order lying outside the cold war framework. They criticized the superpowers for squandering their resources on an expensive arms race when they should be helping the nation-building endeavors in Asia, Africa, the Middle East, and Latin America. Starting with their meeting in Bandung, Indonesia, in 1955, they developed a self-consciousness as members of the Third World, all equally devoted to economic development but wishing to remain nonaligned in the cold war. The sense of solidarity among these countries, and their cooperation in playing a role in international affairs, made the post-1945 years unique; for the first time in the history of international relations, non-Western, less developed countries were defining an alternative global system. Some would establish their own sub-orders: the Association of Southeast Asian Nations (1967), the Organization of Petroleum Exporting Countries (1960), and many others. Each in its own way sought to promote international cooperation by restricting aspects of national sovereignty (for instance, the OPEC decision in 1973 to curtail the production of petroleum), and so was an example of internationalism, albeit quite different in character from the U.S.- or Soviet-promoted world order.

Culturally, too, the Third World's emergence added complexity to international order. To a world already ideologically divided between "free" and socialist nations, the Third World added its own vocabulary, ranging from anticolonialism to cultural autonomy. Some of the vocabulary was universalistic: democracy, human rights, equality, all concepts that had originated in the West. But other ideas were self-consciously anti-Western, whether capitalist or socialist. Indonesia's Sukarno, for instance, talked of an Asian alternative to Western models of Westernization, China's Mao Zedong of "wars of national liberation," and Egypt's Nasser of Islamic revival. While all these countries eagerly subscribed to the United Nations' declaration of human rights, at the same time they often accused the West of having hegemonized human civilization—having so long dominated the way non-Westerners thought about the world and about themselves that the latter had lost a sense of cultural autonomy. The time had come, they argued, to declare their intellectual independence of the West. Given the emergence of such "Third Worldism," an increasingly urgent question was how the new cultural forces could be accommodated into the world order even as the latter remained fundamentally defined by the cold war.

That question became even more urgent after the 1970s, when the world order as defined by the cold war began to erode. How was the world going to be organized if this definition were not to last? Was the passing of the superpower confrontation going to lead to even more numerous attempts at international cooperation, some of which might contradict one another? If no effective pattern of cooperation emerged, would the world revert to nationalistic pursuits of self-interest? Was the nation itself, as a sovereign entity, going to remain a viable unit even when the pressures of cold war confrontation gave way to the self-centered pursuits of individual and group interests?

The history of international relations since the 1970s provides conflicting answers to these questions. On one hand, without the constraints imposed by the cold war, and challenged by new issues, internationalist endeavors have borne some important fruit. During the 1970s, U.S.- and Soviet-bloc countries came together to form the Conference on Security and Cooperation in Europe. When it met in Helsinki in 1975, the member nations adopted a ringing declaration on human rights, including freedom of expression, religion, and migration. Although not immediately applicable, the declaration was important as it bridged the two sides in the cold war for the first time since the late 1940s. And it did so, it should be noted, by adopting the vocabulary of liberal internationalism. That much was a concession on the part of Soviet-bloc nations. Soon, however, this became much more than rhetoric as many individuals and groups in Eastern Europe and within the Soviet Union began calling for more freedom. In this sense, the fall of socialist dictatorships in East Germany, Hungary, Romania, and elsewhere, and the breakup of the Soviet Union, that took place during the late 1980s and the early 1990s were a phenomenon that harkened back to wartime internationalist assumptions.

The international order envisaged during the war but unfulfilled during the cold war appeared now once again a realizable goal. Likewise, educational and cultural exchanges were resumed and initiated between capitalist and socialist countries. Within less than fifteen years after the normalization of diplomatic relations between the United States and the People's Republic of China, for instance, more than thirty thousand students from the mainland came to study at American colleges and universities, among the largest number of foreign students (totaling four hundred thousand in 1992) in the United States. Exchanges between Soviet and Western scholars became common, with academic conferences frequently inviting participants from the countries formerly belonging to the socialist bloc.

Economically, too, there have been important new developments since the 1970s to promote international cooperation. The response on the part of the industrial nations to the first "oil shock" (1973) was significant; instead of reverting to 1930s-type economic nationalism, these countries sought to solve the challenge posed by OPEC through cooperation. Six of them (the United States, Britain, France, West Germany, Italy, Japan) convened a meeting in Rambouillet, outside of Paris, in 1975 to coordinate their policies and pledge not to abandon the spirit of cooperation. These countries, later joined by Canada and thus constituting what came to be known as G-7, would continue to meet once a year, a symbol of their determination to maintain a framework of international cooperation. Although they frequently collided with one another on trade and monetary issues, at least they managed to consult with one another and to adopt common strategies on energy, exchange, and other questions. In time, they would also begin discussing such other global issues as the protection of the natural environment, refugees, and aid to formerly socialist countries. When the president of the Russian republic was invited to the 1992 G-7 meeting, other countries wanted similar participation, indicating that the G-7 gathering of the rich nations might in time evolve into a more global operation.

In the meantime, regional economic arrangements were making progress: in addition to the European Community and ASEAN, there were the Rio Group of thirteen South American countries, and the North American Free Trade Agreement among Canada, the United States, and Mexico. Unlike the trend in the 1930s toward the fragmentation of the world into rigid economic blocs, however, these organizations, while promoting intraregional trade, also contributed to the growth of global economic transactions. Thus the European Community expanded its overall commercial relations with North America and Asia even as its members increased their trade with one another.

Various schemes for expanding ASEAN into a larger association for promoting regional trade often envisaged a huge Asia-Pacific community of nations including the United States and Canada.

By far the most notable developments of the last quarter century, however, have been in the cultural area, broadly defined. The ending of the cold war has unleashed many forces, hitherto suppressed or obscured, that have altered not just the form but also perceptions of international relations. It is no exaggeration to say that the changing consciousness about international order is one of the most remarkable phenomena in the world today. To begin with, concern about the environment has steadily grown in the recent decades. First articulated as a movement against nuclear testing from the late 1950s through the 1960s, the awareness that the air was becoming polluted by atmospheric testing of nuclear weapons, combined with the recognition (dating back to earlier years) of mercury poisoning, adverse physical effects of coal burning and carbon monoxide emissions from cars, and instances of destruction of the ecological balance, brought about a global concern over industrial waste and environmental degradation. It is important to note that the problem was always put in an international framework; there was no such thing as a country's polluting only its own air and waters. Rather, the entire world would be affected. Thus in 1972 the United Nations convened a Conference on the Human Environment, an effort that has continued to this day. To the protection of the natural environment related themes have been added: for instance, the preservation of endangered species and forests, and regulation of the usage of land, oceans, and airspace. Truly, in such matters the destiny of all humanity is involved, and only an international approach will yield significant results.

Equal in importance to the preservation of nature has been the movement for the protection of human rights. Although the United Nations' declaration of human rights started the process, it is in the last decades that rhetoric has become translated into reality through various organizations and conferences, both international and regional. There is little doubt that global awareness of the issue has been strengthened by revolutionary changes in communications technology. Satellite television broadcasting, fax transmissions, computerized mail, and many other innovations have breached national boundaries and made people everywhere aware of what goes on elsewhere. As a result, suppressions of freedom that once might have been little reported abroad now make instant news. The brutal assault on dissidents in China in 1989 called forth a worldwide denunciation of the Beijing regime. Not that the latter was immediately forced to alter its policy, but it could not avoid reckoning with a world environment in which traditional national sovereignty was being modified through the internationalization of national affairs. One could resist this trend, as Beijing did, asserting that a nation's sovereign rights remained the most fundamental, inviolable reality in world affairs; but the very fact that China joined the United Nations and myriad other international organizations as soon as it effected a rapprochement with the United States indicated its recognition that cooperation among nations was just as definite a reality.

The relief of refugees and international migrants has also been an increasingly important item for cooperation among nations. Although the refugee question first became serious in the 1930s, at that time it was mostly a product of the racial policies of Germany and other fascist states. In recent decades, while race prejudice has remained a cause, other factors have been added: interethnic rivalries, religious intolerance, political persecution, economic suffering. They have combined to create a highly volatile situation where millions have left their original homes and still have not found new ones. Especially notable have been the waves of immigration, attempted and successful, into more developed from less developed countries. This demographic dislocation, too, is a matter for an international solution, and the United Nations' office of refugees has never been more active.

The rising importance of cultural issues may be credited with having revitalized internationalism in that all these issues must be solved internationally. That by definition means part of each country's sovereign rights must be compromised. If geopolitical and economic questions often pit nations against one another, at least in the cultural realm it may be hoped that forces of nationalism will be somewhat mitigated and nations will learn to consider not only their respective national interests but also the welfare of the whole world.

## Legacy for the Twenty-First Century

If the twentieth century may be said to have developed a legacy of achievements to be bequeathed to the next century, internationalism will certainly be one. The world circa 1900 was European-centered; internationalism then was interchangeable with intra-European cooperation. Steadily throughout the present century, however, the networks of cooperating countries have widened. At the end of the First World War, a Chinese delegate at the League of Nations made the then-bold suggestion that at least one representative from the Asian world (he meant the whole region from the Middle

East to the Far East) be invited to sit on the council even if its majority might come from Europe and the Americas. That early instance of international affirmative action was not accepted, but the League of Nations took pains to involve non-Western countries in its affairs in many other ways, in particular in the Intellectual Cooperation Organization.

The world has come a long way since then. It has seen another global carnage, racist massacres, religious fanaticism, and totalitarian excesses—in all parts of the globe. "The human condition" as defined by these instances has been an ugly, hopeless one. Yet at the same time, aspirations for freedom for all people have grown steadily. It is sometimes argued that the existence of ethnic, religious, and other minorities and their increasing self-assertiveness are forces for destabilizing world order. They need not be. Indeed, this very phenomenon may be interpreted as evidence that despite all the wars and atrocities of the century, the sovereign power of the nation-state has been steadily checked. If so, it encourages a view of recent and contemporary history as not entirely negative. Moreover, the fact that an increasing number of international cooperative endeavors have been undertaken suggests that diversity and internationalism need not be incompatible. It remains to be seen if, in the next century, these two will somehow reinforce each other and, in so doing, will fundamentally alter the nature of the sovereign state and of the international order.

# 11 War: Institution Without Portfolio

ROBERT L. O'CONNELL

John Lewis Gaddis has recently likened historical process to the titanic subterranean forces which move the continents around the globe "operating with no visible consequences for long periods of time," only to burst forth in cataclysmic upheavals.[1] So it was with war on the verge of the twentieth century. For many, the notion that an institution as apparently fundamental as warfare could have possibly outlived its usefulness was not simply implausible, it was utterly at odds with what they perceived to be happening around them.

The influence of Social Darwinian thinking and a widespread feeling that urban-industrial life was fundamentally enervating led many to see war as a palliative, an equipoise to the tedium and uncertainty of daily existence. Conflicts such as the Franco-Prussian War of 1870–1871 and the Spanish-American War of 1898 allowed citizens at all levels to convince themselves that warfare held out the possibility for adventure in an overcivilized world. It was held up as a short interlude during which young males might test themselves against the traditional code of the warrior, to be delivered back to their former lives purged, hardened, and much the better for the experience. Casualties would always be a regrettable but necessary consequence of the process. But modern weapons, by raising the tempo of military operations, generally were expected to keep the killing to a minimum and confined mostly to the "unfit." While this line of thinking reached a sort of crescendo in the writings of peripheral figures such as German General von Bernhardi, J.A. Cramb in England, and Frenchman Charles Maurras, there is every reason to believe that such notions were widely held, not only among mainstream politicians like Winston Churchill and Theodore Roosevelt (both of whom took the "cure"), but also by broad segments of the populations in every corner of the industrialized world.

This time span also marked the genesis of modern pacifism, and events such as the two disarmament conferences at the Hague in 1899 and 1907 indi-

cate at least some apprehension at fairly high levels as to the potential consequences of modern warfare. But this group remained very much a minority
and not a very insightful one. There was some talk of war's economic futility,
but for the most part the overt rationale for rejecting warfare went no deeper
than its perceived immorality and barbarism. Quite possibly this strain of
pacifism did reflect more profound fears and insights, but they were not
clearly articulated. Meanwhile, judging by the happy crowds that gathered in
Europe's capitals as their respective nations announced their belligerency in
August 1914, humankind had indeed voted with its feet.

Prior to 1939, the term World War I was never used. The conflict was simply
known as the Great War, a monumental and entirely appropriate designation.
For there had never been a conflict remotely like it: two massive field armies
laying siege to each other, locked in a double line of trenches stretching from
the Swiss border to the North Sea like parallel serpents. Until March of 1918
no attack would succeed in moving the lines even ten miles in either direction, while millions of men would die on the narrow band of territory
between the two earthen snakes.

If anything, the war at sea began even more bizarrely, with two enormous
fleets of dreadnought battleships—themselves products of an arms race that
helped to poison the environment leading to war—glowering across the
North Sea but virtually helpless to engage in significant combat. Meanwhile
that pariah among naval weapons, the submarine, feasted on Britain's
seaborne commerce, to be curbed in the end more by the moral reservations
of its German users than by effective countermeasures.

"I don't know what is to be done—this isn't war," moaned Lord Kitchener,
the symbol of Britain's army and soon to go down on a ship struck by a naval
mine. Behind it all loomed military technology, enforcing the stalemate with
a series of weapons, many of which were such newcomers to the battlefield
that opposing forces had little idea how to deal with them. Worse still, armaments did not simply dominate, they did so by making a mockery of the warrior ethic. Skill, strength, swiftness, cunning, and bravery were rendered
nearly irrelevant. Combatants were gassed, torpedoed, mined, bombarded by
unseen artillery, or mowed down by puny-looking machine guns more or less
randomly; there was hardly a heroic death to be had in this sanguinary bur-
lesque. The lesson here—one of the central developments of the twentieth
century—was that weapons were turning against war itself, making it virtually impossible to fight except at a cost far greater than the potential gains.
World War I is etched into our collective memories as much for the quality as

the quantity of the slaughter—the perceived uselessness of the deaths and the fact that the victims were valued members of society instead of the army "inevitably consisting of the scum of the people," as the eighteenth-century French commander Comte de Saint-Germain had decreed.[2] Little productive land or labor was exchanged. And the sheer magnitude of the dead (around ten million), while utterly appalling to public sensibilities, constituted but a small fraction of the combatant states' total populations, and would have only a marginal impact on their future numbers. So war as demographic lever had become merely repugnant.

To understand the importance of these factors one must look at the basis for warfare in most earlier human societies. Many archaeologists, anthropologists, and political theorists now believe that civilization emerged around five thousand years ago through a self-reinforcing process that included among its key drivers increasing populations, agricultural intensification, social stratification, the growth of bureaucracies, and warfare. It was this process that turned simple Neolithic farmers into members of huge social hierarchies, building upon itself until the carrying capacity of the environment and the limits of available technology caused a developmental plateau to be reached.

In the process several basic sources of instability appeared in the system. Very large populations, and the attendant dependence upon labor-intensive irrigated agriculture that focused primarily on a narrow range of cereals, left such societies vulnerable to periodic crop failure and famine. And these, in turn, were to be compounded by the spread of epidemic disease. For in Eurasia the possibility of attack, at first by pastoral nomads and later by better-organized forces from the agricultural sphere, compacted settlement patterns and led to urban centers surrounded by walls—literally nests of pestilence that encouraged the wildfire spread of infection, particularly during times of malnutrition. The population curves that resulted approximated the architecture of roller coasters; disease was a demographic wild card periodically threatening serious dislocation and even collapse.

More than anything else, it was this problem that wars and armies traditionally addressed: not just maintaining social control, but acting as a stabilizer for societies existing at the outer edges of possibility. During periods of overpopulation armies could conquer new lands, or at worst, self-destruct and no longer have to be fed. And when populations fell, new laborers could be appropriated through war. It should be emphasized that warfare was never more than a crude equilibrator, simply the most effective one available. However, this syndrome helps explain the traffic in slaves and repeated transfers of entire peoples, along with military fecklessness and frequency of disaster among empires. For soldiers were the medium of exchange, and battles—orchestrated to produce their death, capture, and enslavement, or return with more labor or land—were key mediums by which energy was transferred from one political entity to another in the traditional agricultural world.

The phenomenon of human beings reduced to the level of tokens to be traded on warfare's version of the marketplace was emblematic of the entire system. But if agriculture-based civilizations operated through compulsion and presented the vast majority with the stark alternatives of starvation or subjugation, this was a matter less of choice than necessity. For populations had grown too large and technology remained too crude to provide any real alternative. So for the great majority of humankind, history was destined basically to repeat itself over the next five thousand or so years and war ground on, the clumsy balance wheel of this rough-hewn clockworks.

But if the pregnant World War I phrase "a war to end all wars" was prophetic conceptually in that war as an institution fundamentally changed in its aftermath, it hardly matched the topography of politics following the Versailles peace treaty. Historians have drawn attention to the phenomenon of the double war,[3] conflicts like the Peloponnesian War and the first two Punic wars, of such magnitude and significance that a respite is required before the fighting is renewed and the issue finally settled. In retrospect, it appears that the two world wars fall into this category, and that the period between 1918 and 1939 was simply an interlude during which the industrialized world girded itself anew. Yet the shock engendered by the Great War was sufficient to cause a radical fragmentation of thought and action, a schism of fundamental significance not simply for the future of organized violence, but also in determining the context for the entire nexus of economic, technological, and political changes that were transforming human existence.

At one level, primarily intellectual and most apparent in the liberal democracies, was a rejection of war and an acceptance that it was increasingly inappropriate to the kind of world that was forming as a result of agriculture's displacement as the primary means of subsistence. However, the pacifism and efforts at arms control that took place during the 1920s and 1930s, while forward looking, were also disembodied from contemporary events—cerebral and moral exercises studiously partitioned from the here and now. Yet the effort was not necessarily fecklessly utopian. For, although the 1925 Geneva Protocol banning poison gas in combat was hedged in by reservations and the 1928 Treaty of Paris outlawed war by fiat and nothing else, they nonetheless registered a growing awareness, soon to be ratified by nuclear weapons, of total warfare's approaching obsolescence and the concept that certain armaments were simply too horrific to use.

The immediate future, however, would be held hostage to a far different way of thinking. As is typical in eras of great change, a refuge was sought in the past. And so large segments of the industrial world, battered by the cumulative impact of the Great War and the oscillations of the business cycle, sought to resurrect the institutions of agricultural tyranny and apply them in an industrial context, giving birth to modern totalitarianism. It was not an entirely illogical accommodation. Given the apparent evolution of machine technology at this point in the direction of economies of scale, centralized management, and the regimentation of huge labor pools, it made a certain sense to conclude that forms corresponding to the great pyramid-shaped hierarchies which had once ruled the ancient world's agricultural river valleys could be superimposed on an environment dominated by machines. For if nothing else, despotism promised an immutable sort of stability and compatibility with military institutions deemed appropriate at a time of great insecurity. Rather than rejecting war, the totalitarian disposition, employing essentially agricultural criteria, reached the opposite conclusion. Aggressive war was to be a key means by which such societies fulfilled their agendas. Thus agricultural despotism's hunger for territory found an analog in the supposed necessity to physically control the mineral and other resources required to run an industrial machine. There was also the same penchant to exploit labor through force of arms—to move and eliminate whole populations both within and without. And implicit in all of this was a willingness to squander large armies in the pursuit of these objectives, a prospect which military technology was eminently capable of accomplishing.

All of this was no aberration, but a logical extrapolation from what many thought was the true course of events. And in this context it should be remembered that important strains of this thinking existed in the liberal democracies, just as elements of individualism, capitalism, and pacifism continued to persist in these supposed fascist and communist monoliths. Ultimately totalitarianism would be shown to be an anachronism based on a profound misreading of human nature, technology, and the role of organized violence; but this was not obvious at the time—nor, it should be added, until very recently.

And so the industrialized world was plunged into another earth-shaking bout of warfare. Only this time the number of deaths—approximately five times those of the Great War—would be far less an accidental result of technologies barely understood than a conscious application of war machinery.

For the major combatants of the Second World War all had worked quietly to perfect and develop the weaponry that had emerged during the Great War, particularly the tank, the airplane, and the submarine. When the time came, all would be employed effectively and promiscuously.

The very devices that had most shocked the respective powers in the former conflict, with the exception of poison gas, tended to become their specialties in the later war. Thus the British, whose cities had suffered at the hands of the German Gotha and Giant bombers during World War I, took to bombing ("dehousing") the Third Reich's population centers with a forthright ruthlessness unmatched by any of the other belligerents. Similarly, the Germans, whose troops had been driven from their trenches by Allied tanks in 1918, were the first to master mechanized tactics epitomized in their armored sweep across France in 1940. So too the Americans, whose anger at unrestricted submarine warfare had driven them into World War I, came to wage World War II's most ruthless and successful underwater campaign against commerce, accounting for roughly three quarters of Japan's merchant tonnage.

In the end, however, it was totalitarianism itself that set the tone for the Second World War, and it was on the Russian front that the issue was ultimately settled. Here, in battles that encompassed hundreds of square miles and millions of participants, human blood would be shed in prodigal quantities as the two exemplars of modern tyranny, Nazi Germany and the Soviet Union, waged an all-out struggle that brought to fruition the possibilities of industrialized warfare. Doubtless both assumed the war and its outcome would provide a blueprint for the future of humanity. But nothing of the kind would occur.

World War II's signal event took place on July 16, 1945, when the first atomic bomb was detonated at Alamogordo, New Mexico—sending, among other things, a mushroom cloud 41,000 feet into the stratosphere, and breaking a window 125 miles away. As the bomb's chief designer J. Robert Oppenheimer watched, he remembered lines from the *Bhagavad Gita* that summed up the moment: "Now I am become death, destroyer of worlds."[4] For the sequence of development that had begun about a century earlier, with the first major improvements in small arms, had finally produced a weapon so powerful that not much more than a generation after this first test it would reduce unlimited warfare between major powers to a logical absurdity.

This time span, however, would be filled with uncertainty of the most fundamental sort. The cold war, with its Manichean struggle between totalitarian communism and democratic capitalism, would mark the climactic chapter in our species' initial efforts to come to grips with a fundamentally new way of living. The stakes were enormous and the outcome by no means assured. For true mismanagement increasingly implied not just victory or defeat, but the probable end of civilization itself. And this, of course, was a function of the spiraling arms competition that would prove the pacesetting event of the entire confrontation.

Viewed retrospectively, it does appear that weapons acquisitions on both sides consistently reflected a commitment to deterrence; but the respective interpretations of this concept diverged radically. For their part the Soviets seem to have taken the Roman military theorist Vegetius ("Let he who desires peace prepare for war.")[5] literally, building weapons that in their quantities and qualities would make them as useful as possible in what were perceived as realistic wartime scenarios. Such a strategy, however, left adversaries no clear criteria by which to differentiate preparation for war from intention to wage war—a very dangerous ambiguity for a generation of Western statesmen deeply influenced by the so-called "Munich syndrome," a fear of appeasing a warmaker as British Prime Minister Neville Chamberlain had Adolf Hitler in the Munich Pact of 1938. Meanwhile, the approach of the other key contestant, the United States, much more clearly reflected what would come to be understood as the primary message of the nuclear age: a major East-West war would be an unmitigated disaster. Thus a central thread of U.S. armaments policy—though often pursued in an unspoken, even unconscious fashion—was intimidation with the aim of making such a war appear utterly futile. In pursuit of this objective and driven by a profound suspicion of their adversaries' intentions, Americans applied their much more vigorous technological and financial institutions to achieve a steady stream of state-of-the-art advances in weapons performance. And the Russians in turn employed a vast scientific and technical espionage network and the heart of their totalitarian command economy in a dogged but hugely inefficient effort to keep up. It was this dynamic which steadily ratcheted up the arms race to undreamed-of heights and set the tone for cold war politics.

Caution was the watchword. And while there is a natural tendency to dwell on the potentially catastrophic consequences of the cold war's several crises, in fact, the degree of moderation consistently shown by both sides was remarkable, and must be attributed to a stark recognition that nuclear weaponry had truly changed the rules of international politics. Philosophically and operationally the Soviets were plainly less predisposed to accept this state of affairs. But multiplying nuclear stockpiles and ever more reliable means of delivery consistently confounded their war planners' efforts to circumvent the grim logic of mutually assured destruction. So at the highest level of engagement it gradually became clear that war on a grand scale had been truly thwarted. Accidents and madness were still possible, but as a premeditated, rational act of policy between nuclear members of the developed community it was defunct.

Less recognized, however, is the stifling effect the standoff had on the cold war participants' attempts to use force at a lower level. The American experience was particularly instructive. In both Korea and Vietnam the United States' unwillingness to apply sufficient force to achieve a victory, that is, to deploy all the weapons in its vast arsenal, can be traced to our fears of provoking general war. In the case of the latter conflict, critics of the American strategy of graduated escalation and of our refusal to invade North Vietnam conveniently overlook the fact that both stemmed from our anxieties—perhaps unwarranted, but still real enough at the time—over drawing in China, and somehow provoking World War III. The desire to be perceived as prudent and as always allowing our adversaries acceptable alternatives came to outweigh the pursuit of victory. Meanwhile, this precarious belligerence would be further undermined by television, which exposed the public to a vision of warfare's brutality never before seen. The metamorphosis of Vietnam from an intervention in an area of relatively minor strategic import into a national tragedy has been blamed on many factors, but relatively little weight has been attached to the inefficacy of modern war itself. Nevertheless, all the signs were there: the public revulsion at the slaughter, the excessive destructiveness of the weaponry, and the inability to articulate what precisely was to be gained from the fighting. The USSR was more successful in steering clear of combat, while sponsoring surrogates in Third World countries like Nicaragua and Malaya to wage so-called "wars of national liberation." However, when the Soviets themselves invaded Afghanistan in 1979, their troops were soon caught in a Vietnam-like quagmire, the first in a series of mishaps leading to the regime's downfall.

Judged by any standard, the collapse of communism and the breakup of the Soviet empire were events of major importance. But they were particularly indicative of the future of warfare and the cumulative effects of militarism. The lumbering Soviet performance in the arms race, by relentlessly prioritizing the military-industrial sector, not only gobbled up much of what was most productive, but choked what little technological creativity the system had to offer. So while Americans were able to tap the same industries that generated arcade games and personal computers to generate advanced weapons, Russian forays into high technology led nowhere. Instead, the Russians were doomed to encounter ever greater costs during their vain efforts to copy Western weapons in sterile defense industries, meticulously segregated from the civilian economy. And by the early eighties, after decades of sacrifice and hard work, the Soviets were truly losing the arms competition, and losing precisely because of what that sacrifice and hard work had built.

It was an allegory of their entire system. The totalitarian superimposition of what were essentially the institutions of traditional despotic agriculture on an industrial economy had managed to produce masses of cement and steel, but little that was truly useful. The instruments of tyranny could run simple societies based on only a few variables; but only systems which left people free to operate on their own initiative could cope effectively with the manifold complexities of truly developed economies. So communism and most of what it stood for failed.

But the manner in which this occurred, the actual outcome, is as important to consider as the nature of the failure. The very fact that a ruling class— armed to the teeth and wedded to an ideology that traditionally lionized coercion and the salutary role of war—would give up without a fight speaks volumes about the obsolete nature of organized violence. For even the most cynical must admit that the peaceful resolution of the cold war was an event basically without historical precedent. That a confrontation this fundamental and dangerous could have come to a close without major warfare is clearly indicative of a basic change in the mechanisms that shape events—not perhaps the end of history, but quite possibly a new beginning.

Among other things, the end of the cold war seems destined to accelerate internationalism, particularly in the developed world, a trend that constitutes the most significant challenge to the monolithic nation-state since that concept formed at the Peace of Westphalia that ended the Thirty Years' War in 1648. Most decidedly, this is not simply a matter of countries voluntarily ceding elements of their sovereignty to supranational bodies, although this is an important development. For the astonishing growth of world trade (a tenfold increase since 1970) and the rise of global corporations are well on the way to creating truly stateless economies within the developed world. And at the same time as the consciousness of far-flung citizenries is being drawn together by the revolutionary force of the electronic media, the traditional transnational claims of organized religion appear to be undergoing something of a renaissance. The state system within the developed world is unlikely to disappear, but its components will be composed of people and institutions with much more divided loyalties and dependencies. This will not preclude certain kinds of organized violence, but war as defined here and traditionally understood will increasingly prove too blunt an instrument to wield effectively in the variegated and sophisticated environments where these trends have progressed the furthest. What, after all, would be the end of such a war: the exclusive possession of land or resources that are largely unusable without the cooperation of international economic institutions? To brutalize obnoxious elements only to be caught red-handed and exposed to world condemnation? To address population problems far better dealt with by economic and health measures? To destroy an enemy only to be destroyed in return? Among the advanced states, this is literally an institution without portfolio.

Nonetheless, there is the phenomenon of intervention into less developed areas. It can certainly be argued that the Falkland Islands campaign (1982) and Desert Storm (1991) constitute examples of advanced societies not only waging war, but doing it successfully. But this misses a larger point. Force was applied primarily to correct naked acts of aggression—as much a matter of principle as anything else. Especially in the latter case, extraordinary moderation was shown. Indeed, the campaign suggests the metaphor of a group of white blood cells surrounding and then eliminating an infection. But significantly, no concerted attempt was made to destroy the source of the infection, the person and regime of Saddam Hussain. Rather, Allied forces wielded their power in the Gulf War in a reticent and contained manner that confounds conventional military logic, and demonstrates instead just how suspect the use of force has become among the stewards of megadeath.

And there are signs that the scope of battle will be narrowed still further. For there is increasing pressure on advanced states to apply military power to simply stop wars—wherever they are and whatever their motivation. Indeed, the logic of peacekeeping grows ever more insistent in its claims that it is the duty of the powerful, and in their interest also, to bring an end to wars. It will be an onerous and in many respects a thankless task. Nor are our armies and weapons particularly well suited to achieve it. But the very fact that it is now demanded of us is telling.

In the meantime, war persists. For we live in a world divided. Perhaps as many as 85 percent of our species' 5.3 billion members continue to subsist in economies either mired in low-efficiency agriculture or only in the process of escaping its leafy grasp. In the case of the latter, consisting of perhaps 3 billion souls and containing giant societies such as India and China, there are numerous signs of development—both governmental and economic—which reflect the earlier paths trod by states in what is now the developed sphere. Today war among such transitional states is still viewed as a viable—though not necessarily preferred—instrument of national aggrandizement. When their strategists talk about the future of war, it is essentially in operational terms; they seldom if ever question the future of the institution itself.

But this is not to concede that those in the transitional sphere are fated to experience cycles of horrific warfare such as those that overtook what are now the advanced societies during the two World Wars. For one thing, should major war come to the transitional sphere, it is destined to be fought with the kinds of modern weapons whose excessive destructiveness gave war such a bad name within the developed sphere. More to the point, the central differ-.ence between then and now with respect to armaments is the specter of nuclear weapons. True enough, these weapons are only gradually spreading among the transitional states; but with that proliferation will come a growing understanding of the incalculable costs that must accompany a substantial nuclear exchange. In the United States political scientists across a broad spectrum are increasingly conceding that nuclear deterrence played a major role in the peaceful end of the cold war, and there is no reason why this logic will not extend itself and have a major moderating effect on the military plans of the transitional states.

Meanwhile, there has been a gradual but steady expansion of democratic principles and government by consent in this venue. While this is no immediate panacea for warlike behavior, there is solid quantitative evidence that, over the long haul, democracies have seldom if ever waged war against other democracies. Thus the spread of consensual politics in the transitional sphere can be expected to coincide ultimately with a contraction of war's sphere of influence. It is unlikely that all transitional societies will manage a prompt or even steady march into the world of the advanced. Moreover, the combination of development's inevitably expanding claims on resources and the huge numbers of people involved are bound to create ecological problems for which there are no ready-made solutions. Yet the transitional sphere remains an environment of hope, and one in which war's grasp can be expected to weaken.

Unfortunately war's vital signs remain strong among the 1.5 billion people who occupy the third of the planet's developmental spheres—the arena where, as in war-waging scenarios from ages past, more than 65 percent of the population is directly engaged in food production, largely on a subsistence basis. Here war continues to play its ancient role of ministering to chronic demographic distortions within agricultural societies, but now compounded by a modern twist. Advanced medicine and emergency food supplies from the developed societies have sent survival rates spiraling so steeply upward that in many areas they threaten the collapse of social services, the devolution of government, and the contravention of virtually all human rights. In this environment, brutality and mass slaughter—frequently inflicted by inchoate bands—increasingly prevail. Much is made of rival warlords and ancient tribal and ethnic hatreds, but just below the surface lurks the age-old need or desire to eliminate excess people. The killing here is typically labeled as senseless; but it is not without purpose. It is simply that the logic behind it is too brutal for most to admit its existence. Nevertheless, it prevails and will continue to prevail until the conditions underlying it are effectively addressed. This will require far more than periodic military intervention to stop the killing. It will demand a fundamental change in economic patterns, along with social and political behavior. It will be a monumental task. But if and when it is achieved, the forces energizing war's last true stronghold will quickly dissipate, and the institution will finally plummet toward extinction.

ENDNOTES

1. John Lewis Gaddis, *International Security* 173:40.
2. Comte de Saint Germain, *Memoires* (Amsterdam: M. M. Rey, 1779), p. 178.
3. See, for example, Arnold Toynbee, *Hannibal's Legacy* (London: Oxford University Press, 1965), 1:1–12.
4. As cited in Len Giovannitti and Fred Freed, *The Decision to Drop the Bomb* (New York: Coward-McCann, 1965), pp. 194–95.
5. Flavius Vegetius Renatus, prologue to *De Re Militari* vol. 3, in T. R. Phillips, ed., *The Roots of Strategy* (Harrisburg, Penn.: Military Service Publishing Co., 1940), p. 14.
6. *Handbook of International Economic Statistics* (Washington, D.C.: The Directorate, 1992), p. 15.

SELECTED REFERENCES

Bloch, I. S. *The Future of War in Its Technical, Economic and Political Relations.* Boston, 1902.
Bundy, McGeorge. *Danger and Survival Choices About the Bomb in the First Fifty Years.* New York, 1988.
Churchill, Winston. *The World Crisis, 1911–1919.* London, 1931.
Dower, John. *War Without Mercy: Race and Power in the Pacific War.* New York, 1986.
Erickson, John. *The Soviet High Command: A Military and Political History.* Boulder, 1984.
Fredette, Raymond. *The Sky on Fire: The First Battle of Britain, 1917–1918.* London, 1976.
Fukuyama, Francis. *The End of History and the Last Man.* New York, 1992.

Fussell, Paul. *The Great War in Modern Memory*. London, 1975.

———. *Wartime: Understanding and Behavior in the Second World War*. New York, 1989.

Gannon, Michael. *Operation Drumbeat*. New York, 1990.

Halberstam, David. *The Best and the Brightest*. New York, 1972.

Herken, Gregg. *The Winning Weapon: The Atomic Bomb in the Cold War, 1945–1950*. New York, 1980.

Herwig, Holger. *Luxury Fleet: The Imperial German Navy, 1888–1918*. London, 1980.

Horne, Alistaire. *To Lose a Battle: France 1940*. Boston, 1969.

Howard, Michael. *The Lesson of History*. New Haven, 1991.

———. *War and the Liberal Conscience*. New Brunswick, N.J.: 1978.

Huntington, Samuel. *The Soldier and the State*. Cambridge, Mass., 1957.

Kagan, Donald. *On the Origins of War and the Preservation of Peace*. New York, 1995.

Kahn, David. *The Codebreakers: The Story of Secret Writing*. London, 1967.

Keegan, John. *The Face of Battle*. New York, 1976.

———. *The Price of Admiralty: The Evolution of Naval Warfare*. New York, 1989.

Kennedy, Paul. *The Rise and Fall of Great Powers: Economic Change and Military Power, 1500–2000*. New York, 1987.

Leed, Eric. *No Man's Land: Combat and Identity in World War I*. Cambridge: 1979.

Marder, Arthur. *From Dreadnought to Scapa Flow*. London, 1961–70.

May, Ernest. *Knowing One's Enemies: Intelligence Assessment Before the Two World Wars*. Princeton, 1984.

McNeill, William. *Plagues and Peoples*. Garden City, N.Y.: 1976.

———. *Pursuit of Power: Technology: Armed Force and Society Since A.D. 1600*. Chicago, 1982.

Mueller, John. *Retreat from Doomsday: The Obsolescence of Major War*. New York, 1989.

Overy, R. J. *The Air War, 1939–1945*. New York, 1980.

O'Connell, Robert. *Of Arms and Men: A History of War, Weapons, and Aggression*. New York, 1989.

———. *Sacred Vessels: The Cult of the Battleship and the Rise of the U.S. Navy*. New York, 1993.

———. *Ride of the Second Horseman: The Birth and Death of War*. New York, 1995.

Powaski, Ronald. *March to Armageddon: The United States and the Nuclear Arms Race, 1939 to the Present*. New York, 1987.

Pynchon, Thomas. *Gravity's Rainbow*. New York, 1973.

Remarque, Erich. *All Quiet on the Western Front*. Boston, 1929.

Rindos, David. *The Origins of Agriculture: An Evolutionary Perspective*. Orlando, Fla.: 1984.

Rosecrace, Richard. *The Rise of the Trading State: Commerce and Conquest in the Modern World*. New York, 1986.

Sherry, Michael. *The Rise of American Air Power*. New York, 1986.

Speer, Albert. *Inside the Third Reich*. New York, 1970.

Stone, Norman. *The Eastern Front, 1914–1917*. New York, 1975.

Snyder, Jack. *The Ideology of the Offensive: Military Decision Making and the Disasters of 1914*. Ithaca, 1984.

Spector, Ronald. *Eagle Against the Sun*. New York, 1985.

Tuchman, Barbara. *The Guns of August*. New York, 1962.

Toland, John. *The Rising Sun: The Decline and Fall of the Japanese Empire, 1936–1945*. New York, 1970.

*United States Strategic Bombing Survey*. Santa Fe, N.M.: 1973.

Weigley, Russell. *The American Way of War: A History of the United States Military Strategy and Policy*. New York, 1973.

———. *Eisenhower's Lieutenants: France and Germany, 1944–1945*. New York, 1981.

Wells. H. G. *A World Set Free*. London, 1926.

Wittfogel, Karl. *Oriental Despotism*. New Haven, 1957.

# 12 Industry and Business

WILLIAM N. PARKER

## Introduction

Early in the twentieth century, the American social critic Thorstein Veblen wrote of a fundamental conflict in modern economic society under the title *The Engineers and the Price System*. The "engineers" he considered to be the modern manifestations of artisans, working industriously out of an instinct for workmanship and creating thereby all that was valuable for the material support of human life. The "price system," Veblen said, was the work of merchants, bankers, and businessmen whose activity preyed on the useful products of industry to create financial wealth. If the engineer was classed with the medieval artisan, thought Veblen, the businessman was the modern counterpart of the robber baron.

Science and capitalism are the two somewhat grander terms in a historian's vocabulary for these two interrelated aspects of modern civilization. The twentieth century has seen an increasingly close connection between science and industry, expressed through the proliferation of the many varieties of engineers. At the same time, growth and change in the forms and organization of business enterprise, not only through the price system but also in large hierarchical structures—the public or private corporations—has formed the social phenomenon which German scholars have called "late" or "organized" capitalism. Together, modern science in the form of technology and capitalism conducted within the modern institutions of finance and corporate management have created a particularly powerful form of human culture whose appeal in the twentieth century transcends any particular locality, race, nation, or preexisting social formation.

Modern capitalist development began in Europe in the Italian city-states in the sixteenth century with the banking and bookkeeping devices of a growing trade. The seventeenth century brought a response to continuing trading opportunities in northern Europe, penetrating the medieval forms of manorial agriculture and commercializing the handicrafts and artisan shops. Late in the eighteenth century and on to the far edge of the nineteenth, these capitalist forms readily extended themselves to accommodate, exploit, and encourage technical changes in the operations of labor in industry and agriculture, made profitable by the proliferation of mechanical inventions and steam power. In these same centuries between the Renaissance and the First World War, both science and engineering in its many applied forms began to grow and flourish in the increasingly class-conscious and nationalistic societies of Europe and the lands settled by Europeans. The nineteenth century then saw the great achievements of "high capitalism," expansive and competitive, within the political containers of complexly developing nation-states and a growing world market. With this material success, the authority of the politically feeble Protestant versions of the Christian religion, in which a full capitalist culture had grown up in northern Europe since the time of John Calvin (died 1564), was extinguished. In the twentieth century science, work, and business have seemed free to rule peoples' lives without obstruction in the "bourgeois democracies." Though the social containers of the national states harbored imperialist aspirations or memories, international markets and business practices took ever deeper root.

In the twentieth century, too, modern technology and capitalist organization, working unimpeded in symbiotic relationship, have shown a power similar to that of an ambitious world religion, able to move from the social contexts in which they originated across oceans and continents to penetrate other lands with other languages, other customs, and other systems of value. In the early part of the century, they seemed European, and were carried around the world behind guns and by migrations and colonizations. But after 1950, Western weaponry was complemented by refined modes of communicating messages and ideas, modes provided by scientific discoveries, electrical engineering, and capitalist investment and organization.

A superficial, far happier account of the twentieth century might ideally have been written if the course of history had moved in the mode fantasized by Adam Smith, within a world where growing trade, expanding markets, and the easy movement of capital, money, and ideas might have created a worldwide division of labor—free from selfish governmental ambitions and restrictions, from war, political oppression, class envy, and ethnic hatred. Instead those flows have moved only against ever stronger counterflows of social movement channeled within traditional or newly created social and political structures: the "state" and the nation, both in their several authoritarian versions and in the less strident, but even more subtly effective, form of the representative but centralized "bourgeois" or "popular" democracies.

Over this political terrain, through the thick vegetation of local, ethnic, regional, and class loyalties, and over the walls of exclusive ideological structures of national power and sentiment, twentieth-century science and international business have struggled to carry on and extend their social life and influence.

## The Engineering of Scientific Knowledge

The penetrative power of modern technology through all the nations and cultures of the world rests on the exploitation of physical nature in the observable aspects of its fundamental character, energy and matter, for the satisfaction of human needs and desires. Technological development has required, then, a careful steering between the potential and the limits of the physical world on the one hand, and the creation, on the other, of the things humans either need, or imagine or may be persuaded to imagine that they need.

The twentieth century inherited from the nineteenth both the structures of acquired knowledge and the social forms and institutions by which that knowledge could be preserved, reproduced, and extended in the minds, thought patterns, and skills of succeeding generations of scientists, engineers, and industrial workers. Its industrial history may begin then with science, and more specifically with three sciences—loose associations of organized thought and observation—that had been moving toward maturity and coalescence from the late seventeenth century. By 1900 they were called physics, chemistry, and biology. Over the following sixty years, they were tumbled together like ice cubes in a shaker, melted down, and fused to one another. Something called science probed into the molecules of the elements of the periodic table, found the sources of their affinities and the energies that combined them, penetrating at last, in the 1930s and 1940s, under the hot lamps of wartime desperation, into the nuclei of the atoms, and by an incomparable engineering achievement confirmed the equations of the physicists in an explosive release of atomic energy, the harbinger of its risky harnessing for peaceful purposes.

Not stopping with new sources of energy, with new modes of communication by wireless transmission of radiant energy, or with new materials shaped by chemical synthesis, the fused power of the sciences broke down at last the reserved provinces of biology, the science of life. The lines between the inorganic and the organic were erased, and the chemistry and physics of the cell, the building blocks of living matter, were exposed. By 1990, science could still not create or reproduce the complex organization of living organisms, but it could control and alter them in the innermost and minute recesses of their being and reproduction.

Starting with the inventor-engineers James Watt and John Smeaton in the late eighteenth century, the succeeding professions of engineers in their many specialized branches, like an electric arc between two terminals, lighted the space between pure science and its practical application in the fields of agriculture, mining, construction, manufacturing, transport, and communications. Under the impulse of the electrifying ideas of science, the dynamo, the internal combustion engine, the new plastic materials were brought on stage. In each developing line of invention a new subprofession of engineers arose to extend and adopt new energies, substances, and modes of transmission.

In agriculture the biochemistry of nature, and in mining the geology of natural mineral depositions were exploited, but with much greater certainty and higher yield in relation to human effort. Wood ceased to be used as a fuel in industrial societies (except at their lowest and highest levels), retaining a use in construction and chemical processing (as a raw material). This latter was also followed by organic matter in its mineralized forms—coal, which had fueled nineteenth-century industrial production, and oil, easily refinable, transportable, and convertible into heat and power. These and the metallic minerals continued to be found in relative abundance: while not in the bonanza strikes of high natural concentrations of the nineteenth century, still enough to satisfy the industrial countries' expanding appetites. Processes of treatment and beneficiation, and the construction of both more powerful and more delicate tools to mine and move the earth kept costs low, just as the mustering of mechanical and chemical technologies cheapened food supplies to nations whose socioeconomic organization put them within reach.

The further working of natural and synthetic materials, still known with increasing anachronism as "manufacture" (literally "hand-made"), availed itself in the latter half of the century of a variety of tools of great power, flexibility, and specialization. With an almost human self-consciousness, self-criticism, and self-control, machine tools—the machine-building foundation of an industrial system—came to work at ever higher speed and finer tolerances and with more nearly complete and self-correcting automaticity. At a few points in the world's factories, mechanical robots replaced human workers in routine operations.

All these accomplishments in the engineering of power transmission were crowned, and in a sense symbolized, by the microchip and an electronic technology of computation and printed record-keeping and communication.

Already, in the 1910s, following the development of long-distance wire transmission of sound, high-energy, high-frequency transmitters had pioneered wireless telegraphy and the radio. The late 1920s brought the first wireless transmission of visual images, and soon the age of television—direct sound and visual communication from all over the earth—dawned, adding to books, newspapers, photographs, and moving pictures an immediate visual and auditory experience, and an intimate—though highly controlled, selective, and unidirectional—view of contemporary events and theatrical entertainment. By these means, the group of human activities dependent on words, pictures and messages—education, entertainment, politics, commerce, i.e., the "service" industries—joined farming, mining, transportation and manufacture in waiting for the deployment of "high tech."

## Demand: A Moving Target

The lines of knowledge and its professional incorporation in the various branches of science and engineering provided a wide range of opportunities for inventions, these in turn being influenced, in step-by-step fashion, by what proved useful and valuable as the processes of technological change moved along. But weakness and instability in the levels of user demand and certain patterns in the evolution of their structure became evident in—and through—the interruptions of depression and war between 1930 and 1945, despite the range of conflicting state policies and the variety of locally and socially conditioned preferences and tastes. Set against the array of alternative possible technologies, materials, styles, and specific product characteristics, demand and the social cultures from which it derived set the lines within which the actual industrial systems of the twentieth century could evolve.

Over the twentieth century as a whole, as new technologies were incorporated, however haltingly and inefficiently, into production in farming and manufacturing, any falling-off of labor productivity, equipment performance, or materials supply due to aging structures and machinery or depleted natural resources and opportunities was either minimized, avoided, or even overbalanced by the abundance of newly discovered raw materials, techniques, and ideas. In the nineteenth century, the world's productive capacity had risen, through geographical and subsoil discoveries and changes in industrial and transport technology—as well as through the absence of destructive war on a world scale. This had made possible huge growth in long-distance trade and massive investments in capital equipment. Industry and business—the increasingly sensitive network of world capitalism—had periodically faltered, experiencing crises such as financial loss, mercantile failure, industrial unemployment, and depressed prices for commercial farm products and raw materials. The century's territorial expansions and technical innovations were launched on successive groundswells of rising prices punctuated by decades of deflation or relative stability. But even the low prices of its "Great Depression" between 1873 and 1896 are best explained as the flow of vigorously growing supplies moving from farms and factories constrained by a relatively constricted monetary base that was determined by an international gold and silver standard. Compared to the next Great Depression in Europe and America in the second quarter of the twentieth century, the first did not reveal any genuine cyclical weakness of investment opportunity or unusual incapacity of demand to keep pace with growth potential.

What was then in the nineteenth century beginning to be called the "world economy" climaxed in a great expansive burst from 1896 to 1914. Then for the next twenty-five years, through the 1930s, the props of nineteenth-century capitalism were knocked away from the industrial countries by organizational disruption at the international level. Germany's violent inflation of 1923 was followed everywhere by volatile capital movements, currency instability, and the domestic political struggles of social classes—all issuing into widespread deflation after 1930, long periods of prolonged and heavy unemployment, and ultimately the resumption of worldwide war. Of the sources of growth so vigorously employed before 1914, only one—developing technological potential—remained alive. That alone might have been sufficient to create growing wealth and incomes, but instead, the system's disorganization revealed itself in an odd form, regarded in the 1930s as a weakened aggregate demand. Societies with great wealth potential, like very wealthy individuals, would have difficulty spending all their incomes, it was argued, but with this difference: when a whole society does not spend, no one can earn; so incomes and wealth will dry up. Bank-financed investment spending, government deficit spending, and even foreign lending must then supply to the income stream what a national economy's excessive and implicit propensity to save puts out of reach.

Two further refinements can be made on this aggregative analysis of the dilemmas of the private capitalist processes in a world of national economies. First, it is important for continued prosperity that the composition of the investment match the composition of demand. This is the sort of problem the private market is designed to solve, but the markets' failures to do so showed up in bankruptcies, abandoned properties, weakened incentives, and so a loss in aggregate demand. Second, it is important that the real investment opportunities for business be divisible into units of appropriate scale to individual enterprises, or to consortia thereof. This had been a notorious problem in nineteenth-century railroad development, but the diffusion of the internal combustion and the jet engine in cars and planes confronted the same barrier—road systems, bridges, and airports were needed on a national scale. The same obstacle was encountered in the marketing of twentieth-century consumer durables—electric refrigerators, washers, sweepers, and all the rest—which required both that electricity be distributed to rural areas and that garage and housing space be available in cities.

World War II temporarily relieved the burden of insufficient demand even before it started, at least in Germany, through rearmament and the "multiplier effects" of increases in employment in the army industries. Then in 1945 all the countries of industrial capitalism came to face the process of postwar reconstruction, with the state taking a new and stronger role, with new social welfare programs and new terms of labor peace and, with the pent-up force of new technologies waiting to burst forth, demand came out of hiding. No one spoke any longer of cyclical weakness or decline, or of an excessive economic potential. Satisfactory international monetary arrangements were devised, and in the various national economies minibooms were on. Roomier suburbs were constructed around the great American and European cities, and unemployment rates were kept low. From 1950 to 1975, in most of the countries of advanced industrial capitalism average incomes doubled even when adjusted for inflation.

At the same time the general growth in labor productivity produced dislocations that could be traced to the structure of demand. For agriculture, the growing incomes bore out Adam Smith's dictum that the growth of demand for food "is limited by the narrow capacity of the human stomach." With labor productivity on farms rising at 3–4 percent a year over long continuous periods, farming's share of the labor force vanished nearly out of sight, falling even in the old peasant countries of Eastern and Southern Europe from 35–45 percent in 1950 to 12–15 percent in 1980. By the 1980s the same fate was overtaking the manufacturing sector, less from an abatement of demand than from the combined effect of mechanization, electrification, and delicate and powerful instrumentation. In these circumstances account must be taken of the increased ingenuity of manufacturers to create product differentiation, and attach imaginary qualities to simple objects through increasingly effective—sometimes subtle, sometimes blatant—salesmanship. What emerged in the high-income countries was a statistical return to the same relatively substantial share of "service" workers in the labor force that had been characteristic of preindustrial societies, though equipped with an array of instruments, buildings, and equipment. No doubt the computer operators in offices, the travel agents and bank clerks, the restaurant workers and entertainers had higher social products and somewhat freer lives than the slaves and domestic servants of the Pharaohs in ancient Egypt.

## The Business of Business: 1900–1970

Technological development and shifting demand set the limits of the world's industrial system. It was then the system's business to break down the aggregates of technologies and markets into bite-size pieces for individuals and their firms, adjusting the structures of markets and hierarchies to produce an efficient result, devising and carrying on routines smoothly and at the same time flexibly, and accepting and utilizing opportunities offered by changes in the parameters of the market and the competition.

### Technological Opportunities and Constraints

Certain tendencies in industrial history appear to be widespread. They are visible in the masses of detailed differences in the technical requirements of the products or services and the local, regional, or international histories and cultures in which business is immersed.

In the nineteenth century, access to water, transport, and ports provided notable cost advantages for the collection and redistribution of minerals and farm-produced foods and raw materials. Thus cities like New York, Liverpool, Rotterdam, New Orleans, Shanghai, Marseilles, Bombay, and Rio de Janeiro were great entrepots. Processing industries clustered near these shipping points as well as in coal-mining districts where mineral fuel—the lifeblood of the industrial system—was cheap. Canals and railroads provided cheap bulk transport to and across the interior of continents, but in rigid patterns set by where the lines ran and where they joined, at centers like Chicago, Paris, or London. The railroad ran like an artificial river, providing cheap hauling along its route, but leaving overland freight still to be carried by wagon over muddy and difficult terrain a few miles from its stations. Raw materials and fuels too were restricted to what nature provided and where nature had planted them. Nineteenth-century technology created rich opportunities for industrial location and commercial activity in a narrow pattern. In the British Midlands, at the Franco-Belgian-German coal fields near the Rhine, and in the Pittsburgh-Cleveland area, the coal-using, steel, and steel-using manufactories arose. In a somewhat more generous pattern related to the availability of water power and local labor, the great textile districts—Manchester, Lille, Alsace, Silesia, New England, and the Southern Piedmont of the United States—were formed.

Similarly, until 1920, and again between 1950 and 1970, many of the developments, linked as they were with tighter, quicker, cheaper transportation and communication and using extensive, expensive equipment of large capacity, also favored the large plant and the large and many-branched centralized organization, as well as urban agglomerations of manufacturers, industrial workers, and business services. Large, multibranched organizations had a technical advantage. There the flow of materials and semifinished parts could move smoothly and undamaged, without losing quality or time, through complex consecutive operations and a set of physical plants and processes. This corresponded to a machinelike human organization with its hierarchically-arranged, multitiered bureaucracy. The saving of time, materials, and energy in such a machinelike material and human mechanism, and the products delivered and sold, could embody a lower cost and a more dependably uniform quality, and so could outcompete the competition of varied and eccentric smaller-scale establishments. Indeed, one of the arguments for a centrally directed socialism controlled by an ideological elite (the Leninist/communist form), or a technocracy run by a managerial elite (the idealized fascist form), lay just here: each claimed to be able to outcompete a system of private, profit-maximizing but myopic producers. Each proposed to eliminate waste, the duplicated efforts of a competitive system. Benito Mussolini claimed even to make Italian trains run on time. A final factor affecting location was the need for research and development efforts, requiring expensive talent and equipment to support the new technologies, as well as systematic linkages with the fundamental sciences.

Twentieth-century technology substantially modified these nineteenth-century technical bases of industrial location and organization. Trucks and, of course, airplanes proved far more flexible than the railroad in choice of route and destination and in handling small cargoes. Oil and electricity vastly widened the range of economical plant locations with respect to power and fuel costs. Plastics, synthetic fibers, and the nonferrous metallic alloys extended the range of raw materials and reduced dependence on natural conditions of deposition or cultivation. A greater efficiency in materials and fuel utilization, and the extraction of by-products of a wide variety enabled manufacture to be "footloose" from materials sources. In short, after 1940, nature no longer dominated the choice of least-cost industrial location for individual industries. More important were access to the skills and brains of a trained or potentially trainable population who unlike land, minerals, harbors, rivers, or mountain passes were rooted to a spot only by cultural conditioning, the opportunity for work, and individual preference.

Geography and geology continued to set some constraints, albeit weaker ones, on the patterns of least-cost location of plants and the industrial agglomerations of plants and populations. But it may be observed that industrial plants still tended to cluster, in some cases with their mates or competitors, near suppliers and complementary service providers. Some small industrial cities declined, but the larger metropolitan industrial districts extended their spread over adjacent rural areas as they grew in numbers and variety to form the characteristic pattern of twentieth-century urban geography.

A similarly mixed conclusion can be drawn regarding how technological changes effected economies of scale and scope for the plant and multiplant organizations, at least after 1970. Even in the heyday of the nineteenth century, factories where many hand operatives were connected like pieces of machinery to a collection of machines around a single power source, as in the spinning mills or on the assembly line for automobiles (or the disassembly line in meat packing), industry offered many places where the small establishment, buying materials in semifinished state and selling a part of a more complex product to be assembled elsewhere, could survive and flourish. Electric power, too, after 1900 ordained generating plants and a distribution network of very large scale. But once the systems were in place, the power was available to homes and small workshops in infinitely small quantities. Some German economic historians hailed the electric motor's arrival as paving the way for the revival of the medieval artisan workshop, since it proved far more amenable to miniaturization than had water power or the steam engine.

Do the new technologies and materials of the late twentieth century enable the organizational separation of the parts of a manufacture or service activity to be conducted without waste by small, independent units of control? New technologies of communication create networks over which information can be widely disseminated. But will information or orders be sent out? Will individual workers, customers, and capitalists be given more informed control over their economic lives, and will those to whom such control is available be equipped to use it? Or do these electronic technologies simply make the centrally controlled structures of decision-making more efficient? If technological knowledge has widened the range of choices in the organization of human productive energies, productivity may prove to be less a matter of some technical or economic optimum than of the psychological adjustment of worker-managers to the culture of the workplace.

### The Corporate Form of Enterprise

In early capitalism, in trade, manufacturing, yeoman farming, or even on the tenant estate or slave plantation, conducting trade or organizing production was done by one man or one family, sometimes with a partner or a few associates, in an informal or very simple contractual or agency relationship. Nineteenth-century business assumed another form, by which funds could be collected for large projects—for example, canals and railroads—chartered by the state. This form, the "corporation, " had developed in the Middle Ages as the legal basis for towns, trading and settlement companies, banks, and even colonies with their proprietors. All were based on charters granted by the royal authority to a group of proprietors or stockholders engaged in a clearly delineated enterprise with a demonstrably public (or royal) purpose. In Britain and America, general incorporation acts passed from 1846 on made this form available to any group of enterprising artisans that wished to invest fixed amounts of capital, divided into specific shares. The terms and conditions of incorporation and of stockholders' liability for the organization's acts and debts were slightly different on the Continent, but essentially, the same pooling of capital was possible, allowing for large-scale, profit-based productive activity. It was no accident that railroads, the earliest example of technical economies of scale and systematic operation, were organized almost from the start by this legal device—first as small local lines then, through purchase and consolidation, as large regional systems.

The corporation as a form of industrial enterprise had several advantages, apart from providing the means to subdivide a large capital requirement into small bits sold as individual shares. It also provided an internal structure of control, forming in effect a double funnel. The nominal ownership of an infinitely large number of shareholders could be funneled into a narrow neck of "directors," and under them, a few officers and managers could sit over a broad, expandable base of salaried and wage employees who could be hired and dismissed at will. This semimilitary, hierarchical command structure made for the smooth, efficient operation of trains or a mill—where purchasing, production, and marketing could be reduced to automatic formulae, timed by machinery, made law in a set of regulations, or channeled into customary practice. Since this structure abolished all individual bargaining transactions in the space between employee and shareholders, it is not surprising that conservative American economists in the 1970s and 1980s found that it "minimized transactions costs," and could account in a perfectly neutral way for the growing dominance of the corporation as a form in industrial organization. The form made it possible for a "strategy" devised by one or a few managers to be sustained over a long period, allowing profits above normal returns (i.e., satisfying to the stockholders) to be used by such a management at its discretion. The form gave the entrepreneur both control and flexibility, to accommodate his or her varied roles of innovator, merchant, manager, hard bargainer, visionary public figure, and industrial statesman or woman. A single boss or close-knit group of colleagues acting as the "brain" of the organism had only to furnish the stockholders with satisfactory profits, taking care that the company's shares sold as well on the basis of those profits—at prices high enough to keep the wolf pack of financial entrepreneurs from buying up control and raiding the treasury. The arrangement gave to the yields on common stock a bit of the guaranteed stability of a bond. This, plus the very size of the corporations reduced risk, or the appearance of risk, for investors.

The corporate form has also been advantageous for lucky and ambitious entrepreneurs through the relative ease by which activities can be extended under the same roof: either backward to suppliers or forward to the market, or sideways by purchasing or driving out competitors, or forging an agreement with them on taking joint action against other elements—workers, suppliers, customers, patent-holders, bankers, or politicians. The form could adapt an internal structure in manufacturing enterprises to entrepreneurs' varying and various strategies; it could dominate small suppliers and distributors, resist labor unions, or create various ways for small groups of corporations to control prices and markets either directly or, by its extra-economic political and legal powers, through the state.

With all its protean quality and flexibility, this ancient form fitted well the engineering- and science-based technologies that developed in Europe and spread to the rest of the world in the nineteenth and early twentieth centuries. They continued into the 1950s and 1960s with the restoration of world capitalism after two decades of depression, political disruption, and war. Indeed, some writers would argue that the corporation itself, through sponsorship of technological and even scientific research, influenced the very direction these technologies took, acting as a kind of "focusing device" for scientific discovery.

For three major industrial countries—Britain, Germany, and the United States—the massive research done by Harvard business administration professor Alfred D. Chandler documents the development of corporate, industrial capitalism over the first half of the twentieth century. The central role of corporate business in the economic growth before 1930 and, with substantial modification, between 1950 and 1975 cannot be missed. In all three countries, new technologies developed in close symbiosis with corporate enterprise; where they developed independently, they were quickly snatched up and incorporated into corporate structures of production. In all three countries the managerial function became professionalized, though British industry's resistance to this impersonalization is blamed for its "falling behind" in the horse race of the industrialized nations. Everywhere in the twentieth century, the large firm extends out like a many-sectioned creature to cover a longer stretch between materials and markets. Particularly striking is the form's accommodation to national peculiarities of legal structure, education, prevailing social values and emphases, and to the differing physical and market circumstances of different industries. Undoubtedly, such a flexible strategy— which preserves a role for leadership to establish and maintain routine while allowing for innovation and growth, and serves varied markets while aiming toward efficiency, service, and profit—accounts for the extraordinary persistence of major firms in all three of the countries that Chandler studied, throughout one of world history's stormiest periods. Unlike the teeming mass of small firms whose success, like that of short-lived insects, is measured by their evolution through a high birth rate and high mortality, the large firm dominated evolution by asserting a limited control of its environment and contriving to accommodate significant structural and functional changes within its carapace.

## Boundary Conditions of Corporate Capitalism Since 1930

So strong a development at the heart of the industrial countries' national economies inevitably also had a negative side. Most of the political and intellectual controversy surrounding business and the economy from 1930 on can be categorized as responses to corporate dominance. These responses either took the form of countervailing power among sectors forming the boundaries of corporate activity, such as labor, the independent professions, farmers, peasantries, consumers, and small businesses, or countervailing ideology—the socialist movement, which, seized by an ideological and political power elite, forcefully and forcibly created by main force an industrial society not only in the Soviet Union but in several Eastern European countries as well. Between capital and labor stood the uneasy political position of the governments in the countries with parliamentary or constitutional democracies pressed by economic instability and war.

On the European continent, fascism, in its successive Italian, German, and Spanish variants from 1925 to 1945, folded the group organizations of both labor and capital into the corporate state. The countries which escaped—Britain, Sweden, the United States, and—except during the German occupation—Benelux (Belgium, the Netherlands, and Luxembourg) and France, still emerged from the war into an environment profoundly altered. Organized labor had become a yet stronger force, and government policies to promote economic stability and programs of social support based on an older German model were either emerging or stronger. The governments, too, increased their regulatory functions, especially in the United States, where the absence of a strong nineteenth-century mercantilist tradition had left business freer than elsewhere. The development of a so-called "middle way" went farthest in Sweden, while a burst of socialism in Britain, and a shot of mercantilism in France, brought a number of major industries—coal, steel, railways—into state ownership. Finally, the huge state war efforts and state-sponsored research projects put governments in the new position of being major customers of industry, and government contracts inevitably involved a degree of state supervision.

Beginning in 1950 the dynamic managerial corporations within the late-capitalist societies continued to grow and expand. As part of their adjustment to their altered environments, they appeared to act, consciously or unconsciously, according to three strategies—strategies aimed not merely at survival, but at handling increases in scope and size. These can be designated as: 1. accommodation and participation; 2. open political struggle; and finally, 3. partial or full exit from the national productive system into the world of finance and/or international business.

The first of these strategies, accommodation, particularly in terms of relations with organized labor, involved changing attitudes and personnel management techniques. A patriarchal feudalism had governed many nineteenth-century establishments, particularly those where the workforce was not far removed from its origins as a servile peasantry. The impersonal twentieth-century corporation could not regain this stance, even when it tried to divert unionization into a company union, or to incite company loyalty by offering various training and fringe benefit programs. The unions forced the corporate employers to the bargaining table under the threat of strike. But as labor's position strengthened after 1950, a strange development occurred, one which had been observed as early as 1900 by the German scholar, Robert Michaels, in the development of the German social democratic movement. As the unions grew in size and administrative functions, with complex interrelations developing among the organizations within and across industries, a professional class of organizers and managers formed relations with workers analogous to those of corporate managers to their stockholders. Without selling out the interests of either party, negotiation became possible among those who shared the problems, ambitions, values, and leadership characteristics of the corporate culture. This rapprochement went farthest in postwar Germany, where union officials were taken alongside bankers onto the boards of directors in some major industries. In Britain and the United States, union leaders and heads of political parties commanding labor moved into a national power elite even while the distinctions among working-class groups based on education and ethnicity and between blue-collar and white-collar workers held fast.

An even more marked accommodation occurred between the corporate bureaucracies and the parallel structures of government agencies—not only in the socialized enterprises, but in various government establishments and regulatory agencies. In France private administration of public duties was as old as the tax farming of the *ancien régime*, and interchange between top technical staffs in government agencies and large private firms in mining, iron and steel, and electricity, for example, was common. Essentially, a technical and managerial elite, all graduates from one of the *grandes écoles* that existed long before the present-day business schools, formed a cohesive professional and social group that distributed itself indifferently between state and private enterprise. Except for some rearrangement of financial assets, Western Europe's brush with nationalization did not make much real difference, except perhaps as a way to allay or control labor problems, and to guide and motivate rationalization and reequipment in some industries. When capitalism has entered its late or organized state, socialization of the structures is not a very revolutionary act. It may disturb such rights and returns as remain to private owners, but it merely assigns other hats and titles to the cadres of corporate management.

To a degree the same phenomenon could be observed in U.S. state regulatory agencies. The American progressive movement from 1880 through the 1920s created structures of industrial regulation, notably of railroads and public utilities, at both state and federal levels. Sporadic efforts were also made to enforce the Sherman Antitrust Act of 1890 and to enact other defining and implementing legislation, and a new wave of such regulation came in in the 1930s with the New Deal. Yet for both periods, such legislation walked a narrow and uncertain path among the fluctuating attitudes of the courts as to its constitutionality. In a great tangle of opinions, federal and state courts appeared to define the corporate charter and the collection of contracts that constituted a business corporation as a legal, or artificial "person," entitled to protection of its property against encroachment by the state, except by due process of law. This was held to apply against state laws under the fourteenth amendment to the U. S. Constitution, which had been adopted to protect the rights and property of freed blacks after the Civil War. In all cases, the distinction between the government agency regulators and the corporations being regulated blurred with the passage of time. In both Britain and the United States, the extent of regulation depended in the last analysis on the prevailing ideology at the top of the national political structure.

Political action as described by the slogans of one of the dominant political parties thus formed more direct means to allow the corporate economy to survive and flourish undisturbed in Western democracies. In this effort, the Right, with its parties of private property and laissez-faire, was strengthened by a curious dialectic, an irony of the economic developments. For the period between 1950 and 1970 formed a kind of Indian summer of high capitalism in the industrial world, made possible by attaching the nineteenth-century dynamism harnessed in large corporations to the various socialist and social welfare pieces of legislation developed since 1930, and in an international economy in which the United States had assumed Britain's mid-nineteenth-century role and achieved its own hegemony. Economically, the partnership of government and business was proving successful: the mixed economy worked. But as incomes rose without undue distortions in their distribution, property became spread more widely, and the prosperity and growth born of recovery and reconstruction, and incorporating staggering technical change within many sectors, pushed the lower limits of the middle class farther down into the working population. Sometime in the mid-1970s, as the prosperous, two-decade American "century" neared its end, the political balance tilted to the right—away from government and toward property. Later, at the turn of the 1980s in Eastern Europe, the same ideological and materialistic force dealt death blows to those corrupt centralized political structures that had founded themselves on the principle of socialized property. In the midst of the political confusion of that counter-revolution against the state, large managerial corporations escaped to continue to expand and flourish, presumably on into the twenty-first century. Competitive advantage in world markets and the selection of the right targets for national industrial policy became a focus of political attention. The outlook as of 1991 was brilliantly limned and strongly researched in Michael Porter's great study, *The Competitive Advantage of Nations*, a notable sequel to Chandler's basic studies and in the same historiographic tradition of the Harvard School of Business Administration.

But at the same time, as Porter appreciated, by 1980 corporate business was able to bring forward another means of protection against the rival power structures of a nation's politics: the resources and markets of the international economy. Capitalism had been founded, of course, on the free movement of capital in trade. Money, like the free knowledge of science, was power, and neither had been long successfully confined to any political unit where power rested merely on military or religious ideology. Beginning in the early nineteenth century, many industrial corporations had been created with foreign capital and the free in-migration of foreign labor. Trade in semimanufactures was common, and from the 1890s on a few corporations began to plant factories abroad. Backward integration to sources of fuels and raw materials, too, had stretched some large corporations across national borders. What was new for the 1960s and increased throughout the rest of the century was the systematic planning of marketing and production without regard to national boundaries, and the moving of materials to and from countries under the ownership of a single large firm, the so-called multinational corporation.

Such a development, of course, appeared to have the greatest prospect in the Economic Community of twelve European powers, where bits of national sovereignty were being melted down into a common pool that would set up no barriers to trade, capital movements, or labor migration within its bounds, and might eventually equalize cost conditions for industry—insofar as national governments could affect them at every point on the West European map. To some quixotic observers, such a merging of economic policies among a group of nations traditionally among the most quarrelsome and competitive in the world raised certain hopes. Perhaps, in all those national policies affecting the production of real wealth, other areas of the world might also join together to pass into the third millennium of what is quaintly called the Christian era in one truly economic unit within which the growth in per capita incomes, regulated so as to stabilize the Earth's natural environment, would be perpetually positive. Under such a regime, the world's wealth differentials, between West and East and between North and South, might even narrow. And could not a single developing body of engineering knowledge and a single price system spreading worldwide thus furnish the foundation at last for a peaceful ordering of human affairs? Despite the worldwide diffusion of science, engineering, and corporate capitalism, it is hard to find hope for any such miracle in the political and spiritual history of the late twentieth century.

The economics of Adam Smith presents two complementary obstacles to any identification of the large, unregulated corporation, however ingenious its engineers or dynamic its management, with automatic increases in the world's welfare. In a world without government economic interference, corporate capitalism with its large, complex units of control increases the risk of monopoly—the shutting down of competitive markets. Islands of higher price, of accumulating unearned rents and profits and an uneven distribution of market power, are the most likely result, countered, as it is argued, by technical economies of scale and scope in production and marketing and the richer harvests of new technologies. But beyond these purely economic features of corporate behavior, as in the old Calvinist view that a comfortable certainty of salvation is the death of the soul, comfortable certainty of profit is death to business enterprise. Even to the most insecure of spirits, a quasi-monopoly position gives a glimpse of certainty, of self-righteousness, of quiet rest.

Against these developments in the 1980s two windows were kept open to allow winds of competition to blow across the corporate world. One was the market for finance. Security markets were violently competitive and endlessly inventive, and access to finance could be gained from corporate treasuries, lightly regulated banks, insurance companies, and trust funds. The market, it might be argued—that is, financial entrepreneurs of the type observed in the 1880s and the late 1920s—would police the corporate managers by means of raids, takeovers, and consolidations, by offering stockholders more for their shares or by promising higher yields on the holdings in a reorganized enterprise. Just as in the finance capitalism of the 1900s and 1920s, but on a far more extensive theater and by a wider accumulation of manipulative devices, entrepreneurial energy in the corporate world was siphoned off in these essentially sterile pursuits. Insecurity was induced, true, but it was an insecurity which no amount of productive skill, no abundance of new technology, no development of new markets, no cleverness of advertising or skill in the arts of corporate management, and no labor policies to develop a workforce loyal to the firm could allay. Ought not a corporate manager interested in the substance of production to have preferred the weak regulation of government bureaucrats to a form of policing through robbery committed by another portion of the managerial class—who knew nothing of production and whose sole superiority lay in the trivial ability to make lightning-fast financial calculations, and in the ruthlessness to enter into the most destructive of risks without regard to either engineering or personnel considerations?

It appears that in the 1980s too, with its conservative free trade policies, competition for a nation's corporations could come from abroad. But in a world of international oligopoly and international finance, that competition would be absent, and now labor, professional workers, property, and all but the managerial power elite would have to look to regulation from international institutions to keep corporations honest. The question still remains,

*"Quis custodiet custodes ipsos?"* (Who will guard the guardians themselves?) Short of the coming of God's kingdom on earth, the question encapsulates a perennial problem of government.

Even if such a reasonable and stimulating regulation could be achieved in human affairs, one last obstacle would remain. For would not its accomplishment entail the melting down not only of economic disparities and political sovereignties but also of all the varied and colorful human cultures—values, beliefs, local pride, ethnic identity—into a single, monotonous, gray, businesslike corporate modernity? Would mankind in a world of rationalized structures not repeat the anguished cry of the Roman pagan to the "pale Galilean" on the proclamation of the Christian faith in Rome:

Thou hast conquered, O Brussels and UNO!
The world has grown gray from thy breath!

Perfection in the regulation of human affairs is the last Faustian impulse of Western culture, its last, impossible dream, its ultimate imperialism. Historians pose such conundrums, confident that they will never be answered but only replaced, after a long historical sequence, by others in the century that is to come.

BIBLIOGRAPHICAL NOTE AND SELECTED REFERENCES

It is impossible to compile a definitive bibliography for the twentieth century while it is still going on. The sources for this essay lie not only in books, but also in countless personal impressions and observations, in newspapers, journals, and conversations with scientists, economists, businessmen, and government officials. The following list of standard library references is organized roughly in the order that the topics are considered in this essay. In each case, bibliographies contained in references on a topic must be further consulted to fill out the subject.

In several cases, notably in the history of twentieth-century science, in its applications to technology, and in the effects of technological change on the location and nature of economic opportunities and the organization of firms and markets to make a response, no simple, single treatment can be found. Recourse must be had to papers given at conferences on one or another aspect of these subjects. See, for example: 1. the collection ably edited by Ross Thomson, published as *Learning and Technological Change*, New York: St. Martin's, 1993; 1. the unpublished papers of the Social Concept Conference, held at the University of Vermont, in Burlington, 13–15 August 1993, under Professor Thomson's direction; 3. the still uncollected and unpublished papers by Paul A. David of Stanford University and All Souls' College (e.g. David and Dasgupta, "Towards a New Economics of Science," reproduced in a series entitled

*MERIT*, by the Maastricht Economic Research Institute on Innovation and Technology (P.O. Box 616, 6200 MD Maastricht, The Netherlands); 4. NAS Colloquium on Science, Technology and the Economy, held at Irvine, Calif., 20–22 October 1995.

Such conference papers are naturally rich in models, theoretical insights, and programs proposed for research with occasional historical insight, but thin in detailed historical reference or continuity.

## Capitalism as a Civilization

Braudel, Fernand. *Afterthoughts on Material Civilization and Capitalism*. Baltimore: The Johns Hopkins University Press, 1977.

Jones, Eric. *The European Miracle: Environments, Economies, and Geopolitics in the History of Europe and Asia*. New York: Cambridge University Press, 1981.

Kindleberger, Charles Poor. *World Economic Primacy: 1500–1900*. New York: Oxford University Press, 1986.

Schumpeter, Joseph Alois. *Capitalism, Socialism, and Democracy*. New York: Harper, 1942.

Sombart, Werner. "Capitalism." In *Encyclopedia of Social Sciences*. New York: Macmillan, 1948.

Veblen, Thorstein. *The Engineers and the Price System*. New York: Viking, 1947.

Weber, Max. *The Protestant Ethic and the Spirit of Capitalism*. New York: Scribners, 1952.

Whitehead, Alfred North. *Science and the Modern World*. New York: Macmillan, 1925.

## Science and Technology: Economic Implications

Abernathy, William J. *Industrial Renaissance: Producing a Competitive Future for America*. Cambridge: Cambridge University Press, 1994.

Mokyr, Joel. *The Lever of Riches: Technological Creativity and Economic Progress*. New York: Oxford University Press, 1990.

Rosenberg, Nathan. *Exploring the Black Box: Technology, Economics, and History*. New York: Oxford University Press, 1990.

Usher, Abbot Payson. *A History of Mechanical Inventions*. 2d ed. Cambridge: Harvard University Press, 1952.

## Twentieth-Century Economic History: 1920–1970

Bernstein, Michael. *The Great Depression: Delayed Recovery and Economic Change in America, 1929–1939*. Cambridge: Cambridge University Press, 1987.

Eichengree, Barry. *Golden Fetters: The Gold Standard and the Great Depression, 1919–1939*. New York: Oxford University Press, 1992.

Hobsbawm, Eric J. *The Age of Extremes: The Short Twentieth Century, 1914–1991*. London: M. Joseph, 1994.

Kindleberger, Charles Poor. *The World in Depression, 1929–1939*. Berkeley: University of California Press, 1973.

Leuchtenberg, William Edward. *Franklin Roosevelt and the New Deal, 1932–1940*. New York: Harper & Row, 1963.

Lewis, Arthur W. *Economic Survey, 1919–1939*. New York: Harper Torchbooks, 1949.

Milward, Alan S. *War, Economy, and Society, 1939–1945*. Berkeley: University of California Press, 1979.

Nelson, Richard R. and Gavin Wright. "The Rise and Fall of American Technological Leadership." *Journal of Economic Literature* 30 (December 1962): 1931–1944.

Van der Wee, Herman. *Prosperity and Upheaval: The World Economy, 1945–1980*. London: G. Selen and Urwin, 1949.

## World Economic Organization: 1970–2000

Calleo, David P. *The Imperious Economy*. Cambridge: Harvard University Press, 1982.

Chandler, Alfred D. Jr. *Scale and Scope: The Dynamics of Industrial Capitalism*. Cambridge: Harvard University Press, 1990.

Galbraith, John Kenneth. *The New Industrial State*. Boston: Houghton Mifflin, 1971.

Hackett, Clifford P. *Cautious Revolution: The European Community Arrives*. New York: Greenwood Press, 1990.

Hannah, Leslie. "The American Miracle, 1875–1950 and After." Paper presented at Business History Society Conference, Ft. Lauderdale, Fla., 17–19 March 1995.

Kennedy, Paul M. *The Age of Diminished Expectations*. Cambridge: MIT Press, 1992.

North, Douglass C. *Institutions, Institutional Change and Economic Performance*. Cambridge: Cambridge University Press, 1990.

Porter, Michael E. *The Competitive Advantage of Nations*. New York: Free Press, 1990.

Reich, Robert B. *The Next American Frontier*. New York: New York Times Books, 1983.

Thurow, Lester C. *The Zero-Sum Society: Distribution and the Possibilities for Economic Change*. New York: Basic Books, 1988.

## The Corporation and the State in Economic Organization.

Berle, Adolf A. and Gardner Means. *The Modern Corporation and Private Property*. New York: Macmillan, 1933.

Chandler, Alfred D. Jr. *The Visible Hand: The Managerial Revolution in American Business*. Cambridge: Belknap Press of Harvard University Press, 1977.

Shonfield, Andrew. *Modern Capitalism: The Changing Balance of Public and Private Power*. London: Oxford University Press, 1965.

# 13  Money and Economic Change

WILLIAM C. MCNEIL

Money can be almost anything. It can be bits of metal, bundles of paper, a string of beads, a plastic card, or even electronic impulses on a computer chip. To an economist, money must act as a unit of account—we must be able to use money to calculate how much we can buy; a medium of exchange—we must be able to use it to buy goods now; and a store of value—we must be able to save it to buy goods in the future. But money is important for more than its role in making the economy work. It has powerful psychological implications as well. It is a symbol for the underlying structures of society. Its evolution in the twentieth century provides a powerful tool for understanding the economic, political, and social transformations that have created the modern world.

## The Gold Standard

By 1900, most of the world had been integrated into a commercial-industrial economy tied together by a monetary system based on gold. Although gold had long been used as a unit of value, its role was clarified and codified in the century after the Napoleonic wars. In 1821, Britain became the first modern nation to adopt gold as its monetary base. For the rest of the nineteenth century, any nation that wanted to participate in the benefits of the emerging British-led world economy had to accept the rules of the gold standard, and they did so in ever-increasing numbers. By 1880, the United States and most of Western Europe had accepted it as the basis of their currencies. By the turn of the century Russia, Japan, and Argentina were on it, and in the first decade of the twentieth century, it became a global system as a host of Latin American and Asian states tied their currencies to gold.

The gold standard, like any monetary system, was a part of a complex web of social relations that defined acceptable behavior and shaped society's moral philosophy. Deeply held beliefs about personal behavior as well as governmental responsibility were embedded within the "rules of the game," as the norms of the gold standard came to be called. The values of the gold standard were those of the new kind of society emerging in Britain, France, and the United States in the late eighteenth and early nineteenth centuries. It was a world that emphasized the rights of the individual over the needs of society and sought to restrain the power of governments while liberating their citizens. The gold standard represented the economic and monetary aspects of the classical liberalism articulated in the writings of such philosophers as John Locke, Adam Smith, and John Stuart Mill, who valued free trade, the preservation of individual freedom, and governments that were chosen by the people and had few responsibilities other than protecting the rights of their citizens.[1]

The gold standard was the monetary counterpart of the industrial, commercial society that came to dominate that classical liberal world. As it spread, it pushed nations toward those values of personal initiative and limited government, since it defined economic success in purely individual and competitive terms. So when those social values changed, it had to change too. As we study the evolution of money, we will also be examining the evolution of society's judgment about the proper relationship between the individual and society.

Every country that accepted the most basic level of the gold standard pledged to freely exchange its currency for a fixed amount of gold. Since each currency could be converted into gold, all money effectively became its equivalent, and all gold standard currencies could be exchanged at fixed rates. Although the actual currency used in day-to-day life could be gold coins, silver coins, or paper notes, central banks of each country were obliged to hold gold as a reserve and were supposed to issue paper currency in a fixed ratio based on their gold holdings. If gold reserves rose, more paper money was supposed to be made available to the economy; if gold holdings fell, the money supply was supposed to be reduced.

These simple features of the idealized gold standard provided remarkable powers for balancing the world economy and helping it operate smoothly. The gold standard promoted world trade while helping each country maintain a balance of trade. If a country began to export more than it imported, the gold standard soon worked to restore an equilibrium. As exporters increased their foreign sales, they brought their profits home and deposited the gold in the bank; the bank gained reserves and issued more money, which stimulated the economy and increased national income. As national income rose, it induced two changes that combined to restore the trade balance. First, as domestic prices rose, foreigners would buy fewer of a country's goods and its citizens would buy more of the now cheaper foreign goods—called the price effect. Second, as national income rose, people would become richer and would buy more of all goods, including more foreign goods—called the income effect. Put together, the price effect and the income effect increased imports and reduced exports, which brought trade back into balance.

The mechanism worked just as well in the face of a trade deficit. As a country lost gold, currency in circulation was reduced, causing prices to fall. This induced foreigners to buy more of the country's goods and caused home income to decline, so people bought fewer imported goods. Thus once again a trade balance would be restored. Since the theoretical gold standard was both automatic and self balancing, it was supposed to allow every nation to participate in a stable, free-trade world economy.

The gold standard had one other virtue: because the size of gold reserves determined the money supply, governments were unable to print excess money or expand the money supply to cover deficit spending. A government that tried to cover deficit spending by issuing more money forced domestic prices up (the price effect) and stimulated the national economy (the income effect). These changes increased imports, with the resultant loss of gold. As a country lost gold, the government had to stop spending money or risk being forced off the gold standard. For a society that wanted to limit the power of government this was a major collateral benefit.

With all these implications, the gold standard theory offered a remarkable system. It protected individual freedom by limiting governmental power, and it always worked to push the international trading system toward stability. However, in reality the gold standard was far more complex and more fragile than the model, and in the course of the twentieth century it underwent profound changes.

Britain dominated the world financial system in the nineteenth century by generating an almost unbelievable flow of investment capital which it lent abroad. In the decades prior to 1914, Britain annually lent abroad nearly 5 percent of its Gross National Product—mostly in the form of long-term bonds. Borrowers used this money to build railroads, canals, mines, factories, armies, and nearly anything else. In the same years, France and Germany also emerged as major international lenders, annually sending between 1.5 and 3.5 percent of their Gross National Product abroad. These loans together clearly represented an extraordinary commitment to the international economy in the classic gold standard period.[2]

At the core of the system lay the Bank of England, its reputation so great that it could confidently preserve the value of the pound sterling while holding only modest reserves of gold. Its power resided in the confidence investors had that it would always be willing and able to supply gold in exchange for pound notes. If investors started selling British securities and caused a run on the pound, the Bank was usually able to protect the value of its currency either by purchasing pound notes on the open market or by raising the discount rate—the interest that it charged for loans to other banks. As the interest or discount rate rose, other banks were more inclined to leave their funds in London or ship them there to take advantage of the higher profits. Because confidence in the Bank of England was so great, it rarely had to force the British economy into recession to preserve the pound's value. The bank's directors liked to boast that at a discount rate of 10 percent, they could draw gold from the moon, and this confidence assured the stability of the pound. The other major money center states, Germany and France, while not as strong as London, were rarely threatened by a run on their currencies. They too were largely freed from following the harsh rules of the gold standard that dictated high interest rates, less money, and falling income in the event of a weakening currency.

Even as the gold standard was becoming established as a worldwide system, it was undergoing important changes. Many states found that holding gold as a reserve was both expensive and inconvenient. Gold hoarded in bank vaults earned no interest and was difficult to move. Bonds, bills, and debts of foreign banks, in contrast, paid interest, were easier to move, and, since they could be converted into gold if presented to the issuing bank, were as good as gold. Given these advantages, around the turn of the century some official national banks began to hold foreign exchange as reserves along with gold. By 1913, about 16 percent of the world's reserves were foreign exchange. Since Britain had been on gold longer than anyone else and had the strongest commitment to the gold standard, the pound sterling was the preferred reserve or "key" currency. Yet it accounted for less than 50 percent of the currency or exchange reserves. The pound was the dominant reserve currency in Asia, but in Europe, the French franc and the German mark were often the major reserve holdings, while in Latin America the United States dollar was the preferred reserve currency. This emerging key currency or gold-exchange system made the real gold standard more complex than its ideal model. Foreign exchange as well as gold was held as reserves and, although London was the core of the system, important local centers in Berlin, Paris, and New York were gaining influence. Even in its classic period, from 1880–1914, the gold standard was far from a fixed or timeless system.

The real gold standard departed from the ideal model not only because some banks held currency as reserves, but also because in practice most central banks did not automatically issue more or less money as their gold reserves rose or fell. Instead, it was common practice for them to keep a fairly stable supply of gold and then, when they attracted more funds, build up a supply of foreign exchange. These funds did not become part of the banks' official gold reserves and banks did not issue more currency based on them. Instead, they "neutralized" or "sterilized" the excess reserves and saved them to cover future trade deficits. By holding excess reserves, banks could avoid expanding and contracting the money supply, thus protecting their national economies from the inflation and deflation that was supposed to make the gold standard work.

Many if not most nations, in effect, were able to escape from the formal rules of the gold standard. Yet this did not mean that the system failed to have any influence or that it did not restrain governments. The fact, for example, that the Bank of England could operate on such low reserve levels reflected the absolute faith bankers and merchants had in the Bank's willingness and ability to preserve the value of the pound. In time of real need, the Bank could and would raise discount rates and impose deflation on the national economy.

It and other central banks were able to deflate their economies because governments prior to the First World War were not held accountable for the prosperity or depression seen as natural products of capitalist economies. Money itself was viewed as legitimately regulated only by the market and not by government action. That was what the gold standard was all about. (The fact that the same bankers who manipulated their exchange holdings could also honestly argue that the system was automatic and natural may tell us more than we want to know about human nature.) What really made the system work was that there were fewer and usually less powerful interest groups pressuring the government for economic support than there would be later in the twentieth century.

We now know that the gold standard worked differently for countries at the periphery of the system than it did for countries at its center. When Britain ran a trade deficit, instead of deflating the economy, the Bank of England could draw large sums of money to London by modest increases in the discount rate. Outlying nations lacked the prestige to win the flexibility granted London.

Many of the peripheral countries, especially those in Latin America, were forced into unstable cycles of boom and bust by the gold standard. When their products were selling well abroad, foreign investors flooded the country with investment capital and pushed their economies into a frantic boom. Then, when a recession came, the foreign money fled back to the stability of London and the local economy was left to collapse into depression. Although the system seemed to work smoothly and almost effortlessly when looked at from the London side, it often whipsawed peripheral states as it drove them from extreme inflationary highs to paralyzing lows.[3] While the Latin American states with heavy trading ties to Britain were harmed most by this erratic flow of money, much larger states could also find themselves in trouble during times of political instability.

Russia and the United States were the two major states to suffer from the destabilizing capital outflows triggered by political unrest. As they faced these pressures, they foreshadowed the problems that would plague the international monetary system in the 1920s and 1930s. In the United States from 1893 to 1896, farmers and silver mine owners in the western states joined to demand that all silver mined in the United States be minted into coins. This "Populist" revolt was the American farmers' last attempt to assert their moral and economic superiority over their East Coast industrial and commercial rivals, part of their struggle to preserve a rural, simpler way of life fought on the battlefields of money.

The farmers, as perpetual debtors, wanted free silver coinage as that would produce a steady inflation, which would in turn increase the price of farm goods while inflating away the value of their debts. Banking and commercial interests wanted to remain on the gold standard and thus assure America's monetary ties to the rest of the world. Their fear of a Populist victory led to repeated monetary crises, as prudent investors sought financial security by sending their money out of the United States. Only after William Jennings Bryan—who supported the free silver platform—was defeated in the 1896 presidential campaign did the Populist threat collapse, and with it the threat of inflation. During the glory years of the free silver movement, the fact that the U. S. Treasury had held larger reserves of both gold and silver than Britain, France, and Germany combined had not been enough to reassure investors that the dollar was stable.[4]

Political instability in the Russian empire undermined its ties to the gold standard just as the Populist revolt undermined the dollar. When Russia was humiliated in its war with Japan in 1905 and then fell into revolution that same year, money fled the country just as it had left the United States in response to the free silver threat. Only the quick restoration of internal order and a two-billion-franc loan arranged by private French, British, and Continental banks saved Russia from being driven off the gold standard.

In the classical gold standard period, as in any other era, political crises like war, revolution, or inflation led to speculative capital flight and undermined the value of money. The fact that there were few such crises prior to 1914 was both a historical accident and the source of much of the gold standard's remarkable stability. Where there was political instability, as in Latin America, the United States, or Russia, the so-called "automatic" stabilizing powers of the gold standard carried little weight.

Just as the international monetary system was evolving in the decades prior to the First World War, money itself was changing forms. In the early nineteenth century, silver coins constituted most of the world's money along with a few gold coins. Paper money made up only about 30 percent of the world's money, divided between bank notes (paper money usually redeemable in gold or silver) and bank deposits. By the 1870s, with the spread of the gold standard, the use of silver declined and gold coins became the most common metallic currency, representing that same approximately 30 percent of the world's money. But the real growth came in the expansion of bank notes and demand deposits. By 1913, 85 percent of the world's money was in the form of bank credits, and instead of being moved from place to place in guarded wagons was most often ordered by telegraph and moved by pen strokes in bank records. In Italy, for example, in 1861, most Italians kept their money as currency and coin at home. By 1913, however, most of their money was held as deposits in banks—ready to be loaned and used.[5] Money was changing form: instead of stashing gold under their mattresses, peasants were hiding their bankbooks.

This paper money or bank credit money emerged with little regulation from governments. In most countries, any number of banks could issue their own notes so long as they were redeemable in gold. In the United States, although only banks chartered by the federal government could issue dollars, by 1905 the government had given charters to 5,668 banks. The only slow transition involved the power to issue money, which was concentrated in the hands of the central banks such as the Federal Reserve System in the United States, the Bank of England, and the Reichsbank in Germany.[6]

## Government Responsibility and the Creation of Fiat Money

In 1914, the outbreak of the First World War brutally ended this brief and fragile world of international monetary order. To protect their gold reserves, all the combatant states de facto suspended the convertibility of their currencies into gold. Although they planned to restore convertibility at war's end, the action proved to be far more difficult to take than any of them had imagined. The war shattered almost all the foundations of the gold standard's order, and even the best of intentions could never put it back together again. Europe's economic dominance, the remarkable domestic and international political stability, and the unusual balance of trade that had all combined to make the gold standard work were now gone. Europe's role as the financial core of the world came to an abrupt and little-understood end with the guns of August 1914.

Although historical boundaries are always fuzzy, the First World War marked a major transformation in both political and monetary history. The gold standard could never be fully restored despite numerous painful and costly attempts. The war forced governments to take control of their economies and money in ways they never had before. To mobilize their entire societies for war, they took on new powers that would never be completely given up. Control of the economy and money became vital to the survival of almost all governments. The political need to use money to create a new kind of society led to the recognition that there was nothing natural or God-given about one kind of money: it was now becoming clear that money was just one tool among many that governments could use to deal with the terrible complexities and instabilities of the modern world.

From 1914 to 1918, as the European nations fought for their survival, they all ran up huge deficits which they financed by issuing more currency, selling bonds at home, and borrowing abroad. By the end of the war, they had all dramatically undermined their prewar monetary positions. France and Germany, which had been major prewar exporters of capital, became desperate seekers of postwar international loans. Britain had sold off perhaps as much as one quarter of its foreign investment in order to pay for imports to keep its war machine going and feed its population. It had also borrowed such large sums abroad, mostly in the United States, that its influence over the international economy was broken. Although London remained an important international credit market and the world continued to look to it for financial leadership, never again would Britain be a major source of international investment. In four years, the Bank of England's power to draw unlimited funds to Britain had been destroyed and with it the freedom from pressure to deflate the economy. After the war, the Bank persistently forced the British economy into recession in an attempt to restore confidence in the pound, but it could never achieve the stability and growth of the prewar years.

The war not only created financial losers, it also created winners—some only for the short run, some for the rest of the century. Asian and Latin American countries, once peripheral to the world economy, now joined the United States in challenging Europe's economic monopoly. During the war, they had exported food and manufactured goods to Europe, and many had enjoyed profound economic growth. With this growth came monetary strength and a diffusion of monetary and economic power away from Europe. Japan emerged as a world economic power in the decade after 1914, Latin America exported more food and manufactured goods than ever before, and India became a major exporter of cotton cloth.

In the 1920s and 1930s, as Europe's farmers and manufacturers fought to regain their markets, the world suffered repeated and prolonged economic crises of overproduction and vicious international competition. Gone was the relative balance and stability of the prewar international economy, as was the benign acceptance or powerless complaint of those hurt by the economic system. A new world of bitter political and economic struggle accompanied the new, more competitive world trading system.

Within Europe, the war changed the fundamental relationships between governments and their people. In the prewar years governments had introduced the first rudimentary reforms to ensure greater social welfare and security for workers. The war gave a massive push to this trend. In England, the government had promised to create "a land fit for heroes" as a reward for its soldiers and workers. New housing, urban improvements, better health care, pensions for widows, orphans, and the wounded, and creation of a more democratic society had all been promised to induce men to accept their fate and continue fighting. In addition, governments all across Europe had learned they had to work with labor unions to win support for the war effort. This increased the influence and legitimacy of labor, and shifted the fundamental sources of power within every state. After the war, governments found themselves seeking votes by promising more social spending. These domestic political changes made it harder to counter trade deficits by raising interest rates, since higher unemployment and increased business failures could translate into defeat at the next election.

By the 1920s governments knew that if they failed to meet at least the minimal welfare demands of their citizens, they would be voted out of office. At the same time, raising taxes became increasingly difficult as interest groups mobilized to fight against higher rates. In Germany, this inability to raise taxes or reduce government support for industry, farmers, labor, or veterans, explosively combined with a determination to end reparations, drove the Reichsmark to a spectacular inflation that would only end in late 1923, when the mark declined to one trillionth of its prewar value. In France, similar politi-

cal pressure led the government to insist that Germany, not the French people, had to pay to rebuild the French economy. In France, as in Germany, the
dogged determination not to raise taxes or cut spending was a direct result of
the new democratization of political life, and undermined French political
independence throughout the first half of the 1920s. Financial weakness made
once-great nations dependent on foreign loans, and made money one of the
most important sources of international power in the modern world.

At the end of World War I governments tried to reduce their spending and
re-create the prewar conditions of the gold standard. But they were never able
to restore the minimalist government of the old classical liberal world. The
war had transformed the responsibilities and power of national governments.
In the prewar years, central governments had only very limited influence over
the economy: on average, European central government spending had
accounted for only 7 percent of national product. During the war, as military
production dominated their economies, government budgets consumed
nearly 50 percent of national production.[7] Despite drastic reductions in military spending after the war, governments could not force their budgets back
into the prewar box. During the 1920s, government spending consumed
about twice the prewar share of national income; about 16 percent in Britain
and slightly less in Germany.[8] By 1950, in response to the pressures of the
Great Depression and the Second World War, both the British and U. S. governments were spending about 25 percent of national income. The final push
to government expansion came from the increased military spending of the
cold war and the social spending of the expanded welfare state. By 1970, 34
percent of national income was spent or transferred by the British and American governments, and this was still lower than that of the Scandinavian
countries.

Economic power was changing places. Governments were gaining power,
and that power was being concentrated in the central government. This and
the increased demand for social welfare not only undermined the prewar economic and monetary system, but also reflected society's changing moral values. Classical liberalism, with its emphasis on individualism and a passive government, no longer seemed to work. In the face of the horror of the First World
War and the catastrophic unemployment of the Great Depression, it became
clear that individuals were unable to defend themselves from the ravages of the
modern world. Instead they demanded that governments act as mediators
between individual citizens and the instability of the market economy.[9]

As the world struggled to come to terms with the collapse of the gold standard and the economic changes brought by the First World War, it also had to

contend with a marked lack of economic leadership. Britain was no longer the world's monetary rudder, and the United States did not have the will or the political inclination to lead.[10]

By 1918, the United States had accumulated a major share of the world's gold, while most other nations found themselves without sufficient reserves to safely convert their currencies into gold. This unequal gold distribution was the final blow to the chances for a successful postwar re-creation of the gold standard. The British government understood that the old gold standard was gone and proposed that central banks be encouraged to use bonds and bills issued in convertible currencies as reserves along with gold. This meant that dollars (and later pounds—when Britain returned to gold) could be used as reserves. This "gold-exchange" standard had been growing informally before the war, and now Britain wanted to make it official. In reality, there were few other options since there was not enough gold to go around, and it was generally believed that money needed some real backing—that it could not simply be pieces of paper issued by a government.

By 1925, most of the European states had once again established stable exchange rates and, for lack of other options, had accepted the gold-exchange standard. But the system was plagued by problems. The British return to a prewar exchange rate of $4.86 to the pound did not account for the fact that British inflation had been greater than that of the United States. British goods were now too expensive to be competitive on the world market. When the Bank of England tried to play by the rules of the gold standard, it found that it could force unemployment up, but could not force wages down. As a result, throughout the second half of the 1920s Britain suffered persistent trade problems and high rates of unemployment.

In contrast to Britain, when France stabilized in 1926, it set the franc at a lower price than was warranted by the international market. Under these conditions, French goods were cheap and France ran a large trade surplus. Instead of inflating its economy as the rules of the gold standard called for, France built up its gold reserves and kept its inflation rate low.

Ten years of war and inflation had affected every state differently, and now uncertainty about the correct price relationship among the world's currencies made the old rules obsolete. The fact that states that ran trade surpluses, like France and the United States, refused to expand their money supply made the problems even worse.

For a brief time in the mid-1920s, cooperation among the central bankers of the United States, Britain, France, and Germany stabilized the system by encouraging capital flows from the surplus countries to countries running trade deficits. But the war had introduced huge volumes of short-term funds to the world money market, and this money could be lent or recalled at a moment's notice. Short-term notes, which had become a mainstay of government finance during the war, could be bought and sold quickly and had to be renewed regularly—often every three months. In the late 1920s and early 1930s, these short-term funds fled any currency that seemed at all weak: these "hot money" flows undermined all efforts to stabilize international finances.

By the end of the 1920s, the entire fragile world economic and monetary system began to unravel. Agriculture and basic goods industries had been in depression throughout much of the decade. In Germany, government subsidies and support for industry, agriculture, and labor had hidden the underlying weakness of the economy from 1926–1929, but the government deficits incurred to finance these policies had in turn been largely covered by foreign borrowing. In 1928–1929, as the rising New York stock market made fortunes overnight, Americans reduced their loans to the rest of the world and invested their money at home. By 1929, Germans were no longer able to cover their deficits by selling bonds in New York and had to raise taxes and cut spending.

Germany was forced to begin its retrenchment policy because it could no longer finance its deficits. But Germans across the political spectrum had come to regard the fiscal deficits as immoral and irresponsible. They had to be ended—and Germany, many believed, would have to pay a price for its weakness. Though the gold standard had failed, that had not eliminated the moral principles of prudent finance, balanced budgets, and limited government responsibility that had been at its core.

In 1929, the German economy was falling into a cyclical business recession, and the new policy of higher taxes and reduced government spending pushed the economy into full-blown depression. In the United States, the stock market crash of October 1929 undermined confidence in an economy already suffering a business slowdown. Since agriculture, other basic industries, and most of the less developed countries were already suffering a long recession, the world economy was extraordinarily fragile in 1930–1931.

In the spring and summer of 1931, a world monetary crisis brought these multiple regional crises together to produce the Great Depression of the 1930s. The immediate cause of the crisis was the failure of the major Austrian bank, the Kredit-Anstalt, in May, whose bankruptcy led investors to worry about the solvency of other Central European banks. Banks all across Central Europe soon suffered huge withdrawals. Then in June it was learned that one of Germany's largest banks—the Darmstaedter und Nationalbank or Danatbank—had invested heavily in Nordwool, a firm speculating on a rise in wool prices. (Wool, like many farm goods, had fallen to what seemed like an impossibly low price.) As wool prices continued to fall, Nordwool went bankrupt and dragged Danatbank down with it. By early July, all German banks had become suspect. Earlier in the 1920s, they had made good profits by borrowing foreign money at short term and lending it with high interest rates at long term. By 1931 many of their German loans were in default, and their foreign creditors were demanding repayment of their loans. Under the pressure of unwise lending and the mounting monetary fears, the entire German banking system collapsed within weeks. No major bank escaped, and the German government was forced to undertake the reconstruction of the banking system.

The shock of the German collapse led investors to worry about other international investments and devaluation of weak currencies. As it turned out, the next weakest currency was the pound sterling. Already facing large-scale withdrawals, the pound was critically undermined when a government committee, the May Committee, reported that Britain would run a large fiscal deficit. In the late summer and fall of 1931, money flowed out of Britain, and the Bank of England refused to try to stem the flow unless the government cut its spending. On September 18, 1931, exhausted by years of struggle to preserve the pound and facing universal domestic opposition to the dramatic raise in the discount needed to draw money to London, Britain ended the pound's century-long tie to gold. With the pound no longer convertible into a fixed sum of gold, its value was left up to the forces of supply and demand. It immediately began to fall in value against the dollar and other currencies still tied to gold.

Over the next three years, the spread of the monetary crisis drew all the smaller, regional economic problems together to consolidate, deepen, and prolong the depression of the 1930s into the greatest economic catastrophe ever to befall modern capitalism. The end of the pound's convertibility may be regarded as the effective end of the gold standard. There was nothing else to replace it.

In the face of the monetary collapse, banks raised their interest rates in a desperate attempt to attract the funds they needed to stay solvent. Government leaders believed that irresponsible fiscal deficits and unstable international speculation had destroyed their ability to govern effectively. Many pledged to adopt responsible, balanced fiscal spending policies and to break their nations free from the instability of the world economy. Businessmen watched all this and concluded that they could not hope to sell more goods, and that therefore they would have to cut back their investment plans. In the

United States, interest rates fell to nearly zero by 1933, and businessmen still refused to borrow because they saw no way to make a profitable investment.

## Putting the World Back Together: The Keynesian Revolution and Command Economies

For much of the world, the political, economic, and monetary disasters of the Great War and the Great Depression destroyed faith in the values of liberal capitalism. The war and diffusion of political power had forced a massive increase in government spending that had undermined the gold standard. Attempts to reverse the trend in 1930 and 1931 had pushed the United States and Germany into the worst depressions suffered by any industrial states. The prospects were grim. The gold standard did not work, free markets led to crises of unemployment, and governments could do nothing to address the problems. The classic liberal value of protecting individual freedom while permitting economic destruction seemed to be the height of immorality. Yet the fascist attempts of Germany, Italy, and Japan to create isolated trading zones subject to their own brutal exploitation presented an even more frightening alternative.

By the late 1930s, as the world moved toward war, leaders in the United States and Britain searched for ways to create a new international monetary and economic system that would be free of the failings of the 1920s and 1930s. To be successful, they had to solve a bundle of complex and interrelated problems. First, they concluded that national governments had to accept much greater responsibility for the economic and social welfare of their citizens. Maintenance of full employment and economic growth were central to this commitment: political stability, the leaders believed, depended on being able to offer people a sense that their government would meet their basic needs.

This commitment to an active government was exactly what the gold standard had made impossible. Preservation of citizens' economic and political freedom was now going to be supplemented by a commitment to assure their economic security. But this meant that governments would have to intrude more in the lives of their citizens. For people such as U.S. President Herbert Hoover, who were committed to democracy and preservation of individual freedom, big government threatened to destroy more than it would save. In his view, liberal capitalism had produced the richest society in human history and had done it by cherishing personal freedom above all: if periodic economic crises were the price society had to pay for freedom, then that was not too high a price. Economist Frederick Hayek voiced the fears of conservatives when he warned that empowering the government to control the economy was putting the country on *The Road to Serfdom*, as he titled his 1944 book on the subject.[11]

Despite these misgivings, in the course of the 1930s government officials in both Britain and the United States slowly accepted the need for an active governmental economic policy. This made returning to the gold standard impossible. From now on, governments had to put domestic stability and security ahead of international monetary commitments—unemployment was more frightening than monetary devaluation. Yet neither British nor American leaders were ready to throw out the gold standard entirely, believing that an open, integrated world trading system would help tie the world together and preserve world peace and prosperity (and the two were intimately linked in their vision). So a world economic and monetary order had to be created that would allow governments to attack unemployment at home while preserving both capitalism and economic integration worldwide. The question was how to build a system that allowed government economic initiative, maintained currency and price stability, and still preserved capitalist freedom for the individual and an open world trading economy.

The man most responsible for providing the intellectual framework for the world's response to this conundrum was British economist John Maynard Keynes. For the two decades since the end of the First World War, Keynes had been struggling to understand the sources of economic instability and depression. In 1936, he put all of his ideas together in a powerful book with the imperious title, *The General Theory of Employment, Interest and Money*, which asserted that for an economy to work efficiently, investment had to be large enough to absorb the savings that people chose to make. He argued that if investment fell, income would have to fall until savings were cut enough to equal the low investment demand. The depression, he said, had been caused by excessive saving and insufficient demand; it would not end until someone or some institution began to invest more. Only government had that capacity, and Keynes therefore called on it to initiate deficit spending programs that could push the economy back to full employment.

Although Keynes's ideas swept through British and American universities and converted the vast majority of academic economists, he was unable to carry government leaders with him. Even though some governments ran fiscal deficits in the 1930s, none did so as a matter of choice. Instead, while the U.S. government under Presidents Herbert Hoover and Franklin D. Roosevelt and the National Socialist Government in Germany ran deficits, they did so reluctantly and kept them to a minimum.[12]

Keynes's frustration came to an end in 1938 after Roosevelt tried to keep his 1936 campaign pledge to balance the budget. In 1936–1937, FDR cut spending and raised taxes and, in the process, sent the American economy into a new and devastating depression. Always a pragmatist, Roosevelt now saw the virtue in Keynes's ideas. In 1938, the American government decided to use deficit spending as a deliberate tool to reduce unemployment—the first time any government had consciously used Keynesian deficits to stimulate demand in an economy. Yet even then, government spending was slow to rise until the outbreak of war in Europe pushed the United States to begin massive rearmament. Now government spending rose sharply; and as it did, unemployment fell. By the end of 1941, American unemployment was no longer a problem and Keynes had been vindicated. During the war, as professional economists came to work for the government, the Keynesian revolution became the new, if sometimes still uncomfortable, orthodoxy in the United States and Britain.

Japan's experience in the 1930s illustrated the ambiguities of the new, more powerful role of government in national economic life. In January of 1930, the nation returned to the gold standard, which it had abandoned in 1917. Like Britain, Japan fixed its currency at the prewar exchange rate and soon found that its goods were too expensive to compete on the international market. Also like Britain, Japan tried to drive its prices down by deflationary monetary policies. And finally, like Britain, Japan suffered terrible economic hardships as it forced its economy to swallow the gold standard medicine.

In December 1931, under the leadership of Finance Minister Korekiyo Takahashi, Japan gave up its gold standard experiment (remember that Britain, too, had gone off the gold standard in September of that year). Japan let its currency float, stopped the export of its gold reserves, cut interest rates to encourage domestic investment, drove the yen down in value so that Japanese goods became cheaper and could be exported, and began to run a fiscal deficit to pay for the rebuilding of the Japanese army.

The Japanese program was a brilliant implementation of Keynesian economic policies before Keynes had articulated them. The Japanese economy grew at a healthy annual rate of 4.3 percent from 1931 to 1936, but its success could not compensate for the political disaster set in play by Takahashi's policies. The low yen rate allowed Japan to dump its cheap goods on trade partners who became increasingly resistant to Japanese economic expansion, which pushed Japan to ever more aggressive policies. The fiscal deficits were popularly supported because they were used to build up the army, which became increasingly independent of government control and then began its conquest of China.

When Takahashi became convinced that the fiscal deficits were crowding out private investment, he tried to rein in military spending. He failed to understand that political expediency now superseded economic rationality. In February 1936, he and other opponents of the military were assassinated by junior army officers determined to prevent any interference with the army. From then on, the army gained ever greater power and pushed Japan into war with China, Britain, France, and ultimately the United States. While Japanese economic policies had been successful in stimulating the economy, they had also stimulated bitter trade confrontations, the militarization of Japanese life, and finally, war and disaster for Japan.

The coming of the Second World War forced American and British leaders to seek new ways to achieve world peace and security. By 1944, as the allies clearly were on their way to victory, British and American leaders deliberately set out to create a new world order that could address all the failings of the interwar economic and monetary system. In July 1944, representatives of more than forty countries met at the New Hampshire mountain resort of Bretton Woods. There, after long debate, they accepted a new international monetary system devised by Harry Dexter White of the U.S. Treasury Department and John Maynard Keynes, representing Britain.

White and Keynes agreed that the world had to find a way for governments to stimulate growth and ease unemployment while preserving free trade and democratic capitalism. But Keynes wanted to go much further and create a powerful new international bank. He wanted to give the bank the power to inflate or deflate the world economy as the situation required and also wanted to create a new form of reserve that would take the place of gold and the dollar and would be controlled by the new bank. Keynes proposed the name "Bancor" for his new reserve unit. Had his plan been accepted, gold would no longer have been the base of the world monetary system. Instead, all money would have been entirely the artificial creation of central banks and this new international bank.

But Keynes lost this fight. White and the Americans were unwilling to give up control of their economy to a supernational bank. Instead, they won approval of a much more limited system that was intended to loosen—but not free—the hands of governments as they tried to manage their national economies. Keynes wanted exchange rates to be more flexible so that governments could spend money to counteract recessions and stimulate faltering demand. But the Americans worried that freeing governments of all restraint would lead to unrestricted fiscal deficits and drive the world toward inflation. So exchange rates were fixed with adjustments possible only in the case of "fundamental" trade imbalance. While not as sweeping as Keynes wanted, the new system was far more flexible than the gold standard.

At the center of the Bretton Woods system were two new international organizations intended to re-create a stable world monetary and economic order. The International Monetary Fund, commonly known as the IMF, was given reserves of currency that it could lend to member countries when they had temporary trade deficits. These loans would allow nations to run short-term fiscal deficits to reduce periodic unemployment without creating the kind of currency crisis so common in the interwar period. Since exchange rates were fixed and the IMF funds were limited, states could run only limited deficits and would, in reality, often face the same kinds of deflationary pressures so common to earlier decades.

While the IMF helped nations address unemployment and short-term trade deficits, it did nothing to solve the problems of long-term capital investment that had been a second source of interwar instability. To provide funds for the reconstruction of Europe after the war, the Bretton Woods conference created the International Bank for Reconstruction and Development, known as the World Bank. After the European economies were on the road to recovery, the World Bank was given the task of providing long-term loans to less advanced nations to help them industrialize.

Nations joining the IMF and the Bretton Woods system were expected to play by the rules of the new international monetary system, and perhaps nowhere was the worldwide influence of the Western European states so clearly demonstrated as in the terms under which the Bretton Woods agreements were accepted. When Great Britain bound itself to the rules, it committed not only itself but all of its colonies and dependencies, a list that, when typed in a single-spaced column, ran for three pages. The lists of colonies and dependencies accepting under the names of France, Belgium, and the Netherlands were similarly impressive. Imperialism may have been dying, but it was far from dead in the years after the Second World War.

When nations committed themselves to the rules of the Bretton Woods agreement, their central banks had to hold gold or a currency convertible into gold as reserves for their national currencies. This re-creation of the gold-exchange standard became in reality a dollar standard. Few countries besides the United States held gold reserves, and no other large countries were able to restore gold convertibility after the traumas of the Second World War. Thus under the Bretton Woods system, the United States held gold as its reserve (although since the 1930s private American citizens had not been allowed to hold monetary gold), and the rest of the world held dollars.

The system officially went into effect in early 1946, but it did not work as expected. The Soviet Union had participated in the conference and had been granted important concessions to win its acceptance of the Anglo-American plan. But as the cold war divided the allies, the Soviets refused to accept the open, capitalistic trading system that Bretton Woods required. Instead, the USSR returned to its pre-WWII monetary and economic structures—a system that used money very differently from the capitalist West.

To understand how money was used in the communist states, we have to consider a function of money in capitalist economies that has not been addressed so far. In market economies, changes in the money price of goods serve as the vehicle for allocating resources. Prices determine what will be produced and what will be bought. Market economies are called markets because it is in the market that buyers and sellers haggle over prices until goods are bought and sold. Changes in price drive changes in supply and demand, which is what makes capitalism work. When people want more of a product, they will bid the price up; when they want less, the price will have to fall to induce them to buy more of it. When prices rise, more people will try to make and sell things, since profits will be higher. Through changes in the price of goods the economy determines how much of every good will be produced. In modern capitalism, money is literally the mechanism that makes the entire system work.

Only in times of national emergency, usually in war, have capitalist governments tried to interfere with money's role as resource allocator. Only during the Second World War did the U.S. government mount a successful attempt to remove price fluctuations as the driving source of production and consumption. On April 28, 1942 the government issued the General Price Regulation, which froze all prices nationwide. The government wanted to be able to buy huge supplies of war materials without driving the economy into a spiral of inflation, and its price freeze was remarkably successful in this way. Consumer prices remained nearly stable throughout the war, despite a tremendous increase in government spending and in employment.

Economist John Kenneth Galbraith has argued that this wartime experience of managed prices is not as rare as Americans choose to believe. He points out that in highly concentrated sectors of the economy—such as oil, steel, automobiles, electricity, and many consumer goods—price is often set by agreements among major producers, sometimes with government involvement. Labor's wages too are often set by union bargaining power or the ability of professional organizations to create a monopoly of supply, as the American Medical Association has done with doctors' services. In the past two decades, some of these formerly protected markets in the United States and Europe have been opened up by international competition. But they remain strong, especially in Japan and France.

The Soviet Union and the Eastern European nations with communist governments took this rejection of the market economy to its extreme. The communist economies used money, but refused to let it or the market determine what would be produced. Instead, the state determined what it needed and wanted and ordered producers to fill its needs. Money played at best a marginal role in these "command" economies.

Since the Soviet state made its primary goal the expansion of national production, it had to reduce consumption in order to make resources available for investment. Under the Soviet system, workers were paid wages in currency and they purchased goods with their money, but only at prices and at stores controlled by the state. With more money, in theory, they could buy more goods. The catch was that because the state was not interested in producing consumer goods, essential products were most often in short supply. The real allocation of goods was not made by the amount of money one had, but by the time one was willing to stand in line to get scarce items.

Only on the margins of agricultural production and on the black market did money play a resource allocation role in the Soviet economy. The black market, or "second economy" as it was called, played a major role in Soviet life and operated at market prices set by supply and demand. In the decades after the Second World War, gasoline, alcohol, and many services essential to a consumer society were commonly purchased on the second market. As much as 10 percent of Soviet earnings may have come from this illegal source.

There was only one legal market sector in the Soviet economy prior to the Gorbachev reforms of the late 1980s, and that was in the production and sale of farm produce. Beginning in the late 1920s and continuing through the Soviet period, farmers were permitted to control small plots of land and sell the goods at market prices in collective-farm markets. Collective-farm market prices were much higher than those at state stores, but better quality and simple availability made them essential for Soviet consumers. Over 60 percent of the potatoes eaten by Soviet citizens as well as 50 percent of the eggs and 35 percent of the meat came from the collective-farm markets.

As important as the second economy may have been, most Soviet prices were set and administered by a complex, overlapping, and competing bureaucracy. Soviet planners tried to set prices that balanced supply with demand while putting the needs of the state above all else. Prices were set by projecting past surpluses and deficits into the future, while trying to take into account changes in needs and problems in supply. Firms producing goods essential to the state were assured of prices that would allow them to continue to operate—obsolete plants and factories were allowed higher prices so that they could compete with more efficient factories. Under these procedures, there were few incentives for innovation or increased efficiency.

In the absence of monetary signals that warned of excess supply or dire shortage, the command economies were successful at meeting the needs of the state (which is, after all, what they were intended to do), but were unable to adjust to changes in consumer demand in a flexible way. Without price changes to signal how much of a specific good was needed or how efficient production was, both industrial and agricultural efficiency deteriorated while consumer demand was left increasingly unsatisfied.

Under these conditions, the communist economies began to falter by the late 1960s. In the aftermath of the subsequent collapse of communism in the Soviet Union and Eastern Europe between 1989 and 1991, absence of a market tradition made the economic adjustment excruciatingly difficult. As the new Russian Republic and the other former communist nations fought to make their economies more responsive and efficient, they finally turned to the World Bank and the IMF, and tried to accept the same Bretton Woods system that they had rejected nearly half a century before.

While the Soviet Union retained a hint of a market-oriented economy even during the Stalin years, China, in the years after the 1949 Communist revolution, all but ended the use of money. For the peasantry, which made up the vast majority of the population, money became virtually unknown. Farmers worked on collective farms where crops were largely taxed away, and in return a living ration of food was provided by the state. The little money that passed through peasant hands had to be spent at state stores to purchase the barest of manufactured supplies. In the cities, while wages were paid to workers, little could be purchased without ration coupons that were provided to workers on the basis of job status and service to the party and state. Until the reforms of the 1980s, no farm market equivalent of the Russian collective-farm market existed. Money was largely a vestige of the earlier capitalist society and had little relevance in this regulated, state-dominated society.

## Systemic Order and Disorder, 1947–1992

In the early years after the Second World War, not only the Soviet Union found the new Bretton Woods order unacceptable. In July 1947, at American insistence and in keeping with its commitments under the new monetary system, Britain tried to return the pound to gold convertibility. But investors, convinced that Britain could not sustain a trade balance, withdrew their money from pound investments. Within weeks the British had to suspend free trade in sterling. They were joined by the rest of the West European countries, Japan, and indeed most of the rest of the world in maintaining government regulation of currency exchange rates. Canada and the Latin American countries were among the few nations besides the United States that could afford to preserve their tie to gold.

The Bretton Woods system had assumed that member states would allow their currencies to be freely convertible into gold or dollars. But the United States economy was so strong and its gold reserves so large that other states could not accumulate sufficient reserves. The flight of money trying to escape the crises in Europe in the 1930s and the fabulous growth of the American economy during the war, in contrast to the devastation of Europe, the Soviet Union, and much of Asia, made the United States by far the world's richest state.

From 1945 to 1958, the United States shipped vast sums of money abroad to finance the reconstruction of the rest of the world. Initially, it also shipped its goods abroad as Europe and Japan rebuilt their economic infrastructures with American resources. In the early 1950s, the American trade surplus declined while capital exports remained strong, allowing the rest of the world to build up their monetary reserves by borrowing money from the United States or by selling its goods.

By 1958, Britain, France, West Germany, and most of the other Western European nations had built up large enough reserves that they could end exchange controls and allow their currencies to be freely convertible into gold or dollars. Since 1950, most of these nations had belonged to a currency clearing system called the European Payments Union. Many of these states, including Britain, France, Holland, and Portugal, retained broad economic ties to their former or current colonies, and this made the EPU a nearly worldwide monetary system outside of the dollar zone. When the Europeans and their associated states made their currencies convertible in December 1958, they transformed the Bretton Woods system into an international reality. It had taken thirteen years for the postwar order, planned so carefully in the mountains of New Hampshire, to achieve the worldwide influence that the gold standard had enjoyed at the turn of the century.

As Europe, then Japan and most of the rest of the noncommunist world joined the International Monetary Fund and accepted the rules of the Bretton Woods system, they tied their money to the American dollar. The United

States maintained its commitment to convert the dollar into gold at the rate of $35 per ounce. Most other central banks held dollars as reserves, although some, especially British Commonwealth countries, held pounds sterling.

For most of the 1950s the dollar was as good as gold, since it was scarce and the United States had huge gold reserves. But beginning in 1958, the flow of American investments and aid abroad began to build up an excess of foreign-held dollars. In 1958, as foreigners began to convert their dollars into gold, the United States began to suffer a steady loss of gold reserves despite the fact that it ran a trade surplus in every year from 1956 to 1973, except for 1972. By 1961, the loss of reserves was worrisome enough that the United States induced its allies to cooperate to preserve the dollar at its par of $35 per ounce of gold. Under this "gold pool," all the central banks agreed to buy and sell gold at the fixed rate and thus ensure that the dollar did not fall in value. But as Americans continued to invest abroad and foreigners continued to convert their dollars into gold, American gold reserves continued to fall, and in 1964 the United States began to impose restraints on capital exports. The dollar exchange system at the core of Bretton Woods was in trouble.

In March 1968, the gold pool central banks agreed that while they would continue to exchange gold among themselves to settle accounts, they would no longer buy or sell gold on the market. Effectively this meant that the major Western nations had ended the link between their currencies and gold. From 1968 onward, money as we know it was worth only the faith we had in it. For private citizens, the currencies of the industrial West were no longer convertible into gold, and increasingly their values were set by supply and demand and not at fixed rates determined by government action. Although the 1968 agreement not to sell gold should have made it clear that the rules were changing, it took half a decade more to sort out how the international monetary system would work once currencies were no longer tied to gold.

Despite the repeated attempts in the late 1960s to protect it, the dollar remained under relentless pressure. Robert Triffin, an American economist, argued that the monetary system itself was the source of the dollar's weakness and that only fundamental reforms could save it. Triffin pointed out that as the Western economies grew and prospered, they needed more and more money to keep the system working. Since the supply of gold was limited, central banks had to increase their holdings of dollars. Eventually, foreigners held more dollars than the United States could cover with its gold reserves. When this happened, faith that the dollar was as good as gold began to erode, and fear grew that the dollar might be devalued. As this fear spread, dollars were turned in for gold and the fear became a reality as gold reserves fell. Triffin argued that for the world economy to continue to grow, some new kind of reserve had to be created that was neither gold nor dollars, but was still limited in supply yet expandable as the world economy grew.

At Bretton Woods Keynes had argued for the creation of just such an artificial reserve currency, and now, in 1969, the International Monetary Fund was given the power to issue what were called "Special Drawing Rights." The members of the IMF agreed to authorize it to issue Special Drawing Rights to each member based on that nation's proportion of IMF reserves. The decision to allocate new reserves in this manner infuriated the world's less developed nations who, having little influence in the IMF, would now get little help from the new plan. The poorer states had argued that they should receive most of the Special Drawing Rights as a form of international aid to allow them to finance more investments and raise their national incomes. But the industrial states, meeting in what was called the Group of Ten (the United States, Britain, France, Italy, West Germany, Belgium, the Netherlands, Sweden, Japan, and Canada), decided that giving larger reserves to the poorer states would only encourage irresponsible spending and larger trade deficits. The decision contributed to the growing division between the "North" and the "South," or the industrial and nonindustrial states of the world. In the end the issue was moot, as few SDRs were issued and the monetary impasse was broken in a quite unexpected way.

In the late 1960s and early 1970s, a new and disturbing money market emerged that brought huge sums of short-term capital into the international financial arena. This new market in what came to be called "Eurodollars," and later "Eurocurrency," had its faint beginnings in the 1950s, when the governments of the People's Republic of China and the Soviet Union began to deposit dollars they held in European banks outside of American control. In the late 1950s and 1960s, private American banks and businesses expanded the practice. These funds, or Eurodollars, were simply short-term dollar deposits that were left in European banks instead of being returned to U.S. banks as had traditionally been the practice. The higher interest rates available in Europe induced banks and businesses to leave their overseas dollars in European banks, which in turn re-lent them on the European market where they earned greater profits. In the 1960s, as the American government tried to stop the outflow of dollars by taxing American foreign loans, the demand for dollars abroad grew. In addition, since the United States regulated interest rates to keep them low, businesses and banks that earned profits abroad had strong incentives to leave the money in European banks and earn higher returns. The government's attempt to regulate money helped create the Eurodollar market, as investors found novel ways to escape government control and move their money instantly around the globe via computer links to wherever they could earn the highest returns. Eventually, not only dollars but other, mostly European currencies entered the market; hence what is now referred to as the Eurocurrency market.

In 1971, as pressure on the dollar mounted, President Richard Nixon faced the prospect of having to raise interest rates and risk a recession just as he was preparing to run for reelection. To free his hands to stimulate the domestic economy, he had to rid himself of the restraints imposed by fixed exchange rates. On August 15, 1971, the United States took the last step in eliminating gold as a measure of money when Nixon announced that the country would no longer buy or sell gold in exchange for dollars. The dollar was freed from its pegged rate of 35 dollars/ounce of gold. By 1975, after several failed attempts to re-create a fixed exchange rate system, all the world's money was left to float without any ties to gold. Even the fiction of a gold standard was finally eliminated.

The Eurodollar market had bred fear that it was re-creating the volatile, short-term capital flows that had destabilized the world economy in the 1920s and 1930s. As long as the dollar and other currencies were fixed to gold yet suffered trade or capital flow deficits that put them at risk of devaluation, this proved true. But when currencies were allowed to float, the market became self-correcting. Small declines in value often led to the expectation that the bottom had been reached and a profit might be made by speculating on currency stability. This set in motion counterflows of funds into the futures market, stabilizing currencies and largely ending the unrelenting downward pressure on weak currencies that had been the bane of the fixed exchange system.

In addition, the Eurodollar market is somewhat more stable than the prewar short-term market, since loans are made in a way that protects the banks. Although the banks hold deposits at very short term (less than three months) and make loans that are medium term (up to five years), the loans carry floating interest rates so that if interest rates rise, the banks can raise their rates. This would tend to protect the banks' income as long as the borrowers could make their payments. Beginning in the late 1970s, that was increasingly not the case.

The Eurodollar market was attractive to banks because it was unregulated by any government and offered higher rates of return than more conventional markets. This meant that it often attracted borrowers who did not have the credit standing that would allow them to borrow on cheaper markets, a factor that became important when, in 1973 and 1979, the Organization of Petroleum Exporting Countries (OPEC) doubled and redoubled the price of oil. Although the industrial countries suffered some distress from the oil shocks, they soon began to export more to the OPEC states and to receive investment funds from them that restored relative stability. Many poorer countries were not so flexible, and the oil price increases sent them scrambling for money to balance their trade deficits. The emerging Eurodollar market was ideal to suit their needs: as Third World countries began to suffer mounting trade deficits and government borrowing mushroomed, the weakest states were drawn most heavily to the Eurodollar market. By the late 1970s, government borrowing accounted for 50 percent of the market.[13]

From 1974 to 1980, OPEC oil profits amounted to 300 billion dollars. Of this sum, $14 billion was loaned by the IMF and World Bank to less developed countries. OPEC states themselves loaned $47 billion to developing countries and deposited most of the rest in Western banks, which lent an additional $147 billion to developing nations—much of that through the Eurocurrency market.

At first, the fluid Eurocurrency market was a godsend, as it provided the funds to keep the world liquid during a massive shift in wealth to the oil-producing nations. The flexible system that had emerged largely as a result of America's inability to maintain the value of the dollar was far better suited to absorb the disequilibrium of the oil shocks than the old fixed-rate system. But for the less developed countries, the virtues of the system soon turned into a nightmare. In 1980, interest rates began a rise that would take them to unprecedented levels, and the short-term loans taken on the Eurocurrency market soon had to be repaid at bankrupting prices. By 1985, Third World debt had reached one thousand billion dollars and many states were forced to chose between crushing deflation or international default. Countries that had enjoyed growth rates on the order of 6 percent per year from 1969 to 1978 suffered declining incomes in the early 1980s and only modest recovery in the later half of the decade. For much of Latin America and most of sub-Sahara Africa, the 1980s were a decade of economic and social crisis without precedent in the twentieth century.

## Mature Consumer Societies and Credit Card Economies

In the same way that the introduction of fiat money reflected the growth of government power in the first half of the twentieth century, the spread of credit cards as a form of money has been an integral part of the maturation of consumer societies. Just as it is artificial, yet useful, to suggest that

World War I represented the birth of government control of the economy and the introduction of fiat money, so too it is useful, if somewhat artificial, to suggest that the first mature consumer society evolved in the United States after the Second World War and has, since then, spread to much of the rest of the world. The credit card and the electronic transfer have revolutionized money just as consumer spending has changed industrial societies.

Even as people were becoming accustomed to using paper and bank accounts in the early twentieth century, they were being introduced to a new and even more elastic form of money. It had long been common practice for stores to allow well-known local customers to buy goods on credit, with the store keeping a book of purchases. In the 1920s, a number of stores in large American cities began to modify this system by issuing charge cards to favored customers in an attempt to win more of their patronage. In the same period, as the automobile industry tried to reach a mass market, it began to promote installment purchases for cars. These new forms of borrowing made credit purchases respectable and transformed the way Americans thought about debt. Instead of being the last resort of the poor, charge cards and automobiles transformed one form of debt into the status symbol of the well-to-do.

Throughout the 1930s, and then especially after the Second World War, as Americans became more mobile, oil companies created the first mass market for credit cards. To win loyal customers, they encouraged credit purchases and issued cards to consumers who had never bought on credit before. These early gasoline credit cards, like the store cards, were marketing tools designed to induce customers to keep buying from one firm. All this changed in 1949.

In 1949, three New York businessmen conceived the idea of a "universal" credit card that would allow business travelers to carry less cash and charge their meals and lodging. Their creation, the Diners Club Card, was the first credit card that was not the marketing tool of an individual company: instead it allowed purchases at a wide range of retail establishments. This was a new form of money, only conceivable in a highly mobile, consumer society with extensive discretionary income. In the 1950s, only the United States could support such an environment. But in the next decades, as consumer societies emerged in Europe, Japan, and much of the rest of the world, universal credit cards grew to become a major new kind of money with new values, benefits, and costs.

In 1958, American Express, which had made its fortune providing travelers checks, entered the credit card business with the added advantage that its card could be used internationally. While still geared to the American consumer, credit cards were introduced to the rest of the world for the first time, though still intended only for the well-heeled business traveler.

In the 1960s and 1970s, universal credit cards were made available to a mass market. As the potential profits of providing credit became apparent, large American banks began to issue their own cards. The two most common were BankAmericard, issued by The Bank of America, and Mastercard, issued by a consortium of banks. The real breakthrough into mass credit came in the late 1960s, when the competing banks mailed unsolicited cards to millions of college graduates all over the United States. By 1986, 55 percent of American families had a universal credit card and it became increasingly common to purchase goods with the order, "charge it."[14]

What began as an American monetary revolution soon spread worldwide. In 1966 the Bank of America began to franchise its credit card abroad and by 1972 it had established affiliates in seventy-one countries. In 1976, its international business had become so great that it changed the name of its card to "Visa"—a word with international recognition.

Visa and Mastercard won access to new international markets by establishing ties to local banks that had often created their own credit card systems. The American banks tied the local markets into the international system. Japan, followed by France, has established the largest credit card business outside of the United States, and both countries have integrated a much larger part of their economies into the credit card system than has the United States. In both countries, local banks have largely been able to control the local credit business.

Americans own over a billion credit cards, or an average of almost four cards for every man, woman, and child in the country. In recent years, the Japanese have taken the cards with almost equal enthusiasm and had two hundred million cards in use in 1992[15]. There even more than in the United States, credit cards have proven very popular with the young, and have allowed easy credit—with an associated increase in personal bankruptcies. The increased use of credit cards is part of a new ethic of the post-World War II generations, who want a better standard of living yet are not as committed to self-sacrifice and traditional values as were their predecessors.

Despite the seemingly universal use of credit cards, they still account for only a small share of consumer purchases. Even in France, where the government has systematically encouraged the use of credit cards, they account for only about 5 percent of consumer spending while bank checks account for another 11 percent, and cash remains the overwhelming way to buy—accounting for 83 percent of all consumer spending.[16]

Compared to cash or checks, credit cards are an expensive way to purchase goods. They create huge accounting problems as millions of individual transactions must be accurately recorded and tabulated. By the end of the 1970s, processing costs were reduced by the introduction of computerized bills. The next step in computerizing the billing process has further reduced costs by using telephone links between each retail outlet and the central computer, allowing the entire billing process to be completed electronically with no paper processing and no human labor costs.

Prepayment cards have become another common way to pay for many consumer services, such as trains, buses, and, in Japan, which has gone furthest in this direction, even meals at McDonald's. In addition, the Japanese have accepted preauthorized payments as the major electronic means of paying their bills. Under this system, customers authorize their banks to automatically pay specific bills each month. Payments are made by computers programmed to subtract funds from one account and add them to another. By the 1980s worldwide, preauthorized payments were used six times more often than payments by check. While Americans have begun to use both of these new forms of money, they continue to prefer to pay their bills by check.

## Conclusion

In the course of the twentieth century, the relationships among money, economic theory, governments, and their people have undergone and continue to undergo profound changes. Under the gold standard in the years before the First World War, the system was assumed to operate automatically without human intervention. During the First World War, governments were forced to take charge of their economies and control money to pursue national goals. Revolution against this all-intrusive government set the framework for the emergence of private banking power in the 1920s. The failure of these private financiers to solve the political problems at the root of the economic instability forced governments to reenter the field in the 1930s. The Bretton Woods system offered a compromise between the restraints of the gold standard and the free hands governments needed to address the economic and political instability that can emerge from modern capitalism. Created by Americans seeking to avoid the instability of the 1920s and 1930s, it was then undermined by Americans no longer willing to suffer the economic constraints of fixed exchange rates. The oil crises of the 1970s brought private bankers back into the picture, but this time within the context of more powerful governments that refused to see their needs subverted. We wait now to see how this new interplay between the private market and governments' political needs will be played out in the twenty-first century.

The ideal of the Bretton Woods system has been largely achieved, but not in a fashion envisioned by John Maynard Keynes or Harry Dexter White. Governments remain liable for the prosperity of their citizens, yet have painfully learned that they do not have the tools to guarantee economic growth. The expectation of the 1960s that the economy could be fine-tuned by careful manipulation of fiscal and monetary policy has given way to seemingly unrestrained fiscal deficits. The international monetary system has come to live with free-floating exchange rates that allow governments to run fiscal deficits, and the earlier belief that deficit spending is immoral and could lead to a currency crisis has given way to a fear that financing the deficits by international loans can only be done by sacrificing sovereign power to foreign lenders.

Our ideas about money and what we can legitimately do have changed; but as the world has become more complex, it is not clear that we have really learned to control our fate or escape from the restraints that appeared so strong in 1900.

ENDNOTES

1. Citizens of the United States rarely use "liberal" in its classical sense. In Europe, "liberal" still refers to the values of Adam Smith, while Americans have taken to using it to describe the welfare state philosophy of John Maynard Keynes, of whom more later.

2. Peter Lindert, *Key Currencies and Gold, 1900–1913* (Princeton: Princeton University Press, 1969), p. 2.

3. A. G. Ford, *The Gold Standard, 1880–1914: Britain and Argentina* (Oxford: Clarendon Press, 1962).

4. Lindert, *Key Currencies and Gold*, p. 12.

5. Michele Fratianni and Franco Spinelli, "Italy in the Gold Standard Period, 1861–1914" in Michael D. Bordo and Anna Schwartz, eds., *A Retrospective on the Classical Gold Standard 1821–1931* (Chicago and London: University of Chicago Press, 1984), p. 443.

6. Karl Erich Born, *International Banking in the 19th and 20th Centuries* (Leamington Spa: Berg, 1983), p. 18.

7. In Britain, which has the clearest records, central government expenditure was 47.6 percent of net national income in 1918. Calculated from B.R. Mitchell, ed. *European Historical Statistics 1750–1975*, 2d ed., rev. (New York: 1980) from series H4: *Total Central Government Expenditure* and series K1: *National Accounts*.

8. Ibid.

9. The classic description of this process is Karl Polanyi, *The Great Transformation* (Boston: Beacon Press, 1985 [1944]).

10. This is the theme of Charles Kindleberger, *The World in Depression 1929–1939* (Berkeley and Los Angeles: University of California Press, 1973).

11. Frederick Hayek, *The Road to Serfdom*. Milton Friedman's work was virtually a replay of Hayek's analysis and became one of the most important economic treatises of the 1970s and 1980s.

12. On United States fiscal policy the clearest survey is still Herbert Stein, *The Fiscal Revolution in America* (Chicago: University of Chicago Press, 1969). On German policy in the 1930s, see Harold James, "What Is Keynesian About Deficit Financing? The Case of Interwar Germany" in Peter Hall, ed., *The Political Power of Economic Ideas* (Princeton: Princeton University Press, 1989). For a more complete discussion, see Richard Overy, *The Nazi Economic Recovery 1932–1939* (London: Macmillan, 1982).

13. M. S. Mendelsohn, *Money on the Move: The Modern International Capital Market* (New York: McGraw-Hill, 1980), p. 80.

14. Lewis Mandell, *The Credit Card Industry: A History* (Boston: Twayne, 1990), p. xiii.

15. "Thrift Is Under Siege in Japan," *The New York Times*, June 16, 1992.

16 Peter Harrop, *The Future of Payment Media* (London: Financial Times Business Information, 1989), p. 7.

# 14 Technology and Invention

CHRISTOPHER FREEMAN

## Introduction

Many accounts of inventions and technology (e.g., Larsen 1960) begin and end by listing, describing, and illustrating the greatest inventions and the most famous inventors. If this review has a different point of departure and a different structure, it is certainly not because the twentieth century was lacking in great inventions, but because a greater depth of understanding can come from a different approach. The twentieth century differed from its predecessors not just in the actual inventions made but in the ways they were made. This difference is the subject of the first part of this review.

The second reason this review differs from earlier accounts is that historians, engineers, economists, and sociologists have increasingly recognized, as the century has progressed, that inventions cannot be satisfactorily treated as isolated, individual events. Rather, they must be treated as part of a continuum of interconnected technical changes. Technologies are systemic in nature—their characteristics often determine the direction of inventive activity and the rate of diffusion of successful inventions and innovations. This is the subject of the second part of this review, which examines the major changes in new technology systems during the course of the twentieth century.

Finally, the rise of new technologies (and the decline of some older ones) is strongly connected to a variety of social institutions. The rise to technological leadership of the United States in the nineteenth and twentieth centuries was a matter not just of great inventors such as Eli Whitney or Thomas Edison but also of a pattern of institutional change—a "national system of innovation."[1] Similarly, the rise of Japan to the front rank of technological powers and the successes of other East Asian countries are related to novel features in their national systems of innovation. This interplay between new technologies and changing social institutions is the subject of the third and final part of this brief review.

# The Changing Scale and Organization of Inventive Activities and Technological Development

## The Rise of the R&D Laboratory

During the twentieth century the main locus of inventive activity shifted away from the individual inventor to the professional Research and Development (R&D) laboratory, whether in industry, government, or academia. The nineteenth century was the heroic period of both invention and entrepreneurship, marked by the "he can make anything" auras of such figures as Eli Whitney, blacksmith, nail-maker, textile and machine tool inventor, and innovator. Henry Thoreau, remembered now as a solitary philosopher, replied—when asked to describe his profession ten years after his graduation—that he was a carpenter, a mason, a glass-pipe maker, a house painter, a farmer, a surveyor, and of course, a writer and pencil-maker. He was, in fact, responsible for numerous inventions in pencil-making, and there was a time when he could think of little else but improving the processes in his little pencil factory.[2] Whitney and Thoreau were not untypical of American and European nineteenth-century inventors, and to people like them Britain's nineteenth-century industrial revolution owed its success.

With an inventive career extending into the twentieth century, Thomas Edison embodied the transition from the "great individualists" to the large-scale R&D laboratories, which he helped to establish. He made a host of inventions and took out more patents (1,093) than any other single individual in patenting history, but this was due, in part, to his setting up large contract research laboratories, first in Newark, New Jersey and later in Menlo Park, California. Among Edison's staff at these laboratories were some of the outstanding engineers and scientists who later helped to build up corporate in-house R&D in Germany and in Britain, as well as in the United States.

By the first decade of the twentieth century, although Edison was still making inventions, the focus of inventive effort was shifting from the contract laboratory typified by Menlo Park, Nicola Tesla's laboratories, or that of Edward Weston to the in-house industrial laboratories established by such firms as Kodak (1895), General Electric (1900), or Du Pont (1902). As Thomas Hughes shows in his 1989 classic study of the "torrent" of American inventions from 1870 to 1940, by the time of the First World War, corporate R&D had displaced the contract laboratory as the center of American inventive activities. An embryonic military-industrial complex had even come into existence, with the sponsorship of industrial research by the U.S. Navy, and especially the strong links established with Sperry Gyroscope.

Joseph Schumpeter,[3] an economist who placed technical change at the center of his analysis, noted that in Europe too the rise of electrical technology led at the turn of the century to a concentration of inventive effort in two giant German firms—AEG (Allgemeine Elektrizitäts Gesellschaft) and Siemens. Already before the First World War, GE in the United States and AEG in Germany had patent-sharing and market-sharing agreements effectively covering all main developments in electrical technology in major world markets. Although some economists still dispute why firms prefer to carry out most of their R&D in-house instead of contracting it out as they do advertising and other services, the answer has always been fairly obvious to sociologists and managers alike. There are clear-cut advantages in terms of trust and internal communications among the R&D, production, and marketing functions in performing R&D in a secure internal environment. It is also a historic fact that the share of contract R&D became relatively less important, now accounting typically for less than 5 percent of industrial R&D expenditures in the leading industrial countries. Governments have made far more use of contracting arrangements with both industry and universities.

German chemical firms such as Bayer, Hoechst and Bädische Anilin und Soda Fabrik (BASF) invented the in-house R&D laboratory in the 1870s, followed by the electrical industry and then, after a several-decade time lag, by firms in other industries. The diffusion of this major social innovation was a fairly slow process: not until more than half a century later did the number of patents ascribed to companies begin to exceed the number taken out by individuals.

In the late nineteenth century, firms in more traditional industries, such as printing, clothing, furniture, and pencil-making, continued to design, manufacture, and sell their products without any formal R&D activity, and most still do so today. But if we ask which are the most typical and fastest-growing industries of the twentieth century, then the answer is clear: those of fairly high R&D intensity (defined by R&D expenditures as a ratio of net output or sales), who conduct formal R&D on a relatively large scale—electronics, pharmaceuticals, aerospace, plastics and other advanced materials, medical and scientific instruments, and automobiles. These industries barely existed in the nineteenth century; the two most R&D-intensive (aerospace and electronics) did not exist at all. They are purely twentieth-century industries, and the scale of their R&D is enormous. In post-WWII United States and Britain, they accounted for about half of all industrial R&D and for an even higher proportion of government R&D. Many firms in these two countries, as well as in other European countries and Japan, spend more on R&D than on fixed investment in plant and equipment.

It seems fairly obvious that it would be difficult to design and develop new types of integrated circuits (now integrating millions of components), digital switches, radar systems, computers, airplane and aerospace engines, computer-controlled machine tools, or robots without significant R&D resources. Not surprisingly, the commonly held view of these industries is that inventive work and the development of new processes and products are less the result of individual genius than of organized teams working with expensive instruments and equipment. However, this view has been contested strongly by one of the most influential books on twentieth-century invention, *The Sources of Invention* (1958),[4] and it is worthwhile to consider this controversy carefully. This will also help to clarify the concepts of "invention," "innovation," and "diffusion of innovations" and so to lay the basis for the subsequent discussion of other major developments in twentieth-century technology.

### The Sources of Invention

Jewkes et al. quote several authors' claims that the age of the individual inventor is over, and that twentieth-century invention became the prerogative of professional teams in large corporations. They then proceed to dispute this view by examining sixty major twentieth-century inventions (six more were added in the second edition of their book). From the short case histories of most of these inventions included in an appendix to the book, they conclude that the majority of the inventions (thirty-three) were actually made by individual inventors, often working on their own or in small firms, without the benefit of large corporate R&D facilities. Among those major twentieth-century inventions that they ascribe mainly to individual inventors are Bakelite, the ball-point pen, the helicopter, the electron microscope, the radio, insulin, xerography, air conditioning, the jet engine, penicillin, the safety razor, quick-freezing, the zip fastener, and (in the second edition of their book) the electronic computer.

Clearly this list includes some of the most characteristic and important inventions of the twentieth century. But the authors' claim is so crucial for the understanding of twentieth-century technology that it deserves closer scrutiny. Of the remaining inventions discussed, twenty-two could be ascribed mainly to corporate R&D departments and the remainder to a mixed category in which government laboratories, industry, and individuals were all involved. The authors acknowledge it is sometimes difficult to classify inventions as either "individual" or "corporate," but if we accept their rough classifications as reasonable (and they make no great claims to statistical precision in an area in which quantification is so hard), then although the list of corporate inventions is also an impressive one, their argument appears at first sight overwhelmingly strong.

However, it is essential to take a historical view. Since the list spans the whole period from 1900 to 1956, it is not without interest to divide their sample into two chronological categories: before and after 1928—the period's halfway mark. It then becomes apparent that, whereas in the early years of the century individual inventions exceeded corporate ones by twenty to eight, in the post-1928 period the number of corporate and "mixed" R&D inventions exceeds the number of individual inventions by nineteen to thirteen. The corporate inventions include nylon, polyethylene, television, DDT, fluorescent lighting, the transistor, acrylic fibers, and hot strip rolling. On the basis of their own sample, therefore, it could be maintained that there was indeed evidence of a movement toward corporate invention during the course of the twentieth century itself. It is necessary to remember that while corporate R&D laboratories originated in German and American chemical and electrical industries late in the nineteenth century, they were still few in number in the first quarter of this century; the most growth of industrial R&D occurred during and after World War II. In 1901, 82 percent of all United States patents were issued to individuals and 18 percent to companies; by 1928, individuals still accounted for 55 percent. Not until 1932 did the number of company patents exceed half the total patents issued.

### The Sources of Innovation

There is a second and even more important observation to be made about the analysis of twentieth-century invention by the authors. As they themselves make clear, their book is about invention, not development or innovation. Yet it is evident that from an economic or social point of view innovation is the more important phenomenon. The need to make this distinction is now generally recognized, but we owe it primarily to the work of Schumpeter,[5] who pointed out that many inventions never actually make it to the marketplace and many patents lapse without ever being used. An invention is the first original concept or idea for a new product or process, but it cannot become an innovation without further development—work which is often time-consuming and expensive. This development phase is necessary to bring the design of the new product to the point of commercial viability or (in military and medical cases) useful application in weapons systems or health care. This often involves further inventions during the course of development.

Innovations, therefore, not only require inventive activity and research, but also design and development work. The "D" of "R&D" usually accounts for more than two thirds of the total financial expenditure. If we examine the sixty inventions on the list of Jewkes et al., we find that many ascribed to individual inventors were in fact developed in the corporate R&D laboratories of large firms, as acknowledged in the chapter on "development." Good examples are color photography, invented by two music students but innovated by Kodak after years of development, or the jet engine, invented by Frank Whittle but developed by Rolls Royce. The authors' sample itself, therefore, actually shows that large corporations accounted for about two thirds of the twentieth century's innovations (or more accurately, those of the first half of the century), even though individuals made a greater contribution to inventions.

Finally, however, we have to observe that some of the inventors described by the authors as "individual" actually worked in university labs and enjoyed the benefits of equipment and support that these labs provided. In fact, some critics would maintain that the entire method of attempting to allocate inventions to an individual inventor is misguided. Gilfillan,[6] the American sociologist who probably contributed most to the sociology of invention, emphasized the innumerable (and often anonymous) small contributions made to any major invention and came close to the position of *The Economist* magazine, which even in the mid-nineteenth century (1851) observed: "Nearly all useful inventions depend less on any individual than on the progress of society." Partly for this reason, the history of invention is full of priority disputes, especially between inventors of different nationalities.

This point leads directly to the issue of "secondary" inventions during the process of any innovation's diffusion. Again, we owe mainly to Schumpeter the distinction between innovation and diffusion. In his view, whereas the first innovation demanded unusual qualities of entrepreneurship and was an act of will as well as imagination, diffusion was mainly a matter of imitating the pioneers and became more and more a matter of routine. Although the invention-innovation-diffusion taxonomy is still widely used by economists and historians, it has been subjected to increasingly strong criticism during the second half of the century. Schumpeter himself recognized that the automobiles made and sold in the later stages of diffusion were very different from those that were being sold in the 1880s. The same point could be made even more forcefully with respect to the electronic computer, the airplane, or the radio. Diffusion of an innovation typically takes several decades, often a century or more, and during all this time, the original innovation is further improved. Hundreds or even thousands of "secondary" or "improvement" patents surround the original "master" patents for any major invention.

With respect to several of the "individual" inventions identified by Jewkes et al., it could be maintained that the later improvement inventions made during diffusion were just as or even more important than the original invention or innovation. Thus, for example, though cellophane was the invention of a French aristocrat, it could be maintained that the work of Du Pont's R&D Department in inventing and developing a moistureproof version was decisive for its widespread acceptance as a packaging material. Similarly the catalytic cracking process of heavy fractions of petroleum is described by Jewkes et al. as the invention of a private French millionaire inventor, Houdry, but his achievement was rapidly superseded by the far superior fluid bed catalytic cracking process developed by several major oil companies and contractors in the 1930s. This joint development was the largest single R&D project before the Manhattan Project which developed the atom bomb.

Thus there are many qualifications to the analysis made by Jewkes et al., though their work nevertheless remains an essential guide to twentieth-century invention. Even if it somewhat overestimates the role of outstanding individuals, it does show beyond any reasonable doubt that such inventors, and very often the small firms they established, continued to make an invaluable contribution to invention during the twentieth century. More recent research has confirmed this was still the case in the 1970s and 1980s. It has generally been recognized by the end of the century that a symbiosis exists between the work of large and small firms, and this book demonstrated the special role iconoclastic inventors and scientists played with their breakthrough inventions and discoveries. The astonishing persistence and determination of such people amply recounted in the book was necessary to overcome the indifference and opposition of those who were wedded to orthodox ideas. Science historian Thomas Kuhn,[7] for instance, demonstrated the same phenomenon in relation to changes of paradigm in science.

However, when all is said and done, despite the undoubted continuing importance of individual and small-firm invention and innovation, the twentieth century is above all remarkable for the growth of large-scale R&D. This was something completely new in the history of the world and, for good or ill, the century is more likely to be remembered for the Manhattan Project, the Sputnik, the moon landing, the Boeing 747, and nuclear reactors than for the safety razor, the zip fastener, or the ball-point pen, useful though these inventions undoubtedly are.

It was above all Hiroshima and the advent of nuclear power that changed the face of human technology. Many might have wished to go back to the days before the Second World War, when the U.S. Department of Agriculture spent more on research than the U.S. Department of Defense. They might also have preferred a world in which small, useful, everyday inventions took precedence over vast weapon systems or nuclear reactors. By the 1970s, the contrast was often made between the human capability to explore space and the failure to solve endemic social problems here on earth, as in Nelson's *The Moon and the Ghetto* (1977).[8] But it was Big Science and Big Technology that stamped their indelible image on the postwar era.

### The Rise of Big Science and Technology

Contrary to popular belief, Big Science and Big Technology did not begin with the Second World War and the Manhattan Project: some very large R&D projects were undertaken in industry long before 1939. The oil and chemical industries in particular were accustomed to scaling up designs for very complex large plants, and it was not surprising that Du Pont was invited to design and construct the Oakridge pilot plant for the Manhattan nuclear weapons project in 1942.[9]

Large laboratories were also being established in universities and in government institutions. Even though "small science" was still overwhelmingly the predominant mode, laboratories such as the Lawrence Radiation Lab at the University of California had made their appearance well before the Second World War. The main reason for the growth of such laboratories was not the size of the government or even the size of firms, but rather the increased complexity and cost of some scientific instruments and new technologies.

One of the reasons for the persistence of individual patents in the nineteenth and twentieth centuries was that mechanical engineering technologies still offered great scope for individual ingenuity and tinkering at very low cost. Many patents were still being taken out for improved horseshoes and can-openers well into the twentieth century. With the rise of electrical engineering and carbon chemistry in the latter part of the nineteenth century, the links between technology and basic science became closer, the role of instrumentation increased, and professionally trained engineers and scientists were usually needed to make further inventions. Atomic accelerators and telescopes were two extreme cases where the enormous increases in the cost of instruments led directly to the need for Big Science institutions.

Historians of science such as Seidel[10] point out that all the main features of Big Science labs could already be identified in the Lawrence Radiation Lab in the 1930s—the role of expensive instruments, the necessity of extramural funding from government and industry, the introduction of bureaucratic management structures, the need for interdisciplinary cooperation, especially between scientists and technologists, and the prestige of sheer size.

Very large groups of scientists and engineers were brought together during the Second World War not only for projects related to nuclear physics and nuclear weapons but also for many other purposes. The Telecommunications Research Establishment at Malvern in England was only one of several government establishments that assembled hundreds of university and industrial engineers, scientists, and technicians to develop such advanced electronic systems as ground, marine, and airborne radar, believed by many to be responsible for the Allied victory in the Second World War. On the German side too, very large teams were engaged in radar development and of course in rocket work, both in private industry and in the military establishment.

The spectacular, if not to say awesome, achievements of the Manhattan Project and of the V-weapons and other weapon systems had a profound and lasting effect not only on the international community of scientists and engineers but also on those responsible for the public funding of science and technology, and on general public opinion. Even before the tensions of the cold war and the Korean War in the 1950s made even greater demands on military R&D, governments in Europe, North America, and Japan had generally accepted the case for a continuous and relatively generous public commitment to the support of scientific research and (in some cases) advanced technology, both for reasons of national security and because it was believed that this would also promote economic prosperity.

Before the war the Irish Marxist physicist Bernal[11] had been almost a lone voice in advocating an order of magnitude increase in the scale of organized R&D activities in Britain and elsewhere. But what had appeared before the Second World War as radical utopianism became quite orthodox thinking in the golden age of economic growth and rapid technical change in the quarter century from 1948 to 1973. The major leading industrial countries, and many smaller ones too, did in fact achieve a tenfold expansion of their R&D systems (or even more) compared with the prewar period. Although it experienced some slowdown and hesitation in the 1970s, this expansion generally continued into the 1980s (table 14.1), and its expenditures were a much larger fraction of the greatly increased GDP in all major industrial countries.

Within the superpowers—the United States and the former USSR—a very high proportion of the enormous R&D spending between 1941 and 1991 was on military R&D and, from the 1950s onward, in the closely related area of space technology. In the USSR this combination probably amounted to more

TABLE 14.1

The Evolution of Gross Expenditures on Research and Development as Percentage of GDP in the Twentieth Century in the Principal Industrial Countries

| COUNTRIES | TOTAL R&D (CIVIL AND MILITARY) AS PERCENTAGE OF GDP | | | CIVIL R&D ONLY |
|---|---|---|---|---|
| | 1934 | 1967 | 1983 | 1983 |
| USA | 0.6 | 3.1 | 2.7 | 2.0 |
| Japan | 0.1 | 1.6 | 2.7 | 2.7 |
| EC | 0.3 | 1.8 | 2.1 | 1.8 |
| USSR | 0.4 | 3.2 | 3.6 | 1.0 |

SOURCE: Author's estimates based on Bernal (1939), and Patel and Pavitt (1987). Estimates for USSR (all years) based on OECD "Frascati" definitions.

than three quarters of what had been a vast overall scientific and technological effort. There can be little doubt that the distortions induced in the economic system by this high bias and the priority given to this type of project were major contributory causes to the collapse of the Soviet system in the late 1980s and early 1990s. In the United States as well as in smaller European powers such as France and Britain, although the distortion was less extreme, it was sufficiently great to give a comparative advantage in manufacturing and trade to those nations fortunate enough to be able to concentrate their scientific and technical resources almost entirely on civil industries. Toward the end of the century there has been a marked contrast between the extraordinary technological virtuosity of the United States armed forces, as demonstrated in the Gulf War against Iraq (1991), and the competitive achievements of Japanese firms in world markets in such industries as automobiles, consumer electronics, robotics, and integrated circuits.

Within the industrialized countries from the 1960s onward, voices have been raised to query the priority of national scientific and technological efforts, whether military or commercial. Some, such as the French philosopher Jacques Ellul,[12] attacked Big Technology root and branch for its destructive effects on humanistic culture.

Others, such as the economist Schumacher,[13] pointed to the many social and economic advantages of small organizations in generating technologies more appropriate to the needs of the majority of the world's population, living in those countries that were variously designated as the "Third World," "underdeveloped," "developing" or simply "the South." Increasingly in the 1970s the Greens developed their critique of mass consumerism, of reckless and irresponsible dumping of pollutants in the atmosphere and the oceans, and of the over-rapid depletion of nonrenewable resources. The image of Big Science and Big Technology became somewhat tarnished.

The Brooks Report, prepared by a distinguished group of scientists chaired by a Harvard physicist, reflected the growth of these concerns in the member countries of the OECD as early as 1971. We shall return to this tarnished image when we consider the problems of reorienting world technology in a cleaner and greener direction. But first we consider the systemic aspects of twentieth-century technologies.

## Technology Systems and Changes of Technoeconomic Paradigm in the Twentieth Century

### A Taxonomy of Technical Change

From the discussion so far it has already become evident that it is useful, indeed essential, to make some distinction between the more radical inventions and innovations and the incremental improvements constantly being made to existing products. It is not as easy to do this precisely as might appear at first sight; some economists who studied inventions and used patent statistics thought it was impossible (e.g. Schmookler in 1966)[14] and it must be accepted that definitional problems are involved, without any clear borderlines, that arise mainly from the systemic nature of technical change. Everyone would agree that the electronic computer and the airplane were among the most important twentieth-century innovations, but most would also agree that the jet engine and the microprocessor were very important too. And what about computerized airline booking systems or the computer-aided design (CAD) system now used to design aircraft and other complex engineering products? The application innovations surrounding a major innovation are often numerous and extremely important.

We need a taxonomy which distinguishes major from minor innovations and also distinguishes the technological systems of interrelated innovations. Ideally we would also like to distinguish the most important systems affecting many industries and activities from those which affect only one area. Although there is no general agreement on such definitions, the distinctions which follow (with some minor variations) have increasingly entered the literature analyzing technical change.

Following the work of Schumpeter (1912) and Mensch (1975),[15] radical or basic innovations are generally defined as those which involve some discontinuity in existing production lines and/or markets. They could not arise simply from improvements in the existing array of products or processes. No matter how much anyone tried to improve a cotton or a woolen factory, they would never get nylon, or as Schumpeter used to say, no matter how many stagecoaches you put together you would never get a railroad. To take another twentieth-century example: however many vacuum tubes you put together you would not get a transistor or an integrated circuit. From this definition of radical innovation it is clear why firms familiar with an established technology often fail to make the transition to a new one, while small new firms may find it easier, as in some of the Jewkes examples. Texas Instruments, Fairchild, Motorola, and Intel were all far more successful with computer microchips than the once more powerful firms who dominated vacuum tube manufacture. Radical innovations necessarily involve structural change in the economy as they require new skills, new equipment, and new components and may give rise to new industries with far-reaching consequences in social and economic life.

Incremental innovations, on the other hand, are all those innumerable small improvements made to existing products and processes as a result of experience in production (described by economists as learning by doing), experience in markets (learning by using), and the exchange between producers and users (learning by interacting). Though these constitute the vast majority of patents that are successfully implemented, even more incremental innovations may go unrecorded, contributing to the accumulation of tacit knowledge within the firm—a factor critical to competitive success. The economic and technical significance of incremental innovations should on no account be underestimated: these are responsible for much of the gradual improvements in productivity recorded in most industries (albeit at varying rates) throughout the twentieth century. The professional R&D laboratory has certainly made a significant contribution to this trend, even though the most spectacular contributions of these institutions have been to radical innovations. It has enabled many firms to understand their existing processes and products in much greater depth and to tackle problems of quality, scale, and maintenance with greater success. An important part of the work of most industrial R&D laboratories involves such incremental improvements and "troubleshooting." However, empirical research has shown that even in firms such as Du Pont which have very strong R&D the majority of incremental improvements actually emerge from other activities, such as production engineering, operations research, marketing, and technical service. For example, one of the widely acknowledged contributions of Japanese management systems has been to further stimulate the flow of suggestions and inventions from the shop floor through such methods as "Quality Circles." Even though many such techniques originated in the United States or Europe, they have been more systematically and widely used in the latter part of the century in Japan, a country that excels in incremental innovation.

So far we have discussed specific inventions and innovations as though they were discrete, individual events. This is useful for many purposes, but in reality of course they form an interconnected web of new knowledge. A "technology" sums up accumulated knowledge, either in a specific field (as in "automobile technology" or "opto-electronic technology"), or in a number of areas (as in "high technology," a somewhat vague term generally referring to expensive, advanced technologies), or in all fields (as in "modern technology" or "stone age" technology). Innovations in any industry may contribute mainly or entirely to the technology of one particular sector, as with the float glass process in the manufacture of plate glass innovated by Pilkington's, a British glass firm, and then licensed worldwide within the glass industry. At the other extreme they may affect the technology in *every* sector, as in the case of the electronic computer. Such pervasive technologies are clearly of the greatest interest alike to the historian and to contemporary observers. While it would take several massive volumes—such as those in the 1978 version of Oxford's *History of Technology*—to describe technological developments in every sector, it is possible to summarize and distill this knowledge if we can identify the most pervasive technologies and the radical innovations with which they were associated. This section will therefore first of all define new technological systems and then distinguish the most pervasive ones, defined as changes of technoeconomic paradigm. Finally, it will briefly outline the diffusion of the most pervasive new technology systems in the twentieth century.

The leading historians of technology, whether American (such as Hughes, 1983)[16] or European (such as Gille, 1975)[17] have increasingly emphasized the *systemic* aspects of technical change. Treating separate inventions and innovations as though they were isolated events does violence to the truly interlocking interdependent nature of any technology. It is indeed obvious that many technologies, such as electric power generation and transmission or telecommunications networks, are inherently systemic. Each of these networks in any industrial country embodies dozens of radical innovations and many thousands of incremental innovations ongoing throughout the twentieth century. Bottlenecks, or "reverse salients," or problem areas within such systems often act as focusing devices to stimulate further innovations. According to many accounts, the limits of the old radio and switching communication devices drew Bell Laboratories into the research program that led to the Germanium transistor.

The systemic aspects of invention and innovation are not confined to networks of hardware installations, with all their associated problems of interconnections, components, materials, and subsystems. They also involve the underlying technologies. Thus, for example, the advances in macromolecular chemistry in the 1920s in Germany and the United States made it possible not only for Wallace Carothers to discover nylon in Du Pont's research laboratories, but for chemists in other R&D laboratories, and especially in the laboratories of the German chemical trust IG Farben, to introduce many other synthetic materials. Moreover this new family of products increasingly gave rise to new machinery for extrusion, injection molding, and other processes common to many synthetic materials, so that an entire constellation of radical and incremental innovations were associated with the diffusion of these new materials from the 1930s to the 1950s.

*New technology systems* may therefore be defined as constellations of radical and incremental innovations that are interrelated both technically and economically.

The concept of new technology systems is needed to take account of these systemic features of technical change. By observing their interconnections we not only simplify and make more intelligible the lists of myriads of inventions and innovations, we can also understand the reasons for the rapid diffusion and success of some innovations compared with the slow progress of others. Polypropylene, diffusing in the 1950s and 1960s, was far more readily accepted than some of the earlier synthetic materials diffusing in the 1930s. Not only were the necessary skills and equipment lacking in those earlier times, but the institutional infrastructure was ill-prepared to cope with new synthetic materials in terms of standards, marketing, regulatory procedures, and so forth. This point leads to the final category of our taxonomy.

Some changes of technology systems affect only one or a few industries, others affect almost every single one. Therefore, it is obviously desirable to distinguish those with very widespread effects from those with purely local consequences. Schumpeter[18] spoke of "successive industrial revolutions" and associated them with Kondratieff's "long waves" in the economy. Rather more precisely the Venezuelan economist Carlota Perez[19] has described the change from one highly pervasive technological system to a new one as a change of "technoeconomic paradigm." Her description has the merit of emphasizing the interdependence of technical, economic, and social change, as well as indicating the nature of this interdependence. In her account the most pervasive technologies have been characterized by the availability of one or more very cheap and abundant inputs, such as coal, steel, oil, or more recently "chips" (microelectronics). In this respect her classification resembles that of archaeologists who distinguish the Stone Age, the Iron Age, the Bronze Age, and so forth. But in a nineteenth- or twentieth-century capitalist system the new technologies are diffused far more rapidly because of the very strong pressures for cost reduction and increased profitability in such economies. Taking advantage of this major change in cost structure, many new interrelated applications of a pervasive new technology can be developed over several decades.

Appearing at first as a revolutionary and unfamiliar way of doing things, the economic and technical advantages of a new technology become increasingly apparent and cumulative. By the time it matures, the economy is locked into a new paradigm. The transition, however, is a painful one, involving the decline of older, established industries, techniques, firms, skills, and other social institutions as well as the rise of new ones. A truly pervasive new technology leads to a new skill profile, a new generation of capital equipment, a new infrastructure, new management procedures and organizations, and even a new lifestyle and *weltanschauung*—a new way of looking at the world—or in Schumpeter's phrase, a "wave of creative destruction." David Nye,[20] in his 1990 study of the electrification of America from 1880 to 1940, points to the numerous changes in language associated with this pervasive change of technology. Expressions such as "he's a live wire," "he has a short fuse," "she gave an electrifying performance," and "he's recharging his batteries" became part of everyday speech.

In the long waves theory (or Kondratieff cycles, as Schumpeter christened them), the periods of boom or high prosperity are associated with the rise to dominance of new technologies, while the periods of prolonged recessions or deep depression are associated with the profound structural changes that occur in the economy when one technoeconomic paradigm is displaced by a new one. How far does the history of the twentieth century conform to Schumpeter's expectations and to Carlota Perez's theory on changes of technoeconomic paradigm? Can these long cycles in the economy be plausibly associated with the rise and decline of pervasive new technologies?

The period before the First World War was generally known in Europe as "la belle epoque" and it was certainly thought of, both there and in the United States, as a time of prosperity and expansion. But from 1950 to 1975 was probably the period of fastest growth that the world economy has ever experienced. Even the communist countries and many Third World countries joined in this expansion. Between these periods of high growth the world experienced the Great Depression and in the closing quarter of this century is once more caught up in what is often called a "crisis of structural adjustment," with stagnation and some prolonged recessions. The cyclical pattern of the century does therefore roughly correspond to the expectations of Kondratieff and Schumpeter. But is this related to the spread of new technologies?

If asked at the beginning of the twentieth century to identify the most pervasive technology, many would probably have singled out electricity, with all its potential and actual applications. Many key innovations in electric motors, transformers, turbogenerators, batteries, lighting systems, and cables had already been made in the nineteenth century, most of them by the 1880s. The decade or so before the First World War witnessed a remarkably rapid diffusion of applications in almost every industry and to millions of households, and this was indeed associated with rapid growth and prosperity.

In the 1890s the newly established profession of electrical engineering had already debated the effects of electrification on factory organization and the layout of machines. By 1914 it was clear that electricity had brought with it (as a result of numerous applications and innovations) a newfound flexibility in most industrial processes, together with far better working conditions. The stand-alone machine tool with its own electric motor was replacing the old complicated (and dangerous) systems of belts and pulleys driven by one large steam engine and characteristic of nineteenth-century industry. Small firms in industries such as printing, diamonds, woodworking, and clothing benefited enormously from the new flexibility in terms of their source of power. Large firms could make big savings in energy consumption and in floor space and capital costs. All involved innumerable incremental inventions and innovations in the electrical industries. This period could reasonably be described as a change of technoeconomic paradigm.

The change also involved new management structures, as vividly described by historians such as Hounshell[21] and Chandler.[22] The new giant electrical firms, such as AEG and Siemens in Europe or GE and Westinghouse in the United States, introduced not only the specialized professional R&D departments but also similarly specialized professional functions in other areas of corporate business such as marketing, accounting, personnel, technical service, and production management. The new pervasive technology did indeed entail a new generation of capital equipment in many diverse industries, a new skills profile, new management structures, and an entirely new infrastructure in the form of utilities generating and distributing electric power to industrial and domestic consumers throughout the world. This universal availability of electricity also led to major changes in lifestyle and social behavior, described so brilliantly by David Nye.[23]

The consumer durable revolution through which most households in the industrialized world acquired vacuum cleaners, electric refrigerators, electric washing machines, electric irons, radios, and later dishwashers, television sets, and video recorders was only just dawning in the United States before the First World War and took the best part of the century to unfold there and later in Europe and Japan. However, its potential was already evident, even if only dimly foreshadowed. We would therefore be quite entitled to regard electrification, with its huge infrastructural network, its universal transmission, and its manifold applications as one of the most pervasive technologies of the twentieth century, even if its roots were clearly present in the nineteenth.

If the same questions about pervasive technologies were to be asked at mid-century, then almost any engineer would mention not only electrification but also the automobile, the airplane, and mass production. The assembly line introduced for the manufacture of Ford's Model T proved to be one of the most revolutionary innovations of the twentieth century and indeed made possible the "consumer durable" revolution referred to above, as it brought many appliances into the range of relatively cheap goods affordable by the average household. While it is true that there were forerunners of mass production technology in the nineteenth century, such as the use of interchangeable components in ordnance and the manufacture of sewing machines or the subdivision and specialization of tasks in the Chicago meatpacking industry, the Ford assembly line established both the philosophy and the practice of mass production as an archetypal twentieth-century American technology. During the Second World War the huge scale of American production of trucks, tanks, aircraft, and landing craft, together with the petroleum products that fueled them, were in the end decisive factors in the Allied landings in Europe and their advance into Italy and Germany. Following the Second World War the mass consumption lifestyle and the mass production of automobiles and other durable goods was not only consolidated in the United States but spread rapidly to Europe and Japan. The quarter century after the Second World War was the most rapid period of economic growth the world has ever known, and it was largely based on oil, automobiles, aircraft, petrochemicals, plastics, and consumer durables.

However, this triumph of mass production was achieved only after a very painful period of worldwide structural adjustment in the 1930s. Mass production capacity for automobiles and other goods had outstripped the absorptive capacity of the (then) very limited market for the new goods. Only with new social institutions and consumer credit arrangements, wage structures, highway infrastructure, and Keynesian-type management of the economy was it possible to harmonize the new technological potential with the existing socioinstitutional frameworks.

Cheap oil not only provided an extremely flexible, universally available source of energy for airplanes as well as cars and trucks, it also provided a very cheap feedstock for the huge new family of chemical products so well-suited to needs of mass consumption: plastic packaging materials, engineering components, throwaway containers, construction materials, and above all components for the mass production of consumer electronics.

Finally, if our hypothetical engineers were to be asked at the end of the twentieth century which were the most pervasive technologies of the century, there can scarcely be any doubt that the electronic computer and associated telecommunications and integrated circuit technologies would be mentioned by every one. Variously called the "information revolution," the "computer revolution" or the "microelectronic revolution," numerous interconnected radical and incremental innovations are once more changing the face of the world economy. Again, as in the 1930s, the economy was experiencing a major crisis of structural adjustment as it painfully adapted to the rise of new industries, the need for a new skill profile, new trading arrangements, and a new worldwide telecommunication infrastructure based on computerized networks and data banks.

As we have seen, a change of technoeconomic paradigm is not just a radical transformation of product and process technology in every industry. It is also a change of managerial "common sense"—the most practical way to achieve profitability and competitive strength. The diffusion of information and communication technology in the last few decades of the twentieth century has reversed many of the most typical principles and practices of the now obsolete mass production paradigm that had been associated with the always controversial mass production ideas and the "scientific management" principles advocated by Henry Ford and by Frederick Taylor.

Such concepts had not always been welcomed by industrial workers, and were brilliantly satirized by Charlie Chaplin in his 1936 film *Modern Times*. Nevertheless they surely have been the dominant management philosophy for a large part of the century, affecting service industries such as tourism (chartered coaches, aircraft; package standardized holidays), catering (self-service; standardized menus) and distribution (supermarkets; standardized, prepackaged products), as well as the typical manufacturing industries making automobiles, washing machines, or standardized components. Perhaps their range and power can best be demonstrated by the fact that even though the communist regimes were dedicated to the destruction of capitalist society and of capitalist social relations, both Lenin and Stalin strongly advocated the application of the principles developed by Ford and Taylor.

It is not easy to change a management style so deeply rooted in worldwide industrial practice for many decades. Yet the main features have almost all been challenged in the closing decades of the century, and in the most advanced firms are being discarded and displaced by quite new principles closely related to the diffusion of information and communication technology (table 14.2).

Whereas firms such as Ford and GM had been characterized by departmental separation of functions and a many-layered hierarchy of managers, they have been obliged to change dramatically in the 1980s and 1990s toward a much more streamlined, integrated structure. The new information technology and its numerous applications in design, data processing, machine control, market feedback, etc. has permitted a far more flexible and fast response to new events, based on more decentralized management systems and the devolution of greater responsibility to the shop floor. Moreover the Taylorist principles of task fragmentation, simplification, and specialization have had to be abandoned in favor of better-educated, "multiskilled" workers. Firms such as Motorola have found it necessary to organize their own "university"—a comprehensive program of educating and retraining their own workers to cope with the new technology, given in collaboration with schools and colleges near their main production sites.

In many of these institutional changes, Japanese industrial practices have appeared to lead the world. While American and European firms had led the wave of innovations in computer technology and transistor technology that made the computer revolution possible, Japanese firms increasingly led in the introduction and worldwide sales of new generations of equipment and circuits in the 1980s. The rapidly falling cost of storing, transmitting, and processing information was the "oil" that facilitated all the innumerable new applications of information and communication technology. Toward the end of the century it appears that Japan and other East Asian countries are in the best position to take advantage of this enormous potential.

Some American commentators have diagnosed the problem as one of failure to change management attitudes and practices still geared to the old mass production paradigm. This was the conclusion, for example, of the 1989 MIT comparative review of American, European, and Japanese companies. *Made in*

TABLE 14.2

Old and New Models of Industrial Organization

| FORDIST MODEL | NEW MODEL |
| --- | --- |
| 1. Rationalization of labor by mechanization | Global optimization of whole production flow |
| 2. Design and then manufacture and organize work | Attempt to integrate R&D, design, production |
| 3. Indirect mediated link to consumers | Close ties between producers and users |
| 4. Low cost by standardization; quality comes second | "Zero defect" objective at each state |
| 5. Mass production for stable rising demand and batch production for unstable | Flexible fast response to market, whether batch or mass |
| 6. Centralization of the production management | Decentralization of production decisions |
| 7. Vertical integration with circles of subcontractors | Networking and joint ventures to reap gains of specialization and coordination |
| 8. Use subcontractors to stabilize cyclical demand fluctuations | Long-run cooperation with chosen subcontractors |
| 9. Divide and specialize production taks for productivity gains | Integrate some production maintenance and management tasks ("recompose") |
| 10. Minimize skill and training and education requirements | Continuous training plus general education to maximize competence |
| 11. Hierarchical control—higher wages to get consent to poor job content | Human resource policies to spur the competence and commitment of workers |
| 12. Adversarial industrial relations; collective agreements to codify provisional armistices | Explicit long-term compromises between management and workers via job tenure and/or sharing dividends |
| 13. "Full employment" | "Active Society" |

SOURCE: Boyer (1990).

*America*[24] describes six fundamental "ills" of the American economy in its failure to adapt. These included lack of industrial training, lack of functional integration, lack of cooperative relationships with subcontractors, government and labor, and management thinking in the old "mass production" style. The book is particularly noteworthy as it was compiled by a combined team of the top MIT engineers and social scientists. These types of misgivings gave rise to much debate on the possible loss of American leadership during the twenty-first century. The final section of this review discusses this question of world technological leadership and the institutional changes associated with it.

## National Systems of Innovation and Globalization of Technology

The discussion of "Fordism" and the institutional changes associated with information technology has served to emphasize the close interdependence of technical and institutional change. Schumpeter always classified organizational innovations and the opening up of new markets as an essential part of the torrent of innovations that were in his view the most characteristic features of capitalist societies. Historians, economists, and sociologists who have concentrated their research on these innovative processes have by the final decade of the twentieth century come to recognize that the national institutional environment can powerfully influence both the rate and direction of inventive activity and the efficiency of innovations and their diffusion.

To historians such as Abramowitz,[25] Landes,[26] or Hughes,[27] it had always been fairly obvious that there have been periods in which technological leadership has passed from one country or region to another, and that such changes have not simply been the result of natural resource endowment and its exploitation. Abramowitz speaks of economic history as a tale of "forging ahead" and "catching up" by various countries. British leadership in the industrial revolution of the eighteenth and nineteenth centuries was not simply based on coal and iron or the climate in Lancashire, but was clearly connected to the inventive activities of British mechanics and engineers and the work of British scientists at that time.[28] Similarly, when the United States (and Germany) overtook Britain in the latter part of the nineteenth century and then during the twentieth century, this again was related to the "torrent of inventions," the work of the new research institutions, the early corporate R&D departments, and new forms of technological education, which left far behind the relatively amateur British system. Finally, the Japanese challenge to American technological leadership and the rapid advance of other East Asian countries in the closing decades of the twentieth century was again clearly related to changes in the organization and management of inventive and innovative activities and to new developments in industrial training.

Contrary to the orthodox mainstream economic theory, with its simplifying assumptions of exogenous technical change and costless dissemination ("manna from heaven"), the new school of neo-Schumpeterian economists[29] stresses (as historians and sociologists had always stressed) the endogenous nature of most invention and innovation activities and the frequently high costs of technology acquisition, accumulation, and transfer. Spurred by this critique, the "new growth theory" in mainstream economics has begun to accept "knowledge accumulation" (expenditures on education, training, and R&D in particular) as central to the process of economic growth. Whereas development economics had previously stressed "tangible" capital investment in fixed assets as the motor of growth for Third World economies, the World

Bank Development Report for 1991 reflected the new thinking on the crucial role of intangible investment:

> ... in practice, technological change has not been equal nor has it been exogenously transmitted in most developing countries, because of import and other restrictions. Furthermore, even if all economies have access to the same technology, national growth rates can differ if human capital and the incentives to adopt new technology differ across countries. The "new" growth theories note that technological change is endogenous and that education and knowledge produce positive externalities or increasing returns.[30]

As a result of this new thinking about economic growth toward the end of the century, "national systems of innovation" have moved to center stage of research interest. In particular, numerous studies of the Japanese system have begun to appear, and many management consultants specialize in transmitting what are believed to be the main features of Japanese management systems, such as "just-in-time" methods of inventory control, "zero defects" and total quality control, integration of research, development, production and marketing functions, and continuous retraining to cope with continuous innovation.

Not everyone, however, is convinced that the Japanese system, which has proved so conspicuously successful in the "catching up" period of the second half of the twentieth century, will be equally successful in enabling Japan to "forge ahead" in the first half of the twenty-first century. Some observers point out that Japanese success is based primarily on excellence in technology and high quality of production rather than original contributions to science. The Japanese share of United States or European Community patents is far higher than the Japanese share of publications and citations in the world's scientific journals.[31] Since the most advanced technologies, whether in materials, in computers, or in biotechnology, are increasingly intertwined with fundamental scientific research in physics, chemistry, and biology, now that Japan has reached the world frontier of technology it may prove much more difficult for it to sustain the pace of technical innovation.

As against this, other researchers point out, the Japanese contribution to world scientific publications, although still relatively small, has been steadily increasing. Furthermore, the major Japanese corporations, whether in electronics or in chemicals, have recognized the need to strengthen their own capabilities in science and in many cases established new research laboratories for this purpose in the 1970s and 1980s. While critics of the Japanese system stress the weaknesses of its universities and its relative dependence on world science, and particularly on American universities, other recent research[32] has cast doubts on this.

In assessing this divergence of views it is important to remember that in the past, world technological leadership has not always been identified with world leadership in science. When the United States overtook all European countries in technology and in productivity between 1870 and 1914, undoubtedly leading the world in invention and innovation activities, Europe nevertheless still led in basic science and, according to some observers, continued to do so until 1939. The links between science and technology have undoubtedly grown closer during the course of the century, and much research has shown that technical innovation in many fields requires the knowledge of very recent science, as well as some active involvement. But then links can be with world as well as national science. Indeed, the stronger the links with world science, the greater the possibilities for technological success.

This leads to consideration of the tendency toward "globalization" more generally in technology as well as in science. Whereas in the first half of the twentieth century when companies established production outside their home country, they rarely established R&D activities abroad, in the second half of the century this has become increasingly common. In the last quarter of the century there has also been a veritable explosion of agreements among American, Japanese, and European companies for joint ventures, technology alliances, and exchanges. The vast majority of these agreements affect the most advanced technologies in electronics, new materials, and biotechnology. Typically now a large Japanese or American company might have more than a hundred such agreements with other firms within the "Triad" of industrialized regions (North America, the European Community, and Japan). Starting in 1992, European companies have been especially active in making arrangements within Europe because of the Single Market, but this prospect has also induced companies from outside Europe to establish technology and marketing arrangements with European partners. The North American Free Trade Area may lead to similar changes.

The motives that have led large corporations to establish R&D activities abroad are varied, but among the most important is the desire to gain access to research in the strongest world centers for science and technology. This was undoubtedly the main motive impelling many Japanese and European companies to start R&D or acquire affiliates in the United States, especially in California's Silicon Valley, both for bio- and information technology. More recently it led both American and European chemical and electronics companies to start research activities in Tsukuba and other Japanese centers. The strength of British basic research in biology and biochemistry was among the factors that persuaded both American drug companies like Pfizer and Swiss or German companies to build up their R&D in Britain. IBM has had major research centers in several European countries for many decades, and was one of the first to develop a worldwide R&D network.

Another motive for locating R&D abroad has been to modify the design of products to suit local specifications and regulations. This has been particularly important in the automobile and engineering industries both for the American multinationals in Europe and more recently for Japanese multinationals in the United States and Europe. According to some estimates, the expenditure of large multinationals on R&D outside their home base amounted to nearly 10 percent of their total R&D by the 1990s, with American and European companies the most internationalized.

These developments have led some commentators to argue that national frontiers and national systems are now no longer important. Kenichi Ohmae, the Japanese management consultant working with McKinsey on his 1990 book *The Borderless World*,[33] maintains that the leading multinationals are now truly international companies. However, although there is a tendency toward globalization, this assessment seems somewhat premature. Even in the early 1990s it was hard to find any Japanese company with foreign directors on its main board, and foreign directors were not at all common in American companies either. Moreover, the most strategically important R&D was still overwhelmingly conducted at the home base, with overseas R&D largely confined to monitoring activities or relatively minor local adaptations. Thus, although national variations in R&D systems, education and training, economic incentives, and other institutions may come to matter less in the twenty-first century, they have certainly still been key throughout the whole of the twentieth century.

This is even more evident if we examine the experience of Third World countries. In the 1960s and 1970s a number of Latin American as well as Asian countries appeared to be breaking away from the vicious circle of poverty, inadequate investment, technological backwardness, and low growth. Brazil, Mexico, and Venezuela as well as South Korea, Taiwan, Singapore, and Hong Kong all achieved very high growth rates (often close to 10 percent of GNP per annum). All became commonly known as the NICs (Newly Industrialized Countries) in the OECD and other international organizations to distinguish them from the general run of Third World countries. Both bankers and governments were very optimistic about their prospects, and lent very large amounts of money through both public and private channels. But with the world economic slowdown in the 1980s, a sharp contrast emerged between the East Asian and the Latin American NICs.

In the 1980s, the East Asian NICs continued or even accelerated this high growth while the whole Latin American continent slowed down to zero or even negative per capita income growth with a vast debt overhang. Of the many factors involved, the contrast between national systems of innovation clearly played an important part in the divergence. Latin American countries generally spend less than 0.5 percent of GDP on R&D (Brazil slightly more at 0.7 percent), but during this period Taiwan and Singapore increased their outlays to more than 1 percent, and South Korea to more than 2 percent. Even more important, in the East Asian countries industry now accounts for the greater part of total R&D, whereas in Latin America in-house R&D in industry is still very low indeed. This is reflected in 1980s patent statistics: Latin America's patent numbers were low, stagnant, or declining in contrast to an explosive growth of patent numbers from Taiwan and South Korea. The education and training system also remains a factor in the East Asian success, with all the "Tigers" actually graduating far more qualified engineers per 100,000 population than Japan, which is itself a country among the international leaders. The contrasting performance of Brazil and South Korea in the 1980s as shown in table 14.3 amply illustrates the difference between technological capabilities in the two countries. The much more rapid diffusion of computerized equipment in South Korea is evident, together with a far stronger infrastructure in telecommunications.

Indeed, the most notable feature of the rapid industrialization of these East Asian countries has been their extraordinary success in electronics. Information technology equipment (ICT equipment), including office machinery, computers, telecommunications, components, and consumer electronics has been by far the fastest growing category of world trade in the last quarter of the twentieth century, as to be expected from the change of technoeconomic paradigm taking place. Any country, therefore, with a substantial stake in the manufacture and export of these goods and services had a strong comparative advantage in international trade. The Latin American and African countries generally were still geared to slow-growing primary commodity exports and simple processed manufactures. The East Asian Tigers, on the other hand, with a total population of less than a third of the European Community's, had in 1989 a combined share of world exports of ICT equipment greater than that of the United States, or of France, Italy, Germany, and the UK combined. ICT equipment accounted for more than 20 percent per annum throughout the 1980s. For the United States these goods

TABLE 14.3

Various Indicators of Technical Capability, 1988

|  | BRAZIL | SOUTH KOREA |
| --- | --- | --- |
| % Age Group in 3rd Level (Higher) Education | 11 | 32 |
|  | (1985) | (1985) |
| Engineering Students as Percent of Population | .13 | .54 |
|  | (1985) | (1985) |
| R&D as % GNP | 0.7 | 2.1 |
|  | (1987) | (1989) |
| Industry R&D as % Total | 30 | 65 |
|  | (1988) | (1987) |
| Robots per Million Employees | 52 | 1060 |
|  | (1987) | (1987) |
| CAD per Million Employees | 422 | 1437 |
|  |  | (1986) |
| NCMT per Million Employees | 2298 | 5176 |
|  | (1987) | (1985) |
| Growth Rate Electronics | 8% | 21% |
|  | (1983–87) | (1985–90) |
| Telephone Lines per 100 | 6 | 25 |
| Per Capita Sales of Telecommunication Equipment | $10 | $77 |
| Patents per $10^6$ Population (U.S. Applications) | 3 | 39 |

SOURCE: Freeman (1992)

accounted for 13 percent of total merchandise exports, for Japan 24 percent, for the EEC only 7 percent, and for Latin America far less.

During the 1980s the rapid growth and prosperity of the Tigers spilled over into the countries of Southeast Asia with Malaysia, Thailand, and Indonesia all enjoying much faster growth and a flow of inward investment not only from Japan but increasingly from South Korea and Taiwan as well. The strong yen of the 1980s drove many Japanese companies to increase their offshore investment in other Asian countries including China, which shared in the general prosperity of the region. All depended increasingly on Japan for imports of capital goods and technology, but at the same time offered increased competition to Japanese firms. Though their success was primarily due to their own "national systems of innovation" and economic and technology policies, the influence of the successful Japanese system was clearly apparent. However, with their high dependence on exports, they remain as yet vulnerable to shocks from the world economy, and the recession of the early 1990s posed new problems for the whole region. At the close of the century it is still not clear whether and how soon the world will be able to embark on a Kondratieff high boom comparable to the earlier spurts of high growth.

Nevertheless the success of the East Asian Tigers in the second half of the twentieth century has given some grounds for hope that other Third World countries might also find the way to raise their living standards through sustained technical change in the twenty-first century. The falling real incomes during the 1980s over most of Africa and Latin America (table 14.4) signaled one of the great failures of the century. Science and technology did indeed help to bring prosperity to the leading industrial countries and raised living standards for the great majority of their populations. But the worldwide distribution of R&D and other scientific and technical activities has remained extremely skewed during the twentieth century. Excluding China and the former communist countries, the Third World has accounted for less than 5 percent of world R&D, and much less than 5 percent of technology transfer agreements, patents, and licensing arrangements. The lesson of the East Asian countries (including China, which has also been growing very rapidly in the closing decades of the century) is surely that successful development imperatively requires autonomous capability in R&D and other technological services. The efficient use of foreign technology (which any country requires) is only possible with independent technological capability and well-educated people. Thus, the import of technology and local R&D are not alternative but complementary activities—both are essential for development.

The prospect that countries as large as China, India, Mexico, and Brazil might successfully industrialize on a far larger scale has aroused fears as well as high

TABLE 14.4

Comparative Growth Rates of GDP in the Third World, 1965–1989

| GDP % P.A | 1965–1980 | 1980–1989 |
|---|---|---|
| East Asia | 7.5 | 7.9 |
| South Asia | 3.9 | 5.1 |
| Africa (sub-Sahara) | 4.0 | 2.1 |
| Latin America | 5.8 | 1.6 |
| GDP PER CAPITA % P.A. | 1965–1980 | 1980–1989 |
| East Asia | 5.0 | 6.3 |
| South Asia | 1.5 | 2.9 |
| Africa (sub-Sahara) | 1.1 | -1.2 |
| Latin America | 3.5 | -0.5 |

SOURCE: World Bank Development Report, 1991.

hopes at the turn of the century. Some environmentalists, such as the MIT team of Meadows et al.,[34] have maintained that the world economy will very likely collapse in the first half of the twenty-first century, either from depletion of nonrenewable resources, the polluting effects of massive industrialization, or the rapid growth of world population. However, in the later version of their book and more recent runs of the computer simulation model upon which it is based, the authors hold out the prospect that an appropriate combination of technical and institutional change might avert these catastrophes.

This has gone some way to meet the arguments of their critics,[35] who maintained that their models underestimated the potential of technical change in averting the most dangerous pollution threats, in economizing in the use of materials (and substitution between them), and in raising agricultural productivity. It has, however, been increasingly apparent toward the close of the century that a further big change in technoeconomic paradigm will be needed if sustainable development is to be achieved for the whole planet in the next century. A new "green" paradigm will have to be based to a far greater extent on renewable energy sources, recycling materials, phasing out dangerous pollutants (after the manner of chlorofluorocarbons in the 1980s and 1990s), massive reduction of carbon emissions in industrial countries, and far more responsible attitudes toward innovation and pollution throughout the world.

The Rio Conference in 1992 marked the first big hopeful step toward a worldwide consensus in this direction but also revealed many of the underlying antagonisms and tensions. It became clear that the poorer countries were not able or willing to bear the full costs of cleaner technology without substantial redistributive aid from the richer countries. At the same time there was encouraging evidence that cleaner technologies could often be both effective and profitable to firms that developed and used them. These economic advantages could be reinforced by appropriate tax regimes and other institutional changes characteristic of the "lock-in" mechanisms of a new paradigm. Public opinion has generally proved rather favorable to cleaner technology even with cost penalties.

One of the constructive results of the critique of mass production technology and of pollution hazards in the 1960s and 1970s was the setting up of various institutions for "Technology Assessment." The United States pioneered this practice with the Office of Technology Assessment (OTA), and a number of European countries have followed suit in the 1980s and 1990s with similar institutions, usually responsible to the relevant parliaments. The TA movement arose from the necessity for democratic institutions to muster sufficient expertise in relation to new (and often complex) technical innovations, to assess their probable, foreseeable costs and benefits, and to redress the bias in public debate inevitably associated with the specialized advocacy for such technologies. The movement toward a green technoeconomic paradigm would certainly lead to a reinforcement of such institutions.

However, it is extremely important that Technology Assessment should not simply become a form of Technology Harassment. New technology has brought enormous benefits as well as hazards and costs, and it will be difficult for future generations to sustain the improvement in living standards and quality of life without irrevocable damage to the environment. Wise technology assessment will be one of the most important functions of the twenty-first century parliamentary institutions. This is a heavy burden that the twentieth century will leave to its successors, but there is one very encouraging feature of the various forms of Technology Assessment that have emerged—the form of TA developed by NOTA (the Netherlands OTA) generally described as "Constructive Technology Assessment." As in other forms of TA it involves assembling the best possible expert evidence on the technologies, but it also involves representation of the main affected interest groups in novel ways. The idea is to sustain a continuous constructive dialogue with the actual or potential innovators so that the perceived risks can be reduced or eliminated before widespread diffusion. The twentieth century has kept Pandora's Box wide open; it will be up to the twenty-first century to check and control what comes out.

ENDNOTES

1. Lundvall, B-A., ed., *National Systems of Innovation* (London: Pinter, 1992).
2. Petroski, H., "H. D., Thoreau, Engineer," *American Heritage of Invention and Technology* (New Haven: Yale University Press, 1989), 8–16.
3. Schumpeter, J. A., *Business Cycles: A Theoretical, Historical and Statistical Analysis*, (New York: McGraw Hill, 1939).
4. Jewkes, J., D. Sawers, and J. Stilleman, *The Sources of Invention* (London: Macmillan, 1958).
5. Schumpeter, J. A., *The Theory of Economic Development*. Leipzig (Duncker and Humboldt, 1912); *Business Cycles: a Theoretical, Historical and Statistical Analysis* (New York: McGraw-Hill, 1939).
6. Gilfillan, S. C., *The Sociology of Invention* (Chicago: Follett, 1935).
7. Kuhn, T. S., *The Structure of Scientific Revolutions* (Chicago: University of Chicago Press, 1970).

8. Nelson, R. R., *The Moon and the Ghetto* (New York: Norton, 1977).

9. Hounshell, D. A., Du Pont and Large-scale R&D," in P. Galison and B. Hevly, eds., *Big Science: The Growth of Large-scale Research* (Stanford: Stanford University Press, 1992).

10. Seidel, R., "The Origins of the Lawrence Berkeley Laboratory," in *Big Science*.

11. Bernal, J. D., *The Social Function of Science* (London: Routledge, 1939).

12. Ellul, J., *The Technological Society* (New York: Knopf, 1964).

13. Schumacher, F., *Small is Beautiful* (London: Abacus, 1975).

14. Schmookler, J., *Invention and Economic Growth* (Cambridge: Harvard University Press, 1966).

15. Mensch G., *Das technologische Patt* (Frankfurt: Umschau Verlag, 1975). English translation *Stalemate in Technology* (Cambridge: Ballinger, 1979).

16. Hughes, T. P., *Networks of Power: Electrification in Western Society, 1880–1930* (Baltimore: John Hopkins University Press, 1983).

17. Gille, C., *Histoire des Techniques* (Paris: Gallimard, 1975).

18. Schumpeter, J. A., *Business Cycles: A Theoretical, Historical and Statistical Analysis* (New York: McGraw Hill, 1939).

19. Perez, C., "Structural Change and the Assimilation of New Technologies in the Economic and Social System," *Futures* 15:5: 357–75.

20. Nye, D., *Electrifying America: Social Meanings of a New Technology, 1880–1940* (Cambridge: MIT Press, 1990).

21. Hounshell, D. A., *From the American System to Mass Production, 1800–1932* (Baltimore: John Hopkins University Press, 1984).

22. Chandler, A. D., *The Visible Hand: The Managerial Revolution in American Business* (Cambridge: Harvard University Press, 1977).

23. Nye, D., *Electrifying America*.

24. Dertouzos, M. L., R. K. Lester, and R. M. Solow, eds., *Made in America: Regaining the Productive Edge* (Cambridge: MIT Press, 1989).

25. Abramowitz, M., "Catching up, Forging Ahead and Falling Behind," *Journal of Economic History* 66: 385–406.

26. Landes, M., *The Unbound Prometheus: Technological and Industrial Development in Western Europe from 1750 to the Present* (Cambridge: Cambridge University Press, 1970).

27. Hughes, T. P., *American Genesis: A Century of Invention and Technological Enthusiasm* (New York: Viking, 1989).

28 Landes, M., *The Unbound Prometheus*.

29. Dosi, G., C. Freeman, R. R. Nelson, G. Silverberg, and L. L. G. eds., *Technical Change and Economic Theory* (London: Pinter, 1988).

30. World Bank, *World Development Report, 1991* (New York: Oxford University Press, 1991).

31. Freeman, C., *Technology Policy and Economic Performance: Lessons from Japan* (London: Pinter, 1987).

32. Hicks, D. and P. Isard, Science in Japanese Companies, *Japan Journal of Science and Technology Studies* 1:1 (May 1987).

33. Ohmae, K., *The Borderless World* (London: Collins, 1990).

34. Meadows, D. H., D. L. Meadows, J. Randers, and W. W. Behrens, *The Limits to Growth* (New York: Universe Books, 1972).

35. Cole, H. S. D., C. Freeman, M. Jahoda, and K. Pavitt, eds., *Thinking About the Future* (London: Chatto and Windus, 1973)..

# 15  Agriculture: Crops, Livestock, and Farmers

B.F. STANTON[1]

This chapter is intended to provide some insights into the incredible achievements experienced in the agricultural sector during the twentieth century. The world's population doubled between 1900 and 1965 and is expected to come close to doubling again by the year 2000. If anything, a larger percentage of the world's people now have access to enough food for subsistence than in 1900. And the impressive gains in agricultural productivity during the twentieth century are what released the labor and capital that would bring about the tremendous growth in the industrial, technical, and service sectors of the world's economy. This chapter seeks to identify some of the great events and developments that have enabled the farm sectors around the world to feed nearly four times as many people at the end of the century as were here in 1900, using a much smaller proportion of the world's labor force.

Viewed from the perspective of the 1990s, most farmers in 1900 had a great deal more in common than modern farmers do today. The basic power used to till the soil, harvest crops, and care for livestock was provided by farmers and their families, some hired labor, and domesticated animals: horses, mules, donkeys, bullocks, and water buffalo. Much of what was produced on each farm was needed to feed themselves and these animals. Any surplus production from one or two key enterprises was marketed or bartered locally in the villages and hamlets where they lived. If they lived in what we now call the "developed" world, the extra wheat, rice, eggs, or butter paid for the clothing or books, tools, or furniture they brought home or ordered by mail. While farmers in Europe and North America commonly had access to schools and learned to read and write, the margin between pure subsistence and surplus was often small: the difference in their standard of living from that of family farmers in India, China, or Central Africa was much smaller than it would become, particularly in the second half of this century.

Most of what farm families everywhere ate in 1900 came from their own farms. Their houses and farm buildings had been built by themselves with the help of neighbors or local craftsmen. Fuel of necessity came largely from local sources. Those who had access to books, newspapers, or magazines read them by daylight or by candles and gas lanterns in the evening. Even those who weren't farmers relied on their own gardens, and livestock for a key portion of their food supply. Those who lived in cities were the minority, and those who lived in town were not far removed from families who made their living in the countryside. Farming, in other words, was the world's primary occupation. Commerce and trade centered around food and fiber: for example, in 1900 in the United States, agricultural exports amounted to $949 million and accounted for 65 percent of the total. Food imports were valued at $418 million and totaled 51 percent of all imports. For the great powers of the world, the quest for more food and new lands in which to produce additional supplies was a driving factor in the push to expand into new territories in Africa, Asia, and Latin America.

## Challenges to Agricultural Resources and Productivity

A growing population poses a particular challenge to agricultural productivity. At the turn of the last century, there were about 1.6 billion people in the world, more than half of them in the great land mass of Asia. The quality of statistics has certainly improved since then, but nearly everyone recognizes that getting a "correct" count in any census is an almost impossible job. Thus, all of the following numbers are approximations, but they nevertheless provide a good overview of the nature of change through time as well as relative magnitudes.

At the midpoint of this century, population had increased by 50 percent. In absolute numbers most of the increase was in Asia; however, more rapid rates of increase had occurred in both North and South America and, to a lesser degree, Africa. Tremendous rates of increase have occurred in the second half of the century, much of it since 1960. A threefold increase in Africa's population between 1950 and 1994 suggests why this is one of the trouble spots in the world; it lacks the internal capacity to produce enough food to meet the burgeoning demands of growing populations. To a lesser degree, the same kinds of problems exist in parts of Latin America and South Asia.

In trying to understand both the triumphs and shortcomings of twentieth-century agriculture, it is important to recognize where the people are relative to the key resources used to feed them. In 1994, Asia still accounted for more than 60 percent of the world's population. Five countries, China with 1,190 million, India with 920 million, Indonesia with 200 million, Bangladesh with 125 million, and Pakistan with 130 million, represented 45 percent of that. In these locations, some of the great advances in agriculture have been made and some of the greatest challenges remain. At the close of this century, much attention is being focused on the problems of meeting the chronic needs of hungry people in several locations across the vast expanse of Africa. Yet, in terms of sheer numbers, some of the greatest challenges of the next century are likely to remain in these five Asian countries.

Particularly during the second half of the twentieth century, substantial effort has been made to try to understand not only the processes of economic development, but also the role of agriculture in these processes. Clearly the economies of some countries have prospered greatly in comparison to others. In the 1990s, in much of Europe and North America, where food is plentiful and agricultural exports are an important component of trade, agriculture accounts for a very small proportion of the Gross Domestic Product. These high-income countries and others like them—such as Australia, New Zealand, and Japan—are commonly referred to as industrialized or "developed" countries. The labor force engaged in agriculture in 1990 made up from 2 to 10 percent of their populations, in substantial contrast to the rates in 1900. For example, in the United States in 1900, the farm population was 30 million, a little less than 40 percent of the national total. In contrast, the farm population of about 5 million in 1990 made up 2 percent of the total.

Another group of countries are often described as developing countries, sometimes called the "LDCs," a broad generalization that includes most of the countries of Latin America, Africa, and Asia. Clearly, any such sweeping description is inadequate to reflect the vast differences within and between countries: Brazil, for instance, encompassing a land area similar in size to the United States, includes a prosperous industrialized region in the south and a large, impoverished agricultural region in the northeast. One of the common ways to show the great contrasts at the end of the century is to list the GNP per capita in some of the most populous of the industrialized and developing countries. Most of the countries of South America, as can be seen, had substantially higher average incomes per capita in the 1990s than those in either Africa or Asia.

During the twentieth century, the degree of difference in economic well-being has grown dramatically, particularly in the years since 1960. The developing nations, particularly the poorest of the poor, have had difficulty even maintaining their low levels of income per capita. Some countries like Ethiopia, Liberia, and Zaire (Congo) saw these meager amounts grow still smaller in

TABLE 15.1
GNP Per Capita

| COUNTRY | POPULATION (millions) | 1985[a] | 1993[a] |
|---|---|---|---|
| INDUSTRIALIZED: | | | |
| United States | 250 | $22,240 | $24,580 |
| Germany | 81 | 21,500 | 21,020 |
| France | 58 | 19,260 | 21,530 |
| Japan | 125 | 26,640 | 34,160 |
| RAPIDLY DEVELOPING: | | | |
| Taiwan | 21 | 6,181 | 10,460 |
| South Korea | 45 | 4,040 | 7,370 |
| Argentina | 34 | 6,180 | 7,500 |
| DEVELOPING: | | | |
| Brazil | 159 | 3,370 | 3,530 |
| China | 1,190 | 965 | 1,738 |
| India | 920 | 230 | 280 |
| Bangladesh | 125 | 175 | 200 |
| Nigeria | 98 | 280 | 340 |
| Ethiopia | 59 | 70 | 66 |

[a.] 1993 dollars

the 1980s, while most others continued to make progress. While the measurement of GNP per capita is at best a poor indicator of true differences, and clearly overstates the size of the gap between rich and poor countries—because so much of production and service in the developing countries' economies does not move through the marketplace at all—it does help to show how large the gap has become. Finding ways to narrow that gap has become one of the major responsibilities of the rich industrialized nations in the post-World War II era.

The availability of natural resources is a perpetual constraint on agricultural production. If the Reverend Thomas Robert Malthus could return to survey the world some 200 years after his famous essay on the impact of population growth[2] was published, he would likely still view the race between man and his food supply with alarm. But the shock would come in the total number of people on the planet and how well they are being fed, not in the millions who fit his dire expectations of starvation and malnutrition. No doubt, he would still come to the same conclusions about the future of the human race, namely, that population increases faster than food supply, leading to poverty, war, and human disaster.

During much of this century, population pressure on domestic resources has been an important factor in determining world events. In the tumultuous years surrounding the two world wars, the need for additional lands to feed people was one of the justifications for military operations in both Asia and Europe. In the postwar era, this need for land provided the impetus for the international funding of both food relief and agricultural development at unparalleled levels.

Harrison Brown, a scientist at the Institute of Nuclear Studies, University of Chicago, reflected both a growing understanding and the associated concern that was building among many citizens around the world in his 1954 book, *The Challenge of Man's Future*.[3] His was a persuasive call to the developed world's relatively affluent countries that new efforts had to be taken to provide more food for the four fifths of the world's people who had, as he wrote, "too little." The timely book reflected the thoughts and fears of many in the immediate postwar years. William Vogt's 1948 book, *The Road to Survival*,[4] was another clarion call. An international effort would be required to feed the world's burgeoning population from limited and finite resources.

One such crucial finite resource is land. In a statistical sense, crop production is a function of area cropped, yields obtained, and cropping intensity. This is an oversimplification of reality, but it speaks to some of the most important constraints that determine how much agricultural product is produced. In his mid-century book, Brown had the benefit of more accurate statistics on world agriculture than were available in 1900. He could thus report that the total land area of the world amounts to about 36 billion acres. Of this, no more than 10 percent is cultivated because the rest is too dry, too steep, too cold, or too inhospitable for cultivation. The challenge at mid-century was how to bring more land under cultivation, how to raise yields efficiently, and how to increase cropping intensity. The impressive result at the end of this century is that with substantial effort, an important part of that challenge has been met. But the easiest gains in productivity have already been achieved. The challenge of the twenty-first century will be more difficult. Malthus's and Brown's dire warnings have not disappeared, despite the great achievements, such as the new improved, high-yielding crop varieties provided by the international agricultural research centers since 1960.

As summarized by the Food and Agriculture Organization (FAO), a measuring arm established by the United Nations to estimate agricultural production worldwide, the most recent estimates of world land use by broad categories are provided in table 15.2. The combination of all cultivated cropland and permanent crops, such as orchards, vineyards, and coffee and tea planta-

TABLE 15.2

World Agricultural Land Use, 1961–65 and 1989

| TYPE OF USE | 1961–65[a] | 1989[a] | 1961–65[b] | 1989[b] |
|---|---|---|---|---|
| Permanent crops[c] | 90 | 104 | 0.7 | 0.8 |
| Cultivated land | 1,313 | 1,373 | 9.8 | 10.3 |
| Permanent pasture | 3,043 | 3,304 | 22.7 | 24.7 |
| Forest and woodland | 4,063 | 4,087 | 30.3 | 30.5 |
| Other land | 4,881 | 4,522 | 36.5 | 33.7 |
| TOTAL | 13,390 | 13,390 | 100.0 | 100.0 |

SOURCE: FAO, Production Yearbooks, 1975 and 1990.
  [a.] Millions of hectares
  [b.] Percent of total
  [c.] Estimated for some countries

tions, accounted for about 10.8 percent of the world's ice-free surface in 1993. In a span of 34 years, only 45 million more acres had been added to the arable base, primarily from land formerly used for permanent pasture and forest. In percentage terms this is a small net addition. In terms of the land that might feasibly be converted to permanent cropland, it represents a large share of what was considered acceptable for agriculture, and some that might rather quickly become a part of "other" land, not suitable for cultivation or pasture because of its fragile nature.

The contrast in arable land per person is greatest for Asia and North America. While 60 percent of the world's people live in Asia, only 32 percent of the cultivated land used for annual and perennial crops is found on this continent. North America accounts for 18.7 percent of the arable land, but only 7 percent of the population. Clearly, the land's capacity to consistently produce large or small amounts of different crops is related to many factors, including access to rainfall, length of growing season, quality and texture of the soil, slope of the land, topography, and the potential for irrigation. Thus, there are relatively large areas of arable land per person in the former USSR, Canada, and the United States which are not able to produce as much per acre as some of the irrigated areas in India, Indonesia, and China, where two and three crops per year are now harvested regularly. Nevertheless, the summary of cropland used by continent (table 15.3) does indicate that additional food production in some of the most densely populated areas of the world cannot be expected to come from additional land in those countries in the next century.

Access to adequate rainfall or to a source of fresh water for irrigation has been important to agriculture from its earliest beginnings. It is commonly believed that irrigation may have been practiced as early as 5000 B.C. Clearly, irrigation

TABLE 15.3
Cultivated Cropland and Permanent Crops
by Continent, 1989 (Millions of Hectares)

| CONTINENT | CULTIVATED CROPLAND | PERMANENT CROPS | TOTAL | CHANGES SINCE 1961–65 |
|---|---|---|---|---|
| Asia | 421 | 32 | 453 | + 5 |
| North and Central America | 267 | 7 | 274 | +17 |
| USSR | 226 | 4 | 230 | + 1 |
| Africa | 168 | 19 | 187 | - 11 |
| Europe | 126 | 14 | 140 | - 12 |
| South America | 116 | 26 | 142 | +59 |
| Oceania | 49 | 2 | 51 | +15 |
| TOTAL | 1373 | 104 | 1477 | +74 |

SOURCE:   FAO, Production Yearbook, 1990.

from either surface or underground sources has grown increasingly crucial over time, particularly in the tropics and subtropics, where it enables the production of two or more crops per year.

Significant growth in the use of irrigation for intensive agriculture is essentially a twentieth-century phenomenon. Without the technical development of irrigated agriculture, new high-yielding crop varieties, and the associated technical inputs in the years following World War II, Malthus's dire predictions might well have become a reality. From 40 million hectares of irrigated land in 1900, the area receiving supplemental water had increased to about 250 million hectares in 1993. For some countries, irrigated land is fundamental to their food supply: Rangeley[5] estimates that 80 percent of food production in Pakistan, for instance, comes from irrigated fields. Of other major countries, China depends on irrigated land for 70 percent of its agricultural output; India, Chile, and Peru for 55 percent each; and Indonesia for 50 percent (table 15.4).

This rapid expansion in irrigation is not without major problems. Water tables must be kept well below the root zone of crops or waterlogging and salt accumulation will occur. The maintenance and productivity of irrigation systems depends on effective drainage systems and water controls. The great structures built to provide electric power, water control, and irrigation around the world are gradually filling with silt; the ecological impacts from impounding fresh water in the great river systems are now beginning to be understood more fully. Demands for changes in the allocation systems for water are being made by society in a number of the richer countries of the world. More and more attention will be paid to underground aquifers and

TABLE 15.4

Irrigated Area by Continent, 1950, 1970, 1985

(Millions of Hectares)

| CONTINENT | 1950 | 1970 | 1985 |
|---|---|---|---|
| Asia, including Asian USSR | 66 | 132 | 184 |
| Europe, including USSR | 8 | 20 | 29 |
| North America | 12 | 29 | 34 |
| Africa | 4 | 9 | 13 |
| South America | 3 | 6 | 9 |
| Oceania | 1 | 2 | 2 |
| World | 94 | 198 | 271 |

SOURCE: Pierce (1990), The Food Resource.

water resources in the twenty-first century, as fresh water is recognized as an increasingly scarce resource, vital to our existence.

How, then, can needed food from crops be produced? Acceptable approximations of world agricultural production levels are a product of the second half of this century—one of the lasting achievements of the United Nations mandating the FAO to gather annual agricultural production estimates for every country using consistent procedures. While the statistical evidence is limited, it seems clear that from 1900 until after World War II there were substantial difficulties in producing enough food in parts of Asia, Africa, and Central America to keep up with their population growth. Brown and Finsterbusch[6] list serious famines with more than half a million deaths in India, in 1899–1900 and again in 1943–1944; in Russia, in 1920–1921 and in 1932–1933; in China, in 1920–1921 and 1929–1930; and in East Africa, in 1918–1919. Japanese military expansion in Korea, North China, and the Pacific was in part motivated by the need for additional land to produce food for Japan's own growing population.

Public and private investment in research and extension services in the first half of the twentieth century, building on the previous century's advances in science and husbandry, set the stage for the great leaps in agricultural productivity which were evidenced after 1950 (see tables 15.5 and 15.6). In a span of forty years, agricultural output has risen faster than the population has increased, with the most dramatic advances in many of the less developed countries of the world. The phrases "green revolution" and "industrialization of agriculture" have been used by many to describe some of this impressive process. First it is important to get an overview of the magnitude of the

TABLE 15.5

World Area and Production of Key Food Crops, 1948-52 and 1990

| | AREA | | PRODUCTION | |
| --- | --- | --- | --- | --- |
| | 1948-52[a] | 1990[a] | 1948-52[b] | 1990[b] |
| GRAINS: | | | | |
| Wheat | 133.2 | 231.5 | 140.1 | 595.1 |
| Rice | 102.4 | 145.8 | 163.9 | 518.5 |
| Barley | 43.5 | 71.5 | 52.5 | 180.4 |
| Maize | 86.3 | 129.1 | 138.6 | 475.4 |
| Millet, sorghum | 87.1 | 82.0 | 54.3 | 88.0 |
| Oats and rye | 51.9 | 38.4 | 69.0 | 80.7 |
| TOTAL | 504.4 | 698.3 | 618.4 | 1938.1 |
| OTHER CROPS: | | | | |
| Potatoes | 14.9 | 17.9 | 167.4 | 269.6 |
| Sweet potatoes, yams | 9.3 | 11.9 | 70.2 | 131.7 |
| Cassava | 5.9 | 15.6 | 52.0 | 157.7 |
| Total pulses | 37.1 | 68.9 | 22.5 | 59.4 |
| Soybeans | 15.5 | 56.3 | 16.4 | 107.8 |
| TOTAL | 82.7 | 170.6 | 328.5 | 726.2 |

SOURCE: FAO, Production Yearbooks, 1959, 1991.
[a.] million hectares
[b.] million metric tons

achievement. Second, I will seek to describe and analyze some of the many factors which brought about such dramatic change.

Between 1950 and 1994, world grain production more than tripled, but the proportion of cropland planted with cereal crops increased by only 36.7 percent. Most of the increases in output were associated with increases in yields and cropping intensity. The increases in output for wheat and rice, the staple food grains for more than half of the world's people, are among the major achievements in agriculture. The gains for maize and barley, food grains in many of the developing countries and major feed grains for animal agriculture in the rest of the world, are no less impressive: barley production at three times its 1950 rate, and maize production up more than four times. But millet, sorghum, oats, and rye, with less land devoted to their production in 1994, did not show the same magnitude of gains.

There were important increases in the land areas devoted to root crops and tubers over the same period—potatoes, yams, and cassava are major sources of calories in many areas where there is a marked population pressure on land resources. But the largest increases were for pulses and soybeans, important sources of vegetable protein and oil.

A major share of the gains in agricultural productivity over the second half

TABLE 15.6

Increases in World Crop Yields, 1948–52, 1990

(Yield Per Hectare)

| | 1948–52 | 1990 | 1990 AS PERCENT OF 1948–52 |
|---|---|---|---|
| Wheat | 1,050[a] | 2,570[a] | 245 |
| Rice | 1,600 | 3,560 | 223 |
| Maize | 1,600 | 3,682 | 230 |
| Barley | 1,210 | 2,520 | 208 |
| Millet, sorghum | 620 | 1,070 | 173 |
| Oats and rye | 1,330 | 2,100 | 158 |
| Potatoes | 11,240 | 15,100 | 134 |
| Sweet potatoes, yams | 7,550 | 11,060 | 146 |
| Cassava | 8,810 | 10,090 | 115 |
| Pulses | 610 | 860 | 141 |
| Soybeans | 1,060 | 1,910 | 180 |

SOURCE: FAO, Production Yearbooks, 1959, 1991.

[a.] Kg per hectare

of the century derives from substantial increases in average yields. All three of the major cereal grains—wheat, rice, and maize—now provide more than twice as much output per unit of land area as they did some forty years ago. Much of the green revolution is associated with the success achieved with these three crops, particularly in irrigated areas in developing countries. The average yields achieved by peasant farmers in 1990 were often three or four times greater than what they achieved in 1970. Yield increases have been important for the root and tuber crops as well, though the initial high yields have made advances somewhat more difficult, and agricultural scientists have devoted substantially less work to improving these yields.

Cropping intensity has also increased dramatically on irrigated lands where population pressure is substantial. In China and India, two and three crops are harvested in favored locations. Vegetable production is particularly important near urban centers, where multiple cropping and intensive agriculture with animal manures and commercial fertilizers are the general rule.

## How Increased Output was Achieved

At the close of World War II, the challenges facing farmers and the agricultural industries around the world were enormous. Any effort such as this to document the important reasons for postwar agriculture's accomplishments will be fragmentary at best. Essentially, many people, organizations, and institutions were involved in individual efforts that added up to a much larger whole. As individuals and nations, in their own best interest, sought ways to alleviate hunger and increase farm productivity, this became a truly international effort.

In making the historic peace after World War II, the victors set about helping the losers reconstruct their economies, providing the food and capital needed to rebuild more stable and peaceful societies. The possibility of establishing new, independent nations was tendered to a number of former territories and protectorates. A successful standard for international cooperation in development was established by the Marshall Plan of 1946–1948, and church groups and private organizations deployed new energy and resources to assist those facing hunger, famine, and deprivation in developing countries and overseas possessions. As mass communications brought the problems of the Third World into graphic focus for a worldwide audience, leaders accepted the challenge of taking a more active role in international assistance. In the 1950s and 1960s, as an international commitment to help the world's disadvantaged began to emerge as the responsibility of the richer nations, special agencies and organizations were established in individual countries to act in cooperation with the United Nations and the World Bank. In nearly all of the wealthier Western countries, funding for "aid" agencies is now an integral part of foreign policy; emergency food shipments and technical assistance for agricultural development are now basic components of these programs.

Agricultural sciences and technology have undergone major advances. In the second half of the nineteenth century, the work of agricultural chemist Justus von Liebig, naturalist Charles Darwin, and others began to change the shape of university education: agricultural chemistry, the natural sciences, and soil studies became part of the curriculum. As stations for agricultural experimenting were founded throughout Europe, agricultural societies and colleges were formed, and public funds allocated—albeit in small amounts at first—for research and education, all dedicated to the new field of agricultural science and technology. Scientific journals reported the results of experiments by estate managers and plantation owners in the tropical and subtropical zones who, starting with promising varieties of native plants, tried out various native propagation and cultivation techniques. The age of modern agriculture had begun.

Mechanization, however, was a key factor—and would remain one in this century. By the second half of the nineteenth century, mechanized agriculture's beginnings were established in the industrialized countries. Such inventions as the reaper, the threshing machine, and the steel moldboard plow began to allow one worker to do more, reducing some of the drudgery of farm labor. With the advent of the the twentieth century, the ability to harness electricity and the gasoline engine instead of a horse or ox saved not only human labor but also the feed required to produce animal power. The tractor in all its sizes and forms—from the power tiller in Asia to the articulated giants of the North American plains—released millions of people from the land for other employment. Mechanization saved not only labor but also much of farming's drudgery, reducing the endless routine of lifting, carrying, and bending while saving steps and speeding up repetitive operations (see table 15.7). In the United States alone, the release of important areas of cropland formerly dedicated to producing feed for horses and draft animals freed up vast areas of land: at least 60 million acres, or more than 15 percent of all the nation's cropland, was released when horses were replaced by cars, trucks, and tractors. If each of these acres produced 1.5 metric tons of grain (60 bushels of corn), they would feed 630 million people in Asia, according to average calorie consumption standards.

While the tractor is primarily a product of the twentieth century, it had its origins in steam plowing and the first internal combustion engines of the late nineteenth century. The first regular tractor use on farms, and the idea of the power takeoff—to transmit power from the tractor engine to run a machine pulled behind it, such as a mowing machine—came between 1910 and 1920. Before 1940 the standard tractor much as we know it today had emerged— with rubber tires, power takeoff, and a high compression engine. In the immediate postwar years, two thirds of the tractors in use were found in

TABLE 15.7

Tractors in Agricultural Uses[a], 1948–52, 1970–71, 1989–90
(in Millions)

| CONTINENT | 1948–52 | 1970–71 | 1989–90 |
| --- | --- | --- | --- |
| Europe | 0.99 | 6.10 | 10.38 |
| USSR | 0.60 | 1.98 | 2.69 |
| North America | 4.04 | 5.57 | 5.73 |
| South America | 0.09 | 0.41 | 1.10 |
| Asia | 0.04 | 0.76 | 5.35 |
| Africa | 0.09 | 0.37 | 0.58 |
| Oceania | 0.16 | 0.43 | 0.42 |
| WORLD TOTAL | 6.01 | 15.56 | 26.24 |

SOURCE: FAO, Production Yearbooks.
   [a.] Excludes power tillers and garden tractors

North America; by 1970 there were more tractors in Europe than the Americas. If one counted power tillers along with wheel tractors, Asia led with the largest number by the 1990s.

Agriculture's mechanization entails much more than tractors, trucks, and electrical power. But the use of these power sources in new machines, as well as engineering advances in other fields, have made possible many of the major advances of the last forty years. Self-propelled mechanical harvesters, for instance, have adapted electronic sensing devices and pneumatic controls to improve the timing of harvest and reduce the need for hand labor. Most crop and livestock operations have benefited from the ingenuity of mechanically minded farmers and engineers, who have found practical ways to adapt engineering principles to carry out repetitive work mechanically. The challenge of the next few decades is to bring mechanization to the small farms of developing countries in ways that improve productivity and reduce risk, a possibility already demonstrated in Japan and Eastern Asia.

The development of the crop sciences has also had a marked impact. In 1900, three different scientists working independently in the Netherlands, Germany, and Austria rediscovered the historic work on peas done in Austria by the Augustinian monk Father Gregor Mendel, as they set about reporting their own research results. Though the import of Mendel's basic work went unrecognized during his lifetime, he is now recognized as the saintly father of genetics. From his research, varietal improvement and plant breeding gained a more solid, scientific base—another building block in the expanding foundation of agricultural science and technology.

The first half of the twentieth century saw important developments in the crop sciences, including the expansion of both public and private funding for scientific work and the establishment, out of botany and biology, of new specializations—plant pathology, entomology, plant physiology, agronomy, genetics, and microbiology. Statistics and biometry became a separate discipline as natural scientists began to require systematic procedures to interpret the results of their experiments. For increasing numbers of scientists, the quest to better understand the workings of nature for the good of humanity became their professional pursuit.

One of these early experimenters was Barbara McClintock, a botanist-plant breeder born in 1900 who spent her lifetime studying corn at Cornell (Ph.D., 1927) and Cold Spring Harbor, Long Island, joining the Carnegie Institution in Washington in 1941. She argued that genes are not necessarily fixed for good in one place along a chromosome, but are "transposable," causing changes in the way genes are expressed. Recognition for her pathbreaking work finally came in 1983, when she became the first American woman to win the Nobel Prize as an individual and not a member of a team. Her comment in *Science* after receiving the prize gives a sense of the incredible advances made during her career:

> I have had the pleasure of witnessing and experiencing the excitement created by revolutionary changes in genetic concepts that have occurred over the past sixty-odd years. I believe we are again experiencing such a revolution. It is altering our concepts of the genome: its component parts, their organizations, mobilities, and their modes of operation.[7]

In the postwar era, the fields of basic biology and agricultural science underwent rapid expansion, with discoveries in one benefiting the other. In *The Double Helix*,[8] James D. Watson's 1968 account of his work individually and with Francis Crick to discover the structure of DNA, one can sense the excitement of biological science. The book reads like a suspense novel, with Linus Pauling at Cal Tech and Watson's group at the University of Cambridge racing to solve the mysterious puzzle of DNA and publish their results first. Their great urge—to understand how and why the fundamental mechanisms of life work as they do—has allowed others to build on their accumulated knowledge, continuing the tide of great practical advances made in twentieth-century agriculture.

One such advance is embodied in the story of the miracle seeds, on which the green revolution of the 1960s was built. It starts with the work of the pioneers, such as Norman Borlaug, who selected and then established the inbred modern cultivars on which advanced breeding lines are constructed. Tissue culture had its beginnings early in the century, when, in 1907, the first successful experiments were completed. As it became a basic technique of agricultural science in the 1960s, through it came the capacity to reproduce plants from single cells, allowing genetic manipulations unthought of in the beginning. The science and experiments of the second half of the twentieth century provided the foundation for biotechnology, which promised to be a mechanism to modify the genetic composition of living organisms. Genetic engineering, as it was defined by the National Research Council in 1987, "the ability to identify a particular gene—one that encodes a desired trait in an organism—isolate the gene, study its function and regulation, modify the gene, and reintroduce it into its natural host or other organism,"[9] is now a reality. The challenges of reaping the benefits of these advances are now receiving the central attention of tens of thousands of scientists worldwide in both the public and private sectors. But the need for plant breeders, plant pathologists, agronomists, and others remains: these potentially new, genetically transformed plants must still be tested and adapted for the many different environments in which they will be grown.

The green revolution, which transformed agriculture in many of the developing countries between 1960 and 1980, resulted from a combination of new seeds, new technology, new agronomic practices, the use of substantial amounts of fertilizer, and new supplies of irrigation water. Supplying the necessary plant nutrients was a crucial part of this success story, founded on the nineteenth-century work of Justus von Liebig at the University of Giessen. Most agricultural scientists consider von Liebig the father of agricultural chemistry, as he demonstrated the importance of different mineral elements in the soil and worked to develop synthetic fertilizers to supplement plant residues and animal manures.

Some of the basic science that recognized the roles of nitrogen, phosphate, and potash in plant nutrition, and the first studies on the importance of magnesium, calcium, sulphur, and iron to plant growth also date from the 1800s. As the industrialization of agriculture began in the developed world, the search for sources of N-P-K (nitrogen-phosphorus-potassium) began to have more than scientific interest. One of the by-products of World War I was the discovery that the same processes used in the manufacture of explosives would also work in the production of ammonia, the basic ingredient of nitrate fertilizer. In the years before World War II, practical methods of soil testing for acidity and fertility were developed, sources of N-P-K were established, and access to cheap energy was acquired: as a result, the commercial fertilizer industry could expand to meet international needs.

World use of commercial fertilizer in the immediate postwar years was modest by 1990 standards (table 15.8): out of the 4.3 million metric tons of nitrogen and 6.3 million metric tons of phosphate applied annually, about three fourths were used in Europe and North America; of the 4.6 million metric tons of potash, 85 percent was used on these two continents. In the next 20 years, the capacity to supply needed nutrients expanded and the use of commercial fertilizer became much more common around the world, particularly in Asia. In 1970, Asian farmers used 12 times as much commercial nitrogen as they had in 1950, and the world consumed more than 7 times more nitrogen, 3.16 times more phosphate, and 3.62 times more potash. The major users of phosphate and potash were still farmers in the developed countries, but the benefits of supplementing existing soil nutrients with commercial fertilizers were becoming understood by more and more people around the world.

TABLE 15.8

Annual Commercial Fertilizer Use, 1948–52, 1970–71, 1989–90
(Million Metric Tons)

| CONTINENT | 1948–52 | 1970–71 | 1989–90 |
|---|---|---|---|
| NITROGEN: | | | |
| Europe | 1.92 | 9.67 | 15.37 |
| USSR | 0.28 | 4.61 | 10.04 |
| North America | 1.25 | 8.29 | 11.24 |
| South America | 0.07 | 0.59 | 3.88 |
| Asia | 0.63 | 7.44 | 37.20 |
| Africa | 0.14 | 0.85 | 0.90 |
| Oceania | 0.04 | 0.16 | 0.45 |
| WORLD TOTAL | 4.33 | 31.61 | 79.08 |
| PHOSPHATE: | | | |
| Europe | 2.64 | 7.82 | 7.44 |
| USSR | 0.44 | 2.21 | 8.14 |
| North America | 2.11 | 4.92 | 4.56 |
| South America | 0.09 | 0.65 | 2.46 |
| Asia | 0.32 | 2.57 | 13.35 |
| Africa | 0.18 | 0.57 | 0.65 |
| Oceania | 0.49 | 1.07 | 0.75 |
| WORLD TOTAL | 6.27 | 19.82 | 37.35 |
| POTASH: | | | |
| Europe | 2.51 | 7.48 | 8.17 |
| USSR | 0.42 | 2.59 | 6.36 |
| North America | 1.34 | 4.26 | 5.08 |
| South America | 0.03 | 0.43 | 2.08 |
| Asia | 0.19 | 1.33 | 4.57 |
| Africa | 0.04 | 0.24 | 0.34 |
| Oceania | 0.03 | 0.20 | 0.25 |
| WORLD TOTAL | 4.56 | 16.53 | 26.85 |

SOURCE: FAO, Production Yearbooks, 1959, 1971, and 1990.

As of 1993–94, the use of nitrogen fertilizer in Asia exceeded consumption in Europe, the former Soviet Union, and North America combined. Plants to produce the needed fertilizer were on line in the major Asian countries. While distribution systems for delivering fertilizer were expanding, the infrastructure—particularly out in the countryside away from major transport systems—still required much more improvement. The ability to test soils, know the quantities of nutrients to apply, and place the fertilizer optimally in relation to the seed is still in the early stages in many developing countries, yet the progress already made in the manufacture and delivery of basic plant nutrients to farmers worldwide is one of the great success stories of the last forty years.

The development of agricultural pesticides to reduce losses of crop production from infestations of disease and insects before and after harvest is another major twentieth-century achievement. Before the turn of the century, cultural and biological controls were the primary options available. At the close of this century, there is a great effort being made to once again use them more heavily. But despite the worldwide emphasis on IPM (integrated pest management), some combination of chemical controls and the biological controls provided by nature and the farmer are still necessary.

In the early 1900s, a number of relatively crude chemical pesticides such as copper, arsenic, and especially hoeing and other forms of mechanical weed control were in general use in the Western world. After World War I, basic chemical science developed in Germany yielded DDT, dieldrin, and aldrin, the latter two named after the scientists who discovered the processes from which these compounds were synthesized. A similar outgrowth of the war years yielded the chemistry underlying the development of insecticide thiophosophates such as malathion and parathion. In the same period the familiar herbicides 2,4-D and 2,4,5-T (agent orange) were synthesized.

But as experience showed, these chemical innovations were not without their costs, and the postwar era has seen the development of more sophisticated and ecologically acceptable pesticides. Rachel Carson, a scientist in the U.S. Fish and Wildlife Service and the 1952 National Book Award winner for *The Sea Around Us*, captured the attention of the world, especially ecologists and the chemical industry, with her final book, *Silent Spring* (1962),[10] which in its first chapter, "A Fable for Tomorrow," starkly portrayed the consequences of the indiscriminate use of chemical pesticides. Carson's plea was that we accommodate ourselves to the planet: her concluding chapter, "The Other Road," proposed a biological, essentially nonchemical approach to pest control. The great efforts of the 1970s and 1980s moved commercial agriculture down the road to that end, and modern chemistry, biological engineering, agroecology, and the agricultural sciences continue to work toward this major objective. But the end of that road is not yet in sight, and this desirable goal remains one of the great quests for the twenty-first century.

At the same time as crop production has increased, so have livestock numbers and production—and with it, the twentieth-century field of animal science, which has made great advances of its own. While the availability of accurate livestock production data from some countries is limited, upward trends since the 1960s in all categories are clear (table 15.9). The greatest growth has been in poultry, generally the most efficient way of converting grains into meat and animal protein, with an increase of 150 percent over 30 years. As incomes rise, the demand for livestock products increases: those with higher incomes in developed and developing countries can bid the cereal crops required for livestock production away from the poor. But in many developing countries, cattle, sheep, and goats provide the only effective way to convert pasture and grass into an important part of local diets.

What was rightly called animal husbandry in the nineteenth century—with an emphasis on what had been learned from experience by farmers—became animal science, as experimentation and applications borrowed from the biological sciences were tested with on-farm trials and experience. Animal nutrition, breeding, reproductive physiology, disease control, and management advanced concurrently with similar scientific discoveries about man and his development. After all, much of what was learned about human health and behavior was based on experiments with laboratory animals.

One of the great steps forward in both human and animal nutrition came from separate studies and work by the British biochemist, Frederick Hopkins, and the Polish scientist, Casimir Funk, between 1906 and 1911. They found that protein, fat, carbohydrates, and minerals were not the only necessary ingredients in the diet. Both people and animals, they postulated, required "vital amines"—soon named vitamins. The findings led to the subsequent discovery of vitamin A and the other fat- and water-soluble vitamins; identification of many of the essential amino acids, trace elements, and fatty acids

TABLE 15.9

World Livestock Numbers, Production FAO, 1961–65, 1990

| DESCRIPTION | PERCENT | | |
| --- | --- | --- | --- |
| | 1961–65 | 1990 | INCREASE |
| **World Numbers: million head** | | | |
| Cattle, all types | 988 | 1,279 | 29 |
| Sheep | 1,015 | 1,190 | 17 |
| Goats | 377 | 557 | 48 |
| Pigs | 531 | 857 | 61 |
| Buffalo | 112 | 141 | 26 |
| Chickens | 4,297 | 10,740 | 150 |
| Ducks | 89 | 573 | 544 |
| Turkeys | 74 | 257 | 247 |
| **Production: million metric tons** | | | |
| Whole milk | 324 | 476 | 47 |
| Cheese, all types | 7.28 | 14.65 | 101 |
| Butter and ghee | 5.57 | 7.76 | 39 |
| Eggs | 16.25 | 35.76 | 120 |

SOURCES: FAO, Production Yearbooks, 1975 and 1990.

came in rapid succession in the next few decades. By 1917 the first books on animal nutrition, such as Henry and Morrison's *Feeds and Feeding*, were published.[11]

In the second half of the century the nutrient requirements of humans and animals were more carefully quantified; ways to analyze the content of feedstuffs were developed; the role of microbes in the digestion of herbivores was elaborated; and the place of urea in the feeding of cows and other ruminant animals was established. Great progress was also made in understanding the biochemical and physiological processes involved in nutrient metabolism. Increasingly, research now focuses on the regulation of nutrient use within the cell, with the expectation that knowledge of these fundamental processes, gained through the application of biotechnology, will permit additional gains in biological efficiency.

Experimentation with artificial insemination by Ivanov and Milanov in Russia eventually led to the practical application and use of this technique in the 1930s and 1940s in both Europe and North America. With the advent of antibiotics, population genetics for sire selection, the ability to freeze and maintain semen, and an improved knowledge of reproductive physiology, great strides were made in animal breeding on farms and ranches around the world. Postwar advances in endocrinology and physiology have since led to successful embryo transfers from selected cows to foster recipients, enabling further progress to be made in selecting both superior males and females. The cloning of superior embryos and the production of transgenic animals are now being done at the experimental level. Most of the gains in milk production efficiency have come from a combination of advances in sire selection methods, artificial insemination, improved nutrition, herd health, milking equipment, and management. In 1900 the average annual milk yield per cow in the United States was 3600 pounds; by 1950 it had increased by 59 percent to 5300 pounds. In the next 25 years the yield essentially doubled—to 10,500 pounds. By 1994 it had increased again, to an average of 16,100 pounds per cow.

Other impressive changes in animal agriculture have been achieved in the poultry industry. The typical rural family in 1900 in Western Europe and North America had a few chickens or ducks of their own to supply eggs and dinners for special occasions. Farm women tended the flocks and traded surplus eggs for supplies when they went to town. But when change came to the poultry industry after World War II, it was dramatic. Because the cycle from fertilized egg to producing adult is so much shorter for poultry than for other animals, the major advances in genetics, nutrition, and animal health were tested and transferred to poultry much more rapidly. With the advent of climate control in housing, the use of antibiotics in feed, and mechanization in feeding and egg handling, poultry meat and egg production was revolutionized around the world between 1950 and 1980. The farm flock essentially disappeared from the Western world. Poultry production is now perhaps the most industrialized of all agricultural enterprises, involving a technology that is transferable to anywhere in the world where consistent access to feed, water, electrical power, and skilled management can be obtained.

In the last two decades of the century, consumer concerns about food safety have added one more element to the criteria used in deciding on the release and use of new technology in agricultural production. At the same time that there has been increased public concern among the richer countries about diet, human health, and food safety, there is also a growing demand for leaner meat containing less cholesterol. The same feed additives and antibiotics that have increased efficiency in the conversion of feed into beef, pork, chicken, eggs, and milk are now under increased scrutiny. The challenge is to ensure that consumer products are free of the "residue" left over from the drugs or additives used with animals. As this chapter is being written, the use of animal growth hormones—developed using recombinant DNA technology—to produce leaner pork and higher milk yields is under rigorous testing and public scrutiny. And wherever large numbers of livestock are concentrated, waste management is now an important concern.

The need to preserve food posed its own challenges, fostering the field of food science. While thermal processing and mechanical refrigeration were developed in nineteenth-century Western Europe, most of the advances in food preservation so widely taken for granted around the world have come about in this century through a combination of private and public research. Advances in packaging; maintaining of basic nutrients, color, and flavor; and controlling microorganisms and spoilage are all outgrowths of the work of bacteriologists, food chemists and technologists, and a wide range of industry workers. In their own self-interest food processors and manufacturers adhere to rigid standards of food safety and quality, not only because of marketplace competition, but also under the very real threat of public censure and court costs if their products are identified as causing ill health. In this century, governments have organized and expanded the agencies that regulate weights and measures, establish standards of sanitation and inspection, and determine procedures for clearance and tolerance for food additives. Because of such steps, high-quality fresh and processed foods now move regularly in international trade. The interdependence of the separate parts of the food industry from farm to market becomes evident as varieties, times of planting and harvest, and cultural practices are determined in concert with food processors, who in turn respond to market demands from buyers and consumers.

A number of new institutions have had a marked impact on agriculture. The Food and Agriculture Organization (FAO) of the United Nations, established in 1945, had its origins in a series of international efforts in the nineteenth and early twentieth centuries. The 1891 International Commission on Agriculture, held at the Hague, issued this stated intent: "to examine the rural economy, to provide technical information of common interest and to promote the international organization of agricultural commodity production and sales."[12] Similar conferences or institutes echoed the sentiment. Following a conference convened by the King of Italy in 1905 involving seventy-four nations, an International Institute of Agriculture was formed in 1908. It began operations by publishing data on traded agricultural commodities, prices, and plant diseases, and was later dissolved to make way for the establishment of the FAO.

The organization of the FAO grew out of a wartime United Nations Conference on food and agriculture convened by President Roosevelt in 1943, and the agency started in earnest in November of 1945, a time of serious food shortages in much of the world. Its success and survival owes much to its dynamic first Director General, Sir John Boyd Orr from Scotland, who brought to the new organization the stamp of an internationally recognized scholar. Orr's 1936 book, *Food, Health and Income*, was acclaimed by the *New York Times* as the most important book of that year. He was a champion of improvements in human nutrition and international cooperation, winning the Nobel Peace Prize in 1949. With the support of Professor André Mayer from France, chairman of the first FAO Executive Committee, and the leaders in Europe and North America, a useful international organization had been established that all countries have since joined. Its charter is much less ambitious than its first leaders had sought, centering on gathering, analyzing, and disseminating agricultural data on a consistent basis; recommending international actions in times of famine, hunger, and distress; and providing member nations with technical assistance on agricultural problems.[13] At the close of the twentieth century, it maintains food balance-sheet information for every country of the world, provides short-term technical assistance for developing countries, and serves as a central clearinghouse of international agricultural data.

Other new institutions developed as well. Between the two world wars, it was widely recognized that the thin line between having enough food to sustain life and having too little was too often overstepped in many places. The severe problems of hardship and famine for the peoples of India and China, for instance, were largely beyond the reach of the modest efforts of agricultural missionaries, private foundations, charitable organizations, and the governments of richer countries. And though experiment stations and agricultural science had already begun in most developing countries before World War II, their efforts were pitifully small.

After the war, international assistance programs to help societies feed themselves were launched on a scale previously unimaginable. Both technical and financial, this assistance came from many sources, both public and private, each in its own way making a difference as man began to recognize some of his responsibilities to fellow man.

Two private foundations, Rockefeller and Ford, took important roles in establishing a major institutional innovation, the International Agricultural Research Institute, now widely acclaimed around the world. The Rockefeller Foundation inaugurated its own division of agricultural sciences in the 1940s, and established country research programs in the crop sciences in Mexico (1943), Colombia (1950), Chile (1955), and India (1956). Seeking to increase India's food production capacity, the Ford Foundation started a program of rural development there in 1951, building on educational programs that used existing agricultural technology through its "package programs." Agricultural scientists working for both foundations at overseas locations learned through experience that it was not ignorance on the part of farmers that limited yields with the technology available to them; rather, they needed new varieties of seed and technology adapted to the specific conditions they faced as producers.

Robert Chandler, the first Director General of the International Rice Research Institute, describes in his 1982 book on the Institute[14] how J. George Harrar at the Rockefeller Foundation and Forrest "Frosty" Hill at the Ford Foundation had the vision and foresight to bring into being an international center in Asia devoted to rice research. Having sold the idea to their respective foundation boards, they established a place where the work could begin and set about building a program of research and outreach that not only could serve rice farmers, but also included mechanisms to ensure the program's survival. Many had a hand in establishing this successful institutional innovation, yet nearly all credit Harrar and Hill, who put the welfare of farmers first and were determined to give this great idea the chance to make a difference in increasing the food supply in Asia.

And make a difference it did. As Chandler assembled an impressive staff of applied scientists from all parts of the world, Harrar and Hill helped to open doors, outline a research program, and build support needed to operate at Los Banos in the Philippines and to work with rice scientists and leaders in all the other countries in Asia. The resulting International Rice Research Institute, organized in 1960 and dedicated in 1962, was distributing the germplasm from its first widely adopted, improved variety, IR-8, by 1966. Building on the pathbreaking work of Rockefeller scientists in Mexico with stiff-strawed, short-stemmed wheat varieties, IRRI scientists developed a combination of agronomic practices and rice varieties that responded extremely well to nitrogen fertilization under irrigation. The much talked-about green revolution in Asia was underway.

The positive experience of success led the two foundations to study the possibility of creating other institutes. The Rockefeller Foundation closed out its formal Mexican Agricultural Program in 1962, inserting in its place a new program with an international mission for corn and wheat in cooperation with the Mexican government. Funded initially by Rockefeller and Ford, CIMMYT (Centro Internacional de Mejoramiento de Maiz y Trigo) was born in 1966 and, building on more than twenty years of research by Rockefeller staff in Mexico, distributed its short, stiff-strawed, disease-resistant, fertilizer-responsive wheat varieties worldwide. In 1970, for these important contributions, Norman Borlaug, director of the CIMMYT wheat program, was awarded the Nobel Peace Prize, and the achievements of both IRRI and CIMMYT were recognized by the UNESCO Science Prize.

Prior to 1970, two other centers had been created—the IITA (International Institute of Tropical Agriculture) in Ibadan, Nigeria and the CIAT (Centro Internacional de Agricultura Tropical) in Cali, Colombia. But as funding them was beyond the resources of the Rockefeller and Ford Foundations, another institutional innovation, the CGIAR (Consultative Group on International Agricultural Research), emerged from negotiations between 1969 and 1971.[15] With the support and leadership of the World Bank, representatives from the Ford, Rockefeller, and Kellogg Foundations were joined in this enterprise by those from the African, Asian, and Inter-American Development Banks, FAO, UNDP (United Nations Development Program), OECD (Organization of Economic Cooperation and Development), and the international aid organizations from Australia, Austria, Belgium, Canada, Denmark, Finland, France, Germany, Italy, Japan, the Netherlands, New Zealand, Norway, Sweden, Switzerland, the United Kingdom, and the United States. Quoting Chandler:

Although Harrar and Wortman of the Rockefeller Foundation and David Bell, Hill and Hardin of the Ford Foundation played important roles in gaining the initial interest of other foreign aid agencies throughout the developed world, it was McNamara of the World Bank who provided the essential impetus to the movement.[15]

As of this writing, CGIAR supports the work of eighteen international centers on five continents, all directed toward strengthening the impact of international agricultural research on economic development in the world's less developed countries. Its two announced imperatives for the 1990s are first, to continue increasing food productivity and second, to improve natural resource management in order to ensure sustainable agriculture in the future. The intended beneficiaries will continue to be, in the words of the organization, "the world's poor and disadvantaged."[16]

Among the many developments CGIAR and other organizations have supported are international gene banks. Decade by decade in this century, agriculturists have become more and more aware that one of this earth's most important natural resources is the germplasm of plants and animals that are fundamental to agriculture and sustaining human life. Nature's genetic resources are one of the building blocks on which the promises of increased productivity from the applications of biotechnology are based, and all the potential of genetic engineering is focused on genes, which are its raw materials. The more diverse and complete these sources of inheritance, the greater the potential to find ways to fix nitrogen, build resistance in plants to disease and insects, and raise tolerance to drought and cold—all the reigning goals of present-day agriculture.

One pioneer of genetic diversity, the Russian botanist and geneticist Nikolai Ivanovich Vavilov, is recognized today as the most prolific plant collector in history. By the early 1930s, he had crossed the globe in search of the wild relatives of many important food crops, such as wheat, rye, barley, lentils, chickpeas, maize, and potatoes. He established more than 400 research centers with some 20,000 employees in the USSR and, from 1920 to 1940, headed the Lenin All-Union Academy of Sciences in Moscow. But besides the seeds he collected and carefully reproduced at a variety of locations, his greatest contribution was a vast "genetics treasure map." On it, he points out the key centers of genetic diversity—the locations that hold the greatest concentration of germplasm important to modern agriculture and world food production. Most of these centers, in both the New and Old Worlds, were unscathed by the intermittent ice ages; thus, in them can be found most of the land races, wild relatives of modern commercial varieties.[17]

Vavilov's original nine "centers of origin," as he called them, have since been expanded to twelve. But his original work and his awareness of genetic diversity's importance have been the foundation for many modern efforts. Tragically, he was arrested in 1940 while on a collecting expedition in the Ukraine and sent to prison, where three years later, in January, he died of malnutrition, alone in his cell. Other Russian scientists maintained his vast collections, and 25 years later he was vindicated and honored posthumously by the Soviet Union. His collections and gene bank became a central part of the N.I. Vavilov All-Union Institute of Plant Industry.

In tandem with the pursuit of collecting plants from foreign lands—an ancient custom to be sure—has been the development of botanic gardens, which not only provide the public with an ever-expanding range of plants, flowers, and fruits, but have a recognized value for medicine as well—a strong impetus for building collections. The venerable Royal Botanic Gardens at Kew in England (1761) has, over a span of two centuries, assembled a diverse range of plants numbering some 50,000 species, sharing germplasm and accurate records of their sources and materials with other botanical gardens. The collecting expeditions organized by these gardens—and financed by national governments, private individuals, and organizations around the world—have contributed much to modern gene banks, particularly since the creation of the international agricultural research centers and the CGIAR.

In 1970, the Southern Corn Leaf Blight struck across the American South, reducing the region's corn crop by 15 percent. Plant breeders and crop scientists across the world were reminded of the costs of relying too heavily on a few key sources of germplasm. As a result, the CGIAR and FAO agreed in 1974 to establish the International Board for Plant Genetic Resources, to coordinate efforts to preserve crop germplasm around the world.

Another issue arose subsequent to this development: with the entry of private corporations into commercial seed production using recombinant DNA techniques, concerns have been raised by nonindustrialized countries about sharing germplasm from within their boundaries with the rest of the world—particularly with private corporations. Patents and intellectual property rights have become an important topic for debate in international trade negotiations, including ownership of agricultural innovations. All agree that the international centers must be the ones to provide leadership and stability to carry out natural resource conservation, though funding for this fundamental activity remains surprisingly small.

The exchange of information and practical experience about the best methods of farming is as old as agriculture itself. When farmers gathered, they naturally talked about the means of their livelihood. Before 1900, agricultural societies, farmers' institutes, fairs, and expositions brought people together from relatively great distances to see what others were doing, to look at each other's produce and livestock, to share information and carry on trade and agricultural business. Agricultural newspapers and magazines had a positive impact, as did farmer organizations in their quest to improve the lot of farmers in the marketplace.

At the beginning of this century, a start was made in agricultural extension, a public sector effort to disseminate the results of research and collective experience in agriculture to improve levels of living and productivity in rural communities. In the United States, this was a somewhat natural outgrowth of efforts in the "people's colleges" of agriculture that were established at each of the land grant universities from the 1860s onward. Out of the experiment stations and demonstration farms came a slow but steady stream of results in applied agricultural science that answered pressing problems of farmers. Farmers' institutes provided one mechanism to distribute this information, but more was needed at the local level.

In 1903 in Texas, Dr. Seamon A. Knapp, an employee of the USDA, organized a team of field supervisors—later known as county agents—to help farmers fight the ravages of the cotton boll weevil. They traveled by train, hiring horses at various locations, and worked with cooperating farmers to demonstrate new practices and hold meetings to share the results. In New York, the first county agent was funded in 1911 by the Binghamton Chamber of Commerce, the USDA, and the Lackawanna Railroad; a year later, the Broome County Board of Supervisors voted to help fund the project as well. The successes of local demonstrations and the work of the first county agents led to the passage of the national Smith-Lever Act of 1914, which established a Washington Office of Cooperative Extension and federal funding for a department of extension in each of the land grant colleges.

In Western Europe, similar experimentation with farm demonstrations, farm advisers, and cooperative programs at the local level occurred in the second half of the nineteenth century, often under the auspices of agricultural societies. Each country evolved its own system and necessary relationships with colleges and experiment stations in the early years of the twentieth century. Public funding for professionally trained advisers came at different times in the early decades of the century. After World War II, publicly funded extension programs to bring the results of applied research to farmers and rural people were put in place in most of the developed countries of the world.

The relative success of these programs in increasing agricultural productivity and raising the quality of rural life led, in the postwar years, to substantial efforts to introduce similar programs for developing countries as an important component of agricultural development and technical assistance. The early extension workers saw their role as a combination of educator and social worker, working to improve rural life by teaching farmers how to save steps, reduce drudgery, and solve technical problems. Extension workers carried the problems they observed in the field to the laboratory, and returned to the field with solutions for the farm and home. In this way and over time, connections to universities and applied science became well established: this concept of extension was introduced to most developing countries as part of international aid programs.

Government has had a role in agriculture for as long as decisions have been made about the distribution of rights to the use of land and water, and as long as taxes have been levied to support the functions of government. Government regulation of trade and protection of producers through tariffs date back hundreds of years. What is different about the twentieth century is the general acceptance throughout the world of an increasing role of national governments in supporting prices and controlling production of storable agricultural commodities. Government market intervention with respect to price and production came in the desperation of world agricultural depressions in the 1920s and 1930s. Simultaneously, there was starvation and hunger in many parts of the world, while agricultural surpluses of storables like wheat, rice, and maize accumulated, for which there were no buyers. Markets by themselves were unable to solve the problems of resource allocation. Governments intervened in North America and Europe out of necessity. Through a process of trial and error, there has evolved a complex role for national governments in the support and regulation of food production and agriculture. That evolution is still far from its final stages as, haltingly, now at the end of the century, more of the decisions on pricing, production, and distribution are being left to market forces.

As K. L. Robinson wrote in his 1989 volume on agricultural price and production policy, one can now view government intervention in agriculture as a response to either a "food problem" or a "farm problem."[18] A food problem arises when output exceeds effective demand and prices fall precipitously. In practice, it has been extremely difficult to match rates of growth in output with rates of growth in demand. Since the restoration of European agricultural production after World War I in 1920, except for brief periods, most industrialized countries have been confronted with problems of excess capacity, leading farmers to demand some kind of floor under the prices of storable commodities. The Japanese and West Europeans, remembering the food shortages and hunger of World War II and the immediate postwar years, constructed agricultural policies between 1960 and 1990 that ensured a strong measure of self-sufficiency in basic food supplies. This produced the following situation: farm prices are supported at high enough levels to encourage added national output; border protection is required to prevent lower-cost producers in other countries from entering domestic markets; and domestic farm production increases in response to guaranteed prices. This produces an accumulating surplus that leads countries to "dump" stored commodities on the world market at reduced prices. While this brief summary is an oversimplification of the complex actions taken in the span of thirty years, it does outline the events and some of the rationale for actions taken.

In rich countries, aggregate demand for food is essentially limited by stomach capacity. Thus, when weather or a change in technology leads to an unexpected increase in supply of a basic, storable agricultural commodity, its farm price falls much more, percentagewise, than its quantity has increased. The reverse is true as well: a short crop will lead to a disproportionate increase in its price. This phenomenon of inelastic demand, as economists call it, requires flexibility in international trade. When international trade in agricultural commodities is relatively free, the stored supply can be shipped to locations experiencing shortfalls, and over time, production can be regulated through international prices. But massive government interventions around the world, in both prices and production, have created distortions. Internal prices for wheat and barley in Europe are well above those in exporting countries like Canada, Argentina, and Australia. When domestic surpluses are dumped on a world market with few hard currency customers, the trade wars begin. In international trade negotiations at the end of this century, most agree that government intervention in agriculture must be reduced and market forces be given a larger role in determining production and price. The questions now revolve around how fast this can be done, and what kinds of supports are necessary to protect farm families and consumers from large swings in prices.

Active intervention by national governments in the production and pricing of agricultural commodities had its beginnings in the industrialized countries in the 1920s and 1930s. In the 1950s and 1960s, governments in the developing countries began to intervene at both the consumer and farm levels, seeking to encourage greater food production while keeping consumer prices for staple foods at "stable and affordable" levels. Subsidization of farm inputs like fertilizer and irrigation water has been common. Government agencies often act as buyers of staples like wheat and rice and distributors of these commodities in consumer markets (China, India, etc.).

Active roles for government agencies in food and agricultural policy have been encouraged by technical assistance agencies from Europe and North America, the World Bank, and FAO. The role of market forces in determining domestic market prices for key commodities has been highly variable depending on the stability of the government itself, urban versus rural pressures, and technical and financial support from international aid agencies.

Though public interest in the conservation of natural resources dates back many years—forest conservation, for instance, had its beginnings in France and England in the seventeenth century—soil conservation became a major concern in the United States in the 1930s, with the great droughts and massive dust storms in the Great Plains that, in 1934 and 1936, even darkened the skies over the cities in the East. In 1936, legislation created the national Soil Conservation Service headed by Hugh Bennet, now thought of as the father of soil conservation in the United States, as well as 2,950 soil conservation districts encompassing 2.2 billion acres across the country. Funds to build shelter belts and subsidize farmers for adopting conservation measures provided the impetus for a conservation component—or requirement—that has been a part of all subsequent agricultural price and production legislation, recognizing that conserving soil and water resources for future generations is a national priority.

Other parts of the world, alerted by North America's misuses of natural resources—such as overgrazing, deforestation, and the slaughter of the buffalo—also took actions to set aside nature reserves. In 1924 the Soviet Union created the extensive *zapovedniki* system. East and South Africa established game parks. Europe undertook a program of conservation management of its forest lands. In the years after World War II, international attention was drawn to the pressure of man on his natural surroundings, particularly in developing countries with soaring population growth. Conservation of soils, water, and forest lands is receiving increased attention from national governments and international agencies.

An important component in the success of agricultural development in this century has been ongoing public investment in roads, bridges, airports, and communication systems. In 1900 agricultural supplies moved chiefly via rail, water, and animal transport to and from farms throughout the world. But with new public investment in the highway systems connecting farms directly to markets, productivity grew, and all-weather farm-to-market roads continue to be one of the keys to agricultural progress. In the developing world, both the building and the maintenance of such roads go hand in hand with delivering the new seeds and modern technology so vital to increased productivity: there must be secure ways to deliver inputs and bring saleable output to market. In many African countries, public investment in infrastructure, and then a commitment to maintain roads, bridges, and communication systems once they are in place, is one of the most pressing requirements for increasing agricultural output and providing a means to reach people with food relief during any kind of disaster.

Investment in human capital is no less crucial. Most twentieth-century investment in the creation and development of the world's agricultural colleges and universities has come out of the public sector. Bringing public schools and educational opportunities to rural people, wherever they are located in the world, is another one of the century's accomplishments. But much remains to be done in many of the developing countries. Improvements in literacy, public health and sanitation, and community stability are all parts of the process by which advances in food production and better living in the countryside can be accomplished. The challenge is to find ways in the coming century to reach rural peoples who remain outside the orbit of most such public investment.

At the same time the farm sector has been gradually moving away from an industry dominated by small household businesses producing in large measure for home consumption, selling any surplus accumulated to improve their standard of living, other sectors of the food industry have undergone significant change. It is no longer unusual to think of the farm sector as but one part of the larger food industry consisting of five components: input supply, farming, processing and manufacture, food retailing, and food away from home, i.e., eating out. This interdependence is linked to the process of development in most industrialized societies, where integration within the larger food industry is increasingly complex and ever changing. Most of the entities in each of the five sectors are privately owned businesses.

Concentration of economic power in the food industry is more diffuse than in such industries as automobiles or air transport. In the farming and food away from home sectors, for example, monopoly power has been almost impossible to achieve except when the land resource has been concentrated in the hands of the state or a ruling family. Historically, food processors and manufacturers have, at times, exercised a degree of power over prices for brief periods, but substitutes within the industry are so numerous that maintaining any degree of monopoly power nearly always requires government assistance. Nearing the end of the century, food retailers have obtained substantial market power in industrialized countries, but the still-vigorous competition within the industry is important to the long-term benefit of consumers.

In almost all societies, government has taken responsibility for assuring food safety and honest weights and measures in the marketplace. In some developing countries, the central government has established monopoly boards or corporations to acquire and distribute food products, conduct international trade in some commodities, and establish prices for some basic staples. In most cases, over time, government roles in pricing and distribution diminish as private sector institutions develop to carry out these functions. Most of the "social experiments" with government pricing and distribution of basic foods in the twentieth century have demonstrated that competition in the marketplace is more efficient in the long run than well-intentioned but state-controlled operations.

In the last two decades, the field of agroecology and calls for sustainable agricultural systems throughout the world have evolved, woven out of the separable strands of ecology in the biological sciences, the conservation movement, and agricultural systems analysis. Agroecology implies a more environmentally and socially sensitive approach to agriculture, one that focuses not only on production, but also on the ecological sustainability of the production systems used.[19] At the heart of agroecology is the notion that a field growing a crop is an ecosystem that, when more fully understood, can be managed to produce greater output in a sustainable manner without danger to the environment. Concerns about establishing sustainable systems have grown apace with increases in human populations and the associated degradation of natural resources, particularly in some of the poorest countries of the world like Nepal, Rwanda, and Haiti.

Some of the fine sustainable agricultural systems are nearly as old as agriculture itself. The irrigated paddy fields and contoured terraces of many parts of Asia have been essentially self-perpetuating and renewable over many centuries, as has been the "slash and burn" agriculture (shifting cultivation) of the tropics practiced in certain parts of Africa where population pressures are not great. Easier to describe in general terms than to define specifically, the intent of sustainable agriculture is, at a minimum, to maintain renewable natural resources in their present state, or to improve them. The depletion of nonrenewable resources is to be avoided as much as possible, especially with respect to such things as fossil fuels, phosphate and potash supplies, and productive agricultural soils. Inherent in this description is a commitment to maintain an acceptable social structure that allows agricultural people to share in the amenities of society around them, and to reward workers and resource owners in agriculture in an equitable manner.

The realm of agroecology and agroecosystems includes diverse forms of agricultural production: relatively primitive shifting cultivation, perennial crops including vines and orchards, pastoral systems, rain-fed arable farming, agroforest systems, and all types of permanent and supplemental irrigation programs. Monoculture and crop rotations are both feasible and sustainable: most agricultural systems have been designed to take advantage of the productivity inherent in the natural resources available. But population pressure, new technology, and ignorance of the long-term consequences of some agricultural practices have led to a recognized degradation of the environment in the form of soil erosion, pesticide pollution, and salinization. The end of this century has witnessed an international emphasis on establishing sustainable agricultural systems, calling attention to the perceived problems in sustaining renewable natural resources, and directing research efforts worldwide to find practical ways to establish high rates of productivity while maintaining or improving the resource base.

Because agroecology's need and logical appeal seem so clear, it is easy to overlook the magnitude of the challenge to design sustainable systems. Even in the rich countries of the world, the task is complex and difficult, requiring a fuller understanding of all the biological processes in an ecosystem and how chemicals, new species, or different practices can affect all the associated interactions. For example, we know that salinization in the irrigated central valley of California is underway, as is true for every other intensively used, highly productive, irrigated agricultural area. The question is how to slow down this accumulation of salts in the soil that will eventually reduce yields and output. How can practical sustainable systems be developed for farmers in the densely populated middle hills of Nepal, where deforestation occurs simply because the poorest of the poor need fuel to cook and to keep warm? Survival today is a difficult reality, with little energy left for saving resources for generations to come. The hope is that farmers themselves, as well as agricultural scientists, will assign greater priority to this effort in coming decades.

In this century, agriculture and the food industry have made dramatic strides in keeping up with population growth, especially since 1960. Estimates made by FAO of the aggregate world food supply in calories per person per day tell the story (table 15.10).

There is enough food produced in the world today to allow minimum diets for all people if mechanisms to deliver supplies where they are most needed can be established and the people have money to obtain the food.

This monumental accomplishment of the second half of the century has been achieved through a combination of scientific advances, new institutions, public and private investment, and substantial international cooperation. It reflects the work of billions of individual farmers along with an increasingly specialized set of partners in food production and distribution. Whether a farmer operates from the air-conditioned cab of a $100,000 tractor in the Corn Belt or in a one-hectare rice paddy in Bangladesh, he is dependent on many other people in an increasingly sophisticated industry—from plant breeders and chemists to credit representatives and truck drivers. A much smaller proportion of the world's population is necessary to produce the world's food than in 1900. Labor released from farming can now be used in producing goods and services that increase the quality of life for more of the world's people.

There remains, however, the humbling challenge of both the present and the future. In many respects, the easiest increases in agricultural production have already been obtained. Most of the arable land and available water for irrigation have been exploited where population pressure is strong. The science and technology that spawned the green revolution cannot be expected to continue to increase yields at the same rates on the same land base. All of the problems of waterlogging, salinization, pollution of soils and ground water, as well as diseases and pesticide resistance by insects must be dealt with just to maintain current levels of productivity. Sustainable agricultural systems must be developed that respond directly to the demands of population growth. In many cases, the natural resource base and local scientific capacity are smallest where population pressure is the greatest. Without political sta-

TABLE 15.10
Calories Per Person, Per Day

| PERIOD | VEGETABLE SOURCES | ANIMAL SOURCES | TOTAL |
|--------|-------------------|----------------|-------|
| 1961–63 | 1924 | 365 | 2289 |
| 1987–89 | 2275 | 428 | 2703 |

bility, it is difficult to make needed agricultural progress. This last constraint may be the single greatest limitation of all in a number of locations in the immediate future.

The richer countries of the world have made a substantial public investment in human capital in applied agricultural science. In large measure, the world's agricultural colleges and experiment stations are a product of this century. The international aid programs and CGIAR centers have been established in response to public awareness and commitment to find ways to feed more of the world's hungry people. This resolve must not be lost even though the difficulty of finding new solutions may increase. Calls to "save the environment" and "preserve our natural resource base" will only have meaning if rural people around the world can also feed and clothe themselves. Reaching out to the poorest of the poor remains a fundamental challenge in the century ahead.

At the beginning of the twentieth century, nearly every family was closely connected to farming or not far removed. In the richer countries of the world, the farm population is today a tiny minority; few of those growing up in urban and suburban environments have a realistic conception of what is involved in providing our daily food supply. But farmers are among the world's primary users and stewards of our natural resources. In an increasingly industrialized world, one wonders who will champion the needs of this basic industry as the farm population shrinks, while its product remains fundamental to human life. The political power of farmers will inevitably be passed on to consumers in the twenty-first century. It is the consumers of the world, not the producers, who will finally make the great decisions about sustainability, global climate change, biodiversity, and harnessing the potential gains from biotechnology. Helping more of mankind understand the demands of farming and the food system may be one of the greatest challenges for farmers in the twenty-first century.

ENDNOTES

1. This chapter benefited substantially from the insightful comments and suggestions of a number of colleagues in different fields in the College of Agriculture and Life Sciences, Cornell University. I am particularly indebted to Randolph Barker, J. Murray Elliot, Robert Herdt, Olaf Larson, Ed Oyer, Robert Plaisted, Kenneth Robinson, Daniel Sisler, Ed Smith, H. David Thurston, and W. G. Tomek. They provided ideas and sources of data, and helped correct errors of fact and judgment. Errors of omission and commission rest finally with the author.

2. Thomas R. Malthus, *An Essay on the Principle of Population as it Affects the Future Improvement of Society with Remarks on the Speculations of Mr. Godwin, M. Condorcet, and other Writers* (London: Everyman's Library, 1798).

3. Harrison Brown, *The Challenge of Man's Future* (New York: Viking, 1954).

4. William Vogt, *The Road to Survival* (New York: W. Sloane Associates, 1948).

5. W. R. Rangeley, "Irrigation and Drainage in the World," in W.R. Jordan, ed., *Water and Water Policy in World Food Supplies* (College Station: Texas A & M University Press, 1987).

6. Lester R. Brown and G. W. Finsterbusch, *Man and His Environment: Food* (New York: Harper & Row, 1972).

7. Barbara McClintock's quote appeared in *Science* 226 (1984): 792.

8. James D. Watson, *The Double Helix* (New York: Atheneum, 1968).

9. National Research Council, 1987.

10. Rachel Carson, *Silent Spring* (New York: Fawcett, 1962). Carson's arresting and poetic vision is not captured in any single quote from the book.

11. W. A. Henry and F. B. Morrison, *Feeds and Feeding* (Madison: Henry-Morrison Co., 1917).

12. Antonietta DiBlase and Sergio Marchisio, *The Food and Agriculture Organization* (Dordrecht: Martinus Nijhoff, 1991).

13. Ibid.

14. Robert F. Chandler Jr., *An Adventure in Applied Science: A History of the International Rice Research Institute* (Manila: IRRI, 1982).

15. Ibid., 161–63.

16. Consultative Group on International Agricultural Research, *CGIAR Annual Report 1990* (Washington, D.C.: October 1991). The CGIAR Secretariat is located at the World Bank, 1818 H Street NW, Washington, D.C.

17. Steven C. Witt, *Biotechnology and Genetic Diversity* (San Francisco: California Agricultural Lands Project, 1985).

18. K. L. Robinson, *Farm and Food Policies and Their Consequences* (Englewood Cliffs: Prentice-Hall, 1989).

19. Miguel Altieri et al., *Agroecology: The Science of Sustainable Agriculture* (Boulder: Westview Press, 1995).

SELECTED REFERENCES

Barker, Randolph, R.W. Herdt, and Beth Rose. *The Rice Economy of Asia.* Washington, D.C.: Resources for the Future, 1985.

Food and Agriculture Organization, United Nations. *Production Yearbooks, 1959, 1971, 1990.* Rome: Food and Agriculture Organization.

Gardner, Bruce L. "Changing Economic Perspective on the Farm Problem." *Journal of Economic Literature* 30:1 (March 1992): 62–101.

Grigg, David. *The Dynamics of Agricultural Change.* New York: St. Martin's Press, 1982.

Hayami, Yujiro and Saburo Yamada. *The Agricultural Development of Japan: A Century's Perspective.* Tokyo: University of Tokyo Press, 1991.

Huffman, Wallace E. and Robert E. Evenson. *Science for Agriculture.* Ames: Iowa State University Press, 1993.

Jensen, N. F. "Limits to Growth in Food Production." *Science* 201 (July 1978): 317–20.

Marco, Gino L., R. W. Hollingworth, and W. Durham, eds. *Silent Spring Revisited.* Washington, D.C.: American Chemical Society, 1987.

McCollum, Elmer V. *A History of Nutrition.* Boston: Houghton Mifflin, 1957.

Orr, John Boyd. *Food, Health, and Income.* London: Macmillan, 1936.

Pierce, John T. *The Food Resource.* New York: Wiley, 1990.

Plucknett, Donald L., N. Smith, J. Williams, and N. Murthianishetty. *Gene Banks and the World's Food.* Princeton: Princeton University Press, 1987.

Robinson, K. L. *Farm and Food Policies and Their Consequences.* Englewood Cliffs: Prentice-Hall, 1989.

Scientific American. *Managing Planet Earth.* New York: W. H. Freeman, 1990.

Shemilt, L. W., ed. *Chemistry and World Food Supplies: The New Frontiers.* New York: Pergamon Press, 1983.

Teranishi, Roy, ed. *Agricultural and Food Chemistry: Past, Present, and Future.* Westport: AVI Publishing, 1978.

Thurston, H. David. *Sustainable Practices for Plant Disease Management in Traditional Farming Systems.* Boulder: Westview Press, 1991.

World Bank. *World Development Report 1991.* New York: Oxford University Press, 1991.

World Resources Institute. *World Resources 1990–91.* Oxford: Oxford University Press, 1990.

# 16 Communications

JAHAN SALEHI AND RICHARD W. BULLIET

Ages are commonly labeled according to defining technologies. Bronze, sailing, gunpowder, clocks, and printing had revolutionary impacts on many facets of society and economy in their respective periods. In this tradition, the twentieth century has rightly been called the Age of Communications, an epithet now evolving into the Information Age. Neither "communications" nor "information" is, properly speaking, a technology, however. Rather, they signify clusters of interrelated technological developments centering in the former case on the telegraph, the telephone, and the radio, and in the latter, on the computer.

The first glimmer of the Age of Communications dawned in the nineteenth century with the invention of the telegraph and telephone, and the first steps in wireless communication by radio. The Information Age began a century or so later with the development of the computer following World War II. Yet these overlapping waves of change can be seen as one insofar as their cumulative effect technologically has been to enable people to communicate cheaply with one another without regard for distance or quantity of information. At the same time, their social and psychological impacts, from the very start, have manifested the same persistent and paradoxical features: 1. they have enhanced anonymity while at the same time invading privacy; 2. they have diminished the importance of geographical distance while making it ever easier for people to avoid dealing with one another face to face; 3. their cost, expanse, and complexity have invited private monopoly, government regulation, or both while the instruments they have placed in private hands have offered unprecedented potential for subverting existing economic and political orders; and 4. they have contributed an essential component to high-density urban living, e.g., by networking high-rise buildings, while also making possible the geographic dispersal of businesses and, by century's end, the phenomenon of telecommuting whereby employees work entirely in their homes by way of continuous computer connection with their employers.

These paradoxical qualities justify a comparison of this century's revolutionary advances in communications and information technology with the industrial revolution of the eighteenth and nineteenth centuries. The balance sheet of benefit and loss for most earlier technological advances was strongly positive: printing, for instance, put thousands of scribes out of work but benefited millions of literate people, and gunpowder wrought horrendous destruction but greatly diminished private war by making possible the centralization of state power. Only with industrialization did serious questions arise as to the value of mass production and inexpensive manufactured goods in comparison to the associated degradation of the physical environment, deadening psychological impact of "dark, satanic mills," and creation of a consumer mentality geared to mass-produced commodities. Nevertheless, from two hundred years' perspective, few would maintain that life in an industrialized society today is markedly inferior to the life of a peasant farmer or urban handicraft worker in a nonindustrialized country.

On communications and information, the jury is still out. Writers of cyberpunk fiction like William Gibson and Bruce Sterling paint disturbing pictures of near-future technological dystopia, of societies where giant corporations spend millions to guard information electronically, where privacy is lost and identity is digitized, and where people not on "the net" are doomed to subsisting in a marginalized underclass. Testifying in 1995 before the House of Representatives Subcommittee on Telecommunications and Finance, Bruce Sterling visualized the following scenario looking back from the year 2015:

> A second major problem has been the growth of unlicensed encryption, which has proven quite unstoppable. Today, some 75 percent of [Internet] archives is material that no one in authority can read. Countries that attempted to control and monitor network traffic have lost market share and service revenue as data processing simply moves offshore. The United States has profited by this phenomenon to a great extent as people worldwide have flocked to the relative liberty of our networks. Unfortunately, many of these electronic virtual immigrants are not simply dissidents looking for free expression, but in fact are organized criminals.[1]

This vision may seem absurd when we actually reach the year 2015, but its current plausibility arises from the same paradoxes of modern telecommunications that have been there from the start.

The telegraph and telephone systems were invented, as so many things are, by many people over many decades. Americans generally acknowledge Samuel Morse as the inventor of the telegraph in 1837 though Sir Charles Wheatstone and Sir William Cooke were working on the same idea in Britain at the same time. Moreover, in France a nationwide system of semaphors on towers, proposed by Claude Chappe in 1793, was by then already providing the government with a visual telegraph system. (Line-of-sight towers for communications would revive with the advent of microwave communications in the 1950s.) The French may have been the first to stress the importance of governmental control over the flow of information, an imperative that seemed headed for obsolescence in the face of technological advance by the late twentieth century, despite its continuing appeal for authoritarian governments.

Telegraph lines were soon spanning continents, and then oceans via undersea cables. The desire to speed private communications and to keep imperialist governments in touch with their colonies was paralleled by newspaper editors competing to scoop rivals. The Associated Press, founded in 1848, fed Lincoln's 1862 inaugural address exclusively to two California newspapers that went together to pay Western Union the then formidable sum of more than $600 in charges. When a successful transatlantic cable was laid in 1866, twenty words cost $150, with additional words at $5 each. The first transpacific cable was completed in 1902 as part of Great Britain's policy of linking all parts of the British empire telegraphically.

The invention of the telephone dates to 1876 and is ascribed, not without controversy, to Alexander Graham Bell. Western Union initially turned down an offer to buy Bell's patent, but three years later, in consideration of the ever more apparent potential competition between the telegraph and the upstart telephone, agreed with Bell's company not to tread on one another's territory. Bell stock skyrocketed from $50 to $995 a share on news of the agreement.

American Telephone and Telegraph (AT&T), using new technology for installing copper wire over long distances, came into being in 1885. Originally the long-distance arm of the American Bell Company, it absorbed the latter in 1900. The resulting Bell System also included the Western Electric Company, an equipment manufacturer bought from Western Union in 1881. Another component, the Bell Laboratories, emerged in 1924 from a 1907 consolidation of research efforts into the Engineering Department of Western Electric.

In 1892, there were 240,000 telephones in use in the United States for the country's 70 million citizens. Private phones cost approximately $250 per year, and public pay phones charged fifteen cents a call—this in the days of penny postage for first-class mail. By 1907, the number of phone users had soared to 6 million. By 1911, Western Union was operating eight transatlantic cables full-time and charging twenty-five cents a word.

Fierce commercial rivalry, combined with government timidity in regulating business in the years before President Theodore Roosevelt championed antitrust legislation, forestalled efforts to establish standards for the burgeoning telecommunications industry. Yet many viewed it as a "natural monopoly," an economic activity like the provision of water or electricity in which the formidable costs of stringing copper wire (increasingly underground in big cities after blizzard disasters in the 1880s) made it implausible that most users would ever have a choice of service providers. Consequently, from 1907 on, state commissions imposed on telegraph and telephone companies an obligation to serve all customers at fair and reasonable rates. They also stipulated rate averaging, which equalized prices between high-cost (i.e., rural) and low-cost markets, with the latter effectively subsidizing the former.

The goal, as expressed in 1908 by AT&T founder Theodore N. Vail (a cousin of Alfred Vail, who had built Morse's first equipment and devised the code that bears Morse's name), was "one policy, one system, universal service." (Vail also coined the term "public relations.") For most countries outside the United States, this meant adopting the new telecommunications technology as a formal government monopoly, usually part of the postal service, in the decades after World War I. But whether privately owned or operated as government agencies, telecommunications monopolies curbed the pace of technological change and kept many new developments in abeyance until after World War II. Their chief goal was to string wire, lay cable, and add customers.

This technological stagnation was quite invisible to most users, however. The increase in telephone subscribers was so phenomenal that the device was increasingly seen as a powerful instrument of change. By 1936, AT&T was servicing almost 34 million phones—93 percent of the world total; and the United States and Canada, the country with the second-greatest density of telephones, were in the throes of a telephone-inspired transformation.

It had not been clear at the outset what direction this transformation might take. Taking a cue from Bell himself in his early demonstrations of the telephone, some entrepreneurs had visualized it as a broadcast device through which a subscriber might hear a concert, a sermon, or a news bulletin: the Telefon-Hirmondo Telephone Newspaper, established by one of Bell's disciples in Budapest, provided regular news reports and special news flashes from

1893 to World War I. Soon, however, telephone advertising featured images of businessmen talking to customers and of housewives ordering meat from the butcher—in other words, engaged in conversation. The key to this use of the technology was the progressive development of a switching system, which allowed the subscriber's line to be connected to any other line going into a central switchboard, or to a long-distance line linking central switchboards.

Switching and party lines, however, raised concerns about the possibility of operators or neighbors listening in on calls. In some of the small local operating systems that multiplied after Bell's patents expired, the operators were assumed to be prime sources of gossip and information. But eventually strict supervision in telephone exchanges, along with laws sharply regulating wiretapping, gave users a greater sense of privacy. This accelerated the use of the telephone for recreational and personal—as opposed to business—calling.

Already by 1890 females had generally supplanted males as telephone operators. They were more diligent, more polite, and more easily subjected to the discipline of the exchange, where they sat for hours on end before long banks of switchboards. Unlike telegraph operators (normally male), they did not require extensive training. Thus the position became one of the most important predominantly female occupations, usually pursued for fairly short periods by poorly paid young women.

Women also became increasingly numerous as telephone users. The telephone not only facilitated shopping, enabling a housewife to phone in an order for delivery, but made possible all sorts of conversation since social calls could be made by phone, alleviating the chore of dressing up to go visiting and reducing the need for preparing the house to receive visitors. Indeed, it liberated many women for the first time from the social confines of their homes and from monitoring by fathers and spouses. Liberation came to teenaged children as well, with the result that youthful monopolization of the family phone became a reliable source of humor. This liberating impact of the telephone was to be replicated again and again around the world, up to the 1990s when, in Saudi Arabia, telephone conversations emerged as teenagers' favorite means of circumventing the strict rules on keeping the genders separate.

As America was being crisscrossed by telephone lines and the world interconnected through telegraphic cables, wireless communication tiptoed onto the stage. AT&T Chief Engineer John Carty had advocated an all-out push for wireless radiotelephony in 1909. Six years later, Bell engineers on the Eiffel Tower heard, for the first time, a voice broadcast across the Atlantic. However, numerous technological developments were needed to make the radiotelephone practical. In 1927, AT&T inaugurated regular service between New York and London at a rate of $75 for a three-minute call. By 1936, the year after the first round-the-world phone call from the president of AT&T to his vice president for long lines in a nearby room, the price had fallen to $25, and all of AT&T's 33.7 million telephones could be interconnected by wire or radio.

Radio transmissions, however, compounded the problem of lack of privacy, since anyone in range with just a receiver could hear whatever was transmitted on a given frequency. Though this did not prevent people from holding radiotelephone conversations, it did make broadcasting, which had failed to catch on as an aspect of telephony, an appealing form of one-way communication. KDKA, the first public radio station, went on the air in Philadelphia in 1920. Three years later, Americans Vladimir K. Zworykin and Philo T. Farnsworth overcame the major technical hurdles in the way of television broadcasting. In 1927, England began public television broadcasts, and sustained public television broadcasting in the United States was inaugurated at the New York World's Fair in 1936, only to be interrupted by the outbreak of World War II. Outside North America and Europe, radio broadcasting spread much more rapidly than telephone use since transmitters and receivers were quite cheap in comparison with stringing thousands of copper wires. Following the pattern of telephone service, most governments determined that radio should be a state rather than a private service.

Competition by private business was the rule in the United States, however. When, in 1927, William S. Paley established the Columbia Broadcasting System to compete with the National Broacasting Company founded the year before, there were 733 private radio stations broadcasting in the United States. While AT&T encouraged the use of its long-distance lines to link stations belonging to a network, the dominating figures in the fledgling radio industry strongly opposed its efforts to enter the broadcast industry on its own behalf.

1927 also saw the crowding of the radio spectrum caused by a multiplying increase in stations, provoking Congress to create the Federal Radio Commission, which became the Federal Communications Commission (FCC) in 1934. The purpose of these organizing bodies was to bring order to the airwaves and assist American business in establishing an American-controlled world communications system via radiotelegraph, yet another aspect of wireless transmission.

World War I had seen the mutual sabotage of undersea cables by Britain and Germany, an action that served to heighten the importance of telegraphic communications by radio. The medium had first achieved notice in 1912, when the stricken luxury liner *Titanic* broadcast an SOS that brought the steamship *Carpathia* to the rescue of the *Titanic*'s surviving passengers. Fearful of seeing the British capture this new communications medium at war's end in 1919, Franklin D. Roosevelt, then the acting secretary of the Navy, asked General Electric to suspend plans to sell crucial equipment to the British Marconi Company and instead establish an American-owned wireless company. The result was RCA, the Radio Corporation of America, originally a collaboration among GE, Westinghouse, and AT&T. Twenty-five years later, the new FCC awarded so many key radiotelegraph circuits to RCA, which was by then free of entanglement with its parent companies, that in effect the company was granted a virtual monopoly.

Assessing the societal impact of telecommunications in the years preceding World War II, the United States was unquestionably the first country to experience a significant transformation. By 1909, a hundred hotels in New York City already had 21,000 telephones in use, more than existed in the entire country of Spain and almost as many as existed on all of the African continent. The Waldorf-Astoria hotel had more telephones under one roof—1,120, carrying more than half a million calls a year—than any other building in the world. The taller the building, the more important the telephone, even in the construction stage when lines were run from the ground level to the working level far above. Engineer John Carty was quoted in 1908 saying, somewhat hyperbolically:

> Take the Singer Building, the Flatiron, the Broad Exchange, the Trinity, or any of the giant office buildings. How many messages do you suppose go in and out of those buildings every day? Suppose there was no telephone and every message had to be carried by a personal messenger. How much room do you think the necessary elevators would leave for offices? Such structures would be an economic impossibility.[2]

The suburbs, too, owed their new popularity to the telephone, along with the streetcar and later the private automobile. Modern architect and visionary José Luis Sert observed in 1942:

> The scale of our cities may change; they may break up into pieces, in the sense that vast suburban zones, developed in these last few decades like parasites, may be segregated from the city proper, giving place to open

areas or green bands. Such a reduction of the area of the city or its limitation to essential elements does not constitute a disappearance of the city. . . . With these changes, the city would be reduced to its essential elements united by a system of networks (streets and highways, telephone and lighting services, and others) to form a vital nucleus corresponding to the vital needs of the country and region.[3]

Telephoning became an American habit. Between the mid-1920s and 1950 the yearly rate of domestic phone calls per person doubled, and doubled again by 1970. By comparison, first-class postal and air mail letters per person rose by only two-thirds over the same time span, and domestic telegraph messages dropped from a nationwide total of just over 200 million in 1930 to under 80 million in 1970. As late as 1975, the number of telephone calls per capita in the United States and Canada was double that of Japan, Denmark, and Switzerland, and four times that of West Germany, Italy, Great Britain, and Greece. Rates of usage beyond Europe and Japan were still lower, yielding an estimate that in the year 2000 more than half the world's adult population will still never have made a telephone call.

Radio, followed by television, became a habit at the same time, particularly in the United States—where the privately owned broadcasting stations produced a greater variety of programming than could the government-owned stations in other countries. The family that in 1945 stared fixedly at the radio while imagining the visual images conjured by the eerie voices on *The Shadow* or *Inner Sanctum* or the comical ones on *The Fred Allen Show* was still staring—a decade later, though somewhat less fixedly—at the often snowy images of Milton Berle or Ed Sullivan on their television set.

Though many voiced opinions on the subject, no consensus emerged regarding the evils or benefits of wired and wireless telecommunications. Tirades against the baleful effects of television and radio far outnumbered complaints about the telephone, but telephony spawned its own brood of annoyances: poor connections (particularly on long-distance calls), obscene callers, intrusive sales pitches, prank calls, interrupted sleep or meals, miscommunication in which the parties afterward had different notions of what had transpired, telephone addictions that led to unpayable bills, etc. Communications analyst Marshall McLuhan's portentous phrase of the 1960s, "the medium is the message," seemed to say a lot; but few people were sure just what it meant.

World War II witnessed the full utilization of wired and wireless communications technology: from tactical commands to military units, to clandestine broadcasts by spies, to personal communications between national leaders, every aspect of the war effort on all sides was affected. Since most messages were in cipher or code after the outbreak of hostilities, cryptography became a strategic weapon. The British cryptanalysis facility at Bletchley Park employed a staff of 1,500 to handle 40,000 German military intercepts per month.

The invention of code machines with almost infinite numbers of combinations, such as the German Enigma, provided an incentive for automatic manipulation of communications data. In 1932, Lieutenant Commander Thomas H. Dyer, the new head of the research desk in the Code and Signal Section of Naval Communications, had installed IBM data processing machines to speed up the process of cryptanalysis; in 1943 the clanking, mechanical card manipulators deciphered the crucial intercept that enabled U.S. war planes to shoot down the plane carrying the Commander-in-Chief of the Combined Fleet, Admiral Isoroku Yamamoto, the ablest of the Japanese naval commanders. Though the age of the electronic computer—beginning with ENIAC, built in 1946 using 18,000 vacuum tubes and weighing thirty tons—was still but a germ in the mind of its architects, the future of massive data processing as a component of communications was already at hand.

A more immediate result of the war was the vast extension of America's hegemony in the telecommunications field. Despite America's precociousness in telephone development and wireless broadcasting, London was the world center of long-distance communications. Guglielmo Marconi, the Italian inventor of practical radio transmissions, had patented his inventions and established his Wireless Company in England in 1896–1897. By 1927 the expansion of shortwave radio was putting competitive pressure on the venerable Eastern and Associated Companies, which had emerged after 1870 as the paramount layer and operator of telegraph cables among the far-flung territories of the British Empire. To resolve the problem, a specially called Imperial Wireless and Cable Conference recommended a merger of all British communications interests into a holding company named Cable and Wireless Ltd. The plan guaranteed that the British Empire would continue to be linked by expensive cables.

Radio traffic being much easier to intercept than cable, Britain thus entered the war with an unmatched worldwide communications network. A war goal expressed in 1940 by the chairman of Cable and Wireless was to seize German, French, and Italian cables and cement Britain's global position in telecommunications. In the United States, James Lawrence Fly, the head of the

FCC and of the Defense Communications Board, sought to persuade the British to allow the United States direct cable communications with South Africa and India. Some of his motives, such as avoiding lines vulnerable to war damage, were practical; but he also visualized a future of direct and unmonitored American communications with the British Empire. America's entry into the war after Pearl Harbor left the British no excuse not to share their communications system with their most important ally. By 1943, the United States was directly connected to British possessions from West Africa's Gold Coast to New Zealand, and new circuits had been opened to Iran, French Equatorial Africa, the Belgian Congo, Algeria, China, and the USSR.

Cable and Wireless warned the government of the inroads being made by American communications companies, but Winston Churchill was in no position to refuse American requests; and in 1945, each Commonwealth country was permitted to nationalize the local assets of the company. Britain continued to concern itself with the postwar fate of Germany's external communications, but the old worldwide communications system centered on London was a thing of the past. The United States had emerged as the dominant force in world telecommunications.

But this was scarcely evident to the average American during the postwar years. Long-distance calls were still uncommon and too expensive for domestic customers, and families would typically cluster around the phone to take turns saying two sentences to distant relatives while the bill-payer gestured to them not to talk too long. Local dial service, first introduced in 1921, became universal, replacing human operators at local switchboards; but the Bell System's female workforce, 223,764 in 1946, fell by only 40 percent over the next three decades because of the continuing need for long-distance operators. Touch tone service began in 1963, but dial, or pulse, telephones have continued in use for some customers into the late 1990s.

The more important changes of the immediate postwar era were in basic technology. Communications scientists had begun experimenting with the ultrahigh frequency, ultrashort wave end of the electromagnetic spectrum in the 1930s. The Bell System pursued the development of high-volume coaxial cables, its first commercial service in 1941 having the capacity for a two-way television channel or six hundred simultaneous telephone conversations. Western Union opted for microwaves that traveled without interference in straight lines between relay towers, linking New York, Philadelphia, Washington, and Pittsburgh in 1948 with a network of twenty-one of them. AT&T, competing with its own microwave system, achieved a dominant position in the transmission of television signals. seventy-five million viewers in seventy-four cities witnessed Dwight Eisenhower's presidential inauguration live in January of 1953 by means of AT&T's microwave towers and coaxial cables. Losing the microwave contest, however, did not deter Western Union from establishing its very successful telex service in 1958. Providing automatic direct-dial communication between typewriterlike terminals, telex cut into the market for long-distance business calling.

Spanning the Atlantic with a microwave beam would have required a mid-ocean relay tower more than four hundred miles high. The feat could be achieved more easily (but not much more) with an orbiting satellite, either a passive reflector—essentially a huge aluminum-coated balloon—or an active receiver and retransmitter. Experimental models of both were launched in 1960, using rocketry developed in the course of the arms race between the United States and the USSR. The science fiction author Arthur C. Clarke had noted in 1945 that an orbit synchronized with the earth's rotation would obviate the problem of a satellite moving out of range of a land transmitting or receiving station. In 1963, Syncom 2 achieved such a geosynchronous orbit over Brazil, the equator then being the optimum location for such a satellite. That same year, seeing the importance of establishing some degree of control over an entirely new field of international communications, the U.S. Congress created the Communications Satellite Corporation (COMSAT), which became the American representative and system manager of INTELSAT, a 100-nation consortium that was soon to own a global network of satellites.

At Bell Laboratories, John Bardeen, Walter Brattain, and William Shockley contributed to the pell-mell pace of communications development with the invention of the transistor in 1947. The device made most vacuum tubes obsolete, and made it possible to shrink the thirty-ton ENIAC computer of 1946 to the tiny fraction of a minuscule silicon chip that supplies the same calculating power today. It had a similar impact on virtually every electronic communications device, making them not only smaller but also more reliable.

National defense against what was then seen as the menace of international communism was a driving force behind almost all of these developments in the United States. Major corporations had begun to lease wires from AT&T or Western Union in the 1930s for the purpose of establishing private communications networks, and the practice mushroomed after the war for everything from airline reservations to money transfers between banks. The U.S. military, however, provided by far the largest market for private wire systems.

Already in the 1960s, when data input was still in the form of punched cards, the Defense Department's computer-controlled AUTODIN (Automatic Digital Information Network) logistics system could network 2,700 substations and process 40 million cards a day. This, and a number of other government systems, was designed by Western Union. AT&T supplied systems for the Strategic Air Command and the Ballistic Missile Early Warning System, along with networks for the U.S. Weather Bureau, the Federal Aviation Agency, the National Aeronautics and Space Administration, the Veterans Administration, and the Social Security Administration.

One Defense Department project of the 1960s, to link the computers of a few research labs and the Pentagon for the purpose of sharing research information, resulted in the formation of the Internet. The objective of the project was to design a system whereby any one of a number of computers could connect to any other computer on a network without going through a centralized control or master computer. Such a system would be able to send packets of information to any address on the internetwork through many different routes, making communication stable and reliable even if portions of the Internet (as it came to be called) stopped operating. Another potential benefit of such a system was that it would be virtually invulnerable to destruction in the case of nuclear attack or sabotage, since the large number of possible data routes guaranteed messages would reach their destinations.

The set of rules that governed communications on the Internet was called IP (Internet Protocol), and the number of universities and companies that were interested in being connected to this Internet grew steadily through the 1970s and 1980s. The power of this system, in which hundreds of smaller computer networks could link to each other using Internet Protocol, led to the creation of new and sophisticated software tools that eased the use of the network.

The most significant piece of software to be developed after IP was the World Wide Web (WWW), a graphical interface to the Internet that enabled nontechnical users to find their way around easily and to display graphics, sound, and motion in addition to ordinary text. With the advent of World Wide Web software, students, businesses, educators, and entertainment companies recognized the potential of a huge new communications medium reaching into millions of homes. Internet use exploded.

The phenomenal proliferation of home and office personal computers, beginning with Apple Computer Company's introduction of its Apple II personal computer in 1977, was a key factor in the Internet explosion. The availability, early in the 1990s, of high-speed modems suitable for transferring large amounts of information over phone lines was another. As a consequence, in 1994 the number of Internet users began doubling every six months, and by 1996, the net included more than 50,000 smaller networks and 40 million users worldwide, with every continent and virtually every country having some connection.

The Internet holds the potential to become the first truly global complete communication network, carrying voice, data, and video signals over the phone and data wiring commonly available in the late 1990s. Because it's not owned or controlled by any government or corporation, but rather loosely guided by organizations such as InterNIC, which advises users on how to conform to IP standards, it's been described as the wild west frontier of communications, a highway with no road signs or traffic cops. National boundaries mean little to the Internet, and governments have encountered serious difficulties in attempts to restrict the transmission of ideas and information throughout the network. The very features that encouraged the development and dissemination of the Internet have made it virtually uncontrollable, leading some observers to refer to this dawning era of telecommunications as the Age of the Internet.

A related area of computer and telecommunications activity has been the growth of "online services," which provide information on privately owned networks in an easily digestible format for millions of users. Companies such as America Online, Compuserve, and Prodigy charge customers a monthly fee to connect to a smorgasbord of information and online activity. By the end of 1996, over 15 million subscribers to online services were spending an average of six hours a month reading magazines, writing electronic mail, doing research, shopping, or chatting with other online users via mouse and keyboard. As the Internet grew in popularity and ease of use, these same online services began moving their proprietary "electronic shopping malls" over to the universally accessible format that the Internet provided.

Telecommunications giants such as AT&T and MCI have gradually taken notice of this phenomenon, and have begun searching for ways to exploit not only the Internet, but also the growing roster of corporations and individuals who want to connect their computers to it. In March 1996, AT&T announced it would offer all of its customers free access to the Internet for five hours a month, or unlimited access for around twenty dollars a month, challenging an industry that had grown up entirely on the premise of metering access to the Internet by the minute. America Online, the most popular online service, responded with a flat monthly charge, thus opening the Internet to greatly increased use.

The early Internet infrastructure of providers, including universities, research labs, and institutions, had agreed to pass along any number of messages that originated anywhere on the Internet for a flat rate based on the size of their connection, the electronic "pipe" that connected them to the Internet. This soon meant that anyone who gained access to the Internet by paying a flat monthly fee to an Internet Service Provider (ISP) could send mail anywhere in the world, staying connected for an unlimited amount of time and at no extra charge. The implications of this new way of competing in the area of long-distance communications were enormous.

Even more startling was the fact that by 1995, voice and video transmissions were possible over the Internet, and "Internet phone calls" were being advertised as flat-fee alternatives to expensive long-distance or international phone service. By paying twenty dollars a month, an Internet user in New York could call Nairobi every hour of every day and videoconference with Paris continuously for twenty-four hours. Local and long-distance telephone providers, needless to say, watched the growth of this activity carefully, considering its possible impact on their own revenues.

But there were other changes as well. A shock wave went through the telecommunications industry in 1984, when the United States government won an antitrust suit against AT&T and finally forced its breakup. AT&T had been the world's largest corporation, grown out of the concept of "natural monopoly" for telephone and telegraph companies established in the early part of the century as a requisite for the development of modern telecommunications services. The Communications Act of 1934 codified this policy, stating that "natural monopolies . . . if properly regulated, could render a superior service at lower cost than that provided by competing companies." At the same time, fears over the dangers of an unchecked monopoly led to assertions of public control. AT&T was barred from offering telegraphic service and Western Union from offering telephone service, while the FCC took on the job of overseeing interstate communications.

For four decades after the FCC's founding, its regulation and implementation of the policy of controlled competition fostered the development in the United States of the world's most efficient telecommunications system. The power and reach of AT&T were checked numerous times by Congress and the FCC through antitrust suits and restrictive legislation, but AT&T's dominance of both local and long-distance service had continued to grow. In 1949, AT&T had been forced to divest itself of Western Electric, the equipment manufacturing arm of its company, to end what the Justice Department considered unfair business practices and a stifling monopoly of the telephone equipment industry.

More significantly, in the late 1960s and early 1970s, the FCC had begun pressuring AT&T to allow connection to its long-distance lines by competitors such as MCI (Microwave Communications, Inc.). While AT&T resisted all such efforts to end its dominance of the telephone industry, in 1975 the FCC responded to legal arguments by MCI and others by ordering the giant to allow long-distance competitors to interconnect. This left pending a broader antitrust suit filed the previous year by the U.S. Department of Justice that would result in a ten-year struggle over the future of the telecommunications industry.

By the early 1980s, AT&T was handling over 200 billion telephone calls a day and making $7 billion a year in profits. The Justice Department argued that it had unfair advantages in both local and long-distance markets, and should be forced to compete on a more level playing field. It had, the government contended, outgrown any need for the right to a "natural monopoly" and was now resisting a return to free-market competition. AT&T responded that it simply excelled at providing telecommunications service to the nation and the world, and that companies such as MCI and U.S. Sprint, a 1983 creation of GTE (General Telephone and Electronics) and United Telecommunications that was designed to exploit the former's leading position in the new field of fiber optics, were using the courts and the FCC to cripple a superior and more efficient competitor.

AT&T lost the lawsuit, and in 1984 the giant telecommunications empire of "Ma Bell" was broken up into seven regional holding companies (RHCs), referred to as the "Baby Bells," which provided local and regional service. AT&T itself was confined henceforth to long-distance service. The regional Bell systems continued to hold monopolies on local service, but AT&T was forced to allow competitors access to their long-distance switches and lines. At the time of the divestment, AT&T argued that service to customers and profits for all segments of the industry would decline sharply if the company were broken up: many shareholders of the Bell operating companies sold their stock, fearing a drop in revenues. But this proved a sad mistake.

Instead of foundering, AT&T and the newly divested regional Bell operating companies, along with the handful of regional holding companies they were part of, entered into a period of frenetic development and expansion. Though the regional Bell companies were precluded from offering long-distance service or manufacturing equipment, nothing prevented them from diversifying into foreign markets. Accordingly, Ameritech and Bell Atlantic acquired the formerly state-owned telephone company of New Zealand; and Southwestern Bell joined with France Telecom and a Mexican mining company to acquire the Mexican telephone system.

These and other opportunities arose because governments around the world, fearful of missing out on the telecommunications revolution or simply eager to raise money by selling government assets, became interested in privatizing their national systems. In 1984, British Telecom was privatized and forced to compete with Mercury Telecommunciations. Japan's Nippon Telegraph and Telephone (NTT) was privatized in 1985 in the interest of greater flexibility and diversification; the Canadian Radio-Television and Telecommunications Commission recommended phone company competition in the long-distance market in 1992. In the meantime, MCI and U.S. Sprint found investors abroad to help them compete with AT&T: Sprint sold a 20 percent interest to Deutsche Telekom and France Telecom and MCI sold a similar interest to British Telecom, with the eventual prospect of complete British control.

Opportunities abounded as new services proliferated. Wireless, portable cellular phone service, offered either by the regional Bell companies or by purely cellular companies, proved exceptionally popular. By the end of 1994 the 24 million subscribers in the United States, representing a 10 percent penetration of the market, faced a dizzying number of service choices. Beeper service, call waiting, caller identification, and a broad variety of discount options confused both cellular and conventional customers, leaving them unsure as to whether the cost of their phone service was actually going up or down; they were further confused by the seemingly arbitrary rates and service options provided by the burgeoning cable television industry, which as early as 1974 counted 4,000 central stations receiving transmissions from orbiting satellites.

The opportunities initially created by the breakup of AT&T led inexorably to growing concern about the limits of competition. Industry leaders had long been aware that by sending digital signals instead of electronic waves, ordinary telephone wiring could convey hundreds of telephone calls simultaneously—a capacity that could be multiplied enormously through the use of coaxial or fiber optic cables. As long as telecommunications services, both wired and wireless, were formally separated by the walls of government regulation, the full potential of the telecommunications revolution could not be realized. This basic constraint, in the heady years following the corporation's breakup, led to visions of totally integrated domestic and business communications systems and to increasing calls for deregulation from many parts of the industry.

The pressure culminated in the U. S. Telecommunications Act of January 1996, which dismantled the regulatory barriers that had kept telecommunications companies out of each other's spheres of operation for over sixty years. The Baby Bells, long-distance companies, and cable television providers would now be able to compete in providing an array of new services, encroaching on markets each had previously had exclusive access to.

Not surprisingly, the first goal for long-distance giants like AT&T and MCI was to gain a foothold in the local calling markets. The Baby Bells and regional cable companies scrambled to strengthen their grip on the phones of their long-time local customers while trying to steal a portion of the $73 billion annual long-distance business away from AT&T, MCI, and U.S. Sprint. All segments of the telecommunications industry believed that merging major companies would give them a competitive advantage in both reach and service offerings.

Offering a combination of local, long-distance, cellular, and even cable services all bundled with package discounts, the various companies competed fiercely for customers' dollars. Even before the Telecommunications Act, attempts to offer comprehensive packages and to cover all the bases of possible future communications sales had led to a rapid series of mergers between service providers from different industries, initiated by AT&T's merger with McCaw Cellular Communications in 1994. It had also led, in 1995, to the voluntary divestiture by AT&T of two of its components: the Network Systems Division (formerly Western Electric), a manufacturer of switching equipment used by local and long-distance companies; and Global Information Solutions (known as NCR before being acquired by AT&T in 1991).

The AT&T–McCaw merger had united the world's largest long-distance telephone provider with the world's leading cellular phone company, and raised the specter of a return to the kind of broad market dominance enjoyed by AT&T prior to the 1984 Baby Bell divestiture. AT&T defended this merger of giants by pointing out that neither had monopoly control of its market, but critics noted that both held preponderant revenue positions in their respective industries. Other companies soon followed AT&T's example, for the 1996 Act signaled an open season for megamergers.

The Act had other impacts as well. It permitted companies to own a greater number of radio and television stations than ever before, and seemed to point toward a relaxation of restrictions regarding foreign ownership of U.S. telecommunications companies. Yet in one area it sought to increase regulation, by seeking to ban obscenity from the Internet, an effort that was overturned by the Supreme Court in 1997 amid predictions of technical impossibility on the basis of protecting free speech.

Overall, the goal of the Act was to promote competition, thus improving service and product offerings while lowering the cost of such services to consumers. Yet it was unclear whether it could accomplish these goals. As of March 1996, Baby Bells controlled almost 100 percent of the local phone markets, along with the switches and wires that gave access to those consumers. The challenge for competitors has been to gain access to those switches or develop alternative pipelines into the homes and offices of customers. Wireless and cable companies have looked to challenge the Baby Bells in major cities, where consumer density warrants an investment in the infrastructure needed to reach them, but coverage of the entire market seems likely to remain the preserve of the copper wires and fiber optic cables of the regional Bell operating companies.

The likely outcome for the remainder of the twentieth century is the creation of deregulated monopolies consisting of huge joint ventures between local, cable, wireless, and long-distance providers, carving out territories based on ownership of the wire (or signal) going into the home or business. Under these conditions, consumers can expect few choices in shopping for telecommunications services, contrary to the hope and intent of the legislators who voted for the 1996 Act.

After a century and a half of an ever-accelerating communications revolution, the paradoxical elements present at the dawn of the age still resist resolution. The conflict between anonymity and invasion of privacy has taken on particular importance. The uncensored Internet has made it possible for anyone with computer access and a little know-how to disseminate his or her views on any subject under the sun, with little likelihood of retribution. To be sure, the clear determination that slanderous or plagiarized postings constitute a form of publication might expose their originator to legal action; but anonymity and pseudonymity are easily arranged, as is posting from a computer source in a foreign country. While would-be regulators rail at the plenitude of pornographic materials available to the casual browser, civil libertarians and advocates of popular culture celebrate the hitherto inconceivable possibilities for personal expression, free from the editorial coercion of commercial publication.

Yet however free a person may be to vent his or her rage, lust, hatred, or contempt from a position of comparative anonymity, the same empowering computer network interconnects massive databases capable of zeroing in on almost any aspect of his or her life, from credit worthiness to records of legal infractions. Even as calls for control of the Internet multiply, computer-violated privacy has become a major theme in movies like *The Net* (1995), in which a woman's entire life is systematically deleted from computer networks, rendering her completely anonymous.

In the words of the Electronic Frontier Foundation, a leading policy research organization,

> While the free flow of information is generally a positive thing, serious problems arise when information flows free—problems such as how to protect children and undesiring adults from exposure to sexually explicit or potentially offensive materials; how to protect intellectual property rights; how to determine which country's laws have jurisdiction over a medium that is nowhere and everywhere at the same time; how best to protect privacy while still permitting recovery for harm; how to ensure that legislators, access providers, and network users do not stifle disagreeable speech.[4]

The second paradox, outlined in the beginning of the chapter, the nullification of the physical space separating people versus the ease of avoiding face to face confrontation, manifests itself ever more strongly in the use of cellular telephones and other two-way wireless communications devices and, again, in the Internet. Automatic switching and satellite relays have for some time been speeding messages from point to point in no time at all, but if the intended recipient was not at the fixed point of reception, the message either did not go through or had to wait for the recipient's arrival. Wireless communication, on the verge of massive expansion in the wake of the telecommunications deregulation of 1996, promises to make the point of reception as mobile as the common citizen.

At the same time, visionary Internet designers are experimenting with avatars—electronic icons that will represent users in cyberspace as they do in disturbingly plausible cyberpunk novels like Neil Stevenson's *Snow Crash* (1992) and William Gibson's *Idoru* (1996). Going a step beyond using "Thor" or "Aphrodite" as a screen name for anonymous conversation, the avatar concept visualizes an image of "Thor" sitting down with an image of "Aphrodite," with neither of the parties thus "communicating" even being sure of the other's gender.

Turning to the third paradox, private monopoly and/or government control versus the vast potential for subverting the social and economic order, the former pole is unpredictable. The communications industry is reentering a period of ferocious competition not unlike that of a century ago, as the interest of many governments in regulating, if not controlling, the flow of information remains strong. Witness the thus far fruitless attempts of Saudi Arabia and Iran to ban home satellite receivers. But the United States—a generation or more ahead of the rest of the world in adapting to the communications revolution—has taken the path of deregulation.

Regardless of whether a new monopoly, government reregulation, or robust and unfettered competition awaits the communications industry in the next century, the subversive power of information technology is here and now. The escapades of hackers and typhoid Marys spreading viruses throughout the computerized world have for some time provided grist for the mill of popular entertainment. More chilling is the seeming reality of public political discourse being reduced to sound bites and paid television advertisements. Some historians attribute the success of the Iranian Revolution of 1979 to the surreptitious distribution of the Ayatollah Khomeini's sermons via audiocassette: imagine if he had been able to post his revolutionary message safely to every person connected to a ubiquitous Internet.

The fourth paradox is less alarming, but potentially more disruptive of social life as it has been lived in this century. Megalopolitan sprawl, facilitated in part by telecommunications, is an accomplished fact in many parts of the world. Its paradoxical counterpart—isolated living in remote locales made possible by instantaneous electronic hookups for business, schooling, entertainment, and socializing—is still a dream for all but a few. However, its appeal remains: imagine your uncrowded, unstressed contemplation of the sun setting over the Green Mountains of Vermont (or, for that matter, of Oman, Libya, or any other place with Green Mountains), confident that your latest effort, finished only minutes before, is already in the electronic in-box of your boss (publisher, agent), that your loved ones are all within easy contact, and that as soon as it gets too cold to stand outside, you will get to choose among thousands of electronic entertainment options, all in quadraphonic sound and large-screen, high-definition picture. Perhaps in the next century.

Finally, one communications paradox at the end of the twentieth century could not have been envisioned a hundred years ago, but is a good indicator of the fact that a revolution has truly taken place. As Secretary of Commerce Ronald Brown put it in a recent article, "How do you create an environment so that once we've built this information infrastructure, you do not create a society of haves and have-nots?" His thought is reinforced by Mitch Kapor, the cofounder of Lotus Development Corporation and president of the Electronic Frontier Foundation, who points out that people who do not have access to the emerging network of computer-based communications "will be highly correlated with the general have-nots. Early in the next century the network will become the major conduit through which we conduct our lives. Any disenfranchisement will be very severe."[5]

What exactly does it mean to be an information "have-not"? The idea is analogous to that of illiteracy in a society overwhelmingly based on print.

When telephonic communication was the preserve of the elite, most people communicated by word of mouth. When the telephone became ubiquitous, as it did by mid-century in the United States, those without were simply considered poor. The implications of the next stage—a massive reorganization of all aspects of daily life around an electronic umbilical cord that attaches individual citizens to the nurturing net—seem more profound. Will those who lack the education, basic skills, or financial resources to participate in this reorganization, be they individuals or whole countries, simply lapse into a limbo of information deprivation? Will lack of connection to the net become akin to a sensual disability like blindness or deafness?

These analogies seem extreme, but the Information Age is still in its infancy. Seventy-one percent of the world's phone lines are located in countries with only 15 percent of the world's population. Throughout most of Asia and Africa, only about one percent of the population has access to phone lines, compared with 56 percent in the United States. The prospect for expanding world communications is almost beyond limit. In 1988, overseas phone calls amounted to 23 billion minutes, a figure that more than doubled in the following decade, with each minute being worth about one dollar to the long-distance carrier.

The question is whether the unequal distribution of high-quality telecommunications will continue to be as extreme as it has been throughout the twentieth century, or whether access to communications will gradually even out with the passage of time and the carriers' never-ending quest for new markets. Unlike technologies such as the internal combustion engine, which seem to be distinctive to the twentieth century, telecommunications is destined to become a shaping influence of the twenty-first century, the true Information Age.

ENDNOTES

1. Idées Fortes, "Life on the Net, 2015: Speaking Truth to Power." Internet posting of *Wired* (4) (1993).

2. John Kimberly Mumford, "This Land of Opportunity," *Harpers Weekly* 52 (Aug 1, 1908):23.

3. José Luis Sert, *Can Our Cities Survive? An ABC of Urban Problems, Their Analysis, and Their Solutions* (Cambridge: Harvard University Press, 1942), 212.

4. Electronic Frontier Foundation, Internet posting, 17 July 1997. http://www.eff.org/EFFdocs/about_eff.html#INTRO

5. Internet posting of Time Inc., 14 March, 1995.

SELECTED REFERENCES

Carey, James W. *Communication as Culture: Essays on Media and Society.* Boston: Unwin Hyman, 1989.

Headrick, Daniel R. *The Invisible Weapon: Telecommunications and International Politics, 1851–1945.* New York: Oxford University Press, 1991.

Hughes, Thomas P. *American Genesis: A Century of Invention and Technological Enthusiasm, 1870–1970.* New York: Viking Penguin, 1989.

Kahn, David. *The Code-Breakers: The Story of Secret Writing.* New York: Macmillan, 1967.

Kerr, Elaine B. and Starr Roxanne Hiltz. *Computer-Mediated Communication Systems: Status and Evaluation.* Orlando: Academic Press, 1982.

Martin, Michèle. *"Hello, Central?": Gender, Technology, and Culture in the Formation of Telephone Systems.* Montreal and Kingston: McGill-Queen's University Press, 1991.

Oslin, George P. *The Story of Telecommunications.* Macon, Ga.: Mercer University Press, 1992.

Pool, Ithiel de Sola, ed. *The Social Impact of the Telephone.* Cambridge: MIT Press, 1977.

Pool, Ithiel de Sola. *Technologies Without Boundaries: On Telecommunications in a Global Age.* Ed. Eli M. Noam. Cambridge: Harvard University Press, 1990.

# 17 Transportation

JOHN C. SPYCHALSKI

Transportation entered the twentieth century in an evolutionary phase of its development, having experienced revolutionary advances in its technology in the 1800s; and the economic, managerial, financial, social, and political changes wrought by their application were well set. Steam propelled most of the traffic on intercity railways, inland waterways, ocean shipping lanes, and pipelines. Electricity, applied to telegraph and telephone communications, played an indispensable role in controlling transport system operations, and also served as the principal form of traction on urban street railways and their nascent short-distance interurban extensions as well.

Viewed on the basis of mode of transport, the steam railway dominated both intercity freight and passenger carriage in Europe, North America, much of Latin America, and parts of Asia and Africa. Inland water transport—on lakes, rivers, and canals—occupied a subordinate, spatially and functionally circumscribed position. Steam navigation enjoyed preeminence on intercontinental transoceanic routes and was significant on numerous intracontinental trade routes, both coastal and intercoastal. Road transport, almost exclusively animal powered, was mainly limited to localized movements of goods and passengers in countries with extensive rail and water networks. Elsewhere, it continued in its centuries-old role as a short and long-distance mode in wheeled, sledded, and pack animal forms. And the pipeline, as an intercity transport medium (i.e., excluding localized gas and water utility distribution systems), carried only crude petroleum. But the seeds were being sown and roots were taking hold for changes in transportation that would prove even more remarkable.

Transportation's great breadth, depth, and complexity offer a wide range of vantage points from which to view its history. In the popular mind, revolutionary changes are associated largely or wholly with technological advances involving the introduction of new modes of transport. However, innovations in the technology of an established mode can also exert significant evolutionary if not revolutionary changes in its capability, performance, and impact. Further, profound changes in a mode's fortunes and influence can result from nontechnological innovations in activities such as managerial practice, methods of financing, labor relations, and government control and promotion. The impact or influence of changes in a transport mode can be either relatively narrow—confined, for instance, to its customers, employees, and equipment suppliers—or broad, posing major sociological, military, environmental, political, and/or public safety implications. This chapter seeks to provide a balanced panorama of twentieth-century transportation, encompassing key events and conditions in each of these areas.

## Air Transport

Orville and Wilbur Wright's four successful flights on December 17, 1903 at Kill Devil Hills near Kitty Hawk, North Carolina verified the technological feasibility of person-carrying, engine-powered, heavier-than-air craft, and stand as twentieth-century transportation's first revolutionary event. Arguably, its singular seminality also places it first among all such events. Within scarcely more than a decade, an ensuing chain of invention and innovation—involving airframe design and construction, aircraft engines, and other components—would initiate radical changes in both offensive and defensive military capabilities and methods, and begin to diminish the isolation of civilian populations from acts of war. Before mid-century, a new mode of transport would be spawned in the form of civilian private and commercial aviation. Finally would come the technology for movement in space beyond the earth's atmosphere.

Electrical engineer P. E. Fansler, in collaboration with Tom Benoist, a plane builder, and Tony Jannus, an early pilot, has been credited with establishment of the world's first scheduled airline. In 1914, Fansler initiated service on a 22-mile route across Tampa Bay between St. Petersburg and Tampa, Florida, using a Benoist-built seaplane piloted by Jannus. The service proved financially unfeasible and, lacking a source of subsidy, ended within months of its inception.

But in the same year, wrought by wartime, aviation technology entered a four-year period of dramatic progress. World War I brought the recognition and exploitation of airborne military applications such as reconnaissance, pursuit, aircraft-to-aircraft combat, and the machine-gunning and bombing of ground targets. In Britain, France, Germany, the United States and Russia, significant government funding accelerated advancements in aircraft structural and propulsion systems. Changes in fuselage, wing, and tail surface design and materials, coupled with engines of greater horsepower, higher speeds, and lower weight, increased top aircraft operating speeds from between 60 and 70 mph in 1914 to 130 mph and above by 1918. Government purchases of military aircraft also fueled the formation of industries for airplane manufacturing, parts supply, and other support materials and services. Last but not least, military training and experience made thousands proficient in piloting, servicing, and maintaining planes.

With the end of hostilities a plethora of aviation equipment and personnel was released for civilian use. In 1919, several airlines began scheduled service in Europe, with equipment that included bombers converted for passenger and mail haulage. Most notable among these new carriers was Netherlands-based Koninklijke Luchvaart Maatschappij (K.L.M.); 75 years later, it would hold the distinction of being the world's oldest continuously operated commercial airline firm. By 1939, it served a route network of more than 20,000 miles, and shared membership in a youthful international airline industry with newer competing and connecting carriers such as Pan American Airways, British Overseas Airways Corporation, Air France, Sabena, Deutsche Lufthansa, and Swissair.

The surplus warplanes offered for sale at bargain prices by the U.S. government were bought by many former military pilots, who went into business for themselves as stunt flyers, tourist pilots, flight instructors, aerial photographers, and crop dusters. In the United States, regular carriage of mail by air began on May 15, 1918, when the Post Office Department started service between New York City, Philadelphia, and Washington. Two years later, Post Office airmail operation was expanded to the New York–San Francisco route. But in the realm of scheduled passenger service, North America lagged behind Europe from 1919 through the late 1920s, delayed by technological barriers to the provision of scheduled air service on a self-supporting (i.e., unsubsidized) basis, and lower levels of political support for government subsidization of such service. That is, the key obstacle to self-supporting scheduled air service was the lack of a cost-effective and properly sized aircraft. To survive without government funding for airline operating expenses, the emerging commercial aviation industry needed an airplane that could produce transport service at a cost less than the revenue generated by its operation at an acceptable load factor (percentage of total seats filled by revenue passengers). This need would not be met until the Douglas DC-3 was introduced in 1936.

But in Europe, the strong political will for government sustenance of scheduled air service between 1919 and 1939 was fired by many desires. For one, Europe wanted speedier passenger and mail links with distant colonial holdings; secondly, it wanted stronger international projections of national interests; thirdly, it wanted a new and vivid symbol of national pride, which a flag-bearing carrier using the latest form of transport technology was uniquely well-suited to provide; and finally, it wanted a means for performing services complementary to military purposes, as with Deutsche Lufthansa's post-1933 Nazi-inspired obligations to cooperate with army maneuvers and carry military officers free of charge.

Methods for providing such sustenance varied in type and with country and time of use. For example, K.L.M. originated as a privately owned airline, operating without financial aid from the Netherlands government until 1923, when it began receiving annual subsidies to cover operating deficits. After 1926, periodic government purchases of new share issues helped to finance its capital asset needs. Service on the company's key colonial route between Amsterdam and Batavia (renamed Djakarta in 1949) was subsidized under the guise of payments for provision of air mail carrying space in aircraft. In contrast to K.L.M., Deutsche Lufthansa was founded in 1926 as a mixed private and government enterprise; the German national and state governments purchased, respectively, 26 and 19 percent of its shares, and other investors bought the remainder. Local governments joined with those at state and national levels in making direct subsidy payments to Lufthansa until 1934, when the national government became the exclusive payer. Lufthansa also received various indirect subsidies, including the remission of airport landing fees and use of government-provided radio communication facilities and meteorological services.

United States policy toward scheduled air passenger service crossed a major threshold in 1925 with passage of the Contract Air Mail Act (commonly known as the Kelly Act), which authorized the Post Office Department to contract with private entities for air mail transportation, and thus phase out the government-operated air mail service begun in 1918. With payments from the Post Office as their primary means for covering operating costs, air mail contractors could carry passengers as a supplementary revenue source. Western Air Express became the first provider of Kelly Act-inspired passenger service when it initiated regularly scheduled mixed mail and passenger operations between Los Angeles and Salt Lake City on April 17, 1926. In the same year, Congress approved the Air Commerce Act, which established an Aeronautics Branch within the U.S. Department of Commerce, charged with promoting aviation through the improvement and expansion of air navigation aids and other forms of assistance.

This substantial government assistance stimulated the formation of commercial air transport firms with private capital, and accelerated technological advances in aircraft. The experimental exploits of noncommercial aviators, such as Charles A. Lindbergh's first nonstop flight across the North Atlantic in 1927, also contributed to creating a climate more hospitable to the idea of expanding air service.

By 1930, the United States had thrust ahead of Europe: 38 domestic airlines operated 30,293 route miles and carried 374,935 revenue passengers—a vast increase from the 5,782 they carried in 1926. In addition, five U.S. flag carriers—that is, airlines incorporated in the United States and of U.S. registry—transported 42,570 passengers on international routes. Air mail traffic reached more than 8 million pounds, increasing tenfold from its 1926 level. And regularly scheduled public air freight service, which had begun in 1926 with the movement of 1.7 million pounds of cargo, increased just as substantially. Air freight service dedicated to the needs of a particular shipper had first appeared in 1925, when Henry Ford's Ford-Stout Air Services began moving freight for the Ford Motor Company between Detroit, Buffalo, Cleveland, and Chicago. Its first-year traffic volume of one million pounds would triple within five years. In September 1927, the American Railway Express Company initiated air express service, a form of premium air freight transport focused on shipments of high time value. The ARE (which became Railway Express Agency, Inc. in 1929) handled the pickup and delivery segments of air express shipments within its established ground transport network, and contracted with airlines for intercity movement segments. Traffic rose from 45,859 pounds in 1927 to 257,443 pounds in 1929, exceeding one million pounds by 1931.

Another significant, multipurpose sector of American aviation to blossom was private or general aviation, including pleasure flying, law enforcement, aerial surveying, air ambulance service, emergency freight movements, and business travel. By 1929, numerous firms in many industries operated aircraft for their own business purposes, ranging upward in size from one- and two-place single-engine biplanes to the single-engine, six-passenger Lockheed Vega and the ten-passenger Ford trimotor also flown by scheduled commercial airlines. Some private business aviators served illicit purposes: airborne prohibition-era rumrunners foreshadowed the pilots flying illegal drugs between South and North America in the 1980s and 1990s. For all purposes, general aviation passenger volume in the United States in 1929 was estimated at about 3 million persons, almost 19 times greater than the total number of passengers carried by scheduled domestic airlines in that year.

Flying, whether as a pilot or passenger, signified adventure, glamour, and ultramodern transport. The worldwide Great Depression did not stall aviation's progress. By 1939, passenger volume on domestic U.S. airline routes stood five times above that of 1930. European carriers continued to expand, particularly on international routes. Most dramatic of the growth among individual carriers was that of Pan American World Airways, which, in addition to further developing its existing U.S.–Caribbean–Latin America links, initiated the successful ongoing operation of the first regularly scheduled year-round transpacific and transatlantic passenger and mail services.

Underpinning this progress were growing commitments by both local and national governments to developing airport and air navigation facilities, and rapid changes in aircraft technology—which greatly advanced the speed, safety, comfort, reliability, and economy of airline operations. Classic 1920s-vintage transports such as the ten-passenger 100 mph Ford trimotor and its Fokker and Junkers-built German competitors, along with the six-passenger, single-engined 135 mph Lockheed Vega and the ten-passenger Boeing 247 of 1933, gave way to the 1936 two-engine Douglas DC-3, capable of carrying up to 21 passengers at 170 mph. With its greater capacity, more powerful and durable engines, and advances in aerodynamic design such as metal skin, monocoque construction in lieu of metal or wood frame and cloth, and cowling-enclosed engines to reduce air drag—aided by research efforts of the National Advisory Committee for Aeronautics and the California Institute of Technology's Guggenheim Aeronautical Laboratory—the DC-3 offered seat-mile operating costs that were one third to one half lower than those of its predecessors. (Cost per seat-mile is calculated by dividing the total cost of operating a flight by the total number of seat-miles produced by the flight's operation.)

While the DC-3 quickly dominated the fleets of most U.S. carriers and several elsewhere, long transoceanic flights demanded something more. Land-based runways for large-sized wheeled aircraft did not yet exist at most foreign destinations or enroute servicing points for such flights. The answer involved flying boats, aircraft with watertight floatable fuselages. In 1935 Pan American began San-Francisco–Honolulu flying boat service using 32-passenger S-42 planes built by the Sikorsky Aircraft Co. A year later, the airline opened its San Francisco–Manila route (via Hawaii, Midway, Wake, and Guam islands) with "China Clippers," four-engine 48-passenger M-130 flying boats with a range of up to 3,200 miles, built by the Glenn L. Martin Aircraft

Company. Pan Am soon supplanted these aircraft with 74-passenger, 183 mph Boeing B-314 Clipper flying boats which, with a range of almost 4,000 miles and amenities such as special dining areas made possible by their relatively spacious interiors, played key roles in Pan Am's 1939 inauguration of New York–Southampton, England and New York–Lisbon–Marseilles flights. Flights took approximately 36 hours (with service stops in Newfoundland on the Southampton route, and in Bermuda and the Azores on the Lisbon route), compared with the five days it took for the day's fastest ocean liners to cross. Imperial Airways, Britain's principal international carrier during the 1930s, also made significant use of four-engined flying boats on long-distance routes such as Southampton–Durban, South Africa, beginning in 1937, and Southampton–Sydney, Australia the next year. The American and British flying boats provided the airline industry with its first truly effective tool for competing with steamship lines in high-value markets such as business travel. After the outbreak of World War II, the large capacity and long-range operating capacity of the flying boats made them invaluable for maintaining vital war-related travel over hostile waters.

1936 to 1941 represented a watershed in the evolution of commercial air transport technology. Although the first year-round scheduled air service across the North Atlantic was provided by heavier-than-air craft in the form of Pan Am's flying boats, regular operation on a seasonal basis had begun three years earlier in 1936, when the *Hindenberg*, a German-owned rigid-frame, lighter-than-air ship operated by Deutsche Zeppelin-Reederei made ten round trips between Frankfurt and Lakehurst, New Jersey. Service was restricted to late spring–early fall because the dirigible's large size (more than 800 feet long, and 100 feet in diameter) and buoyancy made it acutely vulnerable to the winter gales common on the North Atlantic. Even earlier, in 1931, a sister airship, the *Graf Zeppelin*, had begun scheduled service between Europe and Brazil, under the more hospitable climatic conditions of the South Atlantic. But when, in 1937, the *Hindenburg*'s fabric-covered outer surface and hydrogen gas lifting agent ignited as the airship arrived in Lakehurst, New Jersey, killing 36 on board, the use of lighter-than-air craft (LAC) for commercial passenger transport was suspended. Even without this tragedy, however, the LAC's use would have been ended relatively soon by its limited speed (70–80 mph), lower productivity, and greater sensitivity to bad weather vis-à-vis the most advanced flying boats and land planes available in 1939–1940. Henceforth, it was relegated to military and civilian use requiring low and slow overflight and hovering capabilities, such as the famous blimps of the Goodyear Tire & Rubber Company.

The flying boat era on long-distance, over-water routes ensued from the need for a plane that would be both seaworthy if forced down en route by a malfunction, and capable of using harbors and other sheltered waters as take-off and landing surfaces in the years before airports with runway capacities fit for heavy long-range, land-based (wheeled) aircraft became widely available. It was brought to a close by a new generation of pressurized long-range four-engined airliners. Their initial development occurred in the mid-1930s, and a small number of the earliest model among them, the Boeing 307 Stratoliner, entered service on TWA and Pan Am in 1940–1941. After 1945, later models—such as the Lockheed Constellation, Douglas DC-4, DC-6, DC-7, and Boeing Stratocruiser—bearing the fruits of technological advances derived from military aircraft came to dominate the fleets of major carriers in North America, Europe, and elsewhere.

Commercial aviation technology crossed yet another Great Divide—from the piston-engine era to the jet age—in 1952, when British Overseas Airways Corporation (BOAC) introduced the world's first jet-powered airliner, the de Havilland Comet 1, on routes from London to Africa and the Far East. The four-engined, 36-passenger, 500 mph aircraft quickly proved both popular with passengers and profitable to operate. Sadly, this triumph turned to tragedy within two years, when fuselages of three of the new Comets disintegrated in flight. The remaining Comets were grounded pending investigation of the cause, which was traced to metal fatigue. Commercial jet operation next appeared in 1956 in the former Soviet Union, when Aeroflot introduced the Tupolev Tu-104 airliner on the Moscow–Irkutsk route. A strengthened and enlarged Comet 4 entered service on BOAC in 1958, but was immediately eclipsed by two new American-built four-engine jets. First was the 200-seat (approximately), 570-mph Boeing 707, introduced on Pan Am's New York–London route in the same year, then the DC-8 in 1959, when Delta and United placed it in service on long-haul routes within the United States.

Jet service came to shorter-haul markets in Europe and the United States almost simultaneously when both Air France and United began flying the smaller Caravelle, a French-built (Sud-Aviation) plane distinguished by its rear-mounted engines, one on either side of the fuselage. British, U.S., and Soviet aircraft builders soon emulated its aft-mounted engine configuration with designs such as the BAC One-Eleven, Hawker-Siddeley Trident, Boeing 727, DC-9, and Tupolev Tu-134. Their ability to take off and land on relatively short runways brought jet service to medium-sized cities, hastened the retirement of piston-engined planes, and furthered the competitive advantage of air over surface transport.

The 1950s also saw the introduction of turbo-props, planes with jet engine-driven propellers, beginning with the British-built four-engined Vickers Viscount. Similarly, gasoline piston engine-powered rotors gave way to jet-driven rotors on helicopters.

In 1940, Igor Sikorsky flew his design of what is generally considered to be the world's first truly flyable helicopter, which, with vertical takeoff and descent and hovering capabilities, had the greatest spacial accessibility of any transport instrument yet devised. These capabilities soon found wide and successful application in both military and civilian general aviation, but not in regularly scheduled interurban passenger service. Sabena, the Belgian national airline, introduced scheduled helicopter service between Brussels and cities in adjacent countries during the 1950s, but, proving economically unfeasible, the project was abandoned.

After the 1960s commercial aircraft progress fell into three categories. In the first were the wide-body jets led in size by the four-engined 500-passenger 600 mph Boeing 747 introduced in 1970, and the twin-engined Boeing 777, which made its first test flight in 1994. Intermediate-sized wide-bodied planes entering service in the 1970s and 1980s included the Lockheed 1011, DC-10, and Boeing 767, and various models produced by European Airbus Industrie. The second category encompassed the multi-engined turbo-prop aircraft tailored to the needs of air commuter operators. And in the third category was the 1,350 mph, 144-passenger Concorde. Introduced in January of 1976 by BOAC and Air France, it became the only supersonic transport—or SST—to endure in service. The world's first and only other nonmilitary SST, the Soviet-built Tupolev Tu-144, began test flights in 1968, spent ten months in cargo service in the mid-1970s, but never entered regular passenger service for undisclosed reasons.

The results of this chain of technological advances were dramatic for both competitors and users of air transport. By the late 1950s, while still in the piston era, air transport had largely supplanted rail and water carriage for long-distance overland and transoceanic business travel, and had captured sizeable footholds in personal travel among upper-income groups. However, in 1960, even in a country as air-oriented as the United States had become, only 10 percent of people over 18 years of age had ever used scheduled air service.

Thirty years later, the increased productivity and related decline in cost per seat-mile (kilometer) wrought by jet aircraft had transformed airlines into mass passenger carriers in virtually every country with extended borders. In the United States, more than 70 percent of the population age 18 and above had been an airline customers at least once. The total passengers carried on domestic U.S. routes jumped from 56.8 million to 428.8 million, while total passenger-miles increased from 31.7 billion to 345.9 billion. This growth stemmed in part from the government's policy of deregulating and decartelizing airline pricing, and reducing barriers to new competitors. Carriers became free to set fares based solely on their perceptions of market conditions, and service on new routes could be initiated without government judgment of its economic viability.

Tourism mushroomed into a major component of international trade as jet aircraft made long-distance air service both affordable and feasible to widening cross sections of the populations of many countries. In athletics and the performing arts, tours could be created that, in terms of time and distance, could not have been achieved via rail, water, or road. International student exchanges and professional symposia have proliferated, as have domestic and international business travel. Air transport-based package express service networks have appeared that offer delivery times as low as 24–48 hours, whether national or international. Areas near major airports have become business centers in their own right, attracting offices, hotels, and manufacturing and merchandising activities that are sustained by quick access to air passenger and cargo services.

But the jet age explosion in air traffic has also occasioned its costs, in the form of noise and air pollution from engine exhaust. Occupants of land adjacent to airports and beneath airport approach and departure paths have mounted many complaints, at times resulting in curfews on flight operations. Some countries have set deadlines for ending flights by aircraft with older, noisier jet engines, thus accelerating efforts to introduce lower-decibel equipment. Overall, however, these costs, together with the outlays required to remediate them, have been dwarfed by the immense benefit jet air service has brought to passengers and freight shippers. In both developed and developing countries, air transport approaches the threshold of the twenty-first century poised for continued growth.

## Road Transport

In 1901, the streets of cities and towns teemed with horse- and mule-drawn wagons and carts linking intercity rail and water carrier terminals with factories, mills, warehouses, and retail businesses, and vying for street space with horse-drawn cabs, hotel omnibuses, and carriages. However, the predominant mover of nonpedestrian urban passenger traffic was the streetcar or tram, which served virtually all larger cities and numerous medium and smaller communities in North America and Europe, as well as selected localities almost everywhere in the world. Since it operated largely within street space, it was viewed as a form of road transport by British officials. But because it also ran on railway track—a load-bearing running surface and substructure different from the street surface and subbase—North Americans viewed it within the rail mode.

On the principal streets of larger cities, road vehicles ran on strong pavement surfaces. The net loads of as much as 18 tons, carried on steel-tired urban freight wagons, demanded hard paving bricks or granite blocks set on a deep bed of gravel or a concrete base. Stone blocks were often overlaid with asphalt to provide a quieter, lower-friction running surface for wagon and carriage wheels, and better footing for horses and mules. On less important business thoroughfares and residential streets, asphalt would often be applied directly over macadam and gravel. But the typical rural road in 1901 was earth surfaced, often ungraded and unditched, and usually impassable in wet weather. Exceptions existed in some European countries, such as France and England, where improved surface intercity roads had developed over more than a century—only to see their traffic drained away by the post-1825 railway construction boom.

By the 1920s, however, road transport would break out of the perimeters of intraurban and short-distance rural movements to which it had retreated in the face of the nineteenth century's rail expansion. The first thrust in this counterattack was the development of an economically feasible method of mechanized propulsion. Road vehicles powered by steam, electricity, and gasoline-fueled internal combustion engines had been proven technologically feasible and were available commercially in the 1890s, but at production costs and selling prices that severely limited their application. Indeed, early automobiles were seen as little more than pleasure vehicles for the wealthy. A breakthrough in the cost barrier came in the United States in 1901, when Ransom E. Olds initiated assembly line manufacturing: using that method, the Olds Motor Works produced a total of about 9,175 gasoline-engined cars by the end of 1903. The production of Henry Ford's famous Model T, beginning in October of 1908, gave the world its first mass-market automobile. Initially priced at $850, and reduced to $260 by 1925, the Model T moved automobile ownership into the purchasing power range of middle-income earners. Automotive operating costs also became more widely affordable after 1901, when the discovery and exploitation of rich oil deposits in east Texas significantly increased the supply of gasoline and drove down its price. The automobile population in the United States jumped from approximately 78,000 cars in 1905 to more than 5.5 million in 1918.

The number of gasoline and electric-powered trucks in the United States also grew—from about 700 in 1904 to about 250,000 by 1918—as their superior carrying capacity, speed, and durability overwhelmed animal-powered vehicles in both intraurban freight transport and short-distance intercity movements. By the mid-teens, motor trucks offered estimated savings of at least 10 cents per vehicle mile over the horse-and-wagon costs of more than 26 cents a mile. Trucks also offered apparent environmental benefits, as their motor exhaust seemed more sanitary and less offensive than manure deposits from horses and mules.

Successful regular-route motor bus operations debuted in Birmingham, England in 1904, and in New York City, Paris, and London in 1905—where a starting roster of 20 buses soared to 1,066 by July of 1908. Ownership was split among three rival carriers—London General Omnibus Co., London Motor Omnibus Co., and London Road-Car Co.—which typically operated a vehicle with an engine of between 25 and 30 horsepower and a seating capacity of 34 passengers: 16 in a lower-level enclosed deck, and 18 on an open top deck. In Edinburgh, the Scottish Motor Traction Co. (SMT) was founded in June of 1905, operating double-deckers within a year along what became a network of short-distance intercity services by 1914.

The second basic instrument in road transport's recapture of intercity passenger and freight traffic was the provision of an adequate infrastructure in the form of pavement and bridges, sales and service sources for motor vehicles, and food, comfort, and rest facilities for drivers and passengers. America began its quest for improvements in the quality and geographic coverage of the intercity road network.

As motor vehicle ownership and use in the United States proliferated, the miles of roads outside incorporated towns and cities rose from 2,151,379 in 1904 to 2,445,760 in 1914. And the miles of roads surfaced with anything more than plain dirt increased from 153,530 to 257,291. But of this, only 32,180 miles—largely in northeastern states—boasted hard surfaces such as brick, concrete, or bituminous macadam. Overall the road quality in the United States still lagged behind that of several European countries in the pre-World War I years, with relatively unfavorable economic results. A congressional joint committee report issued in January 1915 noted that circa 1912, the average cost of hauling agricultural products from farms to either local markets or railway stations for transshipment was 21 cents per ton-mile in the United States, and 8 cents in France.

Such comparisons supported efforts by federal and state legislators and executives, business groups, and automobile associations to expand the federal government's participation in road development beyond its earlier confines of education, research, and promotion, and assume a prominent role in the planning, funding, and administration of road facilities. The resulting Federal Aid Road Act of 1916 authorized highway improvement grants to states on a 50–50 matching basis up to $10,000 per mile, and required that a state could not receive such grants without first establishing a highway department to administer road construction programs. By 1919, all of the then-48 states had met this requirement, thus setting in place a basic mechanism for joint state-federal development and maintenance of a national highway network that would endure through the remainder of the century.

But as the United States entered World War I, the new act's implementation was disrupted by an abrupt change in priorities. As with aviation, the war gave strong impetus to the advancement of road transport. Allied forces used thousands of trucks to move troops and supplies on the Western Front, and truck production mushroomed. At the same time, war-driven rail freight traffic became extremely congested, giving rise to the intercity trucking industry. To circumvent rail system bottlenecks, manufacturing and merchandising firms that owned trucks for local pickups and deliveries began using them for movements to neighboring communities. Some bought new trucks and initiated even longer hauls such as New York–Boston, Akron–Boston, and Akron–Detroit. Commercial intercity motor freight service also emerged. An early entrant was the Beam Fletcher Corporation, whose fleet of twenty-two five-ton capacity trucks began operating between Philadelphia and New York in November of 1917. Several months later, the Liberty Highway Company began providing daily motor freight service between Toledo and Detroit, using a five-ton capacity four-wheel drive truck which also pulled three five-ton capacity trailers. Running time ranged between 7 1/2 and 9 hours, depending on the weather and condition of a certain 12-mile segment of dirt road within the overall route.

Although wartime trucking costs ranged from 12 to 25 cents per ton-mile compared with rail ton-mile costs of .0025 cents on mainlines and 2–3 cents on branch lines, shippers quickly recognized that the net cost of truck transport could often be less, particularly with shorter-haul movements of package freight. Trucking offered cost-reducing service quality features such as elimination of drayage to and from rail freight stations, less breakage of fragile goods, lighter protective packaging requirements, and lower inventory carrying costs due to faster overall transit time. These and related attractions would fuel continuing growth in motor freight transport in many countries all the way through the 1990s.

The war's end gave an immediate two-pronged boost to road transport, returning large numbers of persons with military-acquired truck driving and maintenance skills to the civilian job market, and rendering huge numbers of trucks superfluous to peacetime military needs. Such conditions aided the early postwar start of extensive commercial road freight haulage in the United Kingdom as individuals purchased surplus vehicles from the British Government and began doing business as owner-drivers. In the United States, the federal government distributed more than 22,000 surplus army trucks along with spare parts and shop equipment to state highway departments for use in road maintenance and construction.

Significant improvements in motor vehicles occurred during the interwar years. As design became a marketing tool for auto manufacturers, streamlined styling and a wide variety of high-gloss paint colors raised the aesthetic appeal of automobiles. In 1919 only 10 percent of all American cars had closed cabs. By 1929, the quest for both greater comfort and better styling had increased the production of fully enclosed models to 90 percent of total output. Other advancements included all-steel bodies, shatterproof glass, radios and heaters, hydraulic four-wheel brakes, power brakes, low-pressure balloon tires, independent wheel suspension, sealed-beam headlights, steering column-mounted gearshift levers, synchromesh manual transmissions, and automatic transmissions. And with increases in engine size and compression ratios, and new formulations for gasoline and lubricants, came rising power and speed capabilities. Luxury models of the 1920s featured eight-cylinder engines. Cadillac unveiled a new 185 horsepower V-16 engine in 1930, and Ford's V-8 of 1932 brought higher power to low-priced cars. Production of steam and electric-powered autos faded during the 1920s, and gasoline power reigned supreme thereafter. A small exception occurred in Germany in the 1930s, when Mercedes-Benz introduced a diesel-engined model. Mercedes also pioneered in the application of superchargers to gasoline engines.

Trucks and buses shared many of these interwar advances, notably those involving engines, transmissions, and tires. The solid rubber tires of the early years were replaced with low-pressure balloon tires during the 1920s, providing a greater cushioning of loads and thus reducing the shock imposed on both truck chassis and the freight and passengers being carried. This cushioning effect, together with balloon tires' larger area of contact between tread and road surface, also reduced damage to pavement and bridge structures, thereby enabling trucks to carry even heavier loads.

Arguably among the most important of basic design changes for commercial freight-hauling trucks was the fifth wheel coupling, essentially a slotted disk mounted behind the cab of a truck tractor. The forward end of a semi-trailer rests on the disk, and a steel kingpin mounted on the bottom of the trailer inserts and locks into the disk, enabling the trailer to pivot on the disk. The simplicity of this innovation belied its economic impact. In a straight truck, about 90 percent of the cargo weight rides on the rear axle(s). In contrast, in a tractor and semi-trailer combination, about 43 percent of the cargo weight rides on the rear axle of the trailer, 43 percent rides on the rear axle of the tractor, and the remainder rides on the front axle of the tractor. By spreading weight over more axles and wheels, the tractor and semi-trailer combination provided a means for doubling or tripling cargo loads without overloading the motor unit and without exceeding legal limits for axle weights and overall vehicle weight. Also, since tractors can be separated from trailers, they can be better utilized, not needing to wait while shipments are being loaded and unloaded, as a straight truck would.

Such improvements were complemented by expansions and improvements in U.S. intercity surfaced roads, which, having covered 387,000 miles in 1921, covered 1.3 million miles in 1940. Several world-famous highway tunnels and bridges also entered service, including the Holland Tunnel under the Hudson River between Jersey City and New York City (1927), the San Francisco–Oakland Bay Bridge (1936), and the Golden Gate Bridge between San Francisco and Marin County, California (1937).

The interwar years hosted many other changes as well. Between 1921 and 1938, the major industrialized countries saw dramatic jumps in total motor vehicles registered—from 10.5 to 29.4 million in the United States, 460,000 to 1.42 million in the United Kingdom, 230,000 to 2.25 million in France, and 9,000 to 1.82 million in Germany. This rise, coupled with increases in size, weight, and speed capabilities and a growing use in intercity transport, illustrated the need for vastly improved design standards on high-density routes, including more controlled access, a minimum of two lanes for traffic in each direction separated by a grass median or barriers, freedom from crossings at grade with intersecting roads and railways, wider lane and shoulder widths, and more moderate gradients and curves. By the onset of World War II, few countries possessed roads with most or all of these superhighway—or motorway—characteristics. Germany, spurred by depression-era job-creation needs and motorized military deployment plans, built the famed 4,200-mile Autobahnen system between 1933 and 1940. Achievements in the United States were more modest, including the Bronx River Parkway in New York, completed in the mid-1920s, the Merritt Parkway in Connecticut, constructed between 1934 and 1940, and the first section of the Pennsylvania Turnpike, opened in 1940.

During World War II, the growth of civilian road transport was stopped by the wartime need to divert critical materials such as steel, rubber, and gasoline to military production. It resumed in the United States in mid-1945, as wartime restrictions were lifted on motor vehicle production, replacement parts, and fuel.

It soon surged. Even with the waning effects of these restrictions, private automobiles and small trucks used for personal travel generated 63.8 percent of the total (220 billion) U.S. intercity passenger-miles in 1945. Fifty years later, their share had risen to about 80 percent, comprising 1.7 trillion passenger miles. Automobiles also provided 98 percent of all intraurban person-trips by the mid-1990s, thus relegating local mass transit service to a residual role in most communities. This growth mirrored America's leadership in automobiles per capita. Indeed, it has been predicted that by the year 2000, the United States will possess one automobile for every person aged 20–64, a level of ownership 25 percent above that forecast for Western Europe and double the projection for Japan.

As they had earlier in countries like Italy and Spain, motorcycles and motor scooters spearheaded the mechanization of road transport in many developing countries. However, automobile (including light van and light truck) use began to grow vigorously in many less-developed areas during the 1980s and 1990s. Much of this use involved new small-scale commercial transport service; the car or van offered a means for earning income from the carriage of other persons and/or their goods as well as providing personal mobility for its owner.

Trucks produced 9.7 percent (81.9 billion) of total U.S. intercity freight ton-miles in 1946, and 28.6 percent (880 billion) in 1993. Market share gain measured in terms of money spent on intercity truck transport was also impressive, rising between 1960 and 1992 from 37.5 percent ($17.9 billion) of total annual outlays for moving freight by all forms of carriage to 47 percent ($176.8 billion). If expenditures on trucking within local areas are added, these shares become 67.5 percent ($32.2 billion) and 78 percent ($292.8 billion), respectively. Similar outcomes occurred elsewhere. By the 1980s, trucking dominated freight transport in virtually every nation outside China and the former Soviet bloc. It also moved toward domination in Central and East Europe after 1989, when shifts to market-based economies brought changes in shippers' needs that called for the flexibility, customer responsiveness, and other qualities of motor freight service.

This resurgence in motor traffic gave renewed impetus to road improvement and expansion, most quickly and extensively in America. Between 1947 and 1957, 20 states built about 2,600 miles of toll roads, much of which was later incorporated into the 42,500-mile Interstate Highway System. Mandated by the Federal-Aid Highway Act of 1956 and built over almost four decades beginning in 1957, the system provided a superhighway network serving more than 90 percent of cities with populations greater than 50,000. Full restoration and expansion of the prewar Autobahnen system occurred relatively quickly in West Germany, but was not accomplished in the East until after German reunification. By the 1990s, France, Italy, Britain, Spain, Austria, and Japan had also connected many or most of their major population centers with motorways. Numerous other countries, ranging from Australia and Canada to Venezuela, built lesser amounts of superhighway mileage, primarily linking major cities with nearby locations. Mexico constructed extensive toll-financed motorways during the 1980s, but set tolls so high that truckers continued to use inferior older roads.

Post-1945 improvements to the U.S. highway infrastructure included notable triumphs over geographic barriers, such as the 29-mile Lake Pontchartrain Causeway in Louisiana (completed in two stages, 1956 and 1969), the 17.6-mile Chesapeake Bay Bridge-Tunnel in Virginia (1964), and the 5-mile Mackinac Bridge in Michigan (1957). The flow of transalpine traffic between France and Italy accelerated with the opening of the 7.5-mile Mount Blanc Tunnel in 1965. Long-distance road movements between Europe and the Middle East, as well as Istanbul-area commuters, were freed from depending on ferryboats in 1973 when the Bosporus Bridge linking European and Asian Turkey was completed.

Viewed overall, the success of mechanized road transport has been mixed in the 1990s. Its inimitable mobility has induced radical changes in social interaction and business methods, and spending on its provision has become a significant if not main driver of economic activity wherever it is adopted. That these qualities and effects have been almost universally perceived as immensely beneficial is underscored by the end-of-century rush to supply automobiles and trucks to nations where their use had long been severely constrained by politically closed economies. Simultaneously, however, both developed and developing countries, in which motor transport has achieved significant growth if not overwhelming dominance, have been struggling with its negative impacts. There is seemingly insurmountable congestion in numerous areas, as traffic growth continually outpaces available space and funds to expand the roads. Other issues demand attention as well, including air quality, noise, urban and suburban land use patterns, and mobility for those who do not have discretionary use of automobiles yet live in locations unserved by public transport.

## Rail Transport

Rail transport entered the century as a growth industry, and would remain so in many countries until the Great Depression. Between 1901 and 1930, intercity railway mileage increased from about 37,500 to 84,400 in Latin America, from 36,500 to 82,500 in Asia (excluding the Soviet Union), and from 12,500 to 42,400 in Africa. Russia completed the Trans-Siberian Railroad in 1916, extending more than 600 miles between Yekaterinburg (later Sverdlovsk) and Vladivostok. Australia's mileage rose from 12,600 to 24,100 in 1920, including a transcontinental line opened in 1919. Canada increased its total railway mileage from 17,900 to 39,000 during the first two decades.

In Western Europe and the United States, rail systems had already acquired the greater portion of their route mileage. However, some additions continued. Most were branch lines, but several were significant main lines. Major projects such as the building of the San Pedro, Los Angeles & Salt Lake between Salt Lake City and Los Angeles; the Western Pacific between Salt Lake City and Oakland; the Milwaukee Road's Pacific Coast extension between Mobridge, South Dakota and Puget Sound; and the Florida East Coast's audacious over-water extension from Miami to Key West helped push U.S. rail route mileage to an all-time peak of 254,037 in 1916.

Even more indicative of the rail industry's growth was track mileage, which included the length of additional tracks on multiple-track mainlines as well as all siding and yard trackage. Between 1900 and 1915, the total track miles in the United States increased 50 percent, from 259,000 to 391,000. Within that time, several large carriers undertook major programs to expand mainline and terminal capacity in an effort to handle steep increases in both freight and passenger traffic. A spectacular example was the Pennsylvania Railroad's Pennsylvania Station project in New York City, which entailed not just the station structure itself, but also the construction of two single-track tunnels under the Hudson River, four single-track tunnels under the East River, the Hell Gate Bridge, and major passenger car servicing and storage facilities. Simultaneously, the competing New York Central Railroad built a new Grand Central Terminal across town, along with making other additions and improvements in its New York operating zone. In the West, the Southern Pacific reduced circuitry on its own route between Oakland, California and

Ogden, Utah by building a new line on a trestle straight across the Great Salt Lake, and the Santa Fe double-tracked its mainlines at a rate of almost 250 miles per year.

The fear of fire in the long tunnels serving the new Pennsylvania Station and Grand Central Terminal accelerated the transition to all-steel passenger cars in the United States, and steel-framed and all-steel freight equipment also became the norm, along with the consequent increases in cubic and weight-carrying capacity. European railways did not follow suit at the same pace. Extensive use of wood in both passenger and freight rolling stock and relatively small two-axle freight cars persisted beyond mid-century on the Continent and in Britain.

Steam ruled the locomotive rosters of the world's intercity railways in 1901, and was destined to continue playing a prominent albeit receding role until the late 1940s, when it would begin to decline more rapidly, approaching extinction by the 1990s. Although the basic characteristics of the reciprocating piston-driven steam locomotive had remained largely unchanged since its introduction in the 1830s and 1840s, it had undergone steady progression in size, weight, power, and speed, particularly between 1901 and the 1940s, in response to continual increases in the length, weight, and speed of both freight and passenger trains. As a case in point, a 4–6–2 (meaning four wheels on its leading pony or pilot truck/wheel assembly, six drive wheels, and two wheels on its rear trailing truck) Pacific-type locomotive (steam locomotives are classified by both their wheel arrangements and commonly used names related thereto) and tender built in 1902 for passenger service in the United States weighed 145.1 tons and generated 25,600 lbs. of tractive effort, while a 1930-vintage locomotive of the same wheel arrangement weighed 309 tons and exerted 51,300 lbs. of tractive effort. The Union Pacific's famous Big Boy, built in 1941 for mountain freight service, weighed 603.5 tons, exerted 135,400 lbs. of tractive effort, and produced more than 6,000 horsepower at 75 mph.

Electric traction posed the first threat to steam's rule. By 1901, it had already displaced horse and cable traction and small steam locomotives on urban street railways and early rail rapid transit lines in North America and Europe, and had sparked a mania for the proliferation of both electric street railways and electric interurban light railways. The latter operated vehicles modeled on streetcar-type technology, but which were heavier, faster, more comfortable, and capable of being operated either singly or in multiple-unit trains. Passenger traffic was their primary aim, but interurbans also developed freight traffic, particularly in package express and less-than-carload (LCL) consignments. Although electric interurbans could be found in several European countries and in Japan, most were built in the United States and Canada, where they reached maximum mileage of about 16,000 in 1916. Their routes typically used in-street trackage within cities and towns, and private right-of-way in suburban and rural areas. This often less-than-ideal infrastructure, together with a concentration on shorter-haul traffic, made the American interurbans early victims of competition from motor transport. Few survived beyond 1940.

Successful electric operation on street and interurban railways did not match the size and capacity conditions of large-scale main line steam railway electrification: additional technological hurdles had to be overcome before main line electrification could proceed. When they were, it did—and within a relatively short time. First to enter service was a three-phase 3,000-volt alternating current overhead wire system in Italy in 1902. The next significant accomplishment occurred in 1906, when the New York Central initiated operation of a 650-volt direct-current third-rail system as part of its Grand Central Terminal reconstruction project. Upon its completion, trains pulled by electric locomotives ran to Harmon, New York—32.6 miles north of Grand Central—where steam power took over. The New York, New Haven & Hartford followed shortly thereafter with the opening of a 25-mile, 11,000-volt alternating-current installation in New York and Connecticut. Its high voltage and an overhead wire (catenary) power distribution method were selected because they promised substantial advantages for long-distance main line use. Unlike the New York Central, the New Haven did not intend to confine its electrification efforts to the New York terminal area; New Haven, Connecticut and Boston were its objectives. Ultimately, New York was reached, but Boston was left for Amtrak to undertake in the 1990s.

The century's first truly long-distance electrification came between 1915 and 1919, when the Milwaukee Road replaced steam locomotives with 3,000-volt direct-current electric ones on about 650 miles of its recently opened Pacific Coast extension. The new electrics featured regenerative braking, a singular innovation particularly for mountain operation: when running downgrade, the locomotive's traction motors could be turned into generators that fed power back into the overhead catenary and created drag to help slow the train, reducing wear on brake shoes and wheels. The additional electricity thus produced was either consumed by other trains moving on upgrade or level track, or credited back to the railway's commercial power supplier.

After World War I, extensive main line electrification programs began in Switzerland, Germany, Austria, Norway, and Sweden, all using 15,000-volt 16 2/3-cycle-single-phase alternating current. The current had actually been used earlier in the 12.5 mile Simplon Tunnel, which opened between Switzerland and Italy in 1913. By 1939, almost every European country had at least some electrified main line trackage, as did Australia, New Zealand, India, Indonesia, South Africa, and Japan. Two notable interwar electrification efforts involved the Southern Railway in England and the Pennsylvania Railroad in the United States. The Southern installed 600-volt direct-current third rail on mainlines to Brighton, Portsmouth, and other points as well as on much of its London-area suburban service network. About 671 route miles came under 11,000-volt 25-cycle alternating current catenary when the Pennsylvania converted its New York–Washington and Harrisburg–Philadelphia lines to electric operation.

Electric propulsion with power supplied from a central generating station offered many operating and environmental advantages over steam. But as it required very high capital investment in power distribution facilities, it was best suited for lines carrying dense traffic, or in long tunnels where engine exhaust from other forms of motive power would be intolerable. This inspired a search for more affordable alternatives to steam involving internal combustion engines. Gasoline-powered rail cars using mechanical transmissions had been used as early as 1905 in light-density passenger service, but the transmissions proved inadequate. In 1908, a gasoline-electric rail motor car—in which the gasoline engine powered a generator that in turn fed electricity to traction motors—appeared, and proved successful enough to be purchased in the hundreds for use on branch lines and on some main line local services. Application of this technology to light freight service followed in 1913–1915, when a Minneapolis-area short line railway bought three gas-electric locomotives.

In 1923, improvements in diesel engines stemming from World War I submarine applications led to the construction of two experimental diesel-electric locomotives, one in Germany and the other in the United States. The American effort resulted in the first commercially viable diesel-electric locomotive, which entered yard switching service on the Central Railroad of New Jersey in 1925. Within ten years, there were 87 small diesel-electric switching locomotives working on 20 American railways. Germany achieved its first success with diesel power in high–speed mainline service in 1933, when the Deutsche Reichsbahn introduced Schnellverbrennungstreibwagen 877 a/b, more commonly called the Fliegender Hamburger, or "Flying Hamburger," a two-car streamlined diesel-electric train running between Berlin and Hamburg on a schedule requiring an average speed of 77 mph, and a maximum speed of 100 mph. Other units, expanded to three cars per train, followed, and the Reichsbahn established an extensive network of fast services. France, Hungary, and other countries pursued the development of similar equipment. By the outbreak of World War II, diesel rail cars and multiple-unit diesel train sets were in passenger service on numerous European railways. However, war-imposed fuel shortages soon forced many of them to suspend operation.

In the 1930s, in an effort to stem if not reverse the growing loss of passenger traffic to road and air transport, American railways also introduced faster services and streamlined equipment, featuring air conditioning, sound-proofing, more comfortable seating, and other advances. The Union Pacific with its City of Salina, and the Chicago, Burlington & Quincy with its Pioneer Zephyr led the way in 1934, followed closely by the Milwaukee Road, the Gulf, Mobile & Northern, the Santa Fe, the Rock Island, and the Baltimore & Ohio. By 1941, many other carriers had followed suit, with generally good results. Most of the streamliners did attract heavy traffic and earn profits. Their often strikingly attractive contours and colors, reflecting the talents of famed industrial designers of the era such as Henry Dreyfuss, Raymond Loewy, and Otto Kuhler, brought an image of modernism to what had become a staid industry.

Diesel power played an important but not exclusive role in this achievement. Some railways opted for improved steam locomotives, which regularly reached speeds of about 100 mph. However, the fate of steam in all categories of use was sealed when advances in diesel engine design made possible two events. In 1935, a diesel-electric locomotive was manufactured (as distinguished from a propulsion unit in a lightweight rail car or train set) with enough power and endurance to replace a steam locomotive on high-speed main line passenger trains composed of conventional-sized cars. And in 1939 a diesel-electric locomotive was produced that could generate total horse-power and tractive effort equal to or greater than that of the most powerful steam freight locomotive. Extensive demonstrations of the new locomotives proved that diesel-electric power could both outperform steam in over-the-road train operation and make possible large savings in operating and maintenance costs. In the face of overwhelming economic evidence, total dieselization was achieved by 1960.

Traffic demands of World War II strained the capacity of railways virtually everywhere. Many continental European systems were also severely damaged by bombing and ground fighting. Maintenance suffered, and shortages of scarce materials placed severe limits on the manufacture of new motive power and rolling stock. When war production restrictions were lifted, a torrent of orders flowed to car and locomotive builders from American railways.

Included in these orders were hundreds of millions of dollars worth of streamlined passenger cars. Most railway executives believed that the success of the prewar streamliners would continue, and that rail transport would capture a profitable share of the postwar passenger market. But their expectations were not fulfilled. The total revenue from rail passengers dropped from 703.2 million in 1947 to 283.8 million in 1970. Under the twin pressures of rising wage rates and inefficient union crew-size and work-rule agreements, labor costs escalated. Rail passenger facilities required large property tax payments, while most road and air transport infrastructure—owned by governmental units—did not. In the 1950s, the Post Office began diverting increasing amounts of mail traffic to air and highway carriers. Historically, mail had moved in "head-end" equipment on passenger trains. In 1971, no longer willing (or in many cases able) to bear the financial losses of the diminished number of intercity passenger trains that remained, most railway companies turned them over to the newly formed, quasi-government owned National Railroad Passenger Corporation (Amtrak). Commuter passenger service passed into the hands of regional public authorities. Thus freed from the burden of passenger deficits, the companies focused on freight traffic, which, being profitable, was the key to their survival without subsidy.

Amtrak and the commuter authorities managed to stabilize the remaining passenger traffic base, and the total number of passengers carried rose from 272.8 million in 1971 to 340.3 million in 1993. With government funding, commuter carriers made significant improvements in their motive power, rolling stock, stations, and other facilities. Amtrak also replaced much of the equipment that it inherited from the (now) freight railways. The streetcar, in the guise of light rail transit, staged a comeback in several cities, including San Diego, Baltimore, San Jose, Los Angeles–Long Beach, Sacramento, Portland (Oregon), St. Louis, Denver, and Dallas, after being largely supplanted by buses in the 1940s and 1950s. However, a seismic shift in the American political climate in the mid-1990s—centered on efforts to reduce and end federal government budget deficits and curtail the role of government in the provision of services—challenged the continuation of this progress.

Though American rail freight traffic also suffered from the post-World War II rise of road, water, and pipeline transport, it did not succumb in the same manner as passenger traffic. Rail freight tonnage remained almost constant, at 1.5 billion in 1947 and 1.6 billion in 1993, while freight ton-miles increased from 654.7 billion to 1.14 trillion within the same time period. This survival can be largely credited to a continual improvement in productivity through ongoing technological change. Horsepower of the largest single-unit diesel-electric locomotives rose from 1,500 in 1950 to 4,000 in 1995, and drive wheel-to-rail adhesion was improved beginning in the 1980s by microprocessor-based controls. Mechanization revolutionized track maintenance and replacement: the drop in route mileage from 226,696 in 1945 to 141,064 in 1992 reflected, among other factors, the more intensive use of remaining track. With the substitution of continuous welded rail for jointed rail, ride quality improved and maintenance costs dropped. Bi- and tri-level cars for the transport of finished automobiles, and trailer and container-on-flatcar equipment—including that for double-stack container operations introduced after 1980—enabled the recapture of traffic lost to long-haul trucking. Long-distance rail movements of low-sulfur coal grew dramatically as coal users sought to comply with more stringent air quality standards. When strong traffic growth revealed bottlenecks in the early 1990s, the Santa Fe and Union Pacific initiated double-tracking programs on some parts of their systems in a manner reminiscent of the early 1900s. Changes in employee work rules and other provisions of labor contracts also contributed to the improved performance of U.S. freight railways during the 1980s and 1990s.

In contrast to North American railways, British rail freight traffic was decimated by road transport and the decline of traditionally rail-dependent industries such as coal and steel, particularly after the 1950s. Most continental Western European rail carriers also suffered heavier freight losses than their American counterparts, as did those in Japan. Post-1989 transitions toward market-driven economies caused drops of 50 percent or more in freight traffic on Central and Eastern European railways. These losses alarmed European governments, which viewed rail freight as less harmful to the environment than road freight and sought policies to reverse them. Switzerland and Austria were particularly aggressive in this regard, forcing truckers to use rail intermodal service for the transalpine international traffic that transited their territory. Also, European rail freight managers became more aggressive in marketing their service. In Britain, the English, Welsh & Scottish Railway Company, which took over most freight operations from British rail after 1995, began to score successes in recapturing traffic from trucking. New infrastructure such as Eurotunnel also improved rail freight's competitiveness. But as of the mid-1990s, the relative and absolute post-1945 success of Western European and Japanese railways rested with passenger rather than freight business.

Foremost among the indicators of this success was the introduction of very high-speed trains, beginning with Japan's Tokaido Shinkansen line between Tokyo and Osaka, which ran at a maximum operating speed of about 130 mph when it opened in 1964. Speeds later increased, and additional lines were added. The French National Railways (SNCF) relentlessly pursued increases in speed for its conventional passenger trains from the late 1940s onward, aided by the wide expansion of electrification and a strong research and development program. During test runs in the 1950s, the SCNF trains achieved speeds in excess of 200 mph.

In 1981, the SNCF opened its first Train à Grande Vitesse (TGV) line, the Sud-Est, between Paris and Lyon, with a maximum top operating speed of about 160 mph on the new specially built track, and slower-speed (e.g., 125 mph maximum) service over conventional trackage to other points. Two additional lines, the TGV Atlantique and the TGV Nord, opened in the 1990s, operating at the higher maximum speed of 186 mph. On May 18, 1990, a test run on the Atlantique line set a new world railway speed record of 320.2 mph. The Nord line, connecting Paris with Lille and the new Eurotunnel, thus provided part of the route for the London–Paris and London–Brussels Eurostar train service that began on November 14, 1994. Thus was activated one of the first significant international routes in a projected 18,000-mile European high-speed rail network planned by the European Community.

Germany started revenue service on June 2, 1991, with its InterCity Express (ICE) train sets, whose top speed ranged from 155 to 175 mph on new lines built specifically for its use, and 125 mph on upgraded stretches of conventional trackage. Like TGV equipment, ICE trainsets were designed to operate over both purpose-built and existing parts of the country's railway network, to reduce the costs of accessing stations in built-up areas with high land values and to increase the range of markets that could be served without changing trains. Spain opened a line between Madrid and Seville in 1992, using trainsets of a modified French TGV design. South Korea also selected TGV technology in 1994 for a line under construction between Seoul and Pusan.

In every market in which it was introduced, high-speed rail service captured significant blocks of traffic from both air and road transport, and generated new traffic involving journeys that would not have been taken in its absence. Thus the transformation of rail transport between 1901 and the 1990s presented a montage of dominance, growth, maturity, decline, and revival. Its new technological characteristics have poised it for continued service after the turn of the century.

## Pipeline Transport

In its broadest sense, pipeline transport encompasses all systems of pipe used to carry gases, liquids, and solids suspended in liquid, including those dedicated to potable water supply and sanitation services. However, the commercial pipeline transport industry has traditionally been viewed in terms of petroleum, natural gas, and coal slurry.

By 1901, petroleum pipelines had already existed in the United States for 39 years, and held unassailable economic superiority vis-à-vis road and rail transport for large-volume movements. They were concentrated in eastern states and linked the nation's principal crude oil-producing fields in Pennsylvania, Ohio, West Virginia, and Kentucky with East Coast refineries. Three events soon expanded their territorial coverage: between 1901 and 1905 there were major oil discoveries in East Texas, Kansas, Louisiana, Oklahoma, and California, while in the eastern fields a decline in production forced eastern refineries to procure crude oil from the new mid-continent sources. The concurrent population growth—and hence increased demand for petroleum products in the Midwest and West—induced the construction of refineries on the shores of the Great Lakes and the Mississippi River and on the Texas Gulf and California coasts. Crude oil trunk pipelines thus were built to link the new oil-producing areas with existing eastern pipelines, new refining locations, and water carrier terminals (to complete movements to refineries by tank ships or barges). Many miles of gathering pipelines also appeared, connecting storage tanks near oil wells with the long-distance trunk pipelines. Growth continued through the teens and 1920s, and by 1931, 50,020 miles of crude-carrying trunk pipelines and 53,640 miles of gathering lines were in service.

Some carriage of refined petroleum by pipeline occurred during the early 1900s, but widespread use of products pipelines did not begin until after 1928, when the production of 40-foot sections of seamless line pipe and the electric arc-welding of pipe joints were perfected. Previously, joints had been screwed together with threaded collars which sufficed for the containment of viscous crude-oil but allowed leakage of low-viscosity liquids like gasoline, causing safety and environmental hazards as well as economic losses. By mid-1931, 3,210 miles of products pipelines had been placed in operation. Pipe diameter at this time typically ranged between 14 and 16 inches, and most lines traversed distances of 200 miles or less, but one ran 1,000 miles from the Texas Panhandle to Chicago. Batching, or the movement of more than one type of refined product through the same line, became a common feature.

Initially, reciprocating steam engines powered the pumps that moved oil through the early pipelines; they were housed in buildings, along with the engines, steam boilers, pumps, and other equipment, sited at intervals along the lines and staffed around the clock by operating and maintenance personnel. Diesel engines of various designs came next, followed by electric motors and gas turbines. These advances in propulsion, complemented by new electronic communications and control technology, enabled remote and automatic controls, and pipeline networks spanning thousands of miles from one location became common.

One of the earliest pipelines outside the United States was an 8-inch crude-oil line about 500 miles long, built in 1905 between Baku, Azerbaijan on the Caspian Sea and Batumi, Adzharia (Georgia) on the Black Sea. Crude-oil lines ranging from 10 to 16 inches in size appeared in Colombia in 1926, Mexico in 1932, and Venezuela in 1939.

World War II accelerated pipeline development in the United States and introduced the improvements elsewhere. Two notable American projects, necessitated by German submarine attacks on coastal tanker ships, were the 24-inch, 1,341-mile Big Inch crude-oil pipeline from Longview, Texas to the Philadelphia and New York areas, and the 20-inch, 1,475-mile Little Big Inch products line between Texas Gulf Coast refineries and the New York area. In Asia, the 6-inch and 8-inch Indo-Burma products pipelines extending almost 3,000 miles were constructed to transport fuel for Allied military operations on the China-Burma-India front. Gasoline for the Allied drive across France and into Germany was supplied by 2,380 miles of 6-inch and 1,440 miles of 4-inch prefabricated pipelines. The British constructed a network of lines between seaports and airports to move aviation gasoline. Also, in Operation Pluto (Pipe Line Under the Ocean), which followed the Normandy invasion, they laid twenty 3-inch submerged pipelines on the floor of the English Channel between England and France.

Wartime experience with pipelines such as the Big Inch demonstrated the economic superiority of larger diameter pipe. After the war, many 6 to 12-inch lines were rebuilt with pipes ranging from 16 to 26 inches. Long-distance installation of 36-inch pipe began in the late 1950s with a 1,643-mile section of a natural gas pipeline linking Texas with East Coast points. Pipe in diameters of up to 40 inches appeared in the early 1960s; up to 64 inches in the 1970s. As supply and demand conditions changed, some American pipelines were converted from crude to products carriage, from oil to gas, and occasionally back to their previous use. Liquefied petroleum gas and anhydrous ammonia began moving in some lines as well. Large oil and gas discoveries triggered the development of extensive pipeline mileage in Canada, North Africa, the Middle East, and the former Soviet Union. Lines for refined products movement appeared between the Netherlands and Germany, France and Germany, and Italy, Switzerland, and Germany, respectively.

Perhaps the century's most audacious and controversial pipeline project was the 48-inch, 800-mile Trans Alaska Pipeline System (TAPS) linking the Prudhoe Bay North Slope oil field with an ocean tanker terminal at Valdez, Alaska. TAPS was originally planned for completion in the early 1970s for $900 million, but construction delays and design changes caused by environmental concerns and safety issues pushed its final cost, when it opened in 1977, to $7.7 billion. Portions of TAPS are laid above ground on special heat-resistant supports to protect delicate permafrost from the warmth of the heated oil moving through it. If left unheated, the viscous crude oil would not flow in the arctic climate. Also unique is the line's zigzag pattern, which accommodates expansion and contraction of the pipe during wide-ranging temperature changes.

Between the 1950s and the 1980s, numerous proposals for the construction of coal slurry pipelines were advanced, but only two materialized. The first was a 108-mile line between a coal mine in southeastern Ohio and an electric power plant near Cleveland, which opened in 1957 and carried more than 6.7 million tons of coal before being mothballed in 1963 after competing railways recaptured its traffic with reduced rates. Second was the Black Mesa Pipeline, which began operation in 1970 on a 273-mile route between a mine in Arizona and a power station in Nevada and remains in continuous service.

Throughout the century, pipeline transport has enjoyed significant success. Its performance has mirrored that of its principal customer groups, the producers and marketers of petroleum and natural gas. However, its role in the treatment of slurried coal and other commodities has remained minuscule.

## Water Transport

Glamour distinguished transoceanic passenger service from all the other players in the complex arena of commercial water transport during the early 1900s. The great age of the ocean liner—symbolized by speed and luxury, particularly on the North Atlantic—had just dawned, spurred by the newly developed marine steam turbine, which greatly surpassed in power and efficiency even the best of the reciprocating steam engines designed for marine use. Another advancement, the conversion from coal- to oil-fired boilers, came about 1920. By the outbreak of World War II, turbine-driven ships had become the basic providers of scheduled passenger, mail, and premium freight service on the world's principal ocean routes.

Ocean liner vessel design and performance reached a pinnacle with the launching of the French-registered *Normandie* and the British-registered

*Queen Mary* and *Queen Elizabeth* in the 1930s, and the American-registered *United States* in 1952. The first three exceeded 1,000 feet in length, while the latter measured 990 feet. All could cross the North Atlantic in slightly more than four days. The *United States* became the final speed record holder among transatlantic liners in its inaugural year, when it achieved 35.59 knots eastbound and 34.51 knots westbound. However, air transport soon rendered this accolade irrelevant. In 1952, North Atlantic sea traffic totaled 842,000 passengers comprising 66 percent of the market, while airlines carried 433,000 passengers (excluding charter flights), or the other 34 percent. By 1965, air traffic had risen to 3.6 million passengers and 84 percent of the market, while sea traffic had dropped to 652,000 passengers—it now only handled a market share of 16 percent. Similar declines set in on other passenger liner routes. The *Queen Mary*, *Queen Elizabeth*, and the *United States* ceased operation in 1967, 1968, and 1969, respectively.

By the 1990s, only the *Queen Elizabeth 2*—better known as the *QE 2*—a somewhat smaller version of the 1930s-vintage *Queen Elizabeth*, offered scheduled North Atlantic passenger service, confined largely to the summer season. In the winter, it served the cruise markets, as was intended when it was built. Cruise ship business to the West Indies, the Mediterranean, and other winter vacation centers burgeoned between the 1960s and the 1990s, yielding annual passenger volumes that dwarfed traffic levels on the erstwhile liner routes during their best years. Large numbers of new vessels specially designed for cruising appeared. Ironically, many cruise passengers reached the ports of departure for their ships by air.

Waterborne passenger traffic also prospered on numerous short-distance routes around the world. Growth in automobile and truck use after the 1940s drew roll-on/roll-off (RO/RO) motor vehicle ferries into service on the English Channel, the Irish Sea, the Baltic and Adriatic Seas, Puget Sound, and numerous other bodies of water. By the 1970s, densely trafficked routes boasted RO/RO ferry ships capable of carrying more than 800 passengers and 350 automobiles.

The desire for shorter travel times brought hydrofoil vessels—capable of regular service speeds of about 50 knots—into commercial transport use; one of the first, the 22-passenger *Albatross*, entered commuter service in 1963 on New York Harbor between lower Manhattan and Long Island. Larger hydrofoils came into regular passenger and cargo use on a wide range of river, lake, harbor, and short-distance sea routes in many parts of the world. Notable applications included cargo movements on the Volga River in Russia and passenger service between France and Italy on the Mediterranean. Another new type of high-speed vessel was the amphibious air cushion vehicle or hover-craft: riding on a cushion of air created by a horizontal fan and driven by air-craft-type propellers, a hovercraft could skim over water or ground at up to about 70 knots. Larger-sized models included the SRN-4 hovercraft, capable of carrying 250 passengers and 30 automobiles, which entered service across the English Channel in the late 1960s.

From the century's beginning through the 1950s, general cargo ranging from food, clothing, beverages, and consumer durables to packaged chemi-cals, motor vehicles, steel, machinery, and a myriad of other items moved in so-called break-bulk freighters. Cargo was loaded and unloaded piece by piece, requiring extensive manual labor and much time in port for vessels. This inefficient process disappeared with the so-called container revolution of the mid-1950s. The revolution was based on a simple concept: door-to-door movement of freight in standard-sized (width and height of 8 feet, length of either 20 or 40 feet) ocean cargo containers, steel or aluminum boxes with doors on one end and reinforced corner posts with locking devices at each top and bottom corner. For land movement, the containers could be secured to rail cars or truck chassis, and could also be stacked at terminals in the meantime. At sea, they would be carried in the cellular holds of specially designed container ships. By the 1990s, break-bulk vessels had largely van-ished from trade lanes between industrialized countries, replaced by con-tainer ships of up to about 1,000 feet in length that could hold around 4000 20-foot containers (20-foot equivalent units, or TEUs). Six or seven container ships could do the work of about 80 break-bulk freighters. Steam turbines propelled the earlier container ships, but sharp increases in fuel oil prices in the 1970s and 1980s prompted a shift to more fuel-efficient but somewhat slower diesel power. Diesels had already captured about 60 percent of total world merchant fleet propulsion by the late 1960s.

Hybrid container-RO/RO and pure RO/RO freighters (as distinguished from ferries) also appeared in the 1960s to accommodate wheeled cargo of all types. Another distinctive innovation was the lighter aboard ship (LASH) freighter, designed to carry up to about seventy 370-ton capacity lighters, or barges. Towboats or tugs moved the lighters on rivers or canals to a port, where they were loaded aboard a LASH vessel by its stern-mounted crane and taken to another port with navigable river access, whence they were unloaded and towed to destinations.

Ocean vessel sizes reached stunning peaks in the 1960s and 1970s with the introduction of supertankers more than 1,000 feet long, including very large crude carriers (VLCCs) with capacities ranging between about 1.2 and 2.1 million barrels of crude oil and ultralarge crude carriers (ULCCs) capable of holding around 3 million barrels. Their huge size and width, or beam, required the modification of harbor and docking facilities to permit loading and unloading.

Cyclical fluctuations in demand for liquid and dry bulk commodities can cause costly idle periods for a specialized vessel like a tanker. In the late 1950s, efforts to combat this produced so-called ore and oil (O/O) ships equipped for hauling either type of commodity. Additional versatility came in the 1960s with the introduction of O/B/O ships designed to handle light bulk cargo, such as grain, as well as either iron ore or coal.

There were also significant improvements in infrastructure. The opening of the Panama Canal in 1914 resulted in major reductions in time, distance, and risk for ships moving between the Atlantic and Pacific Oceans. Other improvements for deep-draft vessels included the Cape Cod Canal and Houston Ship Channel (both in 1914), the enlargement of the Chesapeake and Delaware Canal in the 1920s, and the Welland Ship Canal (1932). The completion of the St. Lawrence Seaway in 1950 opened Great Lakes ports to ocean freighters of up to about 730 feet in length and with a beam of as much as 76 feet. The addition of the Poe Lock to the Soo Locks in 1968 triggered the launching of a new generation of Great Lakes iron ore (taconite) ships. Their length of 1,000 feet and beam of 105 feet enabled them to carry approximately 65,000 short tons (2,000 lbs. equals one short ton) of taconite pellets. Like most Great Lakes dry bulk vessels built after mid-century, they were self-unloading—equipped with an internal conveyor system and a shuttleboom that was extended over the side of the ship when docked to permit discharge of cargo. This eliminated the need for shore-based unloading equipment, thus speeding vessel turnaround. The new superlakers also featured hulls designed for year-round operation through ice-choked waters; traditionally, Great Lakes navigation had ceased during the coldest months.

By the beginning of the century, commercial shallow-draft navigation on rivers and canals everywhere had already lost most passenger traffic and lighter high-value freight wherever rail competition appeared. The remaining traffic, primarily bulk commodities like coal, grain, ores, fertilizer, chemicals, and petroleum, and industrial goods such as steel and large machinery, continued to move throughout the decades. However, trends in amount and relative importance varied by location and time.

Apart from coal shipments on the Monongahela and Ohio rivers, American shallow-draft river and canal traffic was relatively insignificant and in decline until the late teens. At that juncture, World War I-related rail congestion caused the federal government to initiate what soon became an ongoing program for reviving inland waterway freight transport. By the 1980s, the federal government had canalized more than 23,000 miles of river and 2,242 miles of Gulf and Atlantic Intracoastal waterways by constructing lock and dam systems, dredging channels, and installing navigation aids ranging from buoy markers to electronic equipment. It also owned and operated a barge line—administered directly by Executive Branch agencies before 1924, and by the Inland Waterways Corporation thereafter—from 1918 to 1953, using it to demonstrate the feasibility of commercial water transport and encouraging its use by shippers. Earlier, in 1905, the State of New York had also completely reconstructed the famous old Erie Canal and several connecting waterways to create the New York State Barge Canal System.

Infrastructure improvement was complemented by the development of the integrated barge tow, consisting of up to about forty barges lashed rigidly together by steel cables to form a single unit and pushed by a towboat fastened to the rear of the barges. Although a few steam-powered stern wheel towboats survived beyond World War II, diesel-powered screw propeller vessels gained early prominence. Subjected to successive improvements, they became capable of pushing tows carrying upward of 50,000 tons of freight where channel widths permitted—as on the lower Mississippi River. The operating economies of diesel-powered integrated barge tows on canalized rivers drove the total inland water carrier ton-miles from 52 billion in 1950 to 374 billion in 1993. This traffic represented 4.9 percent of all U.S. intercity freight ton-mileage in 1950, and 12.2 percent in 1993.

Unlike the canalized rivers, the New York State Barge Canal system suffered almost complete loss of its commercial traffic by the 1990s, due in part to its relatively narrow width, which barred the use of large tows. It became largely a waterway for inland passenger cruise service vessels and private pleasure craft. After the 1950s, the same fate befell most canal mileage in Britain as well.

Inland water transport remained vibrant in China and in parts of Europe, particularly on rivers such as the Rhine. Some foreign water carriers adopted push towing and integrated barge tow operations after observing American practices. But despite continuing government spending, the extensive network of canals in Belgium, France, Germany, and other European countries lost market share to other modes, particularly trucking.

## Conclusion

Within the twentieth century, transportation moved quickly from an evolutionary interlude in its developmental continuum to another revolutionary phase. The shrinkage in travel time wrought by aviation and the inimitable mobility bestowed by mechanized road transport stood above all other developments. War-driven changes in technology accelerated them, but were not necessary conditions for their emergence. Steam power, triumphant in 1901 on rail, water, and pipeline, is virtually extinct in the late 1990s, swept away by internal combustion and electricity. Diesel-electric locomotives, ocean container ships, liquid and dry bulk vessels, integrated barge tows, and pipelines brought gains in freight transport productivity so huge that they were almost unthinkable in 1901.

Paradoxes abound. Intercity road transport, eclipsed by rail in the nineteenth century, recouped with mechanization and new infrastructure and achieved economic and social importance greater than all other modes. The aircraft vanquished scheduled ocean passenger service but became a major feeder to fleets of ocean cruise ships that carried more passengers than their liner service predecessors. Traditionally bitter road and rail freight competitors have begun to complement one another via the provision of intermodal services. The streetcar, gone from many cities by the late 1950s, has made a reappearance. Intercity rail passenger service, severely eroded by air and road transport after mid-century, has started to reassert itself, with revolutionary advances in speed. There are signs that the twenty-first century could be a new railway age.

SELECTED REFERENCES

Bilstein, Roger E. *Flight in America 1900–1983*. Baltimore and London: The Johns Hopkins University Press, 1984.

Bonavia, Michael R. *Twilight of British Rail?* Newton Abbot, England: David & Charles, Limited, 1985.

Bruce, Alfred W. *The Steam Locomotive in America: Its Development in the Twentieth Century*. New York: Norton, 1952.

Davies, R.E.G. *Airlines of the United States Since 1914*. Rev. ed. Washington, D.C.: Smithsonian Institution Press, 1982.

Eno Transportation Foundation. *Transportation in America: Statistical Analysis of Transportation in the United States*. 12th ed. Lansdowne, Va.: Eno Transportation Foundation, 1994.

European Conference of Ministers of Transport. *Statistical Trends in Transport*. Paris: OECD Publications Service, various years.

Lay, M.G. *Ways of the World*. New Brunswick, N.J.: Rutgers University Press, 1992.

Sampson, Anthony. *Empires of the Sky: The Politics, Contests and Cartels of World Airlines*. New York: Random House, 1984.

Sheppard, Nora, ed. *Introduction to the Oil Pipeline Industry.* 3d ed. Austin: Petroleum Extension Service, Division of Continuing Education, The University of Texas at Austin.

Strohl, Mitchell P. *Europe's High Speed Trains: A Study in Geo-Economics.* Westport, Conn.: Praeger, 1993.

Taff, Charles A. *Commercial Motor Transportation,* 4th ed. Homewood, Ill.: Richard D. Irwin, 1969.

U.S. Department of Transportation, Federal Highway Administration. *America's Highways: 1776–1976.* Washington, D.C.: U.S. Department of Transportation, Federal Highway Administration, 1976.

U.S. Department of Transportation. *National Transportation Strategic Planning Study.* Washington, D.C.: U.S. Department of Transportation, March, 1990.

Wilner, Frank N. *The Amtrak Story.* Omaha, Neb.: Simmons-Boardman Books, 1994.

# 18 Scientific Thought

ERIC HOLTZMAN

The nineteenth century gave considerable momentum, intellectual and institutional, to the central "natural sciences," by which I mean, with unavoidable arbitrariness, physics and astronomy, the earth sciences, chemistry, and biology. As this momentum carried forward to the twentieth century, basic ("pure") science—research without short-term practical goals—continued its fruitful dialectic with applied science. Each has contributed impetus and ideas to the other, and each has profited by the abundance of new scientifically based technologies that have provided research tools as well as marketable products. My concerns will be with the basic-science pole of this dialectic. But I start from the premise that modern basic science in its evolution is most readily understood as one of the means by which societies have grappled with problems of production, explanation, and legitimation, through creating and harnessing human curiosity and mustering a corps of intellectuals and allied technical workers. In this light, the activities of scientists reflect, simultaneously, the needs and resources of the surrounding societies and the ongoing histories of the scientific disciplines.

Twentieth-century basic science expanded to its present large scale through planning and investment, by private corporations and foundations to some extent, but more and more by governments desiring to sustain growth in military and industrial strength, and in medicine and agriculture. The effort has progressed furthest in wealthy, industrialized nations. To a degree it has been characterized by national styles and by competition, which sometimes has been ugly and intense. But the progress also has been grounded in widespread communication and cooperation within international scientific communities. Still, though excellent scientists have come from the less developed countries, most such people have had to migrate, physically or culturally, to the more developed world to join such communities.

The development of the basic research enterprise has required recruiting, educating, and motivating numbers of scientists and technical workers and providing increasingly elaborate experimental and observational facilities. There have been accompanying changes in the articulation of research activities within industrial, military, agricultural, and medical systems. The details of these processes have differed in different periods and places during the century. Britain, and especially the United States during its post-World War II heyday, have experimented with pluralistic mixes of laboratories, large and small, located at research-oriented universities and private and public research institutes; funding in the United States during this period has come principally from the federal government, following agendas designed and administered with substantial participation by working scientists. Continental Europe and Japan have utilized somewhat more traditional models, relying less on the initiatives of the individual investigators and more on centralized control by government ministries, chiefs of departments, and heads of institutes. However, particularly since World War II, the practices of scientific life have converged appreciably, corresponding to growing international intellectual cooperation and reflecting, as well, economic and practical exigencies, imitation of successful programs, and the adoption of English as the international language of several key sciences.

Intensified pressures on scientists to specialize narrowly have come with the growth of the pertinent bodies of information and the increased expense of doing research. Few scientists can avoid limiting their work to short-focus problems—often those suggested by the dominant members of groups, formal and informal, in which they are subordinates. Most master only a very limited technical repertory. But partial solutions to specialization have evolved: new disciplines—such as biochemistry, geochemistry, astrophysics, and geophysics—have flourished at the boundaries between the older ones; habits of collaborative work or sharing information and techniques among otherwise competing groups have become firmly established in many fields; and successful scientists may diversify by heading several groups working on different problems, participating in multiple collectives or even migrating from one field to another. Modern biology, for example, has profited from the involvement of people originally trained as physicists or physical chemists.

What follows is a brief survey of several of the natural sciences, focused on the ways in which their major views have changed during the century. My perspective is that of a research scientist, a biologist with background in the other sciences.

## Physics

### Atoms

A long history, culminating with the successes of chemistry in the nineteenth century, led to the viewpoint that atoms are fundamental building blocks of matter. Nineteenth-century science classified different types of atoms, whose properties were thought to be immutable, and made progress toward understanding how these properties contribute to the features of combinations of atoms, such as molecules, and of the larger aggregates of matter encountered in everyday life. Progress was also made in conceptualizing energy as occurring in different but related forms, including heat, electricity, magnetism, and mechanical energy. The transformations of one form into another were explored in both practical and mathematical terms. Electricity and magnetism were portrayed in terms of fields spreading from energy sources and capable of generating force at a distance from the sources. Light and other forms of radiation came to be pictured as electromagnetic waves that propagate from one place to another. By the century's end physicists had uncovered signs that atoms themselves contained electrically charged particles, such as electrons, and were beginning to study the properties of these "subatomic" particles. And the drastic changes in outlook that were to occur in the twentieth century were foreshadowed in the discovery, in 1896, of radioactivity (Antoine-Henri Bequerel, French)—the fact that some atoms spontaneously disintegrate, releasing energy and undergoing conversion into other types of atoms.

Twentieth-century physics has made extensive use of devices, from early cyclotrons to modern supercolliders, in which atomic structure is dissected by colliding atoms or subatomic particles with one another at high speeds, approaching that of light. The fragments produced in such collisions and the forms of energy released provide clues to atomic organization. One result of this approach was the discovery that certain atoms can be deliberately transmuted into other types—a small-scale fulfillment of the alchemist's dream. Another was the finding that some collisions lead to the release of considerable energy through the splitting (fission) of certain atoms (Austrians Lise Meitner and Otto Frisch, 1939), such as those of uranium, or the fusion of others (Hans Bethe, German, 1939), such as those of hydrogen.

### The Subatomic World

Early in the century, the familiar solar-system-like models of the atom began to evolve (Ernest Rutherford, British, 1911; Niels Bohr, Danish, 1913):

electrons were believed to circle a nucleus made up of other subatomic particles, the protons and neutrons, the system being held together by the attractions between the negatively charged electrons and the positively charged protons. Unsettling problems soon arose, however. For one thing, the insights of nineteenth-century physics predicted that such a system should be unstable—it should collapse in on itself or, when numerous protons are clustered, as they are in the nuclei of many atoms, fly apart from the mutual repulsions of the positive charges. For another, it was discovered that dozens of types of subatomic objects can be produced by collision, and that some of these particle-like objects are quite odd. Many, unlike the protons, neutrons, and electrons, have only ephemeral existences, persisting for small fractions of a second before "decaying"—converting spontaneously into other particles, often with the release of energy.

Much effort has been expended in classifying these particles into families and in tracing their interrelations. Following historical inclinations, many physicists now believe they are progressing toward uncovering a relatively small set of indivisible, fundamental entities (elementary particles) whose combinations generate the observed diversity. Current theories of atomic structure and behavior envisage fundamental entities of only a few types. Of these, some—like electrons—can readily be studied as independent particle-like objects. However, a key class, the quarks, may never assume such existence, or do so only very transiently under extreme experimental conditions; they occur in nature tightly bound as components of composite particles such as protons or neutrons, each of which includes three quarks. Current debate concerns proposals that take things even further, envisioning all of the material objects atomic physicists have studied or inferred thus far, stable or unstable, as derivatives of fundamental entities visualized as roughly analogous to small lengths of string (Yochiro Nambu, Japanese, 1970s).

Another feature of the "grand unified theories" of atomic structure and behavior especially popular in the last quarter century is their characterization of the principal forces within atoms as of three types: electromagnetic interactions, including the attractions between the protons and electrons; strong interactions that help hold the atomic nucleus together; and weak interactions evident in certain features of subatomic behavior. (Some believe all natural forces—these three and the force of gravity as well, which is very weak within atoms—will eventually be found to represent different manifestations of a single more fundamental force.) Rather than picturing forces as conveyed by intangible fields or representing mysterious long-distance attractions and repulsions, the theories attribute them to transfers of particle-like entities between the interacting objects. "Force-carrying particles" are represented by the theorists as having disconcerting attributes that make certain of them exceedingly difficult to observe. Some are said to be "virtual," meaning that they wink into and out of existence almost instantaneously, and because of this can avoid some of the laws that govern more ordinary objects. Others, like the "gluons" that mediate the interactions among quarks, are observable only in combinations with one another or with other types of entities.

### Quantum Theory

Such visions of quasi-existing, particle-like objects whose behavior is assigned seemingly arbitrary characteristics are tied to a way of thinking central to twentieth-century physics. This viewpoint (among others, Max Planck, German, 1960; Erwin Schrödinger, Austrian, 1926; Louis de Broglie, French, 1923)—that of quantum theory (or quantum mechanics)—arises especially from several perplexing features of matter and energy, including the stabilities and instabilities of atoms. The term "quantum" comes from observations that energy, such as light and other forms of radiation, can behave as if comprised of discrete packets with some resemblance to particles of matter; a packet, or quantum, of light energy is called a photon. A related appreciation is that the states in which given types of atoms or subatomic particles exist relate to one another by steplike differences, rather than in smooth, continuous fashion. Some states are "permitted," others are not. For example, features of the rotational behavior of electrons are described by mathematical formulations that include "spin" values; the values for any electron can only be $+ 1/2$ or $- 1/2$. However, though no other values, such as 0 or 1, occur in nature for electrons, there are other particles whose spins do have such values but whose spin values cannot be $1/2$.

### Ambiguities, Uncertainties, and Randomness

That light, regarded by nineteenth-century physics as a wave, also exhibits particle-like properties when examined in suitable experiments, is mirrored by the fact that objects like electrons—classically conceived of as marble-like particles—also exhibit wavelike properties under some conditions of observation. We cannot say that energy, or subatomic objects, *really* are waves or *really* are particles—they can be made to exhibit the attributes of either by the manipulations we put them through in order to detect or measure them (Werner Heisenberg, German, 1927). Another manifestation of nature's elusive tendency to change fundamental aspects of its appearance according to the approach we use in examining it, is the intrinsic uncertainty that limits our capacities to determine where a particular subatomic entity is at a given instant, and how fast it is moving. One way of formulating this dilemma is to say that whatever we do to detect the entity changes its position or its speed or both. But an equivalent viewpoint is that the entity does not really have a definite position and speed, as conventionally conceptualized, at all. When we deal with a population of large numbers of such entities, we can use statistics and related tools from the mathematics of probability to analyze aggregate behavior quite accurately. But when we try to deepen our descriptions, we uncover underlying ambiguities. We can choose formulations that approach the population as though it were a collection of discrete objects that differ, quantitatively, in speed, position, and so forth—resembling particles that can exhibit rather odd behavior, like suddenly appearing far from where we thought them to be. But other mathematical treatments can represent the elements of the same populations as wave-related entities with no fixed boundaries, each somehow having a diffuse, indefinite localization, perhaps even extending, in some sense, toward the infinite. The latter sorts of treatments were devised to deal efficiently with the elusive features of subatomic nature. The price is the loss of our ability to visualize the kind of "substance" that could have such properties and still seem particle-like when properly prodded by experimenters.

A somewhat different problem arises from observations that processes like the decay of radioactive atoms or subatomic particles have random features. One can foretell that over a given period of time, a given proportion of a population of a given species of atoms will decay, but no means are available to predict when a particular individual atom will do so. Though the conceptual dissection of several forms of decay into known or suspected subatomic interactions has been accomplished, the seeming randomness, like considerations about the uncertainty of a particle's location, gnaws at the confidence that underlying causes will prove to be detectable. One line of thought, for instance, holds that conventional concepts of causation cease to be at all useful for such phenomena.

### Relativity

Relativity, the other mainstay of twentieth-century physics, was constructed alongside quantum theory. Though the two approaches look different in initial focus and content, they have interacted productively; in fact, Albert Einstein (1879–1955) was among the founders of both.

The relativistic viewpoint stems, historically, from the recognition that light and other forms of radiation are centrally important carriers of the information we obtain about nature, and from nineteenth-century difficulties in understanding the propagation of light waves. The approach is grounded in familiar experiences, such as the fact that an observer looking out the window of a smoothly moving vehicle may have difficulty deciding for certain whether the vehicle is actually moving or whether the vehicle is stationary and its surroundings—and therefore the objects within—are doing the moving. Einstein developed such considerations into two sets of proposals: the special theory of relativity (1905), which concerns motion at constant velocity, and the general theory (1916), which considers motion altered by gravity or other accelerating influences. He started with the seemingly simple postulates that scientists working in laboratories moving at different speeds will find matter and energy to obey the same laws, and that when these scientists measure the speed of light they will come up with the same values. The relativistic portrait of the universe that emerged is full of challenges to the imagination. Counterintuitive as some of its conclusions are at first glance, and unsettling to certainties about causation and prediction, they accord with a considerable body of experiment and observation: much of this information deals with astronomical phenomena or with extremes of velocity or energy, but the theories are advanced as global statements to clarify and unify our views of all of nature.

### Space-Time

Most strikingly, from the relativistic perspective, space and time lose their status as frameworks that provide conceptual backgrounds, made concrete by rulers, clocks, and so forth, against which we observe objects to move or other phenomena to transpire. The approach asserts that measurements of time and of spatial characteristics such as length are "relative" in the sense that they can be affected by the motion of what is being measured with respect to those doing the measuring. For example, no matter what devices they use, observers measuring the dimensions of an object at rest will obtain different results from the same observers measuring the same object when it has been set into motion. Similar considerations apply to measurements of the timing of phenomena. Perplexing (but verifiable) conclusions follow, such as the prediction that a space-traveling twin who spends part of his or her life in a vehicle moving with respect to the Earth will age at a different rate from his or her Earthbound counterpart. Similarly, the temporal sequence of a set of events can be perceived differently by different observers depending on conditions of motion, that is, one observer may see a given event as occurring earlier than a second event, whereas others may see the two as simultaneous, or even as taking place in the reverse order.

In relativity theory the problems posed by such paradoxes are resolved by abandoning our seemingly obvious and intuitive concepts of space and time as in some sense absolutes, and conceiving instead of the "framework" of the universe in terms of space-time: to describe physical events (bodies or phenomena) in this framework, one must simultaneously specify their locations and behavior both in the three dimensions of space and in time. Mathematically, time represents a kind of fourth "dimension" or coordinate so that the "geometry" of space-time—the mathematical description of the relativistic universe—is often described as four-dimensional, in place of the familiar three-dimensional geometry of space.

### Matter and Energy

Relativity theory also does away with the sharp distinction between matter and energy inherited from classical physics. The obliteration of this boundary is expressed in the well-known equation $E=mc^2$ (energy [E] is equivalent to mass [m], a property of matter basic to classical physics; the two being related, mathematically, by the square of the speed of light [$c^2$]). The liberation of atomic energy through the annihilation of matter, as in a nuclear explosion, is the most familiar practical expression of this relationship. But quantum theory makes use of it as well: the bewildering variety of particles that can appear after atoms or particles collide in an accelerator reflects the plasticity of both matter and energy at the subatomic level. The collisions are to be thought of not simply as separating preexisting particles from one another, but rather as creative processes in which the components of atoms are both separated and altered, with mass converting into energy and energy into mass.

On the other hand, relativity theory and quantum theory treat gravity in rather different ways, both of which are designed to avoid the idea of mysterious forces that operate at a distance. Quantum theory proposes the existence of gravitons—entities with the same ambiguous particle-like and wavelike characteristics associated with photons, whose passage between two bodies accounts for their gravitational interaction. Relativity theory, on the other hand, provides a mathematical formulation in which matter is pictured as affecting the geometry of space-time, "curving" the framework so that bodies we might once have described as attracting one another are instead described as mutually affecting the pathways of one another's passage through space and time. Either theory can be used to account for the fact that even the behavior of light is affected by gravity, though the first experimental tests of light being affected by gravity were based on predictions of such effects by relativity theory.

*Commentary*

In somewhat different ways, both the relativistic and quantum approaches incorporate older and more readily understandable philosophical "discoveries" about the relations of the observer to reality and about the limits of perception. The "real world" has not been abandoned—theories are judged ultimately by whether they predict or account for what is observed in the outcomes of experiments. But more and more, the "explanations" of nature they provide shift us, whether gently or drastically, away from the intuitions derived from ordinary experience. The theories substitute mathematical formulations that often can be neither easily concretely visualized nor imagined in terms of objects, agents, and interactions similar to those we encounter either in everyday life or with instruments like microscopes or telescopes. The names we choose for quantum objects and attributes, like "strangeness," "charm," or "quark"—a nonsense word, with mathematical resonances, borrowed from the Irish writer James Joyce—emphasize the shift. Older words of physics like "force" or "mass" or even "electron" seemed more comfortable because they related to seemingly simpler experiences such as the exertion of muscular effort. When pressed, however, "forces" and "fields," "attractions," and "repulsions" are found to mask their own mysteries.

What preserves our common-sense ideas about how the "real world" operates is the fact that few of the oddities of either the quantum world or the relativistic one are evident in the realm of everyday life—most become prominent only toward the extremes, large and small. Physicists and engineers and mathematicians have collaborated to extricate themselves from the peculiarities of these theories, using mathematical equations to make what amount to useful and precise statements and experimental predictions about, for example, the behavior of atoms, subatomic structure, and energy. A host of practical devices has resulted, ranging from lasers, transistors, and superconductors to microscopes that utilize electrons to obtain pictures of atoms and molecules. Chemists have adapted the theories of atomic structure to develop coherent concepts of the bonds that link atoms into molecules, concepts that expand our abilities to describe and manipulate molecular structure and behavior. Fortunately too, physicists and mathematicians have been improving their handling of complex phenomena closer to everyday life, such as the changing weather or the flow of fluids; chaos theory and fractals (Benoit Mandelbrot, French, 1975), which help us understand seemingly random and irregular phenomena, are among the still somewhat arcane products of this effort beginning to percolate from scientific and mathematical circles.

But, though we have been provided with partial models that enable us to cope with particular features of reality—treating electrons as particles for some purposes and as waves for others—confidence has waned in science's ability, and even in its desire, to construct common-sense portraits that will enable the nonspecialist to achieve an adequate grasp of at least the essentials of the physicist's universe. Science seems to have come up against limits, thus far insurmountable, to what can be said about nature—both about its structure and about the predictable chains of cause and effect that have helped us make sense of the world. Physicists, theorizing now about the precise nature of our world, recognize that the bases for choosing among their competing theories devolve ultimately upon criteria of mathematical elegance, coherence, and simplicity. This situation, with its astringent aftertaste, is, of course, not entirely new. But its starkness seems to have been enhanced.

## Cosmology

Atomic physics and relativity theory powerfully altered the conceptual orientations of physical science. The new ideas, together with spacecraft, telescopes that detect forms of radiation besides light (e.g., radio waves), and other observational devices have driven twentieth-century investigations of the cosmos in exciting directions.

### What's Out There?

The astronomer's catalog of the kinds, distances, and arrangements of the material objects and forms of energy that populate the universe has been considerably enriched. The first major advances, made during the initial third of the century (Edwin Hubble and Harlow Shapley, Americans), completed the displacement of our Earth from the center of things, culminating the progress of several centuries. Not only was it finally accepted that our solar system is located well out toward the edge of our galaxy—a system of stars in which our sun is one among many billions—but it was also established that our galaxy is only one of an immense number of comparable multistar systems. Many of these galaxies have spiral forms similar to ours; in others, the stars are arrayed differently. The old-fashioned stars themselves have been joined by a number of other types of large astronomical objects, a few now well understood, some still not, and several thought, believably, to exist but yet to be definitely confirmed. This last category includes the black holes that have recently attracted the popular imagination, objects expected from physical and astronomical theory to exert gravitational effects strong enough to prevent even light from escaping, and to produce many other bizarre effects.

Space itself seems less of a void separating the interesting objects of the universe than once was thought. It is pervaded by diverse forms of energy and contains diverse types of matter, ranging from rapidly moving subatomic particles to clouds of dust. Some current theories even propose that most of the universe's matter has yet to be described, existing as dark forms, unrecognized by present astronomical methods but detectable by gravitational effects.

### The Universe's Past, Future, and Extent

Changes have occurred as well in the scope and texture of our history of the universe. Once a realm chiefly for philosophical and mystical speculation, the cosmic past has become a fully legitimate focus of study by scientific measurement, inference, and conjecture. For one thing, the life cycles of stars—the sources of their energy and the changes they undergo from birth to death—can now be delineated in terms of the mass-to-energy conversions of atomic physics and the gravitational effects of relativity theory. (Certain black-hole varieties are predicted to develop when aging stars undergo a kind of gravitational collapse, as British physicist Stephen Hawking theorized in the 1970s.) Proposals are being advanced that account, in fair detail, for the formation of the planets of our solar system through the aggregation of smaller bodies, which condensed from the clouds of gas the system originated from. The origins of the various types of atoms of which familiar matter is composed—oxygen, nitrogen, metals, and the like—can be attributed to known atomic reactions taking place, for example, within stars. And realistic theories have been put forth for the formation and accumulation of molecules crucial to life on Earth, such as carbon-containing compounds and water.

But cosmological historians have not restricted themselves to such mundane matters. They have been building a much broader picture of the history of the universe as a whole, seeking evidence by looking back in time. This they do by exploiting the fact that light or other detectable radiation coming from distant astronomical objects is known now to have started its journey billions of years ago; thus it provides evidence of the distant past. Such approaches depend on means that have been devised to determine distances and assess the motion of objects quite far off. Velocities, for example, are estimated from the "red-shift" of the light that comes from astronomical objects moving rapidly away from us. This change in the apparent color of light results from effects similar to those that account for sudden alterations in the pitch of sound made by a rapidly moving vehicle, which rises as it travels toward us, climaxes as it passes us, and then lowers as it moves away.

The insights emerging from such efforts include difficult concepts. Most contending scientific histories describe the universe as having begun 10 to 20 billion years ago. It started as a system containing only elementary particles and radiation, subsequently has evolved through a series of changes, and will end some billions of years in the future. Big-bang models, which are now most widely favored, portray the universe as currently continuing an expansion that began at its origins, an idea that arises from observations that the galaxies are moving rapidly apart. But the concept also incorporates cosmologists' tendency to treat the physical extent of the universe as in some sense limited or finite, though it is not bounded in the conventional sense of having physical edges, and the limits themselves may change in time. One version of such limits relates to a tenet of relativity theory, which conceives of space as being curved by the effects of gravity: anything moving along an uninterrupted path, including the waves of light and other radiation that are our ultimate source of information about the universe, will eventually come back to where it started.

### Time and Direction

Analogous visions see time too as having a beginning and an end. Present-day physics and cosmology have set themselves the derivative task of understanding temporal and spatial "directionality": in one phase of this work, physicists have been grappling with what are called issues of "symmetry." Until recently it was thought, for example, that the same fundamental laws of behavior apply to elementary particles with "spins" in the leftward direction as apply to similar particles with "spins" to the right. And particles of ordinary matter, such as electrons, which carry a negative electric charge were thought to obey laws similar to those governing comparable particles of "antimatter" such as positrons—the positively charged counterparts of electrons. Such expectations have proven false (T. D. Lee and C. N. Yang, Chinese, 1950), found to be violated chiefly in certain subtle atomic phenomena.

The problems with respect to time are more blatant. On the one hand, there is nothing obvious in the known rules describing fundamental atomic events that would permit us, on comparing a motion picture of the behavior of subatomic particles with the same movie run in reverse, to insist that one of the two temporal sequences is "correct." On the other hand, subjective time—the time of ordinary experience—clearly does flow in one direction, in that our experience has taught us to expect that many sequences of events (aging, for example) rarely if ever run backward. Most natural phenomena observed by scientists also exhibit evidence of long-term temporal directionality, which has been codified in thermodynamic laws predicting that over time, the universe tends to become more "disordered." Consequently scientists mostly treat time as intrinsically irreversible. But there is unresolved controversy concerning both the mixture of physical reality and psychological bias that underlies the appearance of directionality, and also what happens to time when the universe reaches its end.

In grappling with such puzzles of cosmological time, space and direction, it is important to keep in mind that, to cosmologists, our universe simply represents all that is observable by reasonably direct means, or about which, from our observations and experiments, we can make certain inferences. In these respects, as in many others, twentieth-century physical science has intensified trends that were already represented in prior times. It is accepted—though not always gracefully, completely, or willingly—that scientific "reality" may not be as broad as the metaphysical reality we can imagine. That is, the ancient quandaries about "everything there is," about infinity and eternity, are not to be solved; they are simply to be sidestepped by declaring them as outside the bounds of science.

## Earth Sciences

The nineteenth century saw intense activity in mapping regions of the earth's land surfaces hitherto "unknown" (to the West). These efforts were associated with colonial penetration, the realignments of control in the Americas, military activities, and the continued search for mineral resources. In the twentieth century, earth sciences such as geology, oceanography, and meteorology have further diversified the scope and aims of their surveys, using an extensive array of devices such as aircraft, satellites, drilling equipment, improved submarines, and seismometers. Applications of the concepts and methods of physics, chemistry, and biology have also gained sophistication. In consequence, our portrait of the earth—its sea bottoms and its atmosphere as well as its land surfaces—is increasingly fine-grained as regards spatial or topographical features and changes over time. Much also continues to be learned about the mechanisms causing mineral, petroleum, and other deposits.

An important feature of recent decades is the increasingly profound appreciation of the interplays between the local and the global, as seen in weather patterns or in the genesis and influences of earthquakes or volcanic eruptions, for example. The predictive facets of the earth sciences have begun to emerge from their infancy so that, for instance, meteorologists are engaged in increasingly realistic debates on both the intrinsic limits to short-range forecasting and what the broad features of global weather are likely to be a century from now. Such enhancements come partly from knowledge accumulating, but in crucial measure they also flow from our capacity to construct mathematical models of the earth, its atmosphere, large segments of its crust, or its oceans by using computers that can handle the volumes of information required. Hypotheses can be tested by suitable manipulations of the mathematical models. This manner of "experimentation" by computer modeling complements earth scientists' physical experiments using apparatuses such as laboratory tanks, in which artificial waves can be created, or chambers in which the pressures and temperatures of the earth's interior can be approximated. Computer modeling is an important twentieth-century feature of many other sciences as well.

### Geological Time

Early in the century (Englishmen John Strutt, 1905, and Arthur Holmes, 1911), geologists resolved one of the nagging problems that arose from the nineteenth-century surmise that the earth must be older than had been previously thought, partly on the basis of biblical revelation. The problem was that a very old earth, heated only by the sun, should be much cooler than it is, and solid to the core. The discovery that the earth's materials include radioactive components—an internal energy supply—provided the "missing" source of heat. That the earth's history actually stretches back over several billion years was also demonstrated by exploiting radioactivity to devise practical methods for determining the ages of geological formations.

The nineteenth-century geological calendar was essentially a relative one—though many sequences of past events were known in some detail, their absolute timing was not, and scientific guesses about the earth's age often ranged from only a few hundred thousand years to several million. But periods of such duration would be too short to account, for example, for the known and suspected processes of biological evolution. The twentieth century established an absolute calendar within which geological epochs, and the paleontological (fossil) record, can be located with reasonable precision and reliability.

### Plates

Plate tectonics, an integrating and unifying theory of the earth's structure, is likely to stand as one of the cardinal scientific accomplishments of this century. This major drama derived from the realization that the list of forces traditionally thought to shape the earth's surface—erosion, volcanism, sedimentation, glaciation, and so forth—was seriously incomplete, and that the surface has a correspondingly surprising history. The set of theories called plate tectonics matured in the second half of the century (Alfred Begner, German, 1912; Harry Hess and Robert Dietz, Americans, 1960s; J. Tuzo Wilson, Canadian, 1960s), stimulated in part by the conclusion that the present-day continents were once parts of a single large continent but have since separated and drifted apart. This idea was advanced to help explain the relations in shape and geology of the modern continents as well as overlaps in the distribution of organisms preserved as fossils. Another key source for the theory was the discovery of enormous trenches, mountain ranges, and regularly patterned magnetic features on the ocean floor. A third was the accumulation of knowledge about the major layers of the earth—the core, mantle, and crust—and particularly about the differences in temperature, density, plasticity, and chemistry among the sublayers of the mantle underlying the earth's surface.

It now is believed that the surface is organized as a set of interlocking segments, or plates. Some of these, like the plates on which each continent rides, are quite large; others are small. Their overall pattern is reasonably stable for long times, but each plate is a dynamic structure. At certain of its borders, a plate acquires new material from the more plastic deeper regions of the earth; this balances the loss of material taking place at its complementary borders. Some of the processes of replenishment and loss can be intermittent, but they are steady enough overall to appear continuous on the geological time scale of many thousands to millions of years. As new material emerges from the depths, it solidifies, is integrated into the surface of the plate, and then is carried slowly away from the plate margins where it emerged. This migration is due to the slidinglike movement of the relatively rigid plate over deeper layers. It may take tens to hundreds of millions of years for this sliding to carry the material across the plate to other borders, at which point it sinks back, via trenches, to rejoin the deeper layers—where it will again be softened by high pressures and temperatures.

Many dramatic features of surface geology—geological faults prone to earthquakes, oceanic ridges, and chains of volcanic ocean islands—can be explained by the properties and behavior of the plates, particularly of the edges at which they form and slide past one another, or at which one plate pushes down below its neighbor. Most of the creation and disappearance of surface material occurs at the ocean floor, with the continents floating on the plates but also moving with them. Plate behavior at the continental edges, and the periodic collision of continents with one another, generates a folding and piling-up of the surface that helps account for structures such as continental volcanoes and mountain chains.

## Biology

In its studies of heredity, twentieth-century biology has also constructed a unifying perspective, resolving long-standing central questions and yielding convincing explanations for disparate observations.

Nineteenth-century biology is best known for its compelling evolutionary account of the history of living organisms. But fundamental advances were made as well in analyzing the microscopic structure of living things: the cell came to be recognized as the fundamental unit of life, analogous to the atom in physics; the reproduction of cells through their division into daughter cells was described; and processes such as fertilization and early embryonic development were analyzed as cellular phenomena. In addition, physiologists and chemists laid the groundwork for the analysis of living systems in chemical and physical terms.

### Genes

The twentieth century began (so to speak—recall that I am a biologist) with the creation of the discipline of genetics. First, the rediscovery in 1902 (Carl Correns, German; Erich Tschermak, Austrian; Hugo De Vries, Dutch) and subsequent extension of the work of Gregor Mendel (1822–1884), a previously unappreciated nineteenth-century investigator, established that the patterns by which many characteristics of organisms were transmitted to offspring could be predicted with simple mathematical rules. These rules, and the explanations they led to, systematized and made sense of common observations such as the fact that, though an offspring often seems overall like a blend of its parents, when one looks at particular characteristics in which the parents differ—the colors of eyes or flowers are traditional examples—the offspring often will resemble only one of the two parents. Such patterns of heredity could be explained by the transmission from parents to offspring of units of heredity—or genes.

At first genes were invoked as purely hypothetical entities of unknown composition, conceived of as underlying determinants of the manifest characteristics of the organism, determinants that could be passed from generation to generation without change. Observations that the offspring of a particular mating shows, say, the eye color of only one of its parents but that the other parent's color can reappear in subsequent generations were explained by the concept that what is inherited is not the eye color itself, but rather the genes whose presence leads to the production of the color. A gene inherited from a parent may have no evident representation (not be expressed, as biologists say) in the features of an offspring, but nonetheless it can pass, intact, from this offspring to the next generation where it may be expressed. This implies that gene expression during the development of a particular individual is a different type of process from the gene transmission from generation to generation.

Though gene transmission has its conservative side, genes soon were also found to change, or mutate. Once this was realized, genetics filled the major gap that remained in the theory of biological evolution: evolution came to be understood in terms of how natural selection affects the frequency and distribution of genes in populations of organisms. Altered genes arise through mutation, and through other processes of change discovered subsequently; new combinations of genes are generated through sexual reproduction; individuals possessing genetic constitutions that lead to traits favorable under prevailing environmental conditions leave more offspring than do other individuals, and therefore have more influence on the genetic constitution of succeeding generations.

Genetics has penetrated deeply into most other arenas of biology as well, providing essential conceptual tools plus means for experimental and practical manipulations of organisms. The genetic study of humans got an early boost from work on hereditary medical disorders—diseases and malformations that, in a manner of speaking, "run in the family." By the last quarter of this century, when the chemistry of heredity had been understood in fair detail, genetic analyses helped unravel previously impenetrable processes such as those underlying immune responses to infection or inoculation. Nowadays, genetic mechanisms or influences are being sought or posited in diverse areas of the study of humans. The analyses are no longer limited to the kinds of yes-no, all-or-none, brown-or-blue, one-gene-specifying-one-characteristic situations with which genetics began: many traits show the coordinated influence of a number of genes, and many genes are known to have effects that spread to multiple characteristics. Considerable interest has awakened regarding genetic influences—established, postulated, or imagined—on mental functions, behavior, and social structure. Related evolutionary and "sociobiological" (that is, biology determining social behaviors and structures, E.O. Wilson, American, 1970s) approaches have become popular in fields that abut biology, such as anthropology and psychology, with ripples being felt more distantly in aesthetics, economics, and politics.

## The Chemistry of Life

Genetics as described thus far is fairly simple in technique. Much of it has been built through naked-eye observations or with tools, like microscopes, that have been around for some time. The mathematical procedures of statistical analysis that emerged in the nineteenth and twentieth centuries helped by guiding the extraction of information about large or complex sets of traits or populations of organisms from samples involving manageable numbers of individuals. Biology, however, has also undergone a methodological upheaval in the twentieth century. The advent of electron microscopes in 1933 and other devices permitted visualizing the organization of life down to the level of the very molecules of which cells are composed. An armory of approaches to the chemistry of life—biochemistry—and to physiology has also accumulated. The pathways by which living organisms metabolize their food, use the gases from the atmosphere, transmit nervous impulses within their brains, and carry out a myriad of other processes have been worked out in detail, or soon will be. Viruses have lost their mystery as entities at the border between the living and the nonliving, having been revealed as efficient parasites that can invade a cell and use it to make more of themselves.

Capping these achievements is the analysis of heredity in biochemical terms, a task that took most of the century and involved a multitude of researchers. First it was realized that genes are transmitted as components of specific structures—chromosomes—that microscopists had found to be passed from parent cells to daughters and, via egg and sperm cells, from parent organisms to offspring. Next the chemistry of chromosomes was analyzed, leading eventually to the realization that the material of which genes are made is DNA (deoxyribonucleic acid). Each DNA molecule has the deceptively simple structure of two long strands coiled around each other (James Watson, American, Francis Crick and Maurice Wilkins, British, 1953). Cells can separate these two strands and make, for each, a partner identical to the original. It is this ability—to generate two perfect copies of what was a single DNA molecule—that accounts for genetic transmission. But the information encoded in DNA's chemical structure also can be copied into other molecules, RNA (ribonucleic acid), and from these the cell can translate the information into the molecular machinery (protein molecules) by which cells carry out their functions, grow, and change. This chain of production—DNA to RNA to proteins—accounts for the expression of genes as the characteristics of organisms. The genetic apparatus is much the same, showing only a few wrinkles, across the entire span of life, from viruses to single-celled organisms such as bacteria to humans. The molecular unity that underlies biological diversity is a powerful testimony to the fact of evolution.

The accomplishments of molecular biology have extended now to the point where the deliberate engineering of genes is a routine laboratory technique, a key procedure in biotechnology, and a central element in plans for the future of medicine and agriculture. At century's end work is well under way on mapping the human genome, the reservoir of human gene capacity.

## Time and the River

### Conservation of Momentum

Overall then, while twentieth-century physicists were prying loose our grips on time, space, causation, and reality, and blurring the boundaries between observer and observed, the other sciences achieved a great deal in delineating the events and timing of our natural history, both earthly and cosmic, and in working out mechanisms and structures of nature. The next century will start, as the present one did, with scientific agendas carrying considerable momentum: physicists are seeking to fill the gaps in their portrait of the subatomic world while continuing the ancient quest for a theory that will unify our view of the span of nature, from the subatomic to the cosmic. One task is to harmonize the relativistic view of gravity as a feature of a space-time framework that can propagate like a wave at the speed of light, with accounts of forces dependent on dynamic exchanges of quantum particles. Astronomers and cosmologists, looking at our distant past and our distant future, are probing the edges of the observable universe, trying to estimate its total content of matter and energy with an eye toward constructing balance sheets adequate for prediction. The ongoing cataloging of stars, galaxies, suspected black holes, and the like is accompanied by increased attention to larger-scale structures, such as recently appreciated patterns in the distribution of galaxies, which should provide important clues to cosmic evolution. Earth scientists too are both improving their predictive capacities and attending to fundamental mechanisms such as those responsible for tectonic plate movements. Biologists are attacking complexity—the development of multicellular organisms, the higher functions of the nervous system, the ecological relations among organisms and environments—while also enriching their picture of biological evolution and composing molecular scenarios for the origins of life.

## Method

A lesson driven home during the twentieth century is that there is no unitary "scientific method" applicable to all phenomena. Still, philosophers of science, historians, sociologists, and anthropologists have been busy describing scientific activities and frames of mind and calling attention to the fact that scientists function within social networks that color all scientific activity. Some of the intellectual features common to many sciences have been usefully captured by reformulating the traditional notions of personal objectivity and dispassionate inquiry in the more realistic terms of community practices and criteria. Science may seek to solve problems by framing them as testable hypotheses, susceptible to experimental or observational verification or falsification; but the problems are posed and dealt with within both historical and personal contexts. And solutions are criticized, accepted, or rejected according to community standards and paradigms. Even apparently neutral research tools like microscopes or electrical meters are freighted with community assumptions about how observations should be interpreted, conventions that have sunk from view during the long histories of their use.

One of the strengths of twentieth-century natural science has been its fluidity—the ability to adapt its strategies to the problems at hand. Old-style reductionism, with its focus on breaking complex systems down into simpler components more amenable to analysis, has retained much of its appeal. But holistic and dialectical traditions, with their efforts to confront complexity and change head-on, have had their impacts. Many of the reductionist "laws of nature" uncovered over the centuries describe repetitive phenomena: chemical reactions, mutual repulsions by bodies with similar electrical charges, the transfer of energy from one body to another. Such phenomena can be observed and dissected under controlled conditions. But the nineteenth and twentieth centuries have expanded science by dealing successfully with biological, geological, and cosmic evolution. These successes have largely stilled the debates as to whether such "historical" phenomena can also be dealt with through "truly scientific" approaches, despite their being observable as complete processes only once. Even explanations invoking prehistoric catastrophes, like the postulated impacts of enormous meteors on earth, have regained scientific respectability after the partial eclipse of such thinking during the struggles between scientific and biblical accounts of the past. Echoes of the old debates as to what constitutes science in the physical sense continue, however, often tinged with political colors, in the area of the "softer" sciences that fall outside my assigned scope—psychology, anthropology, sociology, politics, and economics.

### Autonomy and Community

Critics argue that the pragmatism of basic science, along with the patterns of recruitment, training, socialization, and funding of scientists, facilitates the focusing of the agendas of research, subtly or overtly, on the needs of dominant economic and political groups. This is one corner of the large box of issues related to questions of scientific responsibility and accountability that has filled as the scale and costs of basic research have grown and the seamier effects of scientifically founded technologies have become evident.

Basic scientists view the partial autonomy that characterizes the circumstances under which many of them work as a major contributor to their success, citing experiences such as weapons research; biologist Trofim Lysenko's derailing of genetics through an insistence on nonscientific, ideology-driven theories in Stalin's Soviet Union; or the medical research carried out in Nazi concentration camps as warnings of the baleful effects of outside political intrusion. Autonomy in day-to-day laboratory life is felt to be essential. But scientists also assert the desirability of control by their own community over matters such as decisions about which research projects should be funded, arguing that working scientists are better judges of what is likely to prove important or successful than administrators or planners.

Indeed, scientists and historians of science (Thomas Kuhn, American, 1962) sometimes imagine the history of science to have run almost independently, governed by its own internal laws of curiosity and ingenuity. Such myths of a pristine past could be sustained more easily when both "pure" science and "applied" science were less developed and when "amateur" and "professional," part-time and full-time science graded into each other. Even in the nineteenth century, the scientists working on questions of "purely scientific interest" were few in number. We picture them either as well-situated enough to fund their own research or as working at one of the handful of academic institutions, observatories, or medical establishments where research was tolerated. They relied only on an assistant or two, and communicated with one another chiefly by occasional letter or visit or by the presentation of their work at monthly or annual convocations.

Nowadays there are tens of thousands of basic researchers, working mostly in groups that can be quite large, and communicating feverishly. Funding comes almost entirely from sources outside the community of basic scientists, and while governments, foundations, military agencies, and corporations may accept, sometimes, that scientific independence can contribute to long-term productivity, they do have short-term interests and their own constituents. The inevitable consequent tensions among competing desires and myths are familiar features of twentieth-century science. But in fact, the boundary lines between "basic" and "applied" science have almost always been fragmented and permeable, often amounting to little more than matters of prestige or convention. One need not be much of a historian to trace the current situation back to the nineteenth century, when the experiences of the German chemical industry, British manufacturers, French microbiologists, American inventors and agriculturalists; and of navigators and surveyors, horticulturalists, animal breeders, surgeons, miners, and many others convinced governments, philanthropists, and academic planners of the practical benefits of organized research.

For that matter, though there is reality in the concept of a scientific community whose size, social composition, self-consciousness, and influence have changed dramatically from prior centuries, it is certainly not a cohesive and single-minded grouping, or even a precisely bounded and readily definable set of social entities. Scientists function within heterogeneous contexts and organizations with diverse, often conflicting, programs, priorities, and perspectives. Representation of the scientific community to the outside world is through a meshwork of scientific societies, government panels, national academies of eminent scientists, prestigious journals, science reporters for the mass media, and public relations divisions of universities and corporations. Merit as a scientist, and tokens such as Nobel Prizes, not representativeness or democracy, supposedly govern the choices of spokespeople.

### Is This Science Golden?

As already mentioned, scientists in the United States and elsewhere have established significant influence over the planning of national scientific programs, and retain substantial control over the institutions and practices of basic science. But beyond profiting financially, as a few do, they are generally expected not to press for rights of control over the commercial or military uses to which the products of their work are put. The investment in a large basic science establishment, the related growth and transformation of institutions such as universities into principal loci of scientific research, and the granting or retention of whatever degree of autonomy exists are, of course, predicated upon assumptions that there will be useful products; the partial screening of the basic research enterprise from direct commercial pressures is held to be an effective way of ensuring a continued flow. These assumptions, backed by examples ranging from military weapons to biotechnology and medicine, are frequently advanced as articles of faith by scientists and their allies, seeking maintenance of the status quo or expansion of support.

Riding piggyback, however, upon the expectations that profits are to be had and that life will be made tangibly better are scientific interests, some quite expensive, whose products are more abstract: the benefits of astronomy will take quite some time to reach the marketplace, and many suspect this to be the case for much of recent physics as well. The usual public presentations of this type of situation emphasize that conceptual and technical fluency can yield unanticipated technological benefits. Moreover, knowledge itself is a worthwhile goal, and the infrastructure and industries needed to sustain large scientific projects can yield national prestige or economic benefits. But these generalities provide little guidance to concrete questions about how much should be spent on what kind of science. There has been considerable shifting throughout the century in opinions about the proper roles and "neutrality" of academic institutions, and about the division of labor between knowledge-producing and knowledge-utilizing enterprises and between government-sponsored and privately controlled activities. Even while asserting its need for autonomy, basic science has thus been drawn into synergies and alliances with industry, the military, and other influential forces as it maneuvers within the political systems on which it depends for sustenance.

### Scientists Speak Mainly to Scientists

It is a commonplace that the rise of the sciences over the past few centuries has contributed not only to the prevailing optimism that humankind can solve most problems by technological manipulation of nature, but also to the secularization of Western life, to liberalization and democratization. In the present century, for example, scientists have been among the leading exponents of the international free flow of ideas, and the sciences and closely related professions, such as medicine, have offered expanding employment and career opportunities at many levels. But such impacts of science are mostly diffuse and sporadic. Moreover, they exhibit reciprocal interplays with other influences so that, for instance, the organized basic sciences—having coalesced chiefly in Western Europe and the United States—overemphasize market mechanisms and individual genius, maintain that true merit usually will win out and be appropriately rewarded, and are clumsy in allocating credit to subordinates or to scientists of the past.

In the past few decades, science has penetrated much further into educational curricula and scientists carry considerably more weight in the academic world than they had before. However, the effects on the public's fund of knowledge and the general culture, though perceptible, seem spotty and shallow. Religion certainly has not been vanquished, as some feared it might be. True, a few eminent biologists have set forth their convictions that the biological sciences will provide an enriched basis for our ethical codes by making us skeptical of absolutes while firming up our concepts of human origins, limits, and potentials. But there is not much of an audience for this kind of thinking as compared, say, with the audience for resistance to the idea of biological evolution that has been encountered prominently in the United States, a supposed fountainhead of science and technology. And though we remain optimistic about the powers of technology, a century of experience with advanced technologies of warfare, with environmental degradation, and now with seemingly intractable epidemics has taken some of the gloss off the apple. Predictably but disappointingly, our abilities to diagnose and describe problems still outrun our powers to cure them.

For the most part, scientists function within isolated enclaves that are relatively comfortable and sustaining so that many see little reason to look outside. Some express concern with the scientific literacy of the society at large, but this interest is sporadic and ambivalent. It oscillates between high-minded desires to spread the news about exciting new insights into the natural world and more practical concerns with sustaining funding, deflecting interference, and recruiting and educating the next generation of scientists and technical workers. At the beginning of this century, the conviction was widespread that science would illuminate the world for educated people. The coming century will begin with more puzzlement over where scientific thought fits in. Does it matter that basic physics cannot formulate its central concepts in ways that can be grasped without intense effort? How should policy-makers or voters respond to estimates of risk (e.g., that the ozone layer will thin or that one will contract AIDS) that are presented as statistical probabilities? How should biologists fascinated by the genetic underpinnings of life deal with the beliefs about "bad blood," racial inferiority, and the desirability of eugenic policies that, throughout the century, have surged repeatedly outside the scientific community and sometimes inside as well? Such questions ride near the surface of the intensifying turmoil over how our societies should shape and utilize their technologies. Though basic scientists may hope to float above this surface as they have tended to do in the recent past, aloofness may prove to be a privilege impossible to defend.

# 19 Paths to Discovery

NEIL DEGRASSE TYSON

## Introduction: From the Discovery of Places to the Discovery of Ideas

In how many ways is society today different from yesterday? From last year? From the last century? From the last millennium? An impressive list could be assembled, one rich with medical and scientific achievements—enough to convince nearly everyone that these are special times. While it is easy to notice what is different, the scary part is to look at what has remained the same. Behind all the technology, we are still human beings—no more or less so than those in all of recorded history. Basic forces in organized society change slowly, if at all. Compared with previous centuries, contemporary humans still exhibit primitive behavior: we climb mountains, wage war, look for sex, like to be entertained, and seek economic and political power. Complaints about the demise of society and the "youth of today" also tend to be timeless:

> The earth is degenerating these days. Bribery and corruption abound.
> Children no longer mind parents . . . and it is evident
> that the end of the world is approaching fast.
> —Assyrian Tablet engraved in 2800 B.C.

From the list of unchanging human behaviors, the urge to climb mountains may not be shared by all, but the general human quest to discover, which might drive a person to climb a mountain in the first place, is uniquely responsible for those changes in society that cross centuries. It can be strongly argued that the accumulated history of discovery is all we have to show for our civilizations because discovery is the only enterprise that builds upon itself, passes from generation to generation, and expands human understanding of the universe. This is true whether the boundary of your known world is the other side of the ocean, or the other side of the galaxy.

It is the nature of discovery for comparisons to be made between what you already know to exist and what you have just discovered. The success of prior discovery often helps to dictate the manner in which subsequent forms of discovery unfold. If you find something different, with no analog to your own experience, then it constitutes a personal discovery. If there is no analog to the world's assembly of objects, places, and knowledge, then it constitutes a discovery for all of humanity.

The act of discovery can take many forms beyond the traditional "look what I've found." Historically, discoverers were people who embarked on long voyages to the unknown. When they reached their destinations, they could see, hear, smell, feel, and taste up close what they could not from far away. Such was the age of exploration up to and including the sixteenth century. But once the world was explored and the continents were mapped, human discovery began to be characterized not by oceanic voyages, but by concepts and ideas.

The dawn of the seventeenth century saw the nearly simultaneous invention of what are arguably the two most important scientific instruments ever conceived—the microscope and the telescope. (Not that this should be a measure of importance, but they each have a star pattern named after them among the eighty-eight constellations in the sky: Microscopium and Telescopium.) The Dutch optician Anton van Leeuwenhoek introduced the microscope to the world of biology in 1590, while the Italian physicist and astronomer Galileo Galilei first turned a telescope of his own design to the sky in 1608. They each heralded an era of technology-aided discovery where the human senses were extended to reveal the natural world in unprecedented, even heretical ways. The existence of bacteria and other simple organisms that could only be revealed through a microscope introduced knowledge that transcended human experience. The fact that Galileo revealed the Sun to have spots, the planet Jupiter to have satellites, and Earth to not be the center of all motion was enough to unsettle centuries of Aristotelian teachings. Galileo was arrested, tried, and convicted by the Catholic Church.

Galileo's discoveries defied "common sense"; thus the very nature of discovery, and the paths taken to achieve it, were forever changed: no longer would common sense be the sole effective tool of intellectual investigation. Parts of nature were discovered that are, at least to the human experience, far from common. Our five senses were not only inadequate, but untrustworthy. To understand the world around you required that you trusted your measurements, whether or not they agreed with your preconceptions, providing the experiment was conducted with care and precision. The scientific method of hypothesis—unbiased testing and retesting—would rise to unprecedented significance and continue through the twentieth century. An unavoidable consequence of modern research is that, as an extension of the senses, it renders the act of discovery nearly impossible for the layperson who does not have access to the expensive detectors and laboratory equipment of the day.

## Discovery Incentives

Travel was the obvious method of choice among most historic explorers since technology had not yet progressed to allow other paths of discovery. Perhaps this limitation was known subconsciously, because it was apparently so important for European explorers to discover something that places were declared discovered—complete with flag-planting ceremonies—even when native peoples were already there to greet them on the shores. What drives us to explore? In 1969, the Apollo 11 astronauts Neil Armstrong and Edwin "Buzz" Aldrin, Jr. landed, walked, and frolicked on the Moon, and for the first time in history, humans landed somewhere other than Earth. As Western discoverers, we immediately fell back to our old imperialist ways—a flag was planted, but this time there were no natives to greet us. And, of course, the flag needed a stick inserted along its top edge to simulate a supportive breeze on that barren, airless world.

The lunar missions are generally considered to be humanity's greatest technological achievement. But I felt there should have been one or two modifications to the first words and deeds from the Moon. Upon stepping onto lunar soil, Neil Armstrong said, "That's one small step for [a] man, one giant leap for mankind" and then proceeded to plant the American flag. Perhaps the flag should have been that of the United Nations, if indeed his giant leap was for "mankind." But we all know that if he were politically honest, Armstrong would have said, "one giant leap for the U.S.A." Why? Because the revenue stream for the era of space-age discoveries was fueled by taxpayers and motivated by the prospect of military conflict with the Soviet Union; major funding requires major motivation. For this reason, war serves quite well, for it was largely responsible for projects such as the Great Wall of China, the atomic bomb, and the Soviet and American space programs. Indeed, discovery in the twentieth century was accelerated in the West because of two world wars within thirty years of each other and the protracted cold war that followed.

A close second in incentives for the major funding of projects is the prospect of high economic return. Among the most notable examples are the voyages of Columbus, whose funding level was as large a fraction of Spain's gross national product as the Apollo program was of the United States'. The

Panama Canal fulfilled in the twentieth century what Columbus failed to do in the fifteenth—it provided a shorter trading route to the Far East.

When major projects are driven primarily by the quest for human discovery, they stand the greatest chance of major breakthroughs—this is what they are designed to do—yet they simultaneously stand the worst chance of being successfully funded. The construction in the 1980s and 1990s of the superconducting supercollider, the enormous (and enormously expensive) underground particle accelerator in Texas that was to extend human understanding of the fundamental forces of nature and the conditions in the early universe, never amounted to more than a big hole in the ground. At over $10 billion, its cost was far out of proportion with the expected economic returns from spin-off technologies, with no obvious military benefit.

And when projects are driven by ego or self-promotion, they rarely, if ever, extend beyond architectural monuments. Consider the Hearst Castle in California, the Taj Mahal in India, the Great Pyramids in Egypt, and the Palace of Versailles in France—lavish monuments to individuals that make unsurpassed tourist attractions. They are also monuments to the reality that major funded projects have always been, and remain, a luxury of an either successful or exploitative society.

Most individuals cannot afford to build pyramids, and not everybody gets to be the first on the Moon, or to be the first anywhere. Yet that doesn't seem to stop the need to leave one's mark. Like animals who delineate territory with growls or urine, when flags are unavailable, a carved or painted name is left instead—no matter how sacred or revered the discovered spot may be. If Apollo 11 accidentally forgot to take the flag, what might the astronauts have chiseled into a nearby boulder? How about:

*Neil & Buzz were here*
*7/20/69*

The space program did leave behind plenty of evidence from each visit. There is all manner of hardware and other jetsam, from golf balls to automobiles, scattered about on the Moon from the six Apollo missions. The garbage-strewn lunar surface simultaneously represents the proof and the consequences of discovery.

The prospect of having something named after yourself is a strong motivation for the discoverers of comets. Amateur astronomers, who monitor the sky far more thoroughly than anybody else, are especially good at the task. Whenever you discover a bright comet, the whole world is forced to identify it with your name. Well-known examples include Comet Halley, which needs no introduction; Comet Ikeya-Seki in 1966, which was, perhaps, the most beautiful comet of the twentieth century with its long and graceful tail; Comet Hale-Bopp, discovered in 1995, which was the largest on record; and the late Comet Shoemaker-Levy 9, which plunged and exploded into Jupiter's atmosphere in July 1994 within a few days of the 25th anniversary of the Apollo 11 moon landing. These comets are among the most famous of our times, yet flags were not planted and initials were not carved.

But if money is the most widely recognized reward for achievement, then the twentieth century was off to a good start. A roll call of the world's greatest and most influential scientific discoveries can be found among the recipients of the Nobel Prize, which was endowed in perpetuity by the Swedish chemist Alfred Bernhard Nobel from the wealth he accrued by inventing dynamite. The current impressive size of the prize—approximately a million dollars—serves as an incentive, a discovery carrot for many of the world's scientists in the fields of physics, medicine and physiology, and chemistry. That the awards began in the twentieth century (the first year was 1901, five years after Nobel's death) is fortunate—scientific discovery was just then achieving a rate that could be rewarded annually. But times change. If the published volume of research articles in astrophysics—the field with which I am most familiar—can be used as a barometer, then as much has been discovered in the past fifteen years as in the entire previous history of the subject. Perhaps there will come a day when the Nobel Science Prizes are awarded monthly.

Perhaps it was inevitable, but unlike other awards for scientific achievement, the Nobel has now taken on a level of prestige that often transcends the discoveries themselves.

## Discovery and the Human Senses

If technology extends our muscle and brain power, then science extends the power of our senses beyond our inborn limits. One method to extend your senses is to move closer and get a better look: among humans, the eye is often advertised to be among the most impressive organs, with its ability to focus near and far, to adjust to varying light levels, and to distinguish colors. But if you considered the many bands of light invisible to us, you would be forced to declare humans practically blind, whether or not we can move closer for a better look. How impressive is our hearing? Bats would clearly fly circles around us with a sensitivity to pitch that extends beyond our own by an order of magnitude. And if the human sense of smell were as good as that of dogs, then Fred rather than Fido might be the one who sniffs out contraband from airport customs searches.

If the history of human discovery is characterized by a boundless desire to extend the senses, it is through this desire that we open new windows to the universe. For example, with the early Soviet and NASA probes to the Moon and planets in the 1960s, computer-controlled space probes—which we can rightly call robots—became the standard tools for space exploration. Robots in space have several clear advantages over astronauts: they are cheaper to launch, can be designed to perform experiments of very high precision without the interference of a cumbersome pressure suit, and are not alive in any traditional sense of the word, so they cannot be killed in a space accident. But until computers can simulate a human's curiosity and sparks of insight, and until computers can synthesize information and recognize a serendipitous discovery when it stares them in the face, robots will remain tools designed to discover what we already expect to find. Unfortunately, profound questions about nature can lurk among those that have yet to be asked.

The most significant improvement to our feeble senses has been the extension of our sight into the invisible bands of what is collectively known as the electromagnetic spectrum. In the late nineteenth century the German physicist Heinrich Hertz performed experiments that helped to unify conceptually what were previously considered to be unrelated forms of radiation. Radio waves, infrared light, visible light, and ultraviolet light were all revealed to be cousins in a family that simply differed in energy. The full spectrum—including all parts discovered after Hertz's work—extends from the low-energy segment we call radio waves, and continues in order of increasing energy to microwaves, infrared, visible (comprising the "rainbow seven": red, orange, yellow, green, blue, indigo, and violet), ultraviolet, x-rays, and gamma rays.

Superman, with his x-ray vision, has no special advantage over modern-day scientists. Yes, he is somewhat stronger that your average astrophysicist, but astrophysicists can now "see" into every major part of the electromagnetic spectrum. In the absence of this extended vision we are not only blind but ignorant, since the existence of many astrophysical phenomena is only revealed through some windows and not others. And if we take a selective look at some discoveries made through these windows to the universe, beginning with radio waves, we can see that each requires very different detectors from those found in the human retina.

In 1932 Karl Jansky, in the employ of Bell Telephone Laboratories and armed with a radio antenna, first "saw" radio signals that emanated from somewhere other than Earth. He had discovered the center of the Milky Way galaxy, which emitted a radio signal intense enough that, were the human eye sensitive to radio waves, it would be among the brightest sources in the sky.

Cleverly designed electronics can transmit specially encoded radio waves that can then be transformed into sound. This ingenious apparatus has come to be known as a "radio." So by virtue of extending our sense of sight, we have also in effect managed to extend our sense of hearing. Any source of radio waves, or practically any source of energy, can be channeled to vibrate the cone of a speaker, although this simple fact is occasionally misunderstood by journalists. For example, when radio emission was discovered from Saturn during the Voyager missions of the late 1970s, it was simple enough for astronomers to hook up a radio receiver that was equipped with a speaker. The radio wave signal was then converted to audible sound waves, whereupon one journalist reported that "sounds" were coming from Saturn, and that life on Saturn was trying to tell us something.

With much more sensitive and sophisticated radio detectors than were available to Karl Jansky, we now explore not just the Milky Way but the entire universe. As a testament to our initial seeing-is-believing bias, early detections of radio sources in the universe were often considered untrustworthy until they were confirmed by observations with a conventional telescope. Fortunately, most classes of radio-emitting objects also emit some level of visible light, so blind faith was not always required. Eventually, radio wave telescopes produced a rich parade of discoveries that includes the still-mysterious quasars (the word is a loosely assembled acronym of "quasi-stellar-radio-source")—the most distant objects in the known universe.

Since gas-rich galaxies emit radio waves from their abundance of hydrogen atoms (over 90 percent of all atoms in the universe are hydrogen), large arrays of electronically connected radio telescopes enable us to generate high-resolution images of a galaxy's gas content, revealing such intricate features in the hydrogen gas as twists, blobs, holes, and filaments. In many ways, the task of mapping galaxies is no different from that facing fifteenth- and sixteenth-century cartographers, whose renditions of continents—distorted though they were—represented a noble human attempt to describe worlds beyond physical reach.

If the human eye were sensitive to microwaves, then this window of the spectrum would enable you to see the radar emitted by the radar gun from the highway patrol officer hiding in the bushes, and microwave-emitting telephone relay station towers would be ablaze with light. Note, however, that the inside of your microwave oven would look no different, since the mesh embedded in the door reflects microwaves back into the cavity to prevent their escape. Your eyeball's vitreous humor is thus protected from getting cooked along with your food.

Microwave telescopes, which allow us to peer into cool, dense clouds of interstellar gas that ultimately collapse to form stars and planets, were not actively used to study the universe until the late 1960s. The heavy elements they reveal readily assemble into complex molecules, whose signature in the microwave part of the spectrum is unmistakable. They bear a compelling match to the identical molecules that exist on Earth.

Some cosmic molecules are familiar to the household:

$NH_3$ (ammonia)

$H_2O$ (water)

While some are deadly:

CO (carbon monoxide)

HCN (hydrogen cyanide)

Some remind you of the hospital:

$H_2CO$ (formaldehyde)

$C_2H_5OH$ (ethyl alcohol)

And some don't remind you of anything:

$N_2H^+$ (dinitrogen monohydride ion)

$CHC_3CN$ (cyanodiacetylene)

About 100 molecules are known, including glycine, an amino acid that is a building block for protein and thus for life as we know it. We are, indeed, made of stardust. Anton van Leeuwenhoek would be proud.

Without a doubt, the most important single discovery in astrophysics was made with a microwave telescope. The leftover heat from the big-bang origin of the universe has now cooled to a temperature of about three degrees on the "absolute" temperature scale, which quite reasonably sets the coldest possible temperature to zero degrees, so there are no negative temperatures. Absolute zero corresponds to about -460 degrees Fahrenheit, while 290 degrees absolute corresponds to room temperature. In 1965, this big-bang remnant was serendipitously measured in a Nobel Prize-winning observation conducted at Bell Telephone Laboratories by the physicists Arno Penzias and Robert Wilson. The remnant manifests itself as an omnipresent and omnidirectional ocean of light dominated by microwaves. The measured temperature is approximately 2.7 degrees, and while the light peaks strongly in microwaves, it radiates at all wavelengths.

This discovery was perhaps serendipity at its finest. Penzias and Wilson had humbly set out to find terrestrial sources that interfered with microwave communications, but what they found instead was compelling evidence for the big-bang theory of the origin of the universe—like fishing for a minnow and catching a blue whale.

Moving further along the electromagnetic spectrum, we get to infrared light. Also invisible to humans, it is most familiar to fast food fanatics who may have noticed their french fries bathing in the warmth of infrared lamps (sometimes for hours before purchase). These lamps also emit visible light, but their active ingredient is an abundance of invisible infrared photons that the food readily absorbs. As a child, I knew that at night, with the lights out, infrared vision would discover monsters hiding in the bedroom closet only if they were warm-blooded, but everybody knows that your average bedroom monster is reptilian and cold-blooded. They would thus be missed, simply blending in with the walls and the door.

If the human retina were indeed sensitive to infrared, then an ordinary household scene at night, with all lights out, would reveal all objects that sustain a temperature in excess of room temperature, such as the household iron (provided it was turned on), the metal that surrounds the pilot lights of a gas stove, the hot water pipes, and the exposed skin of any humans who stepped into the scene. Clearly this picture is not more enlightening than what you would see with visible light, but you could imagine one or two creative uses of such vision, such as looking at your home in the winter to spot where heat leaks through the windowpanes or roof.

In the universe, the infrared window is most useful as a probe of dense clouds that contain stellar nurseries. Newly formed stars are often enshrouded by leftover gas and dust. These clouds absorb most of the visible light from their embedded stars and re-radiate it in the infrared, rendering our visible light window quite useless. While visible light gets heavily absorbed by interstellar dust clouds, infrared penetrates with only minimal attenuation, which is especially valuable for studies in the plane of our own Milky Way galaxy—this is where the obscuration of visible light from the Milky Way's stars is at its greatest. Back home, infrared satellite photographs of Earth's surface reveal, among other things, the paths of warm oceanic waters such as the North Atlantic Drift current that swirls 'round the British Isles (which are farther north than the entire state of Maine) and keeps them from becoming a major ski resort.

The energy emitted by the Sun (whose surface temperature is about 6000 degrees absolute) peaks in the visible part of the spectrum, as does the sensitivity of the human retina, which is why our sight is useful in the daytime. If this spectrum match were not so, then we could rightly complain that some of our retinal sensitivity was wasted. We don't normally think of visible light as penetrating, but it passes mostly unhindered through glass and air. Ultraviolet light, however, is summarily absorbed by ordinary glass, so glass windows would not be much different from brick windows if our eyes were sensitive to only ultraviolet.

Stars that are over three or four times hotter than the Sun are prodigious producers of ultraviolet light; fortunately, they are also bright in the visible part of the spectrum, so discovering them has not depended on access to ultraviolet telescopes. Because the ozone layer in our atmosphere absorbs most of the ultraviolet, x-rays, and gamma rays that impinge upon it, a detailed analysis of these hottest stars can best be obtained only from Earth orbit or beyond. These high-energy windows in the spectrum thus represent relatively young subdisciplines of astrophysics.

As if to herald a new century of extended vision, the first Nobel Prize ever awarded in physics went to the German physicist Wilhelm C. Roentgen in 1901 for his discovery of x-rays. Both ultraviolet and x-rays can reveal the presence of one of the most exotic objects in the universe: black holes. Black holes emit no light—their gravity is too strong for even this to escape—so their existence must be inferred from the energy emitted by matter that might spiral in from a companion star (the scene resembles what water looks like as it spirals down a toilet bowl). With temperatures over twenty times that of the Sun's surface, ultraviolet and x-rays are the predominant form of energy released by material just before it descends into the black hole.

The act of discovery does not require that you understand either in advance, or after the fact, what you have discovered. This happened with the cosmic microwave background and it is happening now with gamma ray bursts. The gamma ray window has revealed mysterious, seemingly random bursts of high-energy gamma rays scattered across the sky. Their serendipitous discovery in the 1960s was made possible through the use of space-borne gamma ray detectors that were originally intended to monitor international compliance with the atmospheric test ban treaty. Yet their origin and cause remains unknown.

If we broaden the concept of discovery through vision to include the detection of subatomic particles, then we get to consider neutrinos. This elusive subatomic particle is formed every time a proton transforms into an ordinary neutron and a positron, which is the antimatter partner to an electron. As obscure as the process sounds, it happens in the Sun's core about 100 billion billion billion billion ($10^{38}$) times each second. Neutrinos then pass directly out of the Sun as if it were not there at all. A neutrino "telescope" would allow a direct view of the Sun's core and its ongoing thermonuclear fusion, which no band from the electromagnetic spectrum can reveal. But neutrinos are extraordinarily difficult to capture because they hardly ever interact with matter. So an efficient and effective neutrino telescope is a distant dream, if not an impossibility.

The detection of gravity waves, another elusive window on the universe, would reveal catastrophic cosmic events. But as of this writing, gravity waves, predicted in Einstein's General Theory of Relativity of 1916 as "ripples" in space and time, have never been detected from any source. A good gravity-wave telescope would detect colliding stars over 100 million light years away: one can imagine a future when gravitational events in the universe—collisions, explosions, and collapsed stars—are observed routinely this way. In principle we might one day see beyond the opaque wall of cosmic microwave background radiation to the big bang itself. Like Magellan's crew, who first circumnavigated Earth and saw the limits of the globe, we would then have reached and discovered the limits of the known universe.

## Discovery and Society

As a surfboard rides a wave, the industrial revolution rode the eighteenth and nineteenth centuries on the crest of decade-by-decade advances in our understanding of energy as a physical concept and as a transmutable entity. For example, steam engines convert heat into mechanical energy, dams convert the gravitational potential energy of water into electricity, and dynamite converts chemical energy into explosive shock waves. Engineering technology replaced muscle energy with machine energy. In a remarkable parallel to the way these discoveries transformed society, the twentieth century saw information technology ride the crest of advances in electronics and miniaturization to forge an era that replaced mind power with computer power. Now exploration and discovery occur on wafers of silicon in nations where the work of computers has replaced what would have been lifetimes of calculations. But we may still be groping in the dark: as our area of knowledge grows, so does the perimeter of our ignorance.

What is the influence of all this technology and cosmic discovery on society? Aside from creating more effective instruments of destruction and further excuses to wage war, there are other more lasting effects on the social landscape. For example, the nineteenth and early twentieth centuries saw the development of transportation that did not rely on the energy of domestic animals, including the bicycle, the train, the automobile, and the airplane. The twentieth century also introduced new forms of propulsion with the help of rocket pioneer Robert Goddard, and space ships with the help of the German rocket engineer Werner von Braun when he was transported to the United States to help launch our space program at the conclusion of the Second World War.

The discovery of improved means of transportation was especially crucial to geographically large (and habitable) nations such as the United States So important is transportation to Americans that the disruption of traffic by any means, even if it occurs in another country, can make headlines. For example, on August 7, 1945, the day after Americans killed 50,000 Japanese in the city of Hiroshima, the front page of the *New York Times* read: THE FIRST ATOMIC BOMB DROPPED ON JAPAN. But a smaller headline, also on the front page, read "Trains Canceled in Stricken Area; Traffic Around Hiroshima Is Disrupted." I do not know for sure, but I would bet that the Japanese newspapers of the day did not consider traffic jams to be a front-page aspect of this particular event.

By installing electricity into every domicile, appliances and machines could then be invented to consume this new source of energy: to anthropologists, one of the broad measures of a society's advancement is its per capita consumption of energy. But old traditions die hard: we still measure car engines in "horse" power. While light bulbs are a substitute for candles, we still light candles during dinner, and buy electric chandeliers that hold light bulbs shaped like candle flames. The dependence upon electricity, especially among urban Americans, has reached irreversible levels. Witness New York City during the blackouts of 1966 and 1978, when this decidedly twentieth-century luxury was temporarily removed from the population. In 1966 many thought the world was going to end, and in 1978 there was widespread looting. Apparently, our discoveries and inventions have gone from making life easier to becoming a requirement for survival.

Throughout history, discovery has held risks and dangers for the discoverers themselves. Neither Magellan nor most of his crew lived through their around-the-world voyage in 1575. Most died of disease and starvation. Magellan himself was killed by natives who were not impressed with his attempts to Christianize them. Modern-day risks can be no less devastating: the three crew members of Apollo 1 burned to death on the launch pad in 1966, and the space shuttle Challenger exploded shortly after launch in 1986, killing all seven of its crew. At the end of the nineteenth century, Wilhelm Roentgen and Marie Curie pioneered high-energy radiation— Roentgen explored the properties of x-rays, and Curie the properties of radioactive elements. Each died of cancer.

In some cases, the risks extend far beyond the discoverers. In 1905, Albert Einstein introduced the equation $E=mc^2$, the unprecedented recipe to interchange mass with energy, which ultimately begat atomic bombs. Coincidentally, just two years before the first appearance of Einstein's famous equation, the airplane was invented, which would be the vehicle to deliver the first atomic bombs during warfare. Shortly after the airplane's invention, a letter to the editor in the magazine *Scientific American* expressed concern over possible misuses of the new flying machine. The letter noted that if evil people took command, then they might fly the "aeroplane" over villages and toss canisters of nitroglycerin on innocent people who would have no hope of defense.

Wilbur and Orville Wright are, of course, no more to blame for the deaths by military application of the airplane than Albert Einstein is to blame for the deaths by atomic bombs. These are just examples of discoveries that—for better or for worse—live in the public domain and are thus subject to some of those primitive human behavior patterns that never seem to change.

## Discovery and the Human Ego: A Recent Example

The history of human ideas about our place in the universe has been a long series of letdowns for all those who like to believe we are special. Unfortunately, first impressions have consistently fooled us—the daily motions of the Sun, Moon, and stars all conspire to make it look as though we are the center of everything. But we have learned over the centuries. There is no center of Earth's surface, so no culture can claim (geometrically) to be in the middle of things. Earth is not the center of the solar system; it is just one of nine planets in orbit around the Sun—a revelation secured by Nicolaus Copernicus in the fifteenth century and Galileo in the sixteenth. The Sun is 25,000 light years from the middle of the Milky Way galaxy and revolves anonymously around the galactic center along with hundreds of billions of other stars. The Milky Way is just one of perhaps a hundred billion galaxies in a universe that actually has no center at all. And of course with Charles Darwin's nineteenth-century *Origin of Species* and *The Descent of Man*, the creative act of divinity was no longer necessary to explain human origins.

Rarely is scientific discovery the consequence of an instantaneous act of brilliance. The revelation that our Milky Way galaxy is neither special nor unique was no exception. This generally recognized turning point in human understanding of our place in the cosmos occurred not centuries ago, but in 1920, when a now-famous debate on the extent of the known universe was held in what is now the Baird Auditorium of the Smithsonian Natural History Building at a meeting of the National Academy of Sciences in Washington, D.C. There were two fundamental questions: Was the Milky Way galaxy—

complete with its stars and star clusters, gas clouds and fuzzy spiral things—all there was to the universe? Or were those fuzzy spiral things galaxies unto themselves, just like the Milky Way, dotting the unimaginable vastness of space like "island universes"?

Scientific discovery, unlike political conflict or public policy, does not normally emerge from democratic vote, party-line politics, or public debate. But in this case, the two leading scientists of the day, each armed with some good data, some bad data, and sharpened arguments, went head-to-head over the question. The proponent of the idea that the Milky Way is the full extent of the universe was Harlow Shapley of the Mount Wilson Observatories, who would later forge a visible and influential career as the director of the Harvard College Observatory. The opposing view, which held that the Milky Way galaxy isn't so special, was defended by Heber D. Curtis of the Lick Observatories in California. He later became the director of the Allegheny Observatory and receded from active research.

Both scientists participated in a wave of discoveries in the early twentieth century that were derived primarily from classification schemes for cosmic objects and phenomena. With the help of a spectrograph (which can break up starlight into its component colors the way raindrops can break up sunlight into a rainbow), astrophysicists were able to classify objects not just by their shape or outward appearance but by the detailed features revealed in their spectra. A well-designed classification scheme, one that might include information obtained from an object's spectrum, can allow profound deductions to be made even if the cause or origin of a phenomenon is not fully understood.

The nighttime sky displays a grab-bag of objects whose classifications were not subject to much disagreement in 1920. Among them are three that were especially relevant to the debate: 1. the stars—found in higher concentrations along a narrow band of blended light called the Milky Way, which was by then widely (and correctly) interpreted to be the flattened plane of our galaxy; 2. the hundred or so titanic, globularly shaped star clusters—slightly more common near the plane, and found more toward one direction of the sky than all others; and 3. the inventory of fuzzy nebulae—including the amorphous varieties that predominate near the plane along with the stars, and the spiral nebulae that seem to avoid the plane completely. Both Shapley and Curtis knew that whatever else was argued, these basic observed features of the sky could not be reasoned away.

It is sometimes said that if an argument lasts more than a few minutes, then both sides are wrong. A splendid aphorism, but there are at least two other causes of a protracted disagreement: one is insufficient quality or quantity of data, another, that at least one party is too stubborn to abandon a long-held view. In the published version of the Shapley-Curtis debate, heavily edited from transcripts of the actual event, there was a bit of stubbornness on both sides, but each argued admirably. And what mattered in the end was the relative confidence they each placed on the scant data available. If Harlow Shapley could interpret the available data in such a way that the distances to spiral nebulae placed them within the bounds of the Milky Way, then there would remain no evidence in support of external systems. If Heber Curtis, interpreting the same data, could show that the spiral nebulae were distant island universes, then humanity would be handed the next chapter in its long series of ego-busting discoveries.

Shapley's favorite research topic was globular star clusters, so he had much to say about them. Indeed, he is best remembered for his clever and correct suggestion that the center of the system of globular clusters coincides with the center of the galaxy. The observed excess of globular clusters off to one side of the sky must then reveal the direction, and possibly the distance, to the middle of the Milky Way. Thus he reasoned that the solar system was not in the center, as believed by Curtis and many others, but far out in the plane of the galaxy. Some astronomers counted stars, which suggested that the solar system was in the center of the galaxy. The argument was simple: stars appear uniformly spread in all directions along the Milky Way on the sky. But nobody knew that the Milky Way contains a mixture of stars and obscuring dust clouds, which renders the lines of sight insufficient to see the entire galaxy. In other words, you can't identify where you are in the Milky Way because the Milky Way is in the way. Nothing unusual here: the moment you enter a dense forest, you have no idea where you are (unless, of course, you had carved your initials into tree bark on a previous visit): the extent of the forest is unknown because the trees are in the way.

Noting that globular clusters contain so many stars of nearly all common varieties, Shapley assumed them to be a representative mix of the stars that one might find in our own solar neighborhood, whose properties and distances were well known. Shapley therefore consistently got distances much larger than anybody else. For example, here are some estimates made by leading astronomers (including two from Shapley) of the distance from the solar system to a globular cluster called M13 in the constellation Hercules:

- Shapley 1915: 100,000 light years
- Charlier 1916: 170 light years
- Shapley 1917: 36,000 light years

- Schouten 1918: 4,300 light years
- Lundmark 1920: 21,700 light years

The widely ranging distances to the same cluster demonstrate that astronomers of the day were generally clueless. Shapley felt strongly that the Hercules cluster, with its 100,000 tightly packed stars and its (assumed) representative sample of all stars, would allow him to use M13 as a stepping-stone to more distant globular clusters:

> The great globular cluster in Hercules [is] a vast sidereal organization. When we accept the view that . . . its stellar phenomena are harmonious with local stellar phenomena . . . then it follows that fainter, smaller globular clusters are still more distant.

After computing the distances to globular clusters beyond M13, Shapley ended up with a galactic system over 300,000 light years in extent. This was far and away the largest estimate ever made (before or since) for the size of the Milky Way. Curtis could not specifically fault Shapley's reasoning that the globular clusters might contain stars similar to those found in the local neighborhood, but he remained skeptical nonetheless, stating that "there are many who will regard [this] assumption as a rather drastic one."

Indeed, it was a drastic one. But Shapley's confidence was fueled by the work of Henry Norris Russell and Sir Arthur Eddington, two leading theorists of the day, who proffered compelling ideas about the internal structure of stars and stellar evolution. Shapley was clear and direct about the grim consequences for astrophysics in the 1920s if his opponent's ideas were correct:

> I believe [Henry Norris] Russell's illuminative theory of spectral evolution would have to be largely abandoned, and [Sir Arthur] Eddington's brilliant theory of gaseous giant stars would need to be greatly modified or given up entirely . . . [and] identical spectral characteristics [would] indicate stars differing in [luminosity] by 100 to 1, depending only upon whether the star is in the solar neighborhood or in a distant cluster.

But how was Shapley to know that Russell's theory of spectral evolution would eventually be shown to be completely wrong, and that Eddington's theory of gaseous giants would ultimately require serious modification? How was he to know that the nearest high-luminosity blue stars bear little resemblance to the blue stars in globular clusters? These overestimates in stellar luminosities led him to overestimate the distances to all his globular clusters.

In Shapley's view, if you measure the extent of the globular clusters, then you have measured the extent of the Milky Way galaxy. But Curtis remained convinced that the Milky Way galaxy was much smaller than Shapley suggested:

> Until more definite evidence to the contrary is available, however, I feel that the evidence for the smaller and commonly accepted galactic dimensions is still stronger; and that the postulated diameter of 300,000 light years must quite certainly be divided by five, and perhaps by ten.

Who was right? Along most paths from scientific ignorance to scientific discovery, the correct answer lies somewhere between the extreme estimates collected along the way. Such was the case in the great debate: the generally accepted extent of the stars of the Milky Way galaxy is about 100,000 light years, which is about three times Curtis's 30,000 and one third of Shapley's 300,000.

This famously disagreed-upon extent of the Milky Way still needed to be reconciled with the existence of the spiral nebulae, whose distances were more uncertain than those of any other class of object. Shapley was determined to show that they were no farther than the extent of the Milky Way established by the globular clusters. Both Shapley and Curtis knew that unlike other types of nebulae—which are heavily concentrated toward the plane of the Milky Way—the spirals seem to avoid the plane completely. This recognition earned the Milky Way's appearance in the nighttime sky the alternative and somewhat spooky title, "Zone of Avoidance." The two astronomers also knew that the typical velocities of nebulae near the plane are less than one hundred kilometers per second, while those of the spiral nebulae are thousands of kilometers per second. Shapley was thus forced to suggest that the spiral nebulae had somehow been created in the Milky Way at a regular rate and then forcibly ejected from their birthplace.

Curtis remained the skilled skeptic. He wanted to know why there was no ongoing evidence for spirals being created within the Milky Way. Why weren't at least some of the spirals ejected within the plane of the Milky Way? These were questions to which Shapley had no answer.

And Curtis was convinced that the spiral nebulae were the same class of object as the Milky Way galaxy itself. He assembled a cogent line of reasoning to support this island universe hypothesis, remarking that the spectrum of an entire spiral nebula greatly resembles the combined spectrum of star clusters in the Milky Way. It was a similarity that he uncovered by direct observation rather than by inference:

The spectrum of the average spiral [nebula] is indistinguishable from that given by a star cluster . . . and in general characteristics resembles closely the integrated spectrum of our Milky Way. It is just such a spectrum as would be expected from vast congeries of stars.

Curtis noted next that spiral nebulae on the sky are oriented at all angles to the viewer. Some are seen face-on while others are seen edge-on. The edge-on ones typically reveal dark obscuring patches along their plane. All of this was well known and noncontroversial, but Curtis put it together, arriving at another powerful inference:

So many edgewise spiral [nebulae] show peripheral rings of occulting matter that this dark ring may well be the rule rather than the exception. If our galaxy, itself a spiral in the island universe theory, possesses such a peripheral ring of occulting matter, this would obliterate the distant spirals [from view] in our galactic plane, and would explain the peculiar apparent distribution of spirals.

At this point, had I been the moderator, I might have ended the debate, declared Curtis the winner, and sent everybody home, but there was further evidence at hand. It was well known that in the Milky Way, stars have occasionally been known to appear out of nowhere with tremendous brightness. These new stars were named "novae," derived from the Latin word for "new." Such novae had also been observed in several spiral nebulae, including the most famous spiral of them all, the oversized Great Nebula in Andromeda. Curtis made the assumption that novae form a homogeneous class of objects, which allowed him to draw yet another powerful inference:

Correlations between the novae in the spiral [nebulae] and those in our galaxy indicate distances ranging from perhaps 500,000 light years in the case of the Nebula in Andromeda, to 10,000,000 or more light years for the more remote spirals. . . . At such distances, these island universes would be of the same order of size as our own galaxy.

Perhaps the most commonly invoked evidence against this interpretation (lodged by Shapley and others of the day) was the anomalously bright nova of 1885 in the Andromeda nebula. If the Andromeda nebula were as distant as Curtis suggested, it would imply that this "super" nova must have had the luminosity of nearly a billion suns—a preposterous thought in 1920. Shapley reasoned that if the spiral nebulae were actually the size of the Milky Way, then they must be very distant to appear so small on the sky, and "it would be necessary to ascribe impossibly great [luminosities] to the new stars that have appeared in the spiral nebulae." Only later would the community of astrophysicists discover that there is another variety of "nova" that indeed reaches the luminosity of a billion suns. What do we call them? Supernovae, of course.

Even though Shapley discounted the spiral nebulae as island universes, he no doubt wanted to appear open-minded. In his summary statement, which reads like a disclaimer, Shapley entertained the possibility of other worlds:

> But even if spirals fail as galactic systems, there may be elsewhere in space stellar systems equal to or greater than ours—as yet unrecognized and possibly quite beyond the power of existing optical devices and present measuring scales. The modern telescope, however, with such accessories as high-power spectroscopes and photographic intensifiers, is destined to extend the inquiries relative to the size of the universe.

And Curtis openly conceded that Shapley might be onto something with his hypothesis that spiral nebulae were ejected, especially since the high velocities of the spiral nebulae were not controversial. In his concession, Curtis simultaneously (yet unwittingly) revealed that we live in an expanding universe:

> The repulsion theory, it is true, is given some support by the fact that most of the spirals observed to date are receding from us.

Curtis's views were ultimately shown to be closer to the truth that those of Shapley, in spite of their relative career paths after the debate. By 1929, Edwin Hubble had officially discovered that nearly all galaxies recede from the Milky Way with speeds in direct proportion to their distance. It was self-evident that we, the Milky Way galaxy, were in the center of the expansion of the universe. Hubble was an attorney before becoming an astronomer, so had he debated other scientists, he probably would have won no matter what he argued, but he clearly had the evidence for an expanding universe with us at the center. But in the context of Albert Einstein's 1916 General Theory of Relativity, the illusion of Earth at the center was a natural consequence of a universe that expands in four dimensions, with time as the fourth dimension. In this description, every galaxy would observe all other galaxies to recede as well. Conclusion: We are not alone, and we are not special.

As if all that weren't enough, the onward movement toward our own insignificance continued with a vengeance.

In 1926, the physicist Hans Bethe of Cornell University suggested that the fuel source in the Sun was a thermonuclear fusion of hydrogen into helium, an idea that later would win him the Nobel Prize. In 1948 the astrophysicists Geoffrey Burbidge, Margaret Burbidge, William Fowler, and Fred Hoyle deduced the cosmic abundance of chemical elements by describing in detail the sequence of thermonuclear fusion that unfolds in the cores of high-mass stars. Most of these stars explode as supernovae that enrich the universe with elements from all over the famed Periodic Table. The tally's top five were hydrogen, helium, oxygen, carbon, nitrogen. When we look at the chemical constituents of human life we find precisely that sequence of elements— excluding helium, which is chemically inert. Not only is our existence as human beings not unique, but neither are the ingredients of life itself.

Now that we have good evidence that we were not divinely created and are not in the center of anything, and are not made of special ingredients, there remains one fact that may be the greatest insult of all. Over 90 percent of the gravity in the universe is not attributable to visible matter but to some thing that is yet to be discovered or understood—a dilemma that forms the basis for the famous "dark matter" problem in astrophysics.

The nature of cosmic discovery has descended from glorifying God to glorifying human life to insulting our ego.

## The Future of Discovery

When (or if) space ever becomes our final frontier, it will represent uncharted territories akin to those of the ancient explorers. The voyages may be economically driven with the intent to mine million-ton asteroids for their mineral resources, or the voyages may be survival-motivated with the intent to spread the human species around the galaxy as much as possible, thus avoiding total human extinction from a once-in-thirty-million-years impact catastrophe with a comet.

The golden era of space exploration was no doubt the 1960s, but at that time, the meaning and significance of the space program was somewhat muddled in many urban centers due to widespread poverty, urban riots, and poor educational systems. Many decades later, its meaning and significance remains muddled in many urban centers due to widespread poverty, urban riots, and poor educational systems. But there is a fundamental difference. In the 1960s, the discoveries of the future were something that everybody looked forward to.

For example, I remember the day and the moment when the Apollo 11 astronauts first landed on the Moon. The landing was undoubtedly one of the twentieth century's greatest moments. But I found myself to be somewhat indifferent to the event—not because I couldn't appreciate its rightful place in human history, but because I had every reason to believe that trips to the Moon would become a monthly procession. As a child of the 1960s, this expectation of the future guided my aspirations, my hopes, and my dreams. It started with President John F. Kennedy's speech, when he declared that before the decade was over we would send a man to the Moon and return him safely to Earth. Then there was the ongoing space program, with each mission more ambitious than the next. And then, there was Stanley Kubrick's 1967 visionary film, *2001: A Space Odyssey*, with its space stations and moon bases. When I added all this together, it was perfectly clear to me that voyages to the Moon were simply the next step. Little did I know that they might become our last steps in the twentieth century. In retrospect, I now regret that I did not feel more emotion back on July 20, 1969. I should have reveled in the landing as the singular achievement it has become.

As already noted, the funding stream for the space program had been primarily defense-driven: cosmic dreams and the innate human desire to explore the unknown were of lesser significance. But we can reinterpret the word "defense" to mean something far more important than armies and arsenals. It can mean the defense of the human species itself.

In July of 1994, the equivalent of over two hundred thousand megatons of TNT was deposited in Jupiter's upper atmosphere as comet Shoemaker-Levy 9 slammed into the planet. If this type of collision were to happen on Earth, it would very likely be responsible for the abrupt extinction of the human species.

If we retain "defense of the human species" as a theme, then we have a genuine cosmic vision to save our distant future. The most effective ways to do this are: 1. to acquire the most thorough understanding of Earth's climate and ecosystem that we possibly can, which will minimize risk of self-destruction; and 2. colonize space in as many places as possible, proportionally reducing the chance of species annihilation from a once-in-a-million-years collision between Earth and a comet discovered by an amateur astronomer.

The fossil record teems with extinct species—species of life that thrived far longer than the current Earth-tenure of *Homo sapiens*. Dinosaurs are on this list, extinct today because they did not build spacecraft. Did they not have a space program because there were no funds available? Maybe, but not likely. It was probably because their brains were tiny. Let it be known that if humans become extinct, there would be no greater tragedy in the history of life in the universe—not because we lacked the brain power to build interplanetary spacecraft, not because we lacked an active program of space travel, but because the human species itself chose not to fund such a survival plan. For the first time, the path of discovery found in space exploration could become a necessity rather than an intellectual luxury. The survival of even those who quietly remain unenlightened (or untainted) by the history of discovery depends on it.

# 20 Twentieth-Century Medicine

DAVID ROSNER

The human experience with disease, and expectations regarding the value of curative medicine, have been fundamentally transformed over the course of this century. In the first decades, disease was largely perceived as an inevitable event that could strike anyone at essentially any age. Broad cross sections of the world's population, for example, saw infectious diseases, and particularly tuberculosis, as continual threats whose occurrence could easily lead to death. The medical and public health professions, while depended upon for diagnosis and interventions, were rarely seen as capable of fundamentally altering the natural history of a disease. By mid-century, however, public attitudes and expectations regarding the power of modern medicine had fundamentally altered, as public expectations regarding the ability of science and medicine to cure rose dramatically.

The growing faith in medicine led to paradoxical social results. On the one hand, powerful tools such as antibiotics and sulfa drugs were developed and proved invaluable in treating many of the bacterial diseases. On the other hand, the growing faith in the power of scientific medicine to cure sometimes resulted in harmful social policies and personal activities. For example, despite growing knowledge of the dangers posed by tobacco, many rationalized their smoking by the belief that science would ultimately develop a cure for cancer. Further, enormous social resources were poured into high-technology medical centers despite the fact that for much of the world's population, the major health problems could be addressed through much less costly improvements in nutrition, education, preventive public health measures, and housing.

This essay will outline some of the major changes that have transformed public expectations of medicine during the course of the century, and the changing attitudes toward disease as infectious diseases appeared to be waning and as chronic, noncommunicable diseases gained the attention of the public in industrialized societies. It will also trace the growing belief in the "curability" of most diseases, and the parallel but contradictory evidence that the chronic diseases of the late twentieth century could not be addressed using the same tools and assumptions that had previously governed medical thought. A central focus is the changing relationship of humans to their environment and its impact on conceptions of health in the twentieth century.

## I

In a 1982 essay on what he calls "framing" disease, historian Charles Rosenberg noted that "disease is at once a biological event, a generation-specific repertoire of verbal constructs reflecting medicine's intellectual and institutional history," and "a sanction for cultural values." Pointing out that disease is a "social phenomenon," he illustrates that in large measure, "disease does not exist until we have agreed that it does, by perceiving, naming, and responding to it."[1] Whether they be infectious diseases like tuberculosis, yellow fever, or cholera in the nineteenth century; or cancer, heart disease, or occupational illness in the middle decades of this century; or AIDS (Acquired Immune Deficiency Syndrome) and drug-resistant tuberculosis today, disease is emblematic of the specific society at a particular moment in history. Not only do we define different symptoms as pathological events, we also create the physical environments and social relationships that allow for the emergence of new problems. As we create our physical and intellectual environments, we create the conditions within which diseases thrive and are defined.

Throughout much of world history, differing cultures have shared some basic assumptions about the nature of diseases that plague them. For Western Europeans, Asians, and African peoples, disease has often been understood as a form of divine retribution for the sins of the individual or the community. In East Asian cultures, as Kureyana Shigehisa noted in his 1993 article, "intimations of sickness as punishment can be traced [to] fears of ancestral ire, and the moral failings of more than one emperor . . . would be blamed later for the epidemics that devastated their people."[2] In Western cultures as well, the visitations of plagues were often followed by religious awakenings, days of prayer and introspection. But persecutions came as well—of individuals and groups whose purported gluttony, greed, pride, or transgressions were thought to be responsible for collective suffering. From smallpox to AIDS, from China to the United States, the idea that disease reflects the immorality of the individual and is retribution for the transgressions of the community has been a powerful force in shaping our responses to it.

Throughout much of the nineteenth century, medical thought and therapeutics often reflected the underlying assumption regarding the moral basis
for disease. Individuals were thought to be susceptible to illness when flaws in
their character, behavior, social position, religious beliefs, or physical environment left them vulnerable. When communities were struck by epidemics,
recent disruptions in the life of the community were often seen as responsible. The transformation of an agricultural to a commercial economy in which
new classes emerged or new religious groups assumed more prominent social
positions could be used to explain the appearance of epidemic diseases. The
movement of a new group of people into an older, more established community could inflame ancient hatreds—especially when accompanied by smallpox, fevers, or plagues. In circumstances where different populations experienced dramatically different rates of disease and death, those that survived
understood their experience as an indication of their personal or collective
superiority.

Throughout the twentieth century as well, the underlying assumption that
ties disease and health to sin and virtue has shaped social, institutional, and
political responses. Few of us have not experienced the subtle and not-very-
subtle ways that illness has been used as a type of individual or social judgment. Few have not had a loved one who has been told that his or her cancer
was a result of some real or imagined personal habit. And presently, few suf-
ferers from AIDS have not experienced the power of social opprobrium and
familial judgments.

While the limitations of pre-twentieth-century views of disease are obvious and their continuing impact disturbing, some aspects of the link between
individual circumstance and disease led to important therapeutic perspectives among both physicians and laypeople. Nineteenth-century medical
thought held that diseases were primarily collections of symptoms caused by
a host of different environmental or personal peculiarities and highly idiosyncratic factors. As Morris Vogel and Charles Rosenberg write in their 1979
work on the social history of medicine in America, "the body was seen,
metaphorically, as a system of dynamic interactions with its environment.
Health or disease resulted from a cumulative interaction between constitutional endowment and environmental circumstance."[3]

This emphasis on the importance of individual character and circumstance as a determinant of susceptibility led physicians and patients alike to
believe that disease had to be understood in highly individualized terms. It
was the special circumstance of the patient, or his or her social group, that
determined the type of care provided: therapy itself had to be molded, there-

fore, around the special peculiarities of the individual and his or her community. In Western cultures, rather than seek a uniform or standardized treatment for a given disease, physicians treated symptoms individually and rarely prescribed the same treatments. From the perspective of the diagnosing physician, the collection of symptoms that constituted "hysteria" and "neurasthenia" among Victorian women, for example, varied greatly from patient to patient. The same symptoms could be linked to the ongoing, long-term moral and social environment that predisposed a victim to a disease process, or could be rooted in personal characteristics such as drinking, social position, poor living conditions, or work. Throughout much of the nineteenth century, as John Harley Warner observes in his history of nineteenth-century American therapeutics, "Treatment was to be sensitively gauged not to a disease entity but to such distinctive features of the patient as age, gender, ethnicity, race, socio-economic position, and moral status, and to attributes of place like climate, topography and population density."[4]

Pre-twentieth-century perspectives on the relationship of humans and disease generally emphasized that healthfulness reflected a balance between humans and their environment. Humans in natural settings were healthy—it was assumed—and only spiritual, physical, or social disruptions to that natural state allowed diseases to take their toll. Much of medical practice in both industrial and nonindustrial societies rested on the assumption that the goal of the physician was to reestablish the natural balance between humans and their environments, and much of the discourse among healers as well as laypeople centered on an "ecological" notion of disease. Thus some groups of healers saw their role as a restorative one, aiding nature in the act of healing.

## II

Between 1860 and 1900, medical theory about the causes of disease in human populations underwent profound changes that would ultimately alter both clinical practice and the organization of health-related services throughout much of the world. Traditional beliefs that held disease to be a result of personal, moral, or religious transgressions or reflections of personal characteristics and social circumstances were replaced with what came to be called the "germ theory" of disease. In contrast to seeing disease as a collection of symptoms that might reflect a variety of different causes, the new germ theory sought to identify specific pathogens—what we would now call bacteria or viruses—with specific diseases. Yellow fever, malaria, typhus, and typhoid sometimes share similar symptoms, such as chills, fevers, intense headaches, and jaundice; but with the advent of microscopy, staining techniques, and methods for growing bacterial cultures, they could be identified as different conditions.

The new theory held up the hope that once a particular pathogen was discovered, a specific medicine or treatment could be developed that would cure the disease by destroying the agent that "caused" it. In France in the 1860s Louis Pasteur identified microorganisms as the agents responsible for fermentation; in the mid-1880s, he developed an effective vaccine against rabies. German bacteriologist Robert Koch is credited with "proving" the germ theory in 1877, identifying the microscopic entity associated with anthrax, a deadly and fairly common nineteenth-century disease transmitted from domesticated farm animals to humans. In the following decade, Koch strengthened his reputation as a founder of modern bacteriology by identifying the tuberculosis and cholera bacilli. In 1890, Emil Behring and Shibasaburo Kitasato developed an effective antitoxin for diphtheria, a terrifying disease of children that suffocated between 30 and 50 percent of its victims. With the revolution in bacteriology that followed the discoveries of Pasteur and Koch, a new faith in laboratory science emerged not only among physicians but also among public health workers. "Bacteriology," according to medical historian Elizabeth Fee, writing in 1987, "became an ideological marker, sharply differentiating the 'old' public health . . . from the 'new' . . . which belonged to scientifically trained professionals."[5]

The twentieth century began with enormous optimism about medicine's ability to develop cures for some of the age-old scourges of the human race. Fee quotes William Segewick, an eminent American bacteriologist at the Massachusetts Institute of Technology who looked at the revolution that took over in the universities of Western and Central Europe and the United States: "Before 1880 we knew nothing; after 1890 we knew it all; it was a glorious ten years."[6]

Throughout Europe and the United States, medical and popular literature foresaw a time when prevailing diseases would be but distant memories, with humans expecting to reach old age protected by modern medicines, vaccines, and treatments. It was considered only a matter of time before bacteriologists identified the "cause" of any specific disease, be it tuberculosis, diphtheria, yellow fever, polio, or any other, the only delay in discovering a remedy being the limitations of laboratory techniques.

The bacterial revolution affected the less industrialized world as profoundly as it did Western Europe and North America. Tropical medicine and hygiene, along with military medicine, for example, underwent what medical historian Philip Curtin has described as a "revolutionary change" during the late nineteenth and early twentieth centuries. At the core of this change was, as Curtin writes, "the germ theory of Robert Koch, Louis Pasteur and other microbiologists."[7] Publications on public health practice appearing as late as 1874 in Africa and India were often aimed at informing local public health officials how sanitary science and architecture could be used to protect the public from disease. Open-air structures, for instance, would allow light and dissipate TB bacilli, and proper drainage would protect against cholera and insect-borne diseases. Medical publications of the day often reflected traditional local practices and customs, but by 1894 a more international literature began to dominate the professional communities throughout the world, and local medical and public health literature came to resemble materials that might easily have been found in London and Paris. In the world of public health, the victories of the nineteenth-century emphasis on engineering techniques such as water filtration could now be rationally explained. Yet, as Curtin notes, imperial relationships not only allowed for the development of treatments and preventive techniques, they also caused disease. Grouping large concentrations of men in armies and urban areas helped spawn outbreaks of infectious disease, and created immense sanitary problems that required way more funding than European powers were willing to spend on indigenous populations. But for the armies of Britain and France, Curtin maintains that the germ theory—combined with better nutrition—vastly improved their health experience in the decades immediately surrounding World War I.[8] It also benefited Europeans in general.

As the imagery and metaphors of war began to dominate twentieth-century medical and public health literature, from around 1910 through the 1970s, an internationalizing medical and public health community largely accepted the view that technologies and curative medicine could win "battles" against viruses, bacteria, and other parasites that depended upon human hosts. "Crusades" against tuberculosis, polio, and a host of infectious childhood diseases culminated in "campaigns" and the "March of Dimes"; "magic bullets" were sought to fight venereal diseases such as syphilis and gonorrhea. In the 1920s popular literature hailed the x-ray and radiotherapy, along with radium, as the latest weapons in the fight against disease. In the United States, Superman's x-ray vision was used to thwart evil just as the roentgen ray was used to destroy tumors or identify disease processes invisible to the naked eye. In England, Germany, France, and the United States, parades and propaganda barrages marked the start of popular efforts to wipe out disease just as they might mark the beginning of military actions.

As Susan Sontag points out in her book *Illness as Metaphor*, the prominent metaphor for describing disease became warfare; then attitudes followed suit: rather than seeking to understand disease as a reflection of an imbalance between humans and their environment—or as an ecological issue—people talked about bacteria as entities that had to be "conquered," "vanquished," "obliterated," and even "annihilated," "exterminated" or "destroyed."[9] The patient had to be cured through the use of antidotes that "attacked" the pathogens or the "aggressive" tumors seeking to "invade" healthy tissue. Broad cross sections of professionals and public in European and North American societies shared the assumption that death and disease were products of a hostile nature, which produced enemies in the form of bacteria, viruses, or cancers, and only through equally invasive measures could be stopped. Vast resources were poured into hospitals—the castles where surgeons would cut out disease and doctors analyze the course of the battle—and into laboratories, where the pharmaceutical weapons would be manufactured, bacteria cultured, vaccines produced and diseases identified. One of the best overviews of the history of infectious disease, Harry Dowling's tellingly entitled *Fighting Infection: Conquests of the Twentieth Century* (1977), begins with a chapter on "The Field of Battle" and concludes with "The Continuing War."[10]

The cultural agreement that saw disease as the enemy in Western societies, and particularly the United States, allowed for some of the most striking advances in the fight against it. Paul Ehrlich's magic bullet for syphilis, the drug Salvarsan, along with other treatments of venereal diseases in the early decades are the stuff of medical and popular folklore. Ehrlich's life, in fact, was made into a major motion picture starring Paul Muni. Alexander Fleming, a British bacteriologist, discovered penicillin in 1928, and by mid-century a host of other antibiotics, along with sulfa drugs, became powerful weapons in the battles against bacterial diseases. In the 1950s and 1960s, the development of vaccines for protection against polio, diphtheria, whooping cough, and measles strengthened the post-World War II belief in the powers of science to improve the lives of millions throughout the world. Tuberculosis appeared to be ever decreasing and smallpox—perhaps the most dreaded affliction because of its lethal, epidemic spread and lasting scars—was eradicated by the development and deployment of vaccines in nearly every country.

During the war years of the 1940s and continuing through the 1950s, an explosion of drugs appeared that continually reinforced the belief in the curative powers of medicine and medical science to ultimately control and protect us from age-old scourges. Broad cross sections of the world's professional and dominant classes believed that ultimately, medical science and technology could protect us from widespread devastation. Even in poorer South and Central American countries, scarce resources were poured into curative medicine; their health personnel came to the United States and elsewhere to be trained in the most up-to-date high-technology care.

In contrast to the vastly increasing resources devoted to hospital expansion and care as well as high-technology and diagnostic services, public health agencies throughout the world became chronically underfunded and understaffed. In European and North American societies, public moneys were used to establish medical schools, research institutes, and immense hospital complexes, while insurance agencies, pharmaceutical manufacturers, and medical supply companies reaped enormous profits from the growing demand for medical care. But in poorer countries, the lack of basic immunization services and primary care—combined with malnutrition, impure water supplies, and poor housing—seemed to doom children and adults alike to early death. Furthermore, a generation of public health and medical practitioners were reared in the belief that traditional sanitarian and social approaches to disease prevention were outdated, uninteresting, and unrewarding. Ironically, the success of the postwar decades in developing an ever-widening range of technological innovations left the professional communities and the world's population virtually unprepared for the new scourge of AIDS in the 1980s and early 1990s.

## III

The history of health and society in the twentieth century can be traced along three parallel transformations. The first is the physical and cultural impact of human societies on patterns and types of diseases. The growth of cities, the transformation of rural and urban environments, the mobility of populations, and the growth of commercial and industrial economies all had an impact on disease patterns, while the lack of pure water or sanitation systems in rapidly growing cities, for example, or the political and economic changes that created massive urban slums allowed for the creation of mass epidemics of infectious diseases. The second transformation involves the social response to recognized threats to human health, and the forces that shaped it. Political and public health attempts to reorganize Western European and American cities and to rebuild infrastructures, for example, were concrete attempts to limit the spread of disease. In many societies, the late-nineteenth- and early-twentieth-century social movement surrounding health and welfare insurance—and the parallel attempts to regulate industrial production—were also a response to the dire impact of new economic and industrial relationships in the modern state. Finally, the intellectual conceptualizations that accompanied these broader social changes were important in the development of professions and institutions that would take on the responsibility of treating the ill and caring for the dependent. The history of medical thought, hospital and clinic care, and political programs to aid the dependent all flowed from a logic that evolved during this time.

In contemplating the history of health and disease in the twentieth century, it is worth remembering that both the century's beginning and end have been marked by the importance of infectious, communicable, and occupational diseases that result directly from the changing relationships between humans and their environment. In the middle decades, the specter of epidemic disease appeared to recede in Western Europe and North America; cancers, heart diseases, and other chronic and noninfectious conditions became major factors in shaping disease, disability, and death rates. Throughout most of the rest of the world, including the countries of the former Soviet Union, much of Asia, and Africa, communicable and infectious conditions continued to dominate as the major causes of not only mortality, but also nonfatal illnesses. While chronic, noninfectious conditions emerged as a major focus for health researchers, the model of disease developed in the late nineteenth and early twentieth centuries continued to influence what programs researchers developed to address specific diseases, infectious or not.

## IV

If the health experience has been shaped by the shifting nature of economic, social, and political life, then it has shown some examples more extreme than others. In particular, epidemic disease, whether among women or men, aged or young, rich or poor, has been affected by the isolation of rural communities, the development of commerce-based economies, the growth of large urban centers, the development of extremes in poverty and wealth, and changing housing and work conditions. For example, in Asia, where urbanization and commercial trade routes had been highly developed for millennia, epidemic disease remained a constant threat throughout modern history. Medieval Europe's process of urbanization and economic commercialization led to serious and prolonged outbreaks of bubonic plagues and epidemics of cholera. In the Americas, invasions by Europeans, who brought not only their own diseases but also policies aimed at destroying indigenous peoples and their cultures, led to the native population's virtual destruction by smallpox, tuberculosis, and other contagious diseases. Ironically, the relative isolation of the various colonies tended to limit the damage caused by epidemic disease: for much of their first two centuries, English colonists in New England, for example, had an extremely healthful experience, far better for most portions of the population than that of Europe. But in Africa, European colonization led to the introduction of tuberculosis and other diseases, previously unknown, which had a devastating effect on the African population.

In North America, by the early nineteenth century, an extensive commercial economy, combined with a growing, increasingly urbanized, and poor population, made epidemic diseases a much greater threat. In general, infectious diseases, once primarily local phenomena circumscribed by the relative lack of mobility among self-sufficient and isolated rural communities, began to sweep through continents along the well-established trade routes, propagating in congested urban centers. By the mid-nineteenth century, highly crowded and increasingly poor urban centers in all parts of the world experienced high death rates from endemic infectious diseases; tuberculosis, an ever-present and often chronic and debilitating condition, was undoubtedly responsible for the majority. But fearsome and traumatic epidemics of cholera, dysentery, diphtheria, typhoid, yellow fever, malaria, and a host of other water-, mosquito-, louse-, and airborne infectious conditions were periodic reminders of the enormous threat that infection posed to a teeming city. In the early 1900s, the most common "dread" diseases that affected the world's population were tuberculosis, diarrheas, yellow fever, and pneumonia; as late as 1919, the second-worst pandemic in world history—the influenza epidemic—claimed the lives of upward of 30 million people.

Tuberculosis, a bacterial disease that most often affects the lungs but can attack any region of the body, illustrates the dramatic impact man-made alterations in the environment have had on human health in the twentieth century. Until the growth of urban centers and industrial economies, tuberculosis claimed relatively few lives. But in the 1700s, the disease began to establish itself throughout the world, and by 1900, every region on the globe experienced deaths due to what was called "consumption," or "phthisis." By the 1880s, such deaths far outnumbered deaths from other causes.[11] As noted earlier, throughout much of world history, consumption was understood in highly particularistic terms, with physicians seeing similar symptoms as representing different disease processes in different patients. In the worlds of the public and physicians alike, the origins of the disease could reside in personal characteristics such as poverty and alcohol usage, dissolute living, tobacco usage, or immoral behavior, or more general "predisposing conditions" such as poverty, "damp soil," or miasmas. Significantly, while some physicians were already seeing the varied symptoms of consumption as one disease, two parallel developments changed medical opinion about the possibilities of ultimately improving treatments and cures not specifically tailored to individual patients.

The first was bacteriologist Robert Koch's discovery of the *Mycobacterium tuberculosis* in 1882 and the corresponding rise of bacteriology as a science. This theory, that a specific disease was caused by a specific microorganism infecting a host, was widely seen as the key to unlocking effective treatments for a host of bacterial diseases. By finding specific agents that could weaken or destroy the pathogen responsible for an illness, or by developing vaccines that could prevent the disease in the first place, medical science, it was believed, could finally conquer consumption and other diseases that had devastated people of all ages throughout the world. Through the reasoned and systematic application of principles that developed from an identification of bacteria, diseases that once seemed mysterious and incomprehensible could now be diagnosed more accurately, prevented more effectively, and, for some remarkable conditions, treated. The second event was the steady and continued decline of tuberculosis rates in much of Europe and the United States from the 1880s through the 1970s.

The explanatory power of the bacterial model was great indeed. Yet it could sometimes obscure as well as explain. For example, the growing belief in the germ theory corresponded to the declining prevalence of tuberculosis in much of the industrialized world, leading many to mistakenly believe that there was a direct association between the discovery of the bacteria and the overall decline in mortality from the disease. In the United States and Europe, for example, the age-old practice of quarantining people in sanitaria, often far away from family and friends, was increasingly justified by pointing to quarantine's positive role in protecting the general population from bacteria, as well as the curative value of fresh air and rest for the diseased patients themselves. In 1921, Rhode Island Department of Health's Charles Chapin, one of America's preeminent public health officials, noted the impact of bacteriology on the "Anti-Tuberculosis movement." As he wrote, "Sanitariums are chiefly for cure, but prevention was early recognized as more important that cure. The discovery of the tubercle bacillus by Koch . . . aroused the public to the dangers of contagion, and health officials devoted much attention to spreading information concerning the assumed modes of infection."[12] The causes of tuberculosis' decline in the twentieth century are still obscure, and effective antibiotic treatment for the condition was unavailable until the

1950s—by which time a vast decline in mortality from the disease had already occurred. But sanitaria, which at the height of their popularity only housed a fraction of the infected population worldwide, were credited as effective means of prevention and cure. Practices that today seem inhumane were justified as part of scientifically legitimate programs.

Also, by the beginning of the twentieth century, the growing acceptance of the germ theory shifted the medical and public health community's attentions away from a social explanation of disease, as most directly illustrated by the impact of Koch's discovery of the tuberculosis bacillus on the history of industrial lung disease. An enormous amount of literature on dust's harm to workers' health had already developed, especially in Europe. But Koch's discovery, according to Ludwig Teleky (a noted industrial physician and author of the first history of industrial hygiene), effectively ended the study of dust. In Europe, as this author and Gerald Markowitz relayed in 1991, researchers "mocked at all those . . . quartz lungs, coal lungs, and iron lungs, 'all of which belong in a cabinet of curiosities'" and until the beginning of the twentieth century all forms of consumption or phthisis were mistakenly understood as tuberculosis, caused by a specific organism and spread like other infectious diseases.[13]

Beginning in the mid-twentieth century, a number of scholars began to react to the growing popularity of medical explanations for the rise in life span and apparent lessening of the threat from infectious diseases in the industrial world. They began to reevaluate the importance of medical interventions, emphasizing instead the role of improved nutrition, rising income, environmental improvements like sanitation and clean water, and even genetics as likely causes for the improved vital and health statistics.[14]

Perhaps the most widely read study was René and Jean Dubos's 1952 *The White Plague: Tuberculosis, Man and Society*. The book relates the history of this dread disease, illustrating the enormous toll it exacted in death, disease, and suffering. Written at a time when tuberculosis prevalence and mortality rates were waning in Western societies, the book was optimistic that new antibiotics, combined with a modicum of common sense, portended a future in which tuberculosis would vanish as a major problem for the peoples of the world. At the same time, however, the Duboses warned the medical and public health communities of the dangers inherent in a faulty analysis of the reasons for the disease's apparent decline. Far from reflecting the victory of microbiology or medical science over disease, the decline of tuberculosis rates illustrated for the authors the complex interrelationship among social, economic, and cultural forces in shaping the environment in which the disease had formerly prospered.

The disease's recent sharp decline, they said, required an ecological rather than a purely medical explanation. "Tuberculosis is a social disease, and presents problems that transcend the conventional medical approach," they warned their readers on the first page of the introduction. "Its understanding demands that the impact of social and economic factors on the individual be considered as much as the mechanisms by which tubercle bacilli cause damage to the human body."[15] Written by one of the world's leading microbiologists and his spouse, herself a victim of the disease, the book became a classic of medical history, illustrating the conundrum of twentieth-century medicine. On the one hand, in the middle of the century medical science appeared ready to prove good on its age-old promise of providing effective remedies to serious health problems. On the other hand, as old infectious diseases apparently disappeared, new noninfectious and chronic conditions appeared to be the result of complex ecological imbalances between man-made environments and unknown disease processes. By using tuberculosis, a disease that was familiar to their audience of professionals and laymen but which had many characteristics in common with the arising cancers and chronic conditions, the Duboses hoped to reorient the thinking of experts, politicians, and laymen just at the moment when older analyses were bearing their greatest fruit.

## V

The relationship between human beings and the societies that they create accounts, in large measure, for the diseases and deaths we experience. A major illustration of this fundamental point is the growing importance of occupation as a source of illness and disability, especially in industrializing nations. While at the turn of the century, infectious diseases associated with crowding, impure water, and other bad environmental conditions were undoubtedly responsible for the most deaths throughout the world, industrially related accidents began to take on new importance, especially in Europe and the United States. The mechanical processes used in a variety of growing industries—such as pneumatic tools, jackhammers, and power drills—set the stage for the appearance of chronic lung conditions such as silicosis, white lung or asbestosis, brown lung or byssinosis, and black lung or coal workers' pneumoconiosis. In the growing chemical industries, the dyes and organic solvents produced would later account for previously rare diseases such as bladder and colon cancer. In recent years, occupational diseases have become an area of intense interest to medical officials, public health workers, industry, and labor. Whole new areas of medical and public health specializations have developed since the end of World War II partly in response to the recognition of carcinogens in the workplace, hazardous dust in the air workers breathe, and man-made chemicals that workers touch, taste, or inhale. The latter three would gain international attention, highlighting the role of occupation in the creation of illness. Laborers as well as physicians in a host of industries from steel to construction to petrochemicals have become acutely aware of the dangers posed by substances and materials at work.

The growing attention to the hazards of the industrial workplace has alerted workers even in "clean" worksites to occupational disease. Office workers worry about the physical dangers posed by video display terminals, poorly designed furniture, noise, and vibrations. Stress in the workplace is now seen as key in the creation of modern epidemics, such as high blood pressure, heart disease, and stroke; and the very definition of disease has been altered by rising popular and professional consciousness.

### Occupational Disease and Industrial Society

Attention to the worksite as a source of disease is not new: even the ancients recognized that certain occupations presented special risks. Hippocrates described lead poisoning among metal miners, Pliny the Elder described the dangers that dust posed to tradesmen, and Juvenal wrote of the dangers blacksmiths faced from the soot of "glowing ore."[16] However, the Industrial Revolution fundamentally changed production methods and work relationships throughout the world. The factory system that tore workers from their land and homes created new dangers. In addition to accidents caused by machinery, a faster pace of production, and long hours, the movement of millions of former agrarian workers out of the open air of the fields and into the confined, closed spaces of factories, foundries, and mines created new diseases for the growing industrial workforce. In the nineteenth century, English reformers and physicians quantified, measured, and documented the effects of industrialism and urbanization on the lives of the English working classes, discovering that British workers were suffering from a host of diseases associated with their jobs. In 1832, Charles Turner Thackrah, a Leeds physician, wrote *The Effects of Arts, Trades, and Professions on Health and Longevity*, chronicling the types of diseases and poisonings associated with work among coffee roasters, snuff makers, rag sorters, paper makers, and cotton mill workers.[17] The growing European socialist movements interpreted the workers' disintegrating health as further confirmation that industrial capitalism had unacceptable social costs. In the mid-nineteenth century, Frederick Engels wrote his classic treatise, *The Condition of the Working-Class in England*, devoting two chapters to the conditions of work in a variety of industries, specifically noting effects on the health of workers and most poignantly on child laborers, pointing to the relationship between child mortality and disablement:

> In the manufacture of glass, too, work occurs which seems little injurious to men but cannot be endured by children. The hard labor, the irregularity of the hours, the frequent night work, and especially the great heat of the working place (100 to 130 Farenheit), engender in children general debility and disease, stunted growth, and especially affections of the eye, bowel complaint, and rheumatic and bronchial affections. Many of the children are pale, have red eyes, often blind for weeks at a time, suffer from violent nausea, vomiting, coughs, colds, and rheumatism. . . .The glass-blowers usually die young of debility of chest infections.[18]

By the mid-nineteenth century, physicians, sanitary and social reformers, and radicals recognized the wide variety of occupational diseases that afflicted industrial populations. Medical literature was filled with articles about dust diseases and heavy metal poisonings closely linked to the high heat, poor ventilation, and bad lighting of the early factories. Consonant with much medical theory that associated disease with the social and moral environment of different populations, the medical literature noted the explicit relationship between illnesses and the workplace.[19] In keeping with nineteenth-century ideas about ecological imbalance as causing illness, disease was seen as a reflection of the very unnatural environment of factories, cities, slums, and other manifestations of industrialism that were, by their very existence, forces creating this imbalance. Hence, physicians and public health workers writing about treatments, diagnoses, and cures for disease often framed their arguments in the personal, moral, and social terms that infused medical theory. For example, throughout most of the century impure air, "miasmas," clouds of disease arising from rotting material, and dust were understood to be sources of disease.

In the late nineteenth and early twentieth centuries, as the U.S. medical community narrowed its focus to bacterial diseases, setting back the study of occupational disease for a generation, the nonmedical community was developing a broader view of the relationship between work environment and health. Reformers concerned with the plight of the urban poor saw that the terrible conditions of life and work could not be separated. New York City charity and settlement house workers, for example, documented that nearly one out of every four dwellings in 1890 experienced a death from consumption. In the poor neighborhoods it was clear that the toll was even higher, leaving these communities devastated by the disease. This Progressive Era analysis led reformers and public health workers to emphasize the same intimate connection between work and disease as existed between social conditions and disease. "Where there is dirt and grime and dust, long hours, foul air and bad pay, the community pays for what it calls cheap prices by a little money and many lives sacrificed to greed, ignorance and indifference," said a representative of labor in 1906.

Throughout the industrialized world, governments responded to the impact of industrialization by instituting limited social and health insurance programs. They were aimed at addressing the new forms of dependence created by work-related disability, illness, and/or the death of a family's wage earner. In contrast to the laissez-faire attitudes that marked the pre-industrial era's mechanisms for caring for those made dependent on the larger society, industrialization fostered efforts to address striking social inequalities. By the turn of the twentieth century, in Germany and England, legislation provided for the care of disabled or diseased workers as well as funds for their families in the case of death. In the United States, beginning in 1912, individual states began passing workers' compensation legislation, and New York, California, and Wisconsin had come within two votes of passing compulsory health insurance legislation by the late teens. By 1910, in industrial regions, individual physicians and state public health officials participated in reform movements that led to the banning of phosphorus in matches—the source of a disfiguring and fatal disease called "phossy jaw." But occupational disease was not seen as intrinsic to the mandate of social reformers or the public health profession until the 1920s, when the latter took official notice by organizing special professions dedicated to industrial disease, such as industrial hygiene and occupational medicine.

Reformers and physicians concerned with diseases of occupation focused primarily on acute poisonings, especially from heavy metal and phosphorus exposure. In the early years of the twentieth century, investigators had carried out detailed scientific investigations of lead, phosphorus, and mercury in the United States, while in South Africa, England, and Wales commissions were organized to produce detailed studies of mining diseases. In England in 1902, Thomas Oliver pioneered in the formal study of occupational diseases, producing the first modern comprehensive text on the subject. But from the 1920s onward, industrial hygienists and occupational physicians began to investigate chronic diseases in a number of occupations, including those among painters and battery workers exposed to lead, watch dial makers exposed to radium, and miners exposed to coal, silica, asbestos, and other dusts. The diseases associated with lead mining had been known since antiquity, but the widespread introduction of lead into paint and gasoline, along with the increased smelting of ores associated with the Industrial Revolution, heightened the awareness of its dangers to workers and the public alike.

With the understanding of the increasing importance of industrial sources for disease came an increased awareness that environmental factors could also be held accountable. There were early arguments regarding the dual effect of the modern automobile on both workers' and the public's health: in the early 1920s, workers in petrochemical plants and research centers exhibited signs of acute lead poisoning—hallucinations, seizures, insanity, and death—alerting the public health community to the potential environmental damage of leaded gasoline. Though a major national conference was convened in 1922 by the United States Public Health Service to discuss public policy regarding the use of organic lead in gasoline, not until the late 1960s and early 1970s were systematic efforts made to eliminate lead from both it and indoor paint. Similarly, in the late 1920s women who worked in factories putting luminous radium paint on watch dials came down with symptoms of chronic radiation poisoning, thus engaging occupational disease researchers in one of the first studies of the dangers of radium exposure. But it took until well after World War II for the U. S. government to act on their warnings.

### The Problem of Dust and the Emergence of Chronic Disease

Interestingly, it was tuberculosis and its relationship to industrial dust that spurred the eventual rediscovery of chronic lung disease and the development of the view that exposures to toxins might take years, even decades, to manifest their effects. In the early 1900s, following the introduction of a variety of power tools such as pneumatic drills, sand blasting equipment, jackhammers, high-speed looms, spinning wheels, and the like, there developed an apparent epidemic of what became known as "fibrotic phthisis"—or silicosis—that spurred a host of investigators to identify its cause. Dust was present in virtually every industrial setting, including the mineral and metal dusts found in coal and metal mines, foundries, steel mills, and rubber factories, and the vegetable and animal dusts in granaries, bakeries, textile mills, and footwear factories, thereby presenting an enormous threat to workers and factory owners alike.

Out of this more general concern, industrial hygienists as well as labor and

business began to focus on the effects of silica dust. While this diverted attention from the other dust diseases, it also led to the formulation of general
public policies that were applicable to other chronic industrial diseases in
general. In the decades leading to World War II, politicians, labor, management, insurance company representatives, physicians, and lawyers all raised
questions about responsibility and risk in the new industrial workplaces of
the country. Overall, labor, management, industry, and insurance representatives argued over who defined what we would today call latency, the length of
time between an exposure and the appearance of symptoms. But the issues
were far-ranging, covering everything from accountability to aiding stricken
employees. What was an industrial disease? How could occupational and
environmental diseases be distinguished from each other? How should
responsibility for risk be assigned? Should a worker be compensated for
impairments or for loss of wages due to occupational diseases and disabilities? Should industry be held accountable for chronic illnesses whose symptoms appear years and sometimes decades after exposure? And at what point
in the progress of a disease should compensation be paid? Is diagnosis sufficient for compensation claims, or should inability to work be the criterion?
Then who defines inability to work—the employee, the government, the
physician, or the company?

The first systematic studies of the silica hazard were in Britain, concerning
the experience of British workers in South African gold mines. Researchers such
as Edgar Collis and H.S. Haldane, and the Miners' Phthisis Commission in
South Africa illustrated that phthisis was in reality more than one condition—
that not all dusts resulted in tuberculosis, and that some dusts, particularly silica, could cause serious lung disease in their own right. Shortly after the Boer
War (1899–1902), as the Englishmen who had worked in the South African
mines returned to Great Britain, silicosis gained wider public notice. Thomas
Oliver described the fate of "young miners in the bloom of health" who, after
working in the South African gold fields only a few years, "returned to
Northumberland and elsewhere broken." Due to the unusually hard nature of
the rock from which the gold ore was extracted, dry-drilling and blasting techniques created hazards for native and Welsh workers and their English over-
seers. In 1902, the British-appointed commission studying the situation came to
the conclusion that pathologically victims of "Rand Miners' phthisis"—as it
was called—were not suffering from tuberculosis but from silicosis.

In the United States these reports were picked up by Frederick Hoffman,
the vice president and statistician for Prudential Life Insurance Company,
who published a pathbreaking study in 1908 on "The Mortality from Con-

sumption in Dusty Trades." Hoffman began by pointing out that it required "no extended consideration to prove that human health was much influenced by the character of the air breathed and that its purity is a matter of very considerable sanitary and economic importance."[20] The study's significance lay in its building on the clinical evidence presented in the British material, and on the progressive social analysis subsequently developed by British reformers. It also used statistical materials drawn from the records of Hoffman's insurance company, as well as census materials from both Great Britain and the United States to challenge the medical profession. Although the British, and especially Thomas Oliver, had used statistical and epidemiological data, Hoffman was the first American to use such methods to document the prevalence and scope of industrially created lung diseases and to then use this material to decipher its implications for the work environment. But as the case for dust as a significant cause of pneumoconiosis was also building, Hoffman's 1908 report focused on the impact of industrial dusts on tuberculosis.

By the mid-1930s, with the world in the midst of the Great Depression, the issue of silicosis emerged as a major political, social, and economic crisis. In Europe and the United States, the introduction of power hammers, grinders, cutting instruments, and sand blasters introduced at the turn of the century had by now exposed large numbers of industrial workers to massive quantities of fine silica dust which penetrated deeply into their lungs. Under the financial strains created by massive unemployment, many of these workers, now showing the symptoms of silicosis, began to bring their claims for disability benefits into workers' compensation and court systems. Between 1930 and 1939 the United States saw a massive number of lawsuits brought by diseased workers primarily against foundries and steel mills, which ultimately led to national conferences resulting in the revision of the workers' compensation systems. Through this process, the issue of chronic industrial disease was forced upon the agendas of the medical and public health communities, and the debate mentioned earlier, over responsibility for risk and definitions of the technical and medical means for distinguishing and diagnosing long-term chronic conditions, began. In the ensuing years, the problem of noninfectious, chronic diseases created by the industrial work process would become the centerpiece of industrial medicine. Investigators such as Wilhelm Heuper, Harriet Hardy, Irving Selikoff, Lorin Kerr, and others would begin to link exposures to dusts and toxins at the workplace to a variety of cancers and lung conditions. During the 1950s and 1960s, the medical and public health community officially acknowledged the significance, noted in the 1930s, of the relationship of dust exposure to cancers. In the 1960s and 1970s, the link between devastating industrial lung disease and cancer was brought home through the work of Irving Selikoff, whose investigations of asbestosis, mesothelioma, and lung cancer galvanized popular and professional attention. Due to the widespread dispersal of asbestos throughout the general environment, professionals and the general public became profoundly aware of the dangers of industrial production to the nation's health.

Throughout the twentieth century, the medical and public health activities surrounding occupational health issues were paralleled by social, labor, and political movements. During the Progressive Era, from 1900 to 1917, unions such as the Bakers' and Confectioners' Union, the International Ladies Garment Workers Union, and the Amalgamated Clothing Workers joined with middle-class reform groups such as the National Consumers' League and the American Association for Labor Legislation to press for the reform of working conditions. In the 1920s, activist organizations like the Workers' Health Bureau of America sought to aid labor unions in their investigations of workplace hazards. They joined with the painters, hatters, and petrochemical workers to press for the reform of factory conditions. In the next decade various unions of the Congress of Industrial Organizations used the issue of deplorable health and safety conditions as a vehicle for union organization in heavy industry. Into the 1950s, Left-led unions such as the International Union of Mine, Mill and Smelter Workers pressed for national legislation to protect its members from dust hazards, and by the 1960s, safety and health had become major issues for most unions in the United States and Europe.

With the decline of heavy industry after 1960 and the rise of white-collar and service industries, there was a general belief that occupational diseases would take secondary importance. Though many argued that occupational disease was a legacy of our industrial era, its significance has remained, with its problems taking new forms. With the emergence of a strong environmental movement in the 1970s, attention was once again focused on the dangers associated with industrial production, broadening the scope of what was once seen as a problem for the industrial workforce alone. The emergence of a nuclear power industry—from the production of atomic weapons to nuclear medicine—has heightened awareness of the hazards that radiation poses for workers in even the most highly technical and protected professions. Furthermore, the problems of industrial and atomic waste disposal have forged a link between labor advocates and environmentalists. And as international economic competition has intensified and workers and professionals alike experience intense pressure to increase production speed and improve product quality, the scope of the definition of occupational disease has further broadened. Stress, once considered the problem of executives, is now a major reason for compensation claims in California. Miscarriages, never before defined as an industrial health issue, have been linked to exposures to low-level radiation from video display terminals.

The history of occupational disease reflects the broad history of industrial production and the changing relationship among capital, labor and state. The professionals—physicians, industrial hygienists, and engineers—involved in addressing the problem of industrial disease have often also played auxiliary roles in political and social conflict over the value of workers' lives. Most frequently, the control of industrially related disease has been accomplished through political activities and changing economic conditions rather than through medical or engineering interventions. When professionals have played an important technical role, it has usually been after the issue entered the public's agenda because of industrial or environmental catastrophe or concerted political activity. Like epidemics of infectious illnesses, the recognition of industrial disease has required an understanding of the social roots of illness. But now the questions of responsibility for risk are much more important as the production process and those who own it are increasingly called to account. With the evolution of chronic, noninfectious disease as a major public health problem, an understanding of industrial illness, no longer merely an oddity in a "cabinet of curiosities," has taken on new importance. In the course of studying industrial disease, physicians, government agencies and professionals will be forced to address a host of questions regarding social and political responsibility for society's health. Ultimately, industrial societies will be forced to ask what is the level of acceptable risk we should be willing to assume for industrial progress, and who should bear the cost. At the end of the twentieth century, our focus has once again shifted to worldwide epidemics, this time that of AIDS, as well as the age-old scourge of tuberculosis in a form resistant to treatment by drugs.

## VI

Two categories of illness, the cancers and AIDS, reflect the paradox of much of this century's reaction to disease. As I related earlier, industrialized societies have shaped much of the world's perception of what is the appropriate manner in which to address disease. The development of sophisticated medicines, treatment techniques, and institutions have come to symbolize the possibilities of medical science. Yet in the wake of the breakthroughs in antibiotics and inoculation, fewer and fewer resources have been devoted to maintaining and improving traditional public health measures. Ironically, therefore, much has been lost as well as gained. We have developed the means of addressing infectious diseases through medical interventions, but we have developed them at just the moment when more traditional public health measures—such as sanitation, sewage treatment, food inspection, and housing reforms—were lowering the incidence of infectious illnesses in the first place. Tuberculosis, which had no effective medical treatment until well after its incidence rates were in steep decline, is an example (see table 20.1). This has led to a situation where we have conditioned ourselves to see illness only in terms of treatment and cure rather than prevention. Despite the growing evidence that a significant portion of cancers are due to various environmental factors, such as tobacco smoke, polluted air, and contaminated water, we devote only a fraction of our health budgets to improving the quality of the environment or even identifying those carcinogens that may be causing the epidemic of cancer in the first place. Most of our resources, as well as most public attention, have focused on supporting major medical institutions in the search for a cure for cancer, rather than on environmental reform. And in the least industrialized portions of the world, neither prevention nor cure is a primary focus in nations that are barely able to feed their people.

Perhaps the best illustration of the complex interaction among social, intellectual, and political forces shaping our perceptions of disease is the contemporary epidemic of HIV infection and AIDS. Acquired Immune Deficiency Syndrome caught us unprepared and unable to adequately respond.

TABLE 20.1
Deaths Due to Tuberculosis, United States, 1900–1963

| YEAR | RATE |
| --- | --- |
| 1900 | 194.4 |
| 1905 | 179.9 |
| 1910 | 153.8 |
| 1915 | 140.1 |
| 1920 | 113.1 |
| 1925 | 84.8 |
| 1930 | 71.1 |
| 1935 | 55.1 |
| 1940 | 45.9 |
| 1945 | 39.9 |
| 1950 (Development of effective antibiotic techniques) | 22.5 |
| 1955 | 9.1 |
| 1960 | 6.1 |
| 1963 | 4.9 |

First, prejudices that linked individual morality and infection with AIDS caused inaction and stagnation within the health establishments of the world. The early view that AIDS was only a gay men's disease or a problem afflicting Haitians and Africans probably gave the politically powerful and heterosexual populations both in the United States and elsewhere a sense of security that led to inaction. One need only recall the early descriptions of AIDS victims as immoral, dissolute, and degraded to realize the profound impact of social labeling that affected our response. The later identification of intravenous drug users as another "at-risk" population probably provided further psychological insulation. And the fact that both professionals and the broader public believed that we should engage in a search for a cure for AIDS rather than a massive public health education campaign to encourage safe-sex practice and needle exchanges may have cost precious time in limiting the epidemic's progress. Our faith in curative medicines, in other words, may be costing lives.

The dilemma of modern medicine is tellingly revealed in a very good popular book on the etiology, impact, and treatment of breast cancer. Throughout *Dr. Susan Love's Breast Book*, Dr. Love, a surgeon, repeats the grim statistics on the prevalence of this disease and its ambiguous etiology and even more problematic treatments. Yet the book ends with a classic reiteration of both the power and the problem of modern medicine:

> Though cancer is a complex set of diseases that manifest themselves differently in different organs ... we're well on our way to figuring out what the defect is and how to stop it. ... No matter how "incurable" your cancer is now, the ability of radiation and chemotherapy to help put you in remission may keep you alive until we've discovered more effective treatments, and your remission may become a cure. ... It's nice to think that, in my old age, my expertise won't be that of a practitioner but of an historian, recounting, to a disbelieving audience, what it was like back in the days when breast cancer killed people.[21] To this historian, at least, this approach to disease represents both medicine's power and its folly.[22]

ENDNOTES

1. Charles Rosenberg and Janet Golden, *Framing Disease: Studies in Cultural History* (New Brunswick: Rutgers University Press, 1992), p. xiii.
2. Kuriyama Shigehisa, "Concepts of Disease in East Asia," in K. Kiple, ed., *Cambridge World History of Human Disease* (New York: Cambridge University Press, 1993), pp. 55–56.

3. Charles Rosenberg and Morris Vogel, *The Therapeutic Revolution: Essays in the Social History of American Medicine* (Phiiadelphia: University of Pennsylvania Press, 1979), p. 5.

4. John Harley Warner, *The Therapeutic Perspective: Medical Practice, Knowledge, and Identity in America, 1820–1885* (Cambridge: Harvard University Press, 1986), p. 58.

5. Elizabeth Fee, *Disease and Discovery: A History of the Johns Hopkins School of Hygiene and Public Health, 1916–1939* (Baltimore: Johns Hopkins University Press, 1987), p. 19.

6. Ibid.

7. Philip Curtin, *Death by Migration: Europe's Encounter with the Tropical World in the Nineteenth Century* (New York: Cambridge University Press, 1989), p. 104.

8. Ibid., p. 112.

9. Susan Sontag, *Illness as Metaphor* (New York: Farrar, Straus & Giroux, 1978).

10. Harry Dowling, *Fighting Infection: Conquests of the Twentieth Century* (Cambridge: Harvard University Press, 1977).

11. William D. Johnston, "Tuberculosis," in Kiple, ed., *Cambridge World History of Human Disease.* See pp. 1059–1066 for a review of the literature on tuberculosis.

12. Charles Chapin, "History of State and Municipal Control of Disease," in Mazyk P. Ravenal, ed., *A Half Century of Public Health* (New York: The Nichols Press, 1921), p. 147.

13. See Gerald Markowitz and David Rosner, *Deadly Dust: Silicosis and the Politics of Occupational Disease in Twentieth Century America* (Princeton: Princeton University Press, 1991), as well as their *Dying for Work: Workers' Safety and Health in Twentieth Century America* (Bloomington: Indiana University Press, 1987) and *"Slaves of the Depression": Workers' Letters about Life on the Job* (Ithaca: Cornell University Press, 1987).

14. See, for example, R. G. Brown and T. McKeown, "Medical Evidence Related to English Population Changes in the Eighteenth Century," *Population Studies* 9 (1955): 119–41, and T. McKeown, *The Modern Rise of Population* (New York: Academic Press, 1976).

15. Jean Dubos and René Dubos, *The White Plague: Tuberculosis, Man, and Society* 1952; reprint, New Brunswick: Rutgers University Press, 1987), p. xxxvii (page citations are to reprint edition).

16. In 1700 Bernardino Ramazzini wrote his classic text, *De morbis artificium diatriba* (Diseases of workers). This manuscript, the result of a lifetime of study and observation, was the first systematic treatment of the relationship between the workplace and the occurrence of disease. Ramazzini wrote of the health problems of common laborers, skilled artisans as well as scribes, scholars, tradesmen, and others in the growing commercial classes. He alerted physicians to the significance of the workplace in identifying the source of a patient's illness.

17. Charles Turner Thackrah (1795–1833), a physician in Leeds, paid particular atten-

tion to the diseases of various trades and, in 1832, wrote *The Effects of Arts, Trades, and Professions on Health and Longevity* (1932; reprint, Canton, Mass.: Science History Publications, 1985). In this work, Thackrah organized his text by occupation, listing the diseases and disabilities associated with each trade. Diseases of operatives, dealers, merchants, and master manufacturers and professional men are itemized. Among the operatives who were exposed to harmful substances at work were the corn millers, maltsters, coffee roasters, snuff makers, rag sorters, paper makers, flock-dressers, and feather-dressers. Dangers listed in the section on merchants and manufacturers were "anxiety of mind" and "lack of exercise." Despite the obvious impact of new industrial and urban conditions on the life of the workers and their families, much of this early work is remarkable for its emphasis on the responsibility of the individual worker to both remedy and control those forces destroying his or her life. Edwin Chadwick, Thomas Percival, and William Farr were among a group of Benthamites, Tories, and social reformers who sought to use statistical and quantitative analyses to impose order and expose the horrible working and living conditions that were closely linked to the development of the factory system.

18. Frederick Engels, *The Condition of the Working Class in England*, trans. W. O. Henderson and W. H. Chaloner (New York: Macmillan, 1958).

19. See, for example, Thackrah, *The Effects of Arts, Trades and Professions*.

20. Frederick Hoffman, "The Mortality from Consumption in Dusty Trades," in *U.S. Bureau of Labor Bulletin* 79 (Washington D.C.: GPO, November 1908), 633.

21. Susan Love with Karen Lindsey, *Dr. Susan Love's Breast Book* (Reading, MA: Addison-Wesley, 1991), p. 385.

22. See, for the best account of the experience of the patient, Kathlyn Conway, *Ordinary Life: A Memoir of Illness* (New York: W. H. Freeman, 1997).

# 21 Ecology and the Environment

MARY CORLISS PEARL

## Introduction

The concept of man as belonging to nature—rather than existing in dominion over it—has been the fundamental change in our outlook on the natural environment between the twentieth century and the nineteenth. This new outlook made possible the movement to protect the environment. At the dawn of the twentieth century, most Western leaders saw nature as a set of God-given resources for human use; nearing the end of the century, they have come to the view that humans are merely part of a web of life that has its own intrinsic value. In 1900, religion was seen by most as the source of knowledge about nature; nearing the end of the century, almost 150 years after the first publication of Darwin's tenets of evolutionary biology,[1] his theory has become so widely accepted that most educated people hold the view that humans, like other animals, are a product of randomly generated processes of evolution from earlier life forms. Animals were seen in 1900 as having no rights; nonhuman predators were "varmints" meriting obliteration. At the close of the century, bounty laws have disappeared, and throughout the world, national legislation and international arrangements reflect both the notion that wildlife and wilderness have an intrinsic right to exist and that the future of humanity depends on a healthy environment.

In the 1890s, advances in science and technology seemed to set the stage for limitless economic growth. Yet the negative by-products of growth began to accumulate, and then accelerate after the Second World War. Over the course of the century, widespread concern about the health of the ecosystems that sustain human life and prosperity led to a host of international conventions, UN programs, and organizations. The optimistic view that the European Industrial Revolution had borne many fruits gave way to an awareness of its many costs: land, air, and water pollution; loss of wild lands and loss of community; and conflicts among industrial, agrarian, and subsistence users of resources. Ironically, the new awareness of our biosphere's fragility has been accompanied by a burgeoning rate of human population growth that, for any regime, poses obstacles to sustainable resource use.

## The Legacy of European Colonialism

Because of the huge extent of the British Empire in the nineteenth century, English valuation and use of resources set the stage for the next century's ecological events in much of the world. Areas colonized by Europeans had become part of the great Industrial Revolution, where modes of resource use and transportation changed radically. Resources could be transformed from one form to another, and transported across vast distances. As international markets were created, local limits on consumption became relatively unimportant. And while the British extolled the beauties of their own settled rural landscape, their appreciation of wildlife was minimal, perhaps because after millennia of exploiting their own land they had very few remnants of natural ecosystem left,[2] and because their source of national wealth came from nature transformed. Furthermore, this transformation was the fulfillment of their Christian mandate.[3]

By contrast, the areas they colonized featured characteristics of coherence and stability dependent on local systems of agriculture and subsistence.[4] In pre-Industrial Revolution settings, the emphasis was on resource gathering for subsistence rather than for transformation into commodities; on cooperation among neighbors of long standing rather than atomized societies with individuals acting largely on their own; and—in animist societies—on respect for the souls of natural objects rather than Christian indifference to them. Because resources were collected for use by a relatively small number of local people, resource removal remained sustainable in the absence of population growth.

## Conflicts in Ways of Using Resources

For thousands of years, slash-and-burn agriculture (known variously as shifting cultivation, swidden agriculture, *jhum*, and other terms), where patches of forest land are cleared and cultivated in rotation, was an important means by which people all over the world produced their food. In this method, small plots are burned and cultivated for a few years and then left fallow for more years, allowing the soil to rejuvenate as new plots are burned and cultivated. Over the course of the twentieth century, two factors rendered slash-and-burn agriculture unsustainable: the usurpation of forests by the state and large-scale commercial timber interests, and the growth of local populations. As forests dwindled and numbers to be fed increased, the time land could be left fallow decreased from an ideal of a dozen years or more to as short a time as two or three years—not enough to recover the nutrients lost in food crop cultivation. Throughout the twentieth century, forests have fragmented and disappeared in increasing numbers, and many people who practiced slash-and-burn agriculture have migrated to cities in search of wage labor or have remained in the countryside to work in agricultural settlements—in other words, they have joined the Industrial Revolution.

The British colony of India in the first half of the century provides an example of the clash between pre- and postindustrial cultures in land use. Colonial administrators viewed shifting cultivation as a primitive and nonremunerative form of agriculture in comparison with settled agriculture or timber operations. They created forest reserves to exclude the local villagers, who were traditional resource collectors and slash-and-burn cultivators. Not surprisingly, these new reserves were extremely unpopular, and sometimes local opposition was violent. In the late 1930s, several Saora tribes of northern India invaded reserves and cleared land for cultivation; when the men were jailed, the women continued the work until the men could return to clear the forest again for the next year's crop. As repeated arrests were unsuccessful in stopping Saoras from trying to establish their traditional rights to the land, the forest department forcibly uprooted their crops. Similar scenarios continued all over India.

Losing control over their lands and their means of subsistence, many tribal people were forced into relations of dependence, working as tenants and sharecroppers in the new system of market agriculture or as forest labor in the felling and hauling of timber. As Indian princes sought to emulate their British counterparts in profiting from their forests, they also came in conflict with shifting cultivators. After independence in 1948, the Indian government under Jawaharlal Nehru continued to pursue economic development modeled on the West. As recently as 1993, a group of local tribal people in the Western Ghats set fire to a reserve forest in retaliation for restrictions on their traditional use of it for grazing and collecting.

Now, at the turn of the twenty-first century, clashes continue between traditional users of land—whether hunter-gatherers or shifting cultivators—and resource-as-commodity users, such as large-scale agriculturalists and harvesters for national and international markets. In Papua New Guinea, one of the last countries to remain almost totally (more than 70 percent) forested,[5] timber interests from Malaysia and Japan are conducting massive timber-removal schemes, many illegal.

## American Environmental Values

In an underpopulated continent in the temperate zone, the land use practices and values of Europe fostering an industrial economy and a consumer society were easily replicated by European emigrants as they settled, conquered, and displaced the indigenous population in America. In 1900, some 350 years after the first settlers arrived, the country was still a rural, agricultural society, though the coming century would see its transformation to an urban, industrial nation. America's frontier had only recently ceased to exist, and American society had broken away from important parts of its British inheritance and its own traditional view of the environment. Whereas from the time of initial settlement, American immigrants saw wilderness as repugnant and dangerous, by 1900 it was cities that were viewed with hostility and fear. Rather than viewing human transformation of the environment as a sign of progress or divine will, more observers noticed society's defects reflected in urban centers.

## The End of the Frontier and the Rise of Environmentalism in the United States

To America's pioneers, the notion of preserving wildlife was absurd: in many ways, American character itself was defined by the taming of the frontier, which, once closed, found a substitute in wildlife. However, this was a city-based view, with roots in the European Romanticism of the eighteenth and early nineteenth centuries; the positive view of New World wilderness came from European aesthetic notions. However, by 1900, the descendants of the pioneers, largely of northern European, Protestant extraction, came to view nature study and a strenuous outdoor life as a way to preserve their culture and its virtues for the next generation—largely, city-dwelling non-Northern European immigrants and their children. The surge of immigrants from Southern and Eastern Europe into the cities at the turn of the century, where they manned American factories, was seen by the immigrants of earlier eras as a threat to the character, taste, and morality of the dominant culture. William Hornaday, the director of New York City's zoo, wrote a large reference volume in 1904, *The American Natural History*, in order to enlighten youth and remedy the fact that "fully 95 percent of . . . the great mass of students . . . enter active life ignorant of even the most important forms of the wild life of our own country!"[6] C. Hart Merriam, a Yale University professor, pointed out that "instead of the mental stagnation that naturally follows the automatic performance of a monotonous daily task, [natural history knowledge] stimulates the intellect . . . acquaintance with our common animals and plants appeals to an inherent desire to know more of nature; . . . it promotes the healthy expansion of the intellect and the development of the nobler impulses and sentiments, making better men and better women."[7]

## The Creation of the First National Parks

Motivated by aesthetics and the urge to preserve beautiful landscapes, the world's first national park, Yellowstone, was created in 1872, to provide "a pleasuring ground" for Americans. Citizens were assured that its designation would not place economic progress at risk.[8] A decade later, New York State decreed that an area in the Adirondack Mountains should be kept "forever as wild forest lands"[9] in order to protect New York's water supply. However, the idea of national parks to protect wilderness for its intrinsic value soon followed, with Banff in Canada (1885) and Yosemite (1890). Just before the turn of the century, the U.S. Congress passed a bill empowering the president to create forest reserves out of land in the public domain. Fifteen reserves, totaling more than 13 million acres, were thus established, but within a few years the Forest Management Act of 1897 decreed that the forests be used for economic gain. The debate over protection versus use continued to be played out through legislation, and in 1908, President Theodore Roosevelt set aside the Grand Canyon as a national monument in deference to the wishes of the strict preservationist John Muir.

Although born in the United States, the idea of a national park quickly inspired similar movements around the world. Within a few decades of Yosemite's creation, national parks were decreed in Australia, New Zealand, South Africa, and India. In 1907, the Malleco Forest Reserve was established as the first protected area in Chile, based on concern of recent German, Italian, French, and Swiss immigrants about the depletion of resources in the temperate rain forest zone where most Europeans had settled following homesteading agreements with indigenous chieftains in 1880.[10] By around 1920, the governments of Germany, Russia, Sweden, and Switzerland had set up parks. After Prince Albert of Belgium visited parks in America in 1919, he created two: one in Belgium (the Herzogenwald) and one in the Belgian Congo (Albert National Park, now the Virunga National Park).

## Changing Views of Environmental Conservation: Use Versus Protection

Despite America's early creation of parks, it never resolved their primary purpose: protecting the environment or intact ecosystem, or creating special-use areas of wild resources for cultural, recreational, or economic exploitation. The divergent views appeared soon after the creation of protected areas, epitomized by the personal rift between writer and conservationist John Muir, a champion of preservationism, and Gifford Pinchot, who as chief forester of the U.S. Forest Service in 1905 championed utilitarianism and careful resource development. While most legislation sided with users rather than preservers, Muir represented a groundswell of popular enthusiasm for wilderness that has since been termed a "national cult."[11] The two sides of the nascent environmental movement came to an irrevocable split in 1913 over the decision to dam the Hetch Hetchy valley of Yosemite National Park in order to provide water for the citizens of San Francisco. Despite the fact that the utilitarians won the battle to build the dam, the preservationists ultimately gained as well, having built the framework for a global movement to value wilderness for its own sake. Throughout the century, citizens would found organizations to protect nature—the Bison Society in 1905, the Save the Redwoods League in 1918, the Wilderness Society in 1935, and the Sierra Club in 1949, among others—which would continue to expand the circle of citizens mobilized to protect wilderness. In the 1950s, a dam was proposed for Dinosaur National Monument on the Colorado-Utah border; in contrast to Hetch Hetchy in 1913, preservationists, led by David Brower of the Sierra Club and Howard Zahniser of the Wilderness Society, won a decision against the development. In conceding defeat, Utah congressman William A. Dawson confessed, "We hated to lose it," but proponents of the dam had "neither the money nor the organization to cope with the resources and mailing lists" of the conservation organizations.[12] With this victory in their wake, the conservation community campaigned for a true wilderness preservation system in the United States, and, after seven years of congressional hearings, the Wilderness Act of 1964 was finally established. The act itemized 109 areas in the national forests, parks, wildlife refuges, and Indian reservations to become part of the National Wilderness Preservation System, immune to development pressure, and represented the first positive effort to set aside wilderness, rather than defend it from development.[13] The public resolve to preserve land now came from something more than aesthetic appreciation or concern for individual species of plants or animals—the notion of the ecosystem, a term from a science of the twentieth century, the field of ecology.

## The Emergence of Ecology

Related to the notion that man is a product of evolution, the idea of ecology also first appeared in the middle of the nineteenth century. German biologist Ernst Haeckel coined the term in 1866 from the Greek root *oikos*, meaning household or living relations. He defined ecology as the science of the relations of an organism to the environment, in order to better explain to the German scientific community the significance of Charles Darwin's theory of natural selection.[14] In other words, ecology's real roots lie with Darwin's notion that an "economy of nature"—plants and animals in an ever-changing set of interrelationships—creates an evolutionary process that elaborates and diversifies life forms. Yet the ecological side of Darwin's theories went relatively ignored in comparison with the furor over the idea that humans could be descendants of animals, and not until the twentieth century did ecology mature into a major field of study.

In addition to Darwin's theories, the field of biology in 1900 inherited another legacy from the prior century. Until around 1830, the study of wildlife was contained within the field of "natural history"—geology, zoology, and botany. Naturalists also trained in landscape painting and the aesthetic appreciation of nature. However, by the close of the nineteenth century, the technological breakthrough of dramatically improved microscopes—which made possible the study of minute tissue structures—had made an impact on nature study. Geology split off, and zoology and botany combined into modern biology, comprising physiology, histology, and embryology—all of which would ultimately culminate in the advances of cellular biology such as the discovery and description of DNA in the 1960s. Despite public and religious interest in evolutionary biology, little professional attention focused there. In reaction, in 1893, in a paper entitled, "Biology in Our Colleges: A Plea for a Broader and More Liberal Biology,"[15] C. Hart Merriam called for reinclusion of the material that was the scope of naturalists, writing,

> Is it not as desirable to know something of the life-zones and areas . . . with their principal animals and plants and controlling climatic conditions, as to be trained in the minute structure of a frog? And is not a knowledge of the primary life regions of the earth, with their distinctive types, as important as a knowledge of the embryology of the crayfish?

... The pendulum has swung too far in the direction of exclusive micro-scopic and physiologic work. When it swings back ... the present one-sided study of animals and plants will give place to ... a school of nat-uralists far in advance of those who have passed away.

At the turn of the century, however, only the botanists studied ecology, with such studies as Frederic E. Clements's work on plant formations and cli-max vegetation, and Henry E. Cowles's study of vegetational succession. Not until the late 1980s and early 1990s did programs in the applied fields of con-servation science and policy begin to appear at major universities around the world. At mid-century, however, the field of ecology did take a giant step, albeit outside of academia.

In 1949, the new "school of naturalists," the ecologists, came into their own following Aldo Leopold's book of that year, *A Sand County Almanac*,[16] which popularized the idea that understanding the interrelation of all organisms and their habitats was key to understanding nature. For Leopold, who had practiced wildlife management, ecology was a tool for integrating knowledge in a wide range of disciplines, rather than simply a theoretical construct in botany.[17] In the key essay, "The Land Ethic," Leopold suggests that human beings, as members of the ecological community, relate ethically to the land. His views were in major part a reflection of his personal experience in game management, where he observed the environmental damage done by deer fol-lowing the extermination of their predator, the wolf. Through Leopold's book, the environmental conservation community was introduced to the view that the goal of conservation work was to preserve the health of ecosys-tems rather than protect individual animals or species.

## The Environmental Cost of Development

Despite the growth of the cult of wilderness into a widespread political movement and the political victories of preservationists in the 1950s, most Americans believed that wilderness and development could each make room for the other. Not until the 1962 publication of Rachel Carson's *Silent Spring*[18] did the public awaken to further implications of ecology: that the interrela-tion of living things meant that the by-products of industrial activities could create environmental disasters. "Silent spring" refers to a springtime without bird or insect calls, resulting from poisoning through the food chain because of unchecked use of the dangerous chemical insecticides developed during World War II. Carson exposed the willful ignorance of chemical manufacturers and government agencies who encouraged the indiscriminate use of pesticide, revealing in detail the effects of DDT, dieldrin, and other poisons on soil, water, wildlife, pets and livestock, and ultimately, humans. Beyond the specific alarms about DDT, her book underscored how the view that humanity is apart from and has dominion over nature is increasingly untenable in a society with the technology to produce deadly chemicals. In this, Carson was part of a larger post-World War II shift in world view which challenged the idea that science wedded to technology could lead to human perfectibility and unlimited economic growth. By the late 1980s, evidence accumulated that human activities are of such magnitude that they are destabilizing the global climate and the chemical composition of the atmosphere in ways that are unpredictable and irreversible with current science and technology. Obscure chemicals and pesticide-wielding farmers were not the only villains: the combustion of fossil fuels in nearly every American home and driveway was also to blame. The ecological thinking that emerged post-War, in which events are not isolated and the technology used to solve one problem can have unforeseen effects elsewhere, led ultimately to a vision in the last years of the century of a postindustrial society where science and technology must be informed with an ethic of interdependence, peace, and harmony with nature.

## Legislation to Protect the Environment

The outpouring of concern for the environment that followed the publications of Leopold and Carson created widespread support for stronger conservation policies. On April 22, 1970, more than 20 million people participated in the first declared "Earth Day." In its wake came passage of the Endangered Species Act of 1973, and the Clean Air and Clean Water Acts of 1977. Each of these acts had statutes reflecting ecological concerns; for example, the Clean Air Act specified that wilderness areas larger than 5,000 acres would be assumed to have clean air, that any adverse impacts on the growth and productivity of the plants and animals in the ecosystem would be assumed to affect the air, and therefore that wilderness managers would be empowered to act to prevent these adverse impacts. The Endangered Species Act was the most comprehensive, far-reaching legislation concerning endangered species anywhere in the world, establishing a program to preserve the very ecosystems upon which threatened and endangered species depend.[19] Yet twenty years after its passage, even the legislation's supporters acknowledged that most of the species that should be protected under the Act have not been, while many that are formally protected have continued to decline. Furthermore, the renewal of the Act is so politically volatile that President Bill Clinton chose not to press for it. The century-old divide between use and protection is still reflected in the debate over such legislation. In 1995, an anti-Act extremist posted on the Internet, "Since the sorry day the Endangered Species Act was passed, we have declined from our former greatness as a human civilization. At the same time, the bugs, birds, and other vermin have prospered. . . . [Environmentalists] use endangered species as a gimmick to try to stop growth and progress."[20]

## The Internationalization of Conservation

The past 100 years have witnessed an accelerating array of international laws to govern humanity's use of nature. What was a relatively small cult of wilderness in the West grew, adapted Eastern and animist philosophies as it became more international, and resulted in a major shift from the mainstream view of humans as central and dominant in nature to a view of humanity as a vulnerable part of a web of life. This fundamental change in the mainstream perception of the nature of human life on earth has led to significant actions in public policy on behalf of protecting the environment. During the first part of the century, international arrangements were limited to a consideration of nature as a thing apart from everyday human concerns—a diversion, or an appreciation of a charismatic animal. But in the second half of the century, as the environmental consequences of human actions have begun to become known, international arrangements have flowered into a myriad of commissions, conventions, UN agencies, and other means to monitor the growing impact of human activities on the health of the biosphere.

The first international agreement negotiated on behalf of nature took place in 1900 in London. Although never ratified, it concerned the conservation of African game. Bird hunters and fanciers were the first to negotiate successful arrangements for conservation: sixteen European signatories agreed to protect birds useful to agriculture in 1902, and in 1916, the United States and Canada agreed to cooperate to protect migratory game birds.

After World War II, there was widespread interest in resuming international cooperation for the environment. To that end, Charles Bernard, then president of the Swiss League for the Protection of Nature, and Sir Julian Huxley, the first head of UNESCO (United Nations Educational, Scientific, and Cultural Organization), called a conference of delegates representing 18 governments, 108 institutions and associations, and 7 international organizations. In the fall of 1948 they formally constituted the International Union for the Protection of Nature, or IUPN—changed in 1956 to IUCN when the term "protection" was changed to "conservation," and today, though the acronym remains, called "The World Conservation Union." The IUCN remains the one international body with government agency, NGO, scientific institution, and individual members, all collaborating on conservation work.[21] Through the second half of the century, both it and the UN have held key conferences that have been benchmarks for environmental conservation.

In 1962, the IUCN's new commission on National Parks and Protected Areas met in Seattle, Washington for the first of what would become a decennial world conference on the state of the global protection of nature. The concept of marine parks emerged here; the subsequent conference at Yellowstone in 1972 resulted in recommendations for more and better-managed parks, and protected areas that represented a greater array of ecosystems. Within two months, the World Heritage Convention was ratified by over 100 signatory nations to recognize international interest in the protection of the world's finest natural and cultural sites. Over the next decade, the total amount of protected area grew from 536 to 979 million acres. However, this remains a relatively low number compared to the total amount of 29.7 billion acres of ice-free land on earth.[22] The third meeting, the 1982 World Congress on National Parks, was held in Indonesia—the first parks conference to be held in a developing nation, and a watershed event in that it focused on people as well as wildlife, and on the relationship between economic development and protected areas. The world began to hear the view from developing nations that if parks are to survive, they must be seen as improving human welfare. The fourth parks congress, held in Caracas in 1992, again linked humans and environment with the theme, "Parks for Life: Enhancing the Role of Conservation in Sustaining Society."[23]

In Paris in 1968, UNESCO had sponsored an Intergovernmental Conference of Experts on the Scientific Basis for Rational Use and Conservation of the Biosphere. Unlike any earlier conference, "The Biosphere Conference" reflected ecological values rather than favorite game species or parks. It also culminated in a series of specific recommendations, reflecting international responsibility for the global environment, for action by UNESCO and participating governments.[24] Three years later, UNESCO launched the Man and the Biosphere Program, to support research directed toward problems of accommodating human and wildlife needs. But perhaps the key UN environmental conference of the century was the United Nations Conference on the Human Environment, held in Stockholm in 1972, as it marked the culmination of efforts to place the protection of earth on the official agenda of international policy and law.[25] The conference called for the creation of a major UN agency focused on the environment, and the General Assembly of the UN obliged the following year, creating the United Nations Environmental Program (UNEP).

In 1980, the UNEP commissioned the IUCN to prepare a world conservation strategy, which prescribed maintaining essential ecological processes and life support systems, preserving genetic diversity, and utilizing species and ecosystems sustainably.[26] The five organizations most involved in its preparation, IUCN, UNEP, FAO, UNESCO, and the World Wildlife Fund, all pledged to work cooperatively to encourage its implementation by urging governments to produce national conservation strategies of their own. Over the course of the decade, IUCN published regular reports on the progress of various national strategies. Twelve years later, it launched an updated strategy[27] with UNEP and the World Resources Institute, in consultation with UNESCO and FAO. This time, the document was prepared in anticipation of negotiations leading to a Convention on the Conservation of Biological Diversity as part of the UN Conference on Environment and Development (UNCED) in Rio de Janeiro in June 1992. This was the largest gathering of national political leaders ever, with 106 heads of state and some 35,000 others,[28] including government representatives and nongovernmental organizations ranging from the major international institutions to small tribes and grassroots groups, attending. Immediate outcomes included the biodiversity convention, and a climate treaty which set up a system for international reporting on carbon emissions, though it fell short of listing goals or timetables for reducing emissions. The biodiversity convention was also toothless in that it mandated no actions. But the meeting was an occasion for a global stock-taking of the state of the environment. At the Stockholm meeting 20 years before, developing nations had asserted their right to pollute on their own road to development. By 1992, all countries were united in alarm over the atmospheric concentrations of carbon dioxide and other greenhouse gases, and the risks to life posed by the hole in the ozone layer and the associated rise in ultraviolet radiation.

The late 1980s and 1990s witnessed the entry of a new set of international actors into environmental action: the World Bank and other regional banks added environmental amelioration to their goals, as did the bilateral aid agencies such as the U.S. Agency for International Development (USAID). The World Bank joined with the UNEP and UNDP to create the Global Environment Facility (GEF), to provide governments with significant funding for environmental conservation. USAID developed a number of environmental programs, in 1994 even designing and underwriting the start-up costs for a major, independent, and international foundation for biodiversity conservation based in a developing nation: the Indonesian Biodiversity Foundation. However, the regional development banks, the World Bank, and most international aid agencies maintain as their core goal the rapid deployment of funds for short-term development projects, with environmental concerns added on or considered in terms of the need to mitigate the adverse impacts of traditional development projects. It is unclear whether these major economic institutions are in fact in transition to fully incorporating an environmental ethic into their basic goals.

## The Environment and the Religious Community

People's attitudes and behavior toward the environment are heavily based upon how they view themselves in relation to their nature and their destiny—in other words, upon their religion. During the twentieth century, many people came to be aware of and influenced by religions of other cultures. Animism—the belief that natural objects have souls—is found in different forms throughout the world: Shinto, Japan's first religion, is one example, a form of nature worship where mountains, forests, storms, and torrents in particular are seen as manifestations of the divine in contrast with the more tranquil aspects of nature. Jainism, Buddhism, and Hinduism, which all emerged in India and, in the case of Buddhism, spread throughout Asia, emphasize the underlying unity of all life forms, fostering attitudes of compassion and harmony between humans and other parts of nature.

Though Eastern religions began to be studied more widely in the West during this century, even without exposure to them, some Americans sought in environmental conservation an antidote to godlessness. Joseph Knowles, a popular columnist of his time, wrote in 1913 that "My God is in the wilderness, the great open book of nature is my religion. My church is the church of the forest."[29] In decrying the plan to dam the wild Hetch Hetchy valley of Yosemite, naturalist John Muir wrote that the developers, "these temple destroyers, devotees of ravaging commercialism, seem to have a perfect contempt for Nature, and instead of lifting their eyes to the God of the Mountains, lift them to the Almighty dollar."[30]

During the social upheavals of the late 1960s and early 1970s, many came to question the dogma of the established churches in the West. In a widely influential paper published in 1967, philosopher Lynn White pointed out to the largely Christian readership of the American journal *Science*[31] the link between their belief system and their professional behavior toward nature. He observed that in contrast to Asian and African religions, Christianity establishes a dualism of man and nature, and insists that it is God's will for people to exploit nature for their own ends. Western science and technology, he continued, are so "tinctured with orthodox Christian arrogance toward nature that no solution for our ecologic crisis can be expected from them alone. Since the roots of our trouble are so largely religious, the remedy must also be essentially religious, whether we call it that or not. We must rethink and refeel our nature and destiny."

In trying to do just this, many in the West looked beyond Christian and Jewish orthodoxy to the East. As with Hinduism and Taoism, Buddhist philosophy received fresh scrutiny: the Buddha's view that the earth is also mind inevitably led American adherents to a realization that a similar philosophy could be found closer to home. As one American adherent, finding a symbiosis in Native American traditions, put it,

> Having taken root in the West, Buddhism is following its classical migratory mode—forming a circle with the nature-based wisdom of indigenous cultures. The sophisticated ecological teaching that Native American life represents is grounded in an honorable partnership with a living Mother Earth, from which all life springs. . . . While Native American cosmology is generally centered around harmony, its history is fraught with war. Buddhism helps Native Americans find their path to peace while Native Americans vivify the living Earth for Buddhists. Both traditions share the notion that nature is an active partner in all thought.[32]

Some conservation scientists sought to incorporate nature-based values in their work. James E. Lovelock, an atmospheric scientist from Great Britain, developed in the 1960s analytic techniques to detect trace amounts of chemical substances such as toxic pesticide residues in life forms. He began to pursue astronomy, biology, cosmology, and other disciplines to investigate evidence for biological control of the physical environment. Published in 1979, his resulting Gaia Hypothesis[33] theorizes that the earth's living matter, air, oceans, and land surface form a self-regulating entity, with the capacity to keep our planet healthy by controlling the chemical and physical environment. This control is internal and diffuse, and despite one major effort ("Biosphere II" set up near Tucson, Arizona in the late 1980s), humans have not been able to construct even a simplified biologically controlled life support system. Before the Gaia Hypothesis can be proved, much must be learned about when, where, and at what rate nutrients are recycled and gases exchanged. The search will be long, since so many processes would have to be involved in a control network of such magnitude.[34]

A Western philosophy that combines ecology with sociology, poetry, self-awareness, and political action is the "deep ecology" movement, which appeared in the 1970s and flowered in the 1980s. Mainstream environmentalism focuses on such topics as wilderness preservation, or the mitigation of deleterious environmental impacts based on human valuation of nature. By contrast, deep ecology is based on the premise that all life forms have equal value, and that humans are simply one part of an ecological whole. A practice as well as a philosophy, deep ecology requires its adherents to learn to identify with the diversity of nature.[35] A less radical position has been proposed by conservation biologist and historian David Ehrenfeld, who maintains that once human valuation incorporates diversity, a healthy environment can be conserved. Citing the disastrous effects of what he terms "exploitative generality" in global economic systems, vast forest monocultures, and continent-wide irrigation systems, he posits that until science and society regain a fascination with diversity—with differences, with uniqueness, and with exceptions, all in their own right—there will continue to be accelerating environmental degradation.[36]

## Conclusion

Over the course of the last hundred years, the environment has moved from a peripheral to a central concern of science, of belief systems, and of the global political agenda. The science of ecology and the technology of precise measurements made possible the discovery that our industrial economies have produced toxins that have pervaded every life form on Earth. This realization that we are poisoning our biosphere has in turn galvanized much public opinion to a desire for action, resulting in a large constituency of conservation organizations. It has also caused international agencies such as bilateral aid groups, multilateral banks, and multinational corporations to add environmental goals to their agendas, and has brought about an increasing number of international arrangements for the global regulation of resource use. Western science, with its strong bias toward Cartesian methods, in which wholes are divided into parts for study, has begun to return to a more integrative and holistic consideration of nature, influenced in part by an underlying belief system that has moved away from the traditional Judeo-Christian separation of humanity from other life forms.

Nearing the close of the twentieth century, the concept of environmental protection has begun to take on the same ideological weight that "progress" had in the nineteenth century. In 1990 the executive director of Earth Day commented: "Whereas [the first] Earth Day 1970 awakened people to the issues, 1990 needs to make the environment the screen through which all other decisions are made."[37] This seems to have happened. Gro Harlem Brundtland, the former Norwegian Prime Minister and Chairman of the World Commission on Environment and Development, has commented on the vastly more integrated view of nature that prevailed among leaders in 1985. In 1945, she said, a tree was regarded by most of the world in terms of its economic value and sometimes as a thing of beauty: "Today, a tree is not only a commodity with an economic price, but also a source of fuelwood for poor people outside of the money economy, a form of protection for watersheds and soil erosion, a genetic resource, an aesthetic highpoint in the landscape, and perhaps even a contributor to climatic stability."[38]

Yet despite the vastly increased public will to address environmental problems, from the depletion of the ozone layer and global warming to the growing wave of wildlife extinctions, root problems remain the obstacles to protecting human life on earth as we move into the twenty-first century. First, the industrial nations have failed to acknowledge the role that the overconsumption of resources plays in the destruction of the environment everywhere. Instead, there is a tendency among those who participate in the global economy to exaggerate the deleterious effects of preindustrial resource uses, such as subsistence collection and shifting cultivation. To be sure, population increases have made many of these practices very harmful, but it is also true that subsistence practices became destructive only in the context of an enlarged global market for resource commodities.

Regardless of whether they are traditional or commodity resource collectors, the many people living today on the rural landscape are the ones with the power to maintain or destroy their ecosystems. Yet too often, these people are left out of land use decisions, which are made only at a national or even international level. Without engaging the enlightened self-interest of the people who live alongside wildlands, plans for sustainable resource management will not succeed.

At the global level, international capital pursues short-term gain, even if that means depleting the resources of any one country. Since the long-term self interest of both individual countries and international capital dictates that the global economy cannot flourish with increasingly inequitable distribution of wealth, we clearly need new economic models for global resource management. In addition, we need to account for the terrible price we pay for environmental degradation—species loss in fisheries and elsewhere, deforestation, the drought and heat stress of global warming, and so forth. Mainstream economists and finance ministers have yet to incorporate these costs in their planning.

Another problem facing us is the failure, among politicians from every class and outlook, to move outside traditional political paradigms and recognize the synergistic effect of different groups in environmental destruction. For example, landless peasants and landowners in Ecuador may be political foes, but as agents of deforestation, their interests at times coincide.[39]

Finally, despite the good intentions behind them, arrangements for environmental protection are still too vague in their concepts and toothless in their execution. One much-abused concept is "sustainable development," which has become the stated goal of almost every country, despite the fact that it is a term so loosely defined that it can mean anything from consistent yield over ten years to indefinite productivity. Also, laws of the international commons have been written, but many remain unaccompanied by any enabling legislation or enforcement. Despite the increasing number of UN-sponsored meetings, agreements, and commissions regarding the environment, it is hard to use them as a measure of much more than a growing diversity of good intentions. The Plan of Action to Combat Desertification agreed to at a UN conference in Nairobi in 1977, for example, failed to raise more than .01 percent of the funds it needed.[40]

As we leave the twentieth century, a revolution in information technology presents the possibility of new forms of economic and social organization, much as industrial technology dictated its own economic and social patterns that affected the environment so strongly in the 1900s. But as with the industrial revolution before it, most of the world is not taking part in the information revolution at its inception. A cautionary note is sounded from countries in development. To Indian ecologists Madhav Gadgil and Ramachandra Guha, Western environmentalists appear to be moving toward a postindustrial, postmaterialist perspective in which a forest is central not to economic production but rather to the quality of life. In India, by contrast, debates about the forest, or the environment more generally, are still firmly rooted in considerations of production and use. Gadgil and Guha feel it is too early to say whether these debates will result in a new mode of resource use or new belief system to hold Indian society together.[42] North or South, East or West, pre- or postindustrial, we live on one planet and we all have a stake in fostering a new global mode of resource use, and a new belief system for environmental stewardship that we all can share in the twenty-first century.

ENDNOTES

1. Charles Darwin, *The Origin of Species by Means of Natural Selection, or the Preservation of Favoured Races in the Struggle for Life* (London: 1859).

2. Hugh Green Brynmor, "Great Britain," in Craig W. Allin, ed., *International Handbook of National Parks and Nature Reserves* (Westport, Conn.: Greenwood Press), pp. 141–42

3. Lynn White, Jr., "The Historical Roots of Our Ecologic Crisis," *Science* 155 (3767) (1967): 1203–1206.

4. The following discussion draws on "Ecological Change and Social Conflict in Modern India," in Madhav Gadgil and Ramachandra Guha, eds., *This Fissured Land: An Ecological History of India* (Delhi: Oxford University Press, 1992) 3: 111–245 .

5. Mary Pearl, Allen Allison, Bruce Beehler, and Meg Taylor, eds., *Conservation Research Priorities for Papua New Guinea* (New York: Wildlife Conservation International, 1992).

6. William Hornaday, *The American Natural History* (New York: Charles Scribner's Sons, 1904), p. v.

7. C. Hart Merriam, "Biology in Our Colleges: A Plea for a Broader and More Liberal Biology." *Science* 21 (543) (1893): 354.

8. *Congressional Globe*, 42nd Cong., 2d sess. 1872, 697.

9. New York State laws, 1885, chap. 238, p. 482.

10. Carlos Weber, "Chile," in C. Allin, ed., *International Handbook of National Parks and Nature Reserves* (Westport: Greenwood Press, 1990).

11. Roderick Nash, *Wilderness and the American Mind* (New Haven: Yale University Press, 1967). Also see the third edition, published by the same publisher in 1982.

12. Representative William A. Dawson of Utah, *Congressional Record*, 84th Cong., 1st sess. 101 (June 28, 1955), p. 9386; cited in Nash, 1967, p. 218.

13. Nash, *Wilderness*, pp. 220–24.

14 Ernst Haekel, *Wonders of Nature* (New York: 1903).

15. Merriam, "Biology in Our Colleges," pp. 352–55.

16. Aldo Leopold, *A Sand County Almanac and Sketches Here and There* (New York: Oxford University Press, 1949).

17. Susan L. Flader, *Thinking Like a Mountain* (Madison: University of Wisconsin Press, 1994), pp. 5–6. See also W. C. Allee, A.E. Emberson, O. Park., T. Park, and K.P. Schmidt, *Principles of Animal Ecology* (Philadelphia: Saunders, 1949).

18. Rachel Carson, *Silent Spring* (Boston: Houghton Mifflin, 1962).

19. Michael J. Bean, "Conservation Legislation in the Century Ahead," in David West-

ern and Mary Pearl, eds., *Conservation for the 21st Century* (New York: Oxford University Press, 1987), p. 271.

20. User 1995FOES@aol.com, Internet posting to multiple recipients, 19 January 1995.

21. Despite its importance, IUCN's financial condition has always been precarious: although the World Wildlife Fund was established in 1961 to be the fundraising partner to the IUCN, it quickly split off to become an independent agency with its own action agenda.

22. Craig W. Allin, ed., *International Handbook of National Parks and Nature Reserves* (Westport, Conn.: Greenwood Press, 1990), p. 12; and Norman Myers, ed., *Gaia: An Atlas of Planet Management* (Garden City, N.Y.: Anchor Press/Doubleday, 1984), p. 161.

23. IUCN, *Programme, IVth World Congress on National Parks and Protected Areas* (IUCN, Caracas, Venezuela, 10–21 February 1992).

24. UNESCO, *Final Report on the Biosphere* (United Nations, UNESCO, 1968).

25. Lynton Keith Caldwell, *International Environmental Policy: Emergence and Dimensions* (Durham: Duke University Press, 1984), p. 49.

26. Robert Allen, *How to Save the World: Strategy for World Conservation* (London: Kogan-Page, 1980).

27. WRI, UNEP, IUCN, *Global Biodiversity Strategy: Guidelines for Action to Save, Study, and Use Earth's Biotic Wealth Sustainably and Equitably* (WRI, UNEP, IUCN, 1992).

28. Lester Brown, *State of the World* (New York: Norton, 1993).

29. Joseph Knowles, *Alone in the Wilderness* (Boston: Little, Brown, 1913), pp. 224–25.

30. John Muir (1912) cited in Nash, *Wilderness*.

31. White, Jr., "The Historical Roots," pp. 1203–1206.

32. Allan Hunt Badiner, ed., *Dharma Gaia: A Harvest of Essays in Buddhism and Ecology* (Berkeley: Parallax Press, 1990), p. xv.

33. James Lovelock, *Gaia: A New Look at Life on Earth* (Oxford: Oxford University Press, 1979).

34. Eugene P. Odum, *Ecology and our Endangered Support Systems* (Sunderland, Mass.: Sinauer, 1989), pp. 59–62.

35. Arne Naess, "The Shallow and the Deep: Long-range Ecology Movement, a Summary." *Inquiry* 16 (1973): 95–100.

36. David Ehrenfeld, "Hard Times for Diversity" in Western and Pearl, eds., *Conservation for the 21st Century,* pp. 247–50..

37. As quoted in Badiner, *Dharma Gaia.*

38. Gro Harlem Brundtland, "The World Commission on Environment and Development," (1985) *Journal '86* (Washington: World Resources Institute, 1986), p. 29.

39. Thomas Rudel with Bruce Horowitz, *Tropical Deforestation* (New York: Columbia University Press, 1993).

40. Brundtland, "The World Commission," pp. 25–31.

41.  Gadgil and Guha, *This Fissured Land*, p. 245.

SELECTED REFERENCES

Ehrlich, Anne and Paul Ehrlich. *Extinction: The Causes and Consequences of the Disappearance of Species*. New York: Random House, 1981.
Matthiessen, Peter. *Wildlife in America*. Rev. ed. New York: Viking, 1987.
McKibben, Bill. *The End of Nature*. New York: Random House, 1989.
Rolston, Holmes. *Natural Values*. New York: Columbia University Press, 1994.
Wilson, Edward O. *The Diversity of Life*. Cambridge: Harvard University Press, 1992.

# 22 Cities

KENNETH T. JACKSON

Giant cities dominate the globe. Their lights, their rhythms, and their jobs attract newcomers like magnets attract iron filings. During the twentieth century especially, their growth has been spectacular. In 1900, only 14 percent of the world's population lived in cities; by the year 2000 more than half of the world's people will call some city home. This demographic shift has been most staggering in the so-called Third World. For example, Manila, founded 400 years ago by the Spanish, has mushroomed in the past half century from a bombed-out backwater to a metropolis of 8.5 million people that produces 33 percent of the Philippines' gross domestic product but has only 13 percent of the national population. Mexico City, built on the ruins of an Aztec capital, had only 334,000 inhabitants in 1900; by 1995 it had more than 20 million, and predictions were common that it would soon have more than 25 million. Sao Paulo, surrounded by an agricultural hinterland and now South America's greatest metropolis, was a relatively small city at the beginning of this century; by 1995 its great buildings stretched for miles, reminding visitors of New York or Hong Kong. Cairo, Egypt's capital for a thousand years and now growing at the rate of more than a thousand people per day, has so quickly surpassed its housing supply that cemeteries have become desirable places of habitation. The list could go on. Some cities, like Paris, London, New York, and Tokyo, are famous. Others are known only to the villagers who sacrifice everything to find their way to a bigger place. To all who come there, however, cities suggest power, wealth, competition, achievement, and excitement.

Until about 10,000 B.C. no one lived in cities. Men and women were hunters and gatherers of food, who harvested but did not sow, and wandered but did not stay. Of necessity they lived in impermanent camps. The only people who remained in one place were the dead, and thus the first permanent settlements were cemeteries, the places to which humans returned to be near the remains of their relatives.

The birth of cities for the living altered this nomadic existence. Indeed, the development of concentrated settlements at specific and permanent places was one of the turning points of history because since that time, whenever it was—and no one is sure—cities have been the centers of civilization. In fact, without cities there probably would have been no real civilization, and no real progress on a systematic and sustained basis.

By 4000 B.C., several towns had sprung up in Mesopotamia, especially in the fertile valleys and deltas of the Tigris and the Euphrates Rivers in what is now Iraq. Within 500 years, many prosperous and walled cities dotted the area, each surrounded by irrigated fields and villages.

Mesopotamia was not the only center of ancient urban growth. Other river valleys, such as the Nile in Egypt, the Indus in Pakistan, and the Hwang Ho in China, were also centers of early urban growth. And the Negev in Palestine spawned cities as soon as the residents learned to dig wells for water. The names of these ancient places—Uruk, Ur, Babylon, Nineveh, Mohenjo Daro, Thebes—mean little today, but in their time they were the jewels in the human crown. Individual cities rose and fell with the great empires that were ruled from them, but taken together, concentrations of population moved human beings from a primitive existence to one with written languages, codified laws, and technological achievement. Indeed, the word "metropolis" itself derives from the Greek and means a mother city from which smaller cities (colonies) developed.

Until the first half of the nineteenth century, when London began to grow to unprecedented size, probably no city on earth had ever exceeded a population of one million. Rome reached that size in the first and second centuries A.D., when it was the capital of the Roman Empire and the most sophisticated and powerful city anywhere. In the seventh century, Constantinople, located at the critical junction of Europe and Asia, reached a population that possibly approached one million. The next city to take center stage was Baghdad, which the Muslim ruler al-Mansur chose as his new capital in 765. By 930, it was the largest city on earth, with perhaps one million people. Other great urban complexes before the eighteenth century included Cordoba and Beijing.

In general, however, the world had few important cities and few urban residents in the 1500 years after the death of Jesus Christ. The Holy Roman Empire was too dispersed to sustain a single imperial center, as was feudal Europe, where a deconcentrated system of trading and manufacturing discouraged cities, and they grew only slowly if at all. Whenever struggling villages threatened to become larger towns, disaster often brought an end to such aspirations: the Black Death, for example, wiped out about 80 percent of Europe's urban population in the space of a few years between 1347 and 1350.

The first cities to reach giant size in the modern period were Beijing, Canton, Edo (Tokyo), Paris, and London. By 1750, each had a population of more than a half million, and exercised economic and political sway over a vast hinterland. London, the English capital, soon surpassed the rest, and its rise meant that the capitalist and mercantile economy of Western Europe was generating a new purpose for large metropolises—as coordinators of long-distance networks of exchange. During the eighteenth century, it overtook Paris; by 1801, the year of the first British census, it counted more than 850,000 inhabitants. In the following decades it quickly became the largest city the world had ever known, with a population of more than 5.5 million by 1890. Moreover, as the capital of the British Empire, it had global reach and a preeminent position within the international economy.

In 1800, fewer than ninety places on the planet had even as many as 100,000 inhabitants and, taking Europe as a whole, the level of urbanization (9–11 percent of the total population) was just about the same as in 1700, if not perhaps a little lower. But London's rapid growth in the nineteenth century was indicative of a broad demographic trend that reshaped the Western world and especially Great Britain—the most urbanized nation on earth by 1900, with well over half of its citizens living in cities of at least 10,000. Continental Europe lagged behind Britain, though not by much; and in the nineteenth century, for the first time in human experience, an entire continent rapidly urbanized. On the eve of World War I, of the eight cities in the world with more than two million inhabitants, which included New York, Chicago, and Tokyo, the other five—Berlin, St. Petersburg, London, Paris, and Vienna—were in Europe.

The United States was also unusual in its rapid nineteenth-century urbanization. In fact, the American republic had been an urban place from the time the Pilgrims, the Dutch, and the Puritans had stepped off their boats. They had immediately huddled together in tight little communities—in part because their religion emphasized community, and also because they were terrified of the Indians. As early as 1700, the cities of New Amsterdam (later renamed New York), Boston, Newport, Charleston, and Philadelphia were organizing the economy of the continent.

After 1800, however, American cities exploded in size. Although the cowboy and the farmer captured the public imagination, what was really unusual about the United States was the rapidity of its urbanization, which was exceeded only by Britain. New York was of course the most dramatic example: a colonial outpost of perhaps 60,000 in 1800, by 1900 it was the second largest city in the world and well on the way toward overtaking London. Statistically, Chicago's growth was even more spectacular, inasmuch as the Windy City had not even existed in 1830, yet by the end of the century counted its inhabitants in the millions and dominated the American heartland, an area larger than Europe. Indeed, by 1900, when Philadelphia, San Francisco, Milwaukee, Seattle, Denver, Kansas City, Memphis, Atlanta, Dallas, and Houston, among others, were stretching their muscles, the United States was already more heavily urbanized than Europe, with more cities of a million inhabitants (New York, Chicago, and Philadelphia) than any other nation.

Although the nineteenth century witnessed the initial growth of great cities on a sustained basis, the twentieth century would prove to be a much more dramatic time of urbanization. The concentration of population in large, expanding cities would become the most powerful of the world's demographic trends, and its impact would be especially great on developing nations. As late as 1925, less than 10 percent of the population in the so-called Third World lived in cities. Since World War II, however, urban places in developing countries have grown three times as fast as those in advanced nations. Between 1950 and 1985 the cities of the Third World as a whole, including China, grew by more than 800 million, which is more people than the entire urban world included in 1950. And the growth of urban places may even accelerate with the collapse of communism, if only because those powerful central governments tended to restrict access to metropolitan areas. In mainland China, for example, an urban person was until recently a person with a ration card. People without such a document were not allowed to move to the city, however much they may have wanted to relocate.

Region to region, the experience of cities in the twentieth century has varied considerably. In the developed or advanced world, for example, the growth of urban populations has slowed since 1910. In part, this is statistically inevitable: once a threshold has been reached, the pace of urbanization must slow down. This is because the level of urbanization has an absolute limit of 100 percent of a country's population, and the closer a nation moves toward that figure, the harder it is to raise the proportion.

In Europe, the home of most of the world's great cities in 1900, the twentieth century has not seen the same rapid growth other regions have: urbanization has increased, but by modest amounts, and some metropolitan areas have scarcely grown at all. Vienna began a decline early in the century due to the breakup of the Austro-Hungarian Empire; it reached its peak in population and influence about 1910. Similarly, Berlin, one of the most beautiful and important cities in the world between 1870 and 1940, was virtually destroyed by World War II and has yet to return to its former glory. London, on the other hand, has not experienced any cataclysmic developments, maintaining a roughly stable population for the past half century.

American urbanization, the second-fastest in the world in the nineteenth century, was especially rapid between 1840 and 1930, when New York became the first city in the the world to attain a population of more than ten million—as many as had lived in all the 500 European cities as of 1600. And around 1960, it became the first metropolis to exceed fifteen million. But other cities, especially in the South and West, actually grew much more rapidly: Los Angeles became the quintessential automobile city early in the century, and by 1960 had approximately the same population as London though it sprawled over three times as much land. Meanwhile Las Vegas, Tucson, San Antonio, San Diego, Orlando, and San Jose led a parade of new metropolitan areas that were small in 1900, yet exceeded one million by 1990. Meanwhile, for the nation as a whole, metropolitan areas have continued their dominance at the end of the century. In the 1980s, for example, 90 percent of the nation's population growth and 89 percent of its employment growth took place within the orbit of large cities.

No group in the United States more profoundly affected the urbanization process than African Americans. In 1900, blacks were overwhelmingly southern and rural, with more than 60 percent residing on farms. Even as late as 1960, about 11 percent of the families who operated their own farms were black. By 1990, however, only about 1.5 percent of farmers were black. Quite simply, the African American population has moved from farm to city and from south to north over most of the past century. Only since 1980 have African Americans been returning to the south.

Although Tokyo is geographically far from the great cities of Europe and North America, it is part of the advanced world, and has shown similar growth. By 1990 it had grown together with Yokohama to form one vast metropolis of 23.4 million—the largest agglomeration of people on earth at that time. As a city, Tokyo is perhaps the best manifestation of the shift in economic power toward Asia in the last quarter of the twentieth century because of its incredibly high land values and its rapid modernization.

More than any other country on earth, however, Australia has demonstrated that urbanization is not necessarily dependent upon overall population density. Although the country covers a vast territory—most of it lacking water and extensive vegetation—it has long been among the most urban nations in the world. Its population is concentrated in a few cities—Melbourne, Sydney, Adelaide, Perth, and Brisbane—scattered around the outside edge of the continent, that have grown rapidly in the twentieth century.

In the Americas south of the Rio Grande River, urbanization has a long tradition—nowhere more so than in Mexico City. This vast industrial and trading center grew from 344,000 inhabitants in 1900 to 20.2 million in 1990, when it joined the ranks of one of the three largest metropolises in the world. Built on the ruins of an impressive Aztec capital, the city also increased its share of national production from 29 percent in 1930 to 52 percent in 1983.

In South America, Sao Paulo—the largest city—has grown just as dramatically in the twentieth century, and has become almost as big. But the powerful impact of Latin American urbanization can best be illustrated by smaller countries: in Ecuador, for example, the capital Quito held about 30 percent of the national population by 1952, and 42 percent by 1982. By the year 2000, according to predictions, it will be about 54 percent.

China has had a different history: for a thousand years it has had twice the population and taken up twice the size of all of Europe, and for many centuries was the most sophisticated and technologically advanced civilization on earth. By the thirteenth century, its inhabitants had adopted crop rotation, highly developed plows, and seed selection, and had built a system of internal canals to move goods efficiently throughout the land. Its great cities reflected tremendous economic power and influence: as late as 1650, both Beijing and Canton were among the largest cities in the world, with populations exceeding a half million.

After 1500, however, China went into a long period of decline, and its cities suffered accordingly. By 1900, only about 8 percent of its population was urban, a much lower proportion than in the rest of the world. After the communist takeover of the country in 1949, the growth of cities was further inhibited by a regime that equated great cities with Western decadence. Such places continued to exist—Shanghai had 10.4 million residents in 1950, and Beijing followed with 6.7 million, but 20 million young city residents were forcibly relocated to the countryside for political indoctrination during and after the Great Leap Forward (1958–1960). This massive industrial and agricultural development program was intended to transform China's economy overnight, but it ended in the largest famine in world history.

Like China, India also experienced urbanization early in human history and later became home to some of the world's largest agglomerations. The

Harappa or Indus Valley civilization, which lay near the border of Afghanistan in what is now Pakistan, reached its height sometime around 2100–1750 B.C., with several cities of perhaps 40,000 people. Thereafter, at least up until the tenth century, India had few cities, and those remained small. In the twentieth century the situation changed markedly, and Calcutta, Delhi, and Bombay all currently rank among the few places in the world with more than ten million inhabitants.

The African continent also has a long tradition of great cities, but by 1900 its level of urbanization was less than 5 percent, and only Cairo (at 650,000 persons) could have been considered a true metropolis. The situation was even more stark in sub-Saharan Africa, where Ibadan was the only city in 1900 that had even 100,000 inhabitants. In part, this was the result of a sharp reduction in the slave trade in the nineteenth century, which led to a fall in the population of many port cities.

In the twentieth century, however, Africa has urbanized at an astonishing rate. Between 1930 and 1970, the urban population increased fivefold, growing 4.2 percent a year. Since 1970, urban growth has been even higher—especially in black Africa, where the World Bank has estimated that some cities are growing by more than 10 percent a year, the fastest rate of urbanization ever recorded.

By 1980, more than fifty cities on the continent had populations exceeding 100,000. In addition to the megacities of Cairo and Lagos, Africa's major urban concentrations were at Nairobi in Kenya, Accra in Ghana, Abidjan in the Ivory Coast, Algiers in Algeria, and Kinshasa, the capital of Zaire (Congo), which provides an extraordinary example of the consequences of unbridled urban growth. Only two generations ago, it was a relatively small outpost of Belgium's colonial empire. But by 1995, no one even knew how big it had become—estimates ranged from five to eight million—and it stretches for dozens of miles along the banks of the Congo River. It has become not only ungoverned, but like something out of science fiction, without sufficient food, housing, or health care. Crime is rampant, and with vaccinations against disease practically nonexistent, cholera, dysentery, typhoid, tuberculosis, and malaria reach epidemic levels on an almost annual basis. Armies of rats roam unhindered through the huge mounds of rotting waste that block already inadequate sewage canals. As one observer noted sadly in 1996, Kinshasa is like a giant ant colony, but without the order.

Why have cities in the twentieth century become such a powerful lure? What is it about crowded streets and bustling markets that draws newcomers?

Economists offer a simple answer—urban areas offer a favorable income differential over rural settings and small villages. As urban theorist Lewis Mumford (died 1990), who was not enamored of the modern metropolis, noted many years ago, "the city is a place for multiplying happy chances and making the most of unplanned opportunities."

Rural poverty, then, is the driving force behind urban growth, especially in the developing world. Tourists from the city may fantasize about the quaintness and charm of family farms, or see peace and serenity in native villages in Africa, Asia, or the Americas. Why, they wonder, would anyone swap the glories of nature for the wretchedness of city slums? The answer, of course, is that as visitors, they do not see the underside of rural life—the dirt floors, the lack of running water or flush toilets, the absence of electricity, the boredom and monotony of everyday existence. Four fifths of the world's poorest live in tiny settlements, where, for most people, the migration to the city begins.

With confidence and hope they come.

But the world the migrants find is typically not the world of their dreams. Poverty is not quickly erased because of a move to the city, and the very fact of concentration tends to exacerbate problems that are uncommon in rural areas. In Cairo, for example, children who elsewhere might be in kindergarten can be found digging through clots of ox dung, looking for undigested kernels of corn to eat. Similarly, in Kinshasa, where the jobless rate in 1990 was about 80 percent and the annual rate of inflation was 3,000 percent, thousands of families somehow subsist on one meal every two days. And even in the wealthy and powerful United States, newspapers regularly report on newborn babies dropped into garbage bins by drug-addicted mothers. Perhaps this is because urban problems are more visible than rural poverty.

There are many urban problems: housing, for instance, is no more available to many urban newcomers than food. Typically, the larger the city, the greater the value of the land it sits on. Or as Ashok Khosla, president of the New Delhi-based Society for Development Alternatives, has noted: "Each city contains the seeds of its own destruction because the more attractive it becomes, the more it will attract overwhelming numbers of immigrants." Too often, rapid urban growth leads to overcrowding, tenement dwelling, and eventually homelessness.

Begging, squalor, slums, and misery are of course not unique to our own times or to the developing world: the term "Skid Row" emerged at the end of the nineteenth century in Seattle to describe that part of every American central business district where the homeless, the unattached, and the unemployed congregated. The most famous Skid Row was the Bowery in New York—a one-mile stretch of flophouses, missions, saloons, and shelters inhabited by perhaps 15,000 men in 1900.

And at the end of the twentieth century, homelessness is still an American problem. From Manhattan to Venice Beach, from Seattle to Miami, persons without shelter are commonplace. On a single 1991 weekend in Chicago, despite the availability of 4,000 beds in homeless shelters, two persons were found frozen on the streets. Similarly, the Japanese, the British, and the French have recently become accustomed to the sight of derelicts camped in tunnels, under highways, and inside train stations in Tokyo, Yokohama, Osaka, London, Glasgow, Paris, and Marseille. Even Germany, long known for its affluence and extraordinary level of social services, now experiences beggars on the street.

As late as 1950, however, urban homelessness was rare, and aside from places that had been devastated by World War II, including cities in Europe and China, the phenomenon of street people was associated most notably with India's Calcutta. Then known as "the slum of the world" and "the city of death," Calcutta had a population density rivaling that of New York or Tokyo, but only a few buildings of more than three stories. Families were horribly overcrowded, and several hundred thousand people slept regularly on the pavement. Indeed, so great was the press of humanity that even the border of the garbage dump was occupied.

The explosion of the urban population in the second half of the twentieth century, however, has made homelessness a feature of everyday life in the developing world. In Calcutta, which remains in a crisis situation, the only area with a passable water supply is at the center, where the wealthy live. The depths of squalor can be found in the thousands of legally defined slum districts, known as *bustees*, where a "hotbed" system provides beds for people on a rotation basis, day and night, and migrants who cannot afford to rent a bed or the corner of a room end up living on the street.

The illegal occupation of land in squatter or informal settlements is often the only way for people to get a roof over their heads in the developing world. In Turkey, if a person erects four walls and a roof on vacant land overnight he or she traditionally becomes its owner. As a result, jerry-built houses, or *gecekondu*, have emerged on the edges of Ankara and Istanbul. In the Union of South Africa, the government long forbade the building of houses on the outskirts of major cities, so twenty-five miles north of Pretoria, in an officially unrecognized settlement of more than 500,000 people called Winterveld, a sea of shanties made of scraps and wrappings—sometimes consolidated with metal bars—covers the land.

Every country has its own terms for squatter settlements and they are perceived in ambiguous ways. In Argentina, they are known as *villas meserias*, or townships of misery. In Peru, the term *pueblos jovenos* means young communities, and in Indonesia *kampung* means simply village. In Brazil, the exclusion of slum dwellers from the urban cores is so deeply rooted in the culture that the Portuguese word used to describe them is *marginais*, and the word used to describe their arrival is *invasao*. Pastel-colored squatter settlements—called *favelas* after the name of a flowering tree that grows in profusion on the hillsides—surround Sao Paulo and Recife. In Rio de Janeiro, the coaches full of tourists heading for the Sepetiba Gulf pass the shacks at Rocinha, one of 300 favelas scattered around the city. No one knows for sure how many people inhabit this shantytown of the Cariocas, or common folk, but census takers working from aerial photographs estimate the population at between 100,000 and 120,000. Similarly, in Buenos Aires, Santiago, Mexico City, and Lima, the most degrading poverty exists among the squatter dwellings of the very poor, where flush toilets, sewers, running water, and fire and police protection are unknown.

If anything, the situation in Africa is even worse. The World Housing Survey conducted by the United Nations in 1975 assembled data on sixty-seven large cities, reporting that on average, 44 percent of the population lived in shantytowns, but that in Addis Ababa, Ibadan, Douala, Yaounde, Mogadishu, Lomé, and Buenaventura the proportion exceeded 75 percent. And among megacities, Lagos has recently emerged as the most crowded on earth, with an occupancy rate of 5.8 people per room. By comparison, cities in India average about three people per room, and New York averages only one person for every two rooms.

Cities are inherently unnatural in that they require enormous concentrations of food, water, and materials in a small area, concentrations far beyond anything nature is capable of providing, and in turn generate enormous quantities of garbage and sewage. Just as nature cannot consolidate the resources needed to support urban life, neither can it disperse the waste produced in those cities. Air pollution, water pollution, and garbage pollution are the result.

Air pollution has long been a characteristic of most large communities. In the nineteenth century, city boosters in the United States tried to turn this to their advantage by suggesting that large amounts of carbon in the air actually inhibited rather than caused certain diseases, but no amount of apologetic verbiage could convince most people that a befouled atmosphere added to a city's appeal. Pittsburgh, a major center of heavy industry, was particularly obnoxious in this regard. As Willard Glazer, a travel writer, noted in 1884:

> Failing a night approach, the traveler should reach the Iron City on a dismal day in autumn, when the air is heavy with moisture, and the very atmosphere looks dark. All romance has disappeared. In this nineteenth century the gods of mythology find no place in daylight. There is only a very busy city shrouded in gloom. The buildings, whatever their original material and color, are smoked to a uniform, dirty drab; their smoke stinks, and mingling with the moisture in the air, becomes of a consistency which may almost be felt as well as seen. Under a drab sky a drab twilight hangs over the town, and the gas-lights, which are left burning at mid-day, shine out of the murkiness with a dull, reddish glare. This is Pittsburgh herself.

Although emission controls on factories are typically much stronger in the late twentieth century than in the nineteenth, one fifth of mankind—over one billion people—live in urban areas where the air is not fit to breathe. In the 1990s, atmospheric pollution comes from a variety of sources. Coal, still the major form of household energy in Asia and Eastern Europe, cloaks cities in great plumes of sulphurous smoke. Before the British Clean Air Act of 1952, prompted by the 4,000 people who died from breathing London air, the city was particularly foul and suffered from dense winter smog. At the end of the century, a less visible cocktail of poisonous gases is given off in London by automobiles, factories, refineries, and power stations and causes respiratory diseases in many citizens.

Surrounded by mountains which trap its air in a kind of high bowl, Mexico City is now the world's most polluted metropolis. With more than 35,000 factories and more than three million cars—all using unleaded gasoline— there exists a cloud of smog that cannot disperse. Ozone levels have been pushed to four times the amount considered unsafe in Los Angeles, and to six times that judged acceptable under World Health Organization standards. Yet its population remains.

And what of the water in cities? A secure and safe supply of water is almost a precondition for urbanization: traditionally, most early cities were located on rivers and lakes. But modern cities have often been built in less suitable locations. Southern California, for example, is a desert that has become the home of more than 17 million inhabitants only because pipelines bring water from hundreds of miles away in the Owens Valley in the Sierra Nevada mountains, or the Colorado River. The system worked well enough early in the century, when the population was small and there were few competing cities in the American Southwest. In the 1990s, however, Las Vegas, Phoenix, Tucson, and dozens of smaller places all seek to share a precious resource whose total supply is limited.

Developing countries have an even more serious problem, as they lack the resources to tap into distant supplies. An amount that was sufficient a generation ago is often inadequate now. Karachi, Pakistan, for example, which had 7.7 million people in 1990, provides 30 percent less water than needed, forcing the poor to drink untreated water often contaminated with hepatitis virus. Those taking medicines sometimes get sicker due to unscrupulous local manufacturers boosting profits by adulterating pills and potions with motor oil, sawdust, and tainted tap water, which do not do much to stop hepatitis.

In nature, there is no waste—animal and human excrement goes into the ground and replenishes the farmland. In cities, however, as the urbanization process has accelerated, solid waste has become a sanitation and health issue. The rapidly growing cities of the Third World have been overwhelmed by the amount of sewage they generate: squatter areas are particularly poorly serviced, and people are forced to relieve themselves on the streets. But even the well-managed cities have trouble. Tokyo, for example, has been overwhelmed by its own trash—22,000 tons each day—despite massive recycling and incineration programs. The city has been building artificial islands in Tokyo Bay to hold garbage, but it cannot continue to do so without threatening both the fishing and shipping industries, and will run out of dump sites before the end of the century.

Problems and all, in the short run cities will continue to grow. Sometime around the turn of the millennium, the world will reach a historic milestone. For the first time in human history, half the earth's population, or more than 3 billion people, will be living in cities. By that time, a torrent of migration from the countryside will have created urban agglomerations that dwarf the great capitals of the past. There will be some four hundred cities in the world—compared to only eleven in 1900—with populations of more than one million, including twenty megacities with populations of more than ten million. Although these will include New York, London, Tokyo, and Los Angeles, three fourths of them will be located in the developing world—Bangkok, Beijing, Bombay, Buenos Aires, Cairo, Calcutta, Delhi, Dhaka, Jakarta, Karachi, Lagos, Manila, Mexico City, Rio de Janeiro, Sao Paulo, Seoul, Shanghai, and Tianjin.

But what of the longer term? Will great cities choke on their own size? Will they become so unmanageable that they, like hundreds of places before them, collapse and disappear into the dirt? Who today has ever heard of Calah, or Tikal, or Angkor, or Ur? Who but a tourist to Crete knows anything of Knossos? Who but a biblical scholar knows much of Ephesus?

Even those cities that have survived have sometimes undergone wild swings of fortune. Alexandria, Egypt, for example, had several hundred thousand people at its peak in Roman times, but when Napoleon entered it in 1798, he found only 4000 souls in a squalid and miserable town. Since then it has again boomed to nearly 3 million, but now it faces grave ecological threats. The gleaming port city on the Mediterranean Sea that the medieval Arab writer Ibn Dukmak compared to "a golden crown, set with pearls, shining from East to the West" is now slowly sinking into the unstable, sewage-contaminated Nile delta.

Perhaps the megacities of today will be subject to the same cyclical fate. In Great Britain, for example, which started the modern urbanization process, once-prosperous places like Liverpool and Glasgow have become symbols of decay and decline. And in the United States, stripped automobiles, burned-out buildings, boarded-up houses, and glass-littered streets are so common that a federal official recently noted: "There are some parts of these cities so empty they look as if someone had dropped nerve gas."

St. Louis illustrates this dilemma: once the fourth-largest city in America, called the "Gateway to the West," it is no longer in the top thirty and has become a ghost of its former self. In 1940 it contained 816,000 inhabitants; in 1990 the census counted 397,000. As its suburbs have grown and prospered, many of its old neighborhoods have become dispiriting collections of eviscerated homes and vacant lots. Although the drone of traffic on the nearby interstate highways is constant, there is an eerie remoteness to the pock-marked streets. The air is polluted, the sidewalks are filthy, the juvenile crime rate is horrendous, and the remaining industries are languishing. Grimy warehouses and aging loft factories are landscaped by weed-grown lots adjoining half-used rail yards. Like an elderly couple no longer sure of their purpose in life after their jobs and children are gone, these neighborhoods face an undirected future.

Will the experience of St. Louis, or of Ur, become typical of other places in the twenty-first century? Some futurists argue in the affirmative. In recent years, such prominent futurist authors as Paul Hawkin, John Naisbitt, and Alvin Toffler have created almost a cottage industry out of predicting that cities are doomed and that a new science of telecommunications—led by computers, fax machines, e-mail, and video-telephones—will make personal human interaction unnecessary. In the future, they suggest, we might expect to have breakfast with our spouse (if marriage itself remains a preferred option), kiss good-bye, and then repair to separate rooms or computer stations without leaving home. There, in the comfort of our family rooms, far from the nearest house or grocery store, we will do everything from reporting to work to buying vegetables.

Perhaps the futurists will prove correct, and the great cities of our time, like conquered Carthage, will be plowed with salt before the end of the next century. More likely, however, the great cities of the 1990s will remain great cities in the 2090s. For the same catalytic mixing of people that creates urban problems and fuels urban conflict also spurs the initiative, innovation, and collaboration that move civilization forward. Metropolitan centers are the most complex products of the human mind, and it is unlikely that they will ever lose their roles as marketplaces of ideas, despite the ability of computers to link people over long distances.

Even children, it has been found, want to be where the action is. Most people, secure in the belief that the proper environment for young minds and bodies is a controlled one—and preferably a fenced-in back yard—attempt to keep their offspring away from the street. Yet a German study in 1970 found that children gauge their freedom not by the extent of open areas around them, but by the liberty they have to be among people and things that excite them and fire their imaginations. In scientifically-planned German communities from Kippekausen to Kucknitz, the youngsters evidenced the most contentment when playing near trains and factory smokestacks, poking around the debris of construction, or hanging around busy corners. They felt isolated, regimented, and bored amid shaded walks, fenced-in play areas, and big lawns.

In sum, large concentrations of people still have their virtues and advantages. Cities are places where people of different bents and pursuits rub shoulders, where most of humanity's important achievements and ideas have been born. Whereas village and rural life is characterized by the endless repetition of similar events, cities remain centers of diversity, excitement, creativity, and opportunity. If they express some of the worst tendencies of modern society, they also represent much of the best. As University of Chicago professor Charles E. Merriam told the United States Conference of Mayors in 1934, "The trouble with Lot's wife was that she looked backward and saw Sodom and Gomorrah. If she had looked forward, she would have seen that heaven is also pictured as a city."

REFERENCES

Bairoch, Paul. *Cities and Economic Development: From the Dawn of History to the Present,* translated by Christopher Bruder. Chicago: University of Chicago Press, 1988.

Evenson, Norma. *The Indian Metropolis.* New Haven: Yale University Press, 1989.

Girardet, Herbert. *The GAIA Atlas of Cities: New Directions for Sustainable Urban Living.* London: Gaia Books, Ltd., 1992.

Hall, Peter. *Cities of Tomorrow: An Intellectual History of Urban Planning and Design in the Twentieth Century.* London: Basil Blackwell, 1988.

Hohenberg, Paul M., and Lynn H. Lees. *The Making of Urban Europe, 1000 to 1950.* Cambridge, Mass.: Harvard University Press, 1985.

Jackson, Kenneth T. *Crabgrass Frontier: The Suburbanization of the United States.* New York: Oxford University Press, 1985.

Kirby, R.J.R. *Urbanization in China: Town and Country in a Developing Economy, 1949–2000.* New York: Columbia University Press, 1985.

Mumford, Lewis. *The City in History: Its Origins, Its Transformations, and Its Prospects.* New York: Harcourt Brace, 1961.

Sutcliffe, Anthony, ed. *Metropolis: 1890–1940.* Chicago: University of Chicago Press, 1984.

Vance, J. E. *Urban Morphology in Western Civilization.* Baltimore: Johns Hopkins University Press, 1990.

# 23 Demography and Population Movements

GEORGES SABAGH

The much-publicized United Nations International Conference on Population held in Cairo, Egypt in September 1994 provided an opportunity for the mass media to publicize the world population crisis. Newspapers and magazines featured stories with such titles as: "Reining in the World's Galloping Population"; "Feeding a Booming Population Without Destroying the Planet"; "Battle of the Bulge: Population"; and "Crisis of a Crowded World: And the Fuse Still Sizzles on World Population Bomb." Lester Brown, the president of the World Watch Institute, a private organization in Washington, D.C. that focuses on population, environmental, and ecological issues, warned of "a day of reckoning," with ecosystems breaking down. Even "President Clinton has joined the neo-Malthusian bandwagon," as *U.S. News and World Report* stated on September 12, 1994, referring to the inspiration that pessimists have found in the work of Thomas Malthus, whose *Essay on the Principle of Population as it Affects the Future Improvement of Society* was published in 1798. As can be seen when viewed in the context of his work, the pessimist's vision of the implications of rapid population growth is not new. The so-called neo-Malthusians have warned that there is a need to control population voluntarily in order to bring it into balance with food production and thus avoid the ever-present threat of famines and disease, Malthus's inevitable population checks. More recently, ecologists and biologists have modified the basic neo-Malthusian argument: the earth and its resources, they say, are finite, and rapid population growth will lead to further environmental deterioration.

But, with its inevitable implication that urgent measures—including such methods as sterilization and abortion—must be adopted to control fertility, such pessimism has found opposition in a curious alliance of scholars and religious activists. The Catholic Church in particular has tended to paint a rosy picture of the population problem: interestingly, at the 1994 Cairo conference the Vatican found support in a number of Islamic countries and groups. A Catholic leader provided an example of an extremely optimistic opinion in this statement published in a United Nations press release during the conference:

> If the population of the world has grown from 1 billion to 5 billion in the last 2 centuries, world resources have grown 50 times in the same period. . . . No economy grows without a dynamic demography.

Some economists have also argued that population growth may have a beneficial effect on economic development. But both pessimistic and optimistic views have far-reaching implications for policies pertaining to population growth. The former calls for radical measures to decrease fertility; the latter opposes these measures or is more policy neutral. Both consider technology an important dimension; it can be used to develop new resources, but can also create problems for the environment.

In spite of these bitter debates, most UN delegates from the Third World agreed that rapid population growth could threaten sustainable development. On the other hand, delegates from developed countries, mostly in Europe, were concerned with the possibility of population stagnation and decline. Here history is repeating itself. During the 1930s such fears had been expressed by a number of countries, among them France, at times based on extreme nationalism or even racism, as in Germany, though they were assuaged by the baby boom of the 1940s and 1950s. Unfortunately, we can expect these fears to be heard more frequently in the future.

No matter what perspectives about the implications of population are adopted by governments and nongovernmental organizations, we need to know what course the population of the world will take in the twenty-first century. Population changes in the future will undoubtedly influence the opinions about the implications of these changes.

Thus the main objectives of this chapter are to examine population growth and demographic changes in the world during the second half of the twentieth century, and assess possible population and demographic trends in the twenty-first century.

The estimated population of the world increased by 1 billion in 250 years—from about half a billion in 1650 to 1.6 billion in 1900. The twentieth century saw a rapid acceleration: it took only fifty years to add the next billion to the world's population. The 2.5 billion of 1950 reached 3.7 billion in 1970; 10 years later, in 1985, population had climbed to 4.9 billion. By 1994, the earth's population stood at 5.6 billion.

The annual rate of growth was at its highest ever from 1950–1970. It increased steadily from about 1.8 percent in 1950–1955 to about 2.1 percent in 1965–1970. After that historic peak, the tempo of growth decreased continuously to 1.7 percent in 1985–1990. Even though the rate of growth decreased, the fact that the population was much larger in 1985–1990 than in 1950–1955 meant that the average number of people added annually to the earth nearly doubled from 47 to 99 million during this period.

From a geopolitical perspective, the world's population growth in the twentieth century has been accompanied by significant shifts in the demographic importance of different regions. The demographic share of the more developed countries of the world increased substantially from 21 percent in 1800 to nearly one third in 1900, but then decreased to about 23 percent in 1990, and the opposite was true for the less developed regions. To interpret these patterns of population growth, demographers employ the concept of demographic transition. The demographic transition remains a useful general concept that directs us to examine the relationship between trends in mortality and fertility and the impact of social and economic changes on these trends. Prior to its beginning, both fertility and mortality levels are high, thus yielding little or no population growth. During its early phase, mortality starts to decline while fertility remains high, thus providing an impetus for rapid population growth. In later stages of the transition, as fertility starts to decline, so does the pace of population growth—although this may be forestalled by an accelerating decline in mortality. And at the end of the transition, with both fertility and mortality levels low, population becomes stationary. Western Europe and North America underwent this transition mostly in the nineteenth century and Eastern Europe in the first half of the twentieth century. But this model failed to anticipate the baby boom experienced by both regions after World War II, and also fails to account for the very rapid decline of both fertility and mortality in some developing countries, while in others fertility remains high in spite of a rapid decline in mortality.

In the second half of the twentieth century, the population of less developed regions, including China, surged from about 1.7 billion in 1950 to slightly over 4 billion in 1990, at an annual rate that increased from 2.0 to 2.5 percent and then decreased to 2.1 percent. But if one excludes China, the pace of population growth for the less developed regions increases to 2.3 percent in the late 1980s. By contrast, more developed countries lagged behind, growing from about three quarters of a billion in 1950 to a billion and a quarter in 1990, with an annual rate that plunged by half from a baby boom high of 1.3 percent to a low of 0.6 percent. But the most dramatic demographic changes occurred in the least developed regions where, between 1950 and 1990, the population more than doubled—from 194 million to about half a billion—and the rate of growth jumped from 1.9 to 2.7 percent, the highest anywhere. In 1985–1990, forty-seven countries were defined as being least developed by the United Nations, with thirty-three of these countries in sub-Saharan Africa.

Considering the major regions of the world,[1] what stands out is the enormous and increasing demographic weight of India and China, followed closely by sub-Saharan Africa. The combined population of China and India nearly doubled, reaching 2 billion in 1990—totaling more than one-third of the world; during the same period, the population of sub-Saharan Africa tripled to about half a billion. That of Latin America, Southeast Asia, and the Middle East/North Africa also tripled, reaching 441, 444, and 331 million respectively.

By contrast, Europe grew slowly, experiencing a spectacular loss in demographic prominence. Its 1950 population of 400 million was double that of every major region and somewhat higher than India's—only China exceeded the figure, by about 150 million. By 1990, India and China far surpassed it, sub-Saharan Africa was slightly higher, and Latin America and Southeast Asia were catching up. North America, which had the same population size as Latin America in 1950, gradually lost its demographic edge: by 1990, it was only 60 percent as populous.

Between 1950 and 1990, there were profound changes in mortality and fertility, and by considering them, one can best understand the momentous demographic transformation of this period. Between 1950–1955 and 1965–1970, the world's birth rate declined slightly, from 38 to 34 births for every 1,000 people, while the death rate decreased noticeably from 20 to 13—thus explaining the acceleration of population growth. However, in the next twenty years, this growth slowed down, as a result of the greater decline in birth rates (34 to 27) than in death rates (13 to 10).

A more vivid measure of fertility level is given by considering the number of babies that a woman would bear during her lifetime—the total fertility rate. Similarly, a more graphic gauge of mortality, or more exactly survivorship, is given by life expectancy at birth—the average number of years a newlyborn baby is expected to live under current conditions. From 1950–1955 to 1965–1970, the fertility rate remained high and then, in the next twenty years, plunged from 5 to 3.5 children per woman. While fertility remained almost constant until 1970, 10 years were added to life expectancy; and as fertility declined, another 7 years were added so that life expectancy increased from 46 years in 1950–1955 to 63 years in 1985–1990. 1990–1995 estimates document a further drop in fertility, to 3.1 children, and an increase in life expectancy to 64 years. The early 1970s were thus a turning point, ushering in a major transition in the world's fertility trends. But trends for the world as a whole conceal important regional differences: in the early 1950s, compared to the more developed regions, the less developed regions (including China) had a substantially higher fertility—6.2 versus 2.8 children per woman, and a much lower life expectancy—41 versus 66 years. The least developed countries had even higher fertility and mortality levels.

Since 1970 the developed world has seen its fertility rate drop to a level below that which is needed for replacement of the population (1.9 children per woman), while life expectancy has risen to a new high of 74 years at birth. By contrast, the developing world has seen its fertility level decline but still remain at a high level—particularly if China is excluded—of 4.6 children per woman. In spite of the 20-year gain in life expectancy, the developing countries still lag 13 years behind the developed world. And in the least developed regions, fertility is still more than 6 children per woman, and life expectancy is 20 years lower than in developed countries.

In terms of regional differences, the demographic differentiation of the world in 1950–1955 was fairly simple. The developing regions had high birth rates (40 and over born per every 1,000 people), and relatively high death rates (24 or more dying per 1,000), except in Latin America. Since these death rates were even higher prior to 1950, it is clear that these regions had entered the early stages of the demographic transition. By contrast, in the more developed countries, birth rates were in the range of 20–27 and death rates in the range of 10–15 between 1950 and 1955.

As a result of the momentous changes in the subsequent decades, the demographic profile of the world became increasingly differentiated. In China, in a mere 20 years, the total fertility rate plummeted from 6 to 2.4 children as a result of a drastic population policy. At the same time, its death rate was cut by two thirds and nearly 30 years were added to its expectation of life at birth. By 1985–1990, it had a somewhat lower fertility than did Europe in the 1950s, and also a lower death rate, in part due to its young age structure.

In Latin America, India, and Southeast Asia, birth rates declined to 30 per 1,000, and death rates to about 10 per 1,000. Total fertility rates decreased the most in Latin America, the least in India. While the substantial gains in life expectancy were about the same for the three regions, Latin America's was the highest. The Middle East/North Africa is part of this regional group because its death rate also declined to about 10 per 1,000, but its birth rate remained higher (37 per 1,000). Furthermore, its initial total fertility was very high, declining to only 5.4 children per woman by 1985–1990—though a few Middle Eastern/North African countries reached noticeably lower levels. It is clear, however, that all of these regions were in the second phase of the demographic transition, characterized by rapid population growth.

In a third regional group including South Asia (minus India) and sub-Saharan Africa, there was almost no decline in fertility—which remained at the very high level of 6.6 in sub-Saharan Africa throughout the period—but some decrease in mortality, thus accounting for an increase in the tempo of population growth.

And the rest of the world—Europe, the USSR, North America, and East Asia (mainly Japan and the Koreas)—all experienced a noticeable decline in birth rates, to the lowest level of around 15 per 1,000 in 1985–1990. Total fertility rates, which had been below or nearly below replacement levels in Western Europe and the United States in the 1930s, increased noticeably to around 3.5 in North America and around 2.5 in Europe in the baby boom years of 1950–1965. But by 1985–1990 they had dropped precipitously to below replacement levels. With the exception of East Asia, death rates stayed at about the same level—partly because of an aging population. At the Cairo conference, the delegate from the Russian Federation asserted that "for the Russian Federation and some other developed countries, in which fertility is below replacement levels, problems relating to population are different from problems faced in Africa, Asia, or Latin America."[2]

Clearly, Europe and North America reached their post-transition phase. But this is precisely what had happened to them in the 1930s, and, as already mentioned, the baby boom radically modified this picture. So will history repeat itself and bring about another baby boom? Indeed, this is what one Eastern European delegate at the Cairo conference wished would happen when he stated that "in order not to die out, Estonians must have more children."[3]

There is a vast and multidisciplinary literature on explanations of these complex trends in fertility and mortality, a subject beyond the scope of this chapter. But while there is some agreement on the factors that have led to the decline in mortality, this is not true with respect to fertility. One has to explain not only why fertility declined rapidly in some regions and countries, but also why it did not in other countries. As indicated by population expert Ronald Freedman, "explaining the cause of the transition from low to high fertility" is not so simple since it involves not only tracing the effects of increasing age at marriage, contraception, and abortion[4] but also specifying which social, cultural, and economic changes are responsible for the decline in fertility.[5] As could be expected, an increase in contraceptive use is closely related to a decline in fertility. Thus, China's and Latin America's noticeable increase in contraceptive use between the 1960s and 1990 was accompanied by a sharp reduction in fertility. By contrast, in sub-Saharan Africa, where fertility remained high, contraceptive use remained low. Did family planning programs or the process of social and economic development account for the increase in contraceptive use? Analyses of the differential impact of family planning program efforts and economic development indicate that both have an influence on the extent of fertility decline. Unfortunately, there is no general agreement about which particular economic, social, cultural, or sociopsychological theoretical model best explains the situation.

One of the most important consequences of the mortality and fertility trends described in the previous section is their effect on the age distribution of the population. While people are living to older ages, and this reduction of mortality increases their demographic importance, demographers have shown that the decline in fertility actually has the most impact on the age distribution. Another factor distinguishing this trend is the increasing feminization of the older age groups.

Between 1950 and 1990, the steepness of the age profile did not change appreciably, thus suggesting that the world's population remained young. Reflecting the decline in fertility, the population of children increased less rapidly in 1970–1990 than in 1950–1970, though as a consequence of the earlier higher fertility rates and larger child population, the population of young adults ages 20–39 increased more rapidly in 1970–1990 than earlier. This implies that there was an acceleration in the growth of the younger labor force.

At the same time, the population of those 60 and over was also growing, albeit somewhat more rapidly. As can be expected, there are vast differences in changing age profiles in the different regions.

Sub-Saharan Africa, with its continuously high fertility throughout the period, has the youngest age profile, with a large base of children and relatively few old people. The child population increased more rapidly than any other age group, an age profile that speaks of a high potential for future growth.

In spite of a moderate decline in fertility, Latin America, India, South Asia, Southeast Asia, and the Middle East/North Africa retained a young age profile throughout the period.

Since China experienced a rapid drop in fertility after 1970, its age profile remained young until 1970, but this trend was rapidly reversed by 1990.

The age profiles of Europe and North America show the effects of the baby boom. There is an increase in the number of children between 1950 and 1970 and a decrease between 1970 and 1990, which was particularly sharp in Europe. The baby boom "bulge" translates into a noticeable increase in the childbearing ages 20–38 between 1970–1990. In North America, the surge in international migration during this period has undoubtedly added to the growth of this age group. By the early twenty-first century, the aging "baby boomers" will add substantially to the older population.

As we turn to the future and consider what will happen to the world's population in the twenty-first century, we discover that all projections of future population involve making a series of assumptions or creating scenarios about the future course of total fertility rates and life expectancies. In some of these, assumptions are also made about international migration patterns. Past trends usually guide their selection: for instance, since life expectancy has been increasing in all regions of the world, a continuation of this trend is usually assumed, although the various scenarios differ by only a few years. But some try to account for the negative impact of AIDS on future expectancy. The projection of fertility is more complex. For countries where fertility has started to decline, it is usually assumed that this trend will continue. Assumptions vary with respect to the pace of the decline and the resulting fertility at the end of the period. For countries at or below replacement level, such as the United States, Canada, and all European countries, the scenarios may range from an increase in fertility to a further steep decline.

The most recent and detailed projections takes us only to the year 2025. There are some projections, however, that take us to the end of the twenty-first century: depending on what happens to fertility, the population of the world projected by the United Nations to the year 2100, for instance, will range from a low of 6 billion to a high of 19.2 billion. The figure of 6 billion seems too low since it entails a decline from a projected high of 7.8 billion in 2050. The figure of 19.2 billion also appears unrealistic, and would justify the worst fears of the neo-Malthusians in terms of pressure on world resources. As with most projections, the choice is to arrive at what is called a "medium" or "central" scenario. Projections to the year 2100 have also been prepared by the World Bank[6] and by Wolfgang Lutz, leader of the Population Project of the International Institute for Applied Systems Analysis.[7] Since the medium projection of the United Nations and the World Bank projection assume that all regions would reach a replacement level of fertility by 2100, they both yield about the same figure—slightly over 11 billion. On the other hand, with a somewhat higher fertility rate assumed by 2100, a figure of 12.6 billion was obtained by the International Institute for Applied Systems Analysis. If these scenarios prove to be correct, the world will have 100 years to adjust to the much higher population.

More significant but also more problematic is the diversity of this growth by regions. If the "medium" fertility assumption is correct, the population of Europe, the former USSR, Oceania, and North America will increase slightly to 1.2 billion by 2100, accounting for about 11 percent of the world's population—as compared to 30 percent in 1950. All other regions will have nearly 10 billion and account for 89 percent of the world's population. Even with fertility assumed to reach replacement levels, the population of Africa will soar to an incredible 2.9 billion in 2100, surpassing the entire population of the world in 1950. China, the demographic giant of the late twentieth century and early twenty-first century, will be replaced by India by the end of the twenty-first century.

Regarding the recent detailed projection that lands us in the year 2025, since arriving at a future population figure depends mainly on assumptions about total fertility rates and life expectancy levels, it is crucial to consider first what birth and death rates result from the "medium" assumption. By 2025, total fertility is assumed to be below replacement level (around 1.8–1.9 children) in Europe, North America, East Asia, and China, to be slightly higher than replacement level (around 2.1 children) in the former USSR, Oceania, India, and Southeast Asia, and to be somewhat higher still (around 2.2 children) in Latin America. Between 1990 and 2025, it is assumed that fertility rates will drop sharply—from 5.1 to 2.7 in the Middle East/North Africa and from 5.5 to 2.6 in South Asia (excluding India). While the scenario is similar in sub-Saharan Africa, this region will still have a high fertility rate (3.7 children). This medium scenario also assumes that life expectancy at birth will increase in the future in all sub-Saharan countries. These gains would range from about 5 years for regions with the lowest mortality in 1990 (Europe and North America) to around 14 years in sub-Saharan Africa, which had the highest mortality in 1990.

By 2025, in spite of the assumed increase in life expectancy but because of an aging population, the death rates of Europe, North America, China, and East Asia will increase, becoming nearly equal to birth rates, in a process typical of a post-transition demographic stage. At the other extreme, sub-Saharan Africa, it is assumed, will enter the second phase of the demographic transition, when birth rates start to decrease and death rates continue to drop. For the other Third World regions, the downward trend in birth rates that started before 1990 will continue at an accelerating pace. Since death rates were already quite low in 1990, it is assumed that they will decline only slightly.

From these future trends in birth and death rates it is possible to infer what might happen to both the population size and the age profiles of the various regions between 1990 and 2025. International migration could, of course, modify somewhat these inferences. The populations of the less developed regions would surge from 4.1 billion in 1990 to 7.1 billion in 2025, with the world's population reaching 8.5 billion in 2025. According to the high scenario, this latter figure could go up to 9.1 billion, or, with the low assumption, down to 7.9 billion.

The least developed countries would have the most spectacular growth, from half a billion in 1995 to 1.2 billion in 2025. But unless there is an economic miracle, these will be the countries least able to absorb such a population growth.

The demographic giant of the first quarter of the twenty-first century would still be China, reaching 1.5 billion in 2025, though in the same period, India and sub-Saharan Africa would rapidly catch up on their way to becoming the succeeding era's new demographic giants. Increasing from about 440 to 700 million, Latin America and Southeast Asia would become the other most demographically important regions. Not far behind would be the Middle East/North Africa, whose population would double from 272 to 566 million, surpassing that of Europe, in 2025. For, as could be expected from these trends, Europe would experience very little growth between 1990 and 2025, while North America and the former USSR might have a somewhat higher rate of growth. All three regions would decrease in relative demographic importance, from 20 to 15 percent in the first quarter of the twenty-first century.

The medium assumption about the possible future course of fertility and mortality implies that the age structure of the world's regions would also undergo change. Socially, economically, and politically, the most important future trend is the continuing aging of the population in all regions except sub-Saharan Africa—an aging most pronounced in regions with the lowest fertility and least pronounced in those where fertility would still be relatively higher. It is, therefore, most pronounced in Europe, North America, and East Asia and slightly less pronounced in China. Economically, the most significant trend would be the rapid aging of the labor force and the lack of growth—or even decline—in the age groups 10–29, which provide the new entrants to the labor force. Coupled with the rapid growth of the population in the retirement ages, the trend implies momentous changes in retirement practices and in social security systems.

At the other extreme is the young age profile of sub-Saharan Africa, where with the school population of ages 0–19 projected to more than double, and the age group 10–29 to nearly triple, it will be a real challenge to the region's societies and economies to provide the needed growth in school facilities and new jobs. While the populations of India, South Asia, Southeast Asia, Latin America, and the Middle East/North Africa will show more aging than sub-Saharan Africa—as suggested by a decline or lack of growth of school ages 0–9—they will still have a young age profile. As a result of previous higher levels of fertility, the labor force age groups would still be increasingly appreciably.

The oldest population, ages 70 and over, will double in North America and increase by 60 percent in Europe. This will greatly increase the demand for service workers at a time when the labor force may be shrinking. These workers will have to be recruited from abroad. On the whole, Europe's and North America's need for workers will be even greater than it is now—compounded by projected expanded economies. Thus the medium assumption implies a substantial increase in international labor migration. And not surprisingly, the population projections of the International Institute of Applied Systems Analysis assume that, every year, there may be as many as 2 million migrants from the South to North America, 1 million to Western Europe, 1 million to Eastern Europe, and one-third million to Japan and Australia. Interestingly, the assumed figure for Western Europe is about equal to the average gross immigration from the South for the period 1960–1989. But for North America, the figure of 2 million appears too high.

Is the rapid growth of the world's twentieth-century population a cause for alarm, as the neo-Malthusians would have us believe? While it is beyond the scope of this chapter to analyze the overall social and economic development of the world in this century, a few indicators show that its rapid population growth was not accompanied by a reduction in living standards. In the world as a whole and in the less developed countries, infant mortality, which reflects living standards, was reduced by more than half between 1950 and 1990. But in sub-Saharan Africa, the decrease in infant mortality was less marked, and as of 1990 still remained high. And while there are other measures that suggest that the more populous world of 1990 was better off than in 1950, this was not true for all regions. Between the early 1960s and the early 1990s, per capita food production grew substantially in all developing regions except sub-Saharan Africa, where it declined—particularly between 1969–1971 and 1990–1982. Nevertheless, as Tim Dryson wrote in 1994, data on food production suggest that the "world population growth does not appear to be outpacing food production."[8] From 1965 to 1991, the growth rate of the Gross National Product per capita increased in all developing regions except sub-Saharan Africa, where it decreased. Yet, as suggested by the marked expansion of adult literacy, there was significant social development in all developing regions.

But how about the future? If we are still to believe the prophets of doom, the Malthusian threat will be actualized in the twenty-first century unless something is done to reduce the population of the world to a level even lower than was documented above. One analysis of all the potential for food production shows that the relationships among population, resources, and environment are much more complex and diverse than assumed by the neo-Malthusians. As Vaclav Smil writes, there is "a mix of depressing trends and hopeful possibilities. Worrisome changes include, above all, loss of farmland, soil erosion, overuse of aquifers, salinization of irrigated fields, and declining biodiversity."[9] On the other hand, Smil continues, the optimists could point out that "not only do we understand how to moderate these undesirable trends: we also know how to eventually reverse them with rational agronomic practices." Calculating that agricultural production could be sufficiently increased by 2050 to support a world population of 10–11 billion, Smil's guarded optimism is an answer to the gloomy predictions of the neo-Malthusians. But we should not dismiss the importance of developing a rational population policy. In spite of the acrimonious debate about abortion at the Cairo population conference, the event did achieve a nearly unanimous recognition that the slowing down of population growth and the achievement of sustainable development mutually reinforce each other. Only twenty-some years ago, at the 1974 World Population Conference in Bucharest, a majority of developing countries had favored population growth as a means to economic development: the head of the Chinese delegation had declared that "population is not a problem under socialism." But, as early as 1983, China radically changed its position, and as stated by Prime Minister Xhao Ziyang, the country planned to "continue to lay special stress on population control . . . late marriage and one child per couple."[10]

On the occasion of the Cairo conference and in recognition of the importance of the subject, the Paris Museum of Natural History launched an exhibit to inform the general public about the nature and implications of population growth, looking into the twenty-first century. The organizers of this exhibit provided a succinct and balanced perspective on population growth that can be paraphrased as follows.[11] The world is on its way to mastering its population growth, but, with 11 or 12 billion people, lifestyles will have to be modified, and the resources of the planet will have to be more equitably and better managed. In the long run, the survival of the human species may depend more on the lifestyles of human beings than on their numbers.

This perspective is echoed in a statement made by a delegate at the Cairo conference:

> The number of human beings who can live productively and sustainably on earth is not fixed. It depends on the technologies and capital available, the social organization, and the civic institutions.[12]

## ENDNOTES

1. Some of these regions are defined as follows:
   North America: Canada, United States, Greenland, Bermuda.
   Latin America: all other countries in the Americas.
   Middle East/North Africa: Western Asia, Iran, and North Africa (Algeria, Egypt, Libya, Morocco, Sudan, Tunisia, and Western Sahara).
   Sub-Saharan Africa: all other countries in Africa.
   South Asia (excluding India and Iran): Afghanistan, Bangladesh, Bhutan, Maldives, Nepal, Pakistan, and Sri Lanka.
   East Asia (excluding China): Hong Kong, Japan, Korea (North and South), Macau, and Mongolia.
2. Statement by C. Melikan, Minister of Labor for the Russian Federation, United Nations press release, International Conference on Population and Development, 12 September 1994.
3. Statement by Peeter Olesk, Minister for Culture and Education of Estonia, ibid.
4. According to demographers, these are the proximate determinants of fertility, which also include abstinence and the length of breast feeding.
5. Ronald Freedman, "Family Planning Programs in the Third World," *The Annals* 510 (July 1990): 35.
6. Rodolfo Bulatao, Eduardo Bos, Patience W. Stephens, and My T. Vu, *World Population Projections 1989–1990 Edition* (Washington D.C., 1990).
7. Wolfgang Lutz, "The Future of World Population," *Population Bulletin* 49 (1) (1994). The International Institute for Applied Systems Analysis is an international research organization located in Laxenburg, Austria.

8.  Tim Dryson, "Population Growth and Food Production: Recent Global and Regional Trends," *Population and Development Review* 20 (1994): 407.

9.  Vaclav Smil, "How Many People Can the Earth Feed?" *Population and Development Review* 20 (1994): 280.

10. N. Keyfitz, "Population and Development Within the Ecosphere: One View of the Literature," *Population Index* 57 (1991): 7.

11. "Six Milliards d'Hommes," in *Population et Sociétés* 294 (October 1994): 3. Gilles Pison and Ninian Hubert van Blyenburgh were among the organizers of this exposition.

12. Statement by Fawzi Al-Sultan, president of the International Fund for Agricultural Development, United Nations press release, International Conference on Population and Development, 12 September 1994.

# 24  Epilogue: The Twenty-first Century

RICHARD W. BULLIET

The *Encyclopedia of the Future* is two volumes long and contains almost 500 entries ranging from "Abortion" to "Working Conditions."[1] A crescendo of near-future scenarios is reaching movie screens and paperback novel racks. A new millennium at hand, futurology has become a semiserious profession. So many people, in fact, are already gazing into crystal balls that it would be foolish here to attempt to predict future events or trends. This chapter will confine itself, therefore, to the more modest goal of discussing how the history of the twentieth century may come to be rethought or reimagined from the vantage point of the twenty-first.

If the apocalypse is held in abeyance, one of the few sure things about the twenty-first century is that historians will chronicle its history, and that they will rewrite the history of the twentieth century while they are at it. Assuming the provisional, even evanescent, character of the various master narratives of twentieth-century history currently in vogue, this volume has concentrated on describing fundamental aspects of change in twentieth-century life that are arguably relevant to any approach to its history, giving no special consideration to any particular master narrative of this century's events. Behind this premise is the hope that what has been written here will continue to be germane to histories of the twentieth century written in 2050 or 2090.

Given the manifold rereadings and reinterpretations inflicted on the defenseless nineteenth century by twentieth-century historians, many of the most prominent having dedicated their careers to stamping into the ground the ideology and world view of imperialism that guided so much historical writing before 1900, it must be assumed that many of our own points of view about the twentieth century will be augmented, if not entirely supplanted, by new ones devised to explain the roots of whatever comes next in the twenty-first. That is, the history of our own times and those of our parents and grandparents will, in large measure, be determined by the future, at least for the history-reading or history-viewing public that lives in that future.

The range of possibilities for plausible future rewrites of twentieth-century history is bounded only by the historical imagination, assuming that historians are somewhat more cautious in imagining times they have not personally experienced—whether long ago or future—than, say, science fiction writers. The following sampling of possible future master narratives of twentieth-century history is intended to illustrate the provisional and uncertain nature of our current understanding of our own times. They are couched in the form of proposals submitted to book publishers approximately a century from now—assuming there still are book publishers, and books.

## The Asian Century: Twentieth-Century Foundations (possible copublication with Sony Publishing International)

Historians long maintained that the so-called American Century lasted from 1914, the beginning of the Thirty Years War, when the old order of Europe—the so-called "Long Nineteenth Century"—came crashing down, to 1991 when the United States, economically and politically enervated by its Pyrrhic victory over the Soviet Union, managed one last hurrah by leading a mighty international coalition against the pathetically overmatched forces of Iraq, a country less than a tenth the size of the United States.

This book proposes that the true story of the twentieth century begins in 1905, when Japan defeated Russia in the Russo-Japanese War. Despite the "ten-year setback" (1936–1945) of Japan's midcentury attempt to support its rapid economic growth militarily, the trajectory of Japanese economic growth was steady and inexorable, culminating in the shift of world economic resources to East Asia that is the central fact of our times.

Separate chapters will focus on the emergence of the "Little Tigers," and later the "Middle-Sized Tigers," that followed the Japanese road to prosperity; the saga of China wandering for decades in the trackless wasteland of imported European ideologies before finding itself economically at century's end; and the mysterious inability of Europe and the United States to solve the riddle of international economic competition. Similar special attention will be given, in the Americas, to the historic shift of influence from the Atlantic Coast, fatally infected by nostalgia for a lost era of European connection, to today's burgeoning Pacific coast.

Looking back on our amazing century of Asian development, it is important to brush away the petty historical details of European ideological quarreling—now so clearly perceivable as an irrational episode of civilizational suicide—and refocus public attention on the Asian twentieth century as the precursor of our own era.

## The End of Nationhood: A Reappraisal

This book will examine a series of major writings from the late twentieth century from the standpoint of their assumption that the sovereign nation-state was an inevitable and irreducible component of human society. In light of the great wave of territorial realignment, political amalgamation, and internationalization of responsibility that has marked the last few decades, it is startling to see how little these developments were anticipated by the best minds of that earlier time. Captivated by a supposed seventeenth-century ideological watershed known as the Peace of Westphalia (1648), by which a handful of European principalities agreed to recognize one another's complete sovereignty within fixed borders, these twentieth-century thinkers ardently maintained the eternal verity of sovereign boundaries even in the face of events that were clearly leading to the demise of these archaic notions of sovereignty that we have witnessed in our own time.

The book will begin with a study of precursor movements in the earlier part of the century, notably what was called "communist internationalism" and the institution of the League of Nations. It will then discuss at length the lessons learned from the ill-fated United Nations, which represented the alternative to sovereign nationhood in the second half of the century. Special attention will then be given to concepts like "international sanctions," "humanitarian intervention," and "outlaw state" that emerged toward the end of the century as the theoretical equality of sovereign states clearly began to break down.

The entire argument will be set in the framework of the overarching role of nonsovereign worldwide economic organizations, both public (the International Monetary Fund) and private (AT&T), and of worldwide computer networking, with its intrinsic derogation of the concept of sovereign boundaries.

## The Pacification of Hearts: The New World of Islam

*In the Name of God, the Compassionate, the Merciful*

When the Messenger of God, God's prayers and peace be upon Him, received into the community of Muslims adversaries that had formerly led armies and inspired hatred against God and His Messenger, he greeted them not with punishment and rancor, but with gifts and honors to pacify their hearts. So today, when God's providence, after long travail, has restored unity, power, and prosperity among His people, it is incumbent upon all Muslims to come to a new understanding of times past when Islam was despised and rejected by those who had temporarily gained a dominant position in world affairs. Only by such a revised understanding can we accomplish a contemporary pacification of hearts appropriate to the ever-increasing expansion of the Islamic community throughout the world.

The threshold event of twentieth-century history was the discovery of oil in Iran in 1903. God's providence decreed that the largest petroleum reserve in the world should be located in and around the waters of the Islamic Gulf, then known as the Persian Gulf; that, at the end of the twentieth century, Muslims would similarly control the second-largest pool of oil under and around the Caspian Sea; and, in our own century, that Muslims would gain preponderant positions in exploiting the vast petroleum reserves of the South China Sea and East Turkestan (formerly China's Xinjiang Autonomous Region).

Needless to say, the world transfer of wealth begun in 1974 under the briefly effective Organization of Petroleum Exporting Countries (OPEC) has continued, despite our wars, throughout this century. Our struggles, now thankfully over, have been over who would control this wealth and to what purpose. The sad story of European exploitation of Muslim oil reserves in the first half of the twentieth century was followed by the dual processes of Muslims gaining control of their mineral birthright, and Europeans and Americans jealously conniving to prolong their influence and, that ultimately failing, to cause oil wealth to be spent on Western goods. Western hatred of Islam became rampant, and hundreds of billions of U.S. dollars (then the common international currency) were squandered on weapons aimed at fellow Muslims.

It was God's will that the great war between the believers in God's truth and what the Holy Qur'an calls the Imams of Infidelity should have been fought within living memory. The abode of Islam having been divided against itself to the point of warfare, and those who command the good and suppress the forbidden having emerged victorious, the pacification of hearts must now be extended both to those Muslims who have rejoined the fold, and to the peoples of the West whose twentieth-century efforts to divide and dominate the Muslim community must be forgiven as desperate, fruitless struggles to avoid total energy dependency.

Success is from God, and victory is nigh.

## Una Historia Nueva de los Estados Unidos/A New History of the United States (dual language publication)

Young Americans today look with pride upon the accomplishments of the United States of the Americas, the world's most productive and prosperous confederation of states. Sadly, however, few of them understand the history that led up to the Treaty of Mexico City in 2035. The purpose of this book is to relate the history of the twentieth century from the standpoint of that epochal event.

It will begin in 1898 with the Spanish-American War, the tangible beginning of Washington's unwavering determination, sporadically asserted since the early nineteenth century, to impose its will on the Spanish-speaking countries of the Western Hemisphere. Detailed examinations of the Platt Amendment of 1901–1934, legitimizing the Washington government's intervention in the affairs of Cuba, and the machinations surrounding the building of the Panama Canal (1904–1914), will illustrate government-level intervention. Discussions of the United Fruit Company, the International Telephone and Telegraph Company, and the Guggenheim family's exploitation of Chile's copper resources will serve a parallel purpose for business.

It will then narrate the struggle of the Spanish-speaking peoples living within the territory of the Washington government's jurisdiction to achieve personal respect, equality of opportunity, and language parity within a nation dedicated to denial of its multiethnic character. As amusing as late twentieth-century Latino and Chicano stereotypes (Charlton Heston as a Mexican in *Touch of Evil!*) may seem to today's youth, they should be reminded of the tenacity with which English-speakers defended the cause of language supremacy rather than brotherhood.

The trepidation expressed in 1994—when the North American Free Trade Agreement went into effect—will be recalled as an example of the inability of some thinkers at the end of the twentieth century to understand the potential of a united American economic zone even as they were dreaming of unbounded progress (unfortunately never to be) deriving from peace between technologically advanced Israel and its labor-rich Arab neighbors.

In the spirit of multilingual fraternity and mutual respect that now pervades the American confederation from Montreal to Buenos Aires, this book will be dedicated to an increasingly prosperous future and stand as a warning against the hubris of one government or one people seeking hegemony instead of harmony.

## After the Fall: Portents of Technological Dysfunction

If, at a propitious moment, as much brain power had been devoted to anticipating and forestalling the negative impacts of advanced technologies as to developing the technologies themselves, can anyone doubt that the world would be in much better shape today? I do not mean to suggest that key computer figures like Claude Shannon, John Von Neumann, and William Gates should have been strangled in their cribs to prevent the proliferation of computers, or that as infants automobile magnates Henry Ford, Alfred P. Sloan, and Charles Kettering should have been put in a sack like unwanted kittens and dropped off a bridge to forestall the mass production of cars. Rather, I intend to question why twentieth-century thinkers took so long to recognize the hazards of new technologies.

Part of the answer, I will argue, lies in the time-tested human propensity to let immediate benefit outweigh eventual loss. Another part lies in the ideology of scientific progress that informed so much of twentieth-century thought, whether in the scientific laboratory or at the writing desk of a legion of speculative authors from H.G. Wells to Arthur C. Clarke. Late-twentieth-century Cassandras, like environmentalists Rachel Carson and Paul Ehrlich, while heard, were invariably answered by a legion of learned defenders advocating future technological fixes for impending technogenic problems.

The bulk of the book, however, will examine the "greater fear" hypothesis, the notion that contemplation of a sufficiently calamitous catastrophe exercises a fascination that blinds people to presumed lesser dangers. While stories like graphic novelist Alan Moore's *Watchmen* (1987) or the film *Independence Day* (1996) explored the idea that invasion, or fear of invasion, from outer space might compel the nations of the world to set aside all differences, the end of civilization as we know it through all-out nuclear war became a far more common obsession from 1945 to 1991.

I will discuss imaginative permutations predicated upon nuclear catastrophe, from insignificant early literary efforts like Wilson Tucker's *The Long Loud Silence* (1952); to richly textured stories of civilizational regression like Walter M. Miller's *A Canticle for Liebowitz* (1959), Russell Hoban's *Riddley Walker* (1990), and Alan Moore's *V for Vendetta* (1990); to motion picture realizations like *Road Warrior* (1981).

The final chapter will focus on the birth, in the waning years of cold war nuclear fear, of speculative fiction specifically devoted to technological dysfunction and environmental deterioration, including Neal Stephenson's *Zodiac* (1988), David Brin's *Earth* (1990), and Bruce Sterling's *Heavy Weather*

(1994). I will question whether the greater fear of nuclear annihilation engendered a reduced sensitivity to "lesser" dangers, or even a sort of longing for the worst to occur, thereby forestalling public outcry against runaway technologies until, as we now know, it was too late.

To proceed with this exercise would simply add more opportunities to demonstrate a complete misunderstanding of current trends. Hopefully, the overdrawn scenarios sketched above will not be taken as predictions of the future. Their purpose is immediate, not prospective. They are intended to illustrate a basic truth: that however well we think we understand the times we are living in, or the times just past, the future will surely belie these understandings. History can never be unchanging because it is more than the assembly and narration of past events. It embodies the writer's understanding of those events, and of the bases upon which he or she has assembled and narrated them. As people cannot avoid change in the course of their own lives, and across generations, so history cannot avoid change as stories are reassembled and rewritten under ever-changing circumstances.

It is often maintained that history has moved faster in the twentieth century than ever before. If this is so, master narratives should be falling by the wayside and new interpretations  should be catching on with unprecedented alacrity. The legion of young historians currently embarked on research designed to overturn existing historical landmarks surely hope they are catching this accelerating wave of change.

One may as well argue conversely, however, that the "rate" of historical change should be judged by human factors, rather than by such mechanistic measures as increased speed of communication or transportation. Humans live somewhat longer now than in ages past. Possibly they go through the formative stages of life—adolescence, mating, reproduction, separation from progeny—a bit earlier or later. But fundamentally the human life cycle has remained a constant. Thirty years may see the passage of four generations of computer chip, but they still take an individual person only from infancy to adulthood.

Because there are more people than ever before, there are more human experiences than ever before. As the means of preserving evidence of human experience have vastly expanded through audio and videotape, motion pictures, and digital computer storage, the amount of information available for historians to digest is mountainously greater than ever before. How likely is it, therefore, that the impression of rapid historical change will be validated by the writers of history? Groaning under massive burdens of information, forced into narrower and narrower specializations by the magnitude of their task, and aware that society no longer pays much attention to professorial historians who write mostly for one another's edification, historians may well give place in the twenty-first century to journalists, moviemakers, novelists, literary theorists, or poll takers as shapers of opinion about times present or recently past.

This would be a sad circumstance, for historians know that change is slow, that the future changes the past, and that the present is hostage to the future. These are good things to know, and to remind people of.

ENDNOTE

1. George Thomas Kurian and Graham T.T. Molitor, eds., *The Encyclopedia of the Future* (New York: Macmillan Library Reference USA, Simon & Schuster Macmillan, 1996).

# Index